# JOHN KEATS

# JOHN KEATS
## A NEW LIFE

## NICHOLAS ROE

YALE UNIVERSITY PRESS
NEW HAVEN AND LONDON

DEC 2012

Published with assistance from the Annie Burr Lewis Fund

For information about this and other Yale University Press
publications, please contact:
U.S. Office: sales.press@yale.edu   www.yalebooks.com
Europe Office: sales@yaleup.co.uk   www.yalebooks.co.uk

Set in Arno Pro by IDSUK (DataConnection) Ltd
Printed in Great Britain by TJ International Ltd, Padstow, Cornwall

Library of Congress Cataloging-in-Publication Data

Roe, Nicholas.
   John Keats: a new life/Nicholas Roe.
      p. cm.
   ISBN 978–0–300–12465–1 (cl : alk. paper)
1.   Keats, John, 1795–1821.   2.   Poets, English—19th century—Biography.
   I.   Title.
      PR4836.R525 2012
      821'.7—dc23
      [B]
                                                            2012017299

A catalogue record for this book is available from the British Library.

10   9   8   7   6   5   4   3   2   1

For Matthew

These are not Materials for a Life of our poor Friend which it will do to communicate to the World—they are too wretched to be 'told by a Cavern Wind unto a Forest old'—How strange it seems that such a Creature of the Element as he should have sprung from such gross Realities.

*John Taylor to Richard Woodhouse, reporting*
*Richard Abbey's account of John Keats, 23 April 1827*

# Contents

## Conjunctions, 1819

## Consumption, 1819–1821

# Illustrations and Maps

## Maps

# Preface

J OHN KEATS woke early, roused his friend Charles Brown and stepped outside. Surrounding him was a wild fastness of crags, rocks and rivers: Glen More, remotest heartland of the Isle of Mull. The two men had passed the night here in a shepherd's hut, its air sweet and warm with peat smoke. With their guide singing Jacobite songs in Gaelic, they trudged on six miles across a shoulder of mountain to Derry-na-Cullen, 'the house under the waterfall'. Compared with their last accommodation, this was a mansion – and it still stands, grey and solitary, beside the rushing stream Keats heard as he breakfasted.

Perhaps it was on that very morning that a young Edinburgh lawyer put pen to paper and began an essay on another pretender: 'Johnny Keats', an ignorant and unsettled stripling who had set himself up as a poet. 'Mr. John' was a typical Londoner – a 'Cockney' who kept company with footmen and shopkeepers, while 'foaming abuse' at authority. Eventually this essay would uncover Johnny's seditious secret: he belonged to the Cockney School of Politics as well as the Cockney School of Poetry. Impudent, unmanly and unstable, he was a 'wavering apprentice' of the radical editor Leigh Hunt.

Who was John Keats? The sturdy twenty-two-year-old, who strode six hundred miles around Scotland? Or 'a sickly boy of pretty abilities' who had missed his path in the world?

Few English poets are more widely admired, or more likely to divide opinion. Wordsworth was queasy about his 'pretty Paganism', aware that this young man's questionable beliefs had once been his own. Byron thought his talent overstretched – 'always frigging his imagination' – but was quick to praise *Hyperion*. Eminent Victorians were enthralled and appalled. They loved his melodising, but flinched from the young man – especially when he seemed not man enough. To William Michael Rossetti, his poetry was 'emotional without substance . . . beautiful without control'.[1] Matthew Arnold came to praise a great poet, and found an underbred sensualist.

Yet there was another Keats, altogether more vigorous, colourful and animated, who springs to life in memoirs by contemporaries such as Richard Woodhouse, Leigh Hunt, Charles Brown and Charles Cowden Clarke. For all four of them, Keats was a compellingly restless presence – at one moment mastering complex Shakespearean sonnets, at another doodling nonsense, then commencing an epic to rival Milton. A creature of fits and starts, he was both the lyrical genius of 'Ode to a Nightingale' and the tipsy scribbler of 'Give me women, wine, and snuff'; a stocky schoolboy who 'looked burly and dominant' as he read Spenser, and a mawkish weakling swooning at the thought of his last love, Fanny Brawne.[2]

These double identities of Keats endured well into the twentieth century. Biographies by Sidney Colvin, Amy Lowell and Dorothy Hewlett (1917, 1925, 1937) enriched understanding of his life and works, while professional critics were steadily claiming that his life had nothing to do with his poetry. Walter Jackson Bate's biography (1963) combined both perspectives, displaying an encyclopaedic knowledge of events in Keats's life, then declaring 'To Autumn' to be 'the most nearly perfect poem in English' because its poet was 'completely absent'.[3] Aileen Ward's and Robert Gittings's wonderful biographies (1963, 1968) traced the psychological dramas of his life, and Christopher Ricks's *Keats and Embarrassment* (1974) revealed a poet of humane understanding and searching moral intelligence. In recent decades Keats has seemed more thoroughly at home in his own times – as a freethinker whose melodious plottings are heard throughout Andrew Motion's *Keats* (1997), and as a skilled physician whose training is illuminated in R.S. White's *John Keats: A Literary Life* (2010). As we approach a series of Keats bicentenaries, 'To Autumn' can be enjoyed as one of the supreme lyrical poems in English, and celebrated as a more subtle response to Manchester's Peterloo Massacre than Shelley's *Masque of Anarchy*.

The John Keats readers will encounter in this book is the great Romantic poet and letter-writer, and also a smart, streetwise creature – restless, pugnacious, sexually adventurous. He is Fanny Brawne's jealous, demanding correspondent, and also an astonishingly clear-eyed observer of human behaviour who, had he lived, might have forsaken poetry and reinvented himself as a novelist alongside Charles Dickens. He had suddenly changed course once; to do so again would have been in character.

All of Keats's biographers have confronted the awkward philosophical questions his poems ask about beauty and transience, pleasure and suffering, the claims of art, and mortal fears of ceasing to be. Yet these consummate portraits of genius do not much resemble the feckless orphan, 'five feet hight [*sic*]', whom Geoffrey Matthews once claimed was a 'classic case history of a delinquent'.[4] Matthews's Keats had been brought up in a murky suburban underworld of financial speculation, sexual intrigue, dodgy property deals, booze, quarrels, disease and madness. His mother was a man-hungry teenager; his father – one could never be sure – an innkeeper on the make. Their eldest son, the school bully, grew into a dandy who dressed like Lord Byron, scrawled bawdy rhymes, burned himself with gonorrhoea and tried to cure himself with mercury. Delinquent Keats was in the front row at bloody prize-fights, measuring his poetic 'reach' like a boxer landing a jab.

Nothing in this portrait is fictional. Every detail comes from Keats's letters or contemporary accounts of him. Yet his many self-imposed bouts and trials, physical and imaginative, overlay strikingly different aspects of his personality – undecided, uncertain, in a hurry to be gone. These emotional extremes and instabilities can be traced to his parents' untimely deaths and earlier tragedies and insecurities, and we can sense how those formative deprivations may have shaped the intense ambition and forlorn awareness of his poems. Beyond those events, however, Keats's power as a poet has seemed to draw upon circumstances sealed off in his childhood and lost to posterity. We know a great deal about much of his life, sometimes with day-to-day and even hour-by-hour precision, but there are still significant gaps and puzzles that limit our understanding and appreciation of his achievement.

Those difficulties provided a starting point for my biography. For want of further information, previous biographers have been obliged to repeat a few meagre details about Keats's forebears and childhood, originally assembled by Sidney Colvin nearly a century ago. Whereas Keats's contemporaries William Wordsworth and Samuel Taylor Coleridge revisited their early years to create 'Frost at Midnight', 'Tintern Abbey' and *The Prelude*, Keats has seemed never to have had a childhood. He apparently emerges spontaneously as a poet in adolescence, at some point between quitting Clarke's Academy at Enfield and beginning medical studies at Guy's. We have lacked basic materials to reconstruct how and where Keats lived as a child, and to speculate on how those environments may have fed his imagination. This book begins with a new account of his family and earliest childhood, and finds in London's inner city and shape-shifting edges the beginnings of his life as a poet. Using new archival research, I show how, throughout his life, Keats was obliged to respond to a series of imposed circumstances – reversals of family fortune, deaths, market vagaries, looming poverty, horrific hospital scenes, hostile reviews, the hopelessness of his relationship with Fanny Brawne, persistent

ill-health and the ever-present threat posed by the climate. Poetry for Keats
was from first to last a means of resistance, a way to stand his ground.

A word about form. In recent years there has been a tendency to celebrate
the demise of 'cradle-to-grave' or 'womb-to-tomb' biographies. A new crop of
biographers – and some old hands – have devised lives that begin at the end,
or in which the subject is viewed through lesser-known siblings, imaginary
friends or personal effects (this last trend in the wake of Neil MacGregor's
phenomenally successful *History of the World in a Hundred Objects*).
While there might be reasons for avoiding chronological progression in
lives where little is known about the subject (Shakespeare), there is a very
good case for keeping a more traditional narrative structure for a writer
like – though there is no one like him – John Keats. He tells us repeatedly
that his life had been determined by his origins and early circumstances,
while saying little about what they were. He always felt the pressure of
time, responded to anniversaries, and was careful to alert readers to his
advance as a poet in each of his three books. Ahead of him was an idea of
possible fame, whether as a poet, a playwright or perhaps even as a freedom
fighter in Brazil. If we cannot respond to the contingencies impelling
and distorting those ambitions, we miss an essential dynamic of his life
and creativity. Looking at him through others' eyes cannot make silences
speak, although the scarcity of personal effects known to have belonged to
him tells us of his rootless, and often homeless, way of life. For Keats, dispossession was what mattered, and his response was not to amass property but to
cultivate supportive circles of brothers and friends who would nurture his
rage after fame.

Above all, there is a hunger in all of us to compare the subject with our own
lives: we measure their progress in comparison with our own – what we were
capable of at five, nine, twelve, sixteen and twenty-one. There is no way we
can grasp Keats's extraordinary development – no way we can sense how like
and profoundly unlike others he was – without an apprehension of the arc
connecting his childhood, adolescence and adulthood. We read to know what
being Keats felt like – dogged by misfortune, his future towering impossibly
before him.

Keats tells us little about his own childhood. He says almost nothing about
his parents and early life in his letters, and we are obliged to follow his own
hint that the life of a great writer such as Shakespeare must be discerned figuratively in his works. Much of his poetry comes from real life, and even the
most trivial sights, incidents and encounters provided material for his imagination. As my book developed I became aware of how seemingly slight details
in his correspondence might tell us far more than at first appears. His peculiar

idea that Robert Burns's Scotland was a desolate green in colour, for instance, can be traced to an association laid down when his grandparents moved out of London in the unhappy aftermath of his father's death. As we will see, in suburban North London lay the seed of Keats's idea of Burns's misery as he eked a living from 'a few strips of Green on a cold hill'.[5] At another childhood home in Craven Street, on London's northern edge, the liminal suburban landscape – part city, part open fields – encouraged his imaginative stationings on darkling thresholds and elusive borderlines, as if drawn to recreate scenes of speculation where 'a happy lot' might yet be in prospect.

That medical training at Guy's Hospital held possibilities for a poet was obvious to Keats himself, and the language and techniques of contemporary medicine saturate his letters and poems – most obviously, as we will see, in his heavily opiated months of spring 1819. The cut and thrust of boxing and fencing, his favourite sports, were also re-enacted in combative contests of imagination – in his schoolboy translation of *The Aeneid*, in *Endymion* and his undervalued drama *Otho the Great*. This biography has more to say about Keats as a playwright and theatre critic, and I am concerned throughout the book to highlight the positive influence of Leigh Hunt on his poetry, his ideas of the theatre and that mysterious Shakespearean quality, 'negative capability'.

The sheer physicality of Keats's enjoyment of poetry, apparent from his schoolboy reading of Spenser, shows us how the schoolroom bruiser matured into a poet who was also, we too often forget, a great walker and mountaineer. On his grand pedestrian tour of Scotland in summer 1818 he trekked across Mull to isolated Iona, and set out at dawn to conquer Ben Nevis.[6] From boyhood he was a keen naturalist, up and away early on forays to meadows and brooks. The same inspired curiosity drew him into Dumfriesshire's ruined priories and Iona's Gothic abbey; like Samuel Johnson, who visited Scotland's west coast in 1773, Keats had antiquarian leanings.

His religious beliefs were unorthodox, like the 'pretty Paganism' of Pan's Festival in the first book of *Endymion*. As a boy he loved rhyming and word games, and his lifelong addiction to punning was also a form of pantheism that found meaning and relationships, not blind contingency, in everything. At several points in the narrative I draw attention to the sheer strangeness of some of Keats's behaviour, and his almost clairvoyant habits of composition. Like the gathering swallows of 'To Autumn', his various wanderings around southern counties of England often seem responsive to an obscure homing instinct. On the anniversary night of his father's death he deliberately journeyed to Southampton to commence *Endymion* with a sunrise his father never saw. That poem, like his profoundly unsettling sonnet 'On the Sea', was deliberately framed as an encounter with death – an encounter so unnerving that he fled to Margate and his brother Tom's reassuring company. No less peculiar, his revisions of the four books of *Endymion* early in 1818 followed a monthly cycle, with each corrected book being forwarded to his publisher at the full moon. Coexisting with the radiant masculinity of Apollonian Keats is a lunar poet of enchanted night in thrall to the goddess Hecate.

Several times as I was writing this book Keats gave me an uncanny sense that what I, and other biographers, thought he was doing had no bearing at all on the actuality of his life. Another narrative lay elsewhere, out of sight. In the winter of 1818–19, for instance, figures from his past revived, unbidden, as if trying to reclaim him for an alternative story connected with Keats families at Cheapside. Did their arrival represent a window into his real life as a Londoner, a life not visible in a narrative that focused – as mine was doing – on then-suburban Hampstead? In the following pages I have tried to provide answers where evidence has come to light, or suggest possibilities where facts remain obscure. Like Keats, I have at times left matters open to question.

Literal disconnection from family and friends was the painful experience of Keats's whole life, as they died or left to live elsewhere. Towards the end, as he voyaged to Italy and on to Rome, the actuality of his life was unknown to those who were thinking of him, and hoping for the best, back in England. In the final stages of my narrative I have retraced the tragically dislocated circumstances of his last days, days in which Keats felt he was already leading a 'posthumous existence'.[7] Like many biographers before me, I was moved by Keats's own awareness of the imminent end to a life that had not yet found its intended course. 'Was I born for this end?' he asked Brown in a letter from Naples.[8] There is nothing that can better explain this remorseless intelligence, and in the closing pages of my book I have left Keats and his devoted friend Joseph Severn to speak for themselves.

# Acknowledgements

A S EVERY page of this biography shows, I am indebted to generations of Keats's biographers: Richard Abbey, Richard Woodhouse, Leigh Hunt, Charles Cowden Clarke, Richard Monckton Milnes, W.M. Rossetti, Sidney Colvin, Amy Lowell, Dorothy Hewlett, Aileen Ward, Walter Jackson Bate, Robert Gittings, Andrew Motion and R.S. White. Robert Gittings's *John Keats: The Living Year, The Masks of Keats* and *The Keats Inheritance* have proved indispensable guides to the poet's life and times, alongside Hyder Rollins's editions of *The Keats Circle* and *The Letters of John Keats 1814–1821*. I am grateful to the many contributors to *The Keats-Shelley Memorial Bulletin, Keats-Shelley Review* and the *Keats-Shelley Journal*.

Three stalwarts of Keats family research have added much to my own account. Jean Haynes patiently answered my many questions about the Keats family; her knowledge, gained over long years of first-hand research in parish registers and other records, has been most generously shared. Robert Keats kindly alerted me to his findings about Thomas and James Keates and the Poor House at Lower Bockhampton, and all readers will wish to consult his essay 'John Keats's Father: A New Theory' in the *Keats-Shelley Review*, 26.2 (2012). Lawrence M. Crutcher's masterly study of *The Keats Family* has proved an invaluable source of newly researched information about Keats's siblings and later generations of the family.

John Keats has taken me to many libraries, archives and museums, and I thank the staff of the following institutions: Alexander Turnbull Library, National Archives, Wellington, New Zealand; Bishopsgate Foundation and Institute; The Bodleian Library, Oxford; The Bodleian Library of Commonwealth & African Studies at Rhodes House, Oxford; The British Library; The British Museum; Bethlem Royal Hospital Archives and Museum,

Beckenham; Canterbury Cathedral Archives; Carisbrooke Castle Museum, Isle of Wight; The Courtauld Institute of Art; Derbyshire Record Office, Matlock; Dr. Williams's Library; East Kent Archives, Dover; Enfield Libraries; Exeter Cathedral Archive; The Free Library of Philadelphia; Glasgow University Library; The Guildhall Library, London; Hampshire Record Office; Harrow School; The Houghton Library, Harvard University; Havant Museum; The Huntington Library, Los Angeles; The Isle of Wight Record Office, Newport; Islington Local History Centre; The Jerwood Centre at the Wordsworth Trust, Grasmere; The John Rylands University Library, Manchester; Keats House, Hampstead; The Keats-Shelley House, Rome; Lloyd's Register; London Borough of Hackney Archives; London Metropolitan Archives; Mariam Coffin Canaday Library, Bryn Mawr College, Pennsylvania; The Mercers' Company; Mull Museum, Tobermory; The National Archives, Kew; The National Library of Scotland; The National Maritime Museum, Greenwich; The National Portrait Gallery, London; North Devon Library & Record Office, Barnstaple; Oxford University Archives; The Pierpont Morgan Library; Plymouth Central Library; Portsmouth City Museum; Puke Ariki, New Plymouth; The Royal Academy Library, London; The Royal Bank of Scotland Group Archives, Edinburgh; The Royal Naval Museum, Portsmouth; Stansted Park, Hampshire; The University of St Andrews Library; Tullie House Library, Carlisle; University of Iowa Libraries, Iowa City; The Victoria and Albert Museum; West Sussex Record Office, Chichester; the Worshipful Company of Armourers and Brasiers, Armourers' Hall, London.

I am grateful to the Fellowship Selection Committee at the Houghton Library, Harvard University, for a Joan Nordell Fellowship that allowed me to work for a month in the Houghton's Keats Collection. I also acknowledge the British Academy's award of a small personal grant in the early stages of my research. Thanks go to my colleagues at the School of English, St Andrews University, to Ivan Callus and Peter Vassallo at the University of Malta, and to my fellow trustees at the Keats Foundation, Hampstead, and the Keats-Shelley Memorial Association in London and Rome.

Throughout the writing of this book the following friends and colleagues have offered encouragement and support. Having lived with Leigh Hunt for years, Jane Stabler welcomed John Keats and gave seasonable sweetness to each page of this portrait of him. John Barnard was unfailingly helpful in responding to my ideas and questions; Susan Halpert offered her expert knowledge of the Keats Collection at the Houghton Library; Richard Holmes ensured that the book would be completed at a moment when it might not have been; Jack Stillinger gave trenchant advice about the order of Keats's poems; and Bob White, in print and correspondence, was a welcome source of Keatsian wisdom. Sue Brown, Joseph Severn's excellent biographer, made Keats at home in her apartment in Valletta, Malta, where many of these chapters were written. Ann and Malcolm Wroe, genial hosts, gave good cheer and an inspiring example in Ann's book *Being Shelley: The Poet's Search for Himself*. For specific points of information and advice, I thank the following individuals. Simon Bailey at Oxford University Archives clarified Benjamin Bailey's academic career. Bruce Barker-Benfield's generosity has added significantly to this book. Sue Brown and Grant F. Scott deftly fielded my inquiries about Joseph Severn. Colin Gale, Archivist at Bethlem Royal Hospital Archives and Museum, brought 'Melancholy' and 'Raving Madness' down from their perches. Graham Dalling, Local History Librarian to Enfield Libraries, helped me to map Keats's Enfield and Edmonton. John Gittings gave permission to quote from the Robert Gittings papers at West Sussex Record Office. Stephen Jones of Havant Museum offered information, maps and images relating to the Old Mill House, Bedhampton. Dennis King of New Plymouth has allowed me to reproduce the self-portrait of his great ancestor Charles Brown. Christine Leach explained the topography and history of Derry-na-Cullen on Mull. Lucy Macfarlane, Curator Archives at Puke Ariki, New Plymouth, showed me Charles Brown's remarkable collection of theatrical scripts and his copy of Fairfax's *Tasso*. Ken Page and Mick Scott responded to countless questions about Keats House, Hampstead, and Keatsiana held at London Metropolitan Archives. Fernando Paradinas provided information about the Jennings family bible. Nick Powell advised on Keats's finances and the labyrinth of Chancery proceedings. Nigel Rigby at the National Maritime Museum ensured my ideas of the *Maria Crowther* were in trim. At Rome, Josephine Greywoode and Catherine Payling opened the Keats-Shelley archive. My former student Annalisa Armani corrected my version of Keats's Italian Passport. Glenn Rowe at the Keats Cottage Hotel, formerly Eglantine Cottage, Shanklin, let me explore Keats's rooms. Anthony Da Mancha Stevens sent fascinating information about Sheriff Keats and his family. John Strachan went the extra round in *boxiana*. Heidi and John Thomson made a memorable day in the Charles Brown archive, Puke Ariki, New Plymouth. Carol Kyros Walker revisited her delightful book, *Walking North with Keats*, in answering my questions about Keats's Scottish tour of 1818. Square Sail at Charlestown Harbour, St Austell, enabled me to experience two days at sea on a brig similar to Keats's *Maria Crowther*.

Many individuals have responded to particular points of enquiry. I thank Jeff Abbot, Giuseppe Albano, Alex Alec-Smith, Simon Bainbridge, Helen Baker, Robert Barber, Mike Bevan, John Bidwell, Mike Bishop, Louise Bloomfield, Holly Booth, Rita Boswell, Heather Carson, Richard Childs, Jeff

Cowton, Paul Cox, Anna Delaney, Howard Doble, Angela Doughty, Douglas Dunn, Sally England, Stephen Freeth, Tim Fulford, Deborah Gahan, Marilyn Gaull, Christina Gee, Stephen J. Geertz, Kate Godfrey, Ashley Goodall, Elizabeth Gow, Angus Graham-Campbell, Jim Grisenthwaite, Robyn Gross, Marianne Hansen, Gary Harrison, Martyn Heighton, Stephen Hebron, Sonia Hofkosh, John Houston, Bridget Howlett, Sid Huttner, Noel and Nora Jackson, Steve Jones, Elizabeth King, Sarah Lang, Rhian Light, Brian Livesley, Emma Long, Lucy McCann, Kiyoshi Nishiyama, Michael O'Neill, Margaret O'Sullivan, Don Paterson, Matthew Percival, Karla Pollman, Andrew Potter, Christine Rauer, Alan Richardson, Nigel Rigny Charles Robinson, Jane Ruddell, Cerys Russell, Mary Ruskin, Mark Smith, Richard Smout, Christopher Sweeney, Jane and Simon Taylor, John Thomson, Richard Marggraf Turley, Mark Smith, Damian Walford Davies, Lucinda Walker, Allison Wareham, Timothy Webb, Tim Whelan, Richard White, Jean Whittaker, David Worrall.

David Godwin steered astutely from *Fiery Heart: The First Life of Leigh Hunt* to this new incarnation of Hunt's great protégé. Jeffrey Cox, Hrileena Ghosh, Stacey McDowell, R.S. White and Ann Wroe gave time to read chapters and made countless improvements. The two anonymous readers for the press differed on almost every point, but all of their suggestions have been gratefully received and in various ways incorporated. My excellent editors at Yale University Press, Heather McCallum, Rachael Lonsdale, Heather Nathan, Samantha Cross and Tami Halliday, have been immensely helpful at all stages of this book's production. For my inspired copy-editor Robert Shore, I wish realms of gold.

Matthew Roe braved gadflies and dragonflies to accompany me in Keats's footsteps to that isolated farmhouse Derry-na-Cullen; greeted Iona's pale kings and warriors; and, on a halcyon blue day, voyaged to Staffa and Fingal's Cave. Puffin aerobatics pleased him then, and I hope at some time the swallow-gathering skies of this book will do too.

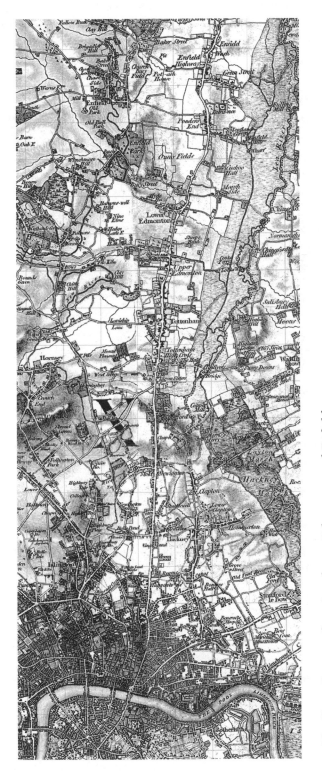

1 The Keats Country, from London to Edmonton and Enfield.

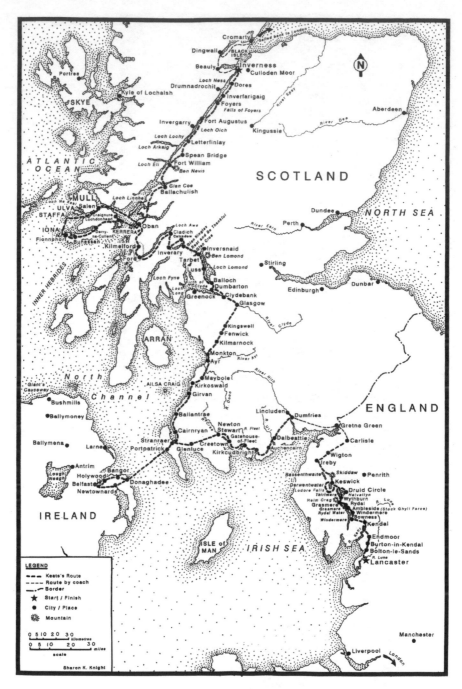

2  Keats's Scottish Tour, 25 June–6 August 1818.

3  John Keats's England. Places visited by or associated with Keats, 1795–1820.

# Early Years, 1795–1814

CHAPTER 1

# Birthplaces

SATURDAY, 14 April 1804. *Dies Saturni*. Thomas Keates called on his sons at
Enfield, dined with friends, then galloped down the long scythe of the
City Road back into London. By day this stretch was crowded with barrows,
carts and stage-wagons. Past midnight, the turnpike was clear. In the dark and
drizzle nobody saw Thomas plunge to the pavement beside Bunhill Fields,
smashing his skull and bleeding heavily – a watchman who found him
remarked on the amount of blood. There was nothing to be done but staunch
his wound and carry him home. Before sunrise, he was dead. For want of
more precise evidence the inquest concluded that 'being riding on a certain
horse it so happened that the said Thomas Keates accidentally casually and by
misfortune fell from the said horse down to and against the ground whereby
he received a mortal bruise in and upon his head.'[1]

John Keats's father knew every stone of the City Road. Aged thirty-one,
Thomas was a professional horseman and lease holder of Keates's Livery
Stables on the Pavement, Moorfields. He could handle an animal that stum-
bled. Could he have been mugged? There were rivals, keen to take over his
flourishing business. Or had he simply been drinking, dozed off and fallen
from the saddle? Whatever happened that night, Thomas's untimely death
remains as mysterious as his early life.

His daughter, Fanny, the poet's sister, recalled being told that her father was
a native of Land's End, Cornwall, a locality that suggested various ancestral
possibilities. Inquiring if her sallow complexion appeared Spanish, Fanny was
reassured that she looked 'English all over'. Perhaps she had cause for asking.
If the family had Cornish origins, her distant forebears might have included a
survivor of the Armada. There was also a well-known family of mariner
Keatses who plied between Poole and the Spanish ports of Alicante and

Cadiz.[2] Spanish blood might explain Thomas Keates's black hair and his daughter's dark looks, her marriage to the Spaniard Valentin Llanos and her long life in Madrid. Keats himself was fascinated by stories of Balboa, Cortez and the Spanish conquistadors and, as we will see, his great poem *The Eve of St Agnes* was, in part, a Spanish inspiration.

Back in England were young Thomas Hardy's neighbours at Higher Bockhampton, Dorset, and we need to be acquainted with them. Immediately next door to Hardy lived the family of James and Rachael Keates and, across the lane, their son William Keates, a carrier. According to Hardy, all of them derived from a family of horse-dealers in the direction of Broadmayne, and he was struck by their resemblance to the poet. Hardy was a man who noticed such things, and perhaps he knew more than he let on. Broadmayne lies to the south-east of Dorchester, and a few miles in that direction – exactly as Hardy said – is the hamlet of Winterborne Came. Here, in December 1736, a John Keats was born. With his wife, Jane, he had two sons – Thomas, born in 1773, and James, 1777 – then tragedy struck the young family.

The father died in 1777, his widow succumbed to an 'ulcerated throat' two years later, and Thomas and James were packed off to Lower Bockhampton poorhouse to work for their keep. Parish records list payments made for 'cloaths' and 'mending shoes' for 'Keates's 2 children'. James eventually married Rachael Talbot and settled at Higher Bockhampton, and – if we take Hardy's hint – his older brother, Thomas, may well have been the father of John Keats the poet. Could Jane Keats's ulcerated larynx, a symptom of tuberculosis, echo in the poet's anxiety about his own 'haunting sore throat'?[3]

All of this, if true, bears out what Leigh Hunt and others said. The poet's 'origin was of the humblest description'; he never spoke of it 'out of a personal soreness which the world had exasperated'; his father was 'a man much above his sphere in life'. What little Keats did say points to his knowledge of 'earlier Misfortunes' that blighted the family long before his own birth. Exactly how Thomas Keates could have escaped from the poorhouse is not apparent; possibly a parish connection led to foster parents in London where there were numerous Keat, Keats and Keates businesses. In the 1770s a John Keat was master of 'Mr. Keat's Livery Stables, Piccadilly'.[4]

Keates or Keats? Thomas used both spellings of his name, and as his poet-son's reputation grew many people tried to claim kinship. Of these, we need to meet just a few. We know that Thomas had a relative named Elizabeth and perhaps a cousin, Joseph, a haberdasher. The haberdasher's son, Joseph Henry, owned himself both 'second cousin' to the poet and a relative of 'Mr. Sheriff Keats' – that is, the grandson of John Keats, vintner, and his wife, Ann Mower. Their sons, Thomas Mower and Joseph, owned hatter's businesses at 14 The Poultry and 74 Cheapside – addresses known to the poet who, in 1816, lived with his brothers at 76 Cheapside. These hatters also claimed descent from 'an ancient and honourable family in the west of England', as *The Times* reported in 1856 when Thomas Mower's son Frederick Keats became sheriff of London. Photographs of Frederick show some resemblance to the poet and, according to *The Times*, the sheriff 'boasted the same ancestry' as 'one of the most distinguished admirals of the navy': Sir Richard Goodwin Keats.[5] Among the sheriff's descendants, family tradition has long held that he was closely related to Keats the poet; and if that was true, John Keats the poet and Admiral Keats came from the same stock too.

Sir Richard Goodwin Keats, commander of the *Superb*, was born on 16 January 1757 at Chalton, Hampshire, eldest son of West Countryman the Rev. Richard Keats and his wife, Elizabeth. Keats the poet was drawn repeatedly to this part of the south coast – to Chichester, Bedhampton, the Isle of Wight, Stansted and Winchester, where Richard Goodwin Keats was educated.[6] Networks of friends help to explain his presence at the consecration of Stansted Chapel in January 1819, and perhaps he was drawn by local Keats associations too – Stansted is just three miles from Sir Richard's birthplace at Chalton. Of course, those three miles might as well be three hundred: Keats was not in Chalton itself, and there is nothing to suggest he was tracking down a relative. However, it is not impossible. Keats had family links with the Royal Navy and Royal Marines, and, as with his other sojourns in South and West England, he may have been drawn to Chalton-by-Stansted by some strange magnetism of family association.

Remember Joseph Keats, Joseph Henry Keats, the hatters Thomas Mower Keats and Joseph Keats, Sheriff Frederick Keats and Sir Richard Goodwin Keats. We shall encounter them again.

\* \* \*

By 1794 Thomas Keates was a young man of twenty-one working at the Swan and Hoop livery stables, Moorgate. His employer, John Jennings, came from a family long established in the parishes of St Stephen, Coleman Street, and St Botolph, Bishopsgate, close to the north flank of London Wall. Spared by the Great Fire of 1666, this part of medieval London was a warren of lanes and alleys winding west from Bishopsgate to the garrets of Grub Street. New arrivals to the city found lodgings here amid a plucky population of actors, balladmongers, coiners and quacks, fortune-tellers, alchemists, beggars and whores. Barred from the city proper, noxious trades such as knackers, blood-boilers and bone-grinders set up alongside gambling dens, taverns and brothels.

* * *

Born in 1730, John Jennings, the son of Martin Jennings and Mary Clementson, was baptised at St Stephen's on 13 October 1730. A sister, Mary, followed in 1733. She married Richard Havers in 1758 and, after his early death, Charles Sweetinburgh. Less is known about her brother's early life. Possibly he was the John Jennings who in 1763 kept the George Inn at Aldersgate before setting up in business himself. The Minute Book of the Worshipful Company of Innholders gives us the details: 'Tuesday 4$^{th}$ January 1774 John Jennings who has taken the Swan and Hoop at Moorgate having purchased his Freedom of this City was sworn and paid £2.14$^s$.4$^d$ and the Officers ffees @ 2$^s$/6$^d$/-.' Now legally established, he married Alice Whalley at St Stephen's, Coleman Street, on 15 February. Six years younger than her husband, Alice was a native of Colne, Lancashire, and retained a North Country thrift and practicality. Their first child, Frances, was born on 1 January 1775 and baptised at home on the 29th. Two sons followed – Midgley John, born 24 October 1777, and Thomas, 10 December 1781. Both were baptised at St Stephen's, on 21 November 1777 and 4 January 1782.[7]

The Swan and Hoop was located immediately outside old Moorgate, opposite Moorfields. For centuries there had been a swamp here, crossed by causeways to Islington and Hoxton. Winter frosts brought citizens to skate; in summer the stench of rubbish hurried them to fresh air and Hampstead. By Shakespeare's day, Moorfields had been drained and laid out as a pleasure garden: bookstalls were set up with ballads and broadsheets; furniture was stacked for sale; and laundrywomen bleached linen in the sun. After the Great Fire, refugees huddled in tents and hovels, and soon the area was notorious for prostitution and 'Sodomites' Walk'. Samuel Pepys came for beer and wrestling, and in the 1730s Old Vinegar's boxing ring drew huge crowds. The Methodists John Wesley and George Whitefield preached here in the open, and in 1785 the Italian aeronaut Vincenzo Lunardi ascended in his balloon. On public holidays aromas of fried sausage, roasted apples and hot gingerbread mingled with the music of fiddles, pipes and drums.[8]

Immediately adjacent to the Swan and Hoop was another awe-inspiring spectacle. Here, in 1675, Robert Hooke built a '*Suburb Wonder*' that immediately entered London folklore – the enormous madhouse, Bedlam. Founded in 1403 at the priory of St Mary of Bethlem, Bishopsgate, the hospital took the bright star of Bethlehem as its symbol. Three centuries later, with those buildings scarcely habitable, Hooke designed a baroque palace as a replacement. Modelled on the Tuileries in Paris, the new Royal Bethlem Hospital was constructed from red London brick with galleries of windows extending for more than 550 feet. In the centre and at each extremity were pavilions of white stone, decorated with Corinthian columns and armorial shields embellished with the Bethlem star. Overhead were three cupolas, a clock in a turret topped with a glittering sphere and, at the pinnacle, a gilded dragon weathervane.[9]

Bedlam and the open space of Moorfields have vanished, although the scene of Thomas Keates's accident is unchanged. Bunhill Fields burial ground is still there on the City Road, and traffic thunders through Moorgate as it did two hundred years ago. The Swan and Hoop succumbed to Victorian improvements, but can still be glimpsed at the edge of eighteenth-century engravings of Bedlam where it appears as a three-storey building with a horizontal stucco cornice. Behind it rise the towers and spires of London's skyline, and Wren's Great Fire memorial. A building resembling the Swan and Hoop survives at 87 Moorgate, and may have stood next door.

On the ground floor of the Swan and Hoop was a tap room. Stairs led up to a parlour, kitchen and drawing room, three bed chambers with dressing rooms and closets, and attics for the servants. Outside, a passage gave access to the stable yard and coach houses – a kind of Georgian car park.[10] Here, amid horse sweat and muck, flourished the lucrative life of a busy livery stable, with ostlers grooming and stable boys polishing bits and brasses. All day and long into the night tides of citizens passed through as they journeyed to and from the city. Lurking in the crowd were petty criminals of all kinds – pickpockets and sharpers, horse-thieves, blacklegs, bubbers and sneaks. Seasoned felons knew the Swan and Hoop as a market for stolen goods – and so did the constables. Richard Richardson, nicknamed 'the one-ey'd Gunner', was arrested here for his enterprising theft of three feather beds and a Persian carpet.[11]

Commercial success brought City connections. Among John Jennings's acquaintances may have been Samuel Brawne of the Coach and Horses on Castle Street, Strand, and John Richards, stable keeper in Oxford Street. Closer to home on Coleman Street lived John Abernethy, father of the great surgeon. Soon Jennings was buying government funds and East India stock, and in 1785 – the year of Lunardi's ascent – he leased the property next door, then sublet it for £46 a year, a sum that nearly covered his rent for the Swan and Hoop.[12] While serving at St Stephen's as senior churchwarden, Jennings also climbed in the City, becoming upper warden and finally, in October 1797, master of the Innholders' Company. To celebrate, he ordered six dozen bottles of white wine, five gallons of rum and five of brandy. There was no claret, but Master Jennings enjoyed a draught of vintage.[13]

Life was good for the Jennings children too. The boys were sent to Clarke's Academy, where the progressive curriculum would prepare them to enter business. Frances was most likely educated at home or in a local dame school. A pleasing figure, oval face and wide mouth made her a 'handsome woman' and she was said to have inherited her father's fondness for good living. Tea-broker Richard Abbey, who enters Keats's story as an acquaintance of Alice Jennings, chatted about Frances with a grocer on Bishopsgate; 'the Man remarked . . . that Miss Jennings always came in dirty Weather, & when she went away, she held up her Clothes very high in crossing the Street, & to be sure, says the Grocer, she has uncommonly handsome Legs.' Abbey linked that recollection to another encounter with Frances, telling Keats's publisher John Taylor that her passionate 'appetites' had made it 'dangerous to be alone with her'.[14] Taylor was the first of many to wonder how Abbey knew this, and glanced at him to see if he could find any traces of the poet's features.

Born in August 1765, Abbey, the son of Jonathan Abbey and Deborah Dodgson, was a Yorkshireman from Skipwith, eight miles south of York. The early deaths of his grandfather and father made him wealthy enough to set up in business in London, where, on 5 February 1786, he married Eleanor Jones, an illiterate city girl. By 1808, he had moved to 4 Pancras Lane, Cheapside, close to Joseph Keats the hatter at number 12 and warehousemen R. and J. Keats at number 1. Most likely acquainted with John and Alice Jennings through the victualling trade, Abbey would be bound up with their family's fortunes, for good and ill, for many decades. Northern roots may explain why Alice Jennings thought well of him, and the esteem was mutual: George Keats remembered Abbey saying 'he never saw a woman of the talents and sense of my Grandmother, except my Mother'. While Abbey let Taylor understand that young Miss Jennings had tried to seduce him, an alternative scenario explains far more about Abbey's subsequent behaviour to Keats and his siblings.[15]

∗ ∗ ∗

When twenty-one-year-old stable hand Thomas Keates caught Frances's eye, she was nineteen. They married on Thursday, 9 October 1794 at St George's, Hanover Square, although Frances was under age and apparently lacked parental consent.[16] They signed the register – Frances swooping impatiently through the 'g' of 'Jennings' – then walked briskly back to the portico, glanced up and down George Street in bright autumn sunshine, and slipped into the crowd. The streets into which they vanished were tense after two years of war with France; just days before their marriage, twelve 'friends of liberty' were locked up in the Tower and Newgate on charges of treason. Among them were shoemaker Thomas Hardy, orator John Thelwall and philologist John Horne Tooke – reformers all, and members of London's democratic Corresponding Society.[17]

It was not supposed to be like this. Thirty years earlier the American Revolution had beamed a beacon of liberty across the Atlantic. National traditions revived in Ireland, Scotland and Wales, while in England Major Cartwright's Society for Constitutional Information recovered the ancient freedoms of Anglo-Saxons and King Alfred. Poetry was in the vanguard of these exciting experiments with tradition: Thomas Percy's *Reliques of Ancient English Poetry* and James Macpherson's 'Ossian' poems breathed fresh life into the languages of Thomas Chatterton and Robert Burns. With the storming of the Bastille in 1789, Tom Paine, England's international rebel, hailed 'an age of revolutions in which everything may be looked for', and William Blake's epic *America* imagined the spirit of freedom, Orc, proclaiming universal liberty in fiery biblical language:

> The morning comes, the night decays, the watchmen leave their stations;
> The grave is burst, the spices shed, the linen wrapped up;
> The bones of death, the covering clay, the sinews shrunk and dried
> Reviving shake, inspiring move, breathing, awakening,
> Spring like redeemed captives when their bonds and bars are burst.
>
> $(37–41)$[18]

Had all that been in vain? When Thomas and Frances Keates married, the captives Hardy, Thelwall and Tooke were languishing behind iron bars in Newgate and the Tower. All three would be tried for their lives, at a moment when memories of Robespierre's Terror were still raw. Was London about to witness identical horrors, with tumbrels clattering to the gallows at Newgate? Many feared that guilty verdicts would lead to mass executions of reformers.

Early on Monday, 26 October 1795, thousands of citizens streamed past the Swan and Hoop towards Islington, where John Thelwall – now an 'acquitted felon' – exhorted the crowd: 'The shopkeeper, the mechanic, the poor ploughman, all suffer together, and to reform the corruption which is destroying us . . . we ought all to unite heart and hand together.' Then, on the following Thursday, George III was jeered and pelted as he made his way to the House of Lords. James Gillray's cartoon shows the royal carriage under a hail of brickbats and dead dogs, its wheels jammed by English sans-culottes while a ruffian discharges a musket at point-blank range. The king suspected an attempt on his life; *The Times* saw an imitation of Gallic insanity.[19]

\* \* \*

Such was the tumultuous world into which Thomas and Frances's first child, John Keats, was born – two months early, according to Leigh Hunt. 'He was a

seven months' child,' Hunt tells us; 'his mother, passionately fond of amusement, is supposed to have hastened her death by too great an inattention to
hours and seasons. Perhaps she hastened that of her son.' His claim has been
doubted, but such seemingly casual remarks from Hunt have usually proved
sound.[20] He knew Keats as well as anyone, and his phrase 'passionately fond
of amusement' – a euphemism for fast living, booze and sex – implies that
Keats was prematurely born because his mother drank. Aspects of Keats's
physiognomy – the small head and projecting upper lip – suggest symptoms
of what we would now call foetal alcohol syndrome which may have rendered
him susceptible to disease.[21] Or is Hunt reminding us that Keats had inherited
a 'passion for amusement' that Richard Abbey also remarked in Miss Jennings,
hinting that a sexually transmitted disease had compromised the poet's health
and left him a prey to consumption? As we shall see, there was more to all of
this than lurid conjecture.

Where and when he was born remain uncertain. In autumn 1795 Frances
and Thomas were most likely at the Swan and Hoop or lodgings nearby. The
baptism register at St Botolph's gives Keats's date of birth as Saturday, 31
October 1795; others give it as the full moon on the 29th – the day of the
attack on the king (Keats's single reference to 'my Birth day' could refer to
either the 29th or the 31st).[22] When young Keats was just two weeks old the
repressive 'Gagging Acts' were published in London. They passed into law on
Friday, 18 December, his baptism day, ensuring that throughout his lifetime
community would be confounded with conspiracy, opinion persecuted and
free speech stifled. A word out of place might mean jail, transportation, even
death. Born too early, if Hunt was right, yet too late to share the exhilarating
first French Revolution, Keats came to believe that Britain was implacably
opposed to all forms of political and social progress.

Revolution and reaction came to the Swan and Hoop too. As Frances began
family life, her youngest brother, Thomas, died of tuberculosis. Midgley John
stayed at Clarke's Academy until he was a tall, skinny youth of sixteen, and is
next heard of seventy miles away at Deal in Kent. Here, on 25 February 1795,
he volunteered for the navy. What evidence we have points to a family quarrel
at around this time, a flare-up of rivalry between brother and sister that drew
in their parents and would eventually divide them all. Midgley John had
embarked decisively on his own life, signalling that he did not intend to follow
his father and run the Swan and Hoop. Dropping his distinctive first name, he
enlisted as Able Seaman John Jennings and joined the man-of-war the
*Leopard*. If he expected action he was disappointed, for the *Leopard* lay quietly
at anchor for the next two months. In April 1796 he was commissioned
second lieutenant in the Royal Marines and was listed on the muster-roll of

the *Russell*, a seventy-four-gun ship of the line. Spring 1797 brought mutinies at Spithead and the Nore as sailors protested over pay and conditions. The Thames was blockaded and officers endured the ritual humiliation of having hot tar poured over them and then a covering of white feathers, an old and brutal punishment for treachery.[23]

That summer the *Russell* patrolled the North Sea with Admiral Duncan, shadowing the Dutch fleet until the squally morning of Wednesday, 11 October.[24] At the Battle of Camperdown, Lieutenant Jennings was said to have been on Duncan's flagship, the *Venerable*, when Admiral De Winter came aboard to surrender, pointed at the tall officer and said he had 'fired several shots at that young man, and always missed'.[25] Jennings's height made him an obvious target and Keats came to regard this story as a touchstone of family honour. Yet Jennings had apparently served bravely aboard another vessel, the *Ardent*, where surgeon Robert Young listed him among the wounded – 'John Jennings – greatly burnt face & hands' – and noted that his injuries had been treated with 'a mixture of olive oil with extract of Saturn', which 'gave great relief very frequently applied with a feather', although Jennings must have suffered agonising pain and disfigurement. Awed by their uncle's heroism, Keats and his brothers 'determined to keep up the family reputation for courage'. Perhaps we can overhear something of Jennings's story in *Hyperion*, as battle-weary Saturn languishes in a scene of awful calm evoked by the image of 'feathered grass'. Possibly, as a child, Keats had overheard talk in which the extraordinary juxtaposition of battle, wounds, Saturn and a feather was lodged in his imagination until called to poetic life.[26]

\* \* \*

In the months after Keats's birth popular discontent seethed along London's streets but, as ever, people also got on with their day-to-day lives. George, a brother for John, was born on Tuesday, 28 February 1797, and by the end of that year Thomas, Frances and their young family were at 12 Craven Street, a new development of terraced brick houses off City Road. Here two more sons were born: Tom on 18 November 1799, Edward on 28 April 1801.

At the start of the nineteenth century Craven Street was a front line where London's expanding suburbs met open fields, a threshold between inner city and surrounding country. The Keatses' new home faced northwards onto the street, with market gardens and meadows stretching beyond. At the back were a kitchen and washhouse, a small yard, more houses and a vinegar factory. Rate books show a constantly changing population, with few staying more than a year or two. The Keatses' neighbours included Joseph Sandall and Frances Grafty, and they were also acquainted with Anne Burch, a relative of 'widow Burch' who lived in Old Street and managed properties throughout the area. Building went on all around, as landowners sold up and developers moved in. We catch a hint of speculative activity in Craven Street from a legal document forbidding tenants to dig 'for making of Bricks or Tiles'.[27]

Across the fields were Hoxton and Hackney, Shoreditch and Newington Green, important centres for religious dissent with meeting-houses and academies. Famous nonconformists like Joseph Priestley, Richard Price and George Dyer had lived there, as did Mary Wollstonecraft's family. William Godwin studied at Hoxton Academy, William Hazlitt attended Hackney Unitarian College, and it is possible that Keats's father was attracted to the area because he, too, had dissenting inclinations. When his youngest son, Edward, died in December 1802, he was buried in Bunhill Fields, close to Daniel Defoe, John Bunyan and John Wesley. In contrast, the inner city was early associated for Keats with the towers and tolling bells of the Established Church – a 'horrid sound' that brought him, he said, a 'chill as from a tomb'.[28]

The house at 12 Craven Street was Keats's birthplace as a poet. Haydon tells us:

> An old Lady (Mrs. Grafty, Craven Street, Finsbury) told his Brother George, when she asked what John was doing, and on his replying that he had determined to become a Poet – that this was very odd, because when he could just speak, instead of answering questions put to him, he would always make a rhyme to the last word people said, and then laugh.

Her memory dated from 1802, when she was a next-door neighbour and knew the family well. Many children play this rhyming game, but few of them go on to become poets – a six-year-old's delight at dodging a question suddenly seemed like a promise of great things to come. Haydon thought the anecdote betokened 'true Genius, innate capacity', and rightly so, for these quick-witted ripostes anticipated every poem Keats would write. When critic John Wilson Croker sneered that *Endymion* was merely a 'game at *bouts-rimés*' – 'rhymed endings' – he unwittingly glimpsed how as a child Keats had rhymed both to baffle what was expected and to lead the story in his own direction. Croker expected rhyming couplets 'to inclose a complete idea', whereas Keats had as if by instinct fastened upon rhyme as a form of contradiction – a way of opening questions to poetry's alternative modes of discovery.[29] It would take time for Keats to recover this original, childish inspiration, and when that happened, soon after he completed *Endymion*, his innate capacity came into its own. Not surprisingly perhaps, many of his poems sought to reconnect with how living at Craven Street had felt.

Raised between the City and rural Middlesex, as a child Keats always lived on an edge. Never fixed, always in flux, that suburban threshold has many counterparts in Keats's poetic topography of borders and prospects. His first published poem, 'To Solitude', effectively locates itself at Craven Street, contemplating the vinegar factory and the city's 'jumbled heap', then scanning north to view 'the steep', dell and river beyond. In later poems Keats, like many contemporary poets and painters, would be drawn to boundaries and limits, beaches, bridges, clifftops, caverns, autumnal mist and darkling dusk, alert to motions of ebb and flow in streams, sky, sea and in his own nature. Formally he would be attracted by the narrow rooms of sonnets yet also lured into the more expansive paths of narrative, in a pattern that corresponds to his physical movements between London and some of the remotest regions of England and Scotland. Exactly as his brave uncle had fought on deck at Camperdown, poetry for Keats was a means to station himself amid a scene of constant change, find his bearings, test his ambition and win through. He was above all a suburban poet, although not in the pejorative senses often implied by that term. The northern suburbs of London were where Keats's life as a poet began and where much of his greatest poetry would be written.

* * *

Late in life John Jennings employed an assistant at the Swan and Hoop: William Wise's appointment was recorded on New Year's Day 1798. Aged sixty-eight, 'excessively fond of the pleasures of the Table', Jennings had made his fortune and wanted others to see it. Keats's poetic feasts and happy vintages may have originated in memories of his grandfather's dinners at the Swan and Hoop, albeit as pleasures often coiled around insecurities. 'Perhaps I eat to persuade myself I am somebody', he reflected gloomily in 1819, aware that his short stature made him feel 'contemptible . . . when . . . sitting by a good looking coachman'.[30] If this was 'comfort eating', those three letters, e – a – t, literally helped make his name: 'Keats'.

Spring 1798 shattered John Jennings. Five years of war had pushed up prices and diminished returns. On Monday, 23 April, *The Times* listed William Wise, 'victualler at the Swan and Hoop', among bankrupts summoned to the Guildhall. Preoccupied with this personal crisis, Jennings could not attend meetings at the Innholders and disappears from the company's minutes. In his absence, the company rallied to the public cause by donating £100 'for the Defence of the Country' and ruled that henceforth guild dinners must be frugal. Possibly Wise was a swindler – George Keats hinted as much when he said his grandfather would have been affluent had he not been gullible.[31] The Swan and Hoop survived as a business, but this shock would have registered with them all. Aged just three, Keats could not have understood what had happened, but, like any child, he would have been able to sense adult anxieties. For Thomas Keates, his father, the misery of the poorhouse would have loomed once again – a shadow that suggests why the poet, too, was so reluctant to look back. In the events of these critical months of 1798 and afterwards, perhaps we can find further reasons why the luxurious feasts in *Lamia*, *The Fall of Hyperion* and *The Eve of St Agnes* were reminders of a formative loss of childhood security; for Keats, the pleasures of food are always as richly and tantalisingly realised as they had been for John Jennings, but they are often indicators of stress, danger and potential damage.

In 1802 John Jennings was seventy-two. His lease had three years to run. At Christmas, Thomas Keates stopped paying land tax on the house at Craven Street, and relocated with his family to the Swan and Hoop, paying rates and an annual rent of £44 to his father-in-law. The business changed hands too, and Thomas was soon advertising chariot horses for sale at 'Keates's Livery Stables' and a horse and gig to be seen at 'Keat's Livery Stables, Pavement, Moorfields'. From now on seven-year-old John would experience life at Keates's Livery Stables hour by hour, noticing how a horse has 'full-veined ears', hearing 'the clang / Of clattering hoofs', watching as 'palfreys twain, / Were slanting out their necks with loosened rein' (*Endymion*, iv.402; 'Calidore', 75–6, 77–8). Sometimes he was allowed to ride a little horse out across Moorfields. Meanwhile, Alice and John moved off to a newly built house on Scotland Green at Ponders End, between Edmonton and Enfield. On 3 February 1803, 'Thomas Keats' was admitted to the Innholders' Company and was 'about to purchase his freedom of the City' when events intervened to prevent him.[32]

Tuesday, 8 February was cold, with flurries of snow. Between ten and eleven o'clock a man walked into the stable yard, announced himself as Captain Thompson and asked to hire a horse for an hour to see a friend at Somers Town. He gave a good address at the Minories, near the Tower, so Thomas let him take a bay mare at five shillings, payable on his return. An hour passed, and the afternoon. By evening, with no sign of the captain's return, there was reason to suspect the worst. Next morning Thomas set off to the Minories, where he discovered that the man was unknown. Thursday, 10 February saw him at Worship Street constabulary office, printing posters to advertise his loss, and after two days word came that his mare was at the Red Lion in Cockspur Street and Captain Thompson under arrest.

A week later, on Wednesday, 16 February, Thomas Keates faced the prisoner at the Old Bailey. Captain Thompson was revealed as Robert Mathews, twenty-nine, 'a Scotsman and a Mariner', charged with 'feloniously stealing a mare', with two similar offences on record. Thomas Keates outlined his loss and, thanks to the Old Bailey's records, we can hear him explaining how he 'went about to all the other stables, thinking [Thompson] might have put it up somewhere else by mistake; that he might, perhaps be intoxicated with liquor'. When Thomas was cross-examined about his business –

Q. You had never seen Captain Thompson before? – A. Never.
Q. And you let Captain Thompson this mare for an hour? – A. I did.

– the lawyer's suggestion that he had been duped drew a forthright response:

Q. Did he give you anything at the time? – A. No.
Q. Do you let horses to any stranger? – A. Yes, if they give me a good address. I would let you one.

Even in this brief exchange we catch hints of his poet-son's zeal for fair play, inherited from his father along with what Charles Cowden Clarke recalled as 'a fine common-sense, and native respectability'.[33] After this exchange, the trial was over quickly. An ostler described Thompson's arrest, then came the prisoner's defence:

I hired the mare, to go to Nottingham-place, about some money; I did not find the person, I came to London, and being intoxicated, I put the mare in a stable, and as I was in want of money, I thought I would sell the mare, and I might go a voyage, and then I should be able to pay the prosecutor for the mare; I sold her for six pounds.

A verdict and judgment followed – 'Guilty. Death' – but 'Captain Thompson' was actually destined to 'go a voyage' as he had hoped. His sentence was commuted, and on 21 April he was delivered to the hulks for exile in Australia.[34]

Horse-stealing was a serious crime, and this sorry episode was also a reminder of a lawless underworld of discharged soldiers and sailors, labourers, drifters and other masterless men who, it was feared, could be lured into revolutionary plots. London in 1804 was a city in turmoil, alarmed by rumours of horrid insurrection, deluded mobs and diabolical conspiracy.[35] Only two years previously, in 1802, there had been an attempt against the British establishment organised by a disgruntled Irishman, Colonel Edward Marcus Despard, formerly one of Nelson's officers. Humiliated by those he had served, Despard embraced radical politics and, after two years' imprisonment for suspected sedition, set about organising a military coup to secure political rights and independence for Ireland. Their plan was to capture the Tower, raze the Bank of England and assassinate King George; across the country others would be awaiting news that the London mail coaches had not arrived, whereupon a mass insurrection would begin. At the last moment Despard's cover was blown and, judged guilty of treason, he was brutally executed at Surrey Gaol on 21 February 1803 – the Monday following Thomas Keates's day in court. Despard was given a hero's burial in St Paul's churchyard, just five minutes' walk from Moorfields. Thomas Keates was not among his mourners, but may well have supported peaceful campaigns for political rights; his eldest son certainly proved receptive to iconoclastic ideas he encountered as a schoolboy.

Thomas and Frances's fifth and last child, Frances Mary (Fanny), was born at Keates's Livery Stables on 3 June 1803. Her oldest brother was now seven years old, and as he gazed across at Moorfields he could see regiments of volunteer soldiers, loyal to King and Country, on parade. With flaring red uniforms and antiquated muskets, these 'Loyal London Volunteers' were preparing to repel a French invasion.[36] Directly opposite, Bedlam was a colossal, unavoidable presence. Day by day Keats watched families pass through the iron gates to seek admission for a patient or to visit a forlorn relative. Presiding over those comings and goings were two massive statues, Caius Cibber's 'Raving Madness' and 'Melancholy Madness', stationed on top of each gatepost. Fashioned from Portland stone, 'Melancholy Madness' showed a naked wretch propped on his forearm, mouth slack and eyes vacant. Atop the opposite gatepost was 'Raving Madness' manacled in torment, a terrifying embodiment of what lay behind Bedlam's elegant façade. For Alexander Pope, these statues had represented the derangement of all that lay *outside* the gates. He located his satirical *Dunciad* in the vicinity of Moorfields because of the district's long association with bookstalls, prostitution and crime, while the proximity of Bedlam's 'Magnific *College*' to the frenzied hack writers of Grub Street spoke volumes.

Aware that poetry's intensities could render him 'not over capable in [his] upper Stories', Keats, too, would find poetic uses for Cibber's gatekeepers. They lingered deep in his memory as gigantic embodiments of anguish, awaiting their summons to reappear as the fallen Titans in *Hyperion*. Like Wordsworth in 'Tintern Abbey' and *The Prelude*, as a poet Keats depended on memories laid down in very early childhood. This is why it is worth trying to reconstruct the environment around Craven Street and Keates's Livery Stables for, as we will see, all of it, even the Pavement which ran alongside Moorfields and on into the City Road, reappears later in his poems.[37]

When Keats stepped out of his father's livery stables, Finsbury Pavement could take him in two directions. Both led to poetry. A turn right across the traffic on London Wall brought him to an unremarkable building packed with wonders. This was the Armourers' Hall on Coleman Street, home to one of the great livery companies of London. Inside, walls were lined with helmets and pikes, swords, spears, daggers, rapiers, gauntlets, gorgets, burgonets, breastplates and chain mail, all sparkling beneath brass chandeliers. Masters of the company appeared in portraits, solemn and official, and small, brightly coloured shields displayed their heraldic arms. The effect was akin to a medieval palace, hung with weapons, armour and trophies. Here, Master John Jennings discussed business while his grandson gazed up at the magnificent trappings for a 'tale of chivalry' – 'Cuisses Herbadgeon spear Casque, Greves, Pauldrons Spurs', and

> that bright lance, against the fretted wall,
> Beneath the shade of stately banneral,
> . . . slung with shining cuirass, sword, and shield.
> ('Specimen of an Induction to a Poem', 37–9)[38]

If Cibber's statues belonged among the mighty forms of epic, here in the Armourers' Hall Keats discovered the colourful, gleaming hardware of Spenserian romance. A few yards further down Coleman Street he would see the church of St Stephen, its grisly gateway capped with a skull and crossbones and a 'Doom', an engraving of Judgement Day. As the years passed, he would get to know every detail on that gate of death as well as he knew the faces of his own family.

A left turn from Keates's Livery Stables led to Finsbury Square and James Lackington's cavernous bookshop, the Temple of the Muses. Inside was a circular counter surrounded by massive bookcases, with a broad staircase leading to 'lounging rooms' and a series of book-lined galleries ascending to a glass dome that lit the whole building. While Bedlam provided Keats with statuesque imagery for *Hyperion*, Lackington's bookshop helped him to the opening of the *Fall of Hyperion* where the poet-dreamer encounters Moneta in another 'eternal domed monument'. Laid down early in Keats's boyhood, too, were his ideas of poetic ambition and fame. 'What a thing to be in the Mouth of Fame,' he wrote to Leigh Hunt on 10 May 1817. 'The Trumpet of Fame is as a tower of Strength,' he told Haydon, 'the Cliff of Poesy Towers above me.'[39] In a few lines Keats sketched the precipitous bookshelves in Lackington's Temple as they had soared over him as a child. He may have been thinking as well of the little halfpenny book tokens Lackington had issued, stamped with the bookseller's portrait and on the reverse a winged figure of Fame, trumpet at her lips, proffering a laurel wreath.

Lackington also gave Keats his publishers. As the little boy gazed up in wonder at bookshelves and radiant dome, perhaps he was noticed by two sales assistants. John Taylor, twenty-two, was a native of East Retford, Nottinghamshire, employed at the Temple of the Muses during 1803–4, where he met another employee, eighteen-year-old James Augustus Hessey. Thus began a lifelong friendship that in 1806 would launch the famous publishing partnership of Taylor and Hessey. Keats wrote to Hunt about 'the Mouth of Fame' just days after Taylor and Hessey had agreed to publish his poetry – perhaps shared memories of Lackington's bookstore had helped bring this about. As Taylor wrote to his father on 15 April 1817: 'I cannot think he will fail to become a great Poet.'[40]

Beyond Lackington's Temple and Islington, the City Road forked into country lanes that wound towards Hornsey and Southgate. The ancient Roman road Ermine Street struck northwards through Tottenham to Edmonton and Ponders End, where John and Alice Jennings were now living in retirement. And from Ponders End it was a short walk across the fields to Enfield, Clarke's Academy, and John Keats's future.

# CHAPTER 2

———————

# School

IT IS August 1803. Thomas, Frances, John and George draw up at a large schoolhouse in Enfield: Clarke's Academy. The façade is of polished brick from local kilns, moulded into fanciful designs of flowers and pomegranates with cherubs' heads peeking over niches.[1] Protruding from the roof are three latticed windows. The rooms are airy and spacious, with the boys accommodated in dormitories of six or eight beds. Across a playground with a pear tree is the schoolroom, and at the back a walled garden with fruit trees, a pond surrounded by strawberry beds and a rustic arbour with a seat. Closer to the house is a drying green with an old morello cherry tree and, beyond this, a paddock for cows that supply the school milk.

During his seven years at the school, Keats came to know this terrain well, overlaying his memories of Moorfields and Craven Street with more rural scenes. The walled garden suggested his idea of a poem as 'a little Region to wander in', where 'antiquated cherries full of sugar cracks' were among pleasures to be tasted while 'lolling on a lawn by a water-lillied pond'.[2] Directly in front of the school was New River, a meandering leat that brought London's water supply from Hertford. Rills and runnels of water ripple through Keats's poems as they did across the meadows of Enfield Wash, Maiden Brook, Marsh Lane, Freezywater Farm and Wet Willows, while the New River was the original of the 'stream of rhyme' that Keats associated with his early attempts at poetry.[3] Wherever Keats was writing the proximity of water in streams, rivers or the sea refreshed his flow of words. East of the school lay a mysterious wooded earthwork known as 'Cæsar's Camp' or 'The Moat' – was it a castle, an encampment or a Roman villa? The aura of romance was irresistible, and if Keats populated it with knights, ladies, dragons, lions, dwarfs and giants he was not the only one to do so.[4] At the centre of Enfield stood a

sixteenth-century 'Pallace' and, across the Market Place, St Andrews Church
and a field of stinking pits for tanning leather. Away to the west was the woodland of Enfield Chase, and to the east lay Edmonton and Ponders End, the
River Lea and the dark ridge of Epping Forest.[5] If Moorfields gave Keats some
of the components for epic, his school helped to form the landscapes of 'Ode
to a Nightingale' and 'To Autumn', becoming a lost paradise or 'faery land
forlorn' with garden-croft, sallows and streams, a castle ruin, and a forest dim.

Keats had enrolled at the most extraordinary school in the country. At
Clarke's Academy he would be taught reading and writing, and also how
England owed its freedoms to the great dissenting tradition, with John Milton
at its head. John Ryland, zealous Baptist, had founded the school at
Northampton and moved it to Enfield in 1786.[6] With him were John Clarke,
principal teacher, his wife, Isabella, and their son, Charles Cowden Clarke. An
'ardent friend of liberty', Ryland cheered the American and French revolutions
and anticipated that there would be similar changes closer to home. Besides
preaching and publishing torrents of tracts and pamphlets, he taught by his
favoured method of 'recreation' – encouraging learning through play. Pupils
were drilled in letters and numbers to prepare them for trade, but, as we will
see, his school also offered numerous other life possibilities. As Ryland shut-
tled between the schoolhouse and the local Zion Chapel, John Clarke set
about recruiting seventy or eighty pupils to fill the schoolroom.

Why Enfield? Removed from, yet in reach of, London, it combined the
attractions of a rural village with ready access to the city – as generations of
radicals and dissenters had discovered. It was Enfield's iconoclastic history
that attracted Ryland and suited the ethos of his school: here, in 1605, Guy
Fawkes hid in a safe house while planning the Gunpowder Plot; forty years
later, Enfield was with Parliament during the Civil War. George Fox, founder
of the Quakers, visited. To cries of 'Wilkes and Liberty!' the flamboyant journalist John Wilkes was twice returned for Enfield and as many times expelled
from the House before a third win, in 1774, secured him the seat for sixteen
years. When the radical Sir Francis Burdett won a fiercely contested hustings
in 1802, his jubilant supporters demolished three hundred bottles of wine and
the Assembly Room – a recent memory when Keats arrived at the school.[7] A
similar hullabaloo greeted Michael Portillo's defeat by Stephen Twigg in 1997.
As Michael Foot observed on that occasion, Enfield is with Runnymede and
Marston Moor in the annals of English liberty.[8]

Ryland and Clarke were thoroughly at home among the voters of Enfield
– indeed, Charles Cowden Clarke said that his father was 'independent-
minded far in advance of his time'.[9] When the French Revolution turned
violent he welcomed a French émigré, Abbé Béliard, who joined the school as

a French teacher (Keats recalled French being 'cramme'd down our Mouths, as if we were young Jack daws').[10] In the dangerous 1790s Clarke was in touch with like-minded individuals such as the brilliant scientist Joseph Priestley, the classicists Alexander Geddes and Gilbert Wakefield, and the poet George Dyer – an eccentric, stammering poet-scholar acquainted with two young firebrands, William Wordsworth and Samuel Taylor Coleridge.

Wordsworth and Coleridge were both Cambridge-educated radicals. Wordsworth, born in 1770, had first-hand experience of the French Revolution, returning to England in 1793 a committed republican; he justified the guillotining of Louis XVI, and wrote a poem of strident social protest, *Salisbury Plain*, exhorting 'Heroes of Truth' to 'uptear/Th'Oppressor's dungeon from its deepest base' (541–2). Two years younger than Wordsworth, Coleridge emerged from university as a Unitarian dissenter. He quickly established himself at Bristol as a charismatic lecturer and poet, convinced that progress in politics, science and religion would bring about a 'blest future' at the millennium. Both were acquainted with John Thelwall, William Godwin and other reformers and freethinkers. As their idealistic hopes were blighted by years of violence and war, Wordsworth and Coleridge were drawn to poetic experiments that might provoke more durable revolutions of thought and feeling. The result was an extraordinary volume of poems mingling traditional forms with experimental techniques: *Lyrical Ballads* (1798).

'The fact is', Cowden Clarke recalled, 'Coleridge had been a Jacobin, and was one of the marked men in the early part of the French Revolution.'[11] He knew of Coleridge's short, misguided career 'as a private in a regiment'. Dyer was an obvious source of information in Enfield, but word of Coleridge could have come from anyone in the dissenting community. Over at Chase Side Chapel was the Baptist minister William Thomas, a tutor long associated with Ryland and Clarke. Major John Cartwright – a veteran reformer from the 1770s and '80s – also made his home at Enfield, as did Holt White, nephew of the great naturalist Gilbert White of Selborne. For all of them, Enfield offered a liberal, tolerant environment hospitable to new ideas and vigorous debate. Talk of English liberties and the natural world filled the schoolhouse, especially in the summer of 1803 when the common land at Enfield was enclosed.

Near to the school on Baker Street lived a young lawyer, J.W. Marriott, who in October 1803 invited Leigh Hunt to his home. Eighteen years old and already a rising man of letters, Hunt had, like Coleridge, attended Christ's Hospital but did not follow him to Cambridge. Publication of his early poems, *Juvenilia*, in 1800 caused a sensation in London literary circles; the book quickly went to four editions, and launched his career like a skyrocket. By day,

Hunt worked at the War Office with another young clerk, John Scott; by night, he did battle in the pit at the Theatre Royal, Drury Lane. When his brother John founded *The News* in 1805, Hunt contributed weekly theatrical reviews; gathered together as *Critical Essays on the Performers of the London Theatres*, they made a genuinely pioneering book that invented modern theatre criticism and had far-reaching influence on Keats's ideas of stagecraft. Marriott also contributed to *The News*, and in 1808 launched his own West Country weekly, *The Taunton Courier*, modelled on the Hunts' new journal, *The Examiner*, with its watchword of 'independence'. Outside the War Office, John Scott also had an impact as editor of John Hunt's newspaper *The Statesman* and, later, of *The Champion* in which Keats's poems and reviews were published.[12] In 1803 all of this lay ahead, but already we can see how Enfield was nurturing an extraordinary generation of poets, journalists and critics.

While Keats and his brother George got to know the school, surveyors were busily reshaping the landscape in the name of 'improvement', which meant much more than fencing in common land. Centuries of traditions patterned on time-honoured boundaries, seasons, saints' days, folklore, fairs and festivals were to be swept away. Further afield the war with France was resumed after the Peace of Amiens, reviving fears of invasion and a global war with Napoleon. Keats had missed the exhilaration of 1789, and grew up in an age of profound local, national and international upheavals. No wonder, then, that his imagination was excited by spectacular struggles, whether in a prize-fight or pitched battle, and was also acutely sensitive to the subtler rhythms and transitions of a natural world that his own eyes told him was vulnerable and vanishing: a gnat's dance, minnows darting, swallows gathering. Arising from nature with a promise of continuity or return, such patterns informed Keats's idea that poetry should come 'as naturally as the Leaves to a tree', while the run-on couplets of his early verse evoked an idyllic 'stream of rhyme' that flowed as blithely as the brooks of Enfield before they were dug into ditches.

School began at seven in the morning and meals were taken at schoolroom tables. Sundays may have seen boys sidle across Market Square to St Andrews, although in religious matters open minds were encouraged. At first Keats took scant notice of school rules – one schoolfellow who recalled his tricks and pranks was surprised that he managed to get through.[13] As the years passed, however, Clarke's regime gradually had a steadying effect on him; instead of the floggings Coleridge and Hunt endured at Christ's Hospital, Enfield boys were encouraged to keep records of their own behaviour and take a lead with 'voluntary' translations from French and Latin. Prizes were awarded at the winter and summer vacations. Unlike the traditional curriculum at Harrow, teaching at Enfield was practical, up to date and ranged through astronomy, botany, the classics, French, gardening, history, mathematics, mechanics and optics. Pupils tended their own garden plots, and on summer evenings 'assiduous boys' were allowed to water the strawberries.

Ryland was acquainted with the famous astronomer William Herschel, discoverer of the 'new planet' *Georgium Sidus* (that is, the 'Georgian Star', Uranus), and taught astronomy as part of a game. In the playground his pupils made a living orrery, with each one of them moving as a planet in orbit around a fellow student standing still as the Sun. Every boy carried a card with information to be learned: 'I represent the grand Georgium Sidus, discovered by Dr. Herschel . . . Above 4,000 times as big as the Earth, I move round the Sun in about 83 years.'[14] Ryland calculated that half an hour at this play would kindle 'sparks of genius' in later life, and with Keats he was right. Two of his most famous lines –

Then felt I like some watcher of the skies
When a new planet swims into his ken
　　　('On First Looking into Chapman's
　　　　　　　Homer', 9–10)

– may recall his excitement at seeing a planet's bright disc through the school telescope. Like the locality of Craven Street, Enfield playground was crucial to the formation of Keats's genius. Here the poet of *Endymion* and *Hyperion* could actually become the moon, or the sun or a planet; he could hurtle across space like a comet, or feel himself a bright star, steadfast while the universe moved round him.

In his first years at school Keats gave no signs of intellectual character beyond demonstrating that when he made up his mind to do something he saw it through with a prize-fighter's determination. In pugilists' slang, 'it's dogged as does it'. Outside classes he fought in the schoolyard, played cricket, swam in the pond and ventured to the mysterious 'Moat'.[15] Now eight, he spent Christmas of 1803 with the family at Keates's Livery Stables, returning to school in January – a month of gales and rain that saw the death of his great-uncle Charles Sweetingburgh.[16] In March, Midgley John Jennings married Margaret Peacock, daughter of a clergyman at Huntingdon.

On Saturday, 14 April, John and George were cheered by their father's arrival on one of his fine horses. Perhaps it was after this visit, up in the dormitory at bedtime, that Keats listened to the Clarkes enjoying a musical evening downstairs and, just as audible, a sudden silence as the hall door shut.

'Your father is dead'. The two boys had been summoned to Mr Clarke's room and given the news. How this took hold of Keats's imagination emerged only gradually; after the first shock he almost certainly felt a sense of childish guilt – if his father hadn't visited, he would be alive now. Later, the numerous valedictions, farewells and adieus in his poems and letters may touch upon their last parting, especially when connected with a word that Keats always uses with extraordinary power, 'gone'. When time passed, the knowledge of his father's death combined with earlier and later misfortunes to 'render every event suspicious'.[17] As events unfolded, he had good reason to suspect that all was not as it should have been.

The funeral was at St Stephen's, Coleman Street on Monday, 23 April, a day traditionally held to be Shakespeare's birthday. With his mother and brothers, and old John and Alice Jennings, Keats followed his father's coffin through the arched gate to the graveyard, peering up at the 'Doom' with its grisly skull and crossbones. As we shall see, when Keats celebrated Shakespeare memories of his father were often awakened, while successive anniversaries of his father's death and funeral summoned Shakespeare to brace and temper his poetry.

Thomas Keates was well known in London and beyond, and his death was reported in *The Times, The Ipswich Journal* and the *Gentleman's Magazine*.[18] At twenty-nine, Frances was now a widow with four young children to care for and Keates's Livery Stables to run. Immediately after the funeral she seems to have vanished while an Elizabeth Keats – presumably one of Thomas's relatives – attended to the business.[19] A temporary arrangement was made for Tom (four) and little Frances (Fanny, now aged ten months) to stay with their grandparents at Ponders End, but we hear nothing of their mother until Wednesday, 20 June, when John Jennings transferred to her the remaining nine months of his lease.[20] In view of what followed, Jennings had obviously acted without knowing what his daughter planned to do next.

On Wednesday, 27 June she married William Rawlings at St George's, Hanover Square without family present – exactly the circumstances of her first marriage ten years earlier, except that this time it was her husband who was under age. So it was that the business at Keates's Livery Stables, steadily built up over thirty years, passed in seven days to William Rawlings – a blow that influenced John Jennings's subsequent actions and hastened his death. If Keats returned at midsummer to what was now effectively Rawlings's Livery Stables, he would have found his mother living with and married to a stranger in the home that had been his father's just two short months before. More likely he went instead with George to their grandparents at Scotland Green, and what had been a temporary arrangement for the two youngest children became permanent. As Keats's sister, Fanny, recalled at the end of her life:

'Upon my Mother's second marriage my Brothers and myself went to live with my Grandmother Mrs Jennings.' And again, thinking of her mother and stepfather: 'My Brothers and myself never lived with them.'[21]

Who was this shadowy figure, William Rawlings, who had taken Thomas Keates's place? Fanny Keats recalled a young man 'not too flush of cash' and with 'no property whatever'.[22] Abbey said that he was a clerk at Smith, Payne and Smith's bank near the Mansion House, and that in time he stood to earn as much as £700 a year. Little else is known except that he had a sister.[23] Perhaps he was the son of William and Eve Rawlings of Crooked Lane, born 16 May 1784 and apprenticed to his father, a tea-dealer and grocer in Gracechurch Street. William Snr was bankrupted in 1801, when Smith, Payne and Smith's records show William Rawlings joined the firm on an annual salary of £70 plus a living allowance of £40 – a good income for a young man.[24] With annual increments of £5 and a chance of becoming a confidential clerk on £700 a year – the figure noted by Abbey – Rawlings had prospects, just as Thomas Keates had had. Suddenly all that changed, however. Having married Frances, he gave the bank three months' notice and drew his last salary payment on 30 September 1804. Aged twenty, with no income of his own and no experience as a victualler or an ostler, he would try to make a go of the stabling business.

The Jenningses 'disapproved of the marriage', and although Frances seems to have hoped to benefit her family the effect of these awful months on her eldest son would be lifelong and damaging.[25] At first he probably felt wounded and rejected, his whole world overturned – who was that man in his father's place? Signs of disturbance had been evident in Keats from an early age. Haydon heard that at five years he had seized a naked sword to prevent his mother going out and 'threatened her so furiously that she burst into tears'.[26] He was 'a most violent and ungovernable child', and this early possessiveness coupled with the experience of being abandoned by his mother left him primed with insecurities.

Frances went on in the same impetuous manner. Seven days after her remarriage, the front page of *The Times* for Wednesday, 4 July 1804 carried this advertisement:

ALL Persons, to whom the late THOMAS KEATS of the Swan and Hoop Moorgate, Stable Keeper, stands indebted, are desired to send the same to Frances Keats, widow and Executrix, that they may be settled, and all persons who have not settled their accounts, are desired to do it immediately, or they will be sued without further Notice. FRANCES KEATS begs leave to return her thanks to her friends, who favoured her late Husband with their custom, informs them she means to continue the business for the benefit of herself and infant family.[27]

Well intentioned but ill advised, Frances mistakenly described herself as an 'Executrix' when her husband had left no will. While it was routine for executors to place such advertisements, the tenor of Frances's invitation to pay up or be sued was not calculated to influence or win over. In the event no legal action ensued, and it was the spring of 1805 before Frances was able to extract almost £2,000 – a considerable sum – from her first husband's estate. What she did with that money is not clear. Her immediate efforts with the livery stables were fruitless, and the Innholders' records show that Rawlings's arrival provoked a rapid turnover of staff.[28] With the lease due to expire at Lady Day, 25 March 1806, events were gathering to a crisis at which Frances's readiness to go to law would bring disaster.

John and George returned to Enfield in September 1804 for the first half of the school year. From now on they stuck together, 'loved, jangled, and fought alternately'.[29] With his 'brisk, winning face', Keats combined personal beauty with extremes of laughter and tears; as passionate and unpredictable as his mother, he was just as likely to get up and go on a whim. In *Sleep and Poetry* there is a bright image of 'A laughing school-boy, without grief or care, / Riding the springy branches of an elm' (94–5). This could have been Keats himself in gleeful mood, surmounting the ups and downs of life with a resilience of spirit that helped keep darker moods in check. Physically he resembled his father, being compact and muscular with fine brown hair and dark hazel eyes.[30] While his character and presence attracted, his esteem could only be won through combat – as fellow pupil Edward Holmes discovered. He would 'fight any one – morning, noon, or night'. At thirteen, he answered a slight by squaring at the assistant master; later he took on a butcher and with a prize-fighter's tenacity landed blows that 'told' until his opponent had to be led home.[31]

Anyone might have fancied he would become great, Holmes recalled, albeit in a military rather than literary capacity.[32] There was a military tradition in the Jennings family. As noted before, the great naval officer Sir John Jennings may have been a distant relative; Midgley John had served at Camperdown; and his grandson would be on the North-West Frontier, retiring in 1906 as General Sir Richard Melville Jennings. As he approached his tenth birthday the prospect of a military career would have delighted Keats – his uncle's heroism was a source of pride, and a measure of what he might himself achieve.

At Christmas 1804, Frances struggled on at the livery stables while her children went to Scotland Green. John Jennings, seventy-four, was now ailing and under the care of a local doctor, Thomas Hammond of Church Street, Edmonton. Feeling his strength fading, on Friday, 1 February 1805 he drew up his will with the assistance of a land surveyor, Joseph Pearson, rather than his lawyer – evidently he had dropped contact with business associates who might have advised on his estate. Just two days after Jennings signed his will, Midgley John's wife gave birth to a little girl, Margaret Alice.

Jennings's will listed his beneficiaries according to the amount of capital needed to provide their legacies. Stocks and annuities amounting to nearly £12,000, plus interest from debts, rents and a mortgage, were divided up so as to leave Alice capital of £6,600, yielding an income of £200 per year. She was also left the household furniture. Investments worth £2,900 went to Midgley John 'for his use during his natural life'; if he died 'without Issue', £500 of this capital was to go to his widow and the rest 'to return to my family'. Frances was left capital for a £50 annuity, to pass at her death to the four Keats children as a supplement to the £1,000 cash plus interest that was to be divided among them 'as they become of Age'.[33] The sum of £5 a year was left to his widowed sister, Mary Sweetingburgh, and there were lesser bequests for relatives and friends.[34] In short, half of John Jennings's estate went to his wife, about a quarter to his son and the balance to provide smaller legacies. His executors were named as Alice Jennings, Midgley John Jennings and Charles Danvers, an ironmonger in Upper Thames Street.[35]

Jennings's intentions are clear. His aim was to benefit his immediate family and ensure his estate would not be squandered at the Swan and Hoop or pass to any family Frances and Rawlings might have. Although the will was vague about the long-term disposal of capital, it was carefully framed to address the present situation. He died on Friday, 8 March 1805 and his funeral followed at St Stephen's, Coleman Street on the 14th. When John Jennings was lowered into the family vault, the lease on the Swan and Hoop had just eleven days to run. And for those eleven days, his three executors did nothing.

While Frances waited impatiently for news, Alice was at Scotland Green and Midgley John sixty-five miles away at Huntingdon. Charles Danvers had been involved in a protracted Chancery case in 1786, and was reluctant to be drawn into another.[36] If he could indeed see trouble looming, his withdrawal only served to bring it on, for the execution of Jennings's estate was now left to two principal beneficiaries – his widow, Alice, and his son, Midgley John. On 25 March, when the last quarter's rent on the Swan and Hoop was due, Midgley John travelled up from Huntingdon with his wife and two-month-old daughter and proceeded to prove the will. The situation was tense, and to Frances it must have appeared that her brother had delayed in order to frustrate her efforts with the business. Midgley John and his family stayed at Scotland Green until Monday, 1 April, when he went to the Swan and Hoop. It was probably now that Frances learned the contents of the will. Her

£50 annuity was by no means a trifling sum, although it was half of Rawlings's final salary at the bank and only just sufficient to clear a year's rent for the livery stable.[37] Compared to her mother and brother, Frances was only a nominal beneficiary, and Rawlings responded by presenting her brother with a bill for £41.4s.9d. owed by John Jennings.[38]

A battle was brewing, and as ambiguities in John Jennings's will became evident his beneficiaries started to manoeuvre for advantage. At issue was an invested fortune of some £9,500. Did Alice Jennings own her capital outright, or for her lifetime only? How was it to be disposed after her death? What was to be the ultimate destination of capital willed to Midgley John? The clause, 'if he should die without Issue', meant that evidence of his baby daughter's existence would strengthen his claim on his capital, and on 3 April little Margaret Alice was baptised at St Andrew's, Enfield, a few yards from her cousins' school. Perhaps the boys attended with their grandmother, at what appeared to be a happy family gathering. Having seen to this, Midgley John paid Rawlings's bill without demur.[39]

Vexed at their comparatively modest annuity, Frances and Rawlings sought an interview with the executors but were rebuffed. Next, they visited Girdlers' Hall in Basinghall Street and consulted a lawyer, William Walton, who briefed as counsel a Chancery barrister, James Trower. It was Trower who drew up and issued the Rawlingses' 'Bill of Complaint' against the executors: that this happened on a Saturday, 6 April, suggests the plaintiffs were in a hurry, with no time to reflect on the notorious delays and procrastinations of Chancery, a court 'where doubt / Leads many in; whence few, or none, get out'.[40]

The 'Complaint' alleged that Jennings's executors had 'combined' to conceal information, 'possessed' stocks, funds and securities not mentioned in his will, and withheld Frances's annuity of £50 (it was typical of Frances that she expected immediate payment). These gripes were preliminaries to the Rawlingses' grand grievance: Alice had insisted that she was 'intitled absolutely' to her capital, while Midgley John was said to 'alledge and insist' that 'in case he should die *leaving issue* he or his said issue will be *intitled absolutely thereto*' (my emphasis). Against her mother and brother Frances and her husband claimed a third share of the capital that produced her mother's annuity, a half-share of her brother's capital after his death, plus the annuity of £50 and any undisposed funds. They now sought to place the will before 'a Court of Equity'.

Midgley John responded immediately, agreeing that the will was as described and submitting disposal of his own capital to the court. He also asserted that his mother was not entitled outright to her capital, and cannily put in his own bid for a share in it after her death while denying that Frances had a similar right to do so. His only concession was to allow that his sister 'may be entitled' to a £50 annuity. Alice next entered the fray, claiming 'absolute' entitlement to her capital 'for her own use and disposal'. Just two months after John Jennings's death, his executors and beneficiaries were at war.[41]

The case was heard on 8 May, a wet Wednesday. A detailed account of Jennings's estate was ordered, and executor Midgley John required to provide it (he had been a purser in the navy, and his records provide almost the only biographical information for this period). Meanwhile, all invested stock in the estate was to be transferred to the accountant general, leaving Midgley John responsible for any unwilled cash. It was now a year since Frances had remarried, and her haste in going to law had trapped all of them in the interminable processes of Chancery. There would be plenty of time for passions to cool.

Midgley John's accounts for 1805 list income from investments and mortgages, rents, debts due, and outgoings for probate, brandy and wine, and costs for putting servants into mourning. The largest outstanding debt was a mortgage of £1,200 held by 'representatives of Hammond deceased', possibly a relative of physician Thomas Hammond, who received £11.17s. 6d. for attending at the deathbed. Rent, poor rates and property tax for Alice's house were paid promptly, as was her servant's wage. She also received £100 in cash on 8 September to meet her expenses in raising the Keats children and to pay the boys' school fees. Frances's half-year annuity of £25, due on 8 September, was 'retained': instead of gaining what she thought rightfully hers, Chancery ensured that she received nothing.[42] Meanwhile Alexander Popham, master of the court, placed an advertisement in the *Morning Chronicle* inviting any 'next of Kin of John Jennings' or their representatives to come forward for possible 'benefit'.[43] As the year wore on into foggy November, Frances's marriage to Rawlings became most unhappy.[44]

So began the legal proceedings that tied up the Jennings estate, leaving Keats with intractable anxieties about money as well as an air of one who had great expectations – such, at least, was Shelley's impression.[45] The rift between the Keats and Jennings families would never be repaired, and as late as the 1880s Fanny Keats, aged eighty-three, was still trying to discover what had happened to their money in Chancery.[46]

While the adults wrangled John, George and Tom were at school, hearing little or nothing of the disputes tearing the family apart. What Keats did know was that his mother now lived with Rawlings, and that his own life was divided between school terms at Enfield and holidays at Scotland Green, where he passed the summer vacation of 1805. It has been assumed that Alice moved to Edmonton this summer, but the land tax register shows 'Jennings' at the Scotland Green property throughout 1805–6.[47] Now aged nine, from

his grandmother's house Keats could venture along the banks of the River Lea
or across meadows to the moated gatehouse at Durance – a remnant of the
mansion where Robert and Mary Wroth had entertained. The absence of their
mother must have been as painful as it was puzzling and, left in the care of
their grandmother, the children clung together as wider family receded. In
later life Fanny said that she did not know her relations; George believed that
they had none at all.

These movements of gathered embrace and energetic stepping-out would be
repeated in Keats's later life, when he alternated between months with his
brothers in London or Hampstead and forays to distant regions. They amount to
strategies of deflection, by which Keats contrived to keep tomorrow his own.
While in London, he imagined being elsewhere; in far-flung parts, his thoughts
turned to town. Obliged in February 1818 to leave for Devon to care for Tom, he
planned a visit to childhood scenes and familiar faces.[48] In far-flung Scotland
later that year he scribbled for his sister a lyric about a 'naughty boy' who had
lived with his 'granny good'. Beginning after the break-up of the family, these
restlessly alternating movements – physical and imaginative – were a way of
ensuring that nothing was irretrievably lost, that there might be, somewhere, a
place or point of equilibrium. Not surprisingly, perhaps, the formal combina-
tions of his poems show a similar tendency, drawn into the sonnet's compact
room while simultaneously attracted to a more expansive stage in the romances,
*Endymion* and *Hyperion*. In many ways the carefully plotted turns and returns of
his 1819 odes represent his most successful assimilation of the contraries that
shaped his life day by day, year by year, gathering with the swallows in 'To
Autumn' for an imminent departure eternally postponed.

After summer had passed, two-year-old Fanny stayed with her grandmother, and her brothers returned to school. Now in his third year, among
Keats's friends were Edward Holmes, Edward Cowper and the schoolmaster's
son, Charles Cowden Clarke. All three boys were extraordinary. With sparkling eyes and masses of curly brown hair, Holmes looked like a young Apollo,
already lit up by literature and music, and ready to shine as Mozart's biographer. Holmes stayed in touch with Keats after leaving school, when they
moved in the same circle of poets, painters and musicians. Where Holmes was
ardent and susceptible, always in love, Cowper had a bright, vigilant manner
and ideas and schemes as profuse as his talk was fluent. He would invent
a mechanical printing press, and had already constructed an ingenious
windmill to spin silk from silkworms he kept at school. Adapting Cowper's
mechanism to the purposes of poetry, Keats was particular in describing how
'the silkworm makes silk from Mulbery leaves'; to evoke the 'soft numbers' of
spoken verse he thought of 'silken ties, that may never be broken'.[49]

At seventeen, Cowden Clarke was eight years older than Keats, an assistant teacher whose jovial presence was felt throughout the school. Bulky and enthusiastic, with a laugh that Hunt likened to 'ten rusty iron gates scraping along gravel', he was a born teacher who became a friend, encourager and confidant.[50] As commanding in the schoolroom as on a cricket pitch, he shared his love of literature by pointing out 'the general beauty of the composition' as well as select 'passionate passages' – a technique that he later adapted in the many books he published during his long life. Keats recalled him reading so as to emphasise the formal qualities of sonnets, odes and epigrams, and how he reached for the skies in describing epic as 'Round, vast, and spanning all like Saturn's ring'.[51] If Mrs Siddons, John Kemble or Edmund Kean were performing in London, star-struck Cowden Clarke would set off to walk twelve miles to see them, returning to Enfield by moonlight. An accomplished pianist, he admired Mozart, Arne and Handel, and taught Edward Holmes the rudiments of music; his pupil's first book would be A Ramble among the Musicians of Germany (1828). Cowden Clarke's influence on Keats was decisive too. Encouraged to read Tasso, Spenser and Chapman's Homer, Keats 'ramped' through whole volumes as if dashing across the meadows.[52] It was Cowden Clarke who did most to nurture Keats's earliest poems and in later years, as a successful lecturer and man of letters, his Recollections of Writers offered heartfelt glimpses of Keats's life at school.

October 1805 brought Keats's tenth birthday and, one week later, word of Nelson's victory and death at Trafalgar.[53] Keats's lifelong interest in Nelson sprang from this moment, aligning the great admiral with his heroic uncle Midgley John who, by chance, witnessed the return of Nelson's body for his state funeral in London. On 23 December he was at his post in Chatham dockyard when Nelson's coffin was taken from his battle-scarred flagship, HMS Victory, and ferried up river to lie in state at Greenwich. Five days later Midgley John went into battle again himself, and submitted his accounts of the Jennings estate to Chancery.[54]

After Trafalgar, Napoleon retaliated by crushing the Austrians and Russians at Austerlitz, an astonishing reversal that hastened Prime Minister Pitt's death in January 1806. A 'Ministry of All the Talents', led by William Wyndham, Charles James Fox and Henry Addington, combined to fill the gap. Hopes of parliamentary reform, the abolition of slavery and Catholic emancipation revived until 13 September, when Fox suddenly died. Wordsworth marked his passing in a magnificent poem, 'Loud is the Vale'; in London, John Hunt kept Fox's reformist campaign alive in The News and congratulated his brother Leigh on his increased interest in public life. Within a year the Hunt brothers announced a new, independent newspaper on politics and the fine arts.

Publication of the first number of *The Examiner* followed on 3 January 1808 and John Clarke, impressed by Leigh Hunt's 'liberty-loving, liberty-advo-cating, liberty-eloquent articles', immediately subscribed.[55] From now on, every Sunday brought a copy of *The Examiner* to Clarke's Academy.

Hunt announced that *The Examiner*'s independent stance would reflect his theatrical columns, that his passion to reform the stage would now extend to performances in the House of Commons. At a time when actors concentrated on 'external habits' of character, Hunt called for a passionate delineation of inner feeling and 'action of the mind', in both of which the great tragedian Sarah Siddons excelled: 'If Mr. Kemble studiously meditates a step or an atti-tude in the midst of passion, Mrs. Siddons never thinks about either and therefore is always natural, because on occasions of great feeling it is the passion should influence the actions.'[56] Siddons seemed able to abandon her own personality, to inhabit another's. While Hazlitt was formulating a theory of disinterested imagination in his 1805 *Essay on the Principles of Human Action*, Hunt was already actively recommending and applying ideas of dramatic conception and the actor's 'passive capacity' in his theatrical reviews for *The News*.[57] Hazlitt has always been brought forward as the critic who stimulated Keats's ideas of 'negative capability' and 'the poetical Character that has no self', but Hazlitt's influence was delayed until 1817, when he published *Characters of Shakespeare's Plays*. When Keats read that book, he would have been aware that Hazlitt was consolidating ideas of sympathetic imagination expounded ten years earlier by Hunt in *The News, The Examiner* and *Critical Essays on the Performers of the London Theatres* to all of which Keats had access at Enfield.

By late March 1806, Frances and Rawlings had left the Swan and Hoop.[58] If they were still together their circumstances must have been straitened, for Frances's modest resources were still locked up in Chancery while the legal costs were accumulating. According to Abbey, she was already addicted to brandy and, with the Chancery case she had initiated against her mother and brother undecided, she could hardly expect a welcome at Scotland Green.

May brought a second hearing in Chancery. Trower had briefed as senior counsel the new solicitor-general, Sir Samuel Romilly, who could be expected to carry weight but would be expensive. Less celebrated lawyers acted for Midgley John and Alice, and on this occasion they proved a match for Romilly. Judgment followed on 29 July: Alice was granted outright ownership of her capital; Midgley John was entitled to his capital for life, with the option for others to apply for a share after his death. Unwilled cash went to the two remaining executors. It would be two more years before Alice and Midgley John actually received their portions of capital, and while stock was to be set aside to provide for Frances's annuity no date was fixed for this. Provision was made to calculate interest on the Keats children's £1,000, and some £230 was earmarked to cover legal costs.[59] For Frances, the judgment was a catastrophe. Two years after her marriage to Rawlings, their legal claim had entirely collapsed. If their parting was not already irrevocable, this was the moment when it became so.

With the judgment in her favour, at midsummer 1806 Alice moved to a large end-terrace house at Church Street, Edmonton, a few yards from Dr Hammond's. Her three grandsons left school at Enfield and walked a couple of miles across the fields to Edmonton, where they joined their sister for the summer holiday. Alice's new home backed onto open fields where Salmons Brook meandered down to form the pool on Edmonton Green – the 'wash' through which Cowper's John Gilpin splashed. To the west along the street was the parish church, Dr Hammond's house and the cottage where Charles Lamb would pass his last months in 1834. A stone's throw across Salmons Brook to the east was the Cross Keys Inn, and the main coach road from London to the north.

Such was the terrain that Keats would range over during school holidays, and he revelled in it. At home the brothers vied with each other to entertain their three-year-old sister, and many years later Keats would recall her standing at the front door to watch coaches go by.[60] In summer the landscape opened up to them, with fields and lanes to explore and brooks to paddle in. Keats would write to his sister of 'how fond I used to be of Goldfinches, Tomtits, Minnows, Mice, Ticklebacks, Dace, Cock salmons and all the whole tribe of the Bushes and the Brooks' – and his love of wild animals accumulated a rich store for his poetry.[61] 'I stood tip-toe' includes precisely caught details dating from this time, such as the minnows

> Staying their wavy bodies 'gainst the streams
> To taste the luxury of sunny beams
> Temper'd with coolness . . .
> If you but scantily hold out the hand,
> That very instant not one will remain;
> But turn your eye, and they are there again.
> 
> (73–5, 78–80)

Then there are goldfinches, glimpsed as they

>                                   drop
> From low hung branches; little space they stop;

But sip, and twitter, and their feathers sleek;
Then off at once, as in a wanton freak:
Or perhaps, to show their black, and golden wings,
Pausing upon their yellow flutterings.

(87–92)

Here is nature close up, as spied by a ten-year-old. We catch Keats's delight in 'sip', 'twitter' and 'sleek', and something much more unusual as well. He is fascinated by nature's freaks and darts, and also by what happens when those impulsive movements meet resistance, a counter-force like the minnows 'Staying their wavy bodies 'gainst the streams' or a laughing schoolboy 'riding the springy branches of an elm'. From such childhood moments – exhilaratingly in touch with the feel of life, pushing against the force of circumstance – sprang poems that often seem at one with the vital permissions and resistances of life. By staying the onward pulse of verse against momentary pauses, for example, Keats's rhymes allow us to take in the mouth-filling vowels of 'taste . . . sunny beams' before turning to savour 'coolness', as if we, too, are tinglingly alive in the mid-stream of sensation. Such moments fore-shadowed Keats's idea of the selfless 'poetical Character' he recognised in himself and Shakespeare, taking as much delight in shade as light, in Iago as Imogen, as the little boy had done in fluttering black and gold, in sunny beams and coolness.

He foraged under hedgerows, across fields, along a dusty lane by a brick-field, laying up a store of sights, sounds and sensations for the future: glistening slug trails, exquisite snail shells, hedge crickets singing, gnats dancing, a pigeon's swoop and tumble, a smashed frog's head and nettle leaves to hide in his brothers' beds. Years afterwards he re-created his Edmonton self in a high-spirited poem for his sister – 'There was a naughty boy' – to which we shall return in Chapter Sixteen.[62]

Keats's summer-morning get-up-and-go was a wakening of the spirit of freedom and adventure that would animate his reading and poetry – and he would bring to those imaginative challenges all of the by-hook-or-by-crook determination that drove him out to sunlit Salmons Brook. Sketching his boyhood for Fanny in brisk short strokes, he links his passion for poetry with his childish rhyme game – both were a way of resisting, contradicting and asserting his independence. '[N]othing would he do / But scribble poetry,' he tells Fanny, and his decision to get his living as a poet was made with the rebellious free spirit of the boy who 'ran . . . / And wrote' because he 'would not stop at home'.[63] When Keats travelled more widely his forays around England often accompanied an impulse to 'venture' into rhyme, continuing the quest for restless self-creation that originated around the age of ten. Even Keats's formal modes of narrative excursion and lyrical introspection, of visionary departure and forlorn return, are akin to boyish venturings and comings home.[64] In time the dauntless spirit of the Keats children would disperse them all – John to Rome, George across the Atlantic to Kentucky, and Fanny to long decades at her married home in Madrid.

And what of Frances, who had broken up her family and left her children to find their own ways? After the judgment of 29 July, her whereabouts are unknown. Her second marriage had failed, she was without money, probably an alcoholic. Abbey claimed that after the break with Rawlings she was 'living *as* the Wife of a Jew at Enfield, named Abraham'.[65] There were a few Jewish residents at Enfield – the D'Israelis had lived there – but none of them fit Abbey's description. Perhaps the person intended was Abraham Wilkinson. Unmarried, and not Jewish, Wilkinson was a wealthy doctor with an imposing house on the Chase Side of Enfield, and there is evidence that he housed distressed women on his estate.[66] It is possible that Wilkinson offered Frances somewhere to live until her annuities were paid; if she was at Enfield her situation can hardly have gone unnoticed at Clarke's Academy, encouraging Keats's protectiveness towards her. Only later did the damage caused by his mother come fully home to him, obliterating the idealised image of women he had cherished as a schoolboy and leaving him vexed and suspicious in female company.[67]

# CHAPTER 3

## Bridge

IDGLEY JOHN Jennings had vexations too. In the ten years since Camperdown he had served dutifully on the home front. The father of three children, he was embroiled with Chancery accounts and the demands of his post at Chatham. What battle and burns failed to do would now be wrought by stress and overwork. Late in 1807 he fell ill and went home to Huntingdon on four months' sick leave. It did him little good. March and April brought sleet and snow, and when he petitioned for a further month's leave his physician noted that his cough was accompanied by a 'discharge of Blood' that 'reduced him very much'.[1] The symptoms of consumption were unmistakable. In July he was promoted captain, and in August received his capital from Chancery. News from the Continent was heartening: Sir Arthur Wellesley had defeated the French at Vimieiro. But for Midgley John all of this came too late. There would be no reconciliation with his sister, and the hot summer of 1808 that his physician hoped would restore him allowed no recovery. He died on 21 November, aged just thirty-one.

His widow, Margaret, was left with three children – Margaret Alice, Midgley John and Mary Ann – a fourth about to be born, and the bitter Chancery legacy. By the judgment reached in 1806 her husband's capital – it had been his for just three months – must now be returned to the court where others might claim upon it. Frances attempted to do so early in 1809, but it was the half-hearted effort of a woman now seriously ill.[2] With the equity that the courts failed to deliver, life had apportioned equal misfortune to the Keats children, their Jennings cousins and their mothers. Margaret's son William was born in February 1809 and, like little Edward Keats, did not thrive.

At Edmonton and Enfield the yearly routine of terms and holidays continued, with frequent visits to and fro along the footpath. Frances was five in 1808, old enough to visit John, George and Tom at school. Long afterwards she remembered happy hours with her brothers and the Clarkes – 'a very young child,' Cowden Clarke said, 'walking round the grass-plot in our garden ... with her brothers; and my mother saying, "That is a very sweetly behaved child!"'[3] Those summer hours passed, and with the death of his uncle in November, Keats lost the hero he might have followed into a military career. That blow was deflected almost immediately, however, when his mother suddenly returned after a five-year absence. Shaken by her brother's death, weary of litigation and illness, Frances was reconciled with Alice and early in 1809 moved into her house at Edmonton. Ailing with 'a rheumatism', she was dosing herself with brandy and opium, but the simple fact of her return encouraged Keats to rise to a challenge unlike anything he had ever faced in the playground.[4] He discovered the school library.

From now on he read steadily along the library shelves as if pacing himself to go the distance. He was an orderly scholar, Cowden Clarke remembered, and read a surprising amount, including William Mavor's *Youth's Miscellany* and his *Historical Account of the Most Celebrated Voyages and Discoveries* and *Universal History*, William Robertson's epic histories of America, Scotland and Charles V, Maria Edgeworth's writings, the seventeenth-century republicans Milton and Algernon Sydney, copies of *The Examiner*, Locke, Campbell's optimistic view of the *Present State of Europe* and Bishop Burnet's *History of his Own Time*.[5] All of these books echo in Keats's poetry. 'Lines Written on 29 May' salutes the English republicans; his 'Chapman's Homer' sonnet recalls Robertson's *History of America*. Mavor's *Youth's Miscellany* depicted a diver taken by a hungry shark, a gruesome scene vividly recalled in *Isabella*. Keats's musings on history in letters and *Hyperion*, like his 'love of civil and religious liberty', grew from the independent ethos of his school and *The Examiner*.[6] In that newspaper Hunt had by now emerged as an eloquent champion of reform, denouncing the shameful Convention of Cintra which squandered the victory at Vimieiro by allowing French soldiers to withdraw and regroup.[7] By 5 November, Napoleon's armies had seized Madrid and regained control of Spain.

Three books particularly fascinated Keats: John Lemprière's *Bibliotheca Classica*, Joseph Spence's *Polymetis* and *The Pantheon* by 'Edward Baldwin' aka William Godwin.[8] These dictionaries of classical literature, history and myth were accessible, vernacular sources of information intended to 'facilitate literature', and for a thirteen-year-old schoolboy they were daringly explicit. At Christ's Hospital, Leigh Hunt had pored over *The Pantheon* because an engraving of Venus resembled his nurse's daughter; Keats looked up from the same page and 'thought a fair Woman a pure Goddess'.[9] Part of the thrill for Hunt was that such books were banned at Christ's Hospital. Lemprière was

suspect for making classical history, literature and myth available to people
who had not mastered the original languages. A standard textbook of the day,
the *Eton Latin Primer*, was written entirely in Latin: given Eton's educational
and social status, to deviate from its methods showed a daringly independent
mind. Besides literature and myth, Lemprière's book was packed with history
and politics including the doctrines of classical republicanism and democracy
that had inspired the revolutions in America and France. In these pages Keats
could read a biography of Aeneas, a plot summary of Virgil's *Aeneid*, and then
turn to the 'celebrated Roman' Caius Cassius dining after Caesar's assassination with Mark Antony 'who asked him whether he had then a dagger in his
bosom; yes, replied he, if you aspire to tyranny'.[10] To some eyes, the *Bibliotheca
Classica* was a primer for sedition like Paine's *Rights of Man*. Hunt got into
trouble for reading it – perhaps it was on this occasion that his brutal teacher,
James Boyer, flung a book that broke his tooth. Under the liberal regime at
Enfield, however, pupils were encouraged to savour Lemprière's book – and
Keats appeared to learn all of it.[11] But the risk of appearing slack and oppor-
tunistic as a result was high. When Keats celebrated George Chapman's
English rendering of Homer, even a well-intentioned critic noted that his
recourse to a translation signalled insufficient 'intellectual acquirement'.[12]
More controversially, by venturing on 'the beautiful mythology of Greece' in
loose rhyming couplets, *Endymion* flaunted his unorthodox education
and idiomatic style in a brazen attack on those 'who lord it o'er their fellow
men' (iii.1).

Keats's friend Joseph Severn lived long enough to understand how the
'modern arcadian world' Keats had created from Lemprière's dictionary
formed the groundwork of English poetry in the mid-nineteenth century. The
Pre-Raphaelites' colourful, highly marketable representations of antiquity
came from Keats, who also opened the way for vernacular reinventions of
classical myth by writers as diverse as Tennyson, Pound, Eliot, Joyce, Walcott
and Heaney.[13] By the time Tony Harrison recalled his own schoolboy reading
of Keats in his poem 'Them and [uz]', 'Cockney' Keats had himself become a
'classic' dubbed into 'r.p.'

Such were some long-term consequences of Keats's first look into Lemprière.
In spring 1809 he determined to impress his mother by winning one of the
school's half-yearly prizes, and to achieve this he devoted every hour to study.
Just as he had formerly got up early to venture into summer fields, he was now
at his books before the morning's first class. While his schoolmates wrangled
in the yard, he wrestled with Latin and French. In the evening he ate his
supper with a book in front of him. And so on the next day, and the next, until
he had to be driven out of the schoolroom to take exercise.

His efforts paid off. At midsummer he stepped out of the ring and carried off his prize: a copy of C.H. Kauffman's *Dictionary of Merchandize and Nomenclature in All Languages*. If this was an obvious award for a boy destined for a life in trade it also proved an invaluable resource for a budding poet. Inside the book's unpromising grey boards was a treasure house of language and imagery – homely, exotic, glowingly vivid and romantically strange. Page after page disgorged cargoes for realms of gold – alabaster, aloe, amber, cassia, cinnamon, coral, diamond, ebony, frankincense, honey, iron, manna, marble, porphyry, silk, silver, slate and vermilion. Keats would raid this book again and again for the rich, material textures of its language, and it was Kauffman that he had in mind when he advised Shelley to 'load every rift'.[14] While Keats idealised poetry that was 'great & unobtrusive', without 'palpable design', Kauffman and the successes of Byron and Scott had alerted him to its commercial value as a commodity that would, he calculated, enable him to gain a living.[15]

The warmth of spring and early summer, with their flowers and healthy air, brought hopes for Frances's recovery. July saw Keats's school prize, and what seemed a turning point when Chancery reported that capital would be assigned to pay annuities for Frances and John Jennings's sister Mary Sweetingburgh. With the large Hammond mortgage settled, £1,000 in cash for the Keats children could also be allocated and their mother's back annuities paid. Solicitor William Walton, now also acting for Alice Jennings, was paid £242 to cover legal costs.[16] The wellbeing of the Edmonton household now seemed assured and yet, as so often in Keats's life, a mite of good fortune was balanced with a remorseless equity that determined worse must follow. Frances's health did not improve. Lassitude and pallor were accompanied by loss of weight, chills and sweats, and a persistent cough that told them the family disease had her in its grip. Away at school, Keats did not see his mother every day and when he walked over to Edmonton his awareness of her decline was all the sharper. His memories of 1809 with spring sunshine and budding green lived on in exalted contrast to the wasted features of his mother – an inexplicable juxtaposition of nature's irrepressible vitality and lingering disease.

Beside her bed were bottles of brandy, and the opium Dr Hammond provided: during the Christmas holiday Keats would let nobody administer her medicine but himself, trusting to this and Hammond's regime of bleeding and cupping to draw off disease. He prepared her meals and read novels to her. At night he kept vigil in his grandfather's great chair, listening to the rattle of her breathing, incessant coughing and, on Christmas Eve, ice pattering against the window pane. So 1810 came in, with no respite for anyone.

In January of 1810, Keats returned uneasily to school, leaving Frances in the care of her mother and Hammond. He clung to hopes of her recovery, but to the others it was clear she could not live. A freezing spell plunged the temperature lower than minus eight degrees, and at this bleak season Chancery gave a shudder that signalled further litigation. As if deliberately seeking to avenge her husband, Midgley John's widow, Margaret, chose this moment to petition that her children Margaret Alice, Midgley John and Mary Ann were 'entitled absolutely' to the whole of his capital. A decision came unusually quickly on 13 February. What had been Midgley John's capital was to be shared equally between Alice and Margaret, giving each nearly £2,000 in stock; this was a valuable inheritance for the Jennings children, but only half of what their mother had hoped for them.

A month later, aged thirty-five, Frances died. On Tuesday, 20 March, six years after Keats had followed his father's coffin through the skull-and-crossboned gate with its image of 'Doom', he buried his mother in the Jennings family vault at St Stephen's. Who attended her funeral? There cannot have been many mourners, and certainly not her sister-in-law, Margaret Jennings. Presumably Alice, now seventy-three, attended her daughter to her grave, and perhaps she brought the three boys from school to bid their mother farewell as she lay shrouded in her coffin. What of Frances's husband, William Rawlings? Abbey said that he died soon after the separation, and in 1809 a William Rawlings aged twenty-five was indeed buried at Bunhill Fields.[17] Something Fanny Keats recalled late in life allows us to see her grieving step-father at St Stephen's: 'he did not long outlive my Mother,' Fanny says, 'whose death affected him greatly.'[18] Given that Fanny knew their marriage had been unhappy, her memory of Rawlings makes him a more sympathetic figure than just another banker who gambled and lost. And Richard Abbey? Perhaps he was in one of the pews too, husbanding his memories.

When Keats heard of his mother's death he withdrew into a nook under the master's desk, hiding from the sympathy of his fellows. In his misery at her loss it must have seemed that all of his efforts to win her back by reading and studying had availed as little as his care for her. From that despair would come his heart-rending realisation that he had 'never known any unalloy'd Happiness for many days together: the death or sickness of some one has always spoilt my hours'.[19] Between the ages of seven and fourteen he had lived through the deaths of his little brother Edward, his great-uncle Charles, his father Thomas, his Jennings grandfather, and his uncle Midgley John. His mother's death left the children in the care of their elderly grandmother, Alice, and it must have preyed on his mind that she, too, could not have long to live. As years passed he became convinced that their lives were blasted by an unlucky star whose malign influence would consume them all. As all of this wrought upon his imagination, the knowledge of his own beleaguered survival may have found a voice in the oracular wisdom of Moneta, mother of the Muses, whose shrine in *The Fall of Hyperion* is sweetened with the perfume of spring flowers and Kauffman's rich spices of cinnamon and frankincense. When Moneta pronounced in softened, maternal tones on the permanence of human suffering and 'an immortal sickness which kills not', she might also have been speaking of what Frances Keats's son had endured by outliving them all.

Frances's death had financial implications too. Held in Chancery for the Keats children was stock bought with the £1,000 cash legacy from their grandfather, plus stock more recently purchased to provide their mother's annuity. In total this amounted to a little over £3,200, so that each child could claim at age twenty-one some £800 capital plus whatever interest had by then accrued. They had only to apply to Chancery and it would be theirs. Secondly, Alice Jennings owned outright over £8,500 stock and some £270 in cash. On 30 July 1810 she acted to ensure that after her death these funds would not vanish into Chancery. All of her capital was placed in a trust for her grandchildren, and two trustees appointed as administrators. Richard Abbey we have met already; now forty-five, he was established as a tea and coffee merchant of Abbey, Cock and Co. at 4 Pancras Lane, Cheapside. John Nowland Sandell, the second trustee, was also a City man. Employed as a clerk to fur merchant John Henry Schneider of Broad Street Buildings – across Moorfields from Keates's Livery Stables – Sandell imported beaver pelts to supply hatmakers such as the Cheapside Keatses.[20] Like many prosperous merchants, both of Alice's trustees owned country houses just outside town, Sandell at Dalston and Abbey at rural Walthamstow.[21] To them, Alice assigned all of her stock and cash 'for the benefit of John Keats George Keats Thomas Keats and Frances Mary Keats', reserving only her income of £200 a year.[22] On the following day, her will divided her capital now held in trust more or less equally between her four Keats grandchildren, meaning that each stood to receive some £2,000 capital; there was an extra legacy for Fanny, including some household goods and the Jennings family Bible. Provision was made for her Jennings grandchildren too. Sandell and Abbey were duly appointed executors and guardians of the Keats children until they came of age. Although Sandell did little as an executor, he seems to have been a kindly man who was well disposed to his wards. Possibly he was an old family friend, related to the Joseph Sandall who was the Keatses' neighbour at Craven Street. At age twelve, Fanny Keats was given a good-humoured testimonial by her guardian: 'This is to certify to whom it may concern, that Frances Mary Keats,

during the time she was on a visit to Mrs. Sandell, was a very good girl. J.S.
14 Jan 1816.'[23] Four months later Sandell died aged forty-six and was buried
at St John's, Hackney. He left a fortune of £20,000.

There were, therefore, two entirely separate funds held for the Keats children: one in Chancery, and another in the trust set up by their grandmother.
By any standards, then, the Keats children were well provided for – had they
actually known what provision had been made for them. Much of their later
anxiety about money stemmed from not knowing their situation or how to go
about claiming funds due to them. There is no evidence that the trustees acted
dishonestly towards Keats and his brothers – as Abbey certainly did, in later
years, towards Fanny – and their first decision regarding Keats himself
suggests practicality and good sense: they started him on a medical career.
The one person who unquestionably knew about the Chancery funds was
solicitor William Walton, and he appears deliberately to have kept others in
the dark.[24]

Following Frances's death, Cowden Clarke may have suggested that Keats
translate some of *The Aeneid* as a distraction from grief. The idea took. Keats
was instantly fascinated by the opening line – 'Arma virumque cano', 'I sing of
arms and of the man' – and Virgil's patriotic epic of battles, voyages and exile
inspired a new and ambitious enterprise of his own. Marshalling his copies of
Lemprière, Tooke and Spence, he set about a prose translation of the complete
poem. Cowden Clarke saw him at work, aged 'under fourteen', revelling in
Virgil's evocations of storm at sea, battles rampaging along Trojan colonnades,
Dido's passion and Aeneas's venture into the underworld.[25] And yet, he
recalled, when his translation was in midstream Keats set aside admiration
and 'hazarded the opinion to me that there was feebleness in the structure of
the work'.[26] While Virgil's poem was packed with striking incidents, its total
effect seemed less assured. Perhaps Keats was thinking of how Virgil directs
Aeneas's destiny through prophecies, flashbacks and divine interventions so
that, as he said later of *Endymion*, 'the Hero . . . is led on' rather than staying
himself against circumstance to shape his own actions, his own future.[27]

Begun now, *The Aeneid* would occupy Keats after he left school until he
finished the 'latter portion' of it.[28] Clarke recognised the importance of this
translation for him: although the manuscript has disappeared there is good
reason to consider it Keats's first major literary achievement, sowing ground
to be harvested in his later encounters with the classical world. In *The Aeneid*
he discovered epic as a test of invention, the supreme achievement of a great
poet.[29] Translation – wording it for himself – gave him practical experience of
narrative possibilities, and what was involved in projecting and writing a long
poem. Above all, Keats framed his translation as a challenge, as a fight he

would have to nerve himself to win. The same combative instinct determined him to set about *Endymion* in spring 1817 as another 'trial' of his imagination, and *The Aeneid* was his model for the episodic structure of his own long poem. Virgil's account of the fiery sack of Troy with Polites 'running through the long porticos of the palace and across the empty halls' gave Keats the idea for Hyperion striding through his embattled palace, 'From stately nave to nave, from vault to vault, / Through . . . diamond-paved lustrous long arcades' (i.218–20). The grief of Dido, queen of Carthage, is noticed in his 'Imitation of Spenser', and Aeneas's visit to the underworld prefigures Endymion's subterranean venture. More generally, Virgil's epic of Rome's founding showed Keats that poetry could address themes of national and historical interest, like the momentous public events that week by week packed Hunt's *Examiner*. As he disciplined himself to long hours of translation, his ambition to achieve greatness was roused with every line. And there were more immediate, tangible rewards too.

'PRIZE MEDAL *AWARDED TO Master J. KEATS*': so read the inscription on one side of Keats's award. On the reverse was a Latin motto, '*Stadium doctrinæ arduum & difficile sit nihilominus Finis gloriosus erit*' – 'The race of scholarship may be steep and difficult, but nevertheless the End shall be glorious' – and the phrase 'AUDIVIT CLARKENEM', 'He listened to Clarke'. This medal passed to George Keats's grandson, then to Amy Lowell, and is now held by the Houghton Library at Harvard; despite that reputable provenance, its authenticity has been questioned.[30] If it is a fake, it has been executed with remarkable skill and the hallmark identifies it as sterling-standard silver from the year May 1810 to May 1811.[31] Its motto is apt for a pupil who was busily translating Virgil, and Cowden Clarke's input is acknowledged. Only Amy Lowell noticed the medal's most puzzling aspect: it was apparently awarded at a school Keats did not attend, 'Rev. William Thomas's Academy Enfield 1810'.[32] What school was this, and who was the Rev. William Thomas?

Born at Bristol in 1767, Thomas was educated at Daventry Dissenting Academy, where Joseph Priestley had studied, then served as pastor at Wellingborough, Northamptonshire. When Ryland and John Clarke relocated from Northampton to Enfield Thomas went too, and it seems likely that he was linked with the school as an assistant master from then on. It was only when the Clarkes retired to Ramsgate at midsummer 1810 that Thomas became principal teacher of what was now 'Rev. William Thomas's Academy Enfield'. Cowden Clarke stayed on as a tutor, hence the medal's 'AUDIVIT CLARKENEM'. As John and Isabella Clarke had taken a close interest in all three Keats boys, their departure from the school was an obvious moment for

John and George to have left as well. Ten-year-old Tom stayed on, his tall and slender frame already showing signs of sickliness.

While Keats's medal dates from a summer full of changes, former associations continued – a contemporary advertisement reads 'WANTED, for a Youth not quite sixteen years of age, brought up at Mr. Clark's Academy, Enfield, a SITUATION . . .'[33] Cowden Clarke remained as a teacher and contact – hence his confusion in dating Keats's departure to both 1810 *and* 1811. When Keats's Victorian biographer Richard Monckton Milnes sent a letter enquiring, 'When did he leave school?' Cowden Clarke immediately jotted '1811' alongside. When he replied formally to Milnes, however, he put 'at fourteen . . . in the summer of 1810'.[34] He admitted to a 'fatal memory' for dates but was confident that, whenever Keats had left, he was aged fourteen. Mistakenly thinking Keats was born in October 1796, Cowden Clarke's first impulse was to add fourteen years and arrive at summer 1811, yet he was troubled by a counter-memory that Keats had left at midsummer 1810 – when he was in fact aged fourteen – and offered that to Milnes. Another reason for Cowden Clarke's confusion also suggests itself. After leaving in 1810, Keats remained close to the school, so close that he received further school prizes (John Bonnycastle's *Introduction to Astronomy* in 1811, and an Ovid in 1812). As Cowden Clarke looked back, it seemed as if he had not actually left until 1811 – and quite possibly later still. With Keats living nearby at Edmonton, the two friends were in constant communication and met frequently. Clarke's timetable at the school gave him afternoons off, and Keats's new career was similarly generous in affording him free time.

The destinies of John and George lay with their guardians. George, now thirteen, was employed at Abbey's counting-house as a junior to a seventeen-year-old clerk, Cadman Hodgkinson,[35] a move that must have been supported by Alice and approved by Abbey himself. Their decision to apprentice Keats to Thomas Hammond, the Jenningses' family doctor at Edmonton, was also taken now. Cowden Clarke was clear that Keats's medical career was not his own inclination but 'had been *chosen for him*'; Joseph Severn alleged that Abbey 'forced him to it gainst his will'.[36] Much has been made of the apprenticeship as an obvious move for Keats: it would lead to a respectable job with a good income, and it would give him an opportunity to cure the disease that had killed his mother.[37] A more likely explanation, however, is that he had no option and accepted apprenticeship as a forced circumstance, a *fait accompli*. The idea of medicine doubtless had some appeal, not least, perhaps, because it allowed him to keep in touch with Cowden Clarke at Enfield. But it was certainly not a decision he made for himself.

Born in 1766, Thomas Hammond belonged to the remarkable dynasty of apothecaries and surgeons descended from John Hammond, parish surgeon at Edmonton.[38] With his two brothers, William and John, Thomas had studied at Guy's and St Thomas's and enrolled in the Royal College of Surgeons. Hammond connections at the London hospitals continued in the next generation, when William Hammond Jnr was a fellow student of Joseph Henry Green, nephew of the eminent surgeon Henry Cline. With old John Hammond's death in May 1790, Thomas and his wife, Susannah, moved into his large country house, 'Wilston', on Church Street, Edmonton – just yards from Alice Jennings's home. Here Thomas took over his father's role as village surgeon and raised six children, four of whom were close to Keats's age. Thomas (born 1791), Henry (1792), Elizabeth (1794) and Edward (1795) were village companions he had known since 1806.[39] To one side of Hammond's house was a separate brick building with a pan-tiled roof. On the ground floor was Hammond's surgery and dispensary, a wood-panelled room with a dresser where medicines were stored and prepared. Above was accommodation for his apprentices, in small rooms with little latticed windows. In many ways Hammond was an obvious choice to oversee Keats's apprenticeship, and his close links with London hospitals would be an advantage later on.

On 17 August 1810 Hammond paid two hundred guineas to bind his son Henry as an apprentice to a London surgeon, and shortly afterwards charged exactly this sum for Keats's five-year apprenticeship. It would cover his board and pupillage, 'Meat, Drink and Lodging . . . and, in case of sickness, proper physik and other necessaries'. Keats would have to promise not to haunt taverns, inns and alehouses and to refrain from gambling.[40] Confident that this was the right move, Abbey and Sandell sold £310 stock from the trust fund to pay the premium.

How did Keats view this new direction in his life? He was on familiar ground and close to friends at Enfield, and yet this in itself may have seemed constricting to a fourteen-year-old in the ferment of adolescence – character undecided, uncertain about his way in life, unable to focus his ambitions. So Keats himself described this 'space of life between' in his 'Preface' to *Endymion* – very likely, I think, recalling the period of his own life that now ensued. That he embarked on apprenticeship while also determined to complete his *Aeneid* translation suggests a division of purpose that was perhaps not yet as evident to him as it soon would be.[41] His mother's death was still searingly recent, and it would be understandable if he was resentful of Hammond – the physician who had failed her. All of these factors, along with Keats's volatile temper, should encourage us to question Cowden Clarke's memory that apprenticeship was the 'most placid period' of his life.[42] What evidence there is suggests that his apprenticeship was shorter and much stormier than Cowden Clarke would admit.

While Keats says almost nothing about his apprenticeship, records of others treading the same path allow us to reconstruct the kind of life he led. Five years older than Keats, John Green Crosse paid £200 and was apprenticed in August 1806 to Thomas Bayly, a surgeon in Stowmarket. His first duties included rolling pills, cleaning the surgery, dusting and arranging bottles, making up medicines, boxing leeches and bookkeeping. We can picture Keats in Hammond's wood-panelled dispensary, busy with similar tasks. Since Crosse was inoculated for smallpox, perhaps Keats was too. Gradually Crosse took on more responsibilities – dressing wounds, drawing teeth, visiting the sick – effectively becoming a junior partner to his master. Over the full course of his apprenticeship, he gained experience in dealing with fractures, dislocations, gunshot wounds, intestinal obstructions, tapeworms, burns and scalds, difficult births, congenital malformations, tumours, convulsions, gout, accidents, diseases, hernias and so on. He became skilled in routine treatments such as bleeding, blistering and cupping, and helped perform the few operations that stood a chance of success in an age without anaesthesia: cutting for stones, mending harelips and amputations. That Crosse greatly enjoyed wine, parties, plays, dances and fair-going suggests his need for a release after stressful days in the surgery.[43] Keats's training with Hammond would have been very similar to Crosse's, and while Crosse seemed to relish all aspects of his life – including opportunities to flirt with his master's daughters – Keats seemingly found his apprenticeship less congenial.

An apprentice was expected to do his master's bidding and, while Thomas Bayly regarded Crosse almost as an equal, Hammond apparently treated Keats as a servant. For an adolescent as spirited and unsettled as Keats, any servile role would have grated – it is surprising that Cowden Clarke's account of his 'placid' apprenticeship gained currency when others offer a markedly different view. One anecdote in particular stands out. It comes from Richard Hengist Horne, a contemporary of Tom's at Clarke's Academy. There are various versions, all to the effect that Hammond's 'visiting carriage (an open chaise with a large hood) was often to be seen by the half-hour at a time standing opposite the front-door of our school-house when the master's lady required attendance'. On these occasions Keats could be seen 'listlessly holding the reins, leaning back immovably', as he waited for his master.[44] In another account Hammond called at the school on a winter's day, possibly in the snowy January of 1812, and Keats was seen minding the horse with 'his head sunken forward in a brown study' – that is, in a gloomy abstracted mood. Horne tells us that he was dared to lob a snowball and hit Keats on the back.[45]

While Keats's characteristic stance was head back with chin raised, his body language on this occasion expressed resentment at attending on his master like a footman – a bitter reminder, perhaps, of his father's early struggles. No longer a prize-winning protégé, he was expected to fetch, carry and wait. The snowball came as a cheeky reminder of his diminished status – and summer weather brought no relief as hot roof tiles made Hammond's surgery intolerable.[46] Each time Hammond gave him a chore it came as a personal slight and provocation, just as he had felt when an assistant master appeared to insult Tom. It was only a matter of time before an order or reprimand so infuriated him that his hand 'clench'd itself against Hammond'.[47]

Cowden Clarke did in fact hint to Richard Monckton Milnes that all was not right with Keats's apprenticeship: 'Hammond had released him from his apprenticeship before his time; and I have some vague recollection that such was the case, for they did not agree; Keats's tastes being totally opposed to his master's.'[48] Horne said that he spent just 'two or three years with Mr. Hammond'.[49]. John Hamilton Reynolds recalled that Keats never referred to his days with Hammond except to regret that he had 'undergone "a one of them"'.[50] And Haydon: 'he was put as apprentice to an Apothecary; here he passed a wretched life . . . His master, at last continually weary of his dislike to the business, gave him up his time.'[51] In short, Keats and Hammond did not get on. Something had to be done.

When Keats recalled clenching his hand at Hammond he was looking back seven years from September 1819 to 1812, and George was clear that 1812 marked a change in his brother's situation that entailed considerable expenditure 'between the time of his getting his indentures [from Hammond] until he was of age, nearly 4 years'.[52] It is important to grasp what George is saying here: Hammond had concluded Keats's apprenticeship in autumn 1812, surrendering his indenture document nearly four years before he came of age in October 1816. As we will see, George's account was later corroborated and amplified by Charles Wentworth Dilke. Both agreed that Keats's connection with Hammond terminated some two years after he began his apprenticeship. Tom had left school at midsummer 1812 aged almost thirteen, and was now working with George at Abbey's counting-house. This was another arrangement that did not last long, and when Tom quit Abbey's Keats lodged with him.[53]

Having broken with Hammond, how did Keats continue his medical studies? Possibly a way was found for him to attend lectures at St Thomas's and Guy's between 1813 and 1815, before he formally enrolled to study. It was customary for some apprentices to do this: Keats's contemporary Charles Thackrah entered himself as a pupil at Leeds Infirmary after three years of an apprenticeship, to prepare for more advanced study at Guy's.[54] John Green

Crosse and John Flint South likewise explored London's hospitals informally before signing on for study.[55] Back in 1793 John Thelwall had received tickets of admission to lectures on anatomy, physiology and chemistry, without actually entering medical training.[56] It is clear that once Hammond gave back his indenture, there were opportunities for informal medical training that might explain Keats's remarkably rapid progress when he registered at Guy's in October 1815. And Hammond, who did not return Keats's premium of 200 guineas, was obliged to fulfil any formalities of his training that remained.

Beyond a failure of personal chemistry, several factors had made Keats's apprenticeship unsatisfactory. Hammond may well have been ill – he died in 1817 – and, while Keats was conscientious up to a point, his mind and energies were principally devoted to his passion for reading and his *Aeneid* translation.[57] With those absorbing literary preoccupations, Cowden Clarke's 'placid' Keats comes into view.[58] As he stepped across the bridge at Salmons Brook, ahead of him lay Enfield, freedom and poetry.

He went to Enfield five or six times a month, usually on a Wednesday or Saturday afternoon when Cowden Clarke was not teaching. His first visits in autumn of 1810 enabled Cowden Clarke to keep abreast of his translation from Virgil (around this time Cowden Clarke made his own translation from *Aeneid* book four)[59] and Keats could browse recent issues of *The Examiner*. Hunt had reprinted an article on brutal punishments in the British army, 'One Thousand Lashes!!', and a charge for seditious libel was imminent. With George III suffering continued bouts of insanity, February 1811 saw the prince of Wales proclaimed regent and, shortly afterwards, the Hunt brothers' trial and rapid acquittal. For a little while it seemed as if the regent might revive the Whigs' hopes for parliamentary reform and emancipation for Catholics in Ireland, but as spring turned into summer that optimism was dashed. Not only did the prince abandon his former friends, he doubled the insult by reinstating his brother, the despised duke of York, as commander-in-chief of the army – in Hunt's view, a matter of 'regret, indignation and contempt'.[60] What better opportunity than St Patrick's Day, 17 March 1812, to reflect on the regent's volte-face? Disgusted by the *Morning Post*'s praise of that 'Adonis in Loveliness', Hunt struggled to find words and symbols adequate to express his scorn:

> What person, unacquainted with the true state of the case, would imagine . . . that this *delightful, blissful, wise, pleasurable, honourable, virtuous, true* and *immortal* PRINCE, was a violator of his word, a libertine over head and ears in debt and disgrace, a despiser of domestic ties, the companion of gamblers and demireps, a man who has just closed half a century with out one single claim on the gratitude of his country or the respect of posterity.

No one was surprised that 'the attorney-general's eye was swiftly on the article' and another indictment for libel was issued. Unabashed, *The Examiner* informed readers that it would 'vindicate the Truth and Necessity of what we have said'.[61]

Hunt's trial, originally set for 27 June 1812, was postponed. In the interim Cowden Clarke encountered him at a party, discovering the scourge of the regent to be a tall young man of twenty-seven with black hair and a sallow complexion. In conversation he was fascinating, animated, cordial and spoke with a sweet baritone voice; he was also as passionate about music as Cowden Clarke.[62] Meeting Hunt extended Cowden Clarke's circle of acquaintants to include Charles Ollier, a twenty-five-year-old bank clerk with literary ambitions, and he also caught up with a former pupil from Enfield, Thomas Richards. With all three Cowden Clarke would prove a vital and not always co-operative intermediary for Keats.

The trial followed on 9 December 1812, and even Henry Brougham's skilful defence of Hunt as a 'rigidly studious man . . . devoted to no Political Party' could not forestall a guilty verdict. The following February the Hunt brothers were fined £500 each and sentenced to two years' imprisonment – John at the notoriously harsh 'House of Correction' at Coldbath Fields, and Leigh across the Thames in Surrey Gaol at Horsemonger Lane, Southwark. Locked up in a cell with bare stone walls and an unglazed window open to the winter air, Hunt was overwhelmed by the sounds of clanking irons, coughing, cursing and shouting. Within days his health collapsed.

Aware that Keats enjoyed poetry, Cowden Clarke had read to him Spenser's 'Epithalamion', the long, song-like poem in which Spenser celebrated his marriage. Its effect was extraordinary. While Spenser's bride resembled Keats's ideal of a 'pure Goddess', it was the poem's sensuality and erotic suggestiveness – 'pure snow with goodly vermill stayne, / Like crimsin dyde in grayne' (227–8) – that seized his imagination. As he listened, the poem's complex rhymes and elaborate structure showed him how the felicity of single lines might be combined with a more general beauty that suffused the whole.[63] Such, at least, was Cowden Clarke's recollection of how Spenser affected him, and echoes of 'Epithalamion' in his later writings suggest Keats was also impressed by how effortlessly Spenser had drawn in classical figures, combining these with 'skyey' references to the planets, moon and a setting sun sinking to its home 'Within the westerne fome'. That night Keats walked back across the bridge with the first volume of Spenser's *Faerie Queene*, and went through it 'as a young horse would through a spring meadow – ramping!'[64]

Hitherto Keats had used punches to make his presence felt. Now language offered a fresh field of action – as if bouts of rhyming and a physically vigorous

'Mr Keats' mutually manifested each other. Cowden Clarke noticed how
Keats loomed physically larger as he recited poetry. One evening he seized on
a line of Spenser, 'hoisted himself up, and looked burly and dominant'
but instead of clenching his hand, he said, 'What an image that is, –
"*Sea-shouldering whales*"!'[65] Clarke and Keats were soon ramping enjoyably
through Shakespeare's *A Midsummer Night's Dream* and *Cymbeline*, Milton's
*Paradise Lost* and Fairfax's translation of Tasso's *Gerusalemme Liberata*.

Summer visits to Enfield extended late into the evenings, with the two
friends sitting reading in the garden until twilight. When it grew dark, they
talked on into the early hours. On one such occasion Cowden Clarke accompanied Keats back as far as the bridge across Salmons Brook, midway between
their homes, where they parted with a cordial handshake. Keats recalled how
their conversation continued as Cowden Clarke retraced his steps, and how
he hung listening

> when I no more
> Could hear your footsteps touch the grav'ly floor.
> Sometimes I lost them, and then found again;
> You chang'd the footpath for the grassy plain.
> ('To Charles Cowden Clarke', 123–6)

As Cowden Clarke's footfall faded in the dark, Keats mentally followed him
back to the school, a scene he now associated with 'all that life endears'.[66]

'An idle loafing fellow, always writing poetry' – so a fellow apprentice at
Hammond's recalled Keats.[67] He destroyed these early attempts at verse,
although the commonplace book kept by Cowden Clarke provides fascinating
hints about what they might have been like – reading it is almost like eaves-
dropping on their conversations. Extracted in Cowden Clarke's notebook are
passages on England's liberties (Locke, Bacon, Selden, Bolingbroke and
Burdett), anti-war polemics by William Crowe and Anna Laetitia Barbauld,
axioms on religious liberty and rotten boroughs, and extracts celebrating
republican heroes like John Hampden, John Milton, Thomas Hollis and
William Penn. Passages from Voltaire suggest that Cowden Clarke encouraged Keats to read the *Philosophical Dictionary* – his ideas about religion
retained Voltaire's sceptical open-minded attitude.[68] Cowden Clarke's taste in
poetry is represented by Barbauld's visionary astronomy in 'A Summer
Evening's Meditation', Collins's 'Ode to Evening', Cowper's 'Yardley Oak',
Chatterton's 'Ode to Freedom', Beattie's 'Minstrel', Byron's 'Windsor Poetics',
Hunt's 'Stanzas on the Death of General Moreau' and three of Wordsworth's
republican sonnets of 1802. All of Cowden Clarke's extracts are touchstones

of liberty, pacifism, reform and religious tolerance, and Keats's epistle 'To Charles Cowden Clarke' echoes their conversations about 'the patriot's stern duty' and heroic figures like King Alfred, William Tell and the bold tyrannicide Brutus (69–72).

Carefully copied into the commonplace book are Cowden Clarke's poems 'On my Birth Day 15.<sup>th</sup> Dec.<sup>r</sup> 1812', 'Sunset. an Irregular Effusion', 'The Nightingale', 'Sonnet on Liberty. Jan<sup>y</sup>. 1814' and 'On my Venerable Grandmother's Attaining her 85.th Year 28.th Jan.<sup>y</sup> 1814'. Keats later addressed similar themes, echoing Cowden Clarke's poems, and a cluster of original poems transcribed in summer 1813 may have been especially significant for him. In addition to his own 'Sunset' and 'Nightingale', Cowden Clarke set down a 'Sonnet on Sunset' by his friend Charles Ollier, and Keats reminded Cowden Clarke of this poem and its author in a letter of 9 October 1816.[69] Ollier's sonnet was memorable not because of any particular literary merit –

> Blest sun! – whether across the eastern height
> Thou rushest forth this nether world to cheer

– but because it showed Keats that poetry was being created here and now. Poetry was something he could try for himself, and it represented a community to which he too might belong. Cowden Clarke's friendship with Ollier and Leigh Hunt already suggested the beginnings of a coterie.

So it was that in August 1813 Keats attempted a poem to stand beside Cowden Clarke's and Ollier's sunsets, albeit as a lesser light; he wrote a 'Sonnet to the Moon', and gave it 'to C.C.C'.[70] This sonnet has been lost but Cowden Clarke's commonplace book, along with Spenser's lines to the moon and Endymion in 'Epithalamion', makes a 'Sonnet to the Moon' an obvious subject for one of Keats's first attempts. Together, 'Sunset' and 'Sonnet to the Moon' announce the solar and lunar motifs that illuminate much of Keats's poetry from his 'Ode to Apollo' of February 1815 to Endymion, 1817–18, and the 'Hyperion' poems of 1818–19.

The Examiner kept the friends up to date with current events. Hunt had now moved into two derelict washrooms of the old prison infirmary, and here he was able to resume editing – his celebrity had increased sales of the paper to eight thousand copies a week. Unlike the majority of felons, Hunt was a 'gentleman', and this brought privileges. He imported his own furniture, improved the walls with rose-trellised paper, painted a sky-blue ceiling with billowy summer clouds, and screened a view to the gallows with green window-blinds. Bookcases, books and busts of the poets came in, and a

furniture carrier arrived with a piano. Flowers and greenery were planted in
the yard outside, and a lute completed a scene of romantic seclusion. Thus
installed, Hunt was able to control his nervous ailments and anxiety attacks.
Rather than disappearing from the public eye, as the authorities had hoped,
he went on supplying copy for *The Examiner* and was spoken of everywhere
as a martyr for liberty. He was also hard at work on his narrative poem *The
Story of Rimini*. His wife, Marianne, and eldest son, Thornton, joined him, but
soon left for Brighton's healthy sea air and bathing. Marianne's place was
taken by Hunt's sister-in-law Elizabeth Kent – Bess – with whom he had a
long, passionate and quarrelsome relationship. Some said that they were
lovers. 'Bess is all attention to me,' Hunt wrote to his wife. Bess kept an eye on
schedules for copy, prepared food, acted as a secretary and helped entertain
visitors. Among the latter were public figures and personal friends such as
Lord Byron, Thomas Moore and Maria Edgeworth, Charles Lamb and his
sister Mary, William Hazlitt, John Hamilton Reynolds, John Scott, Henry
Robertson, Charles Ollier, Thomas Barnes and Thomas Alsager of *The Times*,
and the painter Benjamin Haydon.

Cowden Clarke arrived at the prison with baskets of eggs, vegetables, fruit
and flowers from the Enfield school garden, and Hunt soon regarded him as
an old acquaintance.[71] Cowden Clarke told Keats about these weekly visits,
about Hunt's rose-trellised wallpaper and the little garden embowering his
retreat. For them both, Hunt was a charismatic figure, and they nicknamed
him 'Libertas'. Perhaps Keats hoped for an invitation to accompany Cowden
Clarke on one of his visits to the jail but, if he did, it was not forthcoming.
Instead, he was left to imagine the decorated cell where Libertas was outfacing
tyranny with poetry – a scene that, woven deep into his idea of the imaginative life, would later emerge in his 'Ode to Psyche'.

With winter's approach Keats grew concerned about his grandmother,
Alice, now seventy-seven and increasingly frail. The new year began with
London shrouded in thick fog, and at the end of January 1814 a big freeze had
the country in a lock-down that would last for two months. The Thames froze
over and a grand frost fair was soon under way on the river, with bands,
dancing, merry-go-rounds and fairground stalls. Away from the metropolis at
Edmonton, the coach road north was deserted, fields were masked by snow
and Salmons Brook flowed silently under layers of ice.

# Guy's Hospital, 1814–1817

# CHAPTER 4

# Southwark

A THAW IN mid-March reopened the roads. Keats, no longer apprenticed to Hammond, was free to move to London – or so his friend Charles Wentworth Dilke recalled in the margins of his copy of Milnes's *Life, Letters, and Literary Remains, of John Keats*. Alongside a passage about Keats's apprenticeship Dilke noted that he 'did not serve out his time – They quarrelled & Hammond gave up his indentures. This I believe was in 1814.'[1] He made the point again a few pages later: 'He removed to London before the termination of his apprenticeship. He quarrelled with Hammond who gave up his indentures.'[2] Elsewhere Dilke commented on Keats's living expenses 'for four years nearly before he was of age, owing to his quarrel with the Surgeon & leaving him.'[3]

The decision to bind Keats as an apprentice had been a private matter between his guardians and Hammond. It did not involve the Society of Apothecaries, although when Keats came to be examined by the Society for a licence to practise he would be required to produce a testimonial that he had completed his apprenticeship. Most candidates produced either their indenture or a letter from their master. As Hammond had given the indenture document to Keats himself, the latter left Edmonton in spring 1814 with the documentary evidence required for his formal qualification as an apothecary.[4]

Part of Keats's difficulty was the nature of apprenticeship itself. Throughout his lifetime its value and purpose were in question, especially so in relation to the Apothecaries' Act of 1815. Few had a good word to say about apprenticeship as a system of medical training: a five-year term was deemed too long, and complaints of drudgery were commonplace.[5] Added to these dissatisfactions were personal awkwardnesses between Hammond and Keats. To his credit, Abbey sided with Keats on this: John Taylor reported him saying that

Hammond 'did not . . . conduct himself as [Mr. Abbey] conceived he ought to have done to his young Pupil', and the winter scene with Keats left holding his master's horse bears this out.[6] Still, Abbey remained convinced that medicine was the best way forward and advised him to 'commence Business at Tottenham as a Surgeon'. That this Tottenham plan dated from 1814 turns upon the fact that 'Mrs. Jennings was known & respected in the Neighbourhood, on which Acc[t] her Grandson had a better introduction there than elsewhere'. Abbey's notion that moving Keats to Tottenham was a way to 'punish' Hammond would have had little point in 1817, for he died in February of that year aged fifty.[7] In the event, not going to Tottenham hastened Keats's arrival in the City hospitals where his Hammond connections assisted him.

To understand how this happened we need to catch up with Hammond's nephew William, last glimpsed as a fellow student of Joseph Henry Green. William had introduced Green to his sister Anne Elisha, and on 25 May 1813 they married. By now Green was a senior student and dresser to Henry Cline at St Thomas's; through him, Green was also acquainted with Astley Cooper, the charismatic surgeon who had taught Thomas Hammond at Guy's back in the 1780s.[8] Marriage would obviously have brought Green into the Hammond family circle where Keats was also known, so completing a network of contacts that led from Edmonton to London's teaching hospitals and established figures like Cline and Cooper who could make things happen for a promising student like Keats.[9] These Hammond/Green networks at the hospitals may also have been reinforced by others in the Jennings family: between 1732 and 1795 four Jenningses had studied medicine in London.[10]

Keats's name was already familiar to Green, for the latter's childhood home was at London Wall, just yards from Keates's Livery Stables. Might Green have helped to resolve Keats's difficulties by informally introducing him at St Thomas's and Guy's? Such an introduction was not impossible. John Flint South spent six months in 1813 occasionally attending lectures and dissections as a preliminary to his formal apprenticeship, during which he would meet Green.[11] Keats may well have followed a similar route, dividing his life between City lodgings, his grandmother at Edmonton and Cowden Clarke across the bridge at Enfield. Attending lectures would mean that he kept up his medical training, gained hospital experience and started to make himself known. He also had time to read, complete his version of *The Aeneid* and write his own poetry.

Our next sighting of Keats is at St Thomas's partner institution, Guy's, in mid-1814, where another young student, Charles Aston Key, was also entered as a pupil.[12] It has long been known that Astley Cooper placed Keats in the care of his dresser, George Cooper, who lodged at 28 St Thomas's Street, off the busy Borough Road. Often assumed to date from October 1815, there are good reasons to suspect that this arrangement was actually in place earlier. The obvious moment for Cooper to have intervened was in July 1814, when George began as his dresser and eighteen-year-old Keats had left Hammond and Edmonton.[13] John Flint South says as much: 'George Cooper told me that whilst at Guy's Hospital, where he was dresser to Astley Cooper for eighteen months, he lived in St. Thomas Street, at a tallow chandler's, named Markham, where John Keats, the poet, lived with him, having been placed under his charge by Astley Cooper.'[14] There is nowhere else that Keats is known to have lived at this time, and South offers us a simple and plausible explanation: Keats shared George's lodgings from July 1814 to early 1816 – exactly eighteen months – having been placed there on Astley Cooper's instructions. Another senior student, Frederick Tyrell, shared the apartment, which consisted of a common sitting room with separate bedrooms. St Thomas's Hospital was directly opposite, and Guy's just fifty yards further along the street. They could be at lectures, dissections, operations and the wards in a matter of minutes. And if Keats walked south along the Borough Road, he could visit the coaching inns and taverns that lined the route out of town. The Old George Inn survives today much as Keats knew it in 1814.

If this scenario is correct, a number of otherwise mysterious aspects of Keats's medical career start to make sense. Most obvious of these is why Keats, a freshman student in October 1815, was informed of his imminent elevation to a dressership within a month of registering at the hospital. A dressership was a senior role with responsibilities that called for medical expertise, practical experience, steady nerves and a strong stomach. An obvious explanation is that when Keats enrolled at Guy's his capabilities were already well known – he had been in the neighbourhood for more than a year, in company with students, and had informally attended teaching.

Keats's London sojourn prior to his formal registration at Guy's is also mapped into some of his first poems. His earliest surviving poem, an 'Imitation of Spenser', was written soon after he had completed his eighteenth year, perhaps in spring 1814, as the ice thawed and Salmons Brook started to sing once again:

> Now Morning from her orient chamber came,
> And her first footsteps touch'd a verdant hill,
> Crowning its lawny crest with amber flame,
> Silv'ring the untainted gushes of its rill;
> Which, pure from mossy beds, did down distill,
> And after parting beds of simple flowers,
> By many streams a little lake did fill,

  Which round its marge reflected woven bowers
 And, in its middle space, a sky that never lowers.

  There the king-fisher saw his plumage bright
  Vieing with fish of brilliant dye below;
  Whose silken fins and golden scalès light
  Cast upward, through the waves, a ruby glow:
  There saw the swan his neck of arched snow,
  And oar'd himself along with majesty;
  Sparkled his jetty eyes; his feet did show
  Beneath the waves like Afric's ebony,
 And on his back a fay reclined voluptuously.

  Ah! could I tell the wonders of an isle
  That in that fairest lake had placed been,
  I could e'en Dido of her grief beguile;
  Or rob from aged Lear his bitter teen:
  For sure so fair a place was never seen,
  Of all that ever charm'd romantic eye:
  It seem'd an emerald in the silver sheen
  Of the bright waters; or as when on high,
 Through clouds of fleecy white, laughs the cœrulean sky.

  And all around it dipp'd luxuriously
  Slopings of verdure through the glassy tide,
  Which, as it were in gentle amity,
  Rippled delighted up the flowery side;
  As if to glean the ruddy tears, it tried,
  Which fell profusely from the rose-tree stem!
  Haply it was the workings of its pride,
  In strife to throw upon the shore a gem
 Outvieing all the buds in Flora's diadem.[15]

Beyond Spenser, this owes much to Keats's reading of Milton, Thomson, Beattie, Mary Tighe, Shakespeare and Virgil, yet it also reveals a more individual poetic personality than that list might suggest. Enriched with amber, gold, ruby, jet, ebony, emerald and silver from Kauffman's *Dictionary of Merchandize*, Keats's 'Imitation' also ventures into a less material landscape of transient effects such as sunlight, streams, clouds, flowers, ripples and tides. In his rhyme games and schoolyard fights we have already encountered a vocal, self-assertive Keats hoisting himself up in confrontation. The same instinct for opposition appears in his poem's contrasting textures and tendencies – 'down distill' and 'lake did fill', 'brilliant dye below' and 'Cast upward . . . a ruby glow', 'dipped . . . through the glossy tide' and 'up the flowery side'. Shadows and reflections hint at depth and inwardness as the lake opens itself to 'a sky that never lowers', and a swan contemplates its neck of 'arched snow' reflected like a slender bridge of ice. Amid a changeful scene of incipient conflict, the four stanzas create an ideal landscape of 'gentle amity' to set against grief, age, loss and sorrow. And the keynote is survival. Already alert to his own potential, Keats's phrase 'could I tell' lets us know we will be hearing more from him.

What followed was a group of poems marking his move to London. If 'Imitation of Spenser' grew from secluded garden readings at Enfield, his first London poem tackled momentous international events that were astonishing Hunt in *The Examiner*:

> 'Tis done—but yesterday a King!
>     And arm'd with Kings to strive—
> And now thou art a nameless thing
>     So abject—yet alive![16]

Trapped between the Russians' westerly advance across the Rhine and Wellington's thrust north from Spain, Napoleon had been 'hunted into his last corner'. When Paris was occupied at the end of March, he had no option but to abdicate. From Surrey Gaol, Hunt saw the city sky ablaze with victory celebrations and illuminations, and wrote of 'the first, breathless, pouring forth of the news' and widespread astonishment at 'peace . . . after an interval of twenty years'.[17] Seizing this moment, Keats drafted a sonnet 'On Peace' that echoes *The Examiner*. Proclaiming peace in Britain's 'war-surrounded isle', he urges 'Europa's liberty' against a resurgence of 'sceptred tyrants':

> Keep thy chains burst, and boldly say thou art free;
>     Give thy kings law—leave not uncurbed the great . . .
>                         (12–13)

A similarly declamatory tone reverberates in 'Lines Written on 29 May, the Anniversary of Charles's Restoration, on Hearing the Bells Ringing':

> Infatuate Britons, will you still proclaim
> His memory, your direst, foulest shame?
>     Nor patriots revere?

Ah! when I hear each traitorous lying bell,
'Tis gallant Sydney's, Russell's, Vane's sad knell,
    That pains my wounded ear.

By deploring the fate of English patriots at Charles II's restoration, Keats shames 'infatuate' churchmen and politicians who were readying themselves to welcome a Bourbon revival in France. Sensing ground already lost even as Napoleon was banished to Elba, Keats implies that Britain is incapable of 'boldness'. Cowden Clarke, who had written his own 'Sonnet to Liberty', would have applauded vigorously.

While engaging with public events in his poems, Keats was also enjoying city life. Perhaps it was now that he went to a celebrated attraction south of the river: a bear-baiting. Cowden Clarke remembered how Keats could conjure the whole scene, mimicking the bear like a punch-drunk boxer 'dabbing his fore-paws hither and thither, as the dogs snapped at him'.[18] August 1814 also saw him at Vauxhall Pleasure Gardens, a short distance from his Southwark lodgings. Here were walkways and arcades, fountains, pavilions and groves, with music and dancing brightened by lanterns and fireworks. John Green Crosse's evening at Vauxhall lasted until four the next morning.[19] Whatever Keats's expectations were as he wove tipsily through the throng, the sight of a woman ungloving her hand ignited a passion that possessed him for years. His immediate response was to compose this couplet poem:

Fill for me a brimming bowl,
And let me in it drown my soul:
But put therein some drug design'd
To banish Woman from my mind.
For I want not the stream inspiring,
That heats the sense with lewd desiring;
But I want as deep a draught
As e'er from Lethe's wave was quaft,
From my despairing breast to charm
The image of the fairest form
That e'er my rev'ling eyes beheld,
That e'er my wandering Fancy spell'd!

  'Tis vain—away I cannot chace
The melting softness of that face—
The beaminess of those bright eyes—
That breast, earth's only paradise!

My sight will never more be blest,
For all I see has lost its zest;
Nor with delight can I explore
The classic page – the muse's lore.

Had she but known how beat my heart
And with one smile reliev'd its smart,
I should have felt a sweet relief,
I should have felt 'the joy of grief'!
Yet as the Tuscan 'mid the snow
Of Lapland thinks on sweet Arno;
So for ever shall she be
The halo of my memory.

We learn little of the woman, more about Keats. Seen through his 'rev'ling eyes', her 'fairest form' is coupled with a whore's 'beamy' availability – dosed up with belladonna or eyebright, plying her trade (that she did not even meet his gaze was an unmanning reminder of his short stature and sexual inexperience). At eighteen years old, Keats is left stranded between his adolescent ideal of a 'pure Goddess' and his own 'lewd desiring', while the woman becomes the first of his enthralling *femmes fatales* – a *belle dame sans merci*. His attempt to shake off this experience as lust in a cold climate opens the possibility of a different encounter by 'sweet Arno', while revealing that Keats has not yet understood or resolved his poem's contradictions. Conventional yet disconcerting, the poem's jittery octosyllabics register the self-consciousness of a highly original young poet who has yet to find his own voice.

'Fill for me a brimming bowl' reveals many pointers towards later poems like 'La Belle Dame sans Merci' and 'Ode to a Nightingale', while his allusion to Thomas Campbell's *Pleasures of Hope* – 'the joy of grief' – foreshadows the subtle intersection of emotions in 'Ode on Melancholy'. A sonnet 'To Lord Byron', written around now, responded to the popularity of *Childe Harold*, and Keats had already hit upon an image to express how Byron can 'dress' melancholy 'With a bright halo, shining beamily' (8). The remainder of this sonnet recycles images of a 'golden moon' and 'amber rays', while the warbling of its 'dying swan' is echoed in Keats's sonnet 'To Chatterton' as the voice of doomed genius: 'How soon that voice . . . / Melted in dying murmurs!' (5–6) More personal is a Petrarchan sonnet Keats wrote following the death of his grandmother, Alice, aged seventy-eight. She was buried in the vault at St Stephen's, Coleman Street on 19 December 1814, and Keats's elegiac sonnet 'As from the darkening gloom a silver dove' follows her soul's ascent 'into the realms above' (4). He had been 'tenderly attached to her', and while that tenderness required consolation his sonnet adopted a questioning stance – 'Wherefore does any grief our joy impair?' (14) – influenced by his Enfield schooling and his reading of the sceptical Voltaire.[20]

Alice's death meant that eleven-year-old Fanny was now the responsibility of her guardian, Richard Abbey; he sent her to Susanna Tuckey's boarding school at Walthamstow, close to his country residence in the village. Here she stayed except for holidays spent at Abbey's house, in the Pancras Lane premises, or at kindly John Sandell's home. 'Mr. Abbey was *too* careful of me,' Fanny recalled, 'and always kept me a complete prisoner, having no other acquaintances than my books, birds, and flowers.'[21] She lived isolated from her brothers, who were now expected to make their own way in life. Both Keats and Tom had already done that, although not in the manner their guardian had intended.

Except for Keats's estranged aunt Margaret, older generations of the Keats and Jennings families were now either dead or unknown to him. Had his father not visited his school on that April day in 1804 he would now have been forty-one, proprietor of Keates's Livery Stables and quite possibly master of the Innholders' Company. Keats's brooding on family misfortune is evident in a poem of February 1815, 'To Hope', where a 'solitary hearth' is the scene for reflections on 'sad Despondency', 'Disappointment', 'Despair' and a more resilient ardour of 'Hope' (1, 9, 13, 29). Keats had the opening of another February poem in mind as he began 'To Hope': Coleridge's nocturnal meditation in 'Frost at Midnight'. Whereas Coleridge was snugly installed at his hearth while his family slept, we need to register the full force of the word *solitary* for Keats as it gathers up 'the fate of those I hold most dear' (19). He was writing his poem out of a longing for company, initiating a Coleridgean conversation between solitude and community that would persist in his habits of composition. To write, Keats needed solitude, and the experience of solitude inclined him to seek community. We can trace this pattern in his restless travels during a period of sustained composition, as with *Endymion* in 1817–18, and in the paradoxical circumstance of solitude experienced by '*two* kindred spirits' ('O Solitude!', 14). The idea of companionable solitude in a populated landscape is perhaps typical of a suburban poet: among the pleasures of liberty celebrated in Hunt's 'Hampstead Sonnets' were the Heath's 'haunted solitudes'. In their lyrical shuttlings between solitude and companionship, city and country, Keats and Hunt were alike long before they actually met. This explains why Keats's first published poem, 'To Solitude', spoke so immediately to Hunt that he printed it in *The Examiner*.

Where was Cowden Clarke's cheery presence as Keats sat alone in his lodgings? He had continued his visits to Surrey Gaol, and was gratified to receive a pre-publication copy of Hunt's masque *The Descent of Liberty* (Keats later acquired the first edition).[22] Cowden Clarke's passion for Mozart had brought an introduction to Vincent Novello, his clever wife Mary Sabilla, and their children, among whom was Cowden Clarke's future wife, Mary Victoria. Novello – composer, conductor, organist, pianist and singing master – was impresario of a literary-musical set that gathered in his home at 240 Oxford Road. Among the group were Henry Robertson and Charles Ollier, the jovial Gattie brothers Frederick, William, Henry and John, Thomas Alsager, Arthur and Alistatia Gliddon, John Nyren the cricket historian, Charles and Mary Lamb, and, after his prison term, Leigh Hunt.[23] When Cowden Clarke looked back to this time he was unable to recall exactly when Keats moved to London, arguably a case of tactful amnesia to obscure the fact that his apprenticeship had not worked out. It is clear, however, that early in 1815 they were no longer meeting as frequently as before.

'To Hope' winds up unconvincingly by merging 'dark thoughts' (46) with patriotic well-wishes for Britain, but the poem had registered an abyss of dejection in Keats. His phrase 'morbid fancy' (21) touches a core of genuine anguish and echoes in remarks he later made to the painter Haydon – who endured his own desolate, destructive moods: 'You tell me never to despair', Keats told him: 'I wish it was as easy for me to observe the saying – truth is I have a horrible Morbidity of Temperament which has shown itself at intervals.'[24] He had shaken off the misery of his apprenticeship, but these episodes of mental torment were inescapable. Haydon knew what it meant to descend into paranoia and self-disgust, and for Keats, too, there were 'intervals' that brought back to him the horror of Bedlam and 'Melancholy Madness'. Written after his grandmother's death, overshadowed by Cowden Clarke's absence and his rupture with Hammond, 'To Hope' marks one of the debilitating attacks that George and Tom dreaded in their brother. George in particular recalled Keats's 'nervous morbid temperament' and 'frequent melancholy', and how Tom was the only person who truly understood his character.[25] Keats's behaviour at school – by turns fiercely pugnacious, rigidly studious, tremblingly sensitive, overwhelmed by grief – bears out the observation that he was 'always in extremes', and the gentle wave-like patterns of rising and falling in his poetry from 'Imitation of Spenser' onwards suggest how composition helped temper his volatile moods, enabling him to speak back to himself as he had formerly addressed questions with rhyme. At some time, possibly around the composition of 'To Hope', Keats announced to his brothers that if he failed as a poet he would kill himself. So black were his moods, so intense his identification with the great poets that his brothers knew his resolve to emulate Chatterton and 'die / A half-blown flower, which cold blasts amate' (7–8) was more than mere words.

That moment passed, and on the upswing of feeling it would seem that he had only been half in love with death. Just as 'Despondence' was displaced by patriotism in 'To Hope', Keats's low spirits were cheered by Hunt's release. If he was seeing less of Cowden Clarke, who had not taken him to meet Hunt, it might be possible to contrive an introduction by writing a poem to celebrate Hunt's freedom. He began a sonnet in which he pieced together what Cowden Clarke had told him about Hunt, and invented the rest. The result was a poem that Keats most likely hoped *The Examiner* would accept for publication:

**Written on the Day that Mr. Leigh Hunt left Prison**

What though, for showing truth to flatter'd state,
   Kind Hunt was shut in prison, yet has he
   In his immortal spirit, been as free
As the sky-searching lark, and as elate.
Minion of grandeur! think you he did wait?
   Think you he naught but prison walls did see,
   Till, so unwilling, thou unturn'dst the key?
Ah, no! far happier, nobler was his fate!
In Spenser's halls he strayed, and bowers fair,
   Culling enchanted flowers; and he flew
With daring Milton through the fields of air:
   To regions of his own his genius true
Took happy flights. Who shall his fame impair
When thou art dead, and all thy wretched crew?

The poem has little to say about the reality of Hunt's prison experience, and a good deal to tell us about Keats himself. We need to know more about both.

Sought out by Lord Byron, courted by celebrities, visited by aspirant poets like nineteen-year-old John Hamilton Reynolds, Hunt in prison was at the height of his fame. Release would not be what he anticipated. Constrained to quit his sanctuary on Thursday, 2 February 1815, he was confronted with a public life that now seemed bitterly uncongenial. Once out of prison, he did not hasten to *The Examiner*'s office or Hampstead Heath. Instead, he shuffled just a few yards along Horsemonger Lane to the home of his friend Thomas Alsager, still in sight of the jail. Liberty quickly brought on attacks of agoraphobia, and Thomas Wageman's sketch of Hunt at this moment shows the mental and physical strain of his release. It would be a long time before he got over the shock of freedom, and even then he was often in doubt whether he would not rather be back in prison.

Keats knew none of this – for him, Hunt remained the heroic poet-editor of *The Examiner*. By now he had read Hunt's satire *The Feast of the Poets* and probably also his masque *The Descent of Liberty*, a reminder of what had appeared to be Napoleon's demise in spring 1814. Accordingly, 'Written on the Day that Mr. Leigh Hunt left Prison' is mainly literary in reference, portraying Hunt enjoying the poetic fraternity of Spenser and Milton. Though imprisoned for 'showing truth to flatter'd state', his genius soars into poetic immortality, unlike the 'wretched crew' of the last line. Keats writes blithely of a 'sky-searching lark' and 'happy flights', and his sonnet is in many ways a light thing. But 'Mr. Leigh Hunt' and his 'enchanted flowers' mattered urgently to Keats as inspiring emblems of resistance: *Hyperion* and Apollo's agonies at the threshold of divinity lay years ahead but, already, Keats's sonnet had sketched a myth of the suffering poet that would form the climax of his epic. More immediately, he hoped that his sonnet would produce an introduction to Hunt. Perhaps Cowden Clarke would pass it to him?

Setting out from Southwark, Keats knew that he was likely to meet Cowden Clarke on familiar ground: the path between Edmonton and Enfield. As Cowden Clarke takes up the story, Keats has been waiting for him on the bridge:

> I was walking [to London], and, as I think, to see Leigh Hunt, who had just fulfilled his penalty of confinement in Horsemonger-Lane Prison ... Keats, who was coming over to Enfield, met me, and, turning, accompanied me back part of the way to Edmonton. At the last field-gate, when taking leave, he gave me the sonnet entitled, 'Written on the Day that Mr. Leigh Hunt left Prison'. Unless I am utterly mistaken, this was the first proof I had received of his having committed himself in verse; and how clearly can I recall the conscious look with which he hesitatingly offered it![26]

What Cowden Clarke recalled as a chance encounter was a meeting Keats had contrived: as his 'conscious look' intimated, he intended Cowden Clarke to read his sonnet and invite him to meet Hunt. On being given the sonnet, Cowden Clarke either did not or would not take the hint. Why was this? Quite possibly he was envious of Keats's early attempts at poetry. He had nurtured his own poetic ambitions and cultivated Hunt's friendship – but had then forgotten to write a poem on Hunt's release. Such considerations may explain Cowden Clarke's vagueness about whether 'Written on the Day that Mr. Leigh Hunt left Prison' was his first 'proof' that Keats was writing poetry. He later altered this account, making it hazier still: 'This I feel to be the first proof . . .'.[27] As they parted at the gate, Keats was disappointed Cowden Clarke had not responded as he had hoped, already guessing, perhaps, that he would not show Hunt the sonnet. The friends would not meet again for a while, and it would be longer before Keats was introduced to Hunt. But they all belonged to intersecting circles of friends and acquaintances. It was just a matter of time.

By keeping Keats away from Hunt, Cowden Clarke maintained his position with both – but what might have happened if Hunt had actually met the nineteen-year-old Keats immediately after leaving prison? His sonnet would have pleased him, and he would have responded generously. But Hunt's health quickly deteriorated, and it is unlikely that he would have been able to give him the encouragement he had already shown to another young poet, John Hamilton Reynolds. An introduction now would have had no follow-up. Not meeting Hunt in February 1815 ensured that Keats went on to register at Guy's Hospital, where he continued to write poetry. It would be nearly two years before Cowden Clarke showed Keats's poems to Hunt and introduced him as his own protégé. By then Keats had advanced as a poet, and Hunt was sufficiently recovered to make a decisive impact on his further development. Although 'Written on the Day that Mr. Leigh Hunt left Prison' did not appear in The Examiner, it would be among the stock of poems that Keats accumulated for his first collection. Hunt would read it in due course.

After February's sonnet to Hunt, Keats disappears from sight until summer 1815. Possibly he made a visit to the West Country; certainly he was watching the international scene, along with his fellow lodgers Cooper and Tyrell. March brought astonishing news of Napoleon's escape from Elba, his rapid march north through France and arrival at Paris. 'BONAPARTE RE-INSTATED' proclaimed The Examiner on 26 March, over Hunt's gloomy conjecture that renewed war was 'exceedingly probable'.[28] And there was an imminent conflict in medical practice, too, of which Keats was well aware. The long-debated Apothecaries' Act would become effective on 12 July 1815, granting the Worshipful Company of Apothecaries authority to regulate the profession through training and examinations. Students would be required to complete not less than five years' apprenticeship and at least six months' hospital training before proceeding to examination for the licence. Individuals who passed were formally qualified to practise, on payment of a fee for their certificate (ten guineas in London, six elsewhere). It has been claimed that the new rules were strictly enforced, so Keats *must* have stayed with Hammond for a full five years.[29] All of the evidence suggests otherwise, however: long before the act became law, it was obvious to many that a five-year rule for apprentices was both unworkable and unjust. On 1 September 1815 apprenticeship was the most urgent matter addressed by *The London Medical Repository* in its article 'Questions and Answers on the Apothecaries' Act'. This first enquiry might well have come from Keats himself: 'Whether medical students and assistants, now acting as such, who have *not* served apprenticeship for five years, and apprentices who are *not* bound for so long a term, are or will be accepted as candidates for examination, and a certificate to practise as Apothecaries in England and Wales?' The answer was unequivocal. The five-year requirement was an 'unintended retrospective enactment and unfortunate oversight' rushed into law before Parliament rose for the summer.[30] Moving an amendment to this 'bungling Bill', the aristocratic radical Charles, Earl Stanhope tried unsuccessfully to correct its 'oppressive and incorrect' measures.[31] Nine months later, on 1 June 1816, *The London Medical Repository* announced an imminent parliamentary motion 'with a view to remove [the Act's] restrictive effect . . . from all apprentices who were bound previously to the first of August 1815, for a less term than five years.'[32]

Clearly, then, if Keats felt himself disadvantaged by not having completed a full five-year apprenticeship, others shared his predicament and the authorities were aware of their problem. Many pathways led to the qualifying examination, and while a five-year apprenticeship was emphatically *not* a rigid requirement, the examination itself was compulsory – and this soon raised other pressing issues. Within a year the Examiners' Board had reason to address students on another matter of the utmost gravity:

The COURT OF EXAMINERS OF THE SOCIETY OF APOTHECARIES are extremely anxious to impress upon those persons who may be intending to present themselves for examination, a consideration of the absolute necessity of such knowledge of the Latin language as may enable them to translate the Pharmacopoeia Londoniensis, the prescriptions of Physicians, which they consider as a qualification indispensable to an Apothecary.[33]

There is no comparable announcement about enforcing the five-year rule for apprentices, and everything that happened to Keats after he enrolled at Guy's indicates that the Apothecaries' Act was no barrier to him proceeding. He had his indenture document as a testimonial from Hammond and, in addition, he had translated the whole of *The Aeneid* from the original Latin. Englishing the *Pharmacopoeia Londoniensis* would not be a problem.

# CHAPTER 5

# Bright and Dark

SUMMER OF 1815 brought translations of a different kind. His brothers were acquainted with four sisters, Caroline, Anne, Jane and Helen Mathew, who lived north of the City at Goswell Street. Abbey may have known the girls' father, a wine merchant, and the family was also acquainted with the hatter Keatses of Cheapside. As we will see, John Archer, business partner of Thomas Mower Keats, was frequently at the Mathews' home from 1817 onwards.

Through Caroline and Anne, Keats soon met their lugubrious cousin George Felton Mathew and his sister, Mary Mathew. Now that Keats was seeing less of Cowden Clarke, the Mathews' evenings of readings, dances and concerts offered a hospitable, cultured circle. Another medical student, John Spurgin, may have joined the company, for when he went up to Cambridge in autumn 1815, he soon let Keats know there was 'no female Society' there.[1] At Goswell Street, Keats also encountered a youthful poet, Frederick Leffler, and a lively girl with long dark hair, Mary Frogley. All three Keats brothers promptly fell in love with her, and she later said that Keats had written poems 'to and on me', among them 'Hadst thou lived in days of old' and 'Had I a man's fair form'.[2] It was from Mary that her cousin, twenty-six-year-old lawyer Richard Woodhouse, first heard about Keats. Thoughtful, ascetic and intensely religious, Woodhouse may seem an uncongenial acquaintance for Keats – and it would be some time before they actually met each other. Born in Bath on 11 December 1786, Woodhouse studied at Eton, lived for two years in Spain and Portugal, and then became a lawyer in London. Early in 1811 he had met the publishers Taylor and Hessey, to both of whom he became an informal legal and literary adviser. Although not a published poet himself, Woodhouse had read widely and was convinced that Keats would become a great poet to rival Shakespeare and Milton. Keats came to value the clarity and tact of his literary judgements and discussed plans for poems with him. Their correspondence elicited Keats's fullest account of his own 'poetical Character' and Woodhouse reciprocated by making extensive transcripts from Keats's manuscripts and gathering for posterity a remarkable collection of 'Keatsiana' containing unpublished poems, letters, dates and sources, biographical information and other commentary. Without Woodhouse, our knowledge of Keats's life, writings and habits of composition would be greatly diminished.

They all enjoyed the magazine verse of Tom Moore and Mary Tighe, and George Felton Mathew cultivated the gloomy persona of a suburban Childe Harold – languid, melancholy, thoughtful.[3] Seven months older than Keats, Mathew thought himself Keats's poetic rival, if not his better. Late in 1816 his poems appeared in the *European Magazine, and Literary Review* along with his review of *Christabel* containing a passage on the poetics of contrasts.[4] Keats was much more congenial company. Ebullient and outgoing, he responded to the girls with a winningly 'fine flow of animal spirits'. Caroline remembered his 'very beautiful countenance', his 'warm and enthusiastic character' and that he 'wrote a good deal of poetry at our house', some of which was preserved by Mary Strange Mathew in her album of verses, *The Garland*.[5]

Beauty, warmth and poetry. Overheard in these mid-Victorian reminiscences may be the guarded outlines of an affair between Keats and Caroline, recollected fondly as youthful 'folly' and, more ruefully, a matter of 'our danger'.[6] When Keats could shake off the awkwardness acknowledged in 'Had I a man's fair form', his physical presence was overwhelmingly attractive. For Mathew, Keats's enthusiastically received arrival was probably as dismaying as his independent political views: Keats had been 'of the skeptical and republican school', Mathew recalled, a school that was often associated with scandalously 'loose' sexual behaviour.[7] Still, they had a shared interest in poetry, met on friendly terms, and Keats seems to have admired at least one of Mathew's poems, 'Written in Time of Sickness', an exercise in Gothic gloom. Keats contributed a clutch of sociable verses addressed to his new friends; routinely dismissed as among his worst poems, 'To Some Ladies', 'On Receiving a Curious Shell', 'To Emma Mathew' and 'Woman! when I behold thee' give us a sprightly Keats too often overlooked in accounts of his high calling and epic ambitions. He was adept at light, popular verse and a host of literary references show Mary Tighe's *Psyche* and Wieland's *Oberon* among his recent reading. In upbeat anapaestics Keats flirts with his 'fair nymphs', winks and teases with 'passionate gushes', and shows off with knowingly outrageous rhymes such as 'muse / bedews' and 'smart is / Britomartis'.

Summer 1815 was a good time for Keats. He enjoyed company, and discovered he was a success with women. He had written some accomplished light verse and, displacing Mathews, had established his first 'Keats circle'. As they walked up and down Goswell Street, perhaps Keats and his brothers were noticed by residents at number 128, Sarah Severn and her twenty-one-year-old brother, Joseph. Keen to make his way as a painter and enter the Royal Academy, Joseph Severn was already acquainted with Keats's school friend Edward Holmes. Holmes was taking piano lessons from Vincent Novello, and soon Keats's circle would include all three of them. Feeling himself more a man of the world, he had reason to swagger a little about his enjoyment of 'women, wine and snuff'. He started to dress in fashionably 'Byronic' manner, grew a moustache, turned down his collar and tied a ribbon around his bare neck.[8]

With his brimming 'bowls' of wine and snuff-stained shirts, Keats had the rakish allure of a young poet about town. An unlikely recruit to the mystical doctrines of the Swedish visionary Swedenborg, one might think, but John Spurgin saw possibilities and there is evidence that Keats joined in arguments about how the material and spiritual worlds were related. As an ardent Swedenborgian, Spurgin attended the London Swedenborg Society and was a committee member from 1818. Over the summer of 1815 he tried to convert Keats and, having left for Gonville and Caius College, Cambridge, sent him an elaborate letter recommending Swedenborg's doctrines. His letter also offers tantalising glimpses of their friendship: Keats's interest in the Devonshire prophet Joanna Southcott, their freedom to arrange their lives and studies as they wished, and exchanges of books. By the time Spurgin went to Cambridge he knew Keats well, telling him that Swedenborg would spark 'the brightest and most lucid Flame to the Fire of Poetry'; like one-time Swedenborgian William Blake, Keats would 'wander in Paths amid the Geniuses of old'. Spurgin's allusion to 'that mazy Mist of which you speak' catches exactly Keats's turn of phrase when he felt confused, unsure, in doubt.[9] And Spurgin's vision of 'Geniuses of old' had caught Keats's eye too.

Keats's contact with Mathew continued into 1816, and there would be further exchanges of poetry that were not always competitive – the 'kindred spirits' of Keats's sonnet 'To Solitude' may well refer to Mathew or one of his cousins. A little later on, as we will see, Mathew's verses 'To a Poetical Friend' drew a reply from Keats in his couplet poem 'To George Felton Mathew', the first in a series of increasingly ambitious verse letters to brothers and friends. When Mathew eventually published 'To a Poetical Friend' in the *European Magazine* of October 1816, the acquaintance of summer 1815 had attenuated. Keats had moved on in his medical training and was increasingly confident that light verse was not his true manner. And as his poetry advanced, Mathew responded in the *European Magazine* with a peevish sonnet that begins 'Art thou a Poet?':

> Art thou a Poet?—thou hast learn'd to feign,
>     To mount Parnassus, and enjoy her skies;
>     Whence, as thou tell'st me, aëry deities
> Hold o'er the passions a benignant reign.
> Is't hard the harmonious summit to attain,
>     Is't hard to hear the Muses' silver voice?
> Did ever mortal mount the steep in vain,—
>     Did ever mortal hear and not rejoice?
> Yet talk not of the Muses' mild controul.—
>     The blessings lavish'd on the girl I love,
> Her youth, her beauty, and her unstain'd soul
>     Impart to *me* a blessedness above
> The song,—the lyre,—the voice of fame,—the whole
> Of thy enjoyments in the Muses' grove.[10]

'Did ever mortal hear and not rejoice?' Mathew was deliberately alluding to *Sleep and Poetry*, and Keats's longing

>     to see shapes of light, aerial lymning,
> And catch soft floatings from a faint-heard hymning;
> To see the laurel wreath, on high suspended,
> That is to crown our name when life is ended.
> Sometimes it gives a glory to the voice,
> And from the heart up-springs, rejoice! rejoice!
>                                   (33–8)

Mathew cancels their acquaintance by spurning 'the voice of fame' and claiming that he loves a girl of 'unstain'd soul'. *Unstained*? Perhaps something that had happened between Keats and Mathew's pretty cousins still rankled. With his poems and a review of *Christabel* in the *European Magazine*, Mathew had thought of himself as Keats's patron. 'Art thou a Poet?' shows that his sense of himself as the centre of their literary set was more significant to him, and susceptible to perceived slights, than has previously been suspected.

Keats's high-spirited summer reflected pleasure and passion, as well as the national mood after Napoleon's defeat at Waterloo. But when he paused to reflect on that momentous event, what were his thoughts? Early dispatches about the battle circulated in London on the fine morning of Monday, 19 June and three days later the 'Great and Glorious News' of victory broke in the *Morning Post*. 'What times these are!' Haydon scribbled ecstatically in his diary, 'The more I think of this glorious Conflict, the more I glory in it.'[11] At first Keats shared the general astonishment, for Waterloo was the final act in a world war that had begun before his birth. In his own lifetime – he was now almost twenty – he had watched Napoleon rise from obscurity to bestride the globe as an emperor. There were many, like Haydon, trumpeting Wellington as a 'Great & Glorious Man', but soon reports arrived describing thousands of wounded soldiers and inadequate resources for their care. While Keats's fellow students Tyrell and Key set off for Brussels to offer practical help, his own thoughts turned to Napoleon's situation as his former achievements were demolished.[12] What happens when empire disintegrates? What did it mean for a commanding genius to experience defeat? How did that feel? In years to come Keats would return to these questions, pondering the tides of history until Napoleon's rise and fall started to resemble the mythical wars of the Titans and Olympians. As Keats knew from Lemprière and *The Aeneid*, Virgil had invoked that war of the immortals as a backdrop for his epic of Troy's fall and the founding of Rome, the imperial power on which Napoleon had modelled his own short-lived empire. As he tangled with these intractable issues, perhaps he recalled his uncle Midgley John's heroism at Camperdown and Hunt's outrage at lives destroyed, public money squandered and 'misery of all sorts occasioned to families'.[13] So deep was the family divide, Keats had heard nothing about his estranged Jennings cousins Margaret Alice, Midgley John and Mary Ann, but he knew that, like him, they had grown up without a father. Weakened by his battle wounds, Midgley John had been a victim of war as well as consumption.

Hunt was essential reading at such moments. 'In the speculations that seem most to baffle us regarding good and evil, and the origin of human action,' Hunt writes,

> there is one thing infinitely consoling, which is sure to grow brighter as our sorrow in other respects grows dark—and that is, a charity towards *all* our fellow-creatures, not one excepted. We even begin to think at last, that we are all included in some grand scheme of happiness, which the experience of sorrow in one world is necessary to make us enjoy to the full in another.[14]

In some ways this resembles Keats's elegiac sonnet for his grandmother. It also looks forward to his claims for 'a grand march of intellect' at work in the world, 'a mighty providence' and his less conventional idea of life as a 'vale of

Soul-making' that is gradually darkened until 'we see not the ballance of good and evil'. Whereas Hunt recommended universal charity, Keats, feeling himself 'in a Mist', relied on a knowing passivity: 'Men should bear with each other—there lives not the Man who may not be cut up, aye hashed to pieces on his weakest side'.[15] Mingled here may be memories of wounds he had dressed, Hunt on war 'hacking away', possibly even the sight of a bear's claws ripping dog flesh – all memories, that is, dating from 1814–15 and the Waterloo summer. And the war was closer to Keats than might appear, for his fellow student Tyrell came back from Brussels as an eyewitness of field hospitals and terrible casualties.[16] In the postwar years Keats came to share Hunt's belief that sorrow led to human understanding, and he echoed Hunt when he speculated that 'Misery and Heartbreak, Pain, Sickness and oppression' may be necessary to a 'grander system of salvation than the chrystain religion'.[17] 'Do you not see how necessary a World of Pains and troubles is to school an Intelligence and make it a soul?' he asked in April 1819.[18] Darkened by his tragic passage through life, his insight about 'Soul-making' also represented one of many occasions when he elaborated ideas first encountered in Hunt's journalism. In summer 1815, long before they met, Hunt was already giving impetus to Keats's own speculations; the imminent publication of Hunt's narrative poem *The Story of Rimini* would push Keats's poetry ahead too.

On Sunday, 1 October 1815, a bright morning, Keats walked along St Thomas's Street to the counting-house at Guy's Hospital. Perhaps George Cooper was with him. With lectures due to begin the following day, there was no time to lose. Keats paid the £1.2s. administration charge, and on Monday, 2 October, a hospital fee of £25.4s. – half his mother's annuity – to register for twelve months as a surgeon's pupil.[19] Under the Apothecaries' Act he was required to complete six months' hospital experience in order to take the examination that would qualify him to be a member of the Society of Apothecaries. He enrolled for a full year, indicating that he and his guardians expected him to pursue the longer course of study necessary for membership of the Royal College of Surgeons, and that they were prepared to meet the expense of doing so.[20] In addition to paying his registration fees, Keats equipped himself with a basic set of surgical instruments, most likely purchased from George Reddell, gunmaker, sword-cutler and fine steel-worker at 236 Piccadilly.[21] He paid fees for each course and purchased notebooks. One of these has survived, and it is no ordinary exercise book: bound in skiver – a soft, thin leather – it cost 2s.2d.[22]

Keats was one of 159 students who paid ten guineas for a course on 'Anatomy and the Operations of Surgery', taught by Mr Astley Cooper and Mr Henry Cline.[23] He also signed up for two courses on the Practice of

Medicine, taught by Dr William Babington and Dr James Curry; two on Chemistry taught by Dr Babington, Dr Alexander Marcet and Mr William Allen; and one course on the Theory of Medicine and Materia Medica taught by Dr Curry and Dr Henry Cholmeley. In addition he almost certainly attended Astley Cooper's evening lectures on Principles and Practice of Surgery beginning at 8pm on Monday, 9 October. Like Keats's classes at Enfield, Cooper's teaching had a practical emphasis: he brought along patients from the wards, showed specimens from his own collections and conducted dissections. While these evening lectures were not necessary for Keats to qualify as an apothecary they were vital if he aimed to become a surgeon.[24]

On top of all this, Keats purchased a ticket for William Allen's lectures on Experimental Philosophy. Allen was the 'Spitalfields Genius', a Quaker scientist and philanthropist with so many demands upon his time that he only lectured occasionally: he experimented with anaesthetic gases, campaigned for the abolition of slavery and capital punishment, and, as part-proprietor of the idealistic industrial community at New Lanark, was a factory reformer and entrepreneur. Allen's Experimental Philosophy lectures ranged through some of the topics Keats had learned about at school including astronomy, gravity, electrical fluid, evaporation, organic forms, the speed of light, the light spectrum and human senses.[25] Keats was lucky to catch Allen speaking at Guy's, although if he missed a lecture a note on his ticket said its validity was 'perpetual'. He could attend the following year.

What were Keats's days like? At 10am on Mondays, Wednesdays and Fridays he was at Guy's to hear Babington and Curry on the Practice of Medicine; at the same hour on Tuesdays, Thursdays and Saturdays it was Babington on Chemistry. The Practice of Medicine lecturers made an unlikely pair. Unkempt and with fingers filthy from dissections, Babington delivered clear, practical lectures; Curry performed in a haze of powder, wearing a sand-silver wig, extravagant shirt and neck-cloth, gold watch and a chunky ring on his little finger.[26] On the hour Keats dashed off for hospital rounds, and on Wednesdays and Thursdays helped admit and discharge patients. At two in the afternoons he was ready for Cooper's brisk arrival in the theatre at St Thomas's. Dapper in knee-breeches, Cooper was a showman who knew how to play to a crowd – punning outrageously to fix his audience's attention, then bounding onto the table to show an artery or muscle in his silk-stockinged leg.[27] At four, Keats and the other students busied themselves dissecting the corpses and body parts dug up and supplied by the hospital's 'resurrection men', Ben Crouch (ex-prize-fighter) and Bill Butler (dealer in bones and teeth). Dissections were supervised by Joseph Henry Green, who was younger than the other lecturers. The room itself was spacious but crowded – sometimes as many as two hundred students were dissecting at the same time – and the stench of rotten flesh was overwhelming.[28] Cutting into a resurrected corpse was a stomach-turning exercise. It was also extremely hazardous: Astley Cooper warned his students that a wound to a finger might lead to infection and even death.[29]

Once Keats got used to the stink, maggots and livid colours of decaying flesh, no doubt he joined in the robust jokes that steadied them all to their work. Having rinsed his hands, he would ready himself for Cooper's evening lecture on Surgery and, after that, head back to his lodgings. Here his day ended with snuff, perhaps some wine and talk with Cooper and Tyrell, and so to bed. If he woke at night, he would hear the bell of St Saviour's, Southwark, steadily tolling the hours.[30]

Keats was ideally placed at 28 St Thomas's Street to pursue this intensive programme of lectures, dissections and ward rounds. After a month he learned that on 3 March he would be appointed as one of five dressers to surgeon William Lucas, the son of an older William Lucas who had taught Thomas Hammond surgery. It seems most likely that Astley Cooper was behind Keats's appointment: he had been watching Keats for over a year and Keats, who had lodged with a dresser, knew exactly what the post entailed.[31] George and Tom visited frequently, but Keats had no idea where Cowden Clarke was (he was across town, lodging at Warner Street in Clerkenwell with his sister Isabella and her apothecary husband, John Towers).[32] In Southwark, Keats was close to the sites of Chaucer's Tabard Inn and Shakespeare's Globe Theatre, and just a few hundred yards away was Hunt's old prison on Horsemonger Lane. Having written his sonnet on Hunt's release, perhaps he went to see the prison for himself, discovering similarities between his life in the hospitals and Hunt's in the prison infirmary. Like Hunt he was immured in the inner city, and like Hunt he was drawn to the unconstrained possibilities and permissions of poetry. In these ways Keats's Southwark years marked his closest identification with Hunt as a figure who represented all that he aspired to become himself. With thoughts of Chaucer, Shakespeare and Hunt as inspiring neighbours, even in the midst of his medical studies the claims of poetry were never out of his mind. As the weeks passed he would start to reflect on how the two disciplines might be related. His 'Ode to Apollo' had saluted the 'great God of Bards'; now he was aware of Apollo the healer, to whom physicians bound themselves in the Hippocratic oath.

Cooper and Tyrell completed their qualifications and early in 1816 left Guy's – Cooper to practise at Brentford, Tyrell to pursue further study in Edinburgh. Keats would have to shift for himself. Elsewhere in the same house was a similar set of rooms shared by two students of his own age, Henry Stephens and George Mackereth. Keats may already have encountered them at Cooper's lectures. To reduce costs, he now asked to join them and over the next months they became friends. Stephens and Mackereth had enrolled in the hospital's famous Physical Society, where medical discoveries and advances were announced and discussed. Keats's acquaintance John Spurgin also attended and spoke at meetings, but there is no sign that Keats was a member.[33] While he kept to the hospital's routines, it was poetry, Stephens – himself a poet – remembered, that represented 'the zenith of all his Aspirations'.[34] Keats told him that he favoured Spenser and Byron over Pope, whom he considered 'no poet'. When they compared their own efforts, Stephens's poems were always dismissed by Keats, who prized imagery over more declamatory verse. Keats himself came in for ridicule from Henry Newmark, a student of surgeon John Abernethy at St Bartholomew's Hospital, and possibly an earlier Enfield acquaintance. Stephens recalled Newmark as 'a light-hearted & merry fellow' who mocked Keats's poetry and quarrelled with his brothers.[35] After lectures and grisly dissections they all pitched into the rough-and-tumble of student life, to carouse at the inns and taverns on Borough High Street – The Ship Inn, The King's Head, The White Hart, The George, The Queen's Head and The Spur.

While working towards his dressership, Keats composed one of his most assured and effective sonnets so far. 'To Solitude', dating from dark November evenings, reached out to brighter prospects that show him drawing on the lyrical riches of Wordsworth's recent two-volume *Poetical Works*. Keats's line 'Startles the wild Bee from the Fox-glove bell' echoed Wordsworth's sonnet 'Nuns fret not at their convent's narrow room',

> Bees that soar for bloom,
> High as the highest Peak of Furness Fells,
> Will murmur by the hour in Foxglove bells[36]

– but it would be another year before he felt the full impact of Wordsworth's genius. At present Keats was studying the shorter poems in *Poetical Works*, aware that William Hazlitt's *Examiner* review of Wordsworth's long narrative poem, *The Excursion*, had praised his power as a nature poet while criticising his 'intense intellectual egotism'.

*The Excursion* would be a later discovery for Keats, but a seed had been sown with Hazlitt's idea of Wordsworth's self-absorption and his 'living in the busy solitude of his own heart'.[37] Born in 1778, immediately after the American Revolution, Hazlitt was the son of an itinerant Unitarian minister.

He attended the Unitarian New College, Hackney, where he was taught by the eminent dissenting thinkers Joseph Priestley and Thomas Belsham, read modern philosophy and started to formulate the metaphysical ideas of his *Essay on the Principles of Human Action* (1805). Intellectually and tempera-mentally committed to political reform, in January 1798 he encountered Samuel Taylor Coleridge preaching at a Unitarian meeting in Shrewsbury. That led to an invitation for him to visit Coleridge at Nether Stowey in Somerset, where he also met William and Dorothy Wordsworth. Here Hazlitt read and heard recited poems subsequently published in *Lyrical Ballads*, and sensed a new style and spirit in poetry reflecting former hopes for the French Revolution. It was an experience that he never forgot, and against which he measured both Wordsworth and Coleridge in later years. Having witnessed the extraordinary, inspired achievement of *Lyrical Ballads* in 1798, Hazlitt was appalled by Wordsworth's retreat into an apparently self-satisfied, middle-aged conformity – and he would not allow the poet of *The Excursion* to forget what he once had been.

'To Solitude' grows out of Keats's first encounters with Wordsworth and his assailant Hazlitt. Adapting ideas of 'haunted' and 'busy' solitudes, the sonnet opens with a scene of alienated inner-city life:

> O Solitude! if I must with thee dwell,
>   Let it not be among the jumbled heap
>   Of murky buildings;—climb with me the steep,
> Nature's Observatory—whence the dell,
> Its flowery slopes—its rivers crystal swell,
>   May seem a span: let me thy vigils keep
>   'Mongst boughs pavilioned; where the Deer's swift leap
> Startles the wild Bee from the Fox-glove bell.
> Ah! Fain would I frequent such scenes with thee;
>   But the sweet converse of an innocent mind,
>   Whose words are images of thoughts refin'd,
> Is my soul's pleasure; and it sure must be
>   Almost the highest bliss of humankind,
> When to thy haunts two kindred spirits flee.[38]

Keats revisits the 'solitary hearth' of his poem 'To Hope', draws in the sociable voice of his summer lyrics with 'the sweet converse of an innocent mind', and adopts the rural setting and familiar tone of Hunt's Hampstead sonnets. Transplanted from its remote Wordsworthian summit, Keats's foxglove blooms on a more frequented slope just outside town. By answering

Wordsworth's brand of solitude with a poem of sympathetic suburban 'converse', Keats introduced himself as a 'kindred spirit' of Hunt's and implicitly aligned himself with Hazlitt.

He showed the sonnet to George Felton Mathew, at this time still in touch with Keats. In response Mathew composed his complimentary verses 'To a Poetical Friend', encouraging Keats to persevere with fanciful stories 'of wonder and love' as a release from hospital studies and 'dark spots of disease'. This was a manner Keats had already outgrown, as appears from his next contribution to this poetic dialogue. Written in rhyming couplets over some ninety lines, 'To George Felton Mathew' is altogether more ambitious than Mathew's effort and, while it salutes their 'brotherhood in song' (2), the gesture is one of farewell. Keats reworks pastoral motifs of the 'dark city' and a 'flowery spot' (33, 37), but now his 'different cares' (17) at Guy's brace and animate, bringing thoughts of Shakespeare, Milton and Chatterton as incitements to creativity. Keats's cadences are more complex and sustained than Mathew's routine quatrains, and his couplets have an edgy momentum. When he floated the notion of 'those who in the cause of freedom fell' (66) – 'our own Alfred' (67), William Tell, William Wallace and Robert Burns – he opened a liberal theme to which he knew Mathew would not assent. By the poem's close it must have been obvious to Mathew that last summer's 'poetical friend' had moved on, and Keats made no response to Mathew's irritable sonnet 'Art thou a Poet'. His first 'Keats Circle' was over.

Besides anatomising his poetic and political allegiances, Keats had to attend Cooper's lectures on anatomy, ten more on bones and fractures, then another series on muscles by Henry Cline. A skilful surgeon and a democrat in politics, Cline had visited Horne Tooke at the Tower in 1794 and later gave evidence at John Thelwall's trial for treason. His lectures were less eloquent, delivered in a 'quiet monotonous tone, and very slowly'.[39] Keats kept detailed notes of what Cooper said on anatomy, physiology and pathology, blood, arteries, diseases of veins, absorbents, reticular membranes and the nervous system. There is not a word from Cline's lectures, however. Keats's notebook shows he was struck by Cooper's audacious speculations about whether 'Blood possessed Vitality' and how arteries 'expel Blood in the last Struggles of Life'. He took down an anecdote about the Polish patriot Thaddeus Kosciusko: 'having had the Sciatic Nerve [in his leg] divided by a Pike wound [it] was a long while before his limb recovered its sensibility'. Oddities like 'the Behaviour of a Frog after having been guilloteened' caught his attention, as did Cooper's bright recommendation: 'Snuff to ye Nose, Purgatives to ye intestines.'[40] Keats was making notes for his examinations, but there was matter here for poetry too.

Keats's medical notebook survives as an extraordinary document of his mind and it can stand comparison with his poetry manuscripts. Written in a small fine hand, the impression it gives is of a neat and orderly student. Additional remarks were either written in the margins, or inserted later. As has often been pointed out, Keats embellished the later pages with little drawings of flowers; while Cooper was explaining the structure of a human nose Keats was imagining the perfume of flowers and then, perhaps, the 'halfblown flower' of his own sonnet on Thomas Chatterton's untimely death (perhaps it was now that he sketched two human skulls inside the back cover of his notebook). Like Kauffman's *Dictionary of Merchandize* and *The Aeneid*, Keats's notebook was packed with ideas, images, words and phrases that later surfaced in his poetry. Hitherto his poems had had recourse to conventional figures of 'Despair' and 'Hope' to represent emotions. From now on, his knowledge of anatomy and physiology would enable him to materialise those experiences in the throbbing life of muscles, nerves, arteries, bone and blood – most powerfully so in his haunting lyric 'This living hand, now warm and capable'. This all took time, and developed in parallel with his increasingly profound thinking on pain and suffering, nature and art.

One encouragement in that direction was William Babington's survey of the philosophical merits of art and science. Whereas the artist is 'selfish [and] constantly labouring in his own interest . . . from imitation and without principle', Babington argued tendentiously that a 'Phylosopher or man of Science is in search of truth in order to make a general application of it for the benefit of his fellow creatures'.[41] Babington adopted the terms of eighteenth-century empiricism ('imitation', 'general application') and valued 'some general Law' over the seemingly unprincipled efforts of an individual artist. Here, in his first week of lectures, Keats was challenged with questions about poetic identity and how poetry might 'benefit' others. He would interrogate these problems many times in his letters, and Babington's voice is heard with particular clarity in *The Fall of Hyperion* when Moneta parleys with the poet-dreamer:

> What benefit canst thou do, or all thy tribe,
> To the great world? Thou art a dreaming thing;
> A fever of thyself—think of the earth.

(i.167–9)

William Hazlitt's 1818 lecture 'On Poetry in General' observed that although 'poetry . . . is neither science nor philosophy . . . the progress of knowledge and refinement has a tendency to circumscribe the limits of the imagination, and to clip the wings of poetry'. Hazlitt's phrases distilled for Keats much of what he had already heard in Babington's lectures, capturing poetry's crisis in an age of scientific advances: 'The province of the imagination is principally visionary, the unknown and the undefined: the understanding restores things to their natural boundaries, and strips them of their fanciful pretensions.'[42] Keats would be troubled by fears that his own teeming ideas might never be voiced, that he would never attain the peak of his ambition, that he was living in an age when science had robbed the rainbow of its mystery.[43] For the passionate anti-Newtonian Keats, the cold philosophy of scientific rationalism was like ice to poetry's warm knowledge of life. Clearly the poet and the physician had their respective roles, and both were concerned to benefit their fellow creatures. Were they entirely at odds, or would it prove possible for him to achieve an Apollonian embrace of both?

At the start of 1816 Keats was twenty-one, a student physician and would-be poet, teased by his fellow students when he claimed that poetry alone was worthy of his attention. Poetry was his passion. Fame and greatness were to be achieved through poetry and poetical excellence. The greatest men in the world were poets, and to rank among them was the chief object of his ambition. When, late in life, Henry Stephens looked back on their time at Guy's, he recalled Keats as a swift-witted youth rather under the middle size, with a thin face and prominent cheekbones, well-formed nose and a receding forehead.[44] Keats's usual stance with chin raised could make him appear aloof, and with his Byronic outfit and wispy moustache he cut an improbable figure at lectures, on the wards and along Borough High Street. His brothers were unswerving in their belief in his abilities, while to his fellow medical students he was evidently clever but more likely to be scribbling doggerel than attending to his studies. In short, even as Keats neatly transcribed lectures into his medical notebook, his devotion to poetry was 'absolute'.[45] What would he make of himself?

# CHAPTER 6

---

# 'J.K., and Other Communications'

SUNDAY, 28 April 1816 had the makings of a memorable day. Keats eagerly opened his *Examiner*, skimmed Hunt's poem on Byron's departure for Italy, an article on the Elgin Marbles, news of a suicidal lover and a notice that Mrs John Dickens had given birth to a daughter. Then, in tiny print beneath a list of bankrupts, his eye lighted on this: 'J.K., and other Communications, next week'. For seven days Stephens and Mackereth heard about little else. When the next week's *Examiner* appeared, Keats quickly scanned its columns. There, at the foot of page 282, was his sonnet 'To Solitude' over his initials: 'J.K.' Like any young poet, Keats was 'exceedingly gratified' at seeing his first poem in print.[1]

He had good reason to be. In sending his poem to *The Examiner*, Keats had aimed high. Unlike the *European Magazine* and the *Gentleman's Magazine*, Hunt did not publish gatherings of verse by various hands. Keats had leapt into more exalted company. Already that year *The Examiner* had published Byron's lacerating comment on separating from his wife, Annabella Milbanke,

> Fare thee well!—thus disunited—
>  Torn from every nearer tie—
>  Seared in heart—and lone—and blighted—
> More than this I scarce can die.

and 'A Sketch from Private Life', his coruscating attack on Annabella's maid, Mary Jane Clermont.[2] Three sonnets by Wordsworth had recently appeared: 'How clear, how keen' (28 January), 'While not a leaf seems faded' (11 February) and 'To B.R. Haydon, Painter' (31 March). All of these poems foregrounded the poet's solitude – Byron, blighted and lonely; Wordsworth, a distant 'Enthusiast' hearkening to 'whispers of the lonely Muse'. Hunt had already gone into print to defend Byron against scurrilous accusations of incest and homosexuality, and both Hunt and Hazlitt had long regretted that Wordsworth's remoteness could 'turn our thoughts away from society alto-gether'.[3] After those poems and columns of commentary, the sociable voice of J.K.'s sonnet with its 'two kindred spirits' appeared as a calculated celebration of conversation, pleasure and human company. 'To Solitude' had been written months before it appeared in *The Examiner*, but Keats had seen how it could launch him into a dialogue with Byron, Wordsworth, Hunt and Hazlitt.

He also noted Hunt's care in positioning his sonnet on the page. It appeared between an account of a soldier who bled to death after a botched incision and an article on the 'extreme distress, and absolute ruin' of farmers. *The Examiner* always brought poetry into energetic conversation with public issues, and Keats would have been alert to this. As he surveyed the issue, he heard his poem of social feeling speak out against all that the adjacent columns also deplored: neglect, bankruptcies, seizures, imprisonments and executions. The few poems admitted to *The Examiner* signalled Hunt's particular recommen-dation. This issue for 5 May 1816 flagged 'J.K.' as one to watch.

Keats had Hunt in his sights too. In February 1816, a month before he became a dresser, Hunt had published *The Story of Rimini*. For Keats, this poem was a revelation. Hunt had taken Dante's story of two doomed lovers, Paulo and Francesca, from canto five of *The Inferno* and transformed it into a smart verse narrative in four cantos of loose heroic couplets. From the first page Hunt moved nimbly between colourful spectacle and noisy crowds to more intimate scenes of human feeling. Politically and theologically the poem was attuned to *The Examiner*'s liberal, independent ethos. With a familiar manner, vernacular voice and a dedication to Lord Byron, *Rimini* set before Keats a model of all that he, too, might achieve.

Hunt's poem opens in Ravenna on a festive May morning. Crowds gather. Then, with a 'start of trumpets', Guido, duke of Ravenna, enters with his daughter, Francesca, to await the arrival of Duke Giovanni of Rimini, her 'husband yet to see' in a political marriage arranged by her father. A procession of 'clattering hoofs' follows as trumpeters, heralds, pursuivants, squires and knights arrive, arrayed with escutcheons, shields, scarlet cloaks and caps with dancing feathers. With deft, assured strokes, Hunt sketches horses at a canter:

> The flowing back, firm chest, and fetlocks clean,
> The branching veins ridging the glossy lean,
> The mane hung sleekly, the projecting eye
> That to the stander near looks awfully.[4]

Here as throughout the poem Hunt's language is risky, exciting, making free with adjectival nouns like 'glossy lean', 'purple smearings' and 'glary yellow thickening bright'. No longer confined by couplets, Hunt's cadences hurry his narrative irresistibly forwards. Another figure suddenly 'springs into the square', displaying 'cool mastery' of a 'haughty steed', and what Francesca sees of this prince 'is sufficient for the destined bride'.[5] Full of movement, sound and light, Hunt's opening canto presents suggestive contrasts between liberty and constraint, interweaving passages of vibrant description with glimpses of individuals' inner lives. All seems well, as princess and prince exchange looks of 'sweet gravity' and 'touched respect'.

When Keats turned to canto two, however, something was clearly amiss:

The truth was this:—The bridegroom had not come,
But sent his brother, proxy in his room.[6]

Francesca has fallen in love with the wrong man – Paulo, her future husband's brother:

a creature
Formed in the very poetry of nature,
The effect was perfect, and the future wife
Caught in the elaborate snare, perhaps for life.[7]

In a single line Hunt's poem skips from colour and spectacle to spectacular controversy, for from this patriarchal coercion there is 'no appeal'. Whereas Hunt's first canto is painted on a broad canvas, the second details more subtle human interactions of look and gesture as the snare's destructive conse-quences become apparent.

Less obvious is how the poem spoke to Keats at Guy's. At the start of the third canto, Hunt explains that he wrote in prison to cheer himself with thoughts of 'things far hence', discovering as he did so

—more than what it first designed,—
How little upon earth our home we find,
Or close the intended course of erring human kind.[8]

Hunt had escaped to poetic 'regions of his own', but what was Keats's 'intended course'? He had extricated himself from an apprenticeship that proved an awful snare, only to find that his situation at Guy's had encumbered him all over again. He was about to assume the onerous responsibilities of a dresser, and yet here he was romping through *Rimini* and feeling himself ever more eager to venture a long poem of his own.

Bitter disappointment follows Francesca's discovery

> That she had given, beyond all power to part,
> Her hope, belief, love, passion, to one brother,
> Possession (oh, the misery!) to another![9]

Bound to her 'possessor', Giovanni, she whiles away hours in Paulo's company. As they meet secretly at her pavilion in a 'green garden', Hunt is apparently writing out of his own recent experience:

> There's apt to be, at conscious times like these,
> An affectation of a bright-eyed ease,
> An air of something quite serene and sure,
> As if to seem so, was to be, secure:
> With this the lovers met, with this they spoke.[10]

For Keats, the lovers' fluttering pulses and affected ease may have been a reminder of the Mathew sisters and last summer's pleasures. He had promised George a Valentine poem to send to Mary Frogley, and not a word of it had yet been written.

✳ ✳ ✳

Shortly before 14 February, Keats put *Rimini* aside. Quickly he set down some lines that harked back to Spurgin's letter about 'brightest' poetry and 'Geniuses of old':

> Hadst thou liv'd in days of old,
> O what wonders had been told
> Of thy lively countenance,
> And thy humid eyes that dance
> In the midst of their own brightness.
> (1–5)

No belladonna 'beaminess' here. We can hear Keats trying for Hunt's light touch and tender observation:

> dark hair that extends
> Into many graceful bends,

As the leaves of hellebore
Turn to whence they sprung before,
And behind each ample curl
Peeps the richness of a pearl.
Downward too flows many a tress
With a glossy waviness.

                         (13–20)

While that last phrase catches Hunt's manner, this is inevitably a less daring
poem. A downward glance yields only 'beauties, scarce discern'd, Kept with
such sweet privacy', and Keats ends his valentine by comparing Mary to the
chaste nymph Britomartis.[11]

                        ✳ ✳ ✳

Returning to the risqué third canto of *Rimini*, Keats found Paulo and
Francesca reading 'Launcelot of the Lake, a bright romance', where they
discover a situation that mirrors their own:

As thus they sat, and felt with leaps of heart
Their colour change, they came upon the part
Where fond Geneura, with her flame long nurst,
Smiled upon Launcelot when he kissed her first:—
That touch, at last, through every fibre slid;
And Paulo turned, scarce knowing what he did,
Only he felt he could no more dissemble,
And kissed her, mouth to mouth, all in a tremble.
Sad were those hearts, and sweet was that long kiss:
Sacred be love from sight, whate'er it is.
The world was all forgot, the struggle o'er,
Desperate the joy. – That day they read no more.[12]

Here canto three ends, echoing *Paradise Lost* and Adam and Eve cast out into
wilderness. 'The world was all before them' (xii.646), Milton had written, and
it is a world well forgotten, Hunt suggests, as Paulo and Francesca recover
paradise in each other's arms. Keats was impressed by and learned from the
way Hunt, leaving the rest unsaid, allowed space for his readers' imaginations
to work. He would adopt a similar strategy in his own most frankly sexual
poem, *The Eve of St Agnes*: as Porphyro and Madeline find a consummating
'Solution sweet', Keats cuts away to windowpanes, frosty wind and sharp
sleet pattering.

Canto four concludes Hunt's poem by tracing the lovers' inner pangs and outward calms until Francesca's sleep-talking alerts Giovanni to what has happened. Keats took note of this technique too, and tenderly embroiders Madeline's 'visions of sleep' into the narrative of *The Eve of St Agnes* as she wakes to find Porphyro in her chamber. Whereas Keats's lovers escape, there is no release for Paulo and Francesca: the two brothers fight a duel, Paulo impales himself on his brother's sword and Francesca dies broken-hearted. At autumn's close the lovers are returned in death to Ravenna, and

> buried in one grave, under a tree.
> There side by side, and hand in hand, they lay
> In the green ground:—and on fine nights in May
> Young hearts betrothed used to go there to pray.

With the poem's final triplet gently echoing its opening scene, 'a morn of May / Round old Ravenna's clear-shewn towers and bay', the whole poem has a pleasing symmetry that gathers Paulo and Francesca's tragedy into continuing renewals of love and life.[13] Keats would learn to do this kind of thing too, and decided that his readers needed to be 'flung off' by a less reassuring conclusion than Hunt's.

Having translated *The Aeneid*, Keats was alert to Hunt's skilful shaping of narrative. His idiomatic language impressed too, and his loosening of the heroic couplet tuned his lines to the rhythms and music of spoken English. Aligned with these innovations was the poem's questioning of authority: recommending a more universal understanding than Dante's 'melancholy theology', Hunt affirms human rights and values against institutions of 'authorized selfishness'. The spirit of the poem, in Hunt's view, was 'tolerant and reconciling', looking to the '*first* causes of misfortune' so as to understand 'the danger of confounding forms with justice . . . and making guilt by mistaking innocence'.[14]

Now published, Hunt's poem was soon in circulation. Canto three was Charles Lamb's 'particular favorite'. Byron, who had already read the poem in manuscript, declared it 'devilish good' and urged Tom Moore to 'set it up before the public eye where it ought to be'. Haydon outdid them all: 'my soul is cut in two – and every nerve about me pierced with trembling needles . . . it will establish your genius.'[15]

The public reviews were divided. *The Dublin Examiner,* the *Monthly* and the *Eclectic* favoured *Rimini*'s 'human tone', 'refreshing vigour' and 'easy graceful style of familiar narrative'. Exactly those qualities were abused by the *Quarterly Review* as 'mere vulgarisms', 'fugitive phrases' and 'an unauthorised, chaotic jargon'.[16] Hunt shrugged all of this off, aware that his poem would have drawn no hostility 'if politics had not judged it'.[17]

Others were less accepting. Cowden Clarke replied in a 'fisty-cuffish' pamphlet, damning the *Quarterly Review*'s piece as 'a tissue of falsehood . . . full as malicious as inconsequent'.[18] Enfield connections lay behind his pamphlet's publication. Its publisher, Robert Jennings at 2 The Poultry, was probably the son of John and Arabella Jennings, christened at St Stephen's, Coleman Street in March 1784. To print it, Jennings employed Charles Richards, a former pupil at Enfield School like his brother Thomas; their father, stable-keeper John Richards of Oxford Street, had moved in equestrian circles close to Keats's father and grandfather, and these family associations continued. Charles Richards would print Keats's first collection of poems and, as with *Rimini*, Clarke would go into print to attack Keats's critics. Besides publishing, Robert Jennings was also active in local politics, serving as a councillor for Cheapside in 1818–19 alongside Joseph Keats the hatter.[19]

For Keats, Hunt's poem was an astonishing achievement. As the date for commencing his dressership drew ever closer, he was ambitious to embark on a new poem in the spirit of what Hunt had done. His first attempt, scribbled between lectures and written up at night, tried to capture vivid, impressionistic details like Hunt's knights with 'caps of relvet',

> Each with a dancing feather sweeping it,
> Tumbling its white against their short dark hair . . .[20]

Keats begins,

> Lo! I must tell a tale of chivalry;
> For large white plumes are dancing in mine eye
> ('Specimen of an Induction to a Poem', 1–2)

Writing quickly, he sets up an encounter between a knight and a damsel, who paces 'the worn top of some old battlement' in tearful expectation of her 'stout defender'. This had promise, and could well have led into a narrative like *The Story of Rimini*, although, as we read on, it becomes sidetracked by rhetorical questions that may have been intended to spur the story onwards but fail to do so. The promised 'tale of chivalry' remains obstinately 'far off'. Recollecting his wish to pursue that 'bright path of light' traced by 'Libertas', Keats concludes his poem with an address to Spenser, content to 'rest in hope'.

What he had written turned out to be a 'Specimen of an Induction' to a poem still in prospect. He seems to have made a fresh start right away, beginning a story about a young knight, Calidore, introduced 'paddling o'er a lake' towards an island. Book six of *The Faerie Queene* supplied his hero's name; suburban hedgerows created a landscape of dock leaves, foxgloves, silver birches and 'long grass which hems / A little brook'. Summoned from this pastoral scene by a 'trumpet's silver voice', Calidore dallies with a bevy of maidens until 'brave Sir Gondibert' arrives, whereupon they all retreat into a 'pleasant chamber'. Here Keats abandons Calidore 'burning / To hear of knightly deeds', and drifts into a lyrical evocation of breezes, distant music, the 'moon in ether' and 'soft humming' voices. With the half-line 'Sweet be their sleep . . .', his second attempt at narrative breaks off.

'Calidore. A Fragment' was Keats's most significant poem so far. Following the pattern of his studies at Enfield, he had deliberately set himself the challenge of writing a narrative poem. The results showed he had mastered Hunt's run-on couplets and impressionistic compounds such as 'far clearness', 'easy float' and 'swelling leafiness'. '[I]nto the court he sprang,' we are told, as Calidore emulates the energetic 'spring into the square' with which Paulo got *Rimini* under way. Line by line we can see how Hunt's example was enabling Keats to find a voice and direction of his own. Never a wholly literary poet, Keats also drew deeply on memories of his childhood: if the landscape of 'Calidore' came from Edmonton's meadows, the 'black-wing'd swallow' skimmed in from the Enfield school garden where he used to lie beside the pond,

> Delighting much, to see it half at rest,
> Dip so refreshingly its wings, and breast
> 'Gainst the smooth surface, and to mark anon,
> The widening circles into nothing gone.
>
> (15–18)

Keats's empathic genius delights in that moment half at rest, allowing us to feel the swallow 'Dip so refreshingly its wings, and breast', and also to see its 'breast / 'Gainst the smooth surface' as it darts away. He has a story to tell but those widening circles mark a reflective turn at odds with his narrative's onward development. Here, and in the 'nightingale's first under-song' heard a few lines later, we catch hints of a more introspective voice not yet fully articulated. The 'Induction' and 'Calidore' were never completed but Keats, rightly, thought well of these first attempts and kept them. Both would appear in his first collection.

Henry Stephens recalled that Keats's passion for poetry was all-absorbing, although there was time for a summer excursion to the New River – Keats plunged in immediately.[21] Perhaps this was in June 1816 when he wrote three poems about field-pleasures – 'To one who has been long in city pent', 'Oh, how I love, on a fair summer's eve' and 'To a friend who had sent me some roses' (written to cool a quarrel with Tom's school friend Charles Wells). If Hunt can be believed – and he usually can – Keats passed a summer day walking at Caen Wood near Hampstead, gathering images for a poem that became 'I stood tip-toe upon a little hill'.[22]

Eighteen sixteen brought new acquaintants. In spring George introduced him to William Haslam, a solicitor of about Keats's age who was already acquainted with Joseph Severn.[23] Haslam's father worked for Frampton and Long, wholesale grocers in Leadenhall Street, so possibly George met him through Abbey. From now on Haslam would prove kind, obliging and constant, an 'oak friend'.[24] Severn, nearly two years older than Keats, had recently extricated himself from an unhappy apprenticeship and was now a pupil at the Royal Academy. At their first meetings, around this time, Severn's painterly ambitions would have impressed, while his personality was an attractive mixture of optimism and haplessness, generosity and vulnerability. Severn seems initially to have stood off-centre among Keats's acquaintances – he was busy with his studies – and this may explain why they never quarrelled.[25] Keats and Severn would keep in touch, but their real intimacy lay four years ahead.

From Sunday, 3 March Keats's duties multiplied. For twelve months he was to serve as dresser to surgeon William Lucas, making a team of five with Charles Allen, Charles Egerton, Samuel Harris and Thomas Irish.[26] In financial terms this new role was a mixed blessing: he had a rebate of six guineas from his original registration, but had to pay Lucas a further £50 fee. Every three weeks one of the three Guy's surgeons took his turn on a week's duty, with one of his dressers staying full time at the hospital. Each surgeon would have seventeen duty weeks a year, and each dresser serving for twelve months would have a minimum of four weeks' hospital duty when he lodged full time in the hospital.[27] A duty dresser coped with overnight emergencies, and took charge of surgical cases admitted on Wednesday mornings before the surgeon attended to them. From contemporary accounts we know that Keats would have dealt with accident victims, dressed hosts of outpatients, drawn innumerable teeth and performed countless venesections. He supplied lotions, plasters, linseed-meal and leeches as required, and performed minor operations. *The London Medical Repository* lists the ailments he would have treated: by far the most common was simple indigestion – dyspepsia – followed by asthma, diarrhoea, rheumatism, pneumonia, measles, tonsillitis and scabies.[28] When surgeon Lucas arrived Keats would show him patients that needed further discussion or hospital admission, and then they commenced their ward visits. All five dressers accompanied the surgeon, each carrying the plaster-boxes that denoted seniority over the shoals of other students who followed, pushing and jostling around patients' beds.[29]

Fridays meant scuffles to get to surgical operations, where dressers were in the front line of action. The theatre was cramped, with a wooden operating table surrounded by seats for surgeons, dressers and apprentices. Behind them were steeply stacked galleries where students squeezed together to watch and shout encouragement. In these days before anaesthesia patients were drunk or doped with laudanum to dull the agony of probes, scalpels and saws. Sawdust was scattered to catch blood. Keats and other dressers were responsible for assisting the surgeon, applying tourniquets, dressing wounds and removing amputated limbs. Speed was of the essence, and such was Astley Cooper's dexterity he could complete complex operations in minutes. Lucas was a different kind of operator, neat-handed but reckless with his knife. Tall, ungainly and awkward, he had few surgical skills and his operations were 'generally very badly performed, and accompanied with much bungling, if not worse'. One horror story has Lucas amputating a leg and then absent-mindedly bandaging the severed limb and leaving his patient's living stump raw and uncovered.[30] As dresser, Keats would have had to participate in operations, witnessing harrowing scenes at the operating table and being required to put right any damage inflicted.

What effect did all of this have upon him? Evidently he could cope, and was capable of balancing stressful routines at Guy's with his poetic ambitions – indeed, the intensity of his inward, imaginative life may be the single reason he survived the hospital's testing environment. But that balance was both fragile and fraught. He lived in an age when excruciating agony was a fact of life: the horrific experience of surgery without anaesthetic – effectively human vivisection – was a routine reality. There was no understanding of antisepsis or basic cleanliness, and the hospital's water supply was drawn directly from the sewage-laden Thames. Opium was the only reliably effective treatment, but it was a palliative not a cure. Keats said that although he derived great pleasure from alleviating pain, the medical profession was dreadful because it was witness to so much suffering.[31]

His impulse in 'To Solitude' had been to escape it all. But having listened to patients groaning under the knife as blood poured into sawdust, how could he go back to 28 St Thomas's Street and pen another line about 'the highest bliss of human-kind'? 'Calidore' had sounded a far more sombre note, appropriate to his work as a dresser, in contemplating 'the world's bleak promontory' (107).

The muggy, humid morning of Thursday, 25 July saw Keats walk across London Bridge, turn left into Upper Thames Street, and make his way to Blackfriars and so to the Apothecaries' Hall in Water Lane. Here he notified the Society of Apothecaries that he intended to sit the examination that day. He had the necessary qualifications to do so: he had attended lectures, had gained more than six months' hospital experience and, despite the cancellation of his apprenticeship, was able to provide a testimonial. All was in order. Keats took his place in the Great Hall, where he translated extracts from the *Pharmacopoeia Londoniensis* and physicians' prescriptions, and answered questions on the Theory and Practice of Medicine, Pharmaceutical Chemistry and Materia Medica.[32]

To the surprise of those who thought he had scanted his studies, he passed. Mackereth and Stephens, his fellow lodgers, both failed – a circumstance that explains Stephens's bruised recollection that the examinations were 'more a test of Classical, than Medical – Knowledge'.[33] Keats's route to Apothecaries' Hall may have had its irregularities but he had the necessary medical expertise and, crucially, he understood Latin. *The London Medical Repository* for the following October listed 'John Keats' among recently 'Certificated Apothecaries'.[34]

Summer gave him little respite from his duties – indeed, there is evidence that the weeks from May to August may have been busier than usual. The Guy's 'Admission Book for Women' contains weekly lists written up by the duty dressers. Three entries, for 22 May, 3 July and 28 August, bear some resemblance to Keats's handwriting and the page for 3 July is particularly intriguing in that it contains a doodle of a flower not unlike those in his medical notebook, its radiating fronds or petals suggesting thoughts unfolding while a prescription was prepared. We might conjecture that this was Keats reflecting on how the name 'Calidore' derived from the Latin for heat, *calidum*, used in prescribing treatments like *balneum calidum* – a hot bath. He had been examined on prescriptions and their standard Latin terminology such as 'Mist. Camphor. Spirit. Atheris Nit.', prescribed on 28 August for Mary Polman's hydropsy. The Latin abbreviation 'mist.' for 'mistura', meaning 'a mixture', echoed his own phrase to describe an unsettled mood – 'all in a mist' – a compound of mingled thoughts, feelings and textures like autumn, season of 'mist and mellow fruitfulness', warmth and chill. The medical terms Keats used in his day-to-day routines as a dresser led him irresistibly to the richly compounded language of poetry.

Since 3 March, Keats had combined duties as a dresser with lectures and dissections, writing ever more ambitious poems such as 'Calidore', and making and receiving visits to and from his brothers. Having passed his examination to practise as an apothecary, he badly needed a holiday.

Margate was a popular resort for Londoners in search of sea air, bathing and social amenities, relatively easily reached in ten hours by the newfangled paddle steamers. Perhaps Keats and his brother Tom took the steam-packet 'Regent' that set out from Tower wharf at eight on Saturday and Wednesday mornings. When they disembarked in the evening, they found their lodgings and then explored Margate's elegant New Square, Theatre Royal and Assembly Rooms. Having escaped the city they spent most of their vacation in open fields and walking along clifftops. Keats had long since marvelled at Spenser's 'sea-shouldering whales'; now he celebrated the sea's wonders in a sonnet for George:

Many the wonders I this day have seen:
   The sun, when first he kist away the tears
   That fill'd the eyes of morn;—the laurel'd peers
Who from the feathery gold of evening lean;—
The ocean with its vastness, its blue green,
   Its ships, its rocks, its caves, its hopes, its fears,—
   Its voice mysterious, which whoso hears
Must think on what will be, and what has been.
E'en now, dear George, while this for you I write,
   Cynthia is from her silken curtains peeping
So scantly, that it seems her bridal night,
   And she her half-discover'd revels keeping.
But what, without the social thought of thee,
Would be the wonders of the sky and sea?

Framed by sun and moon, this wonderful seascape introduces two partici-pants in a celestial dance that will reappear throughout his poetry, linking Enfield's 'living orrery' with the 'Dian skies' and 'maturing sun' of 'To Autumn'. Perhaps there was also a recollection here of sonnets on the sun by Cowden Clarke and Ollier and his own early effort at a 'Sonnet to the Moon'. Since Keats notices the moon 'half-discovered' by parting clouds, he may have been writing at the time of the full moon on 8 August; if this is so, it marks the first of many occasions when his creativity responded to celestial and seasonal cycles – in this case when the full moon and sun, Cynthia and Apollo, were balanced in opposition. At other times the moon, sun and their mythical embodiments co-operated to quicken the mists, breezes, clouds, currents and tides of his imagination, as if concerting an interplay of male and female aspects of his own nature. Around now Keats seems to have projected a poem on the Endymion myth; his first attempt at this would form a short episode in 'I stood tip-toe'; his second produced the four-thousand-line poetic romance *Endymion*, and he would return to Margate to make progress with this. Margate's coastline was allowing Keats to recreate himself in other ways too. If the sea's Homeric expanse promised epic possibilities, caves along its shore intimated more inward, oracular discoveries and a 'voice mysterious' like Coleridge's marvellous evocation of 'the stilly murmur of the distant sea'.[35] And all of these wonders, Keats tells his brother George, were underwritten by 'the social thought of thee'.

Social thoughts of a more flirtatious kind were preoccupying Tom: now sixteen, he was eagerly exchanging letters with a mysterious French woman, Amena Bellafilla. Addressed from 'The Square' at Margate, Amena's correspondence was dictated by her to a mutual acquaintance, Tom's high-spirited school friend Charles Wells, also holidaying at the resort. Employed as a trainee solicitor, Wells also had a line in jolly practical jokes. Still, Tom must have inherited all his grandfather Jennings's gullibility to be taken in by Amena's protestations: 'I am the Amazon who is to meet you with open Arms & give you an hundred Kisses remember that & think if I can blush you think me more modest than I really am & yet you shall find me innocent spotless as your own or Cha$^s$. heart'.[36] For Tom, this was apparently hot stuff, quite enough to distract him from the chaos of romantic clichés that made up the rest of this Amazonian billet-doux. At some point the real identity of Tom's Margate lover was revealed, but what Keats remembered later was that his brother had for a time been taken in by Wells's letters – only to have his finer feelings completely dashed. When Keats recovered the 'Amena' letters after Tom's death, the hoax produced an irreparable break with Wells.

Other Enfield acqaintances were close by. Keats's schoolmaster John Clarke and his wife, Isabella, had retired to Bellevue House, Ramsgate, and perhaps he walked over with Tom to visit them. George wrote with news that another school friend, Charles Briggs, had said Cowden Clarke was living with his brother-in-law in North London. It is possible, too, that Keats called on Joshua Waddington, a fellow student who lived at Margate.[37] Although Keats and Tom were far from town, their London connections came with them.

Keats's summer reading came from London too. Week by week Hunt adopted the cheery persona of 'Harry Brown' in verses addressed to friends like William Hazlitt, Barron Field, Charles Lamb and his 'cousin' Tom Brown (that is, the Irish poet Tom Moore, whose 'Twopenny Post Bag' verses were an influence). Written in loose couplets, Hunt's epistles cultivated a bantering address, chattily expansive about Hampstead, poetry, politics, country and city, 'these times and this weather'.[38] Keats's sonnet 'To my Brother George' captured Hunt's voice of affectionate 'social thought' and reflected, like Hunt, 'on what will be, and what has been' (8). Examination success was another encouragement for Keats to take stock of what he had achieved yet, as he did so, he grew despondent. Although his 'Induction' and 'Calidore' had been promising, they had not developed further – perhaps he could make something from feelings of inertia and despondence? A few lines stirred in his head:

> Full many a dreary hour have I past,
> My Brain bewildered, and my Mind o'er cast
> With Heaviness; in seasons, when I've thought
> No spherey strains, by me, could e'er be caught
> From the blue Dome, though I to dimness Gaze
> On the far depth, where sheeted Lightning plays;
> Or, on the wavy Grass out stretch'd supinely,
> Pry 'mong the Stars, to strive to think divinely.[39]

That last rhyme echoes Hunt's 'Harry Brown' manner, but Keats's mood – baffled, brain bewildered – is at first less genially expansive than Hunt's unhurried enjoyment of a season 'half summer, half spring'.[40] More accepting of flickering contradictions, Hunt's imagination was often drawn by an ambiguous middle space to which Keats himself, when less self-absorbed, was also attracted. His lines here struggle on through a series of negatives – 'never hear', 'never teach', 'never make' – and eventually find a way by reflecting on the process of composition itself. By introducing 'Knightly Spenser', 'Libertas' and 'white Coursers', Keats places himself in familiar territory: as his verse gathers momentum, he returns to a striking image in the opening passage, 'the far depth, where sheeted Lightning plays', then strikes forward to imagine sheet lightning as a 'wide Portal' for poetic 'Wonders'.

Poetry's recalcitrance literally gave this verse its occasion, as Keats launched himself into what became an epistle to his brother George, announcing his aspiration for 'Posterity's award'. He touches upon themes of patriotism and the poet's role in society, and concludes by depicting himself in the act of writing his poem: 'E'en now . . . pillow'd on a bed of Flowers / That crown a lofty Cliff'. Initially unpromising, 'To my Brother George' marks a significant advance on his 'Epistle to George Felton Mathew', not least in its announcement of ambitions for posthumous fame. Hunt has often been dismissed as a bad poetic model for Keats, but 'Calidore' and this verse letter to George show how repeatedly and rewardingly he gained and grew from Hunt's example. Yet if Hunt was continuing as a vital force in Keats's poetry, the two had still to meet. To contrive that introduction, Keats would have to go through Cowden Clarke – and now he knew where his old friend was living.

# CHAPTER 7

## An Era

Determined to contact Cowden Clarke, in September 1816 Keats began a verse letter to him:

> Oft have you seen a swan superbly frowning,
> And with proud breast his own white shadow crowning;
> He slants his neck beneath the waters bright
> So silently, it seems a beam of light
> Come from the Galaxy.
>
> ('To Charles Cowden Clarke', 1–5)

The 'Imitation of Spenser' had been full of sparkling light and reflections, as a swan 'oar'd . . . along in majesty'. Now, two years later, that swan 'slants his neck' with a single silent thrust 'beneath the waters bright' into 'his own white shadow'. Fascinated by how such strange transitions seem to merge real and ideal, Keats connects this sight 'oft seen' with something utterly extraordinary – a startling 'beam of light / Come from the Galaxy'. Not 'sent', but 'come': that Keats can recognise and respond to such promptings is a beacon to the future.

More usually, Keats tells Cowden Clarke, poetry has been

> loss of time,
> Whene'er I venture on the stream of rhyme;
> With shatter'd boat, oar snapt, and canvass rent,
> I slowly sail, scarce knowing my intent.
>
> (15–18)

Unwilling for Cowden Clarke to read such poor productions of his 'dull, unlearned quill', Keats confesses he has not yet 'penn'd a line' for his friend and calls on the great eighteenth-century poet William Cowper to explain why. His image of a 'shatter'd boat' reminded Cowden Clarke of Cowper's elegiac lines 'On the Receipt of my Mother's Picture' where that poet, deep in crisis, had imagined himself with 'Sails ript, seams op'ning wide, and compass toss'd'. Perhaps this was a tactful ploy to remind Cowden Clarke of an evening when they read Cowper together at Enfield, hinting that his 'loss of time' as a poet was time spent out of touch with his friend. Almost brought into focus are more far-reaching questions about life and art that will soon preoccupy Keats. What is the poet's role? How does art relate to time? And what is the origin of poetry itself – whence does the 'stream of rhyme' come, and to where does it tend? For the moment 'scarce knowing my intent' appeared to forestall composition of poetry. In a little while Keats, navigating with greater confidence, will recognise how his poetry actually springs from such mists of half-knowledge.

True, Keats had not at that time addressed a poem to Cowden Clarke. But Cowden Clarke had been given the sonnet on Hunt's release, and he can hardly have failed to read 'To Solitude' in *The Examiner*. Could that break-through explain why a silence had fallen between them? Cowden Clarke had sent Hunt his own poems, and not one of them had been published. Keats had succeeded at his first attempt. If Cowden Clarke was piqued, Keats was now writing to restore their friendship. It was Cowden Clarke who had taught him 'all the sweets of song' – Spenser, Milton, the sonnet, ode, epigram and the epic 'of all the king, / Round, vast, and spanning all like Saturn's ring'. It was Cowden Clarke, too, who had pointed out the 'patriot's duty', and introduced him to Mozart, Arne, Handel and Moore's *Irish Melodies*. By setting out this 'friendly debt', Keats did the right thing while obliging Cowden Clarke to recognise and respond to his former pupil's accomplishment. And it was Cowden Clarke who still held the possibility of an introduction to Hunt – although Keats had been published in *The Examiner*, Hunt evidently did not know who 'J.K.' actually was.

'Some weeks have pass'd since last I saw the spires / In lucent Thames reflected': Keats's epistle was carefully contrived to restore their Enfield friendship and bring Cowden Clarke up to date on what he had been doing. Refreshed by his holiday, he closes by remembering evenings of chat among Cowden Clarke's books, suppers taken together, and handshakes and partings on the path '[m]id-way between our homes'. Then, Keats had waited upon the bridge listening as Cowden Clarke's footsteps sounded or fell silent according to whether he walked on gravel or grass.

Recalling the path between Enfield and Edmonton was shrewd, for this was where Keats had handed Cowden Clarke his sonnet 'Written on the Day that Mr. Leigh Hunt left Prison'. Since then a year and a half had elapsed and Keats, still to make Hunt's acquaintance, was in no mood to be put off again. They both admired Hunt, he reminded Cowden Clarke,

> The wrong'd Libertas,—who has told you stories
> Of laurel chaplets, and Apollo's glories;
> Of troops chivalrous prancing through a city,
> And tearful ladies made for love, and pity:
> With many else which I have never known.
>
> (44–8)

'Thus have I thought,' Keats adds, quietly, 'and days on days have flown.' Gently but firmly, Keats directs Cowden Clarke to arrange a meeting with Hunt. Having broken silence by writing, he signs off by staging another farewell to which he trusts his friend will respond:

> These thoughts now come o'er me with all their might:—
> Again I shake your hand,—friend Charles, good night.
>
> (131–2)

As the couplet closed, that handshake clinched the deal.

\* \* \*

Late September brought Keats back to Guy's as the busiest time of year loomed. Early October saw new students arrive with lodgings to find, fees to pay, courses to join and surgeons to contact. Now a senior student and almost twenty-one, Keats would have been sought out for advice. He had also to resume his routines as a dresser, and find somewhere to live himself. Within days he moved into new lodgings at 8 Dean Street, a development to the east of the hospitals, and here he was joined by his brothers and their dog, Wagtail (after a quarrel with Abbey's junior partner, Hodgkinson, George had left his employ).[1] They were living together for the first time since their schooldays, and to complete Keats's satisfaction Cowden Clarke had replied. He would arrange a meeting with Hunt. Could Keats send two or three poems to show him?

Keats did so, and Cowden Clarke took them to Hunt's home at the Vale of Health, Hampstead. Perhaps Cowden Clarke began by explaining that the 'J.K.' of 'To Solitude' had written more than that sonnet, and handed over

'How many bards gild the lapses of time' and 'To Charles Cowden Clarke'.
Hunt read through the longer poem, impressed by its accomplished couplets
and deft references to Tasso, Spenser, Milton, King Alfred, Brutus and Mozart.
If Keats had already known Hunt personally he could not have assembled a
gathering better calculated to win his approval. Nearly forty-five years later,
Cowden Clarke recalled Hunt's

> prompt admiration which broke forth before he had read twenty lines of the first
> poem. Mr. Horace Smith happened to be there . . . and was not less demonstrative
> in his praise of their merits. The piece which he read out, I remember, was the
> sonnet,—
>
> How many bards gild the lapses of time!
>
> marking with particular emphasis and approbation the last six lines:
>
> So the unnumbered sounds that evening store,—
> The songs of birds, the whispering of leaves,
> The voice of waters, the great bell that heaves
> With solemn sound, and thousand others more
> *That distance of recognizance bereaves,*–
> Make pleasing music, and not wild uproar.
>
> Smith repeated, with applause, the line in Italics, saying, 'What a well-condensed
> expression!' After making numerous and eager inquiries about him, personally,
> and with reference to any peculiarities of mind and manner, the visit ended in my
> being requested to bring him over to the Vale of Health.[2]

Horace and James Smith were the authors of *Rejected Addresses*, best-selling
parodies of Wordsworth, Coleridge, Byron and Scott. While Hunt praised
promptly, Smith's instinct as a parodist was to attend to the distinctive tones
of Keats's voice. In a sonnet that evokes the attenuating effects of distance,
Smith fixed upon five remarkably 'condensed' words that proclaimed Keats a
poet. There are all kinds of heraldic, legal and emblematic associations behind
Keats's splendid word 'recognizance' – most importantly the senses of 'known
character' or 'identity' that intersect, through the word 'bereaves', with ideas
of *dis*entitlement or *dis*possession. What Horace Smith apparently heard most
clearly in Keats's voice was its emphatic announcement of deprivation. This
forlorn note is heard throughout Keats's writing, as if summoning the shadows
of his parents and more distant West Country forebears.

'Bring him over to the Vale of Health.' Cowden Clarke passed this good
news to Keats, but there would be further delays. The seven days beginning

on Wednesday, 2 October were almost certainly a duty dresser week when Keats stayed overnight at Guy's.[3] He would have admitted patients on the Wednesday morning, accompanied the surgeon round the wards, assisted at operations on Friday, and for seven days and nights dealt with emergencies. Perhaps it was during these long watches that he set about transcribing more poems for Hunt.

On Wednesday, 9 October – his parents' wedding anniversary – Keats informed Cowden Clarke that he was free to take up Hunt's invitation:

My dear Sir,

    The busy time has just gone by, and I can now devote any time you may mention to the pleasure of seeing Mr. Hunt—'t will be an Era in my existence—I am anxious too to see the author of the Sonnet to the Sun . . . I have coppied [sic] out a sheet or two of Verses which I composed some time ago, and find so much to blame in them that the best part will go into the fire—those to G. Mathew I will suffer to meet the eye of Mr. H. notwithstanding that the Muse is so frequently mentioned.[4]

Mathew's 'To a Poetical Friend' had just appeared in October's *European Magazine*, with its outdated profile of Keats as a poet

Of courteous knights-errant, and high-mettled steeds;
Of forests enchanted, and marvellous streams; –
Of bridges, and castles, and desperate deeds;
And all the bright fictions of fanciful dreams.

Keats responded characteristically by breaking that frame, dismissing past achievements to ready himself for the future. A good number of poems had already gone into the fire. Addressing Cowden Clarke now as an equal, Keats placed himself firmly on London's literary scene: he was anxious to meet the author of a 'Sonnet to the Sun' – either Charles Ollier or Horace Smith, both of whom were acquainted with Cowden Clarke and Hunt – and reminded Cowden Clarke of something in his own 'Portfolio' that he expected to see: 'I will put you in Mind of it—Although the Borough is a beastly place in dirt, turnings and windings; yet No. 8 Dean Street is not difficult to find . . .—At all events let me hear from you soon—I say at all events not excepting the Gout in your fingers'.[5] Keats's tone was genial but commanding. He expected action.

The letter reached Cowden Clarke on the evening of Wednesday, 9 October, or possibly the next morning. Keats was determined to meet Hunt, and Hunt had urged Cowden Clarke to invite him – he would be free at any time after *The Examiner* went to press on Saturday the 12th.[6] But Cowden Clarke, who

was following his own agenda, did nothing. Unknown to Keats, he had passed
his own 'copy books' to Hunt, requesting him to look over his poems. Might
his 'Sonnet to Liberty' find a place in *The Examiner*? Hunt did not reply, and
Cowden Clarke had not fixed when he would bring Keats. Sunday the 13th
passed. Then Monday, Tuesday and Wednesday when Hunt had to start
preparing copy for the next Sunday's *Examiner* – as Cowden Clarke knew. On
Wednesday the 16th he sent Hunt a new edition of Samuel Johnson, possibly
the *Diary of a Journey into Wales* just published by Robert Jennings.[7] Would
Hunt mention it in *The Examiner*? Also enclosed was a letter enquiring if he
had offended Hunt. Why hadn't Hunt replied? Had he read his copy books of
poems? What about the 'Sonnet on Liberty'? Hunt's silence had provoked a
'nervous attack'.[8]

The 'Era' in Keats's existence was postponed. Hunt replied to reassure
Cowden Clarke, offer a criticism of the Johnson and sympathise with his
nerves. He had no recollection of a sonnet – 'When did it come, or by what,
or whom?' In any case it could not appear in next Sunday's *Examiner*, as
Hunt's own sonnet 'To Benjamin Robert Haydon' would appear then. He
sealed the letter and scribbled an afterthought on the inside of the wrapper:
'Will you come & take your chop with us next Saturday – my birthday?
Mr. Haydon I expect will be our guest.'[9]

Cowden Clarke could delay the introduction no longer. On Saturday,
19 October, Keats joined him to walk out to the Vale of Health in the hollow
to the north of Hampstead Heath. Hunt had been living here since late 1815,
at home in a little weather-boarded cottage with his wife, Marianne, and their
three children, sister-in-law Bess Kent and several servants. They kept open
house for all the poets, painters, newspapermen, sculptors, musicians and
radicals attracted by Hunt's convivial company and sparkling conversation.
Among them were Haydon, Hazlitt, Reynolds, the musical Novello family,
Charles and James Ollier, the Gattie brothers, Henry Robertson, Charles and
Mary Lamb, William Godwin, and James and Horace Smith. Shelley and
Mary Godwin would soon be drawn here, and Keats and Clarke were about
to arrive. As they neared the edge of the Heath, Keats walked faster, seeming
to rise with anticipation on every step.[10]

'Libertas' stepped forward and 'J.K.' was introduced to the man he had
admired since his schooldays. If Enfield had initiated Keats's journey to the
Vale of Health, his meeting with Hunt represented another beginning. Up to
now Keats had not encountered an author who wrote for a living; Hunt
earned a precarious income, week by week, as a journalist and a poet. Aged
thirty-two, Hunt was eleven years older than Keats, and at almost six foot he
was as many inches taller. His face had been lined by ill-health and two years'

imprisonment. Cowden Clarke was already familiar with Hunt's manner – he spoke easily and eloquently, in a finely modulated voice that was both welcoming and winning. Keats, who often held back in company, found him approachable and soon felt at ease. Hunt conversed knowledgeably about books, poetry, politics and painting, reviews, theatre, music and opera – he had a light touch, and ranged agreeably over every topic while ignoring the scene of chaos that surrounded them: an old sofa and ramshackle chairs, books, busts, jars filled with flowers from the Heath, grubby children and their toys, a flute and a lute, papers, manuscripts and back copies of *The Examiner*, portfolios of engravings and a large rocking horse. On the wall were portraits of Milton and John Hunt. Keats was shown the tiny parlour where Hunt had set up a study with writing desk, piano, pictures and books. Somewhere among all this was Cowden Clarke's sonnet, and the manuscript of a poem Hunt had announced in *The Examiner* of 6 October and then mislaid: 'The Hymn to Intellectual Beauty' by 'ELFIN-KNIGHT' – aka Percy Bysshe Shelley.[11]

More visible was Hunt's other birthday guest, Benjamin Haydon, historical painter and champion of the then neglected Elgin Marbles. A self-proclaimed genius, Haydon was accepted by many at his own estimate: Wordsworth likened him to Titian; Hunt placed him with Michelangelo and Raphael.[12] Even *The Times* praised the extraordinary perfection of his handling of light and colour.[13] With his colossal canvases, thunderous voice, indefatigable energy and personality as obsessive as it was volatile, Haydon's visions of future glory were on a scale that rivalled Napoleon's.[14] He was also extremely short-sighted.

Born in Plymouth on 28 January 1786, from childhood Haydon was determined to be a painter. Despite the setback of an infection that damaged his sight, he embarked on a mission to reform English art and its misguided audience by restoring the glory of historical painting: 'see or not see, a painter I'll be, and if I am a great one without seeing, I shall be the first.'[15] His poor eyesight explains his microscopic attention to detail – he painted close to the canvas, forehead festooned with spectacles – as well as the grand scale of his work. If he stepped back from a less than gigantic painting, he could not see it. Instead of applying paint in a conventional manner, he said that he 'attacked' his canvases with 'fury'.

Arriving in London in 1804, Haydon made a good start. He studied at the Royal Academy, successfully exhibiting 'Joseph and Mary Resting on the Road to Egypt' (1806) and 'The Assassination of Dentatus' (1809). September 1808 saw his first visit to the Elgin Marbles, then stored in a damp, dirty outhouse on Park Lane. Already a man with a mission, the Greek sculptures redoubled his zeal: 'Oh, how I inwardly thanked God that I was prepared to understand all this! Now I was rewarded . . . I felt the future, I foretold they would prove themselves the finest things on earth . . . I said it then, *when no one would believe me*.'[16] In these marble forms, Haydon believed, earthly nature was united with ideal, heavenly beauty – a notably elusive *mistura* that Keats's Endymion would pursue through four thousand lines of verse.[17] At all hours of day and night Haydon hurried back to study and sketch, and lost no opportunity to trumpet his opinions: 'Such a blast will Fame blow of their grandeur, that its roaring will swell out as time advances.'[18]

After an impressive debut in town, and with several prestigious commissions, Haydon's career would have been set fair were it not that he needed to feel embattled before 'attacking' in paint. A protracted feud with the Royal Academy began when 'Dentatus' was removed from the Great Room to a less prominent location. This slight Haydon never forgave. When he attacked the connoisseur Richard Payne Knight in *The Examiner*, arraigning the Academy as '*a vast organ of bad taste* and *corruption*', his alienation from the art establishment was complete.[19] But Haydon could also warm to those, like Wordsworth, who seemed to share his sense of a high calling. Keats would soon be among them.

If all was going well, Haydon felt 'like a man with air balloons under his arm pits and ether in his soul'; when those highs were punctured, the aeronaut plunged into abysmal depressions. We now recognise those moods as evidence of a bipolar tendency, and Haydon himself was aware of multiple aspects of his own personality. His journals are an astonishingly candid record of his ups and downs, ambitions and checks; of his passionate likings and all-consuming jealousies; of his erotic energy, religious resolve and agonising sexual frustration. His better self, 'B.R. Haydon', was a bright spirit who basked in the anticipation of fame and success. In the shadows of debt, depression and depravity skulked his dismal alter ego, 'John Haydon', a dingy creature who 'painted in imitation of [B.R. Haydon] a few small works . . . and . . . did all those things that men must do who prefer their own degradation to the starvation of their children'.[20] Everything about Haydon appears grotesque and yet, as Aldous Huxley pointed out, his face was delicate – 'as though Mussolini had been strangely blended with Cardinal Newman . . . Haydon had only to look in the glass to realise that he was a great man.'[21] Given Haydon's perilous self-inflation and disastrous volatility, perhaps his greatest achievement was to sustain his self-belief almost as far as the horribly botched suicide that ended his life.

On first meeting Haydon, Keats knew nothing of his egotism and vulnerability. What he saw was a successful painter, well connected in London art circles, whose Elgin Marbles campaign had triumphed with their purchase for the nation. Like Hunt, Haydon was a professional who apparently made his living through his art, and his current work was a gargantuan canvas entitled 'Christ's Entry into Jerusalem'.

The date of 19 October 1816 truly marked an era in Keats's existence. Within a few moments he had met the two men who would shape his life for the foreseeable future. Hunt offered friendship, sociability, conversation and a cultured life organized around poetry, politics, music, paintings and engravings. Haydon apparently embodied the sublimity and selflessness of genius – he had dedicated his life to his art, and 'Christ's Entry into Jerusalem' would eclipse all that he had produced hitherto. Such, at least, were Keats's first impressions. Usually rated among Keats's less successful poems, his verse letter 'To Charles Cowden Clarke' was as momentous in its consequences as anything he ever wrote. But were Hunt and Haydon really as altruistic as he thought?

\* \* \*

Haydon had at first seen Hunt as a like-minded young man – clever, fearless, independent, witty, charming, he was 'one of the most delightful beings'.[22] They took to each other instantly, then discovered how often they quarrelled. Hunt's brio could be insensitive; Haydon's enthusiasm masked a dogged temper and devastating insecurities. Both were depressives. The reef on which they repeatedly foundered was religion. Haydon splintered noisily on Hunt's scepticism; Hunt's cheerful freethinking – his spiritual life raft – was easily overset by Haydonian storms. When Keats first dined with them a long-running quarrel about Voltaire and Christianity gave a tense undertow to the conversation, as Haydon's diary entry for 19 October reveals. Haydon had determined to taunt Hunt by portraying the sceptic Voltaire alongside Newton, a believer, in the crowd that packs 'Christ's Entry into Jerusalem'.[23] Not surprisingly, these quixotic friends quickly divided over Keats and, as we shall see, in the coming months they would vie jealously to become his mentor.

Keats's muscular, physical response to poetry had long been noticed by Cowden Clarke: he seemed to grow as he recited some lines, rather as he had risen on every step as he neared Hunt. Now Hunt, too, registered Keats's promise in terms of his bodily presence and 'fine, fervid countenance'. His compact form and strong, animated features coincided with his 'exuberant specimens of genuine though young poetry'.[24] Ten years later Hunt sketched Keats as he appeared when they first met:

He was under the middle height; and his lower limbs were small in comparison with the upper, but neat and well-turned. His shoulders were very broad for his size: he had a face in which energy and sensibility were remarkably mixed up, an eager power checked and made patient by ill health. Every feature was at once strongly cut, and delicately alive. If there was any faulty expression, it was in the mouth, which was not without something of a character of pugnacity. The face was rather long than otherwise; the upper lip projected a little over the under; the chin was bold, the cheeks sunken; the eyes mellow and glowing; large, dark, and sensitive. At the recital of a noble action, or a beautiful thought, they would suffuse with tears, and his mouth trembled ... His hair, of a brown colour, was fine, and hung in natural ringlets.[25]

Other accounts agree with Hunt's, and it is notable that Hunt apparently detected ill-health in Keats almost from their first meeting.

What did they discuss? Obvious topics would be Keats's poems, Hunt's *Rimini*, *The Examiner* and Haydon's plans for his painting. Their talk most likely touched on Spenser and Byron too – Keats's current favourites coincided with Hunt's – and perhaps Keats's mention of Lemprière called up Hunt's days at Christ's Hospital and afterwards, when he had been 'without a prospect and without a hope, except that of leaving behind ... the promise of something poetical'.[26] Now Keats told Hunt of his own struggles and ambitions, of long nights at Guy's Hospital writing and transcribing his poems, and of weary mornings in the dresser's office or pacing the wards. Across the room, Haydon was so struck by Keats's 'prematurity of intellectual and poetic power' that there and then he 'formed a very high idea of his genius'.[27]

Much of this account of the meeting between Keats, Cowden Clarke, Hunt and Haydon is speculative. One thing beyond doubt, however, is that Keats's passion for poetry had an electrifying effect – Hunt and Haydon were both jolted into admiration of this new prodigy. Neither of them came out and said it, but each had determined to recruit Keats to a new school of young geniuses. The battle was on.

In Haydon's eyes, Keats's dedication to poetry matched his own selfless, Shakespearean pursuit of his own art; both of them were driven by ideas of future greatness and immortal fame, and Haydon knew that he had God on his side. Hunt saw things differently. In Keats he had discovered a youthful poet to cultivate alongside John Hamilton Reynolds, a mainstay of the liberal *Champion* magazine whose latest poem, *The Naiad*, had just been published. Hunt's challenge to existing aesthetics in *The Story of Rimini* had impressed both of these young poets, and now their work would invigorate his campaign for poetic and political reform. 'We became intimate on the spot,' Hunt recalled, and Keats was invited to call again. Three visits followed quickly, on one of which occasions Keats met Reynolds.[28] Hunt's poetic coterie was forming but, as time would show, Haydon had his own plans too.

And what of Cowden Clarke? He would have been watching and listening as his former pupil established himself in Hunt's and Haydon's esteem. Walking back along the lanes to London, perhaps he reflected ruefully that not a single word had been said about his own poems.

CHAPTER 8

———————

# Wild Surmises

'THAT WAS a red-letter day in the young poet's life.' So Cowden Clarke recalled Saturday, 19 October 1816 and it had certainly set Keats forward.[1] Their first Clerkenwell 'symposium' of poetry, as Cowden Clarke termed it, came shortly after their visit to Hunt – most likely on the evening of Friday, 25 October. It was occasioned by Cowden Clarke being loaned the folio edition of George Chapman's Homer. Hunt had recently borrowed this volume from his friend Thomas Alsager, toasting it in *The Examiner* in a manner calculated to appeal to Keats: 'CHAPMAN, whose *Homer*'s a fine rough old wine'.[2] Hunt then passed Chapman to Cowden Clarke. Such spontaneous generosity with another's property was completely in character, and in this instance sprang from the best of motives. Hunt recognised that Keats could learn from what Chapman had done.

In Cowden Clarke's recollection of their wine-warmed evening, they turned to some 'famousest' passages and relished the muscular music of Chapman's couplets. Then, early on the fine morning of Saturday the 26th, Keats left Warner Street to walk back across town to Southwark. As soon as he arrived, he set down fourteen lines on the thrilling discoveries he had made:

**'On the First Looking into Chapman's Homer'**

Much have I travell'd in the Realms of Gold,
    And many goodly states, and kingdoms seen;
    Round many Western islands have I been,
Which Bards in fealty to Apollo hold.
Oft of one wide expanse had I been told
    Which low brow'd Homer ruled as his Demesne;

Yet could I never judge what Men could mean,
Till I heard Chapman speak out loud, and bold.
Then felt I like some Watcher of the Skies
   When a new Planet swims into his ken,
Or like stout Cortez, when with wond'ring eyes
   He star'd at the Pacific, and all his Men
Look'd at each other with a wild surmise—
   Silent, upon a Peak in Darien—[3]

Looking back over what he had written, Keats made one alteration – 'low brow'd Homer' became bardically 'deep brow'd' – then he folded the paper, scribbled the address and sent it to Cowden Clarke, who received it before ten the same morning.

Keats was about to turn twenty-one, and the sonnet magnificently marked his coming of age as a poet. Appropriately, it is located on one of Keats's thresholds, looking into, gazing back, then turning to the future – a juxtaposition that resembles 'To Solitude', where the city's murk had opened to a 'span' beyond. 'Chapman's Homer' is an inner-city poem too, and its 'Realms of Gold' – a glorious panorama of poetic marvels – have disclosed a fresh wonder, Chapman's Homer, boldly and brilliantly encountered as a new planet. 'Then felt I like some Watcher of the Skies,' Keats writes, and on that delighted swim of feeling is carried onwards to imagine further planetary and poetic revelations. Cowden Clarke had long since likened epic to the planet Saturn 'spanning all', and he could be expected to know that Herschel's new planet Uranus had been discovered far beyond Saturn's orbit. It went without saying that the new poet Keats had in mind was himself, for his sonnet eloquently announced his arrival. Its verbal concentration and extraordinary formal intelligence, as 'ken' eddies back in a half-rhyme to 'seen', 'been', and 'demesne', make even the Margate seascape in his earlier sonnet to George seem fussily diffuse:

The ocean with its vastness, its blue green,
   Its ships, its rocks, its caves, its hopes, its fears,—
   Its voice mysterious, which whoso hears
Must think on what will be, and what has been.
         ('To my Brother George', 5–8)

Now, just two months after he wrote that portentous final line, Keats mastered a moment of awed anticipation, 'Silent, upon a Peak in Darien—', and completed a poem of genius.

* * *

Having sent his sonnet to Cowden Clarke, Keats readied himself for an engagement in Hampstead. For most of October, Haydon had been staying at 7 Pond Street, on the edge of Hampstead Heath, to rest his eyes. Immediately after meeting Keats at the Vale of Health, Haydon versified an invitation to John Hamilton Reynolds:

> Come thou Poet!—*free* and *brown*!
> Next Sunday to Hampstead Town
> To meet John Keats, who soon will shine
> The greatest, of this Splendid time
> That e'er has woo'ed the Muses nine.

Reynolds had already met Keats at Hunt's, and told Haydon of his potential greatness.[4] Now Haydon wanted both of them to himself. A whisper might do the trick: 'Now Reynolds it'll be just as well / If that, you don't to others tell . . .' Others, in this context, meant Hunt. Sunday the 27th was fine, and Keats once again stepped out on the Hampstead road, arriving at Haydon's at half past two. Reynolds was already there.

∗ ∗ ∗

Born on 9 September 1794, Reynolds was a little over a year older than Keats, the son of George Reynolds, schoolmaster, and his wife Charlotte. Keats likened his personality to the tang of ginger beer, adding that he was the 'playfullest' of his companions despite suffering recurrent bouts of rheumatic fever.[5] In 1816 the Reynoldses were living at 19 Lamb's Conduit Street, to the east of the British Museum. He had four sisters – Jane (born 1791), Marianne (1797), Eliza (1799) and Charlotte (1802) – and until April 1816 had worked as a clerk at the Amicable Insurance Office. Since then he had pursued a full-time career as a writer and, given his considerable capacity for self-promotion, he looked likely to succeed. He was effectively John Scott's deputy editor at *The Champion*, and his precocious talents had already appeared in poems for the *Gentleman's Magazine* and three published volumes: *Safie, an Eastern Tale* (1814), *The Eden of Imagination* (1814) and *An Ode* (1815). *Safie*, modelled on Byron's eastern tale *The Giaour*, was an auspicious debut. Publisher John Murray sent the manuscript to Byron for comment, and His Lordship's advice for Reynolds led to correspondence and a meeting between the two men. It was most likely Byron who gave Reynolds an introduction to Hunt in Horsemonger Lane, and *Safie* was published with a dedication to Byron 'with every sentiment of gratitude and respect'. *The Eden of Imagination* repeated the trick by emulating Wordsworth's early poem *An*

*Evening Walk* (1793). A copy sent off to Rydal Mount brought a friendly reply. Reynolds's most recent work, *The Naiad*, published by Taylor and Hessey in August 1816, was dedicated to Haydon; it attracted favourable reviews, and by October, Reynolds had embarked on a Spenserian narrative of poetic origins, *The Romance of Youth*, and was well into its first canto. This astonishing productivity put Keats on his mettle: he would soon be following Reynolds's example.

Through the Zetosophian Society, a weekly discussion group dedicated to 'wisdom-seeking', Reynolds was acquainted with several young men about town who would soon meet Keats.[6] Among them was generous James Rice, wisest of Keats's friends, born in January 1795 and now employed in his father's legal offices at 62 Great Marlborough Street, a few yards from Haydon's studio. To Keats, his character had the bouquet of a fine claret – cool, calm, at peace with the world – although this seemingly placid manner may have been the consequence of living with a chronic depressive illness.[7] Serious and scholarly Benjamin Bailey, twenty-five, was studying at Magdalen Hall, Oxford (he matriculated there on Sunday, 19 October, when Keats was meeting Hunt). For a while Keats thought him 'one of the noblest men alive at the present day', and Bailey would prove supportive during the writing of *Endymion*.[8] But there was a taint to his personality. Well intentioned, capable of generosity, Bailey was also devious and self-serving. Destined to take holy orders, this self-confessed 'slave of passion' proposed marriage to Thomasine Leigh (a mutual friend of Reynolds and Rice who lived at Salcombe Regis in Devon). When she declined, Bailey resolved to chase down any young woman who might be snared with an offer. In his curious mixture of naivety and ambition, generosity and self-interest, personal advancement always won through – with damaging consequences for others, including Keats and Reynolds's publisher John Martin. Martin's sister may have been the 'Miss Martin' whom Keats was astonished to learn Bailey had been 'trying at' while making 'impatient Love' to Reynolds's sister Marianne.[9]

Together the Zetosophians had founded *The Inquirer; or, Literary Miscellany*, an occasional journal that involved others with whom Keats would soon be connected. Reynolds contributed articles and poems, while theatrical reviews came from his friend Charles Wentworth Dilke of the Navy Pay Office. As Keats's first acquaintance with Reynolds warmed into a durable friendship, their circle also drew in Keats's brothers, Reynolds's parents and sisters, Dilke's family and Dilke's former school fellow Charles Armitage Brown.[10] Of Dilke and Brown we shall soon hear much more.

Four days after Keats dined at Haydon's, Cowden Clarke forwarded another invitation from him for Sunday, 3 November. Both of them were to breakfast at Haydon's Great Marlborough Street studio. Keats responded in high spirits. Breezily buttonholing Cowden Clarke as 'My daintie Davie' – not 'My dear Sir' as hitherto – Keats promises to be 'as punctual as the Bee to the Clover', puns promptly on his pleasure at seeing 'this glorious Haydon and all his Creation', and moves swiftly to secure another introduction:- 'I pray thee let me know when you go to Ollier's and where he resides—this I forgot to ask you.'[11]

* * *

What did 'daintie Davie' make of this mist of mirth and cajolery? We can sense Keats's excitement at joining London's literary world – Cowden Clarke had led to Hunt and Horace Smith; Hunt to Haydon, who knew Wordsworth, and to Reynolds, who had met Byron. Now there was a prospect of meeting Ollier, and this would prove crucial in the coming months. Keats's social life was buzzing; he was writing poetry at every opportunity; and he was holding down his responsibilities at Guy's. How did he manage to reconcile all of these competing demands? Did he keep them in balance or, as some have suspected, did he whittle back his hospital commitments? The dates and terms of dressers' obligations at Guy's show that it would have been very difficult, if not impossible, for him to reduce his hours. As noted before, as a dresser he is likely to have had four duty weeks per annum; if, as seems likely, the 'busy time' of 2–9 October represented one of these duty weeks, his next such week would have been 25 December–1 January 1817, or 4–11 December if experienced dressers shared the duties of Lucas's newest dresser, Daniel Gossett, who started in October. The upshot is that the weeks Keats actually spent as a duty dresser between October 1816 and March 1817 can only be guessed at from the evidence of what else he was doing. In considering that evidence, we also need to bear in mind his other responsibilities week by week, day by day, at Guy's: assisting at taking-in each Wednesday; accompanying Lucas's ward rounds on Tuesdays and Fridays; attending at theatre while Lucas was operating. On all of these occasions Keats would have been present, performing minor surgery and cleaning and dressing wounds. If he was still going to lectures, they would have had to be fitted into this crowded schedule too.[12]

What is known of Keats's life *outside* Guy's in autumn 1816 shows that most of his meetings with friends were at weekends, with a few encounters on weekday evenings.[13] This means that when Keats was not duty dresser for the week, his intense social life was compatible with daytime hospital duties. That Keats also contrived to keep writing poetry tells us a great deal about his unswerving self-belief; as Cowden Clarke said, when Keats determined to win a school prize he devoted every spare hour with 'close and persevering application'.[14] The same exacting qualities were now seeing him through these demanding months as his ambitions as a poet grew and he set his sights on winning.

∗ ∗ ∗

Late October 1816 marked Keats's twenty-first birthday. Perhaps he celebrated with his brothers; possibly he visited Abbey to ask what remained of his capital. 'Perhaps' and 'possibly' because Keats had first to ascertain that he had in fact come of age. With his brothers he contacted one of their parents' acquaintances, most likely Joshua or Anne Burch. Alice Jennings had died, owing a Joshua Burch £3.15s., and on 13 June the brothers had instructed Abbey to clear this debt from her estate.[15] Anne Burch was briefly drawn into the interminable Chancery case when on 29 June 1825 she gave an affidavit to the effect that 'she was intimately acquainted with Thomas and Frances Keats before and after the birth of John Keats, and "that sd. J.K. was born in the year 1795, viz$^{t.}$ on or about 29th Oct." '[16] If Anne Burch advised on Keats's birthday in October 1816, she was also very likely Tom's source for his story that as a 'most violent and ungovernable child' Keats had threatened his mother with a sword.[17] George, also on a quest to ascertain Keats's age, had called at Craven Street, where he told Mrs Grafty of his brother's determination to be a poet and learned of his rhyme games as a little boy. Both of these encounters with Keats's early life can be dated to October 1816, and they contributed to a developing pattern in which the past revived and influenced his self-fashioning as a poet.

Haydon heard Tom and George's 'interesting particulars' of Keats's boyhood, and on 7 April 1817 noted them carefully in his diary. He mentioned that the brothers had been 'to a Servant . . . to ascertain Keats's age', adding that they did so 'that he might come to his property'. Just seven words, but their import was considerable. Haydon knew that Keats had inherited money – and if Haydon knew, others did too.[18] But exactly how much did Keats stand to inherit in October 1816?

War had already depressed the cash value of stock at Alice Jennings's death, and it sank further during Keats's apprenticeship and time at Guy's. Stock had been sold to pay his premium to Hammond, and interest on the balance generated an annual income of some £55, although this dwindled as more stock was sold to cover his expenses. By October 1816 about two-thirds of his original capital had been sold to raise £1,000 cash for his medical studies, and what remained produced an income from interest of only a few pounds per annum. Either Keats cashed his remaining stock on turning twenty-one, or he took Abbey's advice and waited for the market to recover.[19] Either way, for the next year and a half his resources were limited – although he always gave the impression of being well-off, spent freely, lent generously and generally had an air of affluence.[20] He knew that his brothers' inheritances were intact (neither had yet come of age), but was apparently unaware of his £800 capital still languishing in Chancery – his share of John Jennings's legacy to the Keats children plus their late mother's capital.[21]

His mother's second marriage to a bank clerk seems to have prejudiced Keats against financial dealings of any kind: inheritances, money and misery had long been associated in the Jennings and Keats families, and not enquiring about money was also a way of banishing thoughts of dispossession, pauperism and the poorhouse. Keats's relations with Abbey were often tense and unsatisfactory, and although Abbey seems to have disliked Hammond, the broken apprenticeship may have left a residue of ill-feeling. Any of these factors could explain Keats's curious combination of straitened circumstances and apparent wealth – but perhaps, after all, the simplest explanation is best. Keats was aware that he had funds, but was disinclined to investigate exactly how much: 'I have all my life thought very little of these matters,' he admitted, 'they seem not to belong to me.'[22]

* * *

Keats was calculating in other directions, however. Joseph Severn, first encountered in spring 1816, was now established at the Royal Academy. On Friday, 1 November, Keats heard from him, asking to meet on either Saturday or Sunday, quite possibly to arrange a portrait sitting. 'My dear Sir,' Keats replied by return:

> I am nearly sorry that I have an engagement on Saturday; to which I have looked forward all the Week more especially because I particularly want to look into some beautiful Scenery—for poetical purposes. I am very sensible of your kindness and hope for the pleasure of seeing you ere long at No 8 Dean Street. I know you will congratulate me when I tell you that I shall Breakfast with Haydon on Sunday.

Keats's tone was friendly, his priorities clear. Meeting Severn was not one of them. His eyes were set on a venture out of London – most likely to Hampstead – followed by breakfast at Haydon's. If this was not quite a rebuff for Severn, it does reveal how single-mindedly Keats was now pursuing what appeared to be to his own advantage.

He posted his letter to Severn, walked on to Cowden Clarke's and invited him to his Cheapside lodgings on 17 December – some six weeks ahead. At a time when Keats's social life could alter at a moment's notice, this was an unusually long-term arrangement, and for Keats it was evidently a date of significance: 18 December would mark twenty-one years since his baptism and, although a celebration of that anniversary seems extremely unlikely, his brothers' enquiries about his age had wakened memories of their childhood and early life. Perhaps it was this reflective mood that led Keats to contemplate a long poem surveying his achievements and aims as a poet – a more thoroughgoing treatment of a theme he had already touched upon in verse letters to Mathew, his brother George and Cowden Clarke. Reynolds was at work on *The Romance of Youth*, a quasi-autobiographical account of how a 'youngster boy of golden mind' had developed into a poet. At some time this autumn – Cowden Clarke says it was during a visit to Hunt at the Vale of Health – Keats began to write the autobiographical verses that became *Sleep and Poetry*.[23] As Keats's poetic ambitions became focused with greater clarity, perhaps he felt the need to fix a date when he would announce them to his friends. If my speculation is correct, 17 December would mark a rite of passage that he wished Cowden Clarke and others to witness.

* * *

Murky and wet, Saturday, 2 November brought little prospect of enjoying Hampstead's scenery, but a visit to Hunt at the Vale of Health might nevertheless prove helpful. If Keats took 'On the First Looking into Chapman's Homer' to show to Hunt, as seems likely, that would explain why on the following Sunday morning *The Examiner* announced the future publication of 'The SONNET ON CHAPMAN'S HOMER by J.K., and a selection from the *Naiad*, at the earliest opportunity'.[24] This was more welcome publicity for Keats, and he would have been pleased to be paired with Reynolds. But Hunt was also about his own purposes. As perhaps he knew by now, Haydon had deliberately excluded him from his poetical dinner at Pond Street. *The Examiner* announcement was Hunt's return salvo.

Punctual as bees to clover, on Sunday morning Keats and Cowden Clarke arrived for breakfast at Marlborough Street. Welcomed by Haydon, they settled amicably to their meal, and we can imagine what might have ensued. Haydon already had the morning's *Examiner*, turned over a few pages, started upon Hunt's editorial and – almost choking on a mouthful of sausage – saw the announcement about Keats, Reynolds and 'the earliest opportunity'. Hunt, his rival for the patronage of those two young poets, had poached both of them – and now they would appear together before the public with *The Examiner*'s blessing. It took time for Haydon to subside after any affront; fortunately, there was a distraction on this occasion that would help salve wounded feelings. Breakfast continued beneath Haydon's huge canvas of 'Christ's Entry into Jerusalem', and the painting offered ample opportunity for flattery and other diversions. But what the visitors saw on that Sunday morning was very different from the finished work familiar to later generations.

∗ ∗ ∗

Paintings on heroic and sublime themes had been popularized by Hunt's uncle, Benjamin West, with subjects such as 'General Wolfe', 'The Death of Nelson', 'Achilles' and, most pertinent to Haydon's own ambitions, 'Christ Healing the Sick'. Haydon launched his career by breaking into this market. His 'Macbeth' was a study of acute physical and psychological tension, as was required by his theory of historical painting: 'As a painter has but one moment, first it must be a subject of palpable and gross interest, big with the past and pregnant with the future; next, your actions must be doing, your passions expressing, your lights and shadows fleeting, something must have passed, and something must be coming, and you choose your point of interest – the point between'.[25] Macbeth meditating murder depicts just such a dreadful interim, and Haydon had long planned another such picture that would propel British painting, and Haydon himself, to prominence. It would be comparatively slight in action, a momentous non-event from which, however, everything would flow: Palm Sunday, the point between BC and AD, the end of the pagan world, and the beginning of the Christian age. To everyone who viewed this great work the message would be clear: a new and gloriously Haydonian era in British art was under way. 'Christ's Entry into Jerusalem' was the work that would launch a new academy of artists in which, if Hunt could be deflected, Keats would shortly be enrolled.

As early as 3 September 1809 Haydon was musing about painting Christ the healer, but it was only after four years' study of the Elgin Marbles that he was ready to begin. 'Began my Picture in reality', he noted on 18 August 1814. 'My heart swelled as I touched it'.[26] From now on Haydon's diary recorded his daily progress, with repeated thanks for divine support. Here he is on 8 November 1814: 'I thank God from my Soul, that the head finished this day is an immense advance in my Art . . . Spare my eyes, O God, till I have done all my power can do, till I have reformed the Art & taste of my Country, Amen.'[27] The head just finished was Jairus's, centre right, whose daughter Christ had just restored to life. Not for the first time Haydon dared to compare his own mission to reform art and taste with Christ's: by taking his faithful servant John Sammons as a model for the figure of Christ, the Messiah became a servant to Haydon's artistic ambitions. 'High is our calling, friend,' Wordsworth had proclaimed in his sonnet to Haydon, recognising a spirit whose dauntless self-belief matched his own.

June 1815 saw Haydon take Wordsworth's life mask, reflecting as he did so that 'people find fault with Wordsworth for speaking of his own genius; to be sure they do!' – and then, with a glance at the mirror: 'The World always find fault with a man of genius for speaking of his own genius.' The editor of Haydon's diary notes that the remainder of the page on which Haydon wrote this was torn away, doubtless during one of the painter's terrible depressions. With hindsight it is easy to dismiss Haydon as a deluded failure who tragically misjudged his own gifts, but when he met Keats he genuinely believed he was leading a revolution in British art and eagerly sought new recruits to the cause. Even the Iron Duke was elect. For many years an ardent Bonapartist, after Waterloo Haydon swiftly refreshed his palette to proclaim the duke of Wellington a 'Saviour of the World's intellect' like himself.[28]

January 1816. 'Got the head of Christ in!' Haydon scribbled ecstatically, and as the year advanced he deliberately projected his painting as a personal manifesto. At the Vale of Health, in his lodgings at Pond Street and now in Great Marlborough Street we can see Haydon assembling a group that would appear to the right of Christ's figure – a group purposely established in opposition to Hunt. From 19 October many of his diary entries record his reasons for including Voltaire (the 'sneerer') and Newton ('a Believer'): 'If Newton is right, Voltaire will be as he ought to be, ridiculous. If Newton be wrong, Voltaire will be as he ought to be, reverenced & adored.'[29] In Haydon's canvas Voltaire and Newton embodied the protracted argument with Hunt that would eventually rupture their friendship.

As Keats and Cowden Clarke breakfasted, 'Christ's Entry' still had large areas of blank canvas. Its left and right foregrounds were complete, as was a version of Christ's head, but the remainder of the canvas contained figures sketched in outline only – spaces for surmise. Here Keats would eventually appear, as would Wordsworth. Later that day Hazlitt called and sat for a portrait that would also find its place among the spectators surrounding Christ. He drank a bottle of wine, reminiscing about his early life and how he had given up painting as a possible career. Haydon let him talk, conscious that Hazlitt was capable of 'great good . . . for the great purposes of art', and aware that Keats would further those great purposes too.[30]

\* \* \*

A week at Guy's passed, and on Friday, 8 November, Keats expected to see Haydon again. A note arrived with apologies – he had to attend Drury Lane for a production of *Timon of Athens*. Keats alerted Cowden Clarke and, anticipating a solitary evening, signed off: 'So I rest your Hermit – John Keats.'[31]

The Dean Street hermit did not rest for long. This was very likely the evening that Keats walked across to Thomas Richards's house at 9 Providence Street, Walworth, close to Apollo Buildings. By day Richards worked in the Ordnance Department at the Tower of London; at night he wrote theatre reviews for *The Examiner*. As we have seen, Thomas and his brother Charles were also pupils at Enfield, a connection that helps to explain Keats's decision to call.[32] Charles had printed Cowden Clarke's 'fisty-cuffish' defence of Hunt back in the summer, and if Keats was actively projecting a volume of his poems, the Richards brothers could give him good advice.

The 8th had dawned fine and frosty, and continued well below freezing all day. While Keats was at Richards's house, the barometer suddenly plummeted and a storm prevented him from returning home – 'so whoreson a Night that I stopped there all the next day', he later explained to Cowden Clarke.[33] On Sunday the 10th, the weather again closed in with a blizzard of sleet and snow, followed by a frost that lasted until Monday evening when, as the *The Times* reported, 'the mercury again fell, and was again accompanied with rain, and by a very violent wind'.[34] Change was in the air.

* * *

The following week, 11–18 November, when he was not busy at Guy's, Keats was helping his brothers pack up their lodgings at Dean Street. A move was imminent. At other hours he was at work on two long couplet poems, *Sleep and Poetry* and his poem-in-progress that eventually became 'I stood tip-toe'. Exactly when he composed these poems has proved difficult to establish; no manuscript of *Sleep and Poetry* has survived, and the only evidence for dating 'I stood tip-toe' comes from a phase of concentrated composition and transcription on and after Tuesday, 17 December, when Keats announced that he meant to finish it in one more Haydonian 'attack'.[35]

'I stood tip-toe' is, in part, a catalogue of observations recalled from Keats's childhood ventures at Enfield and Edmonton. As a boy and, now, as a poet, Keats was fascinated by the paradoxical effects of motion – by the way a minnow can 'stay against the stream', resisting the current so as to appear stationary amid moving water, or how on a breezy night the moon appears to glide across the sky,

> lifting her silver rim
> Above a cloud, and with a gradual swim
> Coming into the blue with all her light.
> ('I stood tip-toe upon a little hill', 114–15)

Wordsworth's magical poem 'A Night Piece' has been cited as a 'source' for this image of cloud and moon, but Keats's poetry has the freshness of actual observation – a sense of real things seen as a child, when such strange effects are noticed most strongly. Simultaneously still and in motion, these beautiful images represent the mysterious process through which a poem realises its own potential and comes into being, a process Keats would later identify as 'diligent indolence'. As he was gradually becoming aware, although he had discovered poetry at Enfield, the source of his imaginative power lay much earlier, in a child's delighted stare at the night sky or into the depths of Salmons Brook.

Keats's final 'attack' on 'I stood tip-toe' introduced mythical figures – Cupid and Psyche, Pan and Syrinx, Narcissus and Echo – and a passage describing how a poet had originated the Endymion myth.[36] In closing his poem, he was poised, once again, on the threshold of a further tale, wishing that he, too, 'might / Tell'. After thirty more lines, he breaks off with a glance at his own prospects:

> Was there a Poet born?—but now no more,
> My wand'ring spirit must no further soar.

* * *

'Was there a Poet born?' Keats's preoccupation with what he had done and what was yet to come grew during this autumn, as he proceeded with the frankly autobiographical verses that became *Sleep and Poetry*. James Beattie's story of the progress of Poetical Genius in *The Minstrel* had long been familiar to him, and a more immediate spur to composition was rivalry with Reynolds's work-in-progress, *The Romance of Youth*.

Reynolds's first canto was completed before January 1817, and reveals how closely he had been studying Keats's poetry.[37] Cupid and Psyche are introduced, and Reynolds touches on the Endymion story that concludes 'I stood tip-toe'. 'To such as have been long in chamber pent' (stanza 26) suggests familiarity with Keats's 'To one who has been long in city pent', and his phrase 'heedless Flora's diadem' echoes the last line of 'Imitation of Spenser' (indeed, the whole of Keats's 'Imitation' is loosely paraphrased in Reynolds's stanzas 29–33). The upspring of a 'goldfinch from … covering grass' apparently comes from 'I stood tip-toe', and when Reynolds gestures to 'many marvels of which I may not tell' (compare 'could I tell' from 'Imitation of Spenser', line 19), it is clear that much of *The Romance of Youth* reflected close study of Keats's earlier poems as well as more recent ones. Keats, in turn, appears to have recalled sections of Reynolds's poem in his later writing: 'A silence lean'd along the lifeless air' is distantly echoed at the start of *Hyperion*, and an encounter in stanza 95 with a tall, shadowy woman –

> eyes all dim, and fixed in distress,—
> And sunken cheeks,—and lips of pallidness,—
> Standing with folded arms, and floating hair

– is revisited in Keats's icy confrontation with Moneta in *The Fall of Hyperion*.

✱ ✱ ✱

Exactly how and where Keats composed *Sleep and Poetry* is unknown, although Cowden Clarke said that its 'framework' and many of its lines dated from visits to Hunt from mid-October to mid-December.[38] It opens with the pastoral voice of 'I stood tip-toe', 'What is more gentle than a wind in summer', and is quickly drawn to dream-visions and two contrasting 'realms' of poetry. Pastoral pleasures of 'Flora and old Pan' are displaced by a severer challenge as Keats seeks to write of 'the agonies, the strife/ Of human hearts' (124–5), drawing closer to the actuality of his own experiences and what confronted him each day at Guy's. This 'nobler life' is announced by another of Keats's sky-visions –

> O'er sailing the blue cragginess, a car
> And steeds with streamy manes—the charioteer
> Looks out upon the winds with glorious fear
> (126–8)

– and by a mingled procession of humanity:

> Shapes of delight, of mystery, and fear,
> Passing along before a dusky space.
> (138–9).

When these shadows fade away, 'in their stead / A sense of real things comes doubly strong' (156–7) as Keats contrasts his own 'high Imagination' and the prescriptive codes of French neoclassicism with its Masonic emblems of 'wretched rule / And compass vile' (195–6). Identifying a new and 'fairer season' of contemporary poetry, Keats makes knowing allusions to Chatterton, Byron, Wordsworth, Coleridge and Hunt (who would soon inaugurate that fairer season in a new school of poets). Almost unheard in this crowded scene of 'strange thunders' is Keats's declaration that the 'great end / Of poesy' is 'To soothe the cares and lift the thoughts of man' (231, 245–7), a broadly Wordsworthian sentiment that could easily slide into the naive escapism of 'simply [telling] the most heart-easing things' (268). Keats was writing swiftly, venturing various ideas about poetry, candidly owning his lack of 'spanning wisdom' and steadying himself to touch upon a 'vast idea' that both concentrated his poetic ambitions and freed him for their pursuit (285, 291). At this point he was three-quarters of the way to the four hundred lines that would complete his poem, uncertain how to take it forward. What comes over most strongly in the restless, searching lines he had so far written is the sheer mental, emotional and physical stamina that was driving him onwards throughout this season of high winds and frost, sun and sleet, storms and snow. His poem would be completed, but he needed the right impulse and occasion to do it.

\* \* \*

Monday, 18 November was Tom's seventeenth birthday. By now Keats and his brothers had left Dean Street, moved north across the river and taken an apartment on the second floor of a house at 76 Cheapside, opposite Mercers' Hall.[39] Cheapside, for centuries London's mercantile centre, remained one of its busiest streets: craft guilds clustered in lanes and alleys where bakers, goldsmiths, mercers, haberdashers and saddlers had set up in business. The three brothers knew this terrain well: George and Tom had lived close by at Pancras Lane when working for Abbey. As we have already seen, the hatter Keatses were in business here too – Thomas Mower Keats and his partner, John Archer, at 14 The Poultry, and Joseph Keats at 74 Cheapside, immediately next door to John, George and Tom. Robert Jennings the printer lived at 62 Cheapside, and at the City elections in December 1817 'Mr. Keats' and 'Mr. Jennings' were both returned for the ward of 'Cheap'.[40] It is inconceivable that these near-neighbours were unknown to the brothers, or that the City Keatses were not involved in finding accommodation for them. Yet we hear just once from Keats, a little further in the future, of an unwelcome acquaintance with the hatter Keatses. Possibly that stemmed from some difficulty at this period, or from an earlier family fracas now lost to sight.

That Monday evening, 18 November, Keats composed a sonnet 'To my Brothers' marking Tom's seventeenth birthday and their move to a new home. As rain fell outside, a fresh-laid fire was crackling faintly in the hearth while Keats sought rhymes for his poem and Tom was absorbed in reading. Keats's sonnets this autumn form a lyrical diary marking significant occasions: 'To my Brothers', for instance, tells us that Keats was at home on this evening, and that he had distanced himself from Guy's and Southwark. While Guy's still determined the pattern of his weeks, his life was now also shaped by a different calendar in which sociable occasions and anniversaries made up part of his life as a poet. Unusually, the evening of Tuesday, 19 November saw Keats at Great Marlborough Street, where Haydon sketched his portrait and said he planned to include him in 'Christ's Entry into Jerusalem'. That would explain why Keats returned to Cheapside feeling so 'wrought up' that he had to release his feelings in a sonnet celebrating those 'Great Spirits', Wordsworth, Hunt, and Haydon himself:

> Great Spirits now on Earth are sojourning
>   He of the Cloud, the Cataract, the Lake
>   Who on Helvellyn's summit wide awake
> Catches his freshness from Archangel's wing
> He of the Rose, the Violet, the Spring
>   The social Smile, the Chain for freedom's sake:
>   And lo!—whose stedfastness would never take
> A Meaner Sound than Raphael's Whispering.
> And other Spirits are there standing apart
>   Upon the Forehead of the Age to come;
> These, these will give the World another heart
>   And other pulses—hear ye not the hum
> Of mighty Workings in a distant Mart?
>   Listen awhile ye Nations, and be dumb!
>                       Nov[r] 20—[41]

When this sonnet arrived at Haydon's studio, he replied immediately. That hint of chattering 'in a distant Mart' was unfortunate. He suggested an ellipsis instead, thus inserting an audible half-line space as an awed acknowledgement of genius. Keats took this tip as a matter to 'glory in', and the lines became:

> hear ye not the hum
> Of mighty workings?– – – – – – – –
> Listen awhile ye Nations, and be dumb!

Haydon had indicated that he would send the sonnet to Wordsworth, an idea that put Keats 'out of breath': 'you know with what Reverence—I would send my Wellwishes to him.'[42] It eventually went north on the last day of the year – 'he promises a great deal', Haydon wrote to Wordsworth, passing on Keats's good wishes:

he is quite a Youth, full of eagerness & enthusiasm, and what greatly recommends him to me, he has a very fine head!—he is now writing a longer sort of poem of Diana & Endymion, to publish with his smaller productions, and will send you a copy as soon as it is out—I need not say his reverence for you my dear Sir is unbounded.[43]

Wordsworth was intrigued, acknowledging that Keats's sonnet was indeed 'vigorously conceived and well expressed'.[44]

Haydon had prepared the way for a meeting.

# CHAPTER 9

# Saturnalia

Keats's enthusiasm about Haydon is understandable. He was an established, if controversial, artist and his 'stedfast genius, toiling gallantly' impressed. Soon Keats picked up the inflections of Haydon's voice – 'I glory in it', 'I hope to finish it in one more attack' – and projected his own future in Haydonian terms. 'I begin to fix my eye upon one horizon,' he told Haydon, and that horizon was not the next day's ward round at Guy's.[1] During this autumn, encouraged by his brothers and friends, he determined to make his name and living as a poet; as that horizon grew clearer, he marked his progress towards it with a series of shared anniversaries. He gave particular attention in these months to the fraternal home shared with his brothers, celebrating Tom's seventeenth birthday and George's affection for eighteen-year-old Georgiana Wylie in a pair of sonnets, 'To my Brothers' and 'To G.A.W.'

Georgiana, Keats's 'Nymph of the downward smile, and sidelong glance', is usually said to have been the daughter of Ann Griffin Wylie and James Wylie, an adjutant in the Fifeshire Fencibles (Georgiana kept his commission documents in her scrapbook). James, however, died on 18 October 1795, some two years before Georgiana's birthday in the year between May 1797 and May 1798. A second commission in her scrapbook has an Augustus Thomas Garskill in the North Gloucestershire regiment, and it may be significant that Georgiana's younger brother was named Gaskell, as was a cousin, Frederick Gaskell Griffin. Given the absence of documented birth information, it is likely that Georgiana was illegitimate, and when she met the Keats brothers in 1815 she was living in a fatherless household.[2]

Hunt had said that 'The SONNET on CHAPMAN'S HOMER by J.K.' would be published in *The Examiner* at 'the earliest opportunity', but that could not have prepared Keats for what actually appeared on Sunday,

1 December. Beneath Hazlitt's excoriation of the recently restored French monarchy, Hunt inserted a short article introducing three 'Young Poets': Percy Bysshe Shelley, 'author of a poetical work entitled *Alastor, or the Spirit of Solitude*'; 'John Henry Reynolds' (*sic*), author of *Safie* and 'a small set of poems published by Taylor and Hessey, the principal of which is called the *Naiad*'; and 'youngest of them all, and just of age ... JOHN KEATS'. All three belonged to 'a new school of poetry rising of late' in healthy opposition to French Neoclassicism, Keats in particular being associated with novelty, natural inspiration, and 'truth of ... ambition'. The opening of the *Naiad* was quoted – Keats read these lines carefully – and 'On First Looking into Chapman's Homer' appeared in full, strategically positioned by Hunt so that his article closed with 'a wild surmise' and feelings of powerful and quiet anticipation.[3]

Keats walked out to the Vale of Health to thank Hunt in person; that would explain why Hunt dated his own sonnet 'To John Keats' 1 December 1816, saluting 'Young Keats' and predicting a 'flowering laurel on [his] brow'. For Keats, the 'Young Poets' piece was decisive. As Henry Stephens recalled, 'it sealed his fate and he gave himself up more completely than before to Poetry'. Hunt had publicly associated Keats with his own poetry and politics; at the time this was a matter of immense gratification to Keats. By announcing a 'new school' of young poets, Hunt had also hit upon a winning formula subsequently copied countless times. Chatterton and Burns had been youthful poets too, of course, but no one had thought of them as a school or coterie. Hunt's article in *The Examiner* was influential in that it appeared to launch a concerted movement of poetical youth, initiating a tradition that continues in the burgeoning modern culture of youthful poets, poetry competitions and poetry festivals. Continuing Hunt's role as a cultural impresario in *The Examiner*, innumerable poetry magazines and websites routinely announce the latest generations of 'poetic youth' and 'new voices'.[4] For Keats, youngest of them all, some less happy consequences of being enrolled with Hunt in *The Examiner* were not as yet apparent.

\* \* \*

Hunt's poetic revolution was accompanied by uproar in London. Economic depression after Waterloo had quickly revived unrest; high taxes and the restrictive Corn Laws caused 'general distress'; in the northern counties, industrialising cities endured unemployment, riots and machine-breaking; in rural areas *The Examiner* reported a scene of 'absolute ruin': 'Bankruptcies, seizures, executions, imprisonments, and farmers become parish paupers ... great arrears of rent ... tithes and poor-rates unpaid; improvements of every kind generally discontinued; live stock greatly lessened; tradesmen's bills unpaid; and alarming gangs of poachers and other depredators.' The reform movement, quiescent or underground since the turn of the century, surged back onto the streets. At a mass meeting in Spa Fields, close by Cowden Clarke's home in Warner Street, Henry 'Orator' Hunt challenged the 'impudence' and 'insolence' of Lord Liverpool's profligate government. Originally a farmer from Wiltshire, 'Orator' Hunt had reinvented himself as an independent reformer calling for universal male suffrage and annual parliaments; he gave a voice to widespread discontent at hiked taxes and extortionate prices, and deliberately stirred memories of the French Revolution by calling Coldbath Fields Prison 'the British Bastille'. On the foggy Monday of 2 December, a day after 'Young Poets' appeared, another Spa Fields meeting sparked a riot a few streets away from Keats's Cheapside lodgings. A tricolour flag, hoisted above the turmoil, was emblazoned: 'Nature – Feed the Hungry', 'Truth – Protect the Distressed', 'Justice – Punish Crime.'[5]

Nature. Truth. Justice. *The Examiner* reported these City riots at length, then in the last weeks of 1816 Hunt made space for Hazlitt's explosive essays on 'Modern Apostates'. Prominent among Hazlitt's renegades were William Wordsworth, Samuel Taylor Coleridge, Robert Southey and all those who had backed a revival of Bourbon '*Legitimacy*' in France – a 'monstrous fiction' that 'in England first tottered and fell headless to the ground with the martyred Charles'.[6] Cries of 'Reform!' were being heard again, and in Hunt's new school of poetry 'Nature', 'Truth' and 'Justice' were energetically reviving too.

* * *

At Hunt's on Wednesday, 11 December, Keats met Percy Bysshe Shelley for the first time. Shelley was twenty-four, tall, pale and fashionably dressed – even with his shoulders slumped, his height was considerable. Keats could see at a glance that he represented the world his mother had aspired to when she thought of sending her sons to Harrow. Hunt noticed that Keats did not take to Shelley as kindly as Shelley did to him, putting it down to a sensitivity about social class that inclined Keats 'to see in every man of birth a sort of natural enemy'.[7] Keats often held back in company, and probably felt sidelined as Hunt devoted time to Shelley. For two months he had seen Hunt frequently, sometimes staying overnight at the Vale of Health. A less intense period now ensued; to understand why, we need to know what had brought Shelley to Hunt's.

Born on 4 August 1792 into a wealthy landowning family at Field Place, Sussex, Shelley was the son of the Whig MP Sir Timothy Shelley and his wife, Elizabeth Pilfold. Educated at Syon House, Eton and Oxford, he espoused radical politics and his pamphlet *The Necessity of Atheism*, published in

February 1811, brought banishment from University College. Hunt alluded to his expulsion in an *Examiner* article on court influence at the universities and 'the "necessity" of some vile subserviency to the times'. Sensing an ally, Shelley sought Hunt out. Breakfast at Hunt's – their first meeting – grew into a long, unintelligible argument about deism and atheism that left neither of them inclined to pursue further acquaintance. In August 1811 Shelley suddenly eloped with Harriet Westbrook, the sixteen-year-old daughter of a coffee-house owner, embarking on a restless life of writing and radical agitation that left him without an audience for his poetry. 'An Address to the Irish People', 'A Letter to Lord Ellenborough', *Queen Mab* and *Alastor* had met 'oblivion'. For Shelley as for Keats, Hunt's 'Young Poets' article was crucial in helping to foster a readership he had long craved – and this was not the first time Hunt's words played a crucial role in Shelley's affairs. In summer 1814 Hunt and Hazlitt had argued in *The Examiner* about whether Othello and Desdemona's relationship was a matter of love, lust, intellectual excellence or animal passion. The terms of this argument were echoed chillingly in Shelley's letter to Harriet of 14 July that year, announcing that he was abandoning her and their children, Eliza and Charles. Not explicitly mentioned in this letter was his new, 'all-sufficing passion' for Mary Wollstonecraft Godwin.[8]

\* \* \*

On Sunday, 1 December 1816 – the day 'Young Poets' appeared – Shelley and Mary were at 5 Abbey Churchyard, Bath. Hunt had written, alerting them to the article and announcing some less happy news: he had mislaid the manuscript of Shelley's 'Hymn to Intellectual Beauty' and, as always, was short of money. Realizing that Hunt had given his poetry its first positive notice, Shelley immediately sent £50 with a letter setting out his own difficulties. A few days later Shelley was at Marlow in Buckinghamshire, staying with Thomas Love Peacock and his mother at their home in West Street while looking for a house to lease. Two further letters from Hunt arrived offering 'sympathy & kindness' and a copy of *The Examiner* containing 'Young Poets'. The 'Hymn to Intellectual Beauty' had been found – did Shelley wish his name to appear with it? Hunt also sent £5 as a first payment of interest on the £50. Shelley's reply swept aside preliminaries and addressed Hunt as 'an old friend'. The 'Hymn' might fare best if it was not associated with its author. 'I am an outcast from human society,' he told Hunt, albeit 'an object of compassion to a few more benevolent than the rest'. Shelley mentions his delight at *The Story of Rimini*, anticipates welcoming Hunt to Marlow, and says he is 'strongly tempted' to come to London 'only to spend one evening with you, & if I can I will'. He returned Hunt's £5, encouraged him to spend it on some 'literary luxury' and closed warmly: 'Most affectionately yours P.B. Shelley.' A thoughtful PS added: 'I will send you an Alastor.'[9]

When Keats came to the Vale of Health on Wednesday, 11 December, Shelley was already installed. They dined together, and then Shelley stayed on at Hunt's for three more days. It would be some time before Keats was able to reclaim Hunt's undivided attention, but he had much to occupy him: Guy's dominated his weekdays, and his evenings and weekends were devoted to writing poetry.

On 13 December, Mary Godwin noted in her journal: 'Letter from S. – he is pleased with Hunt', and the next day Shelley arrived back at Bath. Both of them were unaware that on the 12th *The Times* had announced the recovery of the body of 'a respectable female, far advanced in pregnancy', who had drowned in the Serpentine.[10] This was Harriet, Shelley's estranged wife. News reached Shelley from bookseller Thomas Hookham on 15 December, whereupon he took an afternoon coach from Bath and dashed to London, the Vale of Health and Hunt. Mary would soon follow, and Hunt would be preoccupied with this tragedy well into the new year.

✳ ✳ ✳

With Shelley in the ascendant at Hunt's from mid-December onwards, Keats's sonnet 'Keen fitful gusts' most likely records a walk back from Hampstead one evening early in the month – perhaps on the weekend of 7–8 December, when the weather was fine and the nights chilly. Formally assured – it comprises just two sentences, with a rhyme scheme patterned on 'Chapman's Homer' – Keats's sonnet contrasts 'cool bleak air' with 'the friendliness / That in little cottage I have found'. Reynolds's lines about 'yellow leaves all loose and dry', extracted from the *Naiad* in 'Young Poets', may have helped Keats to his 'bushes half leafless, and dry', while the pleasures of *Lycidas* and an engraving of Petrarch and Laura set the scene for the final lines of *Sleep and Poetry*, also written around now (later December is not possible – the Shelleys had taken over at Hunt's, and Keats could not stay overnight). As Hunt recalled, *Sleep and Poetry* closed with 'a description of a parlour that was mine, no bigger than an old mansion's closet'. Here, Cowden Clarke said, 'an extemporary bed had been made up for [Keats] on the sofa':[11]

> and thus, the chimes
> Of friendly voices had just given place
> To as sweet a silence, when I 'gan retrace
> The pleasant day, upon a couch at ease.
> It was a poet's house who keeps the keys

Of pleasure's temple. Round about were hung
The glorious features of the bards who sung
In other ages—cold and sacred busts
Smiled at each other. Happy he who trusts
To clear Futurity his darling fame!
Then there were fauns and satyrs taking aim
At swelling apples with a frisky leap
And reaching fingers, 'mid a luscious heap
Of vine leaves. Then there rose to view a fane
Of liny marble, and thereto a train of nymphs
Approaching fairly o'er the sward:
One, loveliest, holding her white hand toward
The dazzling sun-rise: two sisters sweet
Bending their graceful figures till they meet
Over the trippings of a little child:
And some are hearing, eagerly, the wild
Thrilling liquidity of dewy piping.
See, in another picture, nymphs are wiping
Cherishingly Diana's timorous limbs;—
A fold of lawny mantle dabbling swims
At the bath's edge, and keeps a gentle motion
With the subsiding crystal: as when ocean
Heaves calmly its broad swelling smoothiness o'er
Its rocky marge, and balances once more
The patient weeds; that now unshent by foam
Feel all about their undulating home.

Sappho's meek head was there half smiling down
At nothing; just as though the earnest frown
Of over thinking had that moment gone
From off her brow, and left her all alone.

Great Alfred's too, with anxious, pitying eyes,
As if he always listed to the sighs
Of the goaded world; and Kosciusko's worn
By horrid suffrance—mightily forlorn.

Petrarch, outstepping from the shady green,
Starts at the sight of Laura; nor can wean
His eyes from her sweet face. Most happy they!

For over them was seen a free display
Of out-spread wings, and from between them shone
The face of Poesy: from off her throne
She overlook'd things that I scarce could tell.
The very sense of where I was might well
Keep Sleep aloof: but more that there came
Thought after thought to nourish up the flame
Within my breast; so that the morning light
Surprised me even from a sleepless night;
And up I rose refresh'd, and glad, and gay,
Resolving to begin that very day
These lines.

(350–403)

As those friendly voices recede, silence creates a room for reflection. Keats follows Hunt's example in 'reading' images and scenes on the walls, bringing them to life much as he imagines the ocean's swell frees seaweed to '[f]eel all about' its watery home. His 'train of nymphs' may be an engraving from one of Claude Lorraine's 'Bacchanals' or Poussin's 'Triumph of Flora', while Diana is almost certainly from Titian's 'Diana and Actaeon'.[12] Busts of King Alfred and Thaddeus Kosciusko give us two patriot heroes for Keats since his Enfield days: his sonnet 'To Kosciusko', written this December, also alludes to this scene in Hunt's study. Finally, the print of Petrarch and Laura draws together painting and poetry, enabling Keats to return his poem to its moment of composition. In relatively few lines Keats captures the magic of being 'at ease' in 'a poet's house' – a poet, moreover, who had responded to Keats by opening to him hitherto unimagined vistas of cultural life and opportunity. As in his 'Chapman's Homer' sonnet and 'I stood tip-toe', he concludes his poem on a threshold of anticipation, 'Resolving to begin that very day'.

✶ ✶ ✶

Keats called on Haydon over the weekend of 14–15 December. Reynolds was there too. This was probably the occasion when Haydon took Keats's life mask – an iconic image many, many times reproduced. For the original, Keats had to endure hours of discomfort – Haydon said it was like preparing to cut off a man's head.[13] His hair was swept back under a towel that was then furled tightly around his ears and neck. With his skin greased, eyes and mouth shut, and breathing through straws in his nostrils, he felt Haydon apply the cold, clammy plaster. When his face was entirely covered, Keats had to hold his nerve and wait patiently until the plaster set – a matter of several hours.

Keats's life mask tells us nothing about the colour of his eyes or hair, but we can see strongly cut features, sunken cheeks, a full mouth with a projecting upper lip and the firm chin recalled by Hunt. One nostril is slightly distended by the straw through which Keats breathed – or was this the result of a copious intake of snuff? Most of these features reappear in other likenesses, although none of them captures the power and serenity of Keats's face as it appears in his life mask. Haydon's study for 'Christ's Entry into Jerusalem' has vigorous energy, as does Severn's charcoal sketch of December 1816 – considered by Cowden Clarke as the 'most perfect, and withal the favourite portrait of him'. Severn has Keats's hair long and curly – it was widely reported to have been brown or auburn and his eyes, according to Cowden Clarke, were dark hazel.[14] Severn's later miniature, dating from 1818–19, depicts him looking up from a book, more a conventional man of feeling than the extraordinary presence glimpsed in William Hilton's portrait. Hilton's Keats has his head tossed slightly back, likewise Charles Brown's pencil sketch from 1819 – head resting on his right fist, longish hair in ringlets, eyes a little heavy. What none of these likenesses showed was Keats's full-grown height, just five feet and three-quarters of an inch. Hunt, Shelley and Wordsworth all towered over him.

* * *

'I met Reynolds at Haydon's a few mornings since,' Keats wrote to Cowden Clarke on the morning of Tuesday, 17 December; 'he promised to be with me this evening and Yesterday I had the same promise from Severn and I must put you in mind that on last All hallowmas' day you gave me you word that you would spend this evening with me—so no putting off.'[15] What was this gathering to which Keats was so keen to invite them? He marked festivals and anniversaries with care, and an obvious occasion for this gathering on 17 December was one long known to him from Lemprière – the ancient Roman festival of Saturnalia. Dated by Lemprière to 16 or 17 December, Saturnalia was an ancient festival of Saturnus, supreme god of the Titans in their golden age of power. A precursor of Christmas and Twelfth Night, Saturnalia was a time of feasts, revelry, visits to friends and gift-giving or, in Lemprière's succinct phrase, 'mirth, riot and debauchery'.

Clearly this long-planned evening with brothers and friends was both urgent and important – 'no putting off'. It seems at least possible that it was an evening chosen to announce a change in his life. Several recent events might have encouraged him to do so. Since he had met Reynolds in September, Keats's works-in-progress had included sonnets, 'I stood tip-toe' and *Sleep and Poetry*. After 'Young Poets', *Examiner* readers were expecting more from him. He knew that Thomas Richards's brother Charles had set up as a printer, and on 11 December, when Keats dined with Shelley at the Vale of Health, Hunt had told John Taylor that the Ollier brothers were 'about to commence' as publishers.[16] No doubt Keats and Shelley also heard that directly from Hunt. All of these developments registered a gathering momentum in Keats's creative life, as like-minded poets and publishers joined his circle. His next step was, perhaps, in many ways an obvious one. On the evening of 17 December it seems likely that he assembled his brothers and closest friends and proclaimed a Saturnalian revolution in his life: he was determined to become a full-time poet, and was already preparing his first book. That Cowden Clarke had pictured epic poems 'spanning all like Saturn's ring' made such a Saturnalian evening especially appropriate: George, Tom, Cowden Clarke, Severn and Reynolds were on hand to witness Keats set his course for poetic fame. All of this is necessarily speculation, but if Keats did make such a momentous announcement on 17 December, Severn may well have marked the occasion by making his forceful charcoal sketch of him. Cowden Clarke recalled that this sketch was taken 'when several of [his] friends were there', and it captures perfectly Keats's spirit of dauntless determination.[17]

✳ ✳ ✳

Keats's letter to Cowden Clarke voiced an eager sense of purpose too. After Tuesday's gathering he meant to walk out to Hampstead to tell Hunt of his plans. A 'Sketch of M^r Hunt' was on his mind too, possibly connected with his publishing plans. At Hunt's he encountered Shelley again, just a week after their first meeting. If Keats was indeed brimful with ideas for his book, now may have been the moment when Shelley cautioned him not to hurry his earliest attempts into print. This was not what Keats wanted to hear, but he took note. As he prepared his book he was careful to include a note alerting readers to those poems 'written at an earlier period than the rest'. Years afterwards, wiser with hindsight, Keats would tell Shelley: 'I remember you advising me not to publish my first-blights, on Hampstead Heath'.[18]

What lay behind Shelley's advice? His own publications had not fared well, and perhaps he was thinking of Hunt's high-profile debut as a sixteen-year-old poet in *Juvenilia*. Hunt's book had been published in 1800 behind a glittering list of subscribers, all of whom had parted with six shillings in advance. It went to four editions, the reviews were admiring, and Hunt was touted as a prodigy at literary societies and salons. But as the years passed Hunt came to regret this early praise. One of his subscribers, Edward Law, Lord Ellenborough, had dispatched him to prison.

Keats had the third edition of *Juvenilia*, and came fresh to its contents of 'Miscellanies', 'Translations', 'Sonnets', 'Pastorals', 'Elegies', 'Odes', 'Hymns' and,

1 The Hospital of Bethlem [Bedlam] at Moorfields, London: seen from the north, with people in the foreground. Coloured engraving, c. 1771. Keates's Livery Stables ('The Swan and Hoop') is in the line of houses to the right of the image.

2 The Hospital of Bethlem [Bedlam] at Moorfields, London. Detail of Keates's Livery Stables.

3 Caius Cibber, *Melancholy Madness* c. 1676; statue from the gateway to Bedlam.

4 Caius Cibber, *Raving Madness* c. 1676; statue from the gateway to Bedlam.

a)                                                              b)

5a) James Lackington's bookshop, The Temple of the Muses, Finsbury Square, seen here in 1828. Keats's publishers John Taylor and James Augustus Hessey met here.

5b) Halfpenny book token issued by James Lackington, showing the figure of 'Fame' with her trumpet.

6 *Dooms of the mighty dead*. This 'Doom' depicting the Last Judgment was placed over the gateway to St Stephen's, Coleman Street, London. Having attended numerous funerals at this church, Keats knew this image well.

7 Old houses in Craven Street, off City Road, London. Thomas and Frances Keats lived here with their young family from 1797–1802.

8 Alice Jennings's house in Church Street, Edmonton, Keats's home from 1805 onwards.

9 Clarke's Academy at Enfield. Keats was a pupil here from 1803 to 1810.

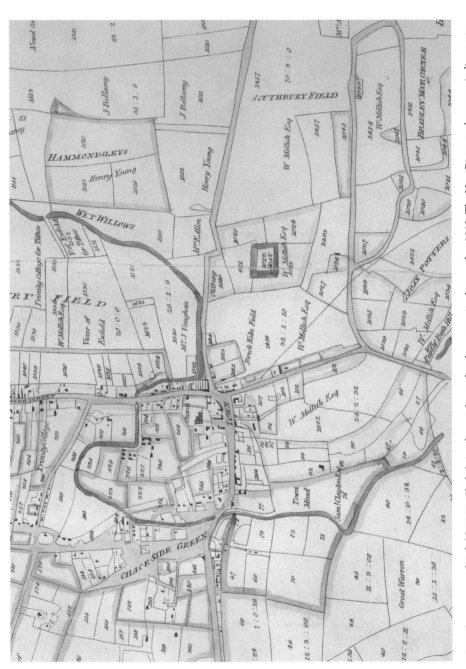

10  Enclosure map of Enfield, 1803. Clarke's Academy is located at the centre, in plot number 1012. The New River can be seen winding past the school and around the village. To the right of the school plot is the mysterious 'Moat'.

11 John Keats's school medal, awarded at midsummer 1810.

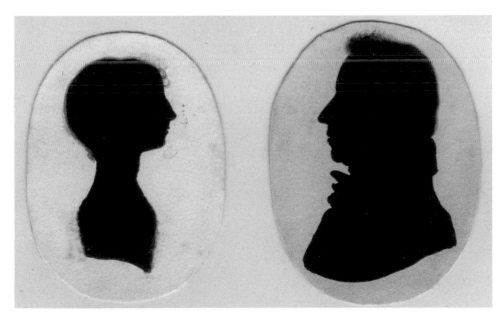

12 Silhouettes of Dr Thomas Hammond and his wife Susanna.

13 Wilston, Dr Thomas Hammond's home in Church Street, Edmonton. The old surgery building where Keats worked as an apprentice can be seen to the right of the house.

14 Footbridge on the path between Edmonton and Enfield. Here Keats and Cowden Clarke parted company after their evenings reading poetry.

15  8 Dean Street, Southwark. Keats
lodged here with his brothers George
and Tom, September–November 1816.

16  *The North Front of Guy's Hospital*, engraving by John Pass, c. 1800.

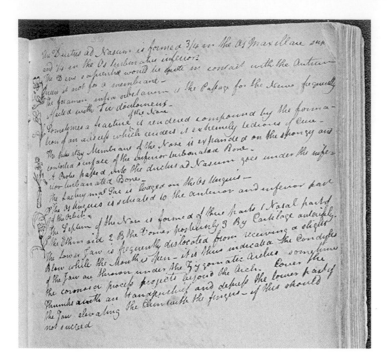

17 A page from Keats's medical and anatomical Notebook, with marginal doodles of flowers.

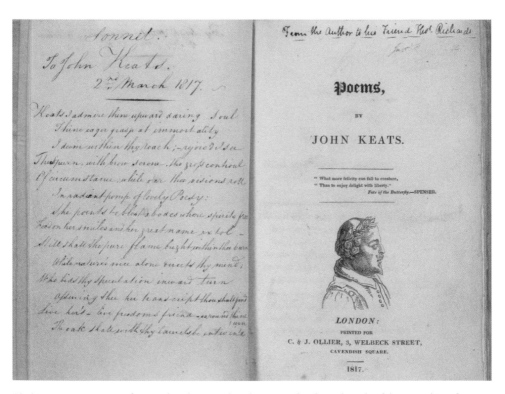

18 A presentation copy of *Poems, by John Keats* for Thomas Richards, with Richards's sonnet 'To John Keats' opposite the title-page.

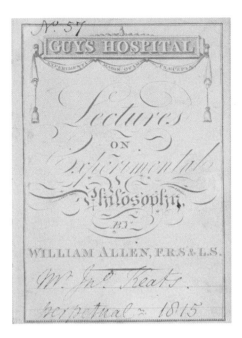

19  Keats's ticket to William Allen's Lectures on Experimental Philosophy at Guy's Hospital, 1815.

20  Keats's fellow student at Guy's Hospital, Henry Stephens (1796–1864).

21  George Wilson Mackereth (1793–1869). A pencil sketch of Keats's fellow medical student at Guy's Hospital. The great collector of Keatsiana, Fred Holland Day, attributed this portrait to Joseph Severn.

22 Apothecaries' Hall, where Keats sat his examination to qualify as an Apothecary, 25 July 1816.

23 2 Well Walk, Hampstead, next door to the house (now demolished) where Keats and his brothers lodged in 1817–18.

24 Sir Astley Cooper (1768–1841), an engraving of the famous surgeon from a portrait by Charles Penny. Keats assiduously transcribed Cooper's lectures on anatomy into his medical notebook.

25 Benjamin Robert Haydon, *Christ's Entry into Jerusalem*. Keats is seen top right, between the pillars, talking to Hazlitt.

26 Montague House, home of the old British Museum. Seen here in the early nineteenth century.

27 G.F. Sergeant, view of Shanklin, Isle of Wight, engraved by J. Woods, early nineteenth century. Keats visited here briefly in April 1817 and again from June to August 1819.

28 The Mitre Inn, Oxford, drawn and engraved by J. Fisher. Defiance, seen here, was the coach Keats took from London to Oxford in September 1817.

29  Magdalen Hall, Oxford, engraved by F. Mackenzie. The image dates from July 1814, just over three years before Keats visited Benjamin Bailey here in September 1817. At Magdalen Hall Keats wrote the third book of *Endymion*.

30  The old Fox and Hounds Inn at Burford Bridge, where Keats stayed in late November 1817. It was here that he finished the fourth book of *Endymion*.

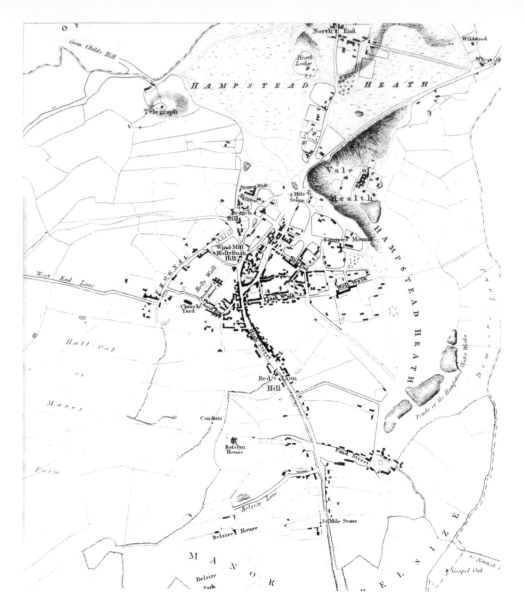

31 Map of Hampstead, published with J.J. Park's *Topography of Hampstead* (1814). Well Walk, where Keats lived from March 1817 to December 1818 can be seen at centre right, just below the Vale of Health.

lastly, 'The Palace of Pleasure' in two cantos of Spenserian stanzas. Hunt's mastery of different genres was on display and, read as a whole, his book told a story of poetic growth. Keats planned his own book in similar fashion. It would comprise a variety of genres and culminate with his longest poem to date, *Sleep and Poetry*, staking a claim on epic and looking to greater achievements in the years ahead. Given Keats's long-standing admiration of Hunt, it is possible that the 'Sketch of M$^r$ Hunt' he mentioned to Clarke may have been an idea for a frontispiece for his book. Above all, Keats was determined to gain his living through poetry as Hunt appeared to do from his writings. And money may have been an additional cause of Shelley's concern about Keats hurrying into print.

He would publish on commission.[19] Having set up as publishers at 3 Welbeck Street, Cavendish Square, with no capital apart from their own brains, Charles and James Ollier were keen to identify new writers. Keats came with recommendations from Hunt and Cowden Clarke. He would cover the production costs of printing, paper and binding; the Olliers would take a percentage of the sales, and the balance would go to Keats. This was the usual way for an unknown author to appear before the public; Shelley would shortly publish 750 copies of *Laon and Cythna*, retitled *The Revolt of Islam*, in exactly this manner. Shelley's production costs, excluding charges for corrections, amounted to £114.5s. Using Shelley's expenditure to estimate Keats's likely outlay for a more modest edition of 250 octavo copies, the maximum cost of production would have been £24.6s.3½d., with a further £4.4s. for a vignette on the title-page. This would cover composing and press work, paper, labels, corrections and boards.[20] If 225 copies sold at six shillings each, the return would be £67.10s., of which the Olliers' 10 per cent would amount to £6.15s. leaving Keats a balance of some £60.15s. – a pleasing margin on his initial outlay. George is most likely to have costed the book beforehand, standing between his brother and 'dealings with the world', and, as we will see, after publication it was George who interrogated the Olliers about sales.[21] Impelled by self-belief and the well-wishes of brothers and friends, Keats's resolve to press on into print is typical of him. Once he had taken a decision he would see it through, and this one was not without hazard. Just as long hours of study had endangered his health at school, his decision to publish on commission brought equally material risks to his wellbeing, as Shelley may have realised.

Many years later the printer Charles Richards was to recall that Shelley went to him 'about the printing a little volume of Keats' first poems'.[22] This has been taken to mean that Shelley paid or attempted to pay for the printing, but it could also be that he was making an equally well-intentioned enquiry about costs or the printer's schedule; his *Proposal for Putting Reform to the Vote* was also due to be published by the Olliers, Keats was not in need of funds, and other evidence points firmly to Keats having paid for publication himself: Abbey was reported to have mentioned 'a little Book which he had got printed'; the Olliers told George that his brother had 'requested us to publish his book'; and, lastly, Keats retained the copyright until September 1820, when he sold the rights for his first book and *Endymion* to Taylor and Hessey.[23]

It was probably now, in the weeks after Saturnalia, that Abbey remembered Keats calling to tell him he did not intend to qualify as a surgeon. In a quiet voice he told his former guardian that he meant in future to rely upon his capacities as a poet, that he 'possessed Abilities greater than most Men' and that he was 'determined to gain [his] living by exercising them'.[24] We have heard those steady tones before, when Thomas Keates was cross-questioned at the Old Bailey.

Abbey told Taylor he had thought Keats 'either Mad or a Fool' and predicted a 'speedy Termination to his inconsiderate Enterprise'. As a businessman he could see that Keats had succeeded at Guy's and to abandon that achievement was, in his eyes, madness. Perhaps Abbey was also conscious that Thomas Mower Keats's business was in trouble at just this time, as his hat manufacturing partnership with John Archer was dissolved at the end of the year.[25] If that Keats enterprise could fail, a Keatsian poetic one was bound to do so too.

His capital held in trust had diminished and, now that he had come of age, just £500 remained in stocks. According to George, over the next two years Keats spent 'at least 200£ per annum' – a large sum, far in excess of routine costs, which shows his reckless generosity in making loans to friends. When he ran out of cash in 1819, he was owed more than £200. In December 1816 his funds were sufficient, and for the remaining weeks of the year he set about preparing his book for the press while also working full time at Guy's, keeping up his social life and writing poems. A sonnet 'Written in Disgust of Vulgar Superstition', composed on Sunday, 22 December, revisits Keats's dislike of church bells, and may echo atheistical conversations at Hunt's house: the 'black spell' of religion is an 'outburnt lamp' destined for 'oblivion'. Cowden Clarke visited the apartment at Cheapside that day, and witnessed Keats writing this sonnet and readying copy for the Olliers.[26] There was no let-up on Christmas Day, a Wednesday, for this was taking-in day as usual at Guy's, and in the evening Keats was back at home transcribing poems. Evidence of his preparation of the manuscript for his book is sparse, but 25 December does offer us some clues.

The printer's copy of the 'Great Spirits' sonnet is headed '14' – it is Sonnet XIV in the published volume – and it has '66' in the upper right-hand corner, the folio number of Keats's manuscript for his book. Below Keats's transcription of the sonnet is written 'Christ Day' and, if this was correct, he transcribed this poem, and had perhaps worked through the planned contents of his book as far as the fourteenth sonnet, on 25 December 1816.[27] That he did in fact work in that way is suggested by a notebook in which Tom transcribed fourteen of the poems while Keats was readying his manuscript for the printer. The poems appear in Tom's notebook as follows:

Page   1 'Specimen of an induction to a Poem'
       3 'Calidore'
      10 'On Receiving a Curious Shell and a Copy of Verses from the Same Ladies'
      12 'Imitation of Spenser'
      14 'To my Brother George' (sonnet)
      15 'Had I a man's fair form'
      16 'To my Brothers'
      17 'Addressed to the Same' ('Great Spirits')
      18 'On First Looking into Chapman's Homer'
      19 'Written in Disgust of Vulgar Superstition'
      20 'To a Friend who sent me some Roses'
      21 'To G.A.W.'
      23 'O Solitude! if I must with thee dwell'
      24 'To one who has been long in city pent'[28]

The earliest poem here is 'Imitation of Spenser', the most recent 'Written in Disgust of Vulgar Superstition' from 22 December (unless the sonnet for Georgiana Wylie was composed after that date). But Tom was not arranging these poems chronologically. The first six poems appear in the order in which they would shortly be published, although Tom's transcription presents 'Specimen' and 'Calidore' as two parts of a single work whereas they would see print as separate poems. 'To a Friend who sent me some Roses', 'To G.A.W.' and 'O Solitude!', written respectively on 29 June 1816, in December 1816, and in October or November 1815, would appear consecutively as Sonnets V, VI and VII. Tom's punctuation of 'To my Brother George' and 'Great Spirits' is almost identical to Keats's marks on his printer's copy where the latter sonnet is dated 'Christ Day'. This suggests that Tom was working alongside Keats, transcribing into his notebook and reproducing some features of the manuscript as it advanced towards publication. Tom's separate transcript of 'I stood tip-toe' also allows us to see that poem taking shape. In December 1816 Keats was intending to give it an epigraph from Spenser's *Muiopotmos*: 'What more felicity can fall to creature, / Than to enjoy delight with liberty.'[29] He would soon change his mind about this.

On Sunday, 29 December, Shelley and Mary Godwin left Hunt's. The next day they were married at St Mildred's, Bread Street, a few blocks from Keats's apartment, and set off for Bath on New Year's Day. While Shelley was undergoing the 'magical effects' of matrimony, Keats set out through the rain for Cowden Clarke's North London home. Together they paced on to the Vale of Health. As night closed in the warmth of the hearth stirred a cricket into unseasonable chirping, and Hunt set Keats the challenge of writing a sonnet about it in fifteen minutes. Cowden Clarke sat quietly with a book at the end of the sofa, glancing up occasionally until 'Keats won, as to time'.[30]

This is Hunt's poem:

> Green little vaulter in the sunny grass,
>     Catching your heart up at the feel of June,
>     Sole voice left stirring midst the lazy noon,
> When ev'n the bees lag at the summoning brass;—
> And you, warm little housekeeper, who class
>     With those who think the candles come too soon,
>     Loving the fire, and with your tricksome tune
> Nick the glad silent moments as they pass;—
> O sweet and tiny cousins, that belong,
>     One to the fields, the other to the hearth,
> Both have your sunshine; both though small are strong
>     At your clear hearts; and both were sent on earth
> To ring in thoughtful ears this natural song,
>     —In doors and out,—summer and winter,—Mirth.[31]

Pressed for time, Hunt adopted a sentimental voice ('little vaulter'; 'warm little housekeeper'), proceeding fluently from 'feel of June' to a candlelit evening and winding up with broad seasonal juxtapositions and a salutary moral. The third and fourth lines suggest that a more tenacious imaginative engagement might have been possible, but the moment passes. There is no such shortfall in Keats's sonnet:

> The poetry of earth is never dead:
>     When all the birds are faint with the hot sun,
>     And hide in cooling trees, a voice will run
> From hedge to hedge about the new-mown mead;
> That is the Grasshopper's:—he takes the lead

In summer luxury,—he has never done
With his delights; for when tired out with fun,
He rests at ease beneath some pleasant weed.
The poetry of earth is ceasing never:
    On a lone winter evening, when the frost
        Has wrought a silence, from the stove there shrills
The Cricket's song, in warmth increasing ever,
    And seems to one, in drowsiness half lost,
        The Grasshopper's among some grassy hills.

Audacious, striking and conceptually daring, Keats's first line launches a sonnet that combines structural simplicity with sustained imaginative engagement. Writing to time, Keats quickly set down two scenes of vivid contrasts that never lapse into 'tricksome' verbiage. His phrasing is tighter than Hunt's, and while his poetry of earth is 'ceasing never' it is open to glimpses of interruption – the birds 'faint', the mead is 'new-mown', the grasshopper tires, a figure hinted at in the penultimate line is 'in drowsiness half lost'. While Hunt's sonnet was a fall-away from his best form, Keats's poem anticipated greater things in the future. Almost coming into view is the landscape of 'To Autumn' when it seems that 'warm days will never cease': in Keats's sonnet, as often in his early poems, ideas and insights are announced that will be more fully articulated in several years' time. Whereas 'To Autumn' takes leave with a 'soft-dying day', the sonnet's refrain 'ever' and 'never' quietly summons the last scene of *King Lear*: 'She's gone for ever. / I know when one is dead and when one lives;/ She's dead as earth' (V.iii.259–61); 'Thou'lt come no more, / Never, never, never, never, never' (V.iii.307–8). Invoking Lear and Cordelia, Keats's mingling of delight and death in this great sonnet announced the extraordinary, Shakespearean ambition that would possess him in the months ahead.

Hunt's praise for Keats's sonnet was unhesitating. He singled out the Coleridgean phrase 'the frost / Has wrought a silence' as 'perfect' and then, Cowden Clarke reports, 'went on in a dilation upon the dumbness of all Nature during the season's suspension and torpidity'. Keats's sonnet had captured all of that in just six words, but Hunt felt it necessary to have his own say too. As they walked back along the dark lanes, Keats told Cowden Clarke that he preferred Hunt's sonnet to his own.[32] For the first time, perhaps, he was finding Hunt's 'era' in his existence trying.

On reflection, Keats thought well of his own work and included it in his book as Sonnet XV. Dated 30 December, it would represent his most recent composition, and he added the earlier 'To Kosciusko' and 'Happy is England' as XVI and XVII. There may have been some personal significance for Keats in the symmetry between his Saturnalian evening on 17 December, Tom's seventeenth birthday and the addition of these three poems to make a group of seventeen sonnets for publication in 1817.

If Keats had already asked Richards to do a cast-off and had received his estimate that the volume would require eight sheets, adding 'On the Grasshopper and the Cricket' meant that an extra leaf would be needed for the last six lines of *Sleep and Poetry*.[33] This is one of several bibliographical oddities that seem to show Keats rethinking and altering his book while it was physically taking shape at the printer. As a result there would be no list of contents, no half-title before the first poem, and the conclusion of *Sleep and Poetry*, isolated on a separate page, would send Keats back to make a last-minute alteration to his title-page in an act of poetic and filial homage.

# CHAPTER 10

# Lancet

THE FROSTS of early 1817 wrought a silence in Keats too. In the first three months of the year we glimpse him only occasionally, and no letters survive for the nine weeks between 1 January and 9 March. There is little hint that a first book is in preparation. What explains this silence? Had he lost confidence in his forthcoming book? Keats was always vocal about self-doubt and self-criticism, and had been notably productive in recent months. Since September he had written his epistle 'To Charles Cowden Clarke', eleven sonnets and two longer poems, 'I stood tip toe' and *Sleep and Poetry*, at 240 and 400 lines respectively. His projected volume would be far more substantial than Reynolds's *Safie* and *Naiad* (ninety-one and sixty-three pages) and closer to Hunt's *Story of Rimini* at 131 pages. One explanation for Keats's silence is that he had no time to spare for correspondence. When not at Guy's, he was absorbed by his book. Cowden Clarke passed many hours at Keats's lodgings; Haydon was attacking his painting or at the Elgin Marbles; and Hunt was once again host to Shelley, who arrived on 6 January to try to secure custody of his children. And with Shelley's return to Hunt's, a further reason for Keats's reticence presents itself.

Keats would encounter Hunt, Shelley and Mary Shelley frequently between January and March, and he must have been aware of the bitter legal battle – Westbrook v. Shelley – reported in the *Morning Chronicle*, *The Times* and *The Examiner*. Commencing immediately after Keats gained his independence from Abbey, Westbrook v. Shelley may well have revived unhappy memories. At issue in court were the custody and guardianship of Shelley's children, Eliza Ianthe and Charles Bysshe, following their mother's suicide; Shelley was represented by Basil Montagu, the Westbrooks by the Chancery lawyer who had acted for Keats's mother, Sir Samuel Romilly. All of this was likely to reawaken early misfortunes: his father's death and mother's remarriage,

Rawlings v. Jennings, Chancery, his mother's and grandmother's deaths, and his misery at Hammond's. Proceedings began on Wednesday, 8 January when the Westbrooks filed a Bill of Complaint: as an infamous adulterer, atheist and republican, the poet of *Queen Mab* was manifestly unfit to take responsibility for his children and their education. The case was summarised in the *Morning Chronicle* on Saturday, 25 January and in Sunday's *Examiner*, where Hunt's witty reference to the prince regent's failed marriage risked contempt of court. The lord chancellor's decision to present judgment in private provoked comment in *The Times*, and the case would drag on for another eighteen months until, in July 1818, the lord chancellor ruled against Shelley.[1]

From Sunday, 9 March 1817 until the end of Keats's life there is no period wholly barren of correspondence. That no letters from Keats survive from these first nine weeks of 1817 may be explained, in part, by Westbrook v. Shelley stirring memories of family history about which we know he was habitually silent. Poetry was implicated too. Shelley's radical ideas in *Queen Mab* were cited as evidence that he was scandalously unqualified to raise his own children, thus entangling him in Chancery; for Keats, however, poetry held the promise of liberation from a miserable past. If his poems sold well, his book might extricate him from Abbey and allow him to set an independent course for his life. Westbrook v. Shelley did not threaten that prospect, but it may well have given Keats cause to reflect on the misfortunes that had followed his father's death. If that was indeed so, it may explain why the memory of his father's death should have affected his first book and some of his subsequent actions in surprising ways.

∗ ∗ ∗

*The Examiner* published 'Hymn to Intellectual Beauty' on Sunday, 19 January over the author's name, 'Percy B. Shelley'. Immediately below was a report of a reformist meeting, carefully positioned there by Hunt to open a dialogue with the poem. As readers took in the whole page, Shelley's celebration of universal beauty –

> never joy illumed my brow
> Unlinked with hope that thou wouldst free
> This world from its dark slavery,
> That thou – O awful LOVELINESS,
> Wouldst give whate'er these words cannot express

– announced a potent response to the reformists' rallying cry quoted beneath it: 'Where is the voice, human or divine, which can preach to the exasperation which famine and oppression produces in the minds of men – (*Applause*) – and I will even add in English minds?'[2] When read in *The Examiner* alongside such articles, Shelley's clarion call to 'love all human kind' rang out all the more forcefully. For Keats, Shelley's 'Hymn' very likely had a more personal impact: its evocation of 'some unseen Power/ . . . Like memory of music fled' would have carried him back to John Clarke's musical evenings at his school in Enfield.

\* \* \*

On 20 March, Keats joined Shelley, Haydon and the Hunts for dinner at Horace Smith's home in Knightsbridge. It was an irritable gathering. Hostilities opened with Shelley's casual remark that Christianity was 'detestable' and, when the servant was gone, Haydon 'resolved to gore without mercy'. When Shelley affirmed Shakespeare no Christian, Haydon and Hunt joined the fray with quotations from *Hamlet*. On religion's 'outburnt lamp' Keats sided with Shelley and Hunt, but he also admired and respected Haydon. All of them were enthusiastic readers of Shakespeare and as their contest raced back and forth between Shelley's atheism, Hunt's deism and Haydon's Christianity, Keats said nothing. On religion he was disinclined to think himself 'more in the right than other people', but he would return to this argument in less heated conversations with both Haydon and Hunt, more interested in what it revealed about Shakespeare than in resolving the issue. In these quieter moments Keats heard Haydon remark that '[n]othing can be gathered from what Shakespeare says'. With Hunt, Keats looked over passages of Shakespeare, and he added 'a word on Shakespeare's Christianity' in a letter the following May.[3] A passage 'in favor [*sic*]' from *Measure for Measure* had already been singled out by Haydon; one against came from *Twelfth Night*. All of this set Keats forward to read and reread Shakespeare for himself, encouraged by Haydon – 'study characters, read Shakespeare' – and attentive to the inscrutability of a genius 'whose Life had been as common in particulars as other Mens'.[4]

\* \* \*

Late January brought cloudy 'thick weather', and it would continue like this until mid-February. Would 1817 be like 1816, another year without a summer? Back home from Guy's on 31 January, a sullen Friday, Keats imagined the arrival of spring:

> After dark vapors have oppress'd our plains
> > For a long dreary season, comes a day
> > Born of the gentle SOUTH, and clears away

From the sick heavens all unseemly stains,
The anxious Month, relieving of its pains,
    Takes as a long lost right the feel of MAY;
    The eyelids with the passing coolness play
Like rose leaves with the drip of Summer rains.

The calmest thoughts come round us; as of leaves
    Budding—fruit ripening in stillness—Autumn Suns
Smiling at Eve upon quiet sheaves—
    Sweet SAPPHO'S Cheek—a smiling infant's breath—
The gradual Sand that through an hour-glass runs—
    A woodland Rivulet—a Poet's death.

May. Summer rains. Autumn suns. Keats's sonnet reflects his recent preoc-cupation with dates and seasons, and extends his fascination with the paradoxical effects of motion to include the constant change of passing time. Autumnal thoughts of 'fruit ripening in stillness' lead naturally to the image of 'gradual Sand that through an hour-glass runs' and then, startlingly, to the idea of 'a Poet's death'. 'I always somehow associate Chatterton with autumn,' Keats said.[5] That doomed genius had outfaced oblivion, and his memory continued to flourish like leaves budding under autumnal sun.

This sonnet came after many anxious months. The regent had been jeered and his carriage pelted with stones as he returned from Parliament; soldiers were called out, magistrates put on alert and a secret committee of ministers convened to suspend habeas corpus. Against this ominous backdrop, Keats welcomed spring as a 'long lost right'. Public in spirit, his sonnet also responded to personal pain: January had been a particularly stressful time for Shelley in Chancery. Those impressionistic images that speak for his 'calmest thoughts' in lines 9–12 owe much to Shelley's own technique in his 'Hymn to Intellectual Beauty' –

Like hues and harmonies of evening,—
    Like clouds in starlight widely spread,—
    Like memory of music fled,—

– as if Keats were seeking to restore to Shelley what suicide and Chancery had violated.[6] Hunt was unwavering in his support for Shelley too, but tensions in the larger ménage at the Vale of Health were becoming more and more dangerous.

* * *

Keats's manuscript went to the printer at some point in January 1817. Visits to the Vale of Health followed. Mary Shelley had returned on 25 January, and Keats and Reynolds met her there on Wednesday, 5 February. Keats was back again with George on Wednesday the 12th when they drank tea and had supper. Throughout these weeks Shelley was shuttling between Hampstead and the court, and when Keats visited conversation must have turned upon recent proceedings – indeed, it is not impossible that the more worldly George tried to advise Shelley on how to proceed.

Saturday the 15th came. Shelley set off for town, and then Keats arrived at the Vale for the second time that week – most likely with proofs of his book to show Hunt.[7] What he found was a house in turmoil, with quarrels, jealousies and rivalries at fever pitch. Looming over everything was Harriet's suicide and the ongoing trial. Hunt's affection for his wife, Marianne, was 'waning', as Haydon icily noted, and his passion for his sister-in-law all too apparent. An explosion was inevitable, and it came on the 15th – possibly while Keats was actually there. After two days of rain and storms, Elizabeth Kent flung herself into one of the Hampstead reservoirs and had to be rescued. 'Miss K. is ill,' Mary Shelley noted.[8] A week later Marianne stayed out late, frightening everyone with hints of another suicide. Hunt's circle has often, and rightly, been seen as a benign bohemian community that welcomed like minded spirits, but in these weeks his house was fractious and ill-tempered in ways that encouraged Keats to break off from him. That would not happen just yet, but the inclination was growing.

The next day Hunt dined with the Shelleys, Hazlitt and his wife, Basil Montagu and William Godwin. Keats's poems were handed round, and 'Chapman's Homer' pronounced extraordinary.[9] Shelley had already corrected proofs of his pamphlet *A Proposal for Putting Reform to the Vote* by 22 February, and was waiting to see revised pages that day. He was impatient, urging the Olliers to print – 'the sooner the better' – and to advertise in '*all* the morning papers of note'. By the time *The Examiner* announced it as 'just published' on 2 March, the Shelleys had left Hampstead and relocated to Albion House, Marlow.[10]

* * *

Keats's book was more complex than Shelley's pamphlet, and its haphazard physical presentation indicates that Charles Richards was not used to setting poetry. The first poem he set in type appears under this heading:

## POEMS.

———————

'Places of nestling green for poets made.'
STORY OF RIMINI.

———————

The poem that follows is 'I stood tip-toe', minus its originally intended epigraph from Spenser; this was now to stand at the front of the book. The heading 'POEMS' and the epigraph from Hunt's *Rimini* are printed directly above the text; it would have been more usual for both to have appeared as a half-title on a separate leaf, followed by a blank, and then the text of 'I stood tip-toe' on a fresh page – as is the arrangement, later in the book, for Keats's 'Epistles', 'Sonnets' and *Sleep and Poetry*.[11] Lastly, there is no contents page listing the book's four sections and thirty titles (as was also the case in Hunt's *Juvenilia*). Had it appeared, Keats's contents page would have looked like this:

## CONTENTS.

———————

Displayed thus, the thirty poems presented in four sections and culminating with *Sleep and Poetry* would have made an impressive statement. The book's ambition or 'reach', as well as its sociable manner, would have been immediately apparent to readers as they opened the book.

Keats read the proofs and then, one evening in late February, a last sheet came with a note saying that if he wished to have a dedication it must be sent forthwith.[12] He stepped to a side table and, while brothers and friends chatted, wrote this dedication sonnet:

**To Leigh Hunt, Esq.**

Glory and loveliness have passed away;
    For if we wander out at early morn,
    No wreathed incense do we see upborne
Into the east, to meet the smiling day:
No crowd of nymphs soft voic'd and young, and gay,
    In woven baskets bringing ears of corn,
    Roses, and pinks, and violets, to adorn
The shrine of Flora in her early May.
But there are left delights as high as these,
    And I shall ever bless my destiny,
That in a time, when under pleasant trees
    Pan is no longer sought, I feel a free,

A leafy luxury, seeing I could please
  With these poor offerings, a man like thee.

Keats was in combative mood. Prefacing his first collection with this sonnet,
he made common cause with Hunt and *The Examiner* in the unsettled weeks
after December's Spa Fields riots. On page 81 was his sonnet on Hunt's release
from prison, and the whole book closed with a celebration of Hunt in *Sleep
and Poetry*. Much as Keats's letters echo Haydon's turns of phrase, 'To Leigh
Hunt, Esq.' picks up Hunt's stylistic mannerisms and populates an English
pastoral scene with classical figures. At a period of acute social unrest – 'a
time, when . . . / Pan is no longer sought' – English liberty survives as a 'leafy
luxury', and from Keats's 'poor offerings' fresh delights and freedoms are
destined to grow. In fourteen lines Keats's dedication repays Hunt's compliments in the 'Young Poets' article, and flings down his own gauntlet for the
'New School'.

   *Poems, by John Keats* would not be published immediately. When Charles
Richards had printed it, the preliminary sheet caused a further complication.
In all copies of Keats's book the title-page is a cancel – that is, a single leaf
pasted in after the other preliminary pages had been printed. There are two
possible explanations for this. Richards had printed a title-page that contained
the title and epigraph from Spenser, the Olliers' address and the date. Having
seen it in proof, however, Keats – who was paying for the book – requested a
replacement with a woodcut vignette of Shakespeare's head in laurelled
profile. This was extremely unusual and expensive to produce, so Keats must
have had compelling reasons for intervening. The image, taken from George
Bullock's reproduction of Shakespeare's bust in Holy Trinity Church, Stratford,
was thought to derive from a life mask. Haydon was convinced of the truth of
the likeness, and may have supplied a sketch from which the woodcut was
taken. That scenario makes good sense – except that, mysteriously, no copies
of an original, cancelled title-page *without* Shakespeare have survived. This
circumstance may indicate that the title-page was not a replacement cancel,
but had been part of the book's design from the outset. Quite possibly
Richards had arranged for it to be set – and perhaps printed – by a specialist
printer who was more skilled in working with woodcuts, and it was then
pasted in when the book was bound.[13]

   However it was created, Keats's title-page had impact. Shakespeare's head
reinforced his epigraph's liberal sentiments, and intersected neatly with Hunt's
presence. *The Examiner* numbered Shakespeare with freedom-loving poets
like Dante and Chaucer: 'nothing stands against him on the score of servility.'[14]
Readers who glanced at Keats's title-page and dedication would immediately

be apprised of his liberal sympathies, and of Shakespeare's ascendancy in his imagination. Less obvious are the vignette's paternal associations. Printing the conclusion of *Sleep and Poetry* on a separate page gave particular emphasis to its final lines, where Keats breaks off with an affectionate farewell to his poem and his book:

> howsoever they be done,
> I leave them as a father does his son.

Perhaps it was these closing lines that decided him to begin *Poems, by John Keats* with an image of Shakespeare, whose imminent anniversary was associated with his father's death. So arranged, his book foregrounds the figure he would soon greet as his poetic 'presider' and concludes, perhaps, with a glance back at Thomas Keates's last farewell.

* * *

Keats had the finished book by Saturday, 1 March and busied himself with presentation copies. Thomas Richards received one, and immediately inscribed an admiring sonnet to Keats opposite the title-page. Hunt was next. Keats set off, found him not at home and was walking along Millfield Lane when he met him returning from the *Examiner* office.[15] Together they went on to the Vale of Health for a celebration dinner followed by libations of wine. Thoughts of 'laurel chaplets, and Apollo's glories' made them giddy and elated – after all, Keats's title-page showed Shakespeare garlanded with green. Suddenly Hunt dashed out to the garden, seized a handful of sprigs and hastily improvised two laureate wreaths – one for Keats, another for himself. Then, solemnly pledging Apollo, they crowned each other before settling down to write sonnets. Hunt's poem has him bowing graciously to his young protégé:

> I submit my head
> To the young hand that gives it,—young, 'tis true,
> But with a right, for 'tis a poet's too.

But when Keats sat down to write, he was so fuddled he found he had nothing to say. That in itself would do for a subject – and a quick reworking of the close of 'Chapman's Homer' would help round the poem off:

> Minutes are flying swiftly; and as yet
> Nothing unearthly has enticed my brain

> Into a Delphic labyrinth. I would fain
> Catch an immortal thought to pay the debt
> I owe to the kind poet who has set
>     Upon my ambitious head a glorious gain—
>     Two bending laurel sprigs—'tis nearly pain
> To be conscious of such a coronet.
> Still time is fleeting, and no dream arises
>     Gorgeous as I would have it—only I see
> A trampling down of what the world most prizes,
>     Turbans and crowns, and blank regality;
> And then I run into most wild surmises
>     Of all the many glories that may be.

With its opening line – 'Minutes are flying' – echoed at the start of the sestet – 'Still time is fleeting' – the sonnet's two-part structure recalls 'On the Grasshopper and Cricket'. Unlike that earlier poem, however, this sonnet is ambiguously divided. The juxtaposition of 'glorious gain' with 'nearly pain' might suggest that Keats was already in two minds about his laurel coronet, although when Reynolds and his sisters arrived he vowed he would not remove it for any human being – and promptly set down a second sonnet, 'To the Ladies who saw me Crowned'. It was addressed to the Reynolds girls, and Keats wrote out both of his laureate sonnets in a presentation copy of his book for their brother.

Later that evening he walked back to the city. In a cloudless spring sky, the stars of the Pleiades were twinkling brightly.[16]

∗ ∗ ∗

Next morning, 2 March, *The Examiner* announced to readers what Keats himself already knew: 'J.K.'s LINES are delayed, owing to the great pressure of temporary matter.' By 'temporary matter', Hunt meant a national emergency. The suspension of the Habeas Corpus Act, a keystone of English liberty, was imminent; the authorities would soon have the power to imprison citizens without trial. Given that dreadful prospect, Hunt's addresses 'To the English People' took precedence, warning of a draconian assault on English freedom. Keats's 'LINES', jostled out on 2 March, would be published two weeks later as a sonnet, 'Written on a Blank Space at the End of Chaucer's Tale of "The Floure and the Lefe"':

> This pleasant Tale is like a little Copse:
>     The honied Lines do freshly interlace

To keep the Reader in so sweet a place,
So that he here and there full-hearted stops;
And oftentimes he feels the dewy drops
    Come cool and suddenly against his face,
    And by the wandering melody may trace
Which way the tender-legged Linnet hops.

O what a power has white Simplicity!
    What mighty power has this gentle story!
    I that do ever feel a thirst for glory,
Could at this moment be content to lie
    Meekly upon the grass, as those whose sobbings
    Were heard of none beside the mournful Robins.[17]

The sonnet is a slight, decorative piece but its appearance in *The Examiner* intersected surprisingly, and powerfully, with Hunt's political campaign. By saluting Chaucer's 'pleasant Tale' at a moment of national crisis, Keats affirmed his Chaucerian lineage as a poet and, by implication, his support for the English liberties Hunt was championing in the same pages. On the intervening Sunday, 9 March, *The Examiner* had recruited Chaucer, Spenser, Shakespeare and Milton to the cause of political reform; all four were great poets who might rouse public opposition to the suspension of habeas corpus. For Hunt, the English people were 'descendants of CHAUCER, one of the great fathers of modern poetry, who was a Reformer in his day, and set his face both against priestly and kingly usurpation; and yet you are told that Reform is essentially a vulgar and foolish thing, and that it is much wiser to let kings and priests settle matters without you'.[18] Just three months had passed since Hunt's 'New School' of poets had been announced in *The Examiner*. Here, in the issue for 9 March, he connected that school of modern poetry with the Chaucerian line and announced loudly and clearly the reformist challenge presented by his coterie of young poets – of whom Keats, youngest of them all, was the foremost. By changing poetic language to a more natural and idiomatic style, Hunt argued, his 'New School' would challenge existing authorities on what constituted 'poetry' and, by extension, the 'authorized selfishness' of Church and State. Their volumes of poetry with spiky politically charged prefaces, promoted by *The Examiner*, represented a potent force for change, and when critics complained about their 'vulgar' and 'foolish' language, their derision acknowledged an irresistible force. If 'Young Poets' had helped to launch Keats's poetic career, the delay of his sonnet on Chaucer highlighted a keen political edge to his poetry – and reviewers were taking notice.

* * *

Laying aside his copy of *The Examiner* on Sunday, 2 March, Keats set off for an appointment with Haydon and Reynolds at the British Museum. They were going to see the Elgin Marbles, and what they encountered was very different from today's Parthenon Gallery.[19] A Temporary Elgin Room had been built onto the Townley Gallery at the back of the old museum in Montagu House, and this meant that Keats would have to walk through the entire building to see them.

Keats, Haydon and Reynolds turned off Great Russell Street, crossed a courtyard containing Alexander the Great's enormous stone coffin and entered the Hallway. Here were Ionic pillars, two Egyptian monuments of black marble covered with hieroglyphs, and a double archway with iron gates to the grand staircase. Overhead was a flat ceiling painted with clouds. At the foot of the staircase a wooden model showed how Blackfriars Bridge was built, and underneath it were fragments from the Giant's Causeway. Lofty walls and high ceilings were decorated with friezes and frescoes, pillars, foliage, trophies and paintings with scenes from classical mythology – Phaëton borrowing Apollo's chariot, Diana and Actaeon, Bacchanalian revels and Roman battles. Keats had entered a palace of the strange and exotic, culled from all ages and quarters of the world. Climbing the grand staircase, he passed three stuffed giraffes and a rhinoceros before wandering through room after room of Etruscan antiquities, marble busts, manuscripts, miniatures, models of a Chinese junk and a Parsee graveyard, serpents, fish, reptiles, birds, dried plants, shells, portraits, fossils, minerals, meteorites, pebbles and crystals, precious stones and a mammoth's gigantic jaw. A visitor in 1786 noted how 'nothing is in order, everything is out of its place; and this assemblage appears rather an immense magazine, in which things have been thrown at random'.[20] All the systematising efforts of the eighteenth century counted for nothing in this vast, disorderly treasure house. Some said it resembled another palace of distraction – Bedlam.

Like Bedlam, the old museum's colonnades and courts, lantern towers, cupolas, saloons, grand staircase, galleries and corridors are another possible prototype for Hyperion's 'palace bright', with its

> thousand courts,
> Arches, and domes, and fiery galleries;
> And all its curtains of Aurorian clouds.

(i.179–81)

As Keats headed towards the Townley Gallery he was also stepping back into classical antiquity, as if passing from his own age of revolutions to the original war between Titans and Olympians. A long gallery of Roman artefacts led to a collection of Egyptian antiquities and more classical sculpture, including 'a fine disco-bolus, or ancient quoit-player'.[21] One Egyptian sculpture displayed here would eventually reappear as the 'Memphian Sphinx' in *Hyperion*, while the athlete with a discus joins a team of 'quoit-pitchers' in book one of *Endymion*.

From this gallery Keats descended a narrow staircase into the Temporary Elgin Room. Perhaps Haydon orchestrated this moment with a rerun of his furious public quarrel with Richard Payne Knight about the sculptures' origin. In brief, Knight had dismissed them as mediocre Roman copies dating from the reign of Emperor Hadrian, whereas for Haydon – like the artists John Flaxman, Thomas Lawrence, and Benjamin West – their Greek antiquity was as unmistakable as their 'union of Nature with ideal beauty'. Keats had walked through room after room packed with centuries of lumber, and now entered a large brick-built chamber with a pine floor and roof, cross-braced with iron girders and pierced with skylights. Metopes and the frieze were arranged on the walls, and in front of these stood huge pediment sculptures, inscriptions and fragments. A recess in the far wall contained several statues and the torso of a god, like a chancel holding the most revered relics. It was here in 1819 that Archibald Archer painted the art establishment of the day led by Benjamin West, president of the Royal Academy, and Joseph Planta, principal librarian of the British Museum. Haydon was relegated to the background to mark his exclusion from Academy circles.

We can picture Keats walking from sculpture to sculpture, hearing Haydon but perhaps not listening to all that he says – gazing up at the skylights, then at shadows across walls and floors. He is impressed, awed, and tries to make sense of how all these individual pieces were formerly combined. How did they fit together? What did this or that fragment mean? What men – or gods – were these?

Back at Cheapside, he drafted thoughts towards a sonnet that became 'On Seeing the Elgin Marbles' – an 'occasional' poem like 'On First Looking into Chapman's Homer':

> My spirit is too weak—Mortality
>     Weighs heavily on me like unwilling sleep,
>     And each imagined pinnacle and steep
> Of godlike hardship, tells me I must die
> Like a sick Eagle looking at the sky.

> Yet 'tis a gentle luxury to weep
>     That I have not the cloudy winds to keep,
> Fresh for the opening of the morning's eye.
> Such dim-conceived glories of the brain
>     Bring round the heart an undescribable feud;
> So do these wonders a most dizzy pain,
>     That mingles Grecian grandeur with the rude
> Wasting of old time—with a billowy main—
>     A sun—a shadow of a magnitude.[22]

Unlike in 'Chapman's Homer', Keats was picking a quarrel here – with himself. Aspiring to 'each imagined pinnacle' and 'dim-conceived glories', he finds himself mortally unequal to the 'steep' of his own ambitions. Quietly acknowledged here are the 'race' and 'steep' of the school medal that saluted one of his earlier encounters with classical antiquity. If initially Keats felt he had failed to measure up, it is striking how Hunt's voice, ''tis a gentle luxury to weep', helped him to the magnificent close of his poem. As with his 'new planet', Keats's skyward glance to 'A sun—a shadow of a magnitude' comprehends the sublimity of 'Grecian grandeur' and, curiously, may foreshadow his idea of 'negative capability' in that the power of a sun, its 'magnitude', is expressed in negative figures.

That Keats sensed he had made a breakthrough in this sonnet is suggested by another written immediately afterwards, 'To Haydon, with a Sonnet Written on Seeing the Elgin Marbles'. He begins by accepting apparent failure:

> HAYDON! Forgive me that I cannot speak
>     Definitively on these mighty things;
>     Forgive me that I have not Eagle's wings—
> That what I want I know not where to seek:
> And think that I would not be overmeek
>     In rolling out upfollow'd thunderings,
>     Even to the steep of Heliconian springs,
> Were I of ample strength for such a freak—
> Think too, that all those numbers should be thine;
>     Whose else? In this who touch thy vesture's hem?
> For when men star'd at what was most divine
>     With browless idiotism—o'erwise phlegm—
> Thou hadst beheld the Hesperean shine
>     Of their star in the East, and gone to worship them.[23]

'I cannot speak / Definitively', 'I have not Eagle's wings', 'what I want I know not where to seek': Keats repeatedly admits, and with renewing confidence actually celebrates, his inability to 'speak definitively'.[24] He offers Haydon a gawky compliment – 'I would not be overmeek', and so on – although his poem is excited and impelled by its discovery that not to know, not to speak 'definitively', can release his imagination to play between possibilities without the prostration implied in Haydon's 'worship'. Suddenly the impasse encountered on beginning his epistle 'To Charles Cowden Clarke' was cleared, and a spring of extraordinary creative energy lay ahead. Keats copied out his two poems, dispatched them to Haydon, then transcribed both into a presentation copy of his book for Reynolds.[25] They were published on the following Sunday, 9 March, in Reynolds's review of *Poems, by John Keats* for *The Champion* and, simultaneously, in *The Examiner*.[26]

* * *

Monday, 3 March dawned fine after a stormy night, one year to the day since Keats had enrolled as Lucas's dresser. A letter arrived from Haydon to acknowledge 'two noble sonnets' and to say he expected to see him with Cowden Clarke and Reynolds that evening. On the front page of the *Morning Chronicle* was an advertisement for Shelley's pamphlet and 'POEMS; by John Keats' to be published priced 6s.6d. 'on Monday next'. Although an exact date of publication is difficult to establish, he already had cause for jubilation, and it seems likely that this was the moment Cowden Clarke later recalled when his first book 'was launched amid the cheers and fond anticipations of all his circle'. It also marked the beginning of the end of his commitments at Guy's, although his hard-won medical knowledge would continue to inform his poetry and his idea that a poet was 'physician to all men'.[27]

Two spectres attended Keats at Haydon's that night. If his mother's illness and death had been decisive at the start of his apprenticeship, it was a memory of his father that encouraged him to make a break for poetry. Charles Brown takes up the story: ' "My last operation", he told me, "was the opening of a man's temporal artery. I did it with the utmost nicety; but, reflecting on what passed through my mind at the time, my dexterity seemed a miracle, and I never took up the lancet again".'[28] At a time when all surgical operations were dangerous, it is significant that this one registered so forcefully with Keats. At risk in that last operation was the misfortune of an arterial wound to his patient's head, identical to the mortal bruise that had killed his father. As Keats swapped his lancet for a quill, his hopes for poetic glory were part of a conversation with his dead parents to whom he could speak in no other way.

\* \* \*

From now on Keats's time was his own. Because he had published on commission, he was entitled to as many copies of *Poems* as he wished. Thomas Richards, Hunt and Reynolds already had theirs, and inscribed copies also went to Cowden Clarke, John Byng Gattie, Haydon, Fanny Keats (inscribed by George from 'the Author and his Brother'), George Keats, George Felton Mathew, the Misses Reynolds, Joseph Severn, Charles Wells, Charles Wilkinson and William Wordsworth.[29] It is inconceivable that Tom Keats did not have one, and among other likely recipients are Edward Holmes, Vincent Novello, Horace Smith and Henry Stephens. Bailey received a copy, and a passing reference to 'Mrs Dilk' at this time suggests Keats had now met Reynolds's friends Charles Wentworth Dilke and his wife, Maria. Perhaps they had a copy too. On 10 April, John Scott wrote from Paris to acknowledge his extraordinary poems. Abbey certainly had a copy, and John Taylor heard that he told Keats it was 'hard to understand & good for nothing when it is understood'.[30] He could not have known that Taylor was also among the book's first readers, and that he formed a very different idea of its merits. Now is the moment to find out why.

Born on 31 July 1781, John Taylor was the son of bookseller James Taylor of East Retford and his wife, Sarah Drury. Trained up by his father in the book trade, he migrated to London and by 1802 was working at Lackington's Temple of the Muses, where he met James Hessey. From April 1804 Taylor was working for Vernor and Hood, booksellers, at 31 The Poultry – a few yards from Thomas Mower Keats's premises at number 14. Two years later Taylor and Hessey set up in partnership as booksellers at 93 Fleet Street, from where they published S.T. Coleridge, John Clare, William Hazlitt, Thomas Hood, Leigh Hunt, Charles Lamb, Thomas De Quincey, John Hamilton Reynolds, John Scott and the influential *London Magazine*. Always scouting for new talent, they commissioned illustrations for Goldsmith's *Citizen of the World* from a young painter, William Hilton. As the business grew, their network of friends drew in Richard Woodhouse, lawyer in the Temple, as a legal adviser, and a skilful physician, Dr George Darling. Both would figure significantly in Keats's life, and there is evidence to suggest that Taylor and Hessey may have been aware of Keats's family long before they met him.

While at Lackington's, Taylor and Hessey would have passed the Swan and Hoop many times, and could easily have encountered Thomas and Frances Keates; as enterprising booksellers, they would have scanned newspapers and the *Gentleman's Magazine* where, in April 1804, Thomas Keates's death was reported. Edmund Blunden notes an odd coincidence that in the earliest letter from Hessey to his partner, dated 19 August 1806, the name Keats occurs: 'Pray what is become of John White? is he still with Keats or is he removed with Sir John Duckworth to the Royal George?' This is Richard Goodwin Keats of the *Superb* – a relative, apparently, of Thomas Keates – so Taylor already knew the name and some of the wider Keats family when, early in 1817, Reynolds introduced him to the poet. By mid-March, Taylor had read *Poems, by John Keats* and was writing excitedly to his brother about the book and the poet's idiosyncratic appearance; no longer affecting Byronic dress, he was now sporting 'some sort of sailor costume' akin to the uniform of his naval relative.[31]

Reviews soon appeared. First into print was Reynolds's welcome in *The Champion* for poems graceful and genuine, 'fresh from nature' and with a 'natural freedom of versification'. A short notice in *The Monthly* likewise noted 'sweetness and beauty of composition', a 'fertile fancy' and a 'careless and profuse magnificence' that had seemed to Reynolds 'occasionally overwrought'. Then came George Felton Mathew's grudging estimate in the *European Magazine*. No longer close to Keats, he drew attention to his loose couplets and, instead of finding a pleasingly 'natural freedom', faulted them for a 'slovenly independence of versification' akin to Hunt's. Soured by Keats's success, Mathew claimed that earlier poems, dating from their friendship, were 'superior to the rest'. 'Till I heard Chapman speak out loud and bold' was a 'bad line' that inflated the sonnet into 'unseemly hyperbole'.[32] In all of these references to 'natural freedom' and 'independence', reviewers were responding to language, versification and, implicitly, politics. Much harsher words would follow.

Keats wrote to thank Reynolds. They met one evening the following week, and Haydon joined them 'latish' to talk about future plans. Keats's brothers were anxious that he should break his sociable city routine and go by himself to the country. Haydon agreed. Keats must be alone to improve himself.[33] Hunt's absence from these conversations is noticeable. There may have been talk of a plan, encouraged by Hunt, that Keats should compete with Shelley to write a long poem in six months. Hunt had been invited to visit Shelley at Marlow, and perhaps Keats was too; he would have enjoyed the Thames Valley with its woods and water meadows, but Haydon was desperate to keep him away from Shelley and Hunt. And Keats, determined to have his own unfettered scope, refused to go anyway.[34]

As a first step out of town the brothers determined to quit Cheapside and move to Hampstead's quiet and clear air. They flitted in the week of fine weather between Monday, 17 March, when Keats wrote to Reynolds from

Lombard Street, and Tuesday, 25 March, when he addressed Cowden Clarke from Hampstead. Keats and Hunt were invited to a musical evening at Novello's on Wednesday – would Cowden Clarke join them? He tells Cowden Clarke he has written a sonnet on Hunt's 'sweet tale', *The Story of Rimini*, and will make a copy for him 'against tomorrow'.[35]

They rented rooms at 1 Well Walk, home of the village postman Benjamin Bentley, his wife and children.[36] A photograph of an identical adjacent property from 1889 shows a three-storey terraced house with a basement, next door to the Green Man tavern. Shaded by lime trees, Well Walk extended east of Hampstead to the Heath. Opposite Bentley's house was a fountain, pouring out gallons of the rusty, unpalatable water that had transformed Hampstead into a fashionable spa. A few yards further along was the old Long Room where the waters were taken: Addison and Steele came here early in the eighteenth century; Pope, Goldsmith, Dr Johnson and Fanny Burney followed later. By Keats's time the spa was disused, although the spring continued to flow beside Well Walk. As always, living close to water connected him with childhood scenes, awakening his thirst for fame. 'Keats said to me today as we were walking along "Byron, Scott, Southey, & Shelley think they are to lead the age but . . ."' – so Haydon began his journal entry for 7 April, but Keats's further thoughts have been erased. When the passage is resumed, we hear him 'talking of some mean People. "What a pity", said Keats, "there is not a *human dust hole*".' Haydon reflected that Keats was the only man he had met 'who is conscious of a high call', and in this Haydon deemed him wholly unlike Hunt and Shelley.[37]

The circle of friends who welcomed Keats's first book was fragmenting. Ironically, given that Keats was now Hunt's near-neighbour at Hampstead, there would be no further gatherings at the Vale of Health, certainly no more antics with laurel crowns. Ashamed, now, by the silliness of that evening, Keats had drafted an apology to Apollo,

> God of the golden bow,
>     And of the golden lyre,
> And of the golden hair,
>     And of the golden fire,
>         Charioteer
>         Round the patient year—
>             ('God of the golden bow', 1–6)

and renewed his vow to 'Delphic Apollo', whose inspiration he had acknowledged in *Sleep and Poetry*:

I will strive

Against all doubtings, and will keep alive

The thought of that same chariot, and the strange

Journey it went.

(159–62)


One auspicious development was an agreement with Taylor and Hessey to publish his next book. Another was Keats's purchase of Whittingham's seven-volume set of Shakespeare's works – the edition was sold by Robert Jennings at 62 Cheapside. In the first volume, opposite an engraving of Shakespeare's birthplace, he wrote 'John Keats—April 1817'. Turning over two pages he saw Shakespeare's portrait 'from the Bust in Stratford Church' like the vignette in his own book. The volumes were compact and portable. This was an important consideration, for Keats, encouraged by his brothers, was now planning his own strange journey out of London to begin *Endymion*. As many as six coaches left for Southampton each day, so he had plenty of choice as to date and time for this venture towards a new poem, and what they all hoped would be 'a great good' that would follow.[38] It was Keats's own decision to book a seat on the mail coach to Southampton on the night of 14–15 April.

# The Year of *Endymion*, 1817

# CHAPTER 11

---

# Strange Journeys

THE BROTHERS gathered at the Bell and Crown, Holborn, in good time for Keats's leave-taking. With box stowed and farewells said, he clambered up to his seat and wrapped himself in a plaid. At four-thirty sharp, the coach clattered along Holborn, weaving west and south through Hyde Park, Knightsbridge and rural Hammersmith.[1] Night fell clear, moonless and chilly, so at the King's Arms, Bagshot, he paid for an inside seat. As he gazed out his world contracted to a bright hoop cast by the coach lamps. Hurdles and palings. The glitter of a window. Lopped trees. A cow. A donkey. Night-faring countryfolk. Towns with strange names – Alton, Chawton, Alresford. A barber's pole. A doctor's shop. He tried to doze. The last stretch from Winchester lay through woods and across heathland as dawn broke over bright yellow furze.

After fourteen hours they entered Southampton through medieval Brandgate and pulled up at the Coach and Horses. Keats could smell sea air. Gulls shrieked from rooftops. The streets were awake and busy, so he collected his box and set off in search of breakfast. Seventy-seven sleepless miles now separated him from his brothers. Muzzy with weariness, he took out one of the Shakespeare volumes – the first, containing *The Tempest*. That play would run in his head throughout the following days. Enquiring for a boat to the Isle of Wight, he was told to come back at three that afternoon. He wandered through back streets, then settled to write to his brothers: 'I am safe at Southampton . . .'

\* \* \*

Alone for the first time in many months, Keats confronted the formidable challenge that he had set himself. From the 'bare circumstance' of Endymion's story he would write four thousand lines of poetry – he thought of it as a 'test' and 'trial' of his imagination, like his translation of *The Aeneid*.[2] From Lemprière's outline – 'Diana saw [Endymion] naked as he slept on mount Latmos, and was so struck with his beauty that she came down from heaven every night to enjoy his company' – he elaborated the full story:

> Many Years ago there was a young handsome Shepherd who fed his flocks on a Mountain's Side called Latmus—he was a very contemplative sort of a Person and lived solitry among the trees and Plains little thinking—that such a beautiful Creature as the Moon was growing mad in Love with him . . . and when he was asleep on the Grass, she used to come down from heaven and admire him excessively from a long time; and at last could not refrain from carrying him away in her arms to the top of that high Mountain Latmus while he was dreaming—[3]

He had arranged his travel with purpose: on the morning of 15 April, he would set about his task. Somewhat oddly, he tells his brothers: '*N.B. this tuesday Morn saw the Sun rise*—of which I shall say nothing at present.' And, indeed, nothing more was said. One meaning of this opaque remark, however, may be found in the long night of 14–15 April thirteen years before, and a sunrise their father did not live to see. Keats had survived that dark transit, and from now on would be possessed by thoughts of posthumous fame and his own 'brazen tomb'.[4]

✱ ✱ ✱

At three, the ferry cast off, slipped down Southampton Water on an ebb tide and entered the Solent. Ahead lay the Isle of Wight with its low hills, and when they moored at Cowes three vessels, the *Kinnersley Castle, Pomona* and *Hussaren*, were loading troops for North America. All of the south coast had been heavily garrisoned during the Napoleonic Wars, and Albany Barracks on Newport Road struck Keats as 'a Nest of Debauchery in so beautiful a place'. Others felt the same: at Newport that night he discovered that someone had engraved on the window, 'O Isle spoilt by the Mil*a*tary', but on reflection he decided there might be advantages in the local women being 'a little profligate'.[5]

Next day he walked seven miles to Shanklin, attracted by its coastal location and the precipitous tree-lined cleft of the Chine. Down he clambered nearly three hundred feet, and followed the stream to the sea. Shanklin was a beautiful place, but it was expensive and out of the way and he planned to roam across the entire island. A central location would be cheaper and more convenient. Thursday the 17th saw him settling into lodgings at Mrs Cook's house in the new village, Carisbrooke. From his window he could see the castle where Charles I had been imprisoned, its battlements rising above wood-alleys and copses. There were 'quick freshes' – streams and runnels that danced across meadows, under hedges and alongside paths. Close by was a little hill, Mount Joy, from where he could scan the Solent.

If the landscape was auspicious, so was his new home. He unpacked his volumes of Shakespeare and Spenser, then pinned up pictures of Haydon, Mary, Queen of Scots and 'Milton, with his daughters in a row'. Above these he hung a portrait of Shakespeare he had found in the passage – 'I like it extremely,' he told Reynolds, adding: 'From want of regular rest, I have been rather *narvus* – and the passage in Lear – "Do you not hear the Sea?" – has haunted me intensely.' An overnight journey, scant sleep and his friends' expectations had all combined to make him overwrought. Keats's word '*narvus*' was a reminder of Astley Cooper's lecture on 'nerves' at Guy's, and also echoes a word heard long ago at Keates's Livery Stables. A 'narve' was taut animal sinew used to tension a saddle-tree or to make bowstring – 'the nerve of Phoebus' golden bow'.[6] After the laurel crown episode, would his new poem, *Endymion*, be sufficient to appease Apollo?

*Narvus*, Keats had misremembered Shakespeare. 'Do you not hear the Sea?' is not a line in *King Lear*, but a mixture of Edgar's question to his father, 'Hark! do you hear the sea?' (IV.vi.4), and the opening of *The Tempest*:

Antonio: Where is the master, boson?
Boatswain: Do you not hear him?
(I.i.11–12)

Both passages create dramatic tension, and Keats's spliced line 'Do you not hear the Sea?' captures his own feelings of trepidation – 'in a taking' and 'all in a Tremble' – until he could begin to direct his nervous energy into composition:[7]

**On the Sea**

It keeps eternal Whisperings around
    Desolate shores, and with its mighty swell
    Gluts twice ten thousand Caverns; till the spell
Of Hecate leaves them their old shadowy sound.
Often 'tis in such gentle temper found
    That scarcely will the very smallest shell
    Be moved for days from whence it sometime fell
When last the winds of Heaven were unbound.

> O ye who have your eyeballs vext and tir'd
> 　Feast them upon the wideness of the Sea
> O ye whose Ears are dinned with uproar rude
> 　Or fed too much with cloying melody—
> Sit ye near some old Cavern's Mouth and brood
> Until ye start as if the Sea Nymphs quired—[8]

The words 'gluts', 'feast' and 'fed' are typical of Keats's gourmandising vocabulary when under stress, although with the sea in 'gentle temper found' this haunted sonnet marked an eerily apprehensive interim. But awaiting what? Moments of quiet in Keats's poems often presage a sudden transition, as in the ominously tranquil opening of *Hyperion* or halcyon calm of his poem 'Dear Reynolds'.[9] Tennyson's 'Nature, red in tooth and claw / With Ravine' would prove to be at deadly work in that poem, like the voracious 'throat of Orcus' engulfing Aeneas as he descended to greet his father.[10]

Ruling over rapacious nature was Hecate, familiar to Keats from Lemprière. His sonnet invokes just two of her many roles, as moon-goddess of the sea's 'mighty swell' and in her daemonic guise as guardian of the gates of Hades. Casting back to his Margate sonnet, Keats reimagines the sea's 'voice mysterious' as an entrancing 'shadowy sound', like the songs of Orpheus as he entered the infernal regions to charm the king of hell and rescue Eurydice. Possessed by poetry's oceanic command over life and death, Keats's last, magical line echoes the sea-nymphs' 'hourly knell' for Ferdinand's father in *The Tempest* – a father who will eventually return as if from the dead. There could be no such return for Thomas Keates although, following his son's strange overnight journey to Southampton, perhaps his voice echoes in those 'eternal Whisperings' as they announce a new master whom Keats would from now on associate with the sea: Shakespeare.

* * *

Continuing his letter to Reynolds the next day, Keats mentions an imminent birthday. 'On the 23rd was Shakespeare born.' He looks to receive a letter on that day from Reynolds, requesting 'a Word or two on some Passage in Shakespeare that may have come rather new to you; which must be continually happening, notwithstand^g that we read the same Play forty times'.[11] As protean and 'continually happening' as the sea, Shakespeare resurfaces in a subsequent letter to Reynolds's sisters when Keats mentions the 'varying (though selfsame)' music of the sea, and asks: 'Which is the best of Shakspeare's Plays?—I mean in what mood and with what accompaniment do you like the Sea best?'[12]

'On the Sea' brought Keats temporary respite, but *narvus* feelings soon revived. '[T]his Morning . . . I am nearly as bad again,' he tells Reynolds. 'I find that I cannot exist without poetry.' He had one option. 'I shall forthwith begin my Endymion, which I hope I shall have got some way into by the time you come, when we shall read our verses in a delightful place I have set my heart upon near the Castle.' And then he signs off: 'Give my Love to your Sisters severally—To George and Tom—Remember me to Rice M^r & M^rs Dilk and all we know.'[13]

And that is the last we hear from him on this visit to the Isle of Wight. Exactly how much of *Endymion* he composed there is unknown, but some guesses are possible. In describing Carisbrooke Castle for Reynolds, he made two slips of the pen: 'The trench is o'ergrown with the smoothest turf, and the walls with 'Joy' ivy—The Keep within side is one Bower of 'Joy' ivy.'[14] 'Bower of Joy': perhaps this was a bawdy joke for Reynolds, in keeping with the profligate women mentioned a few lines later. Possibly Keats was thinking of Virgin's Bower and Traveller's Joy, popular terms for clematis; or maybe he had the local hill, Mount Joy, in view as he was writing. Whatever the reason, his deleted references to 'Joy' also echo the opening lines of *Endymion*:

A thing of beauty is a joy forever:
Its loveliness increases; it will never
Pass into nothingness; but still will keep
A bower quiet for us, and a sleep
Full of sweet dreams, and health, and quiet breathing.
Therefore, on every morrow, are we wreathing
A flowery band to bind us to the earth,
Spite of despondence, of the inhuman dearth
Of noble natures, of the gloomy days,
Of all the unhealthy and o'er-darkened days,
Made for our searching: yes, in spite of all,
Some shape of beauty moves away the pall
From our dark spirits. Such the sun, the moon,
Trees old, and young sprouting a shady boon
For simple sheep; and such are daffodils
With the green world they live in; and clear rills
That for themselves a cooling covert make
'Gainst the hot season; the mid forest brake,
Rich with a sprinkling of fair musk-rose blooms:
And such too is the grandeur of the dooms
We have imagined for the mighty dead.

(i.1–21)

*Endymion* gets under way on an April morning at Carisbrooke, with its landscape of 'clear rills', 'rushes fenny', 'ivy banks' and 'copse-clad vallies'. The phrases 'whisper round' and 'city's din' echo 'On the Sea', and 'surgy murmurs of the lonely sea' (121) is a reminder of the beach at Shanklin and that favourite line – Coleridge's 'stilly murmur of the distant sea'. These intersections of phrase, echo, and landscape suggest that Keats composed the first 120 lines or so of *Endymion* at Carisbrooke. Alone, not eating properly and with little sleep, he was soon mentally and physically exhausted – as he told Hunt, not 'over capable' in his 'upper Stories'.[15] Perhaps this explains a more sombre aspect of the poem's opening, harking back to 'unhealthy and o'erdarkened ways' along which Keats had followed his parents' coffins to the gateway of St Stephen's, with its carving of 'dooms / . . . imagined for the mighty dead'. Margate had been on his mind in recent days, and on the 23rd or 24th he dashed 'pell mell' to meet Tom at their old lodging there – across country, via London, or possibly by sea. Somewhere on his journey he acquired a copy of Scott's poem *Marmion*, a gift for his brother.

By Thursday, 8 May, Haydon had heard of his move and wrote encouragingly: 'you did quite right. . . . Do not give way to any forebodings they are nothing more than the over eager anxieties of a great Spirit.' Wordsworth's head was now in 'Christ's Entry to Jerusalem', and if Keats came to town 'for a day or two' his own would be, 'with glory & honor'.[16]

Two days later he told Hunt how he had been 'down in the Mouth' at *Endymion*, but now felt more confident: 'I have asked myself so often why I should be a Poet more than other Men,—seeing how great a thing it is,—how great things are to be gained by it—What a thing to be in the Mouth of Fame.' That evening Keats wrote again to Haydon, still preoccupied with the idea of fame: 'The Trumpet of Fame is as a tower of Strength the ambitious bloweth it and is safe.' The biblical phrasing was calculated to appeal to Haydon, as was his allusion to Dover Cliff in *King Lear*: 'I am "one that gathers Samphire dreadful trade" the Cliff of Poesy Towers above me—yet when, Tom who meets with some of Pope's Homer in Plutarch's Lives reads some of those to me they seem like Mice to mine.' Having read *Love's Labour's Lost, King Lear* and *Antony and Cleopatra*, Keats had been wondering if his 'good genius' might be Shakespeare: 'Is it too daring to fancy Shakspeare this presider?' When he left Carisbrooke his landlady had given him the Shakespeare portrait. 'Do you not think this is ominous of good?'[17]

With that question Keats broke off. News of more financial difficulties had come from George and, with it, the Olliers' irritable reply to his enquiry about sales:

3 Wellbeck Street, 29th April, 1817.

Sir,—We regret that your brother ever requested us to publish his book, or that our opinion of its talent should have led us to acquiesce in undertaking it. We are, however, much obliged to you for relieving us from the unpleasant necessity of declining any further connexion with it, which we must have done, as we think the curiosity is satisfied, and the sale has dropped. By far the greater number of persons who have purchased it from us have found fault with it in such plain terms, that we have in many cases offered to take the book back rather than be annoyed with the ridicule which has, time after time, been showered upon it. In fact, it was only on Saturday last that we were under the mortification of having our own opinion of its merits flatly contradicted by a gentleman, who told us he considered it 'no better than a take in'. These are unpleasant imputations for any one in business to labour under, but we should have borne them and concealed their existence from you had not the style of your note shown us that such delicacy would be quite thrown away. We shall take means without delay for ascertaining the number of copies on hand, and you shall be informed accordingly.

Your most, & c.

C. & J. Ollier.[18]

This was bluster. Sales of the book were limited to 'some dozens', as Keats put it, so the 'greater number' of fault-finders were few indeed. The first reviews had been welcoming, and echoed the Olliers' sense of the book's merits; no one went into print claiming it was a 'take in' – a swindle. As ambitious for his brother's *Poems* as the Olliers were for their new business, George had reproached the publishers for not promoting sales. Stung by this, the Olliers had responded in kind and Keats's phrase 'rather like a nettle leaf or two in your bed' catches their tone exactly. The book was readvertised in *The Times* on 26 July, and unsold stock was eventually transferred to Taylor and Hessey, from whom the book could still be purchased as late as 1824.[19]

George's letter plunged Keats back into gloomy apprehensions. Resuming his letter to Haydon on 11 May, he revoked hopes of finishing *Endymion* by autumn and mused on his 'horrid Morbidity of Temperament'. Haydon alone would understand the turmoil, anxiety and sacrifice he had already endured, and the suffering he anticipated in years ahead 'could plans be brought to conclusions'.[20] Hunt could have no conception of 'greater things—that is to say ethereal things', for he had deluded himself into the idea that he was a great poet. Just six months had passed since the 'Era' of their first meeting.

What did Keats mean when he said that a 'morbid temperament' was his 'greatest Enemy and stumbling block'?[21] Much more than depression or low spirits. In his essay 'On Mr. Kean's Iago', Hazlitt associated 'morbid sensibility' with the corrosive effects of personal ambition mingled with feelings of social disadvantage. Iago, for Hazlitt, was a proto-Jacobin, convinced that 'talents ought to decide the place', irked that he 'could not be supposed to assume it as a matter of course, as if . . . entitled to it from his birth'.[22] As Keats read this, he recognised himself. He had told Abbey that he 'possessed Abilities greater than most Men', and was 'determined to gain [his] living by exercising them'. Haydon heard how he was 'proud of being the lowest of the human race', Bailey that he had 'suspected every Body'.[23] Years later Hunt attributed Keats's suspiciousness, particularly in relation to the aristocratic Shelley, to 'an irritable morbidity'.[24] His 'horrid Morbidity of Temperament' was the rankling of a self-made young man who felt himself frustrated by the prejudice of others and hampered by his own self-doubt. If Keats could overcome both, he would be at liberty to create himself. Would *Endymion* enable him to do so?

In his ambition for 'towering poetical fame', *Endymion* became a test of his poetic powers – a summation of his life so far. A passage from a lost letter to George, written at this time, mentions his plan for *Endymion* and describes a long poem as 'a little Region to wander in where [readers] may pick and choose', an analogy that recalls the school garden at Enfield. Lingering in that neighbourhood, Keats's thoughts turned to the New River and ventures on the stream of rhyme: 'a long Poem is a test of Invention which I take to be the Polar Star of Poetry, as Fancy is the Sails, and Imagination the Rudder.'[25] These references, along with the 'Trumpet of Fame' and the 'Temple of Fame', show him plotting *Endymion* in relation to childhood scenes and associations that he knew George would recognise: their school, the New River and, earlier, the Temple of the Muses with its cliffs of books and the figure of 'Fame', trumpet to her lips, on Lackington's tokens. Seeking to answer his own question in 'I stood tip-toe' – 'Was there a Poet born?' – Keats developed *Endymion* as a verse autobiography in which he scrutinised his own abilities in the process of writing his poem. When he finished it, he would have his answer.

We next hear from Keats on 16 May acknowledging a loan of £20 from Lackington's former employees Taylor and Hessey.[26] He had given up *Endymion* on Sunday, 11 May, and his subsequent attempts to resume it had been fruitless. Disclosing no 'new planet', the 'swimming in [his] head' had been as unproductive as 'the effects of a Mental Debauch' – low spirits and lassitude. Self-absorbed, anxious, obsessed by thoughts of profligate women and bowers of joy, Keats's lack of sexual experience compounded his feelings of inadequacy. Still, his publishers would welcome something positive about

*Endymion*: 'This Evening I go to Cantrerbury [sic]—having got tired of Margate—I was not right in my head when I came—At Cant[y] I hope the Remembrance of Chaucer will set me forward like a Billiard-Ball.'[27] Adding that he had some idea of seeing the Continent in the summer, he signed off.

\* \* \*

Canterbury's Chaucerian associations were encouraging, although Keats did not linger long in the cathedral city. When Tom returned to London Keats turned south to the coast, hoping to push on with his poem. At Haydon's recommendation he stayed at Bo-Peep, now St Leonards-on-Sea, a tiny hamlet with an inn called The New England Bank. Haydon had thoroughly enjoyed himself here in 1814. He had bathed before breakfast, then sketched pigs, ducks, chickens and geese, shot seagulls, spiked eels, ridden twenty miles before dinner, and walked along the beach under the stars' 'steadfast gaze'.[28]

Keats enjoyed less strenuous pleasures. Soon after he arrived he met a beautiful woman, Isabella Jones, who immediately attracted and intrigued him. Isabella was clever, talented, sociable, witty and tantalisingly enigmatic. In her late thirties, she was at Hastings with Donal O'Callaghan, elderly brother of Cornelius O'Callaghan, MP, 1st Baron Lismore. But who was she? This Keats was never able to establish, although Donal's connections in Whig circles offer what appears to be a clue. These included his cousin James O'Callaghan, MP, and Frances, Lady Lismore of Clifden House, Tunbridge Wells.[29] Among Lady Lismore's acquaintants were Frances, Lady Clermont and her sister Anne, widow of the Rt Hon Theophilus Jones, MP for Leitrim.[30]

Following her husband's death in 1811, Mrs Theophilus Jones migrated between fashionable addresses; her comings and goings were noted among other 'Fashionable Changes' of the day. Well known at Hastings, she subscribed to a history of the town and and was noted as '*An admirer and encourager of the fine Arts*'. Among her summer residences was Lady Lismore's home at Clifden House, from where Isabella Jones also dated a letter of 31 May 1819 to Keats's publisher John Taylor.[31]

Edmund Blunden knew all of this. A note that survives in Robert Gittings's papers reads:

Mr. Gittings
    Isabella Jones stayed at
        Clifden House
            Mount Sion
                Tunbridge Wells.[32]

In his book *Keats's Publisher*, Blunden quotes from Isabella's letter to John Taylor:

> Then (May 31st, 1819) [Isabella Jones] goes to Tunbridge Wells as an invalid, and in the usual Italian hand she makes a request: 'You once favoured me with the most amusing and delightful letter I ever read (Love epistles excepted) and that at a time when perhaps I did not feel its value, being blest then with better health; now I request that you will in charity write, and if you are at a loss for a subject walk to Somerset House and give me your candid opinion upon my likeness by Chalon, n. 895, and moreover tell me who Barry Cornwall is and rely upon my secrecy and discretion tho' a woman—*Lysander and Ione* reminded me very often of *our* favourite *Endymion* and I fancy I discern Mr. Taylor in the well selected motto's to each poem—the *Magdalen* and *Woman* are my favourites among the smaller poems'.[33]

Unfortunately, this letter in Isabella's Italian hand has disappeared. It is clear, however, that her affectionate references to *Endymion* and another young poet, Barry Cornwall, locate her at Clifden House in company with Lady Lismore – and possibly with her acquaintance the artistic Mrs Theophilus Jones. When in London, Isabella lived in rooms at Gloucester Street, Queen's Square and, later, at 57 Lamb's Conduit Street, close to John Hamilton Reynolds's home; Mrs Theophilus Jones's town address was the upmarket Conduit Street in Mayfair.[34]

Socially the two women were apparently miles apart, yet they had aristo-cratic friends and acquaintances in common as well as the same name. All of this suggests that they may have been related in some way. Possibly Isabella was illegitimate; perhaps acknowledged by the family, she may have had an allowance and followed fashionable seasons while maintaining a home of her own. Such a scenario might explain her presence in Hastings and Tunbridge Wells, and also the elusiveness that perplexed and beguiled Keats. But there are other possible identities for Isabella too, as we shall see.

Brought together at Hastings in May 1817, Keats and Isabella attracted each other and within a few days he 'warmed with her . . . and kissed her'. To 'warm with' might have been merely a flirtation, or a more explicitly sexual affair – as suggested by Keats's later phrase 'warm on amorous theft'.[35] Although the precise nature of their relationship is unclear, Isabella apparently offered Keats the passionate experience he needed for his first book of *Endymion*. Meeting her one breezy morning, he noticed how

> wind out-blows
> Her scarf into a fluttering pavilion;

'Tis blue, and over-spangled with a million
Of little eyes.

(i.627–30)

Those four lines give the moon-goddess, Diana, a more vital presence than
the 'pearl round ears', 'orbed brow' and 'hovering feet' that Keats lifted from
Hunt's lexicon of female beauty. Endymion's first kiss may well have been
Keats's, too:

I ev'n dared to press
Her very cheek against my crowned lip,
And, at that moment, felt my body dip
Into a warmer air.

(i.661–4)

Isabella is associated with a group of sprightly lyrics written this summer and
afterwards. If 'Unfelt, unheard, unseen', 'Hither, hither, love' and (later) 'Hush,
hush! tread softly!' marked the pleasures of their 'warming', then 'You say you
love' with its contrary refrain 'You say you love, *but . . .*' hints that she was both
more experienced and less impetuous than Keats.[36]

Richard Woodhouse's collection of Keatsiana contains a version of this
poem that Keats wrote especially for Isabella, with a variant line that runs 'You
say you love, and then you smile . . .'. If her smile was meant to cool another
'warming', Isabella had good reason to be discreet. As Keats would shortly
discover, she lived in a succession of comfortably furnished apartments in
North London. She had friends and possibly relatives in prominent Whig
families. And she was publicly visible too: in May 1819 her portrait by the
soon-to-be-fashionable A.E. Chalon was on exhibit at the Royal Academy.
Later that year she invited John Taylor to a party at 57 Lamb's Conduit Street:
'you shall have pretty women to look at—sensible men to talk with—the
*cosiest* corner in the room—a tass of real Farentosh'.[37] Either Isabella had an
independent income, or someone else was paying for all of this. In January
1819 *The Times* listed a Captain Jones among those dead of fever in Ceylon,
and commented 'Poor . . . Mrs. Jones' – cause enough for Isabella to be at
Clifden House as an 'invalid' the following May.[38] She certainly had army
acquaintances, among them 'Mrs. Colonel Green', wife of Lieutenant Colonel
Thomas Green of the Indian Army, whom she visited with Keats on 24
October 1818. But perhaps her circumstances and behaviour can best be
explained if she was the widow of Lieutenant William Jones, killed on Nelson's
*Victory* at Trafalgar on 21 October 1805. This Isabella Jones lived on until

1843, when she was tragically burnt to death aged sixty-four.[39] She would have been around thirty-eight years old when Keats met her, under the protection of the O'Callaghans as the widow of a war hero. For them, her liaison with a twenty-one-year-old poet who published in *The Examiner* would have been unthinkable. Or did Isabella deliberately appear enigmatic, sensing that if Keats knew of her aristocratic connections he would drop a relationship that she was determined to continue?

* * *

Back in London, Keats wrote to Taylor and Hessey on 10 June to request a further loan of £30, bantering about 'virginity' and his 'Maidenhead with respect to money', and leaving them to read between the lines. Wherever Keats wrote this letter, he posted it at Lamb's Conduit Street at 2pm on Tuesday 10 June, probably while visiting Reynolds and his family – they lived at number 19. Reynolds had just returned from a visit to John Scott in Paris, so Keats had reason to call and show him the first book of *Endymion*. Another explanation for him being in that neighbourhood was that he knew it was where Isabella Jones lived – in 1818 she had lodgings at Gloucester Street, Queen Square, just a block away. George and Reynolds would both meet Isabella, and in 1821 she donated two guineas to a subscription for John Scott's widow 'per Messrs. Taylor and Hessey'. By then, having attended her party, John Taylor had fallen unhappily in love with 'Isabel' and wrote rueful sonnets to this 'Inconstant Lady'.[40]

Part of the awkwardness of the situation was that, while Isabella knew Keats's brothers, publishers and other friends, she wanted her liaison with him to be confidential: 'she wishes we should be acquainted without any of our common acquaintance knowing it.'[41] Edmund Blunden surmised that 'Taylor, if anybody, was Mrs. J's interest', but this was by no means evident to Keats or, for that matter, Taylor. By contriving to be both available and aloof, known and unknown, Isabella Jones enthralled Keats as completely as the woman he had glimpsed at Vauxhall, and with more momentous consequences for English poetry. And having kept her relationships in separate compartments, beautiful Mrs Jones would vanish from Keats's circle as suddenly and mysteriously as she had arrived.

# CHAPTER 12

# Fellowship

Hunt's promised review of *Poems* was a puzzle too. When it eventually appeared on 1 June, it said nothing about the book. Instead, having introduced Keats as 'a personal friend', 'a young poet indeed', Hunt digressed onto the poetic revolution that was establishing a 'true taste for nature'.[1] When *The Examiner* continued this review on 6 July, Keats must have been dismayed to see a discussion of his 'poetical faults' and 'errors' – mainly inherited from Hunt – filling a column and a half before any 'beauties' were noticed. Most of the latter were routine – 'sensitiveness', 'fancy', 'imagination', 'warm and social feelings' – but Hunt also grasped what was essential in Keats: 'a strong sense of what really exists or occurs', 'close observation' and a progress from 'phys ical associations to mental' as when, in the sonnet 'To my Brother George', Keats writes of the seashore as if it were 'a border . . . of existence'.[2]

\* \* \*

The first book of *Endymion* was finished. After its *narvus* nativity in the Isle of Wight, Keats had continued, 'adventuresome / . . . and . . . uncertain' (i.58–61), always on the cusp of poetic possibility as rhyme led him onwards. Its three sections comprised an introduction (i.1–62); a description of an ideal pastoral community celebrating with a 'Hymn to Pan' (i.63–406); and Endymion's forlorn interview with his sister Peona (i.407–993). Phrases imported from the verse epistle to Cowden Clarke – Endymion's 'little boat' (i.47) with 'canvas tatter'd' (i.773–5) – helped sustain Keats in the mid-stream of fresh composition. Deep in the book, Endymion's encounters with Diana may well be warmed by thoughts of Isabella Jones 'blushing, waning, willing, and afraid' (i.635), and Keats's closing cadences circle back to childhood meadows and streams at Enfield and Edmonton. While every page shows

Keats's strong sense of what has really occurred, his poem is not naively retro-spective: in Endymion's struggles we can trace Keats's own anxieties as he watches himself undergo this self-imposed trial. Endymion, like Keats, is afflicted by vacillating moods, consumed with 'thirst for the world's praises' (i.771) and 'endeavour after fame' (i.848). His sudden swings of temper mirror Keats's too, veering between 'slumbrous rest', 'endearing love' and the demons of 'heavier grief' and 'down-sunken hours' (i.442, 467, 527, 708). As if fulfilling Keats's wish to salve his continual 'burning of thought', Endymion wakes with a 'healthier brain' and Peona urges him onwards with Keats's own fameful hope to be 'in the trumpet's mouth' (i.465, 737).

In this acutely self-conscious narrative Endymion/Keats considers how sympathetic feeling may enable us to subdue selfishness, freeing us to 'blend' and 'mingle', much as Antony – a commanding genius 'who might have tower'd in the van' – surrendered to his passion for Cleopatra and 'let occasion die' (i.770–843). Not to struggle, not to assert, not to know – in such moods of 'ardent listlessness', or passionate capitulation, may be found poetry's power to 'bless / The world with benefits unknowingly' (i.826–8); in such moods even an egotist can merge with other identities through 'fellowship', 'sympa-thetic touch', 'a sort of oneness' and 'enthralments self-destroying', as was evident in a set of draft lines that Keats deleted:

> Wherein lies happiness? In that which becks
> Our ready minds to blending pleasureable:
> And that delight is the most treasureable
> That makes the richest Alchymy. Behold
> The clear Religion of Heaven! Fold . . .

Dissatisfied with this passage, Keats tried again:

> Wherein lies Happiness? In that which becks
> Our ready Minds to fellowship divine;
> A fellowship with essence, till we shine
> Full and free of space. Behold
> The clear Religion of heaven—fold &c—[3]

Writing to John Taylor in late January 1818, he described this 'Argument' as 'a regular stepping of the Imagination towards a Truth', displaying 'gradations of Happiness even like a Pleasure Thermometer'. For obvious reasons, comment on this passage has identified the 'Pleasure Thermometer' as an idealistic or neo-Platonic ascent from the physical world to an exquisitely immaterial 'fellowship with essence'.[4] But, as we saw just now, Keats's allusion to *Antony and Cleopatra* had also given a theatrical, as well as transcendental, sense to this 'stepping of the Imagination' – as if to be 'alchemiz'd, and free of space' (i.780) was also a dramatic process of transmutation into another's identity. In his *Critical Essays on the London Theatres*, Hunt praised the great actress Sarah Siddons for rendering – or *fellowing* – the feelings of dramatic characters on stage; only an accomplished actor can master such quicksilver 'transitions . . . as the passion fluctuates', Hunt had observed, in a phrase that prefigured Keats's 'gradations of Happiness' – that is, the full range of emotions, from lust to lambent spirituality. Keats's word 'gradations' comes directly from Hunt's *Critical Essays* too. 'It is not in the simple passions,' Hunt claimed, 'but in their gradations and changes that the actor is most admirable.'[5] Hazlitt's praise for Shakespeare's genius in creating 'ebbs and flows of passion' in *Antony and Cleopatra* was available to Keats in 1817, although Hunt supplied the alchemical concept of 'gradations' that Keats seized on to describe his 'stepping' from base selfhood to more sublime 'empyreal' insights.

Keats thought his 'Pleasure Thermometer' was of 'greatest Service' as his 'first Step towards the chief Attempt in the Drama' – a form of imaginative alchemy that might indeed yield gold from box-office or book sales.[6] This may have meant a long-term plan to write a successful play or simply the next step in *Endymion*'s unfolding 'drama'. Either way, throughout this first book Keats marks his own progress and turns all occasions to account, nowhere more so than in daring to describe poetic creativity as a paradoxical process of 'ardent listlessness'. Animated yet inert, ardent listlessness intensifies those mingled sensations, or 'luxuries', that we know had fascinated him as a child. In such misty moments of vital indolence, Keats now suggests he is most creatively engaged while also 'free of space' – at liberty to 'reach back to boy-hood' and greet one source of his imaginative life: Salmons Brook, another stream of rhyme where he floated 'ships / Of moulted feathers, touchwood, alder chips, / With leaves stuck in them' (i.881–4).

* * *

Back at home in Well Walk, with Hunt and Haydon out of town Keats saw a good deal of Reynolds. They walked and read poetry on Hampstead Heath, with Keats reciting *Endymion* and Reynolds responding with his new poem, *Devon*, a blank-verse meditation vaguely recalling Wordsworth's *Tintern Abbey*. Reynolds's image of the Ocean 'playing on loose rocks, / Lifting the idle sea-weed carelessly' was taken from *Sleep and Poetry*, while the closing lines of *Devon* owe much to 'On the Sea' and what had so far been written of *Endymion*. Their friendship was at its closest over this summer, with both equally placed in terms of poetic achievement and future ambition. It also brought Keats the acquaintance of two slightly older men who would soon be among his most loyal friends and supporters.

By March 1817 Reynolds had introduced Keats and his brothers to Charles Wentworth Dilke, his beautiful wife, Maria, and their son, Charley.[7] Born at Bedhampton, Hampshire on 8 December 1789, Dilke was the son of Charles Wentworth Dilke Snr, a clerk at the Admiralty, and his wife, Sarah. Now a bulky man of twenty-seven with receding black hair and large dark eyes, Dilke was opinionated, outspoken and quick-tempered, yet he also doted on his son and would be a zealous champion of Keats's reputation. He despised his post in the Navy Pay Office (although he kept it for more than thirty years) and aspired to a cultured life of literature and philosophy. He was acquainted with John Dickens, father of the novelist, and met Charles once, briefly, when he was working in the blacking factory. Dilke had recently published six volumes of *Old English Plays, Being a Selection from the Early Dramatic Writers*, and his unswerving belief in a progressive 'march of intellect' – based on William Godwin's theories of human perfectibility – would influence Keats's vision of a 'grand march of intellect' and the trajectory of 'undeviating' advance intended for *Hyperion*. 'John George & Tom were with me three times a week, often three times a day', Dilke recalled, and it was through these visits to his newly built home at Wentworth Place, a large house in the Lower Heath Quarter, that Keats eventually met Dilke's school friend and neighbour Charles Armitage Brown.[8]

Wentworth Place was actually two semi-detached houses, containing Dilke's family home and, separated by a wall, Brown's residence. Dilke recalled that Brown and Keats 'were *drawn together* by force of circumstances & position'. Brown himself recollected a different first encounter.[9] Gadding pleasurably between Well Walk and Wentworth Place one day in late summer, Keats encountered him on the Hampstead Road. They struck up a conversation that led to a close friendship of immense importance to Keats – and us.

\* \* \*

Brown's character appears most clearly in writing palindromes, sentences that read identically forwards and backwards. Whenever one encounters him, the same obsessive, palindromic traits appear, whether in his unswerving daily and annual routines, his resolute support for Keats or, later, his undeviating disdain for George. Born at Lambeth on 14 April 1787, Brown was the sixth son of William Brown, a Scotsman, and his Welsh wife, Jane Armitage. Little is known about his early life, although his son Carlino said that he attended school with Charles Wentworth Dilke.[10] At fourteen, he was working like George and Tom in a counting-house, then joined his brother John at

St Petersburg where he traded bristles for the London market. With prosperity came an engagement – to a Miss Kennedy – but then a speculation failed and he left Russia aged twenty-one, bankrupt and single. For four years he lived in penury, being too independent or stubborn to seek assistance from family or friends, until he became a London representative of the East India Company, for another brother, James. In 1814 his comic opera *Narensky* was staged successfully at Drury Lane, netting him £300 and a 'silver ticket' granting free entry to the venue for life. When James died in 1815 his legacies amounted to £41,000 – although the value of his estate had been grossly overestimated. Initial hopes of a windfall quickly receded, and in 1816–17 Brown was surviving from month to month by tutoring; in summer he let his half of Wentworth Place and moved out. When James's legacy was paid in spring 1818, Brown received £3,333, just sufficient to repay an outstanding debt to his brother's estate of £3,041.8s.9d.[11] He was nevertheless now a man of leisure, free to cultivate literary pursuits and indulge a taste for gin and brandy. Having been jilted once, he viewed women as being only for flirtation and sex – for which he was willing to pay.[12]

Brown's self-portrait, depicting him around the time he first met Keats, shows a young man of about thirty with reddish-brown hair brushed over a wide forehead, pale blue eyes, forthright nose and firm mouth with a flicker of a smile. However one reads this face, it expresses a robust presence with more than a hint of Celtic *craic*, qualities that Keats gleefully reversed in his satirical sketch of Brown as a thin-waisted, melancholy ascetic. In 1828, aged forty-one, Brown sat for a bust by Andrew Wilson at Florence; by now his hair had receded but a high forehead and rugged features convey the same determined presence. It was Brown who became the champion of Keats's fame after his death, when his bitter quarrel with Dilke over the Keats brothers' finances led to an irreversible break in what should have been a lifelong friendship.

From now on Keats was often at Wentworth Place. In due course he would meet Brown's noisy nephews James and John; Dilke's elderly parents, Charles and Sarah; his brother William, and sister and brother-in-law Letitia and John Snook of the Old Mill House, Bedhampton. Even 'old Philips' the gardener was among this summer's acquaintance.[13] Did he also find time to visit the Continent, as he had hoped? Not a jot of evidence for this survives, although his description of Adonis's Bower, written for *Endymion*'s second book, was based on Poussin's 'Echo and Narcissus' and suggests familiarity with the painting's colour. In 1817 'Echo and Narcissus' was exhibited at the Louvre, where it still hangs today.

Others found Keats elusive. Hunt, back from his stay with the Shelleys at Marlow, was living at 13 Lisson Grove, where Haydon would soon be a quarrelsome neighbour. He sought out Keats, but found no trace of him. 'What has become of Junkets, I know not', Hunt wrote to Cowden Clarke. 'I suppose Queen Mab has eaten him'. Haydon's letters to Keats had lingered over Hunt's 'self delusions', and Cowden Clarke recalled that 'Reynolds poisoned [Keats] against Hunt—who never varied towards [him]'. Was Keats simply avoiding Hunt? Or did Hunt's jest about Milton's line in 'L'Allegro', 'Faery Mab the junkets eat', reflect his awareness that Shelley's Chancery case had unsettled Keats in the spring? Now Chancery lumbered back into the headlines: on 27 August the Morning Chronicle reported under 'Law Intelligence': 'PRIVATE HEARINGS—QUEEN MAB. WESTBROOK V. SHELLEY ESQ.' Shelley's controversial poem was again at issue, ensnaring him in Chancery as lawyers contested whether it was 'subversive of every moral feeling' for advocating that humans should 'act and live in the state of nature'.[14] By suggesting sexual passion as a 'chief intensity' of life, Endymion was every bit as provocative as Queen Mab – yet Keats was hoping that his poem would draw the world's praises, and open purses.

'On the Sea' appeared in The Champion on 17 August, and shortly afterwards Keats passed a Sunday at Well Walk with Cowden Clarke and Severn. From Endymion he recited his 'Hymn to Pan' and, from more recent work, the 'Bower of Adonis' episode commencing 'After a thousand mazes overgone' (ii.387).[15] Mazes are certainly what readers experience in the footloose second book of Endymion. Opening with an invocation of love's 'sovereign power' over 'pageant history' and a 'universe of deeds', Keats tracks his hero 'wandering in uncertain ways' (ii.1, 14, 15, 48) that are, in fact, deeply grounded in landscapes and localities of England. Shanklin Chine is revisited as a 'wooded cleft, [with], far away, the blue/Of ocean' (ii.75–6); Canterbury and 'dusk places . . . / Cathedrals call'd' reappear midway through the book (ii.626–7); the 'heath', 'woodland dun' and 'shady spring' give us Keats's Hampstead and the fountain along Well Walk. Endymion's venturing into the underworld, recalling Aeneas's quest for his father, Anchises, also seems to draw on an actual event: Keats's overnight journey to Southampton. Like sights fleetingly glimpsed by lamplight, Endymion experiences Hades as a 'dusky empire' of mingled impressions where – like Keats on the night coach – he feels '[c]hilly and numb' and sets his eyes on 'an orbed diamond . . . / . . . like the sun / Uprisen o'er chaos' (ii.220–48). Endymion passes next into a 'marble gallery' that resembles the Townley Gallery and Temporary Elgin Room of the British Museum,

A mimic temple, so complete and true
In sacred custom, that he well nigh fear'd
To search it inwards; whence far off appear'd,

Through a long pillar'd vista, a fair shrine,
And, just beyond, on light tiptoe divine,
A quiver'd Dian. Stepping awfully,
The youth approach'd; oft turning his veil'd eye
Down sidelong aisles, and into niches old.
And when, more near against the marble cold
He had touch'd his forehead, he began to thread
All courts and passages, whence silence dead
Rous'd by his whispering footsteps murmured faint:
And long he travers'd to and fro, to acquaint
Himself with every mystery, and awe.

(ii.258–71)

In this 'mimic temple' Endymion petitions Diana's 'airy form' as if 'he would o'erleap / His destiny', only to be left 'Desponding o'er the marble floor's cold thrill' (ii.333–4, 338). Flickering throughout are hints of a scene that Keats will revisit in *The Fall of Hyperion*, when his poet-dreamer ascends icily from the 'paved level' to learn that he has 'felt / What 'tis to die and live again before / [His] fated hour' (i.123, 142–3). So that dark night of 14–15 April 1804 continued to haunt Keats's poetry – as an episode in Endymion's 'fairy journey' (ii.352), and in *The Fall of Hyperion* as a death-or-life struggle to attain a vision of 'high tragedy' (i.277). To succeed in that, Keats, too, must lie on the cold pavement of Moorfields, raise himself up and climb away.

The second book's wayward narrative eventually arrives at Adonis's bower where a 'youth / Of fondest beauty' with 'faint damask mouth' slumbers, careless of an 'unseiz'd heaven' embodied by his lover, Venus (ii.393–4, 405, 464). Another unconsummated tryst between Endymion and Diana follows, lubricated with 'slippery blisses' and 'milky sovereignties', yet doomed to slide into nothing more than casual chat. Byron objected that 'such writing is a sort of mental masturbation', its climax postponed by Keats having to stretch his narrative to four thousand lines. Endymion and Diana warm and kiss as Keats had done with Isabella Jones – only to part until their next encounter.[16] If there was feebleness in the structure of *The Aeneid*, as Keats thought, at least Virgil was organised towards an end. Aware from the outset of the need to 'make an end' (i.57), the narrative of *Endymion* proceeds on a tantalising principle of delay.

The full moon of 26 August saw the second book finished. When Haydon proposed a convivial evening, Keats was up for 'one of our right Sort meetings' but Reynolds had been taken ill. To rally his friend, Keats was often at Lamb's Conduit Street in a gold-blue haze of snuff and cigar smoke. He saw a good

deal there of the Zetosophians Bailey and Rice, while John Martin had just
returned from Wordsworth's house at Rydal Mount.[17] Bailey would soon
resume his studies at Magdalen Hall, Oxford, and suggested that Keats should
join him there – he was about to begin his third book, and distance from
London's distractions would help. With George and Tom holidaying at Paris,
there was little to detain him at Well Walk, and on Wednesday, 3 September
he was at the Belle Sauvage by eight to board the fast mail coach the 'Defiance'.
At a quarter past, they set off under glorious skies along the Thames Valley to
Maidenhead, Henley and so to Oxford and the Mitre Inn where Bailey was
waiting to greet him. Soon Keats met Bailey's college friends Charles
Whitehead and George Gleig, son of the bishop of Brechin, recently returned
after serving with Wellington in Spain. In an earlier stint at Oxford, Gleig had
been Snell Scholar at Balliol College; there he began a lifelong friendship with
a fellow graduate of Glasgow University, John Gibson Lockhart, who in turn
had met Jonathan Christie at Balliol in 1809.[18] By a curious coincidence Gleig,
Lockhart and Christie would all be in touch with each other, and Keats, in
November 1817.

At Magdalen Hall, Keats composed his third book. College routines helped
and, as usual, his poetry flowed more readily with water nearby in the rivers
Cherwell and Isis. Each day Keats sat down to complete fifty lines, working
until two or three in the afternoon when they went out for a walk – Keats
reflecting on his progress, Bailey grumbling about his difficulties gaining a
curacy.[19] Book three takes its cue from Bailey, opening with a rant against
those 'who lord it o'er their fellow men', especially the 'empurpled vests' of the
bishops blocking Bailey's preferment (iii.1, 11). Spurning such worldly 'regali-
ties', Keats speculates on elemental powers that 'keep religious state, / In water,
fiery realms, and airy bourne', enriching our senses with 'spiritual sweets' – at
which point he dated his manuscript 'Oxford Sept[r] 5' (iii.30–1, 39).[20] A paean
to the moon follows, as Keats steers his narrative towards Endymion, who is
eventually discovered – after some two days' composition – roaming the 'deep,
deep water-world' of 'things / More dead than Morpheus' imaginings' (iii.101,
121–2). In this oceanic junkyard are 'rusted anchors' and 'Rudders that for a
hundred years had lost / The sway of human hand', with several items Keats
recalled from the British Museum – 'gold vase emboss'd / With long-forgotten
story', 'mouldering scrolls' and 'skeletons of man, / Of beast, behemoth, and
leviathan, / And elephant, and eagle, and huge jaw / Of nameless monster'
(ii.123, 125–36).[21] This grotesque gathering is in keeping with the sardonic
mood of the book as a whole, a mood that reflected Keats's uneasiness as the
consequences of some recent 'gadding' became apparent.

A first letter to Jane and Marianne Reynolds on Friday, 5 September is full
of his pleasure at life 'among Colleges, Halls Stalls plenty of Trees thank
God—plenty of Water thank heaven—plenty of Books thank the Muses—
plenty of snuff—thank Sir Walter Raleigh—plenty of Sagars, ditto ... I'm on
the Sofa—Buonaparte is on the Snuff Box.' In 1795 Coleridge outraged
audiences at his lectures by claiming that Robespierre was a good man; in
1817, that image of Napoleon on Keats's snuffbox was similarly provocative.
To his sister, Fanny, he wrote of 'the finest City in the world – it is full of old
Gothic buildings – Spires – towers – Quadrangles – Cloisters Groves & ... is
surrounded with more Clear streams than ever I saw together – I take a Walk
by the Side of one of them every evening and thank God, we have not
had a drop of rain these many days.' He had heard from George and Tom –
they lost money gambling at *rouge et noir* in the Palais-Royal – and from
Haydon with a request to track down a young artist, Charles Cripps, with a
view to training him 'in the Art'. Keats reported Cripps 'anxious to avail
himself of your offer'.[22]

With Bailey – 'so real a fellow' – he went on the Isis and explored streams
and inlets including 'Reynolds's Cove', where they read Wordsworth. They
were 'naturalized riverfolks', he told Reynolds, and then plunged into gossip
about London, the theatre, bluestockings and poetry by Katherine Fowler
('Mrs. Philips'). A surer sense of his own independence was mellowing Keats
towards Hunt: 'What a very pleasant fellow he is, if he would give up the
sovereignty of a Room pro bono—What Evenings we might pass with him,
could we have him from M^rs H—.'[23]

Proceeding at 'a pretty good rate', by Sunday, 21 September his third book
amounted to eight hundred lines and, with a full moon on the 25th, he pushed
on to a full thousand.[24] This was good progress, by far Keats's most productive
period of composition since the previous autumn, and the shape of the
complete poem was now becoming evident. His first book had presented
passion as a 'chief intensity', an ideal essence (i.800); now book three explored
its poisonous counterpart in Glaucus's enthrallment by Circe, enchantress and
'arbitrary queen of sense' (iii.459). Her 'delusive banquet' is unmasked in a
'haggard scene' where 'Groanings swell'd / Poisonous', where brutishly
deformed embodiments of sensuality are medicined from 'a black dull-
gurgling phial' of 'sooty oil'

Until their grieved bodies 'gan to bloat
And puff from the tail's end to stifled throat.
      (iii.490–1, 497, 521, 525–6)

Encountering Glaucus after his thousand years' bondage, Endymion is greeted as a liberator of doomed lovers – among whom Keats and Bailey at this time numbered themselves (thrown over by Thomasine Leigh, Bailey was now pursuing Marianne Reynolds).[25] Book three's preoccupation with 'arbitrary sense', 'cumbrous flesh', 'fever'd parchings' and 'poisonous' effects of passion (iii. 459, 551, 636, 491) may well reflect the fact that at Oxford Keats was treating himself with mercury. The nature of his illness was never explicitly stated, but the word 'poisonous', heard insistently in book three and nowhere else in *Endymion*, is a reminder that in 1817 a standard medical term for both gonorrhoea and syphilis was 'venereal poison'.

Keats and Bailey walked thirty miles to Stratford on a two-day visit to Shakespeare's birthplace, inscribing their names among thousands that already blackened the walls. They looked into Holy Trinity church and sought the 'simple statue' that also adorned the title-page of Keats's book.[26] After two weeks of unbroken fine weather Keats returned to London on Sunday, 5 October, changing from coach to coach as far as Hampstead, where George and Tom had already arrived back from France.

Next morning, finding himself 'tolerably well', he set off to see Reynolds's family in Lamb's Conduit Street. Here he delivered a parcel from Bailey, found Jane and Marianne 'greatly improved', and heard that Rice was very ill, as he told Bailey in a letter. Walking west, he called on Hunt and Haydon, now uneasy neighbours at Lisson Grove, and found Shelley there. Everybody seemed irritable and at odds. On Tuesday the 7th Keats was with Brown at Wentworth Place when Reynolds arrived 'pretty Bobbish' (i.e. in good spirits). They passed a pleasant day, then Reynolds left to walk into town 'that cursed cold distance' – this was perverse, for he knew he was expected at Brown's again on the 8th with Keats, his brothers and possibly the Dilkes. To Bailey, Keats confided that he was 'quite disgusted with literary Men' – Hunt, Haydon and even Byron. Particularly galling was a buzz about town that *Endymion* was indebted to Hunt, when Hunt had not yet seen a single line of it. The whole of this letter shows that Keats, too, was out of sorts, and his glancing remarks about being 'tolerably well', Rice being very ill, Reynolds being 'Bobbish' and the 'cursed cold distance' to town all point to an underlying concern about health – Tom's, and his own.[27]

# CHAPTER 13

# 'Z'

KEATS HAD been unwell at Oxford. On returning to Hampstead, his first letter let Bailey know '[t]he little Mercury I have taken has corrected the Poison and improved my Health'. To W.M. Rossetti, this spoke for itself.[1] For others, including Keats's contemporaries, the matter does not appear so straightforward. Once widely prescribed for venereal disease, by 1817 mercury was a less obvious recourse; there had been surprisingly successful cures without it. As Keats may have known, Astley Cooper held that mercury was not always necessary, although in small doses it could alleviate secondary symptoms of syphilis (fever, rash, muscle aches and joint pains like rheumatism). The nature of venereal infection was also in question. If Cooper's views represented the enlightened consensus on mercury, disputes about pathology showed that some physicians believed gonorrhoea was an early stage of syphilis.[2] 'It would be madness to say the two diseases are alike', Cooper thought, but Dr Solomon Sawrey – who specialised in venereology – held that a small dose of mercury to treat gonorrhoea would prevent syphilis developing. Mistakenly believing that Sawrey was Keats's doctor in October 1817, and citing his *Inquiry into the Effects of the Venereal Poison*, Keats's biographers have concluded that his 'little Mercury' signalled a mild venereal infection of gonorrhoea – no great threat to health, and socially insignificant.[3]

A different diagnosis is possible. When Keats wrote to Bailey his reference to mercury was an update on a course of treatment Bailey was already aware of. This mercury was not prescribed by Sawrey, who first appears in Keats's story in January 1818, but most likely by Keats himself for symptoms he understood. While Keats assured Bailey he was 'tolerably well' a second letter on 29 October said that he had been indoors for a fortnight, 'not . . . well enough to stand the chance of a Wet night'. The implication is that he had confined himself, not on someone else's orders, although without a more explicit account of his symptoms it is impossible to say what was wrong. While gonorrhoea and the primary symptoms of syphilis are unpleasant but painless (a discharge and ulceration), Keats had been feeling so poorly that he was unable to go out for two weeks. Also confined with him at Well Walk was Tom, whose cough was now showing signs of being pulmonary consumption. With cold weather coming, Tom's best option would be to winter in Lisbon, and Keats was inclined to join him there.[4]

From this fragmentary picture of Well Walk in October 1817, several speculations arise. Tom's illness would have stirred memories of their mother's sickbed – George recalled she had been confined 'by a rheumatism and at last died of a consumption'. Feeling debilitated, living in close proximity to his consumptive brother, Keats was careful not to risk going to London and stayed in Hampstead. Or was he aware of an altogether darker scenario, now brought painfully home to him by his own illness and its treatment? Whatever George's vague term 'a rheumatism' signified, Frances Rawlings was a desperately sick woman and a known secondary symptom of syphilis was said to be 'pains in the larger joints, resembling rheumatism'. Some of what Abbey said about Frances's 'strange Irregularities – or rather Immorality of her after-Life' may gesture glumly at what her 'rheumatism' actually signified, as might Leigh Hunt's disturbing observation: '[Keats's] mother, who was a lively woman, passionately fond of amusement, is supposed to have hastened her death by too great an inattention to hours and seasons. Perhaps she hastened that of her son.'[5]

Keats could be as wayward and impulsive as his mother and, on the face of it, that may be all that Hunt meant: careless of hours and seasons like her, Keats had fallen ill. Or was Hunt signalling that her fondness for passionate 'amusement' led to a complaint 'resembling rheumatism', and that her lively son had followed a similar path? That Keats was still dosing himself with mercury in September 1818, by which time a superficial infection should have cleared, has been attributed to Dr Sawrey's intervention. By then treating Tom, Sawrey, it is said, prescribed mercury as a precaution lest Keats's painfully ulcerated throat was a symptom of syphilis.[6] An alternative view might be that venereal infection and protracted doses of mercury had by then weakened Keats's immune system, and that his sore throat was a first symptom of tuberculosis taking hold. Back in 1779, an 'ulcerated throat' had killed Jane Keats, as the poet may have known. Amy Lowell rightly dated the first indications of Keats's broken health to autumn 1817, and when she speculated that Keats had contracted syphilis she may have been closer to the truth than she was willing to allow; certainly Keats's symptoms and repeated doses of mercury might indicate as much, and some aspects of his distorted behaviour and perceptions towards the end of his life may be attributed to an awareness of this secret 'core of disease' rather than to tuberculosis.[7]

\* \* \*

His fortnight's confinement over, Keats saw a good deal of the kindly solicitor James Rice. A full moon on the 25th lit his attendance at a first meeting of a sociable 'Saturday Club' at Rice's house, 50 Poland Street, and a couple of days later Rice called at Well Walk. From Oxford, Bailey sent word of a vacant curacy in Lincolnshire – to try to secure it he had attended 'Responsions', the first oral examinations for a BA degree, but was quickly disappointed. The bishop of Lincoln required ordinands to have a degree, and Bailey's application was turned down flat. Keats, no admirer of bishops, can hardly have been shocked and wrote to express indignation at this 'yawning impudence in the shape of conscience'. His school in Enfield had taught him to expect as much, and his repellent image of the bishop as a 'smashed frog putrifying' is a schoolboy memory of how a crushed frog's head resembles a mitre.[8]

Bailey eventually gained his curacy without graduating: the register of students passing 'Responsions' up to 1821 does not list his name.[9] Thirty years later, established as archdeacon of Colombo (in modern Sri Lanka) and forgetful of his former friend's support, he announced to Richard Monckton Milnes that Keats's 'religious education seems to have been greatly or wholly neglected'.[10] Ironically, had Keats been alive, this nonsense would not have surprised him. He might be prickly and standoffish but, unlike Bailey, pompous and paranoid in middle age, he could also be patient. 'The sure way Bailey', Keats counselled, 'is first to know a Man's faults, and then be passive.'[11]

William Hazlitt, first mentioned by Keats in a letter of March 1817, has routinely and rightly been cited as a powerful influence on him. While in Oxford, Keats had read his early *Essay on the Principles of Human Action*, noting its claim that the human mind was 'naturally disinterested': 'the love of others has the same necessary foundation in the human mind as the love of ourselves.'[12] But why should Keats have been hospitable to Hazlitt's ideas, and did their relationship consist of a more complex exchange of ideas than might at first appear? Part of Hazlitt's appeal for Keats lay in helping him to articulate the sympathetic or 'disinterested' imagination that had been his since boyhood, qualities for which Hunt's theatrical reviews had already provided the concept of 'passive capacity'. Temperamentally attuned to Hazlitt, and primed with ideas from Hunt, Keats was also ready to question. He pointed Bailey to Wordsworth's poem 'Gipseys', written in 'one of the most comfortable Moods of [Wordsworth's] Life'. Hazlitt had claimed that Wordsworth's poem was an 'attack' on gipsies' way of life, while Keats finds no incisive engagement or imaginative understanding in it: the poem is merely a 'sketchy intellectual Landscape – not a search after Truth'.[13] Like the poet, so his critic: had Hazlitt thought longer and deeper, he would never have detected an imaginary fault – it would have been better, Keats implies, had both he and Wordsworth adopted a wise passivity and said nothing.

Together, Hunt, Hazlitt and Wordsworth were impelling Keats to his first great creative insights: 'one thing that has pressed upon me lately and encreased my Humility and capability of submission and that is this truth— Men of Genius are great as certain ethereal Chemicals operating on the Mass of neutral intellect—[but] they have not any individuality, any determined Character.'[14] The phrase 'ethereal Chemicals' suggests he is thinking again of imagination's alchemical transmutations and sublimations. Developing concepts of 'passive capacity', or a 'capability of submission' that annuls individuality, Keats's letter offers this marvellous speculation about imagination and truth:

> What the imagination seizes as Beauty must be truth—whether it existed before or not—for I have the same Idea of all our Passions as of Love they are all in their sublime, creative of essential Beauty ... The Imagination may be likened to Adam's dream—he awoke and found it truth. I am the more zealous in this affair, because I have never yet been able to perceive how any thing can be known for truth by consequitive reasoning—and yet it must be—Can it be that even the greatest Philosopher ever arrived at his goal without putting aside numerous objections—However it may be, O for a Life of Sensations rather than of Thoughts! It is 'a Vision in the form of Youth' a Shadow of reality to come—and this consideration has further convinced me for it has come as auxiliary to another favorite Speculation of mine, that we shall enjoy ourselves here after by having what we called happiness on Earth repeated in a finer tone and so repeated—And yet such a fate can only befall those who delight in sensation rather than hunger as you do after Truth—Adam's dream will do here and seems to be a conviction that Imagination and its empyreal reflection is the same as human Life and its spiritual repetition.[15]

This striking coalescence of ideas and experiences marks an extraordinary advance in Keats's conceptions of the poet, poetry and poetic life. Passion and sensation when seized by the imagination are as 'True' as Adam's dream of Eve when he wakes to 'behold her, not far off / Such as I saw her in my dream' (*Paradise Lost*, viii.478–9). By analogy, in another 'favorite Speculation', the imagination's 'empyreal reflection' of reality can be likened to a spiritual repetition of earthly existence in the afterlife. Echoes of *Paradise Lost*, *Endymion* and the 'Pleasure Thermometer' ring clear, and Keats's speculations also summoned resources laid down in distant childhood and now forming part of his intuitive nature. His Elgin Marbles sonnets had shown how not speaking definitively, not knowing his intent, yielded creative insights in ways that 'consequitive reasoning' never would; and as far back as Craven Street, his game of deflecting questions into rhyme could spark discoveries more profound than a merely 'correct' answer. When Keats wrote of 'a vision in the form of Youth', he might have been thinking of how his own early childhood had shaped the poet he was now becoming – sympathetic yet sceptical, a creature of passions and sensations inclined to live for 'now': 'I scarcely remember counting upon any Happiness—I look not for it if it be not in the present hour—nothing startles me beyond the Moment.'[16]

\* \* \*

Straws in the wind. Recent weeks had seen two further reviews of *Poems, by John Keats*, both warning against Hunt's influence while detecting an 'immature promise of possible excellence'. Then came a shock. A 'flaming attack upon Hunt', entitled 'On the Cockney School of Poetry', appeared in October's *Blackwood's Magazine* over the initial 'Z'. Keats told Bailey he had 'never read anything so virulent'.[17] Z's riposte to Hunt's 'Young Poets' article pilloried the poet of *Rimini* as a man of little education, questionable morals and sour Jacobinical politics. Low-born and with low habits, Hunt 'labours to be genteel' while his poetry, 'always on the stretch to be grand', is vulgar and indecent.[18] Such was the 'moral depravity of the Cockney School', Z contended, that *The Story of Rimini* coupled 'simple seduction' with 'all the details of adultery and incest'.

Heading this article was a verse by Cornelius Webb, an acquaintance of Hunt's, prominently enrolling 'KEATS' as 'The Muses' son of promise'. Not surprisingly, Keats suspected that a subsequent 'Cockney School' essay would attack him. Legal action by the Hunts and, later, Hazlitt might forestall further essays, but as yet they had no idea who Z was. 'I don't mind the thing much,' Keats told Bailey, but he did. Since April he had worked steadily to assert his independence from Hunt. Z had reversed that, associating Keats with a 'Cockney' coterie whose 'wretched taste' in poetry stemmed from inadequate education, unsettled opinions and social ambition – three components of the 'morbid temperament' that Hazlitt associated with Jacobinism.

Z's abuse in *Blackwood's* could be seen as a kind of backhanded recognition, even a compliment, and it was variously motivated. First published in April 1817, the magazine had not flourished until William Blackwood contracted two fresh contributors, John Wilson and George Gleig's Balliol friend Lockhart, to give his magazine a more incisive anti-Whig edge. Both were graduates of Glasgow and Oxford universities, excellent classical scholars and brilliant polemicists. Rising above Edinburgh's backbiting political cliques, they pitched their quarrel on the national stage by attacking – among others – Hunt and his associates. Hiding behind the cipher Z, they ridiculed and slandered with impunity. Protracted rivalry between Edinburgh and London was a further incitement, and for Wilson, an early admirer of Wordsworth, there was real alarm and disquiet at a new generation of poets, educated outside the establishment, whose experimental poetry and polemical prefaces were pitched squarely against the status quo. Perceived as a genuine threat to the nation's political, cultural and moral fabric, Hunt, Keats and Hazlitt were treated accordingly. Only Reynolds escaped the onslaught. Lockhart admired his poems.[19]

Z's essays generated shock, outrage and hurt, although their long-term effect was not what the authors anticipated. Instead of shaming Hunt, Keats and the others into silence, a colourfully disreputable 'Cockney' identity showed how 'young poets' thrive outside the establishment – in a word, Z gave them what we would call 'street cred'. Two hundred years on, we can see how Hunt's 'New School' anticipated modern ideas of poetry as a form of self-expression open to and enjoyed by all. The prototypes of today's poetry festivals were Hunt's noisy gatherings at the Vale of Health, while Z's vulgar and iconoclastic 'Cockney School' prefigured equally 'disreputable' coteries such as the Pre-Raphaelites, the Surrealists, the Group, the Martians and even the 'Punk' poets of the 1970s and '80s. Poetry has always invited popular participation: together, Hunt and Z ensured that tradition's survival.

But at the time no one knew who Z was – and *Blackwood's* wasn't telling. For a while Keats suspected Charles Ollier, his nettled publisher. In *The Examiner*, Hunt called for Z's address and was said to be 'nearly sure' that the culprit was his old acquaintance John Scott, with whom he had quarrelled about Byron.[20]

Scott vehemently denied responsibility. By now he had sold *The Champion*, and Reynolds's lucrative source of income was no longer secure. Sunday, 2 November saw Keats and Rice at Reynolds's, a last visit before their friend was articled as a legal pupil to solicitor Francis Fladgate. Rice had paid for Reynolds's legal training, and promised that he would employ him as a partner in the family firm at Poland Street. On succeeding to this business, Rice kept his word and later transferred the entire firm to Reynolds, handing him a fortune that enabled him to further his poetic ambitions while building a legal career.

Keats had just passed his twenty-second birthday. Tired of *Endymion*, looking to write something of 'greater moment', he was easily distracted. His lyric 'O Sorrow', tender and poignant as Feste's songs, indicates one fresh direction of growth:

> O Sorrow
> Why dost borrow
> The natural hue of health from vermil Lips?
> To give maiden blushes
> To the white Rose bushes
> Or ist thy dewy hand the daisy tips?[21]

He sent this to cheer Jane Reynolds, who had been ill, and it proved curiously appropriate to the city's mood too. News that the Polish patriot Thaddeus Kosciusko was dead arrived from Switzerland and then, on Thursday 6 November, Princess Charlotte, the regent's only child and heir, died during childbirth.[22] Unlike her father, Charlotte was popular and public mourning was declared. Between black borders *The Examiner* deplored this 'visitation of a darkness'; Keats's request to the Dilkes for a copy of Coleridge's *Sybilline Leaves* adds a laconic footnote; 'Vivant Rex et Regina—amen—'.[23]

Up from Marlow, the Shelleys were at lodgings in Mabledon Place, Islington, where Keats, Hunt and Godwin met them on Tuesday 18 November.[24] Three days afterwards Keats was again at Reynolds's, with Rice and Martin, to meet Jonathan Christie – Lockhart's college friend and, now, William Blackwood's London agent. At this gathering an intricate network was completed, through which Reynolds, Christie, Keats, Bailey and his Oxford connections George Gleig and John Lockhart variously came into contact with each other and became linked, through Christie and Lockhart, with *Blackwood's Magazine*. Furthermore, all of them were well disposed towards Keats – even, at this stage, Lockhart – and there may have been a plan, of which Keats was unaware, to try and influence *Blackwood's* in his favour. Shortly after meeting Keats, Christie wrote to Lockhart about him. Most unluckily, this important intervention has been lost. 'What you say of Keates is pleasing', Lockhart responded on 27 January 1818, inviting Christie to write a genial review 'in admonition to leave his ways &c., and in praise of his natural genius'.[25] The intention was to counsel Keats against Hunt – routine in most reviews of *Poems, by John Keats* – and then bring him before the public in a favourable light. Christie's article – if it was ever written – did not appear and by 1818, when Lockhart and Wilson were actually in command of *Blackwood's*, Keats had been selected for attack.[26]

Fifty-five years after encountering Keats, Christie added this supplement: 'I never saw the poet Keats but once, but he then read some lines from (I think) the "Bristowe Tragedy" with an enthusiasm of admiration such as could only be felt by a poet.'[27] Keats always associated Chatterton with autumn, and his ballad of Syr Charles Bawdin's brutal execution by Edward the 'traytor kynge' caught the temper of the times. Week by week *The Examiner* was reporting violent events in the North of England. After the Spa Fields riots of 1816 there had been sporadic unrest across the country as economic depression, unemployment and high prices led to clashes and arrests in Taunton, Yorkshire and Nottingham. Then, on 9 June 1817, came an insurrection at Pentrich in Derbyshire by ironworkers and labourers incited by the notorious *agent provocateur* and spy 'Oliver'. When this 'conspiracy to overthrow the Government' was suppressed, its leaders were imprisoned and prosecuted for high treason. On 7 November three of them, Jeremiah Brandreth, William Turner and Isaac Ludlam, were dragged on a hurdle to the scaffold, hanged, then cut down and beheaded. Brandishing each head, the executioner exclaimed, 'Behold the head of the traitor', whereupon *'there was a burst of horror from the crowd'*:[28]

> And oute the bloude beganne to flowe,
> And round the scaffolde twyne;
> And teares, enow to washe't awaie,
> Dydde flowe fromme each mann's eyne.[29]

Such were the words Christie recalled Keats reciting with 'an enthusiasm of admiration'. Further violence would follow in the late summer of 1819, and Chatterton would again be in Keats's thoughts as he began 'To Autumn'.

✳ ✳ ✳

Tom had recovered sufficiently to travel to the West Country, where he planned to winter at Teignmouth with George. Keats needed a change of scene too, as a spur to finish the last five hundred lines of *Endymion*. Saturday, 22 November saw him take a coach to Dorking, a mile from where he planned to stay at the old Fox and Hounds Inn by Box Hill.

As soon as he arrived a letter went off to Bailey, telling him that Jane and Marianne Reynolds suspected his illness was related to Tom's consumption. Keats himself saw no such connection, and Bailey knew 'more of the real Cause than they do'. He did not have any chance of being 'rack'd' with unsuccessful love affairs, as Bailey had been, for he had schooled himself to look for a different kind of happiness: 'I look not for it if it be not in the present hour—nothing startles me beyond the Moment. The setting sun will always set me to rights—or if a Sparrow come before my Window I take part in its existence and pick about the Gravel.'[30] Often read as a touchstone of Keats's 'negative capability', these reflections – following upon the 'real Cause' of his recourse to mercury – give us a less passive Keats. He accepts things as they happen and, by implication, 'takes part' in other existences as they present themselves. The 'real Cause' of his illness was that he was sexually adventurous, and had looked to chance encounters and casual sex rather than the 'rack' of courtship or, he might have added, Endymion's unconsummated romance protracted over four thousand lines.

A letter to Reynolds followed. 'I like this place very much—There is Hill & Dale and a little River—I went up Box hill this Evening after the Moon.' Tomorrow, Sunday, 23 November, was the full moon – a good omen. His volume of Shakespeare's poems had struck him as 'full of fine things said unintentionally – in the intensity of working out conceits', so that Shakespeare had 'left nothing to say about nothing or any thing'. Climbing Box Hill now, one can see thousands of tiny snail shells on the chalky slope. Perhaps it was these that put Keats in mind of what Shakespeare had said about snails: he quoted 'the tender horns of cockled snails' from *Love's Labour's Lost* and lines from *Venus and Adonis* on 'the snail, whose tender horns being hit, / Shrinks back into his shelly cave with pain'.[31] Shakespeare's seventeenth sonnet had suggested a 'capital Motto' for *Endymion*:

a poet's rage
And stretched metre of an antique song.

In this sonnet, Shakespeare anticipates posterity's scorn for his poetry and, in high spirits, Keats followed his motto with an invocation to Aquarius recently composed for *Endymion*: 'give your vote, pro or con.—'. Whether Reynolds pro'd or con'd, these lines duly appeared in print (iv.581–90) and are among the worst Keats ever wrote.

He was in a hurry to finish and, like Shakespeare's snails, found poetic materials immediately to hand: the Mole River with its wooded banks, precipitous paths up Box Hill, and groves of box and yew on its summit. So far, Endymion's wanderings had accompanied Keats's restless ventures across the South of England, and now book four brought into focus his poem's themes of dislocation and exile, nativeness and home. 'Muse of my native land! Loftiest muse!' Keats begins, then introduces an Indian Maid who has parted from her native land and 'bade / Adieu to Ganges' (iv.1, 30–1, 33). As Endymion falls in love with her, 'heart cut in twain', we can see how his story reflects Keats's wish to write of human passion with 'no more of dreaming' (iv.673). Juxtapositions of sense and essence, waking and dreaming, mortal and spiritual, real and empyreal, had preoccupied Keats in recent letters. Following his move to Burford Bridge, he now set about resolving these against a backdrop of scenes through which he rambled on these late November days. Believing himself abandoned by the Indian Maid and his moon-goddess, Endymion enters a Cave of Quietude – a space of 'content' beyond 'grief and woe', of quiet after conflict. Here, promisingly, Endymion 'knew not whither he was going', like Keats 'not knowing his intent'. Drawn by trumpets to a 'bright array' – Cynthia's wedding – Endymion is borne down 'to the green head of a misty hill', where, forsaking 'cloudy phantasms', 'airy voices' and 'daintiest Dream', he seeks an earthly home for human love:

> Now,
> Where shall our dwelling be? Under the brow
> Of some steep mossy hill, where ivy dun
> Would hide us up, although spring leaves were none;
> And where dark yew trees, as we rustle through,
> Will drop their scarlet berry cups of dew?
> O thou wouldst joy to live in such a place;
> Dusk for our loves, yet light enough to grace
> Those gentle limbs on mossy bed reclin'd:
> For one by one the blue sky shouldst thou find,
> And by another, in deep dell below,
> See, through the trees, a little river go
> All in its mid-day gold and glimmering.
>
> (iv.673–85)

Endymion's idyllic life is located among the ancient yew, oak, beech and box trees that still cover the summit of Box Hill, from where the River Mole may be glimpsed as it winds towards Dorking. Up here, too, Keats would have noticed the curious grave of Major Peter La Billiere, whose tragic story intersected with Endymion's and possibly with Isabella Jones's.

Born in 1726, La Billiere was a marine officer who, as a young man, 'fell in love with a lady, who, although he was remarkably handsome in person, eventually rejected his addresses; a circumstance which could not fail to inflict a deep wound on his delicate mind'. Settled in later life at Dorking, his many eccentricities culminated in a request to be buried without church rites, head downwards on Box Hill, reasoning 'that the world was turned topsy-turvy, and, therefore, at the end of it he should be right'.[32] La Billiere died in 1800, and

Keats would have seen the stump of wood marking his grave. As Endymion woos the Indian Maid, he too is wounded by her words of rejection:

'Ah, bitter strife!
I may not be thy love: I am forbidden—
Indeed I am—thwarted, affrighted, chidden,
By things I trembled at, and gorgon wrath.
Twice hast thou ask'd whither I went: henceforth
Ask me no more! I may not utter it,
Nor may I be thy love. We might commit
Ourselves at once to vengeance ...'

(iv.756–63)

Passionately direct, bafflingly enigmatic, her words have a pressure of feeling unfelt in preceding pages, as if Keats were recalling an actual exchange between two lovers. Had La Billiere's story sent him back to a tryst with Isabella Jones, when Keats had been rebuffed? 'I may not be thy love: I am forbidden. Twice hast thou ask'd whither I went: henceforth, ask me no more! I may not utter it, nor may I be thy love.' That has to be conjecture, although the possibility that Keats was attempting to work through his feelings about Isabella Jones – and an illness that made him 'thwarted, affrighted, chidden' – would link these anguished lines with his poem's equally traumatic beginning back in April.

With Endymion forsaken and alone, Keats needed around two hundred lines to make a total of four thousand, thus fulfilling the 'test' he had set himself. As in the first book, he gathered impetus for this last effort by resorting to familiar scenes – 'the old garden-ground of boyish days' and 'little onward ... the very stream' (iv.784, 791). Endymion's sister Peona is summoned from the first book to accompany him through the poem's final pages. Here they will meet the 'dark-eyed stranger' once again, and discover that his earthly love, the Indian Maid, and her ethereal counterpart, Cynthia, are identical. With kisses and 'blissful swoon', the lovers vanish (iv.999); Peona goes home; and Keats's parallel worlds of sense and essence, waking and dreaming, mortal and spiritual, real and ideal, are at last 'alchemiz'd' and reconciled together.

* * *

His trial was over. Six months after he began *Endymion* at Carisbrooke, Keats wrote under his poem's final line: 'Burford Bridge Nov. 28. 1817.' Book four had been hurried to a close but elsewhere, despite mystification and mawkishness, his poem launched poetic and philosophic speculations of considerable daring and from these he had grown intellectually and imaginatively. Those six months had also seen Keats crisscross the South of England as he sought congenial environments for composition at Shanklin, Carisbrooke, Margate, Canterbury, Bo-Peep, Hampstead, Oxford, Hampstead again and, finally, Burford Bridge and Box Hill. Landscapes where he wrote supplied local habitations for the Endymion myth, and his own experiences and moods are felt along every line: ambitious and insecure in book one; wandering and wayless in book two; poisonously afflicted in book three; eager to make an end in book four. Led by his instinct for rhyme since early childhood, in *Endymion* Keats made a heroically sustained effort to imagine 'the agonies, the strife / Of human hearts' (*Sleep and Poetry*, ii.124–5) and to fulfil ambitions he had set for himself in his first collection: 'Was there a Poet born?' he had asked at the end of 'I stood tip-toe'.

With his manuscript stowed alongside his volumes of Shakespeare, Keats leapt on the coach back to London.

## CHAPTER 14

# Immortal Dinners

LONDON WAS covered with a thick yellow fog, but for Keats December was a month of parties, pantomimes and plays. On Sunday the 14th he was at the Swan with Two Necks in Lad Lane to see George and Tom off to Teignmouth. It would do Tom good to winter there, for the mild air was renowned as a cure for pulmonary complaints.[1] That night Keats dined with Haydon, and would pass nine of the next ten evenings at theatres or with friends. He avoided Hunt, but his *Examiner* essays on 'Christmas and Other Old National Merry-Makings' were fine seasonal reading – as were reports of bookseller William Hone's trials for writing and publishing parodies of the Scriptures. The charge brought against him at each of his three trials was 'blasphemy'.

Momentous news came from Haydon: Wordsworth was in town on business. A year before, Haydon had forwarded Keats's well-wishes to him, and Keats had inscribed a copy of his *Poems* 'To W. Wordsworth with the Author's sincere Reverence'.[2] Book four of *The Excursion* had influenced 'I stood tip-toe' and *Endymion*, and Wordsworth was now at a zenith in Keats's esteem. Along with Haydon's pictures and Hazlitt's depth of taste, *The Excursion* was a thing 'to rejoice at'.[3]

Haydon seized the moment. He fired off a note to Thomas Monkhouse, cousin of Wordsworth's wife, Mary, at his home at 28 Queen Anne Street:

Dear Sir,

Will Mr. Wordsworth be at home to-morrow morning at Lambeth as Keats is down and very anxious to see him—or will he do you think be so occupied with business as not to be able for a few minutes to see us?—Yours most truly,

B.R. Haydon.[4]

Keats's hectic schedule and Wordsworth's comings and goings make it difficult to identify when the meeting actually took place. Certainly it was not in the week after Keats's dinner at Haydon's: from 13 to 18 December, Wordsworth was in Kent with his brother Christopher.[5] Most likely it occurred between Monday the 22nd and Saturday the 27th at Monkhouse's Queen Anne Street home. Haydon witnessed what happened:

> Wordsworth received him kindly, & after a few minutes, Wordsworth asked him what he had been lately doing, *I* said he has just finished an exquisite ode to Pan— and as he had not a copy I begged Keats to repeat it—which he did in his usual half chant, (most touching) walking up & down the room—when he had done I felt really, as if I had heard a young Apollo—Wordsworth drily said
> 'a Very pretty piece of Paganism'—
> This was unfeeling, & unworthy of his high Genius to a young Worshipper like Keats—& Keats felt it *deeply*—so that if Keats has said any thing severe about our Friend; it was because he was wounded—and though he dined with Wordsworth after at my table—he never forgave him.[6]

Written twenty-eight years after the event, Haydon's account repeats what he had already said in a letter of 12 February 1824: 'When poor Keats repeated his exquisite ode to Pan . . . "a very pretty piece of Paganism" said Wordsworth.'[7] If this was the calculated snub that Haydon reports, Keats himself seems not to have noticed and in the weeks ahead would meet Wordsworth at least five times. Quite possibly Keats took Wordsworth's comment as a compliment: the older poet recognised that Keats, too, had been inspired by the myths of 'pagan Greece'.[8] Paganism's contemporary associations with political and sexual freedom are celebrated in the benign natural religion of Keats's 'Hymn to Pan' in *Endymion* and, twenty years before, those ideals had appealed to a younger, radical Wordsworth and his friends – as the older poet, now forty-eight, had recently been reminded. In the second of his trials for blasphemy, William Hone claimed that government, not religion, had been the target of his scorn. He quoted numerous texts, including one from the *Anti-Jacobin* for July 1798 calculated to make Wordsworth shudder when it was reprinted in the *Morning Chronicle* on Friday, 19 December. This was an extract from 'New Morality', a satirical poem lampooning devotees of 'Theophilanthropy' – a natural religion not unlike the Cult of Pan celebrated in Keats's 'Hymn'. Corralled in 'New Morality' along with Marat, Mirabeau and Voltaire were the English Jacobins 'Coleridge and Southey, Lloyd and Lamb, and Co.'[9] In the context of this roster from 1798, the phrase 'and Co.' meant William Wordsworth, whose challenge to poetical prejudice in *Lyrical Ballads* grew out of the revolutionary republicanism he had formerly embraced. Twenty years on Wordsworth had become a rock of the establishment. As 'Distributor of Stamps' for Westmorland, he was a tax officer, and he was also a close friend of the local Tory grandee Lord Lowther. Both men were alarmed at resurgent 'Jacobinical principles' in the forthcoming general election. When the Whigs adopted Henry Brougham, a champion of reform, to contest the Westmorland election Wordsworth threw himself into six months' vigorous campaigning for Lowther, likening Brougham to 'one of the French Demagogues of the Tribunal of Terror'.[10] If Wordsworth had reason to be worried by Brougham's oratory and popular appeal, he was also aware that Brougham stood for liberal ideals like those celebrated in Keats's 'pretty piece of Paganism', ideals that he had once espoused himself. Given Wordsworth's political views in 1817 his comments on *Endymion* were understandable, but Keats would not forgive his support for Lowther against Brougham.

'Now is the winter of our discontent / Made glorious summer by this sun of York . . .' With habeas corpus suspended and Hone on trial for blasphemy, London was in need of Shakespeare's words. Monday, 15 December saw Edmund Kean, the greatest actor of the day, return to Drury Lane as Richard III – and Keats was there to see him. Debilitated by drink and venereal disease, Kean had been absent for three weeks. Now recovered and in good voice, he stormed back on stage in a thunderous rendition of Richard's hypocrisy, sarcasm, boldness, cruelty and ambition. As Keats told his brothers, Kean did it 'finely'.[11]

\* \* \*

Wednesday was the 17th, Saturnalia, and exactly a year since Keats – as I conjecture – had committed himself to poetry. In the evening he dined with witty Horace Smith and his brothers James and Leonard. Also present were Thomas Hill, dry-salter, book collector, *bon vivant*; Edward Dubois, proprietor-editor of the *Monthly Mirror*; and John Kingston, a 'Comptroller of Stamps' in the tax office. Like Leigh Hunt, Smith and Dubois were veterans of the literary circle that used to meet at Hill's residence in Sydenham where 'wine flowed merrily and long'.[12] Keats, who had felt at home in Hunt's bohemian household, was uneasy among these older men. When their smart talk turned to 'Kean & his low company' he knew these acquaintances would 'never do'.[13]

\* \* \*

Thursday the 18th brought him back to Drury Lane, tasked to review Kean as Luke in Sir James Bland Burges's comedy *Riches* (an adaptation of Philip

Massinger's *City Madam* of 1632). Bankrupted by his follies, Luke, a former gallant, is living disguised as a servant to his brother, Sir John Traffic, where he is abused by Lady Traffic and pitied by her daughter, Maria. Duped into believing Sir John has died leaving him a fortune, Luke emerges as his true self – a tyrant, now courted and flattered by his former oppressors. As the ruse that exposes them all is uncovered, Lady Traffic is chastened and Luke dispatched into exile. The plot is simple, the comedy leaden, yet *Riches* struck Keats as powerfully as *Richard III*. The play's sudden reversals connected with his own experiences of misfortune and dependence, particularly in this scene where Maria and her mother are discussing Luke:

> Maria. Poor creature! I don't wonder he feels his change of fortune.
> Lady Traffic. Feel indeed? What right has he to feel?
> Maria. The same that we ourselves would have, were we like him reduc'd to sudden misery.
> Lady Traffic. When that season comes we may begin to think on't.[14]

Keats would have been alert to how this scrap echoes the tempestuous third act of *King Lear* where the old king discovers that even wretches can feel. But how would it feel to have no 'right to feel'? With some such question turning in his mind, Keats left the theatre. Later, he drafted this poem as a Shakespearean pendant to the play:

> In drear nighted December,
>     Too happy, happy tree,
> Thy branches ne'er remember
>     Their green felicity—
> The north cannot undo them
> With a sleety whistle through them,
> Nor frozen thawings glue them
>     From budding at the prime.
>
> In drear nighted December,
>     Too happy, happy brook,
> Thy bubblings ne'er remember
>     Apollo's summer look;
> But with a sweet forgetting
> They stay their crystal fretting,
> Never, never petting
>     About the frozen time.

Ah! would 'twere so with many
  A gentle girl and boy—
But were there ever any
  Writh'd not of passed joy?
The feel of not to feel it,
When there is none to heal it,
Nor numbed sense to steel it,
  Was never said in rhyme.

Ne'er, ne'er, never, never, never. Gently, insistently, Keats's poem reminds us of the final scene of *King Lear* and of all those, unlike the seasons, irrevocably gone. With nature frozen and silent, the pains of memory are captured by that agonisingly physical word 'writh'd' – 'were there ever any / Writh'd not of passed joy?' Perhaps Keats's icy tree and brook were associated with the traumatic losses of his boyhood, particularly his mother's death in the bitter winter of 1809. In the landscape of his childhood, they endured year by year as sentinels of grief that Keats may well have experienced as a kind of shocked numbness: 'The feel of not to feel.' Early publications of this poem corrupted its final stanza to read 'To know the change and feel it, / When there is none to heal it', so that it chimed with Maria's sentiment, 'Poor creature! I don't wonder he feels his change of fortune.'[15] But Keats was actually led by his poem in a contrary direction, to the startling reflection that grief may comprehend 'The feel of not to feel' as well as what can more readily be 'said in rhyme'.

On Friday morning, as Keats set about his review 'On Edmund Kean as a Shakespearean Actor' for *The Champion*, the second of Hone's three trials for blasphemy began at the Guildhall. This attempt to silence opinion, contrasted with Kean's glorious volubility, gave Keats his opening: '"In our unimaginative days",—*Habeas Corpus'd* as we are, out of all wonder, uncertainty and fear;—in these fireside, delicate, gilded days,—these days of sickly safety and comfort, we feel very grateful to Mr. Kean for giving us some excitement by his old passion in one of the old plays.'[16] Kean's excitement of 'old passion' echoed Hunt's call for a revival of old merry-makings: to Keats, Kean was a 'relict of romance', a passionate remembrancer of Old England's liberties. His idea of Kean's 'gusto' – the intensity of his stage presence – echoes Hazlitt in *The Round Table* and suggests how, for Keats, Kean appeared to embody Shakespeare's sensual and spiritual grandeur. As always with Keats, however, Hazlitt's *Round Table* co-author, Hunt, proves a touchstone too – especially Hunt's observation that on stage Sarah Siddons 'never thinks . . . and therefore is always natural'.[17] So, in *Riches*, Kean had acted Luke perfectly, seeming to embody 'a man incapable of imagining to the extreme heinousness of crimes'; and, now, Keats mentions how, in playing Richard III, 'Kean delivers himself up to the instant feeling, without a shadow of thought'. The sickness that had kept him off stage had been as much of a national disaster as the suspension of habeas corpus: 'Kean! Kean! Have a carefulness of thy health, an in-nursed respect for thy own genius, a pity for us in these cold and enfeebling times! Cheer us a little in the failure of our days! For romance lives but in books. The goblin is driven from the heath, and the rainbow is robbed of its mystery!' Just a week before Keats wrote his review, Benjamin West had lectured to the Royal Academy on the rainbow's prismatic principles 'as a rule for the distribution of colours in a picture'.[18] No hearts leapt at that news, but Keats apparently took note of newspaper reports of what West had said. Having sent his review to John Scott at *The Champion*, he passed the evening with Tom's old schoolfellow, Charles Wells, at Featherstone Buildings, Holborn. Amusing and mischievous, Wells was good company. Keats saw him often this winter, forgetful for the moment of his 'Amena Bellafilla' hoax on Tom.

Next morning West's lecture was still on his mind. He went to see the painter's iconic work, 'Death on the Pale Horse', exhibited in West's gallery at 125, Pall Mall, and by evening was with Dilke at Wentworth Place. Sunday brought time to begin a letter to his brothers, musing on the week's events and West's painting. 'Death on the Pale Horse' was wonderful 'when West's age is considered' but Keats found 'nothing to be intense upon'.[19] Depicting the Four Horsemen of the Apocalypse, with Death at the centre clutching bolts of lightning, West's painting strove for sublimity and, in Keats's view, fell short. Its lurid colours, seething clouds and anguished figures met all the requirements of contemporary aesthetic theory, yet remained disappointingly inert. The excellence of art, Keats had decided in *Sleep and Poetry*, is not a matter of 'wretched rule'. True genius is an imaginative intensity 'capable of making all disagreeables evaporate', like one of Shakespeare's characters 'swelling into reality' in performance or in a reader's mind. West's 'age' was indeed the problem. A creature of the previous century with a rational, empirical outlook, West, like Newton, had contrived to reduce the rainbow's glorious colours to an arid list of 'principles'. He could smooth, inlay, clip and fit, but a finished work like 'Death on the Pale Horse' would never excite a 'momentous depth of speculation' like *King Lear*.

Keats was at Lamb's Conduit Street on Christmas Eve. Reynolds would shortly leave for Exeter and asked Keats to review a pantomime, *Harlequin's Vision*, and a new tragedy, *Retribution*. Benjamin Bailey was assiduously courting Marianne Reynolds during this vacation but, sensing that they did not like George, Keats had cooled his affection for the Reynolds girls some-what.[20] For Christmas, Keats headed back to Hampstead, meeting William Godwin on the way, and passed the evening at Wentworth Place with Dilke and Brown. Next day all three set off for Drury Lane and the first performance of *Harlequin's Vision*.[21] As they walked afterwards back up the cold lanes to Hampstead, Keats and Dilke had a 'disquisition' in which we might conjecture Keats touched on habeas corpus, wonder, uncertainty and fear; Shakespeare and gusto; the 'feel of not to feel'; and the intensity of Kean's performances. All of these topics dovetailed with Hunt's idea that imagination was a 'passive capacity'. As Keats picks up the story in his letter to his brothers: 'at once it struck me, what quality went to form a Man of Achievement especially in Literature & which Shakespeare possessed so enormously—I mean *Negative Capability*, that is when a man is capable of being in uncertainties, Mysteries, doubts, without any irritable reaching after fact & reason.'[22] A month earlier he had said that genius had no individuality, no determined character. Now he was imagining what it meant to exist without individuality, to live with uncertainties and doubts without 'irritable reaching'. Hazlitt had said that Shakespeare scarcely had an individual existence, that he had lived in and through the emotions of his dramatic characters.[23] Perhaps the 'feel of not to feel' was what it meant to be Shakespeare, a man who could feel only by imag-ining how all other men and women might feel.

* * *

Back at Well Walk, Keats found an invitation to Haydon's on Sunday the 28th.[24] That afternoon he set off through a cold winter twilight to join the company in Lisson Grove. Wordsworth and Monkhouse were already there with Charles Lamb, and looming over them was the canvas of 'Christ's Entry into Jerusalem'. As Haydon had said, Wordsworth now appeared in a group that included Voltaire and Newton. Over dinner they set to on Homer, Shakespeare, Milton and Virgil, with Keats drinking enthusiastically and Lamb quickly getting drunk. The latter joshed Wordsworth for calling Voltaire a 'dull fellow' in *The Excursion*, then took Haydon to task for putting Newton into his painting. Keats weighed in, agreeing with Lamb that Newton 'had destroyed all the Poetry of the rainbow, by reducing it to a prism', where-upon they all drank 'Newton's health, and confusion to mathematics!'[25]

Another guest arrived. Joseph Ritchie, a former surgeon at Lock's Hospital, had already met George and Tom at John Scott's apartment in Paris. Tom had taken his copybook of Keats's poems to Paris and, as we have seen, Scott was one of Keats's early admirers.[26] Within days of meeting the poet's brothers, Ritchie was writing to a friend: 'If you have not seen the Poems of J. Keats a lad of 19 or 20 they are worth your reading. If I am not mistaken he is to be the great poetical luminary of the age to come.' Reading the attack on Boileau in *Sleep and Poetry*, Ritchie was heartened that English poetry had broken 'the trammels of French taste & French Criticism'.[27] At Haydon's, Ritchie met Keats in person, asked politely about his brothers and confided his own romantic plan: he would voyage to Tripoli, cross the desert and discover the source of the Niger. Talk turned to *Endymion*. Perhaps it was now that Keats recited his 'Hymn to Pan', then made Ritchie promise to take a copy of his poem to the Sahara and fling it into the sands.[28] On hearing this, Lamb stirred to ask 'who is the Gentleman we are going *to lose?*' – a prophetic feeling, Haydon noted in 1819, for Ritchie died at Murzuq on 19 November that year.

Relaxed and convivial, the company retired to another room for tea, where-upon Lamb fell asleep. In came John Kingston, whom Keats had recently met and disliked at Horace Smith's. That morning Kingston had asked Haydon, whom he had not previously known, if he might call to meet Wordsworth. As he joined the company, 'frilled, dressed, & official', he announced himself as the poet's superior at the government's stamp office and then launched into a conversation about poetry. Stirring from his doze, Lamb said: ' "What did you say, Sir?" "Why, Sir", said the Comptroller, in his milk & water insipidity, "I was saying &c., &c., &c." "Do you say so, Sir?" "Yes, Sir" was the reply. "Why then, Sir, I say, hiccup, you are—you are a silly fellow." ' Bewildered by these remarks, and unaware of Lamb's 'previous tipsiness', Kingston persevered by asking Wordsworth, 'Pray, Sir, don't you think Milton a very *great genius?*' With this, Lamb 'blew up Kingston', Keats told his brothers, 'proceeding so far as to take the Candle across the Room hold it to his face and show us wh-a-at-sor$^t$-fellow he-waas'.[29] Copious quantities of wine had been taken and Lamb was hurried away 'by force' to Haydon's painting room, where he continued struggling and calling.[30] Supper followed, with Keats determined to astonish Kingston by 'keeping my two glasses at work in a knowing way'.[31]

Written immediately after that dinner, Haydon's diary entry gives us a portrait of Lamb as a drunken clown and Wordsworth frozen into formality by the sudden arrival of his supervisor. To prevent further offence to Kingston, Lamb was rapidly bundled off stage – or was it for his own good? Two months afterwards, Lamb reflected on their boisterous evening. Writing to Mary Wordsworth of 'that Gentleman concern'd in the Stamp office that I so strangely coiled up from at Haydons', he explained: 'I think I had an instinct he was the head of an office. I hate all such people—Accountants, Deputy Accountants. The dear abstract notion of the east India Company, as long as she is unseen, is pretty, rather Poetical; but as SHE makes herself manifest by the persons of such Beasts, I loathe and detest her.'[32] That turn from instinct to an 'abstract notion' of the East India Company seems odd, until one realises that when Kingston arrived Lamb – as well as Wordsworth – had been confronted with his superior. Since 1792 Lamb had worked at the East India Company as a clerk in the accountant's office. As controller of stamps and an accountant at the East India Company, Kingston appeared frequently before Parliament to report the company directors' resolutions 'concerning Salaries to their Servants'.[33] Kingston was thus Lamb's paymaster, as well as Wordsworth's. Shortly after the dinner Wordsworth had a tense exchange with Kingston's office about his failure to submit accounts.[34] And Lamb? He kept his post at East India House, and revisited its poetical qualities in his Elia essay 'The South Sea House' where Kingston does not appear among clerks of 'a curious and speculative turn of mind'.[35] The outrageous events at Haydon's on 28 December 1817 have come down to us as 'The Immortal Dinner', but what started as a congenial gathering almost ended in catastrophe.

The last days of the year were freezing and foggy. On New Year's Day, Keats saw John Dillon's new tragedy, *Retribution, or the Chieftain's Daughter*, at Covent Garden. His reviews of this production ('most wretched') and *Harlequin's Vision* ('a child should write a critique upon it') appeared in the first *Champion* of 1818 and marked Keats's swansong as a theatrical reviewer.[36] He was seeing a good deal of James Rice, picking up his city slang, and enjoyed a noisy supper-dance at the home of 'uncle' George Reddell who had supplied surgical knives at Guy's.[37] Bottles of wine were ranged on the stairs. Keats 'drank deep' and won 10s.6d. at cutting cards for half-guineas. Also there were Bailey and Rice, 'dancing as if he were deaf'. Winey chat about the derivation of the word 'cunt' was interrupted by Frank Fladgate bawling about piss-pots. 'Hoollo! Here's an opposition pot—Ay, says Rice in one you have a Yard for your pot, and in the other a pot for your Yard.'[38]

* * *

Keats's sister was staying with Abbey for the school holiday. On one of his visits to see her, Mrs Abbey declared that 'the Keatses were ever indolent— that they would ever be so and that it was born in them'. Fanny whispered to her brother, 'If it is born with us how can we help it.' Alert to the slight on their father, Keats made no comment when reporting this exchange to his brothers, but it had begun one of his webs of speculation. Coming after months of intense work on *Endymion*, Eleanor Abbey's gabble about the Keatses'

birthright eventually found a different form of words in his wonderful idea
of imaginative life as 'delicious diligent Indolence'. Pursuing this speculation,
he tells Reynolds: 'let us our open our leaves like a flower and be passive
and receptive—budding patiently under the eye of Apollo', adding further that
'I was led into these thoughts . . . by the beauty of the morning operating on a
sense of Idleness.'[39] In this mood he wrote 'O thou whose face hath felt the
winter's wind', an unrhymed sonnet with a Shakespearean refrain – 'O fret
not after knowledge' – echoed by a thrush's song that comes 'native with
the warmth'. This, Keats says, returning to Mrs Abbey's words, is mere sophis-
tication to excuse his own indolence.[40] By March 1818 the suggestion that the
Keatses' indolence was innate, 'born with us', had passed effortlessly into
Keats's axiom that 'if Poetry comes not as naturally as Leaves to a tree it
had better not come at all' and from there to his 'demon Poesy' in 'Ode
on Indolence' where

> The open casement press'd a new-leaved vine,
> Let in the budding warmth and throstle's lay.[41]
>
> (47–8)

∗ ∗ ∗

Calling on Wordsworth on Saturday, 3 January, Keats found him in a stiff
collar ready to dine at Kingston's – Keats had been invited too but had
declined, 'not liking that place'.[42] Claret and Sunday dinner with Wells and
Severn were more to his taste, followed by a hilarious six-hour impromptu
concert imitating sounds of musical instruments. Next morning Keats went to
Solomon Sawrey to give an account of Tom's renewed blood-spitting. Sawrey
was reassuring and asked for further information about his palpitations and
cough, but Keats's mood was subdued – there was now no mistaking the
signs of tuberculosis. He went to Rice's home at Featherstone Buildings and
began a letter to his brothers. That night he was supposed to dine with
Wordsworth, but the weather was so bad he thought of cancelling. In the
event he went, meeting Wordsworth's 'beautiful Wife and his enchanting
Sister' – that is, his sister-in-law, Sara Hutchinson, Coleridge's beloved 'Asra'.
This was an altogether more sober occasion than Sunday's party. Keats does
not tell us what they talked about, but his later remark about Wordsworth
having 'damned the lakes' – spoiling the Lake District by association, as
Hunt had Hampstead – suggests one possible topic of conversation. When
Keats attempted to disagree with the author of *The Excursion*, Cowden
Clarke recalled, Mrs Wordsworth 'put her hand upon his arm, saying, –

"Mr. Wordsworth is never interrupted". One senses that this was a some-what stilted evening with Wordsworth's admiring wife and sister-in-law forming what Keats later termed his 'fireside Divan'. 'Little Keats too I see is in the publishing line,' Sara Hutchinson noted a few weeks later, commenting dismissively of *Endymion*: 'however beautiful it may be I am sure it cannot awaken my interest or sympathies – I wonder anybody should take such subjects now-a-days.'[43] Preoccupied with Tom's problems and the need to start revising his poem, on this occasion Keats had not warmed to the Wordsworths' company either.

* * *

As 1818 began John Taylor was discovering the erratic side of his young poet, who had yet to deliver anything for publication. Five weeks had passed since Keats had finished *Endymion*. He retreated to Well Walk, and on 6 January began corrections with the first new moon of the year. A letter informed Taylor he was not especially well, but to expect the first book in four days. In closing, Keats asked to be remembered to the Hessey household, and sent his regards to 10 Percy Street, home of the artist Peter De Wint, his wife, Harriet, and her brother William Hilton. Taylor had introduced him to this artistic household, and both men would prove loyal friends.

The fall-out from Haydon's Immortal Dinner continued. Reynolds had been invited but had not responded, and Haydon was piqued. A sharp note from Haydon, followed by another in palliation, drew a lacerating response from Reynolds. Haydon was also at odds with the Hunts over borrowed silverware. Endeavouring to bear up with them all, Keats decided to keep clear of Haydon for a while. He excused himself on the 10th because of the Saturday Club with James Rice, and, to head off a second invitation, said he had already accepted for an 'insuperable engagement' on the Sunday.[44]

Monday the 12th began another hectic week. With Wells he went to see George Colman's comedy *John Bull* performed at a private theatre, The Minor, in Catherine Street, Covent Garden. They had a box at the stage edge but, like most of these unlicensed establishments, the theatre was a dirty hole 'all greasy & oily'. After the first act they hightailed it for Kean in *Richard III* at Drury Lane, and with Brown's silver ticket they got in for free. Back at The Minor to catch the end of *John Bull*, they went below stage to the green room. Here, in narrow candle-lit passages – Keats told his brothers – were actors and scene–shifters, 'a little painted Trollop' dressed as a Quaker, 'damned if she'd play a serious part again, as long as she lived', and 'a fat good natured looking girl' in soldier's clothes. An actor 'dressed to kill' was waiting 'in the very sweat of anxiety' while the overture played three times over without the curtain drawing up. Keats relished these colourful backstage encounters and his evocation of London's theatrical demi-monde has all the wit and sharp-eyed detail of Dickens's essay on 'Private Theatres' in *Sketches by Boz*.[45]

∗ ∗ ∗

Back at Hampstead, Keats began a letter to his brothers, only to be distracted by a dance at Dilke's and another at the London Coffee House. On Friday the 16th he was at the Reynoldses' new home in Little Britain where he wrote a sonnet 'To Mrs Reynolds' Cat', the first in a remarkable outpouring of occasional poems during the next month. On Sunday he met Hunt, then dined at Haydon's with Hazlitt and the artist William Bewick, who afterwards wrote of meeting 'Keats the poet'.[46] It was 19 January before he got back to his letter, confessing that he was only able to write in 'scraps & patches'. Progress on *Endymion* was slow too. The four days to correct its first book had stretched to fourteen, and the moon was now almost full. He would 'take it to Taylor's tomorrow—intend to persevere'.[47]

His mood was now more inward, 'perplexed in a world of doubts and fancies', living 'squat at Hampstead' (i.e. hidden from sight).[48] In this mist he had been projecting another poem, *Hyperion*, to contrast with what he had done hitherto. Like Bonaparte, Endymion, being a mortal, had been led on by circumstance, he told Haydon; as a foreseeing god, Apollo in *Hyperion* would shape his own actions.[49] In planning this epic poem, Keats was once again aiming high, but there were more immediate contingencies to deal with too. Taylor's suggestion that Haydon should illustrate *Endymion* had come to nothing, and the recriminations between Hunt, Haydon and Reynolds were continuing. 'Men should bear up with each other', Keats wrote to Bailey; 'there lives not the Man who may not be cut up, aye hashed to pieces on his weakest side'.[50]

As if prompted by that caution, on Wednesday the 21st Keats visited Hunt for the first time in many weeks.[51] Trying to rekindle their rapport, Hunt showed him a 'real authenticated Lock of *Milton's Hair*' and suggested they should compose on it – Keats must draft his poem in one of Hunt's notebooks. That Hunt intended that this should be a moment of friendly intimacy is suggested by the opening of his own poem:

> It lies before me there, and my own breath
>   Stirs its thin outer threads, as though beside
>   The living head I stood in honoured pride.
>                    ('To the Same', 1–3)

Hunt can be quaint and sentimental, but here he surprises us with the pleasure of tender human contact. Across the room Keats was out in space, reaching for a grandeur appropriate to the poet of *Paradise Lost*:

> Chief of organic numbers
>     Old scholar of the spheres
> Thy spirit never slumbers
>     But rolls about our ears
> For ever and for ever.
> Ah what a mad endeavour
>     Macketh he
> Who to thy sacred and ennobled
>                             hearse
> Would offer a burnt sacrifice of
>                             verse
>     And Melody—
> ('Lines on Seeing a Lock of Milton's Hair', 1–10)[52]

A few lines later, Keats's 'presumptuous tongue' fell silent: while the sight of Milton's hair had startled him, he had not been moved to anything like Hunt's sensation of affectionate familiarity. Back at Hampstead, he transcribed his poem, then copied it into his letter for Bailey. In the quieter, more reflective lines that now completed his poem, he delayed his encounter with Milton to an 'after-time' grown 'high-rife / With Old Philosophy'. This would not be the only occasion when his idea of Milton's poetic power – 'Father of organic numbers' – would prove an obstacle to his own creativity.[53]

Shakespeare was no such barrier. Correcting *Endymion* and seeing Kean had forced on Keats the contrast between decorative romance and Shakespeare's poetry of passion, sending him back to *King Lear*. He had recently been passing his evenings with Dilke, and it was at Wentworth Place on the wintry night of 22 January, before he read *King Lear* once again, that he wrote this sonnet:

> O golden tongued Romance, with serene Lute!
> Fair plumed syren! Queen! if far away!
> Leave melodizing on this wintry day,
> Shut up thine olden volume & be mute.
> Adieu! for once again the fierce dispute,
> Betwixt Hell torment & impassioned Clay
> Must I burn through; once more assay

The bitter sweet of this Shakespeareian fruit
Cheif Poet! & ye clouds of Albion.
Begetters of our deep eternal theme,
When I am through the old oak forest gone
Let me not wander in a barren dream
But when I am consumed with the Fire,
Give me new Pheonix-wings [*sic*] to fly at my desire.[54]

As Keats bids adieu to the romance verse of Spenser and Hunt, his fiery reincarnation shatters the formal constraints of the sonnet. Hitherto he had
worked within the octet and sestet structure of the Petrarchan sonnet. Here,
he adopts a more Shakespearean rhyme scheme, leaping out of the final
couplet and off that last, long Alexandrine line as a poet of 'impassioned clay'
and 'Albion' – the ancient England of *King Lear*. His energy was suddenly
formidable. 'I think a little change has taken place in my intellect lately,' he
tells his brothers, 'I cannot bear to be uninterested or unemployed, I, who for
so long a time, have been addicted to passiveness.'[55] *Endymion* was essentially
a portrait of passiveness, a 'barren dream', whereas now Keats was conscious
of a ripening of intellectual powers, impatient to soar into new skies.

* * *

Tuesday the 23rd took him across Blackfriars Bridge to the 'Rotunda' auditorium at the Surrey Institution, where at 7pm Hazlitt commenced his third
lecture on the English poets. In looking back to 'genius in former times',
Hazlitt claimed that Chaucer, Spenser and Shakespeare were poets writing
'near the beginning of their arts'. Whereas Shakespeare had seemed to write
effortlessly from nature, Milton's belatedness appeared in 'quantity of art'.
Here, in a single observation, Hazlitt explained Keats's recoil from Milton: to
write like Milton was to imitate his art, whereas to emulate Shakespeare was
to embrace nature. By announcing that Shakespeare was 'the least of an egotist
that it was possible to be', Hazlitt might have been echoing Keats on 'negative
capability' and poetic character – and it is possible that Keats had talked of
such matters when he met Hazlitt at Haydon's a week before the lecture. We
are so used to hearing of Hazlitt's influence on Keats that other exchanges, in
which Keats shaped Hazlitt's ideas, have been overlooked. Back in 1807 Hunt's
*Critical Essays* recommended actors to master how 'passion fluctuates', and, a
few months before Hazlitt's lecture, Keats had compared Shakespeare to the
sea. Now, as he sat in the Surrey Institution, he heard Hazlitt talking of the
'dramatic fluctuation of passion' in Shakespeare as being 'like the sea, agitated
this way and that, and loud-lashed by furious storms'.[56] That observation may

well have given Keats his cue for the 'perilous seas' of 'Ode to a Nightingale'; equally, Hazlitt's remarks on Shakespeare were part of wider conversations in print and in private to which Hunt and Keats also contributed.

∗ ∗ ∗

Hunt had been writing on the genius of former times too. Three *Examiner* essays on 'Old National Merry-Makings' sought to revive the festive traditions of Christmas, Twelfth Day and May Day as celebrated by those 'lovers of old English pleasures', Shakespeare, Sydney and Herrick. Such enjoyments included song and dance, Christmas greens and gambols, maypoles, wassail bowls of wine or mead or metheglin mixed with spices, and 'spicy nut-brown ale'. For Hunt, those former times were associated with the kind impulses, liberal views and humane sociability recommended week by week in *The Examiner*. Among ensuing correspondence about the season was a letter arguing that Christmas 'is not a Christian institution; that it is the Saturnalia of ancient days—the Feast of Saturn, the Father of the Gods'.[57] If Keats had already been thinking of Saturn's role in his projected epic *Hyperion*, here, in the first issue of *The Examiner* for 1818 was a suggestion of how his poem based in pagan antiquity might speak directly to the modern world.

∗ ∗ ∗

For two months Keats had written little. Then, in the last week of January, he was suddenly teeming with ideas and four poems came in quick succession. 'O blush not so' is an erotic lyric of 'amorous nipping', much in the pleasureful spirit of Hunt's old merry-makings. Two verses to Apollo followed. 'Hence burgundy, claret and port' reflected the brightness of a 'sun-shiny day', while 'God of the Meridian' was shadowed by more personal worries that carried over into the sonnet 'When I have fears that I may cease to be'. Together these poems capture an edgy Keats, excited and unsettled at Hunt's and Hazlitt's ideas, awed by the sheer abundance of his own imagination. It was thoughts of Tom's illness that darkened the most powerful of these late January lyrics, as Keats confronted the possibility that his own life could be cut short too:

> When I have fears that I may cease to be
>   Before my pen has glean'd my teeming brain,
> Before high piled Books in charactery
>   Hold like full garners the full ripen'd grain—
> When I behold upon the night's starr'd face
>   Huge cloudy symbols of a high romance

And feel that I may never live to trace
  Their shadows with the magic hand of Chance:
And when I feel, fair creature of an hour,
  That I shall never look upon thee more
Never have relish in the fairy power
  Of unreflecting Love: then on the Shore
    Of the wide world I stand alone and think
    Till Love and Fame to Nothingness do sink.—[58]

'When . . . When . . . and when': the single long sentence of this sonnet locates Keats on the cusp between doubt and hope, waste and fulfilment, nothingness and a future that might harvest his imagination's ripening richness. He echoes two of Shakespeare's most famous sonnets, 'When I do count the clock that tells the time' and 'Not mine own fears, nor the prophetic soul', attuning himself to Shakespeare's poetry of love, ambition, life's brevity and death. This, for Hazlitt, was the instinctive poetry of nature, and Keats would go on to attempt a series of sonnets explicitly in the Shakespearean manner and form. Those 'cloudy symbols of a high romance' are misty forms of other poems yet to be written, ghostly Ossianic epics that he fears he may not live to write, while the 'fair creature of an hour' is like the woman at Vauxhall, a spectral beauty glimpsed once, then lost for ever.[59] For twelve lines the sonnet keeps Keats's possible destinies in precarious balance, until the heartbreaking Shakespearean refrain 'never . . . never . . . never' leads to that desolate promontory 'on the Shore / Of the wide world', where no sea-nymphs quire and 'Love and Fame to Nothingness do sink'.

 'I cannot write sense this morning', he told Reynolds on the morning of the 31st, as if overcome by the *narvus* feelings that had troubled him on the Isle of Wight. There he had found release in writing to Reynolds, while the tidal whisperings of his sonnet 'On the Sea' had brought intimations of Shakespeare. 'When I have fears' is a much bleaker poem and, unable to write better sense in prose, he copied the verses out for his friend instead.

* * *

The rebound came three days later. A more upbeat letter to Reynolds thanks him for two sonnets on Robin Hood, whimsically likened to a woodlander's 'dish of Filberts'. Joseph Ritson's ballad anthology *Robin Hood*, Scott's *Ivanhoe*, and Peacock's *Maid Marian* had shown the potent appeal of an outlaw 'spirit of freedom and independence' in years of economic depression.[60] Reynolds's first sonnet also displayed a wishfully romantic imagining of the past:

**To a Friend: On Robin Hood**

The trees in Sherwood Forest are old and good,—
The grass beneath them now is dimly green;
Are they deserted all? Is no young mien,
With loose slung bugle met within the wood?
No arrow found,—foil'd of its antler'd food,—
Struck in the oak's rude side?—Is there nought seen,
To mark the revelries which there have been,
In the sweet days of merry Robin Hood?
Go there with summer, and with evening,—go
In the soft shadows, like some wandering man,—
And thou shalt far amid the Forest know
The archer-men in green, with belt and bow,
Feasting on pheasant, river-fowl, and swan,
With Robin at their head, and Marian.

When Keats recalled Reynolds's forest of 'soft shadows' in 'Ode to a Nightingale', his labyrinth of 'verdurous glooms' offered an 'outlaw' escape from 'The weariness, the fever, and the fret / Here, where men sit and hear each other groan'. He started towards that 'forest dim' in 'Robin Hood: To a Friend', responding to Reynolds with a brisk unsentimental lyric in seven-syllable lines:

No! those days are gone away,
And their hours are old and gray,
And their minutes buried all
Under the down-trodden pall
Of the leaves of many years:
Many times have winter's shears,
Frozen north, and chilling east,
Sounded tempests to the feast
Of the forest's whispering fleeces,
Since men knew nor rent nor leases.

No, the bugle sounds no more,
And the twanging bow no more;
Silent is the ivory shrill
Past the heath and up the hill.

Time has undone romance. The old oak forest has been felled to construct warships. Honey can't be got without 'hard money'. Keats was now writing, he tells Reynolds, 'in the Spirit of Outlawry':

> So it is: yet let us sing,
> Honour to the old bow-string!
> Honour to the bugle-horn!
> Honour to the woods unshorn!
> Honour to the Lincoln green!
> Honour to the archer keen!
> Honour to tight little John,
> And the horse he rode upon!
> Honour to bold Robin Hood,
> Sleeping in the underwood!
> Honour to maid Marian,
> And to all the Sherwood-clan!
> Though their days have hurried by
> Let us two a burden try.

Less nostalgic than Hunt on the subject of Old England, Keats thought the bold genius of former times could nevertheless be reclaimed by poets of the present. He continues this idea in a second poem for Reynolds. He had recently been at Cheapside to drink at the Mermaid Tavern, meeting place of Shakespeare's contemporaries Francis Beaumont and John Fletcher:

> Souls of poets dead and gone,
> What elysium have ye known,
> Happy field or mossy cavern,
> Choicer than the Mermaid Tavern?
> Have ye tippled drink more fine
> Than mine host's Canary wine?
> Or are fruits of Paradise
> Sweeter than those dainty pies
> Of venison? O generous food!
> Drest as though bold Robin Hood
> Would, with his maid Marian,
> Sup and bowse from horn and can.

Convivial and bowsey, Keats's feast of 'poets dead and gone' actually sprang from a quarrel with his contemporaries, especially Wordsworth and Hunt, for writing egotistical verse with a 'palpable design' on readers. 'Poetry should be great & unobtrusive,' he counsels Reynolds. 'Let us have the old Poets, & robin Hood.' Keats, like Hazlitt, was an 'outlaw', enrolling the old poets as 'generous food' for modern readers, against the self-interested coercions of contemporary writers. In three weeks' time Hazlitt would conclude his Surrey Institution lecture 'On Burns, and the Old Ballads' by invoking Robin Hood 'who still, in imagination, haunts Sherwood Forest'.[61]

Keats was feeling haunted too. It was the Vauxhall woman. On Wednesday, 4 February he addressed her again in a sonnet, 'Time's sea', recounting in Shakespearean cadences the bittersweet sensation of being 'tangled in [her] beauty's web':

> Thou dost eclipse
> Every delight with sweet remembering,
> And grief unto my darling joys dost bring.

A powerful erotic urge overwhelms sight, hearing and taste to 'devour / Its sweets in the wrong sense', and in this riot of desire Keats endures something of 'the strife / Of human hearts' he had sought in *Sleep and Poetry*. His recent rereading of Shakespeare was now enabling him to articulate a poignant threshold between joy and sorrow, desire and disappointment. Partly this was because Shakespeare had put him more completely in touch with his own feelings. These included traumatic alternations of happiness and grief, elation and depression, and gentler collisions too – since his early Edmonton days he had relished 'the luxury of sunny beams / Temper'd with coolness'. Hunt had shown him how to render that kind of 'luxurious' experience in poetry. Now Shakespeare was teaching him how to orchestrate the sunlit pleasures and dejected depths of his life in poetry of a more universal, human understanding. In this respect the change that Keats remarked in his intellect was both transparently simple and richly profound. He had started to make sense of himself, as these lines on his own 'camelion' nature suggest:

> Welcome joy, and welcome sorrow,
>     Lethe's weed, and Hermes' feather,
> Come to-day, and come to-morrow,
>     I do love you both together!
>     I love to mark sad faces in fair weather,
> And hear a merry laugh amid the thunder;
>     Fair and foul I love together.
>     ('Welcome joy, and welcome sorrow', 1–7)

* * *

Later on the 4th Keats dined with Shelley at Hunt's. Egyptian sculpture at the British Museum had inspired Shelley's sonnet 'Ozymandias', recently published in *The Examiner*, and Hunt now suggested sonnets on 'The Nile' in fifteen minutes. Keats's effort – 'Son of the old moon-mountains African!' – was a Petrarchan sonnet echoing recent talk of the Sahara with Ritchie, and containing one of his worst lines: 'Oh, may dark fancies err! they surely do.' Still, he had good reason to suspect the motives behind one piece of gossip that reached him at Hunt's: Mrs Hunt told him he was to be invited to a party at Charles Ollier's to keep Shakespeare's birthday.[62]

For the moment Keats was busy 'copying on the Hill'. By the new moon of Thursday, 5 February he had revised *Endymion*'s second book, and his schedule so far suggests that the third would be ready around the full moon on the 21st. Taylor heard on the 27th that he had already 'coppied the 3rd Book' and begun the fourth. He was anxious to get his poem printed so that he could 'forget it and proceed' – a sentiment soon to be echoed in a preface he promised to supply in good time.[63]

Hazlitt's lectures offered him a way forward. On 3 February, in closing remarks on Dryden and Pope, Hazlitt observed that a modern translation of tales in Boccaccio and Chaucer – such as 'that of Isabella' – could not fail to succeed.[64] This registered with both Reynolds and Keats, who were in the audience, and sometime afterwards Reynolds suggested they should collaborate to modernise Boccaccio's tales in verse.

Even when Hazlitt's lectures missed their mark they proved fertile for listeners. In his peroration about Swift, Gray and Collins on the 17th, Hazlitt dismissed Chatterton as a poet not of genius but 'extraordinary precocity'. Keats was immensely disappointed. Word of this seems to have reached Hazlitt, for his next lecture addressed this particular dissatisfaction. He had intended less to question Chatterton's genius, he explained, than object to attempts to estimate it solely by his youth and singular circumstances. Hazlitt's remarks most likely prompted Keats to dedicate *Endymion* to Chatterton's memory, and his quotation of Herbert Croft on the Chatterton phenomenon also helped shape Keats's idea of *Hyperion*. Likening Chatterton to a young Apollo, Croft had remarked: 'Superstition and admiration would have explained all by bringing Apollo on earth; nor would the God ever have descended with more credit to himself.'[65] Keats's young Apollo, 'anguish'd' into eternal life at the close of *Hyperion*, is in effect his golden reincarnation of Chatterton – the child of sorrow in whose premature death Keats had recognised a 'fair morning' of poetic immortality.[66]

If Keats was sometimes disappointed by Hazlitt's lectures, he wrote to George and Tom at Teignmouth that Wordsworth had left a bad impression 'by his egotism, Vanity, and bigotry'. Here Keats was almost certainly echoing Hazlitt's attack on Wordsworth's egotism; 'Vanity' recalled Mary Wordsworth silencing Keats while her husband talked; and 'bigotry' alluded to Wordsworth's increasingly vocal opposition to Brougham. Yet, leaving aside these detractions, Keats continued to think the author of *Lyrical Ballads* and *The Excursion* 'a great poet if not a Philosopher'. And there were other great poets to read. A fourth canto of *Childe Harold* was imminent. He had not yet seen Shelley's *Revolt of Islam* – the Olliers' reissue of *Laon and Cythna* – but his brothers might be able to help: 'I don't suppose you have it in the Teignmouth Libraries'? The suggestion that Shelley's controversial poem might have been stocked in that fashionable resort was not unreasonable, for Croydon's library subscribed to *The Examiner* in which Shelley's poetry had been praised. At the close of Keats's letter he suddenly leaps from books to money worries: 'I hope you have a moderate portion of Cash—but don't fret at all if you have not.'[67] On 28 February, George would turn twenty-one, and stood to inherit £2,010 in stock.[68]

\* \* \*

Keats's winter racketing was at an end too, and with the unsettled weather of fog, cloud, rain, high winds and snow he grew restless. For a moment he thought of returning to childhood scenes and acquaintances at Edmonton, although as it turned out the coming months would take him far from the city where he had wintered, to Teignmouth, Liverpool, the Lake District, Burns's Dumfries and the Scottish Highlands.[69] As he prepared to leave town, on most evenings he was 'very thick' with Brown and Dilke. Tuesday, 3 March was an exception, for he attended Drury Lane to see Frederick Reynolds's popular play *The Will*, a comedy of disinheritance set in Devonshire.[70] Keats and his brothers still had no inkling of the further £800 stock plus interest held for each of them in Chancery; had Keats known of those funds, the course of life he was about to start on might have turned to laughter too.

# Roads of the Dead, 1818

# CHAPTER 15

## Dark Passages

Tom seemed to be getting better. George would return to London, and to keep Tom company Keats would join him at Teignmouth. He booked an outside seat on the 'Royal Mail' to Exeter for 7.30pm on Wednesday, 4 March. Usually this journey took around twenty-seven hours but, heading westwards, the coach was overwhelmed by a terrific storm: houses were wrecked, rivers flooded, and between Honiton and Exeter sixteen large elms were torn up and flung across the road. Keats escaped 'being blown over and blown under & trees & houses being toppled', although travelling outside, cold and wet through, was still dangerous to his health. When he reached the New London Inn, Exeter, on Thursday night, there was time to rest and warm himself before taking a coach over Haldon Hill to Teignmouth. Tom greeted him in streets littered with tiles, branches and other debris.[1]

Together they walked to their lodging at 20 Strand, a compact townhouse some fifty yards from Teignmouth's busy port. With a population of four thousand, Teignmouth in 1818 was a fashionable watering-place: there were twelve bathing machines, hot baths, an assembly room, a public library that took the London papers and a theatre where Kean had scratched his name on the green room wall. Temperate air carried by sea and land breezes was believed to 'waft off all injurious particles', but what Keats experienced were days of rain that made it 'a splashy, rainy, misty snowy, foggy, haily floody, muddy slipshod County'.[2]

Confined by abominable weather, he passed an afternoon writing to Bailey of the greatness of England and Englishmen, especially Shakespeare, compared with the 'dwindled' Devonshire men he had encountered. He soon met his brothers' friends Marian and Sarah Jeffrey and their mother, and declared the local women 'passable'. Gloomy and uneasy, his letter is vexed by thoughts that a mental pursuit like poetry may be a 'mere Jack a lantern', taking 'value and worth from the ardour of the pursuer'.[3] He had composed a sonnet on the four seasons of 'the mind of Man' and copied it out for Bailey; in conception and structure it is Shakespearean, its 'ports' and 'havens', 'mists' and 'threshold brook' reflecting life at Teignmouth. With no sign of the rain abating, Keats wrote to tell Reynolds he had finished the fourth book of *Endymion* and would draft a preface 'soon'. 'Soon' proved to be sooner than he anticipated. Letters from George and Brown advised that the printer wanted copy immediately.[4]

The eight-paragraph preface Keats set down on Thursday the 19th caught his doleful mood and doubts about *Endymion*. Readers should be aware, he began, that, as an individual in a 'great nation', Keats himself is 'a nothing'. He has 'fought under disadvantages' – *Endymion* is an 'endeavour', not a 'thing accomplished' – and promises to 'redeem' himself with a new poem written out of 'love of fame'. With an eye to critics, he seeks to pre-empt hostility by alluding to his 'self-hindering labours'. Ambitious, anxious and defensive, this first attempt at a preface is shot through with symptoms of 'morbid sensibility'. He dispatched it on the 21st with the fourth book and a resounding upper-case dedication: 'INSCRIBED, / WITH EVERY FEELING OF PRIDE AND REGRET / AND WITH A "BOWED MIND", / TO THE MEMORY OF / THE MOST ENGLISH OF POETS EXCEPT SHAKESPEARE, / THOMAS CHATTERTON.' Under a bright full moon, his package sped to London by the night mail.

The weather lifted. A walk along the Teign Estuary led Keats through Bishopsteignton to Kingsteignton, and back along the opposite shore via Combteignhead to Shaldon. These local associations reappear in some lively 'doggrel' and 'bitchrell' he sent to Haydon about the 'maidens sweet / Of the Market Street'.[5] Later, after clambering six miles along the rocky undercliff, he came to Babbacombe Bay and ventured as far as Kent's Cavern – a reminder, for Keats, of *Lear*'s stoical earl outfacing adversity: 'Nothing almost sees miracles, / But misery . . . / Fortune, good night; smile once more; turn thy wheel' (II.ii.160–61, 168).

Favourable first impressions notwithstanding, Tom's recovery would have been a miracle indeed. On 23 March, Easter Monday, Keats set out 'over the bourn' to Dawlish fair, glad to be away from their dark rooms at Teignmouth yet unable to forget Tom's continual blood-spitting. Reynolds was ill too, confined in London with 'a heavy cold & fever, leading a life of pain, sleeplessness & bleeding'.[6] Next day a letter to Rice mingled jests with speculations culled from Keats's close reading of Milton and Wordsworth. Study of these poets would, he hoped, enable him to 'philosophize', which, in turn, would be preparatory to an attempt at epic. But, like Teignmouth's weather, Keats's feelings never settled for long; his letter skips from philosophy to sexual slang to a rueful sigh 'Oh! for a day and all well!' – then launches into a bawdy lyric about Dawlish fair and rumpling the daisies with 'Rantipole Betty'.[7] Throughout these days, he was at work on *Isabella*, swiftly mastering the narrative possibilities of its Italian *ottava rima* verse. The plan now was for Keats and Reynolds to collaborate on a volume of Boccaccio translations, and Keats had set to by composing some opening stanzas before he left London.

Restless juxtapositions also chequered a verse letter to Reynolds begun on 25 March:

Dear Reynolds, as last night I lay in bed,
There came before my eyes that wonted thread
Of Shapes, and Shadows and Remembrances,
That every other minute vex and please.[8]

This scene resembles the close of *Sleep and Poetry* – 'upon a couch at ease . . .' – except that here the images are 'all disjointed' until Keats settles into an evocation of Claude's painting 'The Enchanted Castle'. Perhaps he had seen this in Hunt's or Haydon's print collections, for he named it from William Woollett's 1782 engraving rather than giving its correct title, 'Landscape with Psyche and the Palace of Amor'. In April 1819, when Claude's painting was exhibited at the British Institution, Keats would revisit the Cupid and Psyche myth in his 'Ode to Psyche'. That return also brought back this passage, abruptly introduced some twenty lines into his verse letter:

The sacrifice goes on; the pontif knife
Gloams in the sun, the milk-white heifer lows,
The pipes go shrilly, the libation flows.[9]

Marooned in a 'slipshod County', Keats seems to have been daydreaming about another of Claude's masterpieces, 'Landscape with the Father of Psyche Sacrificing', overlaying this with a reminiscence of the Elgin Marbles to form a scene that would reappear in the 'green altar', 'mysterious priest' and 'heifer lowing at the skies' of 'Ode on a Grecian Urn'. Such pleasurable 'dreamings . . . of sleep and wake', Keats now realises, 'shadow our own Soul's daytime' by reminding us that life is continually forced by circumstance, that 'Things cannot to the will / Be settled, but they tease us out of thought' (another phrase that would reappear in 'Ode on a Grecian Urn'). Forlorn, perplexed

that without human wisdom or 'philosophy' life is 'a sort of purgatory blind',
he is confronted with this bitter realisation:

> —It is a flaw
> In happiness to see beyond our bourn—
> It forces us in Summer skies to mourn:
> It spoils the singing of the Nightingale.[10]

His imagination is precociously active, but as yet lacks a necessary ballast of
knowledge and wisdom. When Keats revisited these juxtapositions in his odes
of spring 1819, his epistle's abrupt swerves between dream and actuality, pain
and pleasure, would be tempered by more sustained cadences and less
febrile speculations. Impelling him towards those profound understandings
of humanity's 'flawed happiness' was this terrifying vision, with which he
closed his epistle to Reynolds:

> Dear Reynolds. I have a mysterious tale
> And cannot speak it. The first page I read
> Upon a Lampit Rock of green sea weed
> Among the breakers—'Twas a quiet Eve;
> The rocks were silent—the wide sea did weave
> An untumultuous fringe of silver foam
> Along the flat brown sand. I was at home,
> And should have been most happy—but I saw
> Too far into the sea; where every maw
> The greater on the less feeds evermore:—
> But I saw too distinct into the core
> Of an eternal fierce destruction,
> And so from Happiness I far was gone.
> Still am I sick of it: and though to day
> I've gathered young spring-leaves, and flowers gay
> Of Periwinkle and wild strawberry,
> Still do I that most fierce destruction see,
> The shark at savage prey—the hawk at pounce,
> The gentle Robin, like a pard or ounce,
> Ravening a worm—Away ye horrid moods,
> Moods of one's mind![11]

An eternal fierce destruction: here, at last, is the horror that stalked the
'eternal Whisperings' and desolate shores of his sonnet 'On the Sea'. *Narvus*,

haunted by thoughts of his father's death, Keats had fled the Isle of Wight and sought Tom's company at Margate. Now, at Teignmouth, all sense of being happy and at home was banished by the disease consuming Tom's life, inexorable as the rhyme engulfing 'saw' and 'maw' with 'evermore'. Agonising experience had taught Keats the limitations of contemporary medicine; as a surgeon he was terrified that his scalpel might slip and sever an artery. Was poetry, like medicine, utterly helpless in the face of nature's fierce destruction? A fleeting jack-o-lantern? Keats had long known himself implicated in a world 'at savage prey', for, years ago, as he gazed into the depths of Salmons Brook, his looming shadow had scattered tiny creatures for cover. He, too, lived in a world where 'greater on the less feeds evermore', and his closing thoughts – pivoting on that Wordsworthian phrase, 'Moods of one's mind' – turn to poetry and his own voracious ambition. He had deliberately 'leapt into the sea' with *Endymion*, risking what he knew would be a fierce struggle for poetic fame or destruction – a struggle that was by no means finished.

In signing off, he reminded Reynolds of his 'new Romance', *Isabella, or, the Pot of Basil*, a poem that melds 'purple phantasies' of passion with murder, exhumation, and 'green and livid' stains of decay he recalled from dissecting corpses at Guy's. At one moment 'at home . . . and happy', in the next 'at savage prey', every stanza of *Isabella* was attuned to the sharp contingencies of Keats's life. As the anniversary of his father's death approached in mid-April, he was once again drawn back to the terrible events that had initiated his life as a poet; from now on we are increasingly aware that, beneath its warm textures and rich colours, Keats's greatest poetry enfolds a shattered skull.

Haydon wrote. Keats must see his own native country near Plymouth: 'Stay till the Summer, and then bask in its deep blue summer Sky, and lush grass, & tawny banks, and silver bubbling rivers—you must not leave Devonshire without seeing some of its Scenery rocky, mossy, craggy with roaring rivers & as clear as crystal—it will do your mind good.' But Keats's thoughts were elsewhere. By 8 April, with Tom seeming better again, he was anxious to be back in London; further ahead lay the prospect of a pedestrian tour to the north; it would prepare him for a life of writing, study and seeing 'all of Europe at the lowest expense'. After the mist and rain of recent days Keats hoped to clear himself of anxieties and doubts. 'I will clamber through the Clouds and exist,' he tells Haydon, looking to accumulate a stock of imagery that will sustain him on 'the labyrinthian path' to poetic eminence, aware of 'innumerable compositions and decompositions which take place between the intellect and its thousand materials before it arrives at that trembling delicate and snail-horn perception of Beauty'.[12] At Box Hill, Keats had associated Shakespeare with the tender 'snail-horn'; now, as took stock of his own aspirations, he would have to prove himself as tactful – and resilient too.

For a moment he had seen his future clear, then cloud closed in again. Experienced publishers, Taylor and Hessey saw at a glance that his wheedling preface would not do and wrote to tell him so. Keats's response in a letter to Reynolds emphasised his high motives, 'the Principle of Beauty' and 'public Good' – this, too, was in line with Hazlitt on 'morbid sensibility'. He has 'no feel of stooping' to the public and hates 'the idea of humility to them': his claim for public attention springs from talent alone.[13] He packed off a revised preface on 10 April. Its manner is steady and direct: doubts about his poem's 'mawkishness' are mentioned now not to forestall criticism but to conciliate informed opinion.

The two prefaces demonstrate Keats's different stances before the public. If his first attempt had been muddled, vulnerable, the second proved comparatively assured. Keats achieved this by adapting a strategy from his 1817 volume, where a note had alerted readers to his earlier poems by way of pointing to more recent achievements and, by implication, the promise of what was to come. That narrative of growth now extended to *Endymion*. 'It is just that this youngster should die away,' Keats writes, 'a sad thought for me, if I had not some hope that while it is dwindling I may be plotting, and fitting myself for verses fit to live.' As always, Keats looked to posterity to resolve present dilemmas, poetic and personal. Transposing the dwindling and dying of a consumptive onto the 'youngster' *Endymion* was a way of coping with Tom's sickness; by the same token, 'verses fit to live', for which Keats said he was assiduously 'fitting [him]self', would be a healthy earnest of the future. As Keats listened to Tom's rattling breath and rasping cough, his own physical wellbeing and hopes of poetic fame became inseparably entwined.

Confined to the 'labyrinthe' of Teignmouth – so Tom called it – Keats found release in composing *Isabella*, projecting his northern tour and venturing to nearby villages. Then, around the weekend of 18–19 April, James Rice arrived. It was a year since Keats had begun *Endymion* on the Isle of Wight: on 18 April 1817 he had written to Reynolds that he would begin 'forthwith' and asked to be remembered to Rice. Perhaps Rice brought an advance copy of *Endymion* from London, for the poem was now in print in an edition of five hundred or 750 copies.[14] Certainly he gave Keats a folio copy of Mateo Alemán's comic romance, translated from the Spanish as *The Rogue: or, The Life of Guzman de Alfarache*, and inscribed 'John Keats From his Friend J$^s$ Rxxx 20th April 1818'.[15] It was exactly the tonic Keats needed; spicy and titillating, the book opened with Guzman's conception in an elaborately illicit affair. Keats read these lurid pages immediately, then turned to celebrate his 'warm meeting' with Rice in a sonnet that alludes to Guzman's ancestral home in 'the rich Levant'. As we shall see, Keats would return to Guzman's story, reading intensively and underlining passages that struck him as significant. Here, at Teignmouth, he had found in *The Life of Guzman de Alfarache* a source for what would prove to be his greatest narrative poem.

A letter went off to John Taylor on 24 April. Keats was 'pleased much' by *Endymion*, and was already making fresh plans: he would 'travel over the north this Summer', then retire to study 'for some years'. Taylor heard how he had been 'hovering for some time between an exquisite sense of the luxurious and a love of Philosophy' – that is, between a 'life of sensations' and one of reading and thought. In *Isabella*, he was already moving decisively away from the luxuries and couplets of his early verse, but, as he had told Reynolds, he 'dared not' philosophise until he acquired further insight into the 'lore of good and ill'.[16] Closing his letter with errata for *Endymion*, Keats asked for the first time to be remembered to his publisher's lawyer, Richard Woodhouse.

He had been studying Milton and had thoughts of learning Greek and Italian. Travel might be another way of learning philosophic 'lore', but much depended on Tom: for the moment, he seemed content in the care of a local physician, Dr William Turton.[17] With summer and the north still some way off, Keats turned to Wordsworth's poetry, seeking to cure his own 'high Sensations' with a more 'extensive knowledge': 'it takes away the heat and the fever,' he told Reynolds on 3 May, 'and helps, by widening speculation, to ease the Burden of the Mystery.' Paraphrasing passages of 'Tintern Abbey', Keats was looking to Wordsworth to help him confront 'the ill "that flesh is heir to"'. At this point he broke off and copied out for Reynolds fourteen lines he had written on May Day, the beginning of what seems to have been a projected 'Ode to Maia':

Mother of Hermes! And still youthful Maia!
    May I sing to thee
As thou wast hymned on the shores of Baiæ?
    Or may I woo thee
In earlier Sicilian? Or thy smiles
Seek, as they were once sought, in Grecian Isles,
By bards who died content in pleasant sward,
    Leaving great verse unto a little clan?
O give me their old vigour, and unheard,
    Save of the quiet Primrose, and the span
      Of heaven, a few ears

Rounded by thee, my song should die away,
        Content as theirs,
Rich in the simple worship of a day.[18]

This unfinished ode survives as an irregular sonnet, a fourteen-line fragment
of a more capacious poem that might have explored the strange coincidence
of Maia's maternal 'smiles', resurgent spring and Tom's wasting illness. If that
was indeed what Keats had in mind, he may already have been looking for a
poetic form that would be both more concentrated and expansive than
anything he had yet written – a quest that would, eventually, lead him to the
commanding synthesis of opposites in his fully achieved odes of spring 1819.

Throughout this letter of 3 May to Reynolds, Wordsworth and Shakespeare
are cited as representing a comprehensive human understanding as far as
Keats himself had experienced life: 'axioms in philosophy are not axioms until
they are proved upon our pulses', he told Reynolds. 'We read fine things but
never feel them to thee full until we have gone the same steps with the Author
. . . you will know exactly my meaning when I say, that now I shall relish
Hamlet more than I ever have done.'[19] While Keats's exact meaning is not
quite evident, he was apparently saying that he had lived through the experiences of Hamlet – that he too had 'gone the same steps' in a life he had recently
described as 'all disjointed'. An obvious similarity between Keats and Hamlet
was his mother's hasty remarriage after his father's death. Had Frances, like
Gertrude, been keeping two men – Thomas Keates and William Rawlings –
on the go at the same time? Keats's identification with Hamlet might suggest
as much and, if he did indeed have suspicions about his mother, as Robert
Gittings conjectured, there are further ramifications that intersect with his
idea of himself as a poet.[20]

That Keats was indeed foraging back through some of the darkest passages
of his memory is suggested by a sinister aspect of Isabella, hitherto overlooked. Ostensibly Keats's poem tells the tragic story of two young lovers,
Lorenzo and Isabella. Isabella is the sister of two avaricious Florentine
merchants, who, when they discover the affair, murder Lorenzo and bury his
body in a wood. Warned by Lorenzo's spirit where his corpse lies, Isabella
retrieves it and reburies his head beneath a basil plant, until her weeping alerts
her brothers, who contrive 'to steal the basil-pot, / And to examine it in secret
place' (473–4). Aware that their guilt has been discovered, they make their
escape while Isabella, denied her relic, pines to death. Keats came to think
Isabella a 'weak-sided' sentimental poem that would be laughed at. 'There are
very few', he explained, 'would look to the reality.'[21] But what is 'the reality' of
Isabella? An obvious 'reality' would be to recognise how the brothers' greedy,

bourgeois principles are destructive of romance. Or did Keats mean that there were very few who would see a more personal reality behind his poem's critique of murderous money-getting?

He was close to finishing *Isabella* at the anniversaries marking his father's death on the night of 14–15 April and his funeral a week later. His mother's remarriage had been hasty, so hasty in fact that to some eyes it might appear to have been planned in advance. As Frances's husband and as manager at Keates's Livery Stables, Thomas Keates would have been ideally placed to renew the lease in March 1805 and then to continue his business for many years. Could his eldest son have imagined that, like Lorenzo in *Isabella*, the former stable hand, raised in the poorhouse, had jealous rivals in London 'well nigh mad / That he, the servant of their trade designs' (164–5) had moved 'much above his sphere in life'?[22] There is some evidence that Keats came to suspect as much, principally in the way that he altered Boccaccio's story in framing his poem. In Boccaccio, Lorenzo's murder arises from his 'scandalous' love for Isabella, and occurs when he merely 'fortuned' to be riding with her brothers. In Keats's version his murder is actively plotted by the brothers with 'pride and gainful cowardice', and Keats even inserts an apology to Boccaccio 'For venturing syllables that ill beseem / The quiet glooms of such a piteous theme' (151–2).[23] It is as if Keats hijacked Boccaccio's story in order to relay his suspicions of a family tragedy that involved a clandestine affair – like that of Guzman's parents   and a conspiracy to do away with his father. The symmetries between his poem and the events of 1804 are of course not exact, but perhaps they are sufficiently close to indicate how early misfortunes were continuing to shadow his imagination.

Six weeks after he completed *Isabella*, Keats made his only overt reference to 'the early loss of our parents and . . . earlier Misfortunes' while explaining to Bailey how his intense attachment to his brothers had 'stifled the impression that any woman might otherwise have made upon me'. 'I am certain I have not a right feeling towards Women', he confided in July 1818, explaining that he was 'full of Suspicions' on account of 'being disappointed since Boyhood' – a reference to his small stature, 'Mister John Keats five feet hight'. Much later in the year he returned to the idea of 'stifled' responses when he said that he had been obliged to 'smother' his feelings, that he lived 'under an everlasting restraint', that he had 'suspected every Body'.[24] Taken together, these circumstances and suspicions might, if true, explain why the outwardly charming and engaging John Keats had depths within him of rancorous, Hamlet-like brooding, why he could plummet from periods intense activity into weeks of helpless lassitude. Of the Keats children, he was the only one who resembled his father in looks, and he admitted to a 'gordian complication of feelings' about women 'which must take time to unravel and care to keep unravelled', adding darkly: 'I could say a good deal about this.' He had already hinted that the 'only way' to 'unravel' this complication was 'to find the root of evil, and cure it, "with backward mutters of dissevering Power"'. Evidently the 'cure' he had in mind related to circumstances in the past, while his salutary quotation was drawn from Milton's masque, *Comus*, in which a 'false enchanter' ensnares a virtuous woman. Perhaps this was his way of acknowledging what he could not bring himself to confront directly – that his adored mother, Frances, had been entangled in an affair while married to his father. Joseph Severn remembered: 'Keats used to say that his great misfortune had been that from his infancy he had no mother.' Taken literally, this hints at some very early desertion by Frances, before her husband's untimely death.[25]

As Keats drew to the end of his 3 May letter to Reynolds, he compared life to a 'large Mansion of many Apartments', an allusion to the Gospel of St John and also a reminder of that mansion of knowledge – the British Museum. From an 'infant or thoughtless Chamber', we are impelled by an 'awakening of the thinking principle' into a second 'Chamber of Maiden-Thought' where we become 'intoxicated with the light and atmosphere'. This 'breathing', Keats says, is 'father' of a tremendous effect, that of 'sharpening one's vision into the head and nature of Man – of convincing ones nerves that the World is full of Misery and Heartbreak, Pain, Sickness and oppression'. Keats immediately deleted 'head' and inserted 'heart', but the close juxtaposition of 'breathing', 'father', 'head' and 'Heartbreak' gathers the circumstances and consequences of his parents' early deaths into a vision of life as he had so far experienced it. Life, Keats says, is a gloaming advance that reveals 'many doors . . . set open— but all dark—all leading to dark passages—We see not the ballance of good and evil.'[26] And then, recollecting perhaps what he had written about going 'the same steps as the Author', he leads Reynolds back to Wordsworth and 'Tintern Abbey':

> We are in a Mist—*We* are now in that state—We feel the 'burden of the Mystery.' To this point was Wordsworth come, as far as I can conceive when he wrote 'Tintern Abbey' and it seems to me that his Genius is explorative of those dark Passages. Now if we live, and go on thinking we too shall explore them. He is a Genius and superior [to] us, in so far as he can, more than we, make discoveries, and shed a light in them—Here I must think Wordsworth is deeper than Milton.[27]

As Keats moves from 'dark Passages' of Wordsworth's genius to the idea of living or voyaging in a 'Mist', he suggests our present inability to analyse life's compounding of good and evil. That he returns to the language of his medical training, and ideas of *mist.* and *mistura* to diagnose the ills of existence, is significant, for it suggests he is already thinking of poems as a form of therapy and of the poet as a physician. He goes on to contrast the historical circumstances of Milton and Wordsworth, arguing that the latter's genius – appearing in the present age – is evidence of a 'grand march of intellect', and then winds up this extraordinary letter of intense, imaginative speculation with a promise to copy out *Isabella* for Reynolds.

Wordsworth had been on Keats's mind throughout his weeks at Teignmouth, and this final letter for Reynolds from there sets out his intellectual and poetic allegiance to the older poet while pointing to a deeper, more personal identification. He was literally claiming that he had followed the same path as Wordsworth, lived through similar experiences, and so could explain for Reynolds his understanding of the point at which Wordsworth had arrived in 'Tintern Abbey' ('*We* are now in that state'). Keats thinks he has attained a kind of existential platform – as Wordsworth had done – from which he too might make poetical forays into the 'dark Passages' of his own life. As Keats knew, in his 'Preface' to *The Excursion*, Wordsworth had identified his minor poems as 'little cells, oratories, and sepulchral recesses' that formed parts of a much larger and more ambitious work. That masterwork was Wordsworth's unfinished philosophical magnum opus, *The Recluse*; for Keats, by analogy, poetical forays into the 'dark Passages' of his life would be preparatory to his attempt on the epic in *Hyperion*.

Unmentioned in this letter is a real, tragic resemblance between the two poets of which Keats, I suspect, may have been aware from their recent meetings in London. Like Keats, Wordsworth had been orphaned while a schoolboy. His mother, Ann, had died in March 1778 of pneumonia and his father, John, five years later at Christmas 1783. Like Thomas Keates, John Wordsworth was taken ill while riding at night, and their sons had learned of their deaths at school. Keats could not have known that Wordsworth had transformed his father's death into one of the strangest 'spots of time' in his autobiographical epic, *The Prelude*. But if he had indeed been aware of the heart-rending losses they had in common, it would have brought home to him the similarity between his own circumstances in May 1818 – fourteen years after Thomas Keates's death – and Wordsworth's in July 1798, when he wrote 'Tintern Abbey' fourteen years after his own father had died.

Keats and Tom left Teignmouth on Monday, 4 May. Their parting from Sarah and Marian Jeffrey was more formal than it might have been had Dr Turton not come along too to bid his patient farewell.[28] The Jeffrey girls had been close to all three brothers, and may have hoped for more; years later Marian – now Mrs Prowse – published a poem, 'Autumnal Musings', that echoed Keats and alluded sadly to 'first aspirings of the Poet's mind' and a 'tardy Spring' that led only to polite friendship.[29] At Honiton, Keats sent a note thanking Mrs Jeffrey and reporting that, so far, Tom had borne the journey well. As they continued their long haul to London they had hopes of being there within a day – but that was not to be. After a few miles of cold air and jolting roads Tom coughed up so much blood that they were forced to get off the coach at Bridport and rest until he recovered. They would not arrive back at Well Walk until Sunday the 10th, almost a week after they had set off. 'Lord what a Journey I had and what a relief at the end of it,' Keats wrote. 'I'm sure I could not have stood it many more days.'[30] He flung himself into visits and dinners with friends not seen for two months: Reynolds, Brown, Dilke, Haydon, Hazlitt, Thomas Barnes (editor of *The Times*), Taylor and Hessey, and the painters David Wilkie and Severn.

If Keats was not already aware, it was now that he heard that George and Georgiana Wylie would marry. Unemployed since quitting Abbey's, George had turned twenty-one and come into his inheritance. America was an attractive prospect: property could be bought cheaply, and George planned to become a farmer.[31] This was no wild and wonderful project like Coleridge and Southey's plan to establish Pantisocracy in Pennsylvania. Morris Birkbeck's practical handbook for emigrants, *Letters from Illinois*, had just been published by Taylor and Hessey; George borrowed a copy, and in it he discovered both the 'power of capital' in America and Birkbeck's 'liberal plan' for a settlement of 1,440 acres. Keats echoed this in a letter informing Bailey that George, who was 'too independent and liberal' to get on in London, would purchase '1400 hundred Acres of the American Government'.[32] George had a good head for figures and a businesslike mind. For him, the romance of emigration was completely realistic.

The three brothers had supported each other since November 1816, when John joined George and Tom at Cheapside; for longer if one counts their time together at school in Enfield. Keats's earliest poems were fraternal addresses to his brothers, and their belief in his genius had been unwavering. They had helped see his first book through the press and George, in particular, had always shielded him from worldly demands, protecting him for poetry. Now all that would change. George's future lay across the Atlantic. Tom, who was in a 'lingering state', also talked of travelling – he would go to Pavia to acquire 'knowledge and strength', although it was obvious that he was destined for the grave.[33]

Keats felt numb. About George's wedding he was 'stony-hearted'. Even Bailey's news that he had written a review of *Endymion* stirred no interest. If the immediate wrench was George's marriage and departure, his depression also stemmed from the emotional and physical exhaustion of caring for Tom at Teignmouth and their gruelling journey back. He still planned a four-month walking tour of Scotland as far as 'John o Grots', and Brown had agreed to go with him. But Keats was not in good health or spirits, scarcely able to do more than lounge under the trees that lined Well Walk. By early June he was positively ill and confined to the house. From now on, he would display signs of a chronic tendency to chest infections – a consequence of travelling outside on coaches, and weeks shut inside with Tom. 'I have been too often in a state of health that made me think it prudent not to hazard the night air,' he later admitted, aware that he should be more careful.[34] With Tom sinking under the family disease, his own symptoms gave cause for urgent concern. Evidently he was worried by his lungs' susceptibility to cold night air, and, as we have seen, Hunt was convinced that he had inherited this and other weaknesses from his mother.

Deep in lethargy, Keats did not mention *Endymion*'s first favourable review in his correspondence. It appeared in the *Literary Journal* for 17 and 24 May, and praised his poem's 'beautiful simplicity', 'warmth of feeling' and 'tender-ness of expression'. A 'vivid imagination and refined mind' were acknowl-edged, and Hunt's influence noted and not faulted. All of this amounted to 'most unqualified approbation', but clouds were gathering.[35] 'I have been calling this Morning on Mr. Gifford,' Taylor reported on 15 May. He had heard that this notorious Tory satirist was working on an article about Keats and Shelley and, fearing the worst, had attempted to defend Keats from attack because of his 'Connexion with Hunt'.[36] But Taylor had been misinformed. John Murray, publisher of the *Quarterly Review*, had in fact commissioned John Wilson Croker, sent him both of Keats's books and advised him that Keats's talent had been 'misdirected if not destroyed by Hunt'.[37] Poet, politi-cian and man of letters, Croker had tastes that were staunchly traditional; for him, Pope and Dryden, giants of earlier epochs, represented an apex of poetic achievement. The stakes were clear, and Croker had already set to work.

In the event publication of April's *Quarterly Review* would be delayed until the autumn and, meanwhile, Bailey placed two enthusiastic notices of Keats's 'rising genius' in *The Oxford University and City Herald*. Bailey's assiduous correspondence with Taylor this spring mingled acclaim for Keats with his own attempts at rising to 'a Curacy ... in the Diocese of Carlisle'. His praise for Keats was not disinterested: 'the Bishop of C— has promised to ordain me,' Taylor heard. 'Could you serve me at all in this?'[38] As usual Bailey had his own agenda and Keats, gratified by his 'honourable simplicity', was also clear-sighted about what lay ahead: 'another blow up against Hunt' in May's issue of *Blackwood's* had made slighting reference to that 'amiable but infatuated bardling, Mister John Keats'.[39] *Blackwood's* 'blow up' was already against him too.

There were some brighter prospects. An attempt to ridicule *Endymion's* 'demi-celestial amour' in the *British Critic* coincided with a genuinely perceptive review in *The Champion*. While 'modern poets' like Wordsworth are a 'universal presence in their poems', Keats 'goes out of himself': 'his passions, feelings, are all as much imaginative as his situations. Neither is it the mere outward signs of passions that are given: there seems ever present some being that was equally conscious of its internal and most secret imaginings.' A few lines later came this more audacious suggestion: 'When [Keats] writes of passion, it seems to have possessed him. This, however, is what Shakespeare did, and if *Endymion* bears any general resemblance to any other poem in the language, it is to *Venus and Adonis* on this very account'.[40] The reviewer was evidently familiar with *Endymion* before publication, and had paused to assess other reviews before venturing on his own. There is evidence as well that this reviewer may have discussed poetry directly with Keats or with his publishers Taylor and Hessey. All of these factors point to Reynolds or, more likely, Woodhouse as the author. Others might blame the 'voluptuousness' of Keats's poems and his connection with Hunt, but in *The Champion* Keats was already with Shakespeare.

For Keats, Shakespeare and Scotland were strikingly combined in London's most popular theatrical attraction. Throughout May, comedian Charles Mathews was packing the English Opera House with his annual one-man show and an entertainment called 'Mail-Coach Adventures during a Journey to the North'. Got up in Scottish garb, Mathews mimicked

> an old Scotch woman . . . and while she tells her story of 'the poor dear mon', her late husband . . . you might really think you were sitting with her in an inn-room, and attending to the calm old gossiping of a grey-haired Scotch-woman, with her failing memory, her kindly noddings and winkings, and her feeble up and down tone, half faltering, and half decided.[41]

In the audience with George, Keats was impressed by Mathew's knack with character and turns of phrase. Witnessing the performance just days before he set off for Scotland, what he saw suggested how he might write up his Scottish tour. The long journal-letters he planned to send to Tom, George and Georgiana would display all the dramatic variety of songs, poems, mimicry and local colour he had seen on stage. And he anticipated that his correspondence would circulate among a wider audience of friends.[42] Keats's journal-letters are, in effect, his own one-man show – a narrative by turns comic, descriptive, political, lyrical, sublime – and he actually transposes Mathew's phrase 'poor dear mon' into the 'good MONY sensible things' that Burns wrote. In transcribing this letter long afterwards, Woodhouse underlined 'MONY' to show it was correct.

As they walked through Bloomsbury down to the Strand, Keats had encountered Isabella Jones. It was a year since their liaison at Hastings, and since then she had extended her contacts among Keats's circle of friends. George and Reynolds had met her while Keats was away at Teignmouth, and she had had a copy of *Endymion* from John Taylor. Occurring close to her home in Gloucester Street, this encounter was a coincidence like their first meeting at Hastings. But perhaps Keats noticed that George's presence seemed to make Isabella wary, for he later remarked on how assiduous she was in keeping her various acquaintances separate.[43]

George and Georgiana were married at St Margaret's, Westminster on Thursday, 28 May, then pushed ahead with their plan to emigrate. A week later George cashed the stock willed to him by his grandmother; prices had risen since the postwar slump of 1815–16 and George's share realised more than £1,600. He immediately deposited £500 cash in Keats's account with Abbey, some of which was to clear his own debts and the balance to go to his brothers. 'Life must be undergone,' Keats wrote grimly to Bailey on 10 June, but a playful letter to the two Jeffrey girls reveals he now had sufficient funds to joke about taking 'a pinch of snuff every five Minutes'. Despite 'a little indisposition', he had been able to call on George and Georgiana in their temporary home at 28 Judd Street, Brunswick Square.[44]

Preparing for his Scottish tour was proving a 'hard run' as the day for setting out drew closer. On 19 and 20 June, a Friday and Saturday, he was at Abbey's twice to draw £170 cash for himself and Tom, then on Sunday evening he dashed off two farewell notes. One went to Taylor: 'Au revoir! God keep us all well.—I start tomorrow morning. My Brother Tom will I am afraid be lonely.' He requested books and copies of *Endymion* for Tom and Reynolds's mother, and asked to be remembered to Hilton, De Wint and Woodhouse. A second message went to Thomas Monkhouse, gratified by his pleasure at *Endymion* and anticipating a visit to Wordsworth at Rydal Mount: 'I shall set out tomorrow morning.'[45] There were departures on the public scene too. Parliament had been dissolved for the general election.

* * *

At Wentworth Place, Brown made arrangements to let his house over the summer. His tenant would be Mrs Frances Brawne, widow of Samuel Brawne of West End, Hampstead, and her three children. By birth and marriage Mrs Brawne was well connected. Her family, the Ricketts, were colonial administrators in Jamaica and Barbados, and her father, wealthy John Ricketts, had City concerns and estates in Kent. Her brother had prospered as a cheesemonger, and her two sisters both married to advantage. Samuel Brawne's father had kept the Coach and Horses on Castle Street, off the Strand, and, like John Jennings, he had invested in property. As Frances's future husband, however, Samuel did not meet with approval and when they married at Hampstead on 13 November 1799 her father did not attend. For ten years they lived variously at West End (a hamlet near Hampstead), Ealing and Kentish Town, where in April 1810 Samuel died of consumption. Left in the care of their mother were three children: Frances (Fanny), born on 9 August 1800; Samuel, born on 26 July 1804; and Margaret, born on 10 April 1809. Thereafter the young family stayed with relatives at Croydon, Ashurst and Stoke Newington, gaining financial security when the cheesemonger left £1,100 to his sisters and £1,500 in trust for the Brawne children. They are next heard of in June 1818, arriving to summer at Wentworth Place. By now Fanny was eighteen, young Samuel fourteen, and Margaret nine.[46]

∗ ∗ ∗

On Monday the 22nd Keats, Brown, George and Georgiana were at the Swan with Two Necks to wait for the Liverpool coach. They made an odd group. George in business clothes and Georgiana in girlish dress were busy loading packages. Alongside Keats's stocky fur-capped figure, Brown stood tall and outlandish in white hat, glasses, and tartan coat and trousers. Both men were equipped with a walking stick, strong shoes and a knapsack containing pens, ink and paper. To these Keats added Cary's translation of *The Divine Comedy* – three tiny volumes, recently reissued by Taylor and Hessey – a shirt, some towels, a cap, hairbrush, comb, new stockings and a supply of snuff.[47]

Back at Well Walk, ill and alone, Tom scribbled a note to Taylor. Keats had forgotten to request a copy of *Endymion* for Severn: 'M$^r$ S. will call at your house for one.'[48] Tom would be cared for by the Bentleys and visited by the Dilkes, Haslam and other acquaintances. On one occasion, hearing that Dilke had a minor ailment, Tom walked into Hampstead and bought cherries for him. He tried to keep himself occupied, neatly endorsing Keats's letters with the dates they were received and answered.[49] But as his brothers left variously for Scotland and America, Tom must have wondered if he would see either of them again.

# CHAPTER 16

---

# Walking North

I: *Sad work at Appleby!*

THIRTY MILES from Tom and Hampstead, the party paused at the Bull Inn, Redbourn. Henry Stephens had set up a medical practice here, and there was just time enough for him and Keats to meet and discover how sharply their lives had diverged.[1] One was settled, respectable, beginning to make a living; the other was a bohemian poet on the highway north, confronting the country surgeon he might himself have become. Their encounter highlighted Keats's decision to commit himself to poetry, and that ambition would set the tone for the tour ahead. In many ways this extraordinary adventure was an epic projection of boyhood rambles around Edmonton, and as he moved further north memories of his childhood would revive in his letters and poems as never before.

One reason for this was that the brothers were separating. By turning to the past, Keats kept in touch with the survival group that had sustained him up to now, and by sharing his memories with Fanny and Georgiana, he drew them both into the circle too. An acrostic he composed for Georgiana, 'Give me your patience', begins each line with the letters of GEORGIANA AUGUSTA KEATS and turns in a final stanza to the origin of her new surname:

> Kind sister! aye, this third name says you are;
> Enchanted has it been the Lord knows where.
> And may it taste to you like good old wine,
> Take you to real happiness and give
> Sons, daughters, and a home like honied hive.
> (17–21)

Nourishing wine and honey alert us to what Keats felt had been withdrawn from his childhood – a home of 'real happiness' that he now wishes for Georgiana as she begins life with his brother. As Keats headed north he would be looking to his own future, too, and poetic possibilities that might indeed make the name 'Keats' savour as richly as the old wine of Chapman's Homer.

Their coach rattled on overnight through Towcester, Coventry and Lichfield, and throughout the next day until they arrived, shaken and weary, at the Crown Inn, Liverpool. That night they dined together and said their farewells. Keats and Brown would rise early and take a coach for Lancaster.

Next day, Wednesday the 24th, George set about booking a passage to America. For some weeks *Gore's General Advertiser* had been announcing the 'fine first-class American Ship TELEGRAPH', captain Hector Coffin: a streamlined copper hull ensured a swift transatlantic crossing, and accommodation on board was 'very superior', with two cabins and twelve state rooms. George secured one of the cabins and, with the ship already cleared to sail, he and Georgiana went aboard with their bed, bedding and five packages of possessions. Also joining the *Telegraph* were another fifty-two emigrants and a cargo of iron.[2] They remained at anchor for thirteen days before a fair wind on 7 July enabled them to hoist sail for Philadelphia.

At Lancaster, Keats and Brown mingled with crowds of voters. With polls due to open there was not a bed to be had until they found a private house that would take them in. Next morning their energetic 4am start was stalled for three hours because of heavy rain. Under grey clouds they read Milton's *Samson Agonistes*, then set off on a dismal four-mile trek to breakfast at Bolton-le-Sands. Brown seems to have had a guidebook, possibly the two-volume *Traveller's Guide through Scotland, and its Islands* in the recent edition of 1818. This had a helpful appendix on the roads and sights of the English Lake District, and there are similarities of phrasing in the *Guide* and Keats's and Brown's letters.[3] From now on their daily and weekly routines and steady progress indicate that they were following an itinerary, making detours to visit waterfalls and the shattered remains of medieval castles and abbeys. If sublime mountain scenery had been a strong inducement to make this tour, the Gothic ruins they encountered would prove helpful for Keats's poetry too – perhaps more so than the natural landscape.

Through deluges of rain they trudged on to Burton and found the landlady of the King's Arms in high dudgeon: 'Ah! gentlemen, the soldiers are upon us! The Lowthers had brought 'em here to be in readiness. There'll be sad work at Appleby! There's Mr. Brougham, a great speaker in the house, I understand, comes down to oppose the Lowthers. Dear me! dear me!—at this election time to have soldiers upon us, when we ought to be making a bit of money.'[4]

More than party was at issue, for this election would test family prestige. Backed by William Wordsworth, Robert Southey and the editor of the *Westmorland Gazette,* Thomas De Quincey, Lord Lonsdale was contesting two seats for the Tories against Henry Brougham's challenge for the Whigs. Hitherto Lonsdale's candidates had been returned as a matter of course, and in 1818 his sons Viscount William Lowther and Colonel Henry Lowther were standing. But Brougham was a force to be reckoned with. Who would win?

Like the Lowthers, Brougham belonged to an ancient Westmorland family. Born at Edinburgh on 19 September 1778, he was a precocious child, excelling at the high school in Edinburgh and matriculating at the university aged just fourteen. Study of humanity, philosophy and law led to an uncongenial stint at the Scottish Bar during which he helped launch *The Edinburgh Review.* His notice of Byron's first volume, *Hours of Idleness,* ridiculing the 'young lord' for 'pleading minority', was one of many critical salvoes he would unleash over three decades. Unsuccessful on the Scottish circuit, Brougham set off for London, read Law at Lincoln's Inn and was called to the English Bar. His legal reputation was established in February 1811 by his brilliant defence of the Hunt brothers, on trial for seditious libel in an article about the horrors of military flogging. That acquittal was followed in 1812 by a guilty verdict for Hunt's 'Adonis in loveliness' libel on the regent. Treating this outcome as 'a victory in the circumstances' (there was no doubt about what Hunt had written and printed), Brougham shifted his relationship with the brothers from law to letters, and supplied so much material for *The Story of Rimini* that he was almost a co-author.

As an *Examiner* reader, Keats's sympathies were firmly with Brougham in this contest between privilege and the people. 'The LOWTHERS ... can represent none but themselves and the tax-gatherers,' Hunt warned the Westmorland electors: 'Brougham will represent *you*.'[5] But *The Examiner's* connection with Brougham also reminded Keats of the trouble his own connection with Hunt had brought, and the onslaught he anticipated from Z.[6]

That night they found an inn at the village of Endmoor, and passed an evening talking with a local drunk, Richard Radshaw, who 'ballanced himself as well as he could saying with his nose right in M[r] Brown's face "Do—you sell Spect—ta—cles?"' Brown later related this man's tragic history at length.[7] The next day, Friday the 26th, they breakfasted at Kendal and walked west to fashionable Bowness, Windermere, and the mountains: 'they surpass my expectation,' Keats wrote to Tom, 'beautiful water—shores and islands green to the marge—mountains all around up to the clouds.' Enquiring after Wordsworth, Keats was informed that he had been there canvassing for the Lowthers. 'What think you of that—,' he continued to Tom, 'Wordsworth versus Brougham!! Sad—sad—sad.' More disappointed than surprised, Keats tried to make allowance: 'and yet the family has been his friend always. What can we say?' He still hoped to see Wordsworth in person and, after dining on fresh trout, he and Brown set off along a winding lakeside lane to Ambleside and the Salutation Inn. Here Keats attempted to describe for Tom the extraordinary effect of Windermere, sighted first from Bowness and now from Ambleside at the lake's northern extremity: 'the two views we have had of it are of the most noble tenderness—they can never fade away—they make one forget the divisions of life; age, youth, poverty and riches; and refine one's vision into a sort of north star which can never cease to be open lidded and stedfast over the wonders of the great Power.'[8] Harking back to the opening lines of *Endymion* while also looking forward to 'Ode to a Nightingale', Keats's letter acknowledges the locality's genius, Wordsworth, whose *Excursion* contained an image of 'the Polar Star ... / ... that never closed / His steadfast eye'.[9] This letter suggests how Wordsworth's influence was helping Keats 'refine' his vision of an ideal constancy. Although his 'Bright Star' sonnet was not composed now, that poem does recall the 'noble tenderness', human feeling and star-like steadfastness he associated with this first day at the Lakes.

Saturday the 27th saw them make a late start at 6am – 'we call it a day of rest', Keats explained. They walked out before breakfast to Stock Ghyll waterfalls and Keats later sketched the scene for Tom:

We, I may say, fortunately, missed the direct path, and after wandering a little, found it out by the noise—for, mark you, it is buried in trees, in the bottom of the valley—the stream itself is interesting throughout with 'mazy error over pendant shades'. Milton meant a smooth river—this is buffeting all the way on a rocky bed ever various—but the waterfall itself, which I came suddenly upon, gave me a pleasant twinge. First we stood a little below the head about half way down the first fall, buried deep in trees, and saw it streaming down two or more descents to the depth of near fifty feet—then we went on a jut of rock nearly level with the second fall-head, where the first fall was above us, and the third below our feet still—at the same time we saw that the water was divided by a sort of cataract island on whose other side burst out a glorious stream—then the thunder and the freshness. At the same time the different falls have as different characters; the first darting down the slate-rock like an arrow; the second spreading out like a fan—the third dashed into a mist—and the one on the other side of the rock a sort of mixture of all these. We afterwards moved away a space, and saw nearly the whole more mild and silverly through the trees.[10]

Owing little to conventional picturesque description, Keats's account conveys his delight at water buffeting, streaming, darting and 'dashed into a mist'. Brown recalled how Keats 'scrambled down lightly and quickly' amid the rocks and cataracts, just as he clambered along rubbly undercliff at Teignmouth.[11] As always with Keats, water created a glorious torrent of poetry too. Here, he reminded Tom of the river that flows through Eden in *Paradise Lost*, caught Hunt's voice in 'thunder and freshness' and also, perhaps, young Wordsworth in quest of a cuckoo's wandering voice – a voice that Keats would echo in the song of his own nightingale, 'buried deep', like this magnificent waterfall, in 'the next valley-glades'.

As Keats walked back to a 'Monstrous Breakfast', he reflected on 'the tone, the coloring, the slate, the stone, the moss, the rock weed' and what he termed 'the intellect, the countenance of the place'. Far from being overawed by its grandeur, he felt he learned poetry there and would 'write more than ever' from his wish to add 'a mite to that mass of beauty'. In a telling reversal of the moment when he had 'hoisted himself up' in burly salute to Spenser, amid mountains and lakes he was no longer self-conscious about his height. 'I never forgot my stature so completely—I live in the eye; and my imagination, surpassed, is at rest'.[12]

With breakfast done and the letter to Tom dispatched, they set off for Wordsworth's house, turned up the steep lane to Rydal Mount, knocked at the door and were admitted. Wordsworth was away at Lowther Hall for the election. Keats 'looked thoughtful' at this news, wrote a note for the poet of 'Resolution and Independence', and left it on the parlour mantelpiece.[13]

After viewing Rydal Falls, they took the road along the shores of Rydal Water and Grasmere, crossed Dunmail Raise – then, as now, 'a defile of tree-less mountains' – and dropped down to the Nag's Head, Wythburn, where they slept in flea-ridden beds.[14] Long since drowned by Thirlmere reservoir, Wythburn has vanished except for a chapel that still stands at the beginning of the path up Helvellyn. After rain in the night, Sunday the 28th dawned misty and drizzling. To climb Helvellyn was impossible, so they quick-marched eight miles on to Keswick, breakfasted at the Oak Inn and made a twelve-mile circuit of Derwentwater taking in the Falls of Lodore. They were back at Keswick for dinner, then set out again a mile and a half uphill to see the 'Druid temple' at Castlerigg. Although Keats knew Southey's poems well, especially *Thalaba the Destroyer*, he expressed no inclination to call on him at Greta Hall, and retired to bed 'rather fatigued'.[15] Perhaps it was now that he opened his copy of Dante's *Inferno* and read in canto five of Minos presiding over the torment of those 'carnal sinners' Cleopatra, Helen and Francesca of Rimini. This canto was Hunt's source for *The Story of Rimini* and it would haunt Keats in coming days, influencing his response to Robert Burns's Dumfries.

He got little rest. Rising at four to climb Skiddaw, Brown and Keats 'fagged and tugged nearly to the top', from where they could see Dumfries and Galloway, the Irish Sea, Helvellyn, Scafell and as far south as Lancaster and the Pennines. It grew colder as they ascended, stirruped up with rum, until mist shut out the view. Although they did not gain the summit, Keats was elated: mountain air had produced 'that same elevation, which a cold bath gives one—I felt as if I were going to a Tournament.' After Skiddaw they walked on to Ireby, said to be Cumberland's oldest market town, where they were entertained by a country dancing school at the Sun Inn: 'they kickit & jumpit with mettle extraordinary, & whiskit, & fleckit, & toe'd it, & go'd it, & twirl'd it, & wheel'd it, & stampt it, & sweated it, tattooing the floor like mad.' There were 'some beautiful faces, & one exquisite mouth'.[16] Hunt's image of Francesca of Rimini, 'lips / All trembling kissed', was still haunting him.

Tuesday the 30th. They pressed on through Wigton to Carlisle, where Keats found a letter from Georgiana. The castle and cathedral did not impress, and on the next day they took a coach thirty-eight miles across the border to Dumfries. Keats's coat was torn and his thighs were aching and feet blistered, so the respite was welcome. As they sped through the Solway landscape, his mood darkened. Barefooted girls and hovels with smoke drifting from doors were signs of Scotland's poverty, but what shocked most was a pervasive, sullen mood of oppression. Bailey's yawning bishops were bad enough, but the dour Presbyterian 'kirkmen' who had banished merriment and had persecuted Burns were worse still.

## II: *In the Bardies Country*

At Dumfries they visited the Bard's domed mausoleum in its corner of St Michael's churchyard, and had hopes of seeing his widow. They had anticipated little difference between English and Scottish towns, but Dumfries seemed curiously alien: 'the Clouds, the sky, the Houses, all seem anti Grecian & anti Charlemagnish.'[17] The place was cold and solemn, Brown thought, and Keats's uneasy mood found expression in a sonnet, 'On Visiting the Tomb of Burns':

> The Town, the churchyard, & the setting sun,
> The Clouds, the trees, the rounded hills all seem
> Though beautiful, Cold—strange—as in a dream,
> I dreamed long ago, now new begun

The shortlived, paly summer is but won
From winters ague, for one hours gleam;
Through saphire warm, their stars do never beam,
All is cold Beauty; pain is never done.
For who has mind to relish Minos-wise,
The real of Beauty, free from that dead hue
Fickly imagination & sick pride
Cast wan upon it! Burns! With honor due
I have oft honoured thee. Great shadow; hide
Thy face, I sin against thy native skies.[18]

Burns's personality was 'southern', Keats felt – warm, sensual, luxurious. His misfortune was to live in a nation dominated by a kirk that persecuted human passion exactly as Dante's vision of judgement had damned Francesca and her lover, Paulo. Keats's identification with Burns arose partly from his own sense of displacement. Dilke heard from Brown that Keats spent 'five hours abusing the Scotch', yet this prejudice was not a thoroughgoing antipathy and a more considered analysis of Scottish character would follow.[19] His letters show him delighting in the Scottish landscape, while his ballad 'Old Meg she was a Gipsey' celebrated a woman who was as free a spirit as the Scottish patriot William Wallace. Just once Keats allows us to glimpse a formative association from his childhood, when he mentions how he had thought Burns's landscape was 'desolate . . . but a few strips of Green on a cold hill'.[20] It seems likely that as a boy Keats linked Scotland with 'strips of Green' because of his grandparents' home at Scotland Green, an association later overlaid with feelings of orphaned misery that now coloured his ideas of Scotland and Burns.

Early on Thursday, 2 July, Keats left his tattered coat at the menders and went two miles out of town to view Lincluden Priory – the first of many such visits on their tour. What he found beside Burns's River Nith was a crumbling sandstone ruin, all that was left of a Benedictine nunnery founded in 1160. Overhead were high Gothic windows let into walls with recessed tombs and other niches, narrow doorways framed by carved tracery and deep vaulted cells. Wrecked during the Reformation in 1560, Lincluden was rebuilt as a domestic residence, becoming a private mansion with an elaborate pleasure garden. Abbey and priory ruins usually included cloisters and domestic quarters, but here at Lincluden the juxtapositions of spirituality and worldliness, austerity and delight, were more sharply delineated. Already inspired by the passionate contraries of Burns's life and work, Keats found at Lincluden a complex Gothic structure that physically embodied them. It would be some months before these associations took possession of Keats's imagination but already, under Burns's native skies, the structure, textures and tones of *The Eve of St Agnes* were starting to form.

On returning to Dumfries, Keats started a letter to his sister telling her that he and Brown had been variously mistaken for travelling jewellers, razor-sellers and spectacle-vendors. He broke off when his coat returned 'fortified at all points', and the two men immediately set out for Dalbeattie. Here – despite a fast day appointed by the Kirk – they met with a hospitable welcome from Mr Murray, a one-legged publican who advised them on their route to Kirkcudbright. They would be 'enchanted with it'.[21]

He was right. Brown records that on Friday, 3 July they walked through corn-fields and forests, turning aside to explore the twelfth-century Cistercian abbey at Dundrennan with its finely executed door in the north transept and massive bundled-shaft pillars – a structure that Keats studied carefully. Back on the road, they headed on to Kirkcudbright's winding bay, woody hills, blue moun-tains and fertile valley.[22] Their bleak impressions of Dumfries lightened. Keats in buoyant mood continued his letter to Fanny with 'a song about myself' that shows how this venture north had put him back in touch with his childhood. He scribbled these lines one evening, with a new moon low in the western sky:

> There was a naughty Boy
>     A naughty boy was he
> He would not stop at home
>     He could not quiet be—
>         He took
>         In his knapsack
>         A Book
>         Full of vowels
>         And a shirt
>         With some towels—
>         A slight cap
>         For night cap—
>         A hair brush
>         Comb ditto
>         New Stockings
>         For old ones
>         Would split O!
>         This knapsack
>         Tight at 's back

He revetted close
And followe'd his Nose
To the North
To the North
And follow'd his nose
To the North—

There was a naughty boy
And a naughty boy was he
For nothing would he do
But scribble poetry—
He took
An inkstand
In his hand
And a Pen
Big as ten
In the other
And away
In a Pother
He ran
To the mountains
And fountains
And ghostes
And Postes
And witches
And ditches
And wrote
In his coat
When the weather
Was cool
Fear of gout
And without
When the weather
Was warm—
Och the charm
When we choose
To follow ones nose
To the north
To the north

To follow one's nose to the north!

There was a naughty boy
   And a naughty boy was he
He kept little fishes
   In washing tubs three
      In spite
      Of the might
      Of the Maid
      Nor affraid
      Of his Granny-good—
      He often would
      Hurly burly
      Get up early
      And go
      By hook or crook
      To the brook
      And bring home
      Miller's thumb
      Tittle bat
      Not over fat
      Minnows small
      As the stall
      Of a glove
      Not above
      The size
      Of a nice
      Little Baby's
      Little finger—
      O he made
      'T was his trade
      Of Fish a pretty kettle
      A kettle—a kettle
      Of Fish a pretty kettle
      A kettle!

There was a naughty Boy
   And a naughty Boy was he
He ran away to Scotland
   The people for to see—
      And he found

That the ground
Was as hard
That a yard
Was as long,
That a song
Was as merry,
That a cherry
Was as red—
That lead
Was as weighty
That fourscore
Was as eighty
That a door
Was as wooden
As in england—
So he stood in
His shoes
And he wonderd
He wonderd
He stood in his
Shoes and he wonder'd—[23]

This delightful 'song about myself' gives us the exuberant Keats who partied, played in scatty, improvised orchestras with his friends, and 'worked' glasses of wine – sparkling, tipsy, unpredictable, marvellous company. Separating from his brothers, meeting with Stephens and the Brougham–Hunt link had all encouraged him to glance back, and now his foray into Scotland and memories of Scotland Green had revived Alice Jennings, his 'Granny-good'. Brown tells us that the scenery at Kirkcudbright impressed Keats as 'equal and similar to the best parts of his favourite Devon'. The previous spring Keats had endured weeks of dreadful weather at Teignmouth, and while he enjoyed some days they hardly suggest the phrase 'his favourite Devon'. Could Brown's words mean that he had visited Devon more than once, and that those other visits had established Devon as a favourite? Exactly when these may have occurred is unclear, but his poem for Fanny might indicate the Edmonton and Enfield years, roughly 1805–10. It may be significant, too, that the first chapter of Brown's *Life of John Keats*, drafted at Plymouth and delivered there as a lecture, claimed that his father was 'a native of Devonshire'.[24]

Keats seized any opportunity to add to his journal-letters; his voice has an off-the-cuff immediacy, whereas Brown composed more considered recollections. Their writing habits were different too: Keats set down sentences at odd moments and at any angle whereas Brown, to Keats's amusement, methodically extracted paper, pens and ink from his knapsack, always in that order, before proceeding to write.[25] Like one of Brown's palindromes, no doubt they were scrupulously returned to his knapsack in identical order.

Saturday, 4 July was another day of rest. Perhaps they set off for Gatehouse around six, and then on by the coast road to Creetown, a village with a small port where the landlady confided that 'very few Southrens passed these ways'.[26] Brown was impressed by rows of neat cottages here but to Keats they looked primitive, unlike ones 'up the Devonshire vallies'.[27] Meals did not go far to stave off hunger: Keats mentions a diet of ham, chicken, bread and pork sausages, 'dirty bacon dirtier eggs and dirtiest Potatoes with a slice of Salmon', and water 'diluted with wiskey'.[28] From now on their food would be less nutritious, at times little more than eggs, oatcakes and whisky, and this would soon begin to tell on Keats's health.

Leaving Creetown on 5 July, they walked four miles to Newton Stewart, then followed a military road to a surprisingly comfortable inn at Glenluce. Breakfast next morning was served in a carpeted chamber with upholstered chairs, afterwards they went to see the twelfth-century abbey nearby. Set in a wide, secluded valley were a few fragments of a chapterhouse – at the time Keats visited, the extensive foundations visible today were completely overgrown. Keats judged it not worth going to see and, returning to the main road, they turned right towards Stranraer. After six miles in hot sun a mail coach took them up, spun on to Portpatrick and set them down at the mail packet for Ireland. That night they slept across the water at Mr Kelly's Inn, Donaghadee.

Hearing it was just forty-eight miles to the Giant's Causeway, they determined to scud up to Antrim and back in a week. On Tuesday the 7th as George and Georgiana sailed from Liverpool, Keats and Brown took off on the Belfast road, but what ensued was little more than a 'peep' at the country. Ireland was expensive, the landscape dreary, and the rags, dirt and drunken misery of the poor were too much to bear. A Scottish cottage with smoke coming from its door was a palace compared to an Irish hovel. Turning back, they encountered a figure that seemed to embody the country's wretchedness:

the Duchess of Dunghill—It is no laughing matter tho—Imagine the worst dog kennel you ever saw placed upon two poles from a mouldy fencing—In such a wretched thing sat a squalid old Woman squat like an ape . . . with a pipe in her mouth and looking out with a round-eyed skinny lidded, inanity—with a sort of horizontal idiotic movement of her head—squab and lean she sat and puff'd out the smoke while two ragged tattered Girls carried her along—What a thing would be a history of her Life and sensations.[29]

Fascinated by the woman's grotesque appearance, Keats leapt to the possibility of relating her life and sensations as if aware of his own capacity to write a 'history' utterly different from anything he had yet attempted: perhaps a sketch like Mathews's old Scottish woman, possibly an episode in a novel? Not seeing the Giant's Causeway had freed him to imagine other stories, alternative conclusions, and their sixteen miles back along the shore of Belfast Lough took no time at all. By 8 July they were at Donaghadee, where they crossed with a fair wind to Portpatrick and spent the night there.

Ahead lay the Highlands and the short, gloaming nights of a Scottish summer. From Stranraer their road led along Loch Ryan, dipped inland into pastoral Glen App, then climbed steeply up Carlock Hill. From its crest, Keats was astonished to see the immense rock of Ailsa Craig rearing out of the sea like a submerged mountain. Looming sublime through misty rain, it gave Keats 'a complete Idea of a deluge'. That night they slept badly at Ballantrae – the inn was dirty, the weather stormy – and on Friday, 10 July hurried on thirteen miles to more comfortable quarters at the King's Arms, Girvan.[30] Here Keats wrote for Tom a sonnet depicting Ailsa Craig as a sleeping giant with 'broad forehead' heaved by some mighty power from 'fathom dreams' to 'eagle skies'. *Hyperion* was still only an idea, but this sonnet shows Keats already excited by mythical beings of 'giant size' and elemental forces of earthquake and deluge that had shaped the earth. Exactly as he had hoped, Scotland's landscape was strengthening his 'reach' in poetry. How was it, he wondered, that the wild sea and black mountains of Arran had not beckoned Burns to a 'grand attempt at Epic'?[31] Less obvious to Keats, perhaps, was how Scotland's ruined priories and abbeys were also infiltrating his imagination with their winding passageways, aisles and galleries, cloisters, pillars, effigies, shattered casements and arched doorways.

Saturday, 11 July. Their weekly day of 'rest'. The two men began later than usual, breakfasting after eight miles at the hamlet of Kirkoswald. A few miles further on they explored the remains of thirteenth-century Crossraguel Abbey and nearby Baltersan Castle. There was more to see here than at Glenluce – a gatehouse, chapterhouse, dovecote, abbey church and abbot's residence with what Keats described as 'a winding Staircase to the top of a little Watch Tower'.[32] After dinner at Maybole he began a letter to Reynolds – 'I am approaching Burns's Cottage very fast' – then left off to go nine more miles to Ayr through 'the Bardies Country' and scenes of his great comic poem 'Tam o' Shanter'. Arriving from the south, they came suddenly to the beautiful Auld Brig O' Doon that Tam O'Shanter crossed to escape the witches – 'A running stream they dare na cross'. Keats was amazed by this ancient bridge, 'surrounded by every Phantasy of Green in tree, Meadow, and Hill'; to celebrate, Brown and Keats each took a pinch of snuff on the keystone.[33] Perhaps as Keats stood on this poet's bridge high above a famous salmon river, he recalled his own modest span across Salmons Brook, where he would part from Cowden Clarke after their evenings of poetry.

From the brig they sauntered happily a few yards to the ruin of Kirk-Alloway, 'Where ghaists and houlets nightly cry' and Tam saw 'Warlocks and witches in a dance'. Senses tingling with snuff, Keats contemplated the grave of William Burns and Agnes Brown – the Bard's parents – then went on to the low, thatched cottage where Burns was born. In 1818 this clay-walled farmhouse was still surrounded by the fields Burns had worked with his father.[34]

Keats had looked back with pleasure on his day with Bailey at Shakespeare's Stratford, and anticipated similar feelings now. It was the sense of 'annulling self' at the shrine of a literary giant that particularly pleased, but what confronted him on entering the cottage took him aback. Burns's birthplace, built by his father, was now a 'whiskey-shop' with a drunken custodian who claimed to have known the Bard – a 'great Bore with his Anecdotes'. Keats had determined to write a 'merry' sonnet here, and he succeeded:

> This mortal body of a thousand days
>     Now fills, O Burns, a space in thine own room,
> Where thou didst dream alone on budded bays,
>     Happy and thoughtless of thy day of doom!
> My pulse is warm with thine old barley-bree,
>     My head is light with pledging a great soul,
> My eyes are wandering, and I cannot see,
>     Fancy is dead and drunken at its goal;
> Yet can I stamp my foot upon thy floor,
>     Yet can I ope thy window-sash to find
> The meadow thou hast tramped o'er and o'er,—
>     Yet can I think of thee till thought is blind,—
> Yet can I gulp a bumper to thy name,—
> O smile among the shades, for this is fame!

He came to think this sonnet disappointingly 'flat' because it speaks less of Burns's 'honour due' than of his own high spirits – 'pledging a great soul' over and over until, head reeling, he opened a sash for fresh air and discovered a meadow Burns had 'tramped o'er'. His elation was genuine, however. Only later did it come to resemble his giddy coronation with laurels, prompting a more sober reflection on his ambitions and prospects.

After they left Burns's cottage, Keats, addled with whisky, added nothing to his letters for Reynolds and Tom. They visited Ayr, slept, and the next day – Sunday the 12th – went on to Kilmarnock. Monday morning saw them twelve miles along the Glasgow road before a rainstorm caused them to pause at Kingswell, where Keats resumed his letter to Reynolds. That curator was a drunken jackass who 'ought to be kicked' – imagine Burns attempting to live, and write, in such dismal company:

> His Misery is a dead weight upon the nimbleness of one's quill—I tried to forget it—to drink Toddy without any Care—to write a merry Sonnet—it wont do—he talked with Bitches—he drank with Blackguards, he was miserable—We can see horribly clear in the works of such a man his whole life, as if we were God's spies.[35]

Such was the mystery of things: Burns, a genius of abundant and passionate humanity, had been constrained to live among a pack of narrow-minded drunkards. Significantly, all that Keats recollected of what the curator had said was 'his description of Burns's melancholy the last time he saw him'. Shadowing this idea of the Bard was Wordsworth's depiction of him in 'Resolution and Independence' – a poet who began in 'gladness', now among 'mighty Poets in their misery dead'.[36] And with Wordsworth's lines in mind, Keats was surely also thinking of his own destiny. The grave of William Burns and his poet-son's 'day of doom' had announced with horrible clarity what lay ahead for Keats too, bringing home to him the fickle nature of 'fame' which might amount to no more than a drunkard's trashy chatter. Seen in that bleak light, the inspiring associations of any poet's birthplace were sheer 'flummery'.

Musing on the stark contrasts between Burns's life and his works, Keats was reassessing his own life. He had spoken vehemently against marriage, he tells Reynolds, because his own marriage prospects had seemed 'blank'. Yet he had also felt pleasure in loving his sister-in-law Georgiana, had yearned for Reynolds's happiness and, despite contrary appearances and expressions, had in fact been getting closer to Reynolds every day. He had resolved to care for his own health and advised Reynolds to do so too.[37]

Here, in Keats's letter to Reynolds, is a tentative approach to what he would eventually describe as a 'life of allegory'. It is an enigmatic phrase, suggesting how a life – like Burns's – squandered among bitches and blackguards is not to be taken 'literal'; in the poetry that flowed from it we see – as if we were God's spies – into the mystery of a great human spirit:

> Is there, for honest Poverty
>   That hings his head, an' a' that,

The coward-slave, we pass him by,
   We dare be poor for a' that!
For a' that, an' a' that,
   Our toils obscure, and a' that,
The rank is but the guinea's stamp,
   The Man's the gowd [gold] for a' that.
                ('For a' that and a' that', 1–8)

Keats's father, like Burns's, had been born to honest poverty; and like Burns, Keats, too, had 'Commenc'd a Fornicator'.[38] Feelings of personal inadequacy and lack of experience, coupled with an overwhelming sexual appetite, had driven him to visit whores. Despite those squalid facts, Keats wants Reynolds to know that he, too, is as warm-hearted, enlightened and humane as Burns. He would return to this idea of a life lived figuratively in attempting to characterise another genius – his 'presider', Shakespeare.

### III: *Footsore and Fly-Bitten*

Glasgow came into view on the evening of 13 July – 'very fine', Keats thought it, although its citizens 'turned to wonder at us'.[39] It was probably here that Brown bought a new pair of shoes to help him slog through the Highlands. For two days they footed along the Clyde, through Dumbarton and so to the shores of Loch Lomond where fashionable barouches and hissing steamboats spoiled the silver water and dark purple mountains. Early on the morning of Friday the 17th they turned west around the head of Loch Long, up steep Glen Croe to the stone seat inscribed 'Rest and Be Thankful', then down Glen Kinglass to Cairndow on Loch Fyne. By the time they settled to breakfast they had walked fifteen miles.[40]

There was time to relax. Keats bathed, 'quite pat and fresh', until a gadfly bite unleashed a torrent of 'dudgeon' in his letter to Tom. Election results had been national news since the 7th when the Westmorland poll was printed in the *Morning Chronicle*: Viscount Lowther, 1,211; Colonel Lowther, 1,159; Brougham 889. Writing fast, Keats set down a poem about some better uses for the gadflies bite:

Has any here an old grey Mare
   With three Legs all her store
O put it to her Buttocks bare
   And Straight she'll run on four

Has any here a Lawyer suit
  Of 17, 43
Take Lawyer's nose and put it to 't
  And you the end will see

Is there a Man in Parliament
  Dum founder'd in his speech
O let his neighbour make a rent
  And put one in his breech

O Lowther how much better thou
  Hadst figur'd to'ther day
When to the folks thou madst a bow
  And hadst no more to say

If lucky gad fly had but ta'en
  His seat upon thine A—e
And put thee to a little pain
  To save thee from a worse.

Better than Southey it had been
  Better than M$^r$ D—
Better than Wordsworth too I ween
  Better than M$^r$ V— [41]

Angry and scurrilous, Keats's poem brilliantly bandies numbers, figures, 'seats' and 'measures' to mock Lowther's inept speechmaking and the dismal election outcome. 'Lawyer suit / Of 17, 43' is a witty metrical joke – one is obliged to read 'Of one seven, four three' – which may refer to the 'Broughton Rules' of 1743 to regulate boxing: the match at Appleby was rigged, Keats hints, both unfair and illegal.[42] Southey and Wordsworth had been diminished by association. So had Robert Dundas, First Lord of the Admiralty, and Nicholas Vansittart, Chancellor of the Exchequer – their names vanish into dashes. As a taxing chancellor, 'M$^r$ V—' was an obvious target, and Brougham had been obliged to appeal to 'M$^r$ D—' about electoral bribery.[43]

With Keats smarting from his gadfly bite and Brown's feet badly blistered, they trudged on another eight miles to Inverary where they stopped for the night. While Brown rested Keats went to see August von Kotzebue's popular comedy of seduction and betrayal *The Stranger* acted in a barn, with bagpipe music 'at the heartrending, shoemending reconciliation'. Reynolds had panned this play in *The Champion*, as Keats was aware: 'thank heaven it has been scoffed at lately almost to a fashion.' In this beautiful Highland setting beside Loch Fyne, the play's strangest aspect was its suburban setting near Enfield.[44]

It was now twenty-three days since they had set out from Lancaster. Although Keats did not know it, the full moon on this Friday evening, 17 July, marked the midpoint of their tour. With Brown lamed by new shoes and Keats complaining about 'coarse food', long days on the road had tested their stamina and resolve. Luckily, a thunderstorm prevented an early start the next morning, so Keats began a letter for Bailey until the rain let up and they could pace slowly through Glen Aray. This was a 'complete mountain road' with 'not a sound but that of Mountain Streams' – and the approach to Loch Awe 'very solemn towards nightfall' with two castled islands visible in the gloaming.[45] At Cladich the accommodation and food were awful, and they may have been tempted to take a ferry and follow the direct route to Oban. But Brown rallied on the morning of Sunday the 19th, and they set out to cover twenty miles down Loch Awe, every ten steps 'creating a new and beautiful picture'. It was a tough day. The weather was unsettled, and there was nothing to eat but eggs from roadside cottages. Brown recalled this day as 'one of our pleasantest', but by the time they came to the inn at Ford he was 'scarcely able to walk'.[46] Supper was more eggs with oatcake.

✳ ✳ ✳

Back in Carlisle, Bailey was savouring success. The Bishops' Register reads: 'At a public ordination held at the Chapel, Rose Castle on the 19th July 1818, the Lord Bishop of Carlisle did admit the following persons into Holy Orders viz: Benjamin Bailey entitled to perform the office of Curate of Orton in the County of Cumberland.'[47] Within days Bailey would be dining with another bishop, with momentous consequences for Keats.

✳ ✳ ✳

The next day Keats and Brown fared better. Fortified by roast chicken and a bottle of port, they tracked the craggy coast of Loch Melfort with eagles circling overhead and glimpses of distant mountains.[48] Keats's description of Highland life took flight, too, in this remarkable account of the inn at Kilmelford that night:

> The Inn or public is by far the best house in the immediate neighbourhood—It has a white front with tolerable windows—the table I am writing on suprises me as being a nice flapped Mehogany one; at the same time the place has no water-closet nor anything like it. You may if you peep see through the floor chinks into

the ground rooms. The old Grandmother of the house seems intelligent though not over clean. N.B. No snuff being to be had in the village, she made us some. The Guid Man is a rough looking hardy stout Man who I think does not speak so much English as the Guid wife who is very obliging and sensible and moreover though stockingless, has a pair of old Shoes—Last night some Whisky Men sat up clattering Gælic till I am sure one o'Clock to our great annoyance—There is a Gælic testament on the Drawers in the next room—White and blue China ware has crept all about here—Yesterday there passed a Donkey laden with tin-pots— opposite the Window there are hills in a Mist—a few Ash trees and a mountain stream at a little distance—They possess a few head of Cattle—If you had gone round the back of the House just now—you would have seen more hills in a Mist—some dozen wretched black Cottages Scented of peat smoke which finds its way by the door or a hole in the roof—a girl here and there barefoot.[49]

Keats notices all the noisy material contrasts between native life and London fashions: a mahogany table, floor chinks, old shoes, 'clattering Gælic' and fashionable Chinese-style porcelain that has 'crept all about' like Keats himself – 'gone round the back' to whatever functioned as a lavatory.

The next morning Keats and Brown covered a rainy fifteen miles to Oban, thinking to cross to Mull until – talking with local men – they learned the extortionate cost of doing so: seven guineas.[50] This was like 'paying sixpence for an apple at the playhouse', so they resolved to go on to Fort William the following day. Keats had finished his letter to Tom and posted it, when one of the men came back and after 'a little talk' agreed to guide them to Mull and across the island as far as Iona.

## IV: *The Road of the Dead*

Early on Wednesday, 22 July they crossed the Firth of Lorne to Grass Point on Mull. From the old Drover's Inn the winding 'Pilgrim's Road' led inland to Lochdon, and turned left onto the track up Glen More – 'the most dreary you can think of—between dreary Mountains—over bog and rock and river with our Breeches tucked up and our Stockings in hand'.[51] Glen More is now partly forested, and the cottages where they encountered Mull's kindly, Gaelic-speaking inhabitants are piles of ruined stone. Brown believed that his ancestors came from the Western Isles and 'got a parcel of people about him at a Cottage door [and] chatted with ane who had been a Miss Brown'. Keats thought from her likeness that she must have been a relative, and noticed how amid Mull's wild, elemental landscape the local people handled Brown's spectacles 'as we do a sensitive leaf'.

They spent their first night on Mull in a shepherd's hut under 'rafters and turf thatch blackened with smoke—the earth floor full of Hills and Dales'. Here Keats finished his letter to Bailey by transcribing a peripatetic poem, 'There is a joy in footing slow across a silent plain', looking back over his journey and recasting it as a quest 'To find a Bard's low Cradle place about the silent north'. His buoyant mood brought Wordsworth's 'Resolution and Independence' to mind again:

> I was a Traveller then upon the moor;
> I saw the Hare that raced about with joy;
> I heard the woods, and distant waters, roar;
> Or heard them not, as happy as a Boy:
> The pleasant season did my heart employ:
> My old remembrances went from me wholly;
> And all the ways of men, so vain and melancholy.
>
> (15–21)

Wordsworth's happiness had been disturbed by thoughts of poets succumbing to 'despondency and madness', and Keats was aware, too, of the risks entailed by living too completely in his imagination. With that dismaying reflection came memories of all that might be lost to him 'beyond the Bourn of Care':

> O horrible! To lose the sight of well remember'd face,
> Of Brother's eyes, Of Sister's Brow, constant to every place;
> Filling the Air as on we move with Portraiture intense
> More warm than those heroic tints that fill a Painter's sense—
> When Shapes of old come striding by and visages of old,
> Locks shining black, hair scanty grey and passions manifold.[52]

Keats had started this letter to Bailey with Hamlet-style broodings about women.[53] As he closes it with an echo of Hamlet's 'undiscover'd country from whose bourn/No traveller returns' (III.i.79–80), his poem turns, appropriately, to those among whom he felt no such insecurities. He ranges over what close family still remained to him as well as some ghostly 'visages of old' from times when despondency and madness had been near-neighbours to his own 'low Cradle place' at Keates's Livery Stables. 'Footing slow about the silent north', Keats was also on a journey through his own past and, having visited Burns's cottage, perhaps he almost began to wonder whether posterity would regard Keates's Livery Stables as a bard's 'great birthplace'.

That night Keats and Brown supped on white bread, then tried to sleep while their guide snored 'on another little bed about an Arm's length off'.[54]

*  *  *

While Keats was writing to Bailey about poetic fame, Bailey himself was in Scotland as a guest of the bishop of Brechin, father of his Oxford acquaintance George Gleig. The bishop had helped Bailey to his curacy, and now Bailey would deliver his maiden sermon at his private chapel – he had already met the bishop's daughter, Hamilton, and as usual hoped to impress. At dinner a further introduction followed. Gleig presented a twenty-four-year-old lawyer, John Lockhart, who, Bailey afterwards wrote to Taylor, 'abused poor Keats in a way that, although it was at the Bishop's table, I could hardly keep my temper'. But keep it he did. 'I said I supposed [that Keats] would be attacked in Blackwood's. He replied "not by *me*"; which would carry the insinuation he would by someone else.'[55] Bailey assured Taylor that he could place a defence of Keats if he was '*grossly* attacked', although the tenor of his letter suggests that, led on by his antagonist and overawed by his host, Bailey actually went half way to agreeing with Lockhart. Established in his curacy, Bailey, despite his protestations, was changing his mind about Keats. In April he lauded *Endymion* in the *Oxford Herald*, and Taylor heard of copies sold 'upon the strength of my recommendation'.[56] Now he informed Taylor there were 'two great blotches in it' – an 'indelicacy' sufficient to 'offend *every* one of proper feelings', and 'that abominable principle of Shelley's – that *Sensual Love* is the principle of *things*'. 'I feel convinced *now*', Bailey told Taylor, 'the Poem will not sell'.[57]

Whatever Bailey actually said at the bishop's table, it proved a gift for Keats's assailants. A possible reconstruction of what happened runs like this. Anxious to appear favourably disposed to all present, Bailey had conceded on *Blackwood's* slanders about the 'Cockneys'. Hunt's *Story of Rimini* was 'indelicate', 'unhealthy' and 'diseased', *Blackwood's* had claimed, and – glancing from Lockhart to the bishop and his daughter – Bailey agreed that *Endymion* was 'blotched' too.

The most recent 'Cockney School Essay' had bragged that 'Leigh Hunt is delivered into our hands to do with . . . as we will'. Bailey had done the same for Keats and then, in a blundering attempt to rescue the situation, did further damage. Apprised by Lockhart of an impending attack, Bailey attempted to disentangle Keats from Hunt and the 'Cockney School' while simultaneously inviting Bishop Gleig's interest in him. In doing so, he blabbed out more. Keats's family was 'humble' but 'respectable', the company heard. He was orphaned, had brothers and a sister, and 'had been brought up to the profession of medicine and then abandoned it for the pursuit of Literature'.[58]

Taking pleasure at this 'accident' that had enabled him to defend Keats, Bailey let Taylor know that he would not 'give up any names on the opposite side of the question'.[59] When fellow guest Lockhart set off back to Edinburgh, he was no doubt congratulating himself too. Quizzed a little about rhymes in *Endymion* and Keats's association with Hunt, Bailey had blabbed all that he needed for the August issue of *Blackwood's*.

$$* * *$$

The next day was Thursday, 23 July. Lockhart was back in Edinburgh and Keats was breakfasting at that remote 'mansion' Derry-na-Cullen, where he began a letter to Tom. Fortified for the next stretch of their journey, he and Brown walked west along Loch Scridain to the village of Bunessan, where they bedded down. From here it was just six miles to Fionnphort and a boat across to Iona. Since landing at Grass Point, they had covered thirty-seven miles – 'a most wretched walk', Keats called it.[60]

Iona astonished him. The third book of *Endymion*, set in the depths of the ocean, was written among the colleges and quadrangles of Oxford. Now, here on this tiny island, surrounded by the stormy Atlantic, were 'the ruins of a fine Cathedral Church, of Cloisters, Colleges, Monastaries and Nunneries'. Keats gave Tom a quick history of 'would-be Bishop-saint' Columba's arrival, and how Iona was considered 'the most holy ground of the north'. A well-whiskied schoolmaster showed them

> a spot in the Churchyard where they say 61 kings are buried 48 Scotch from Fergus 2nd to Macbeth 8 Irish 4 Norwegian and 1 french—they lie in rows compact—Then we were shown other matters of later date but still very ancient— many tombs of Highland Chieftains—their effigies in armour face upwards— black and moss covered—Abbots and Bishops of the island always one of the chief Clans ... There have been 300 Crosses in the Island but the Presbyterains destroyed all but two, one of which is a very fine one and completely covered with a shaggy coarse Moss.[61]

The tumbled buildings, cobbled road of the dead and two lichened crosses all contributed to a desolate atmosphere reminiscent of James Macpherson's mournful 'Poems of Ossian'. Surrounding Keats and Brown was an Ossianic landscape of heathland, keening reeds, windswept trees and sea-foam, and here, too, in front of them lay carved stone effigies of kings and warriors – Ossian's 'chiefs of old, the race that are no more'.[62] The Presbyterians' fanatical demolition of the abbey had been as thoroughgoing as the extinction of Ossian's mighty ancestors. In months to come Iona's warriors – valiant men-at-arms who embraced death as eagerly as Burns did women – would make an uncanny reappearance in 'La Belle Dame sans Merci'.

Keats pocketed some pebbles for Fanny, and they hired a boat to take them to Staffa. As the dark entrance of Fingal's Cave came into view between its soaring columns of black basalt rock, it brought to mind the Celtic warrior Fingal – father of bard Ossian, 'last of all his race'. Approaching more closely, Keats noticed a homely detail: 'one may compare the surface of the Island to a roof'. What he meant was that, viewed from the sea, Staffa's peculiar rock formations immediately below the turf looked (and still look) like carefully dressed edges of a thatched roof. Burns's cottage was thatched, and Fingal's Cave would prove to be a poet's house too. They landed and, with the sea dashing below, stepped gingerly along a ledge of broken pillars as far as the cave's inmost point where a gap led into another cavern. 'For solemnity and grandeur it far surpasses the finest Cathedrall,' Keats informed Tom. So extraordinary were the rock formations, they seemed carved by 'Giants who rebelled against Jove', a reference that suggests he was thinking of his projected epic, *Hyperion*. Also on his mind – as we will see – was the tremendous influence of poets' fathers: of Fingal, father of Ossian; Jupiter, father of the Nine Muses; William Burns, father of Robert; and of his own father, Thomas Keates.[63]

They sailed onwards to the head of Loch na Keal and, back on Mull, walked to Salen, a little port where they stayed before crossing back to Oban. The next day, Sunday the 26th, Keats completed his letter to Tom with an account of their island-hopping. He finished it with an extraordinary poem about Fingal's Cave in which Milton's 'young poet', Lycidas, drowned and swept by 'sounding Seas / . . . beyond the stormy Hebrides', is discovered

>     sleeping there
> On the marble cold and bare
> While the surges washed his feet
> And his garments white did beat
> Drench'd about the sombre rocks.

Once again Keats had been lured to an Orphic threshold, 'some old cavern's mouth', and the 'shadowy sound' of a mighty poet. Lycidas revives to relate how the cave 'was architected thus / By the great Oceanus'; its 'Mass of black Columns . . . bound . . . together like bunches of matches' resembled the bundle-shafted pillars Keats had seen at Dundrennan. Now, though, this 'Cathedrall of the Sea' had been desecrated by hordes of tourists, 'cutters . . . and fashion boats / . . . cravats and . . . Petticoats'; like the rainbow's colours, its magic had been undone by modernity.[64] By implication Keats was also suggesting that, since Milton's time, English poetry had diminished too – just as Wordsworth had dwindled in his estimate at the Westmorland election. This would not be Keats's only encounter with Milton on his tour of Scotland.

Slipped in at the end of his letter was this news: 'I have a slight sore throat and think it best to stay a day or two at Oban.' Keats makes light of this for Tom, and may have thought rest would cure it. His symptoms were a resurgence of the ailment that first appeared on his return from Oxford in autumn 1817. For four weeks he had tackled tough walks and climbs, got soaked day after day, eaten badly, slept in damp beds. Now, exhausted and tired, he realised an infection had taken hold – and there was no option but to go on. After they had rested at Oban, bad weather hindered their progress over fifty-two miles towards Fort William, although Keats seems to have felt his throat 'in a fair way of getting quite well'.[65] Their aim was Inverness, at the northern extremity of the Great Glen that cuts diagonally across the Highlands. And then, as they had originally planned, on to John o'Groats.

By Saturday, 1 August they were at Fort William, with Keats determined to ignore his sore throat. At five on Sunday morning they set out with another guide and his dog to climb Ben Nevis by the Mountain Track, a strenuous but straightforward ascent from Glen Nevis. After a first pull up, they arrived at 'a heath valley in which there was a Loch' – that is, Loch Meall an t-Suidhe – and then, fuelled with whisky, came a formidable scramble through scree, snow and mist to the summit 'above 4000 feet above the Sea'. Later Keats described for Tom how the mountain's 'immense head … is composed of large stones', with chasms 'the finest wonder of the whole—they appear great rents in the very heart of the mountain'. Throwing down rocks 'set the echoes at work in fine style', and then Keats sat a few feet from a precipice and wrote this sonnet:

Read me a Lesson muse, and speak it loud
Upon the top of Nevis blind in Mist!
I look into the Chasms and a Shroud
Vaprous doth hide them; just so much I wist
Mankind do know of Hell: I look o'erhead
    And there is sullen Mist; even so much
Mankind can tell of Heaven: Mist is spread
    Before the Earth beneath me—even such
Even so vague is Man's sight of himself.
    Here are the craggy Stones beneath my feet;
Thus much I know, that a poor witless elf

   I tread on them; that all my eye doth meet
     Is mist and Crag—not only on this height
     But in the World of thought and mental might—[66]

'We see not the ballance of good and evil. We are in a Mist,' Keats had
explained to Reynolds. That was at Teignmouth, back in the spring. Here,
now, 'blind in Mist', Keats's poem had come to him while he was as sightless
as the poet of *Paradise Lost*. What was his muse's 'lesson'? That our origin and
our destiny, whether Heaven or Hell, are shrouded in mist. Milton's Adam and
Eve were expelled from Paradise with the 'world . . . all before them', the same
world in which Keats, with mist 'spread / Before the Earth beneath me', knows
only 'craggy Stones' where he takes a chance 'sometimes on two sometimes on
three, sometimes four legs—sometimes two and stick, sometimes three and
stick, then four again, then two, then a jump, so that we kept on ringing
changes on foot, hand, Stick, jump boggle, stumble, foot, hand, foot, (very
gingerly) stick again, and then again a game at all fours'.[67] Like life itself, each
step was a gamble at risk of slip and fall – hence, perhaps, Keats's wonderful
word 'boggle'. To 'boggle' is to start with fright, as his father's horse had done
when he plunged to the pavement: 'jump boggle, stumble'. Gathered into the
'witless' wisdom of his sonnet are all the uncertainties and insecurities Keats
had felt since childhood, when he too had been abandoned to find his way
through a misty world. In his poem's ringing, Shakespearean cadences there
is also the assurance of someone stepping steadily, gingerly, onwards to
confront whatever lay ahead. On the summit of 'old Ben' he had discovered
what it meant to 'clamber through the Clouds and exist', unaware as yet that
he, too, was stepping on the road of the dead.[68]

   Like Ailsa Craig, Ben Nevis's 'huge crags', 'shattered heart' and 'cloud-veils'
challenged his epic ambitions. His response to those sublime sights was characteristic: Keats, who had stood 'tip-toe upon a little hill', climbed on a cairn
of stones 'done pointedly by some soldiers of artillery . . . and so got a little
higher than old Ben himself'. That urge to reach higher and outclimb the peak
of Ben Nevis is a reminder of the fearless schoolboy who might have become
a soldier too, who had once gazed up ambitiously at an unclimbable cliff of
poesy. As he leapt down, the poet who had conquered Scotland's highest peak
felt almost ready to tackle a poem as surprising as the prospect from that
summit – 'the sudden leap of the eye . . . into so vast a distance'.[69]

   The descent was 'vile'. Once down, there was no let-up to allow the two men
to recover from their twelve-mile climb. On 3 August they were en route to
Inverness, crossing the High Bridge with which General Wade had spanned
the River Spean in 1736. Their route lay along the old military road between

Fort William and Inverness, constructed by Wade as part of a military network to suppress Jacobite rebellion. Early in the nineteenth century Wade's roads, bridges and barracks endured as reminders of recent wars, as they had been for William and Dorothy Wordsworth on their Scottish tour of 1803. Across the Great Glen, Keats and Brown could see a major civil engineering project of more recent years, Thomas Telford's Caledonian Canal connecting south-west and north-east Scotland, to provide a shorter, safer route for vessels than around stormy Cape Wrath.

By the evening of 3 August they had reached the inn at Letterfinlay, midway along Loch Lochy's eastern shore. Keats now had time to write to Tom, recounting his climbing of Ben Nevis and adding a humorous extempore verse dialogue between 'one M$^{rs}$ Cameron of 50 years of age and the fattest woman in all inverness shire who got up this Mountain some few years ago' and old 'ungrateful Nevis' for whom she has deserted her pickles, preserves and 'China closet' (Keats means dainty blue and white china *and* a comfortable water closet). This is light stuff in jogging couplets, but gigantic shadows were stirring: Ben Nevis 'disturb'd [in] Slumber of a thousand years' harks back to Keats's slumbering giant Ailsa Craig, and looks forward to 'grey-haired Saturn' in *Hyperion* whom 'no force could wake'.[70] Keats finished his letter for Tom on Thursday the 6th at Inverness. 'My Sore throat is not quite well and I intend stopping here a few days,' he told his brother, then folded his letter, and sealed and posted it.

Brown gave Dilke a different view of the situation. 'M$^r$ Keats ... is too unwell for fatigue and privation. He caught a violent cold on the Island of Mull, which far from leaving him, has become worse, and the Physician here thinks him too thin and fevered to proceed on our journey.'[71] Instead of going to John o'Groats, Keats would return immediately to London. A possible route was by sea from the busy port of Cromarty – the *George*, a small coaster or 'smack', would sail on 8 August.

Keats and Brown took a coach eleven miles to Beauly, where they paused to view the thirteenth-century priory and its monuments engraved with skulls. As they journeyed on to Dingwall and along the west coast of the Black Isle, they began a comic poem in Burns's stanza on the skulls of Beauly's long-dead monks. It helped pass the time and lightened their mood, and two stanzas contributed by Keats anticipated some of his more celebrated poems yet to be written. After Brown's typically robust stanzas on clerical hypocrisy and self-indulgence comes a first complete stanza by Keats:

Poor skull, thy fingers set ablaze,
With silver saint in golden rays,

The holy missal; thou didst craze
  'Mid bead and spangle,
While others pass'd their idle days
  In coil and wrangle.

This figure of a solitary monk illuminating manuscripts and fingering beads is a first sketch of the Beadsman in *The Eve of St Agnes*, who patiently tells his rosary while others 'coil and wrangle' in 'argent revelry'.[72] Here too are the richness and austerity, inspiration and idleness, penance and profligacy that will surround Porphyro's meeting with Madeline. Keats's encounters with the medieval and Gothic in Scotland shaped his narrative poem in other ways, but here we should also notice how Keats's second complete stanza in the Beauly poem seems to foreshadow 'La Belle Dame sans Merci':

This lily colour'd skull, with all
The teeth complete, so white and small,
Belong'd to one whose early pall
  A lover shaded;
He died ere superstition's gall
  His heart invaded.

This youthful lover's 'lily colour'd skull' will also belong to Keats's knight-at-arms in 'La Belle Dame', glimpsed beneath the 'lily on [his] brow' and 'fading rose' of his cheek, while the rhymes 'all', 'small', 'pall' and 'gall' seem to lead inexorably to the later poem's fatal surmise: 'La Belle dame sans merci / Thee hath in thrall.'

At Cromarty they found a bustling, prosperous town with fine houses, a courthouse, a brewery, a hemp factory beside the harbour, and elegant streets lined with shops. This was an obvious place for Keats to purchase provisions for his voyage, and with these he parted from Brown and went on board.

Together they had walked over 640 miles, averaging around fifteen miles for each of the forty-three days they were on foot. Now Brown would complete the remainder of the tour on his own.[73] Eventually he came back south to Edinburgh, then to Carlisle, where he stayed some days with Bailey, and so back to Wentworth Place in the autumn.[74]

Why Keats went by sea is unknown. A coach south to Edinburgh and another to London would certainly have been quicker and better for his health (the letter Keats posted at Inverness on the 6th was delivered to Tom just six days later – it can take longer today). Perhaps it was too expensive or Keats, after weeks of open space, could not bear the prospect of close confinement. Possibly he hoped sea air would cure his throat. As the *George* cleared the Firth of Cromarty, a nine-day voyage lay ahead, with Keats passing the time wrapped up in his coat on deck or in a small cabin below. Unable to stomach the staple fare of thick porridge, he ate beef the whole way.

Putting in at Leith on around 10 or 11 August, the *George* took on additional passengers, cargo and, as was usual, packages of journals destined for London booksellers. So it was that Keats may well have sailed back from Scotland not only with the sore throat that would eventually kill him, but also with copies of *Blackwood's* containing the article with which Z intended to destroy him as a poet.

CHAPTER 17

# Sleepless Nights

SUNDAY, 16 August. Wentworth Place. Maria Dilke began a letter to her father-in-law: 'John Keats' brother is extremely ill, and the doctor begged that his brother might be sent for.' Her husband had written to recall him from Scotland, then Brown's letter from Inverness had arrived. Keats was unwell too, and already en route for London. 'How Brown will get on alone I know not,' Maria continued, 'as he loses a cheerful, good-tempered, clever companion.'[1]

By his own account Keats landed on Monday, 17 August – high water at London Bridge was at 3.30pm. That evening the coach set him down at Hampstead in time to call at Wentworth Place before going up to Well Walk. 'John Keats arrived here . . . as brown and shabby as you can imagine; scarcely any shoes left, his jacket all torn at the back, a fur cap, a great plaid, and his knapsack. I cannot tell what he looked like.'[2] As yet Keats knew nothing of Tom's grave condition. After greetings and exclamations at his appearance, Dilke passed on Sawrey's warning and Keats hurried home.

As soon as he saw Tom's emaciated face he must have known it was all over. Memories of their mother's death and 'family disease' surged back, banishing the independence and exhilaration of recent weeks. Pulmonary tuberculosis, the disease that had afflicted Tom for nearly a year, was in its final stages and from now on Keats would be confined almost continuously to rooms where he would nurse his dying brother. By day he would have to be vigilant, for the slightest agitation made Tom haemorrhage blood. At night he would lie awake listening to Tom restless and feverish with night sweats, until laudanum – tincture of opium in alcohol – helped both of them to sleep.[3] Throughout these weeks Keats devoted himself to his brother and wrote reassuring letters to their sister, Fanny, reporting the slightest indication that 'poor Tom is a little better'.[4] Abbey gave permission for her to come over from Walthamstow several times during September, but thereafter she did not visit again. Keats found it easier not to tell George and Georgiana – there was no good news, or he found other reasons not to write. Yet, however carefully Keats tried to conceal Tom's condition, family knowledge 'of one great, solitary grief' meant that they could not be deceived. The reality surfaces in almost all of Keats's letters this autumn: 'Tom has not been getting better'; 'Tom . . . has lately been much worse'; 'I wish I could say Tom was any better'; 'Poor Tom is about the same'; 'Tom gets weaker every day'. Eventually he forced himself to write to America, 'to say the truth . . . he is no better, but much worse'.[5]

Keats was in a poor way too. Plagued by his sore throat and a raging tooth, he was particularly oppressed by the sudden transition to the confines of a sick room. For toothache a standard painkiller was laudanum, and Keats was almost certainly dosing himself, as well as Tom, to dull pain and quell anxiety. After weeks of free-ranging and climbing through clouds, he was now restricted to errands and an occasional foray to town. Skiddaw's clear cold air had bucked him up, as if going to joust at a tournament; now he was inhaling tubercular bacteria exhaled with Tom's every breath. Although the pathology of disease transmission was not properly understood, Keats's instinct as a physician told him that living 'in a continual fever' was 'poisonous to life'. There was no let-up for him, confronted by Tom's 'countenance his voice and feebleness' and aware that he 'looks upon me as his only comfort'. No wonder the urge to escape became overpowering. 'His identity presses upon me so all day,' he told Dilke, 'that I am obliged to go out'.[6]

But who could he go to see, to talk through his worries and forebodings? Brown, his closest friend, was not yet back from Scotland and everyone else was ill or convalescing. Dilke, unwell, had left for the seaside; Reynolds, having narrowly escaped injury in a coach accident, was in Devon; Haydon had retreated to his sister's at Bridgwater, his eyes so bad that he had to dictate a letter to Keats. Only Severn was in town, recuperating from a bout of typhus fever.[7] The second half of August saw gloriously fine weather, perfect for walking on Hampstead Heath, but on Sawrey's orders Keats remained indoors.

Two weeks passed, and then on Tuesday, 1 September he went to London. This was his first opportunity to call on the Reynolds family at Little Britain, where he found the sisters in a 'bustle' about their Anglo-Indian cousin Jane Cox. When Keats arrived she was in conversation upstairs with Mrs Reynolds, and the sisters were 'warm in her praises'. As this remarkable woman did not appear Keats took no heed, 'not being partial to 9 days wonders', but he did note another transitory phenomenon. Bailey, who had once been as warm in his praises of Marianne Reynolds, was 'not quite so much spoken of'.[8]

Bailey was easily put out of mind, but the most recent issue of *Blackwood's* could not be ignored. By early September, Z's fourth 'Cockney School' essay was on sale. After three attacks on Hunt, this was an assault Keats had long anticipated – but nothing could have prepared him for how venomous it would prove to be. Lockhart went straight for his tenderest spot, and with gleeful malevolence caricatured him as an ignorant upstart – a 'bantling' who had only learned from Hunt how 'to lisp sedition'.[9] Destined by his friends for a respectable medical career until seized by 'poetical mania', this 'wavering apprentice' was no better than a 'farm servant' or 'footman' with ideas above his station. As for 'Johnny Keats's' poems, they were 'drivelling idiocy' fit only for a madhouse. Ignoring Bailey's attempts to detach Keats from Hunt, Z quoted long extracts of 'raving' from *Sleep and Poetry* and *Endymion* by way of identifying Keats with 'the rising brood of Cockneys' and dismissing him as of no significance whatsoever.

In reality, Z – or Lockhart – took Keats and his poetry very seriously indeed: Napoleon had been routed at Waterloo and now the enemy lurked within, assiduously plotting a cultural revolution that would, Lockhart feared, prove as damaging as an invading army. Poems were their weapons of choice, not pikestaffs, and the battle was for cultural authority. Looking south from Edinburgh, Lockhart saw how Keats's challenge to existing poetic paradigms and aesthetics, notably the neoclassicism of Pope and Boileau, was inherently and – to his eyes – dangerously political. A change in poetic idiom towards a more natural, vernacular style might well anticipate a transformation of political realities; loosening the heroic couplet, as Keats had done in *Endymion*, might help undo the bonds of society too. The 'Cockney School of Poetry' and the 'Cockney School of Politics' were one and the same, and Keats had allies. Hunt, Haydon, Hazlitt and other 'unsettled pretenders' were active in London, challenging the establishment on a broad front – hence Lockhart's need to rehabilitate William Wordsworth, former republican, as the 'purest, the loftiest, and ... most classical of living English poets'. Twenty years after the explosive combination of tradition and experiment in *Lyrical Ballads*, Wordsworth had become a bulwark against a poetical-political revolution he had himself initiated. And 'Johnny Keats'. He must be made to look ridiculous: 'It is a better and a wiser thing to be a starved apothecary than a starved poet; so back to the shop, Mr. John.' Silencing Keats would save the status quo.

In all of this we can hear a garbled version of what Bailey had told Lockhart, but there seem to have been other informants at work too. Z knew about Keats's height. Mixing physical stature with poetic abilities, he called Hunt 'small' and Keats 'a still smaller poet'. Z's innuendos about 'unmarried ladies' and illegitimate 'bantlings' would be echoed in some of Abbey's suspicions about Keats's mother – so perhaps those rumours had a wider currency. Similarly Z's emphasis on infection, ridiculing Keats's move from medicine to poetry, may indicate a separate source on family history and family disease – possibly George Gleig, or Christie's elusive letter to Lockhart of late 1817. Ironically, as Keats read over Z's words at Well Walk, he was shut away with a brother who was actually enduring the 'terrible symptoms' of a real disease that was genuinely incurable. I suspect the fact that poor Tom's predicament was so overwhelmingly more awful than his own gave Keats, like Lear, strength to survive the storm. (We know that Keats was reading *King Lear* in these unhappy autumn weeks, for he ringed the words 'poor Tom' in his copy, and wrote the date alongside: 'Sunday Evening Oct. 4. 1818.')

Z so infuriated Hazlitt that he began legal action, prompting John Murray to withdraw from business collaborations with Blackwood – ironically, both publishers had put Hunt's *Story of Rimini* into print in 1816.[10] But there was no violent reaction in Keats's letters, no expression of fury or dismay. Hearing nothing from Keats, James Hessey decided to find out more.

Under the full moon of Monday, 14 September, Keats dined at 93 Fleet Street. With Taylor away at Retford to see his family, Hessey had rounded up Hazlitt, Woodhouse and three others. All seemed 'well pleased', Hessey reported, with Keats in such good spirits that he stayed all night and some of the next morning. Hessey's impression was that he 'does not seem to care at all about Blackwood, he thinks it so poorly done, and as he does not mean to publish any thing more at present he says it affects him less'. With studied sang-froid, Keats announced that he had been 'recovering' his Latin and preparing to learn Greek, but, wary and watchful, Hessey was not taken in. About Keats, Hessey appears to have been more undecided than Taylor, and with reason. Their exchanges over the preface to *Endymion* had shown Keats could be moody and volatile, 'a man of fits and starts' who was 'not much to be depended on' – like his present air of equanimity. Hessey was willing to allow that 'sometime or other he will ... do something valuable', but when would that be?[11] In September 1818 no one could foresee what Keats would do next. Observing him in company, Hessey was trying to gauge the likely effect of the *Blackwood's* essay on him, concerned for his future as a writer. For Richard Woodhouse, what Keats said at the dinner was thoroughly alarming.

Towards the end of that week, Keats called again at Little Britain. This time as he chatted with Reynolds's sisters about their brother's engagement, the door opened and their cousin Jane Cox came in. She had a 'rich eastern look', 'fine eyes and fine manners' and the feline poise of a 'Leopardess'. She might not be a 'Cleopatra', Keats decided, but she was certainly a 'Charmian' – Cleopatra's worldly, experienced, unillusioned servant. He could see she was conscious of his admiration, relieved that 'from habit she thinks that nothing *particular*'. There was no sneer at his height, no embarrassment, no hurry to be gone. Her self-possession put him at ease, too, for 'what we both are is taken for granted'. 'I am at such times too much occupied in admiring to be awkward or on a tremble,' he later admitted. 'I forget myself entirely because I live in her.' 'They call her a flirt to me,' he wrote afterwards to America: 'What a want of knowledge? She walks across a room in such a manner that a Man is drawn towards her with a magnetic Power.' The woman at Vauxhall, Mathew's sisters and the envious Reynolds girls suddenly belonged to an unsatisfactory past; in Jane Cox, he had met the first woman who appeared to accept him. 'I like her and her like,' he told George, confident for the first time of 'right feeling' about a woman.[12]

That moment of self-possession passed. Back at Well Walk on Tuesday, 22 September 'by Sawrey's mandate', he wrote to Reynolds that 'the voice and shape of a woman' had haunted him for two days and kept him awake at night.[13] This has been said to be Fanny Brawne, still living with her family in Brown's half of Wentworth Place. But there is nothing in Keats's letters to indicate they had yet met, and mention of the haunting voice and shape evokes Jane Cox's 'rich talk' and 'magnetic' presence. Overcome with guilt that his feelings for a woman had preoccupied him while Tom lay dying, he tells Reynolds that 'the relief, the feverous relief of Poetry seems a much less crime—This morning Poetry has conquered ... I feel escaped from a new strange and threatening sorrow.' Reynolds's engagement appeared like a happy dream after what Keats seems to have glimpsed, when laudanum- and mercury-induced 'nervousness' distorted the obsessions of his waking life. 'Poor Tom—that woman—and Poetry were ringing changes in my senses,' he told Reynolds, as if all three were aspects of a single dark anxiety. Taking shape in the infected rooms of Well Walk was Keats's less benign idea that a woman's 'magnetic Power' was associated with entrapment, disease and death. His response to Jane Cox, he now saw, was a new and potent form of self-immolation, as feverishly all-consuming as poetry or the tuberculosis destroying Tom. Equally disturbing was his realisation that this was what he almost wished for. 'I should like her to ruin me,' he winked at Georgiana, only half in jest.[14] For Reynolds, marriage to Eliza Drewe lay ahead. Awaiting Keats were his lyrical embodiments of Jane Cox in the fatal charisma of two women – La Belle Dame sans Merci and Lamia, who, like Jane, appears as 'a pard' (i.e. a leopardess). Through these narratives of erotic enchantment, Keats would also express his ambivalent feelings of desire for and fear of Fanny Brawne. And in Keats's fantasies about Jane Cox, feverously indulged while his brother lay dying, lurked the origins of his tormented idea that unconsummated sexual passion and consumption's onset were linked.

Poetry had conquered, he told Reynolds. But what had he written? Over the troubled weekend of 19–20 September he made a free translation of a sonnet by the sixteenth-century French poet Ronsard. Three lines ablaze with sexual energy recall his reading of Dante's *Inferno*:

> My heart took fire—and only burning pains
> They were my pleasure—they my life's sad end—
> Love poured her beauty into my warm veins.[15]

Release also came through poetic 'abstraction' related to his earliest work on *Hyperion*. For months he had been preparing this attempt at epic, beginning as far back as his visit to the British Museum and its awe-inspiring fragments of 'Grecian grandeur'. There had been further hints and anticipations in *Endymion*, and his letter to Haydon on 23 January 1818 announced that, unlike his 'mawkish' poetical romance, *Hyperion* would be written in 'a more naked and Grecian Manner— . . . the march of passion and endeavour will be undeviating.'[16] He had made intensive study of the masters: Shakespeare, Milton, Cary's Dante and *The Excursion*, as well as Lemprière's *Classical Dictionary* and Baldwin's *Pantheon*. And he had just returned from a trek around Scotland in quest of appropriately sublime imagery. Even with these resources assembled, however, he found this long-meditated work beset with difficulties. As he looked back, he saw himself setting about *Endymion* in a spirit of dauntless independence, whereas now he was paralysed by misgivings. 'In Endymion, I leaped headlong into the Sea,' he told Hessey, all too aware of his present hesitation.[17] Since that poem, his intensive reading and speculations about the 'poetical character' had combined to make him pause. There was a social dimension too: back then George and Tom had given him staunch support, and fellow poets like Hunt, Reynolds, Cowden Clarke and Mathew had all encouraged him at one time or another. Now that nurturing community had broken up, leaving Keats – confronted by the achievements of Dante, Shakespeare and Milton – suspecting that there was 'nothing original to be written in poetry'. Its riches were 'already exhausted,—and all its beauties forestalled'. Such at least was what Woodhouse understood him to have said over dinner at Hessey's.[18]

Perhaps this was simply the effect of Hessey's wine, as Keats unwound after weeks of tension. And there might have been further delay had he not found himself 'obliged to write' on Monday, 21 September to ease his constant worry about Tom. As rain scattered leaves along Well Walk he set down the opening paragraph of *Hyperion*, in fourteen lines so subdued they seem to question the possibility of his poem proceeding:

> Deep in the shady sadness of a vale
> Far sunken from the healthy breath of morn,
> Far from the fiery noon, and eve's one star,
> Sat grey-haired Saturn, quiet as a stone,
> Still as the silence round about his lair;
> Forest on forest hung above his head
> Like cloud on cloud. No stir of air was there,
> Not so much life as on a summer's day
> Robs not one light seed from the feathered grass,
> But where the dead leaf fell, there did it rest.
> A stream went voiceless by, still deadened more
> By reason of his fallen divinity
> Spreading a shade: the Naiad 'mid her reeds
> Press'd her cold finger closer to her lips.

(i.1–14)

Commencing his epic with an experimental blank-verse sonnet, Keats rose to the challenge of his new poem while signalling a wish to discover a better sonnet stanza.[19] Banishing Hunt's run-on couplets – as predicted in his 'Lines on Seeing a Lock of Milton's Hair' – Keats now began to master the 'organic numbers' of Miltonic blank verse, their resonant cadences tempered to an austere announcement of 'fallen divinity'. More intricately inward than anything he had written hitherto, these lines form a complex lattice interwoven by alliteration, assonance and half-rhymes until the sibilant hush is broken by ten bleak monosyllables: 'But where the dead leaf fell, there did it rest.' The 'voiceless stream' is rendered so by Saturn's fallen divinity and by Keats's anxiety as he ventures into the flow of unrhymed verse, where 'the Naiad 'mid her reeds / Press'd her cold finger closer to her lips' in a gesture of conscious complicity. He intended these fourteen lines to announce an expansive epic narrative, yet they might equally well suggest a more introspective path. As he embarked on his long-projected poem, Keats's imagination was being drawn in two directions.

Encountering Saturn fallen and 'quiet as a stone', readers immediately understand that, by epic convention, *Hyperion* has opened at a late stage in the war between ancient gods. Led by Saturn, the Titans – offspring of Heaven

(Coelus) and Earth (Tellus) – have been overthrown by the next generation of Olympian gods. Saturn has been displaced by his son Jupiter, and Neptune has defeated Oceanus. Having languished as a 'frozen God' through four 'silver seasons' of the moon, Saturn 'at length . . . lifted up / His faded eyes, and saw his kingdom gone'. Like Lear and Satan, without his kingdom Saturn has no sense of 'real self' and, with his followers, struggles to comprehend his new identity and circumstances. Only Hyperion, Saturn's brother and god of the sun, remains in place – undefeated 'yet unsecure':

> His palace bright,
> Bastion'd with pyramids of glowing gold,
> And touch'd with shade of bronzed obelisks,
> Glar'd a blood-red through all its thousand courts,
> Arches and domes, and fiery galleries.
> (i.176–80)

Keats planned that his poem would trace Hyperion's downfall and Apollo's accession as his successor. A second book would introduce defeated Titans debating the reasons for their overthrow, like Milton's fallen angels in *Paradise Lost*. Apollo would be introduced in a third book, wandering the world until his encounter with Mnemosyne, mother of the Muses, initiates his transformation into the Olympian god of the sun, medicine and poetry.

By opening his poem in an anxious, uncertain interval between Saturn's defeat and Hyperion's fall, Keats tapped into the national mood of 1818. After the victory at Waterloo, the Bourbon *ancien régime* had returned to the French throne and Britain, exhausted by twenty-five years of war, had sunk into a brooding calm. 'It is quiet,' Hunt wrote in *The Examiner*, 'it seems peaceable to us here in Europe; it may even continue so, as far as any great warfare is concerned' – but he detected in the spread of knowledge a potent agent for further change, an enlightenment as irresistible as the force that swept away the Titans.[20] The present, according to Hunt, was merely a lull before further momentous events – as Keats suggests when Hyperion's wife, Thea, contemplates Saturn with

> a listening fear in her regard,
> As if calamity had but begun;
> As if the vanward clouds of evil days
> Had spent their malice, and the sullen rear
> Was with its stored thunder labouring up.
> (i.37–41)

Thea's gloomy prospect of 'evil days' emerges from defeat, whereas Keats had already indicated that his poem would follow an 'undeviating' trajectory of progress in the realm of myth and, by implication, in the modern world. He had not been much in Hunt's company lately but, as always, he was attentive to Hunt's arguments in *The Examiner*.

Pursuing Saturn and Thea to 'that sad place / Where Cybele and the bruised Titans mourn'd' (ii.3–4), Keats opens his second book with recollections of Rydal Falls and the Highlands:

> the solid roar
> Of thunderous waterfalls and torrents hoarse,
> Pouring a constant bulk, uncertain where.
> Crag jutting forth to crag, and rocks that seem'd
> Ever as if just rising from a sleep.
>
> (ii.7–11)

Back in July he had imagined Ailsa Craig's giant forehead traversing 'two dead eternities'. Now that 'craggy pyramid' and all the gulfs, chasms, heights, sullen depths, 'loud tormented streams: / And . . . everlasting cataracts' (ii.362–3) of his Scottish tour came together in a sublime backdrop to scenes of power eternally vanquished.

Less obvious are his poem's more private autobiographical references in the aftermath of George's departure. If Keats captured England's ominous paralysis in 1818 he also evoked the dreadful interim into which his own life had sunk as he awaited the inevitable outcome of tuberculosis. During those dark days it was perhaps natural that he should have remembered scenes associated with their early family life together at Craven Street and Keates's Livery Stables before their parents' deaths. That was a time when inner-city buildings had loomed over him, colossal as old Ben's cloudy summit; now, memories of Bedlam, the British Museum and Lackington's Temple of the Muses were summoned to poetic life by the demise of mythical parents, and we overhear in the 'solitary sorrow' and 'lonely grief' that 'best befits' Keats's muse an echo of the 'one great, solitary grief' that united Thomas and Frances Keates's orphaned children.[21] Certainly he had been thinking about poets' fathers, poets' birthplaces and poetic fame in the summer, reflecting on his own origins and ambitions. *Hyperion*, he quickly realised, offered an opportunity to refashion the tragic history of his own family as poetic myth. In this archetypal story of parental downfall and the rise of a divine poet-physician, Apollo, he would rebuff *Blackwood's* slanders by presenting his own life as a triumphant ascent of genius from the ruins of its forebears.

Composition this autumn was only possible as momentary distraction from his awful situation with Tom. At best his opportunities were fleeting, soon interrupted, and it is difficult to assess how much he was able to write and when. More evident is the sustained draw of retrospection, as Keats consciously recovered his own past in fashioning his myth of Apollo. With its lustrous courts and galleries, Hyperion's 'palace bright' is a celestial counterpart to the cavernous old British Museum where the rise and fall of earthly civilisations, reflecting the original revolution in Keats's poem, were embodied in exhibits such as the

> Memphian sphinx,
> Pedestal'd haply in a palace court,
> When sages look'd to Egypt for their lore.
> (i.31–4)

Hyperion's radiant home also recalls that glowing red-brick palace adjacent to Keates's Livery Stables, the formative setting of Keats's life from which he too had soon been expelled – eventually to find his own way as a poet. In bright sunlight Bedlam's bricks and stonework shimmered and shone; its grand cupola surmounted with a glittering sun-like sphere almost certainly suggested Keats's idea of a sun-god flaring from nave to vault, and onwards 'until he reach'd the great main cupola' (i.217–21). Like the 'bruisèd Titans', Hyperion will be compelled to experience

> all the frailty of grief,
> Of rage, of fear, anxiety, revenge,
> Remorse, spleen, hope, but most of all despair.
> (ii.93–5)

Disanointed by 'mortal oil', fallen divinity becomes vulnerable to the 'mortal bruise' that had felled Thomas Keates, and undergoes something of the anguish that awaited his sons on that awful day in April 1804:

> As with us mortal men, the laden heart
> Is persecuted more, and fever'd more,
> When it is nighing to the mournful house
> Where other hearts are sick of the same bruise;
> So Saturn, as he walk'd into the midst . . .
> (ii.101–5)

As he contemplates the fallen Titans, Keats likens them to 'a dismal cirque / Of Druid stones, upon a forlorn moor' (ii.34–5) – another summer recollection, this time from Castlerigg stone circle  and also to more statuesque embodiments of anguish in Cibber's studies of 'Melancholy Madness' and 'Raving Madness' above the Bedlam gate:

> Instead of thrones, hard flint they sat upon,
> Couches of rugged stone, and slaty ridge
> Stubborn'd with iron.
>
> (ii.15–18)

As Keats begins his catalogue of the fallen Titans all 'pent in regions of laborious breath', Cibber's figure of manacled torment in 'Raving Madness' came powerfully into focus:

> Dungeon'd in opaque element, to keep
> Their clenched teeth still clench'd, and all their limbs
> Lock'd up like veins of metal, crampt and screw'd;
> Without a motion, save of their big hearts,
> Heaving in pain, and horribly convuls'd . . .
>
> (ii.23–7)

Enduring a Dantesque torment, the Titan Cottus is postured like 'Melancholy Madness'–

> prone he lay, chin uppermost,
> As though in pain; for still upon the flint
> He ground severe his skull, with open mouth
> And eyes at horrid working
>
> (ii.49–52)

– as is Enceladus, formerly most powerful of the Titans,

> on a crag's uneasy shelve,
> Upon his elbow rais'd, all prostrate else.
>
> (ii.64–5)

Unfolded in Keats's second book are the Titans' various attempts to explain their defeat. Rallied by Saturn, Oceanus proclaims a *fait accompli*. They have fallen in due succession 'by course of Nature's law' (ii.181):

'... as thou wast not the first of powers,
So art thou not the last ...
And as we show beyond that Heaven and Earth
In form and shape compact and beautiful,
In will, in action free, companionship,
And thousand other signs of purer life;
So on our heels a fresh perfection treads,
A power more strong in beauty, born of us
And fated to excel us.'

(ii.188–9, 208–14)

Next, Clymene – in one tradition mother of Mnemosyne – bears witness to Apollo's music as 'that new blissful golden melody' (ii.280) before her voice is overwhelmed by the fierce declamations of Enceladus. All are silenced by Hyperion's arrival, as his brightness amid 'darkness and huge shade' discloses the Titans' 'misery . . . To the most hateful seeing of itself' (ii. 369–70).

Cutting away from this scene of 'alternate uproar and sad peace' (iii.1), book three would trace Apollo's path to divine – and poetic – power. So Keats's delineation of 'the march of passion and endeavour' served a double purpose. It enabled him to confront urgent contemporary questions about historical and intellectual progress and the fortunes of empire, and also to shadow tragic revolutions in the house of Keats as he advanced towards poetic fame amid the wreckage.

\* \* \*

After his letter to Reynolds on 22 September we hear nothing further from Keats for more than two weeks. His routine went on as before, with full-time care of Tom and snatched moments at *Hyperion*. Each Sunday's *Examiner* came as a lifeline from the world beyond. Perhaps he noticed on Sunday the 27th an article on a young clerk called Roberts, reported missing and taken up by a constable at Woolwich. Sick of his sedentary office occupation, he had determined to join Simon Bolivar's liberation movement in South America. That campaign was reported in depth by *The Examiner*, and large numbers of British and Irish volunteers had rallied to Bolivar's cause. Keats kept his eye on these reports, and may not immediately have noticed another publication this weekend. The long-promised April issue of the *Quarterly Review* had just appeared, with Croker's review of *Endymion*.[22]

Brazenly admitting that he had read only the first book, Croker, like Z, foregrounded Keats's association with the new school of Cockney poetry: he is a 'copyist' of Hunt. Having mauled the Preface – as Keats's friends expected – he produced extracts to demonstrate that *Endymion*'s sentences, lines and dangerously 'new words' were unintelligible and that its couplets did not 'inclose a complete idea'. But while this review was facetious and patronising, it was not entirely dismissive nor was it unperceptive. Croker found 'powers of language, rays of fancy, and gleams of genius', and, as we have seen, his attempt to ridicule the poem as 'an immeasureable game at *bouts-rimés*' unwittingly located a source of its quirky, capricious vitality. Keats had used rhyme to direct narrative since early childhood, and his verse epistles and *Endymion* grew from those formative games at rhyming. Disdaining the pleasures of play, however, Croker declared himself 'perplexed and puzzled' by *Endymion* and, in more ways than one, the poem 'altogether escaped' him.[23]

Within a week a letter defending Keats against the *Quarterly Review*'s 'malice' and 'injustice' appeared in the *Morning Chronicle*. The author, 'J.S.', encouraged Keats to break with Leigh Hunt – a reliable pointer to John Scott as the identity of the writer. A second, shorter letter followed from 'R.B.' with extracts from *Endymion* to repair Keats's 'injured merit'.[24] At Exeter, Reynolds published an admiring review of *Endymion* in *The Alfred*, showing how Keats excelled in Milton's power of 'breathing a spirit of life and novelty' into pagan mythology. That link with Milton defiantly connected Keats with English republicanism and an impeccable poetic pedigree, and Reynolds's review was immediately reprinted in *The Examiner* under a headnote informing 'J.S.' that even when under attack by the critics Keats and Hunt had spirit enough to 'stand by [a] friend'. Belatedly trying to make amends, Bailey had sent a defence of Keats to *Blackwood's* and the *Scots Magazine*. It was not printed.[25]

Exhausted though he was by his Scottish tour and Tom's shocking illness, Keats had nevertheless risen above the *Blackwood's* assault. *Hyperion* was, at last, under way. But the stress of caring for his brother, his own persistent sore throat, continuing doses of mercury and confinement at Well Walk had made him increasingly overwrought. The *Quarterly Review*'s sneers proved more than he could take. By Friday, 2 October, Keats, in despair, had contacted his oldest friend, Charles Cowden Clarke. Responding to his distress, Cowden Clarke went to see him sometime during a period of exceptionally heavy rain from Sunday the 4th to Tuesday the 6th – bad weather gave him an excuse to stay overnight rather than return home the same evening. In a letter to the *Morning Chronicle* of 27 July 1821, Cowden Clarke described what happened on that long, sleepless night. Going back over the *Quarterly Review*'s 'discomfort of a generous mind', Cowden Clarke recalled 'that Keats [had] lain awake through the whole night talking with sensative-bitterness [*sic*] of the unfair treatment he had experienced'. Forty years later in the *Atlantic Monthly*,

Cowden Clarke returned to the sleepless night at Well Walk, adding: 'He felt the insult, but more the injustice of the treatment he had received; he told me so, as we lay awake one night, when I slept in his brother's bed.' This can only have been Keats's room at Well Walk, when the spare bed had recently been vacated by George and the sheer physical burden of caring for Tom was such that 'his friends could see distinctly that his own health had suffered in the exertion'.[26]

After his sleepless night Keats, steadied by Cowden Clarke's companion-ship, gathered himself again to outface his critics. Within days he was writing confidently to Hessey, thanking him for forwarding J.S.'s letter from the *Chronicle* and assuring him that his own self-criticism was far sharper than anything the reviews could inflict. Independence was all: 'The Genius of Poetry must work out its own salvation in a man: It cannot be matured by law & precept, but by sensation and watchfulness in itself.' Then, with an intuitive leap of genius, came his insight about the self-generative nature of imagina-tion: 'That which is creative must create itself.'[27] The poetic imagination, whether of an egotist like Wordsworth or an enigma like Shakespeare, must create the taste by which it is appreciated. In the circumstances, his renewed confidence that his own poetry would be further matured was a triumphant rebuff to the reviews.

Such swings of mood between despair and self-belief were typical of Keats and, understandably, it is his upbeat account of himself in his letter to Hessey that posterity has preferred. But Cowden Clarke's 1821 letter shows us that he was much more deeply wounded by attacks on *Endymion* than his friends and biographers were subsequently willing to admit. Unfortunately, in later years Cowden Clarke – concerned, like Keats's biographers, to discredit Shelley's and Byron's stories that Keats succumbed to a review – omitted the sleepless night passage from his *Recollections of Writers* (1878).[28] As a result, the traumatic effect of reviews was lost to sight, surviving only in Byron's quip that Keats was 'snuff'd out by an article'. We need to remember that Cowden Clarke was closest to what had really happened, and his account of Keats's restless 'sensa-tive-bitterness' is a reminder of how agitated thoughts of 'Poor Tom—that woman—and Poetry' had also banished sleep a few nights before. Cowden Clarke's considered view was that 'It is not impossible that [Keats's] premature death may have been brought on by his performing the office of nurse to a younger brother, who also died of a decline . . . To *what* extent the treatment he received from those writers operated on his mind, I cannot say.' Cowden Clarke's italics indicate that, in his view, 'those writers' – hostile critics – had indeed helped to bring on the fatal illness, and that Keats was more volatile, and less assured, than his letters would have had their recipients believe.[29]

Back from Devon, Reynolds met Keats on Tuesday, 13 October. He borrowed the manuscript of *Isabella*, read it immediately and encouraged Keats to publish it to 'annul' the *Quarterly Review*. Reynolds knew that even bad reviews aroused interest, and during this month alone the *Morning Chronicle* and *The Examiner* kept Keats in the public eye on the 11th, 13th, 22nd, 25th and 30th. Hessey, noting that a 'stir' about *Endymion* had improved sales, readvertised it, and by mid-December Keats himself acknowledged that the *Quarterly Review*'s attack had done 'some service'.[30]

A letter from George arrived. Georgiana was expecting their first child next spring. Cheered by a moon 'now shining full and brilliant', on 14 October, Keats began a second journal-letter to America describing Tom's condition, his own return from Scotland, reviewers' attacks and his belief that he would be 'among the English poets after [his] death'. His attraction to Jane Cox is unpersuasively downplayed as a 'passtime and . . . amuzement'; 'sleepy' British politics are recounted at some length; and then Keats breaks into an extempore lullaby for their baby:

'Tis 'the witching time of night'
Orbed is the Moon and bright
And the Stars they glisten, glisten.[31]

He called on Georgiana's family on Thursday the 15th, and walked with Hazlitt to Covent Garden. Around mid-October he added to his letter visits to Dilke, Brown, Haydon, Rice and Hunt, mentioning how on one foray to town he had encountered Isabella Jones on Theobald's Road, Bloomsbury and accompanied her to see a genteel friend – Mrs Henry Green, who ran a boarding school at Islington.[32] Then, with Keats wondering what might ensue, they walked back to her home on an upper floor of 34 Gloucester Street, Queen's Square. This house has now gone, but others of the same period remain and give us some idea of Isabella's spacious and comfortable apartment. It was 'a very tasty sort of place with Books, Pictures a bronze statue of Buonaparte, Music, æolian Harp; a Parrot a Linnet—A Case of choice Liquers &c &c'.[33] Prominent amid fashionable clutter, the statue of Bonaparte signalled Mrs Jones's Whiggish views (in 1818 Lady Holland erected a bust of Napoleon in the garden of Holland House, London's famous Whig salon).[34] Keats continues: 'she behaved in the kindest manner—made me take home a Grouse for Tom's dinner—Asked for my address for the purpose of sending more game.' Taking this as an encouragement, and recalling that he had 'warmed with her before and kissed her', he thought it would be 'living backwards not to do so again'. In the letter this scene develops as a delicate comedy of embarrassment, with Isabella contriving to disappoint him 'in a way which made me feel more pleasure than a simple kiss could do'. Unlike Jane Cox, who needed no props, Isabella was surrounded by *objets* that spoke for her 'good taste' in saying Keats would please her if he would 'press her hand and go away'.[35]

Others were concerned about Keats too, and less pleased to see him leaving. Sensing that he was more troubled than appeared, Woodhouse had written to persuade him not to think of abandoning poetry.

> I may have misconceived you,—but I understood you to say, you thought there was now nothing original to be written in poetry; that its riches were already exhausted, & all its beauties forestalled—& That you should, consequently, write no more: but continue increasing your knowledge, merely for your own gratification without any attempt to make use of your Stores.

This was clearly a well-rehearsed argument. With legalistic precision, Woodhouse informed Keats that he could not agree his premises, and deprecated his conclusion:

> the true born Son of Genius, who creates for himself the world in which his own fancy ranges who culls from it fair forms of truth beauty & purity & apparels them in hues chosen by himself, should hold a different language—he need never fear that the treasury he draws on can be exhausted, nor despair of being always able to make an original selection.[36]

The significance of Woodhouse's intervention can hardly be overstated. It drew from Keats a careful reply, feeling his way forward as he discriminated his own poetry from 'the wordsworthian or egotistical sublime'. Hunt's theatrical reviews, negative capability and Hazlitt on art's intensity all streamed into Keats's next statement about the poetical character, which is uniquely and eloquently his own: 'it is not itself—it has no self—it is everything and nothing—It has no character—it enjoys light and shade; it lives in gusto, be it foul or fair, high or low, rich or poor, mean or elevated—It has as much delight in conceiving an Iago as an Imogen. What shocks the virtuous philosopher, delights the camelion Poet.' A poet 'has no Identity', he tells Woodhouse, because he is continually assuming other identities such as the sun, moon, sea, other men and women, all creatures that have 'an unchangeable attribute'.[37] Here, in few words, Keats condensed the essence of his own art since his early Margate sonnet to George. From this remarkable letter sprang four new lyrics in the manner of Milton's 'L'Allegro' and 'Il Penseroso' on the pleasures of opposites: 'Welcome joy and welcome sorrow', 'Where's the poet?', 'Bards of Passion and of Mirth' and 'Fancy'. Woodhouse's well-meaning correspondence had successfully reconnected Keats with the poetics of contrast – 'Muses bright and Muses pale' – and by so doing helped ready him for great achievements in the year ahead.

On receiving Keats's reply, Woodhouse immediately sent Taylor an incisive analysis of the ideas in Keats's letter, his distinction between himself and the 'Wordsworth School', and various types of poetry and poets. Woodhouse's advocacy of Keats, with its attentive argument for his poetry and references to *Endymion*, indicates that he was acting as Taylor's literary-legal adviser.[38] Indeed, it is possible that Taylor and Hessey had actually encouraged Woodhouse to write to Keats in the first place, and that Woodhouse and the publishers shared anxieties about Keats despite his good humour at Hessey's recent dinner. Woodhouse's idea that Keats 'creates for himself the world in which his own fancy ranges' suggests he had perused Keats's earlier remark to Hessey: 'The Genius of Poetry must work out its own salvation in a man . . . That which is creative must create itself.'[39] Woodhouse's response had made Keats think more acutely about his own poetical character and – as important – inspired him to fresh composition. As poet of a world in which his own fancy ranges, Keats could write wherever Fancy led. Rather than thinking of Coleridge's quasi-religious definitions of Imagination and Fancy in *Biographia Literaria*, Keats had in mind those restless aficionados of boxing, 'The Fancy', who roamed the countryside to spectate at prize fights: 'Ever let the Fancy roam, / Pleasure never is at home' ('Fancy', 1–2). In such poems he felt 'you have one idea amplified with greater ease and freedom than in the sonnet'. That sense of dissatisfaction and fresh poetic possibility would encourage his sparring with sonnet forms in the coming winter, strengthening his poetry's reach towards the odes of spring 1819.

At the end of October, Keats told Woodhouse he was 'cogitating on the Characters of Saturn and Ops', possibly indicating he was back at work on the second book of *Hyperion* where Saturn's wife, Ops, or Cybele, is introduced with other 'bruisèd Titans'.[40] He called at Abbey's on Tuesday the 27th, drew £20 cash and made another fruitless attempt to persuade Fanny's guardian to let her visit Tom. A few days later, on Sunday the 31st, Keats signed his journal-letter to America, 'Your anxious and affectionate Brother John', and added a vague postscript: 'This day is my Birth day.'[41]

We hear little from him in November. Dilke's recollection was that he made another visit to Teignmouth around now, leaving Tom in the care of the Bentleys and Mrs Davenport of Church Row, Hampstead.[42] If he was in fact in Devon, then a £25 note and complimentary sonnet, forwarded from

Teignmouth by 'P. Fenbank' on 9 November, was a fortunate outcome of this second visit. Apart from two letters to his sister and a note to thank Mrs Davenport, the only letter that survives from this month is to James Rice on the 24th. Rice was not one of Keats's frequent correspondents, but he had visited Keats at Teignmouth back in April. Perhaps the 'one or two rather pleasant occasions' Keats says he wishes to tell him about alluded to a more recent visit when he had seen the Jeffrey girls. Such happy occasions were otherwise scarce for Keats this autumn.[43]

Tom died on the morning of Tuesday, 1 December, his passing eased by laudanum. Overnight Keats had written to prepare Fanny and, while the Bentleys made arrangements for an undertaker, he went to post the letter before walking down to Wentworth Place. Brown was still in bed, so Keats woke him and gave him the news. They both remained silent for a while, and then Brown spoke: 'Have nothing more to do with those lodgings,—and alone too. Had you not better live with me?' Keats pressed his hand, and replied: 'I think it would be better.'[44]

# Conjunctions, 1819

CHAPTER 18

# ditto, ditto

'BROWN DETAINED me at his House.' So Keats reported to America, two weeks after Tom's death. Their plan to 'keep house together' had advantages: although Keats would have to pay £15 rent quarterly plus day-to-day expenses, he would enjoy Brown's robust company and escape Bentley's noisy children.[1] A door at the side of Wentworth Place led into a narrow hallway with Brown's parlour on the right and Keats's to the left, accessible only when the front door was shut. Both rooms were light, with high ceilings and large windows. Furnishings included modern Regency chairs, a sofa-bed, a sideboard with books and a box of James Tassie's 'gems' – reproductions of classical cameos made with paste and enamel. On Brown's walls hung prints of Hogarth's 'The Rake's Progress', 'The Harlot's Progress' and 'Credulity, Superstition, and Fanaticism'. From the hallway a steep staircase led up with a short return flight of stairs at the top, and a stairway disappeared down to a basement kitchen and extensive wine cellar. On the first floor Brown's bedroom was at the front and Keats's at the back. All rooms had open fireplaces, and Keats's bedroom was also warmed by pale pink walls. The Hampstead Ponds were close by, and there were two domestic water supplies: rain from the roof was piped down to a small lead basin that survives today, and hard water from Hampstead's springs came to the house through pipes of elm.[2] There was most likely an earth closet adjacent to the house.

Surrounding Wentworth Place was a large garden planted with fruit trees, a vegetable plot with a toolshed, and fields to the back and towards the Heath.[3] This open country would not remain so for long, as speculative building was rapidly changing the landscape. In 1820 the Freemasons Arms opened on an extension of Downshire Hill that ran eastwards to the Heath, and three years later St John's Church was consecrated. George Crutchley's 'New Plan of London' shows that the country lanes that had led Keats from Well Walk to Wentworth Place were, by 1835, lined with villas. When he moved in with Brown he did not relocate to the idyllic pastoral haven glimpsed in Joseph Severn's portraits of 'Keats Reading at Wentworth Place' and 'Keats Listening to the Nightingale'; he was in the middle of a suburban building site. Surrounded by this dismaying evidence of 'progress', Keats faltered in his commitment to *Hyperion*'s 'march of endeavour'. As he did so, he was increasingly drawn by memories of the romantic medievalism of remote Scottish abbeys with their intricate interior spaces and, across the Heath, by Caen Wood with its 'verdurous glooms and winding mossy ways'. Together, they make up the entwined, introspective spaces of poems that he would write in the coming spring.

Brown put the word round about Tom, and Haslam wrote to George. On 2 December a letter went off to Cowden Clarke telling him that Tom's funeral was arranged for Monday the 7th at St Stephen's, Coleman Street. Then, encouraged by Brown, Keats began a flurry of social engagements calculated to distract him from his grief. At the theatre for the first time since May, he saw Howard Payne's *Brutus*. 'Kean was excellent, the play was very bad.'[4] In town or at Hampstead he called on or was visited by his sister Fanny, Abbey, the Bentleys, Brawnes and Dilkes, Hazlitt, John and Leigh Hunt, Haslam, Haydon, Mrs Reynolds and her daughters, Lamb, the Novellos, Wylies and a kindly Hampstead neighbour David Lewis. Bailey and Rice were out of touch, and Reynolds was again in Devon. Woodhouse wrote of a 'set' of ladies who admired *Endymion*, including the novelists Jane and Anna Maria Porter and Woodhouse's cousin Mary Frogley (to whom Keats had dedicated 'Hadst thou lived in days of old'). Might they have the pleasure of an introduction? Flattered, Keats left the matter to chance.[5]

In gambling mood, on Friday the 4th he joined a huge crowd of 'the Fancy' heading out of town to Crawley for a keenly anticipated contest between two celebrated boxers: Jack Randall and Ned Turner. The roads were clogged in all directions, and the *Morning Post* reported a '*bang-up* set out altogether'. The fight started at 1pm on a wet Saturday, and after a '*ruffianing*' eighteenth round to '*tumultuous applause*', Randall 'broke out with fresh energy' and '*peppered* the face of his opponent, like a footman's stylish knock at a door—it was ditto, ditto, ditto, ditto, till Turner went down covered with blood'. The fight went to thirty-four rounds before 'a flush knock-down blow' to Turner's head '*floored* him'. Randall clasped his fallen foe's hand 'with much zeal and friendship', and Turner acknowledged he 'had won the battle nobly'.[6] Afterwards Keats described the rapidity of Randall's blows by tapping his fingers on a windowpane, an idea that would return to him in *The Eve of St Agnes* where

the frost-wind blows
Like Love's alarum pattering the sharp sleet
Against the window-panes

(322–4)

– as if warning the lovers to keep up their guard.[7] Footmen could be poets too.

On Monday the 7th he followed Tom's coffin to St Stephen's, once again stepping through the skull-and-crossboned gate. Inside were the tombs of his father, mother and Jennings grandparents. A few yards away was the Armourers' Hall and, across London Wall, Keates's Livery Stables, now trading once again as the Swan and Hoop. Tom's funeral had drawn Keats to a part of London sure to awaken memories of his childhood, parents, brothers and sister – he would have been mournfully aware that, of Thomas and Frances's five children, only fifteen-year-old Fanny and himself remained in London. Anxious about his sister's wellbeing – Abbey planned to withdraw her from school – Keats called at Walthamstow three times before Christmas, on one occasion cutting across frosty fields near their former home at Edmonton. Supported by friends, he had coped bravely with Tom's death, although there were signs of agitation in muddled dinner arrangements with the Reynoldses and Haydon. Work on *Hyperion* remained at a standstill.[8]

Thursday, 17 December was a quiet day at Wentworth Place. Brown had taken his nephews to see the lions at the Tower, and Bentley called with a clothes basket of books from Well Walk. After weeks when he had been unable to settle to *Hyperion*, Keats now went on a little, but it was clear that further composition would require 'a new leaf to turn over' and a fresh start.[9] Perhaps the clear days of hard frost at mid-month were when he wrote his poem 'Fancy'. Two weeks of 'traipsing' since the prize-fight had readied him to write a poem that captured his own restless bouts of high spirits and melancholy, as even visits from well-meaning friends grew wearisome:

Ever let the Fancy roam,
Pleasure never is at home:
At a touch sweet Pleasure melteth,
Like to bubbles when rain pelteth.

(1–4)

The four-stress rhyming couplets of 'Robin Hood' and 'Lines on the Mermaid Tavern' were perfectly adapted to Keats's double purpose. If the steady ditto-ditto of paired rhymes can seem to bear down on human pleasures –

Every thing is spoilt by use:
Where's the cheek that doth not fade,
Too much gaz'd at? Where's the maid
Whose lip mature is ever new?
Where's the eye, however blue,
Doth not weary?

(68–73)

– the same bang-up counterpointing of rhythm and rhyme can also

bring thee, all together,
All delights of summer weather;
All the buds and bells of May,
From dewy sward or thorny spray;
All the heaped autumn's wealth,
With a still, mysterious stealth:
She will mix these pleasures up
Like three fit wines in a cup,
And thou shalt quaff it.

(31–9)

With the weather veering likewise between hazy sun, frosts, fog and rain, his sore throat had returned. Brown left to spend Christmas with Dilke's parents at Chichester but Keats, who had hoped to go too, was again restricted to Hampstead.[10] This brought an unwelcome dilemma. He had received two invitations for dinner on Christmas Day, one from Mrs Brawne and another from Mrs Reynolds, and he seems to have accepted both. Both women were concerned for his wellbeing, and Keats handled this awkward situation uncharacteristically badly. He had already accepted for Mrs Brawne's dinner *not* expecting to be in Hampstead – or so he told Mrs Reynolds on 15 December, thereby disingenuously extracting himself from the latter's invitation and initiating a protracted feud between the Reynolds sisters and Fanny Brawne. His health would have made a more plausible excuse, for the Brawnes' home at Elm Cottage was just a short walk from Wentworth Place up Downshire Hill.

Some thoughts added to his letter for America the next day give a more honest explanation: Mrs Brawne 'is a very nice woman – and her daughter senior is I think beautiful and elegant, graceful, silly, fashionable and strange we have a little tiff now and then—and she behaves a little better, or I must have sheered off.'[11] By now Keats and Fanny Brawne had known each other for some time, although exactly how long is impossible to ascertain. Dilke recalled that they met at his house, possibly as early as August 1818 on Keats's return from Scotland.[12] After that Mr and Mrs Dilke were away from Hampstead until 16 October, when Keats and Brown (just back from the north) visited them. A first meeting with Fanny in late October or November was also a possibility, although Keats – caring for Tom when he was not ill himself – was often unable to leave Well Walk. All one can say is that by December 1818 Keats and Fanny were fairly well acquainted, and that he already felt himself interested in this eighteen-year-old. Fashionably dressed, with a clear complexion, lustrous blue eyes and braids of fine brown hair, Fanny had a bright manner; her aquiline nose and firm mouth suggested a strong personality, mingling resolve with good humour. If Keats found her silly, fashionable and strange, a more steady character appears from the clarity and poise of her first letter to his sister.[13] She played the piano and danced, and among her favourite works was *The New London and Country Songster*, a collection of popular songs that included one Keats knew well, 'Water Parted from the Sea'. She said she enjoyed 'trumpery' novels and, although 'by no means a great poetry reader', had been swept up like Keats by Byron.[14] Fanny Brawne's considerable literary intelligence should not be judged at her own self-deprecating estimate.

In most respects utterly unlike secretive Isabella Jones and the 'eastern' beauty Jane Cox, Fanny Brawne's quick wit and capriciousness were a welcome contrast to Keats's own cares. Living nearby, she was frequently encountered in Hampstead and she had one quality that drew Keats especially strongly: she did not look down on him. Having sketched her character in his letter for America on 16 December, he filled out her portrait two days later:

> Shall I give you Miss Brawn? She is about my height—with a fine style of counte-nance of the lengthen'd sort—she wants sentiment in every feature—she manages to make her hair look well—her nostrills are fine—though a little painful—her mouth is bad and good—her Profil is better than her full-face which indeed is not full but pale and thin and without showing any bone—Her shape is very graceful and so are her movements—her Arms are good her hands badish—her feet toler-able—she is not seventeen—but she is ignorant—monstrous in her behaviour flying out in all directions, calling people such names—that I was forced lately to make use of the term *Minx*—this is I think not from any innate vice but from a penchant she has for acting stylishly. I am however tired of such style and shall decline any more of it.[15]

Fanny was about Keats's height, and she measured up in other respects too. Noting qualities bad, tolerable and good, Keats wishes to appear appreciative but uncommitted and quite possibly about to 'sheer off' with her – although what he actually wrote suggests the beginning of a different story. Probably many of the first encounters between Keats and Fanny took place in the context of parlour games or evenings of music overseen by Mrs Brawne. In such playful settings no one, perhaps not even Keats himself, noticed how he had caught the tones of her voice – including her 'monstrous' habit of calling people 'such names'.

'What a Stupe' was Keats's verdict on Fanny's affection for a less well-favoured friend, 'a downright Miss without one set off'. 'Stupe', meaning a fool, is exactly the kind of 'minxy' insult Keats heard from Fanny. And while 'stupe' is not a Keatsian word, the two occasions when he uses it are both associated with mimicry. We hear it a second time when he describes short-sighted Richard Woodhouse contorting his face into a 'stupe' – here meaning a piece of twisted fabric – while looking into a shop window. In doing so, Woodhouse appeared to be mimicking someone else: 'I stood by in doubt whether it was him or his brother, if he has one.'[16] To 'give' Miss Brawne for George and Georgiana, Keats took on her voice too and, now in a vein for mimicking, went on with a comic scene between Hunt, Hazlitt, Ollier and others. His tone throughout is affectionate, a merging of his own identity with those of his acquaintances and Fanny who, as time passed, would come to mean much more to him. For the moment he could see eye to eye with her, describe her figure and voice, unaware as yet how much she fascinated him.[17]

After three days of thick fog and dark moonless nights, Keats joined the Brawnes at Elm Cottage for Christmas Day. Fanny later wrote to Keats's sister that this was 'the happiest day [she] had ever then spent', a statement variously taken to mean that Keats declared his love for her or that they became engaged – despite the fact that elsewhere she says explicitly that this momen-tous event occurred later.[18] Most likely this was 'the happiest day' simply because of Keats's convivial company. There was no further mention of Fanny in his letter for America, and when Keats began his next journal on St Valentine's Day their relationship had not moved beyond 'every now and then a chat and a tiff'.[19] A few days after that Keats mentioned that he had been seeing Isabella Jones, who supplied him with more game, and later reported an enjoyable conversation with one of the most beautiful girls he had ever seen.[20] Other women were still very much in the frame as potential companions, lovers and muses.

Strapped for cash as usual, Haydon was pressing for a loan. Most unwisely, Keats had let him believe he 'would sacrifice everything . . . to [his] service'.[21] He applied to Taylor for £30 and forwarded it, aware that Haydon's expecta-tions were very much greater. Payback of a kind came on Sunday the 27th when Keats dined at Lisson Grove. He read a letter from Ritchie at Tripoli 'among Camels, Turbans, Palm Trees and sands', inspected architectural details on 'Christ's Entry' and pored over Carlo Lasinio's engravings of the fourteenth-century frescoes in the Campo Santo, Pisa. 'I do not think I ever had a greater treat out of Shakespeare,' he remarked, an extraordinary statement given that he had long regarded Shakespeare as his 'presider'. In these frescoes Keats had found a source for speculation as continually fresh as passages from the plays: 'Full of Romance and the most tender feeling— magnificence of draperies beyond any I ever yet saw not excepting Raphael's— But Grotesque to a curious pitch—yet still making up a fine whole—even finer to me than more accomplish'd works—as there was left so much room for Imagination'.[22] Keats's excitement is understandable. As he turned the large folio pages, what he saw were images corresponding to his own recent experiences of delight and despondency, for Lasinio's frescoes combined scenes of extraordinary beauty and conviviality with harrowing, wormy circumstances of bodily decay, death, judgement and doom. Here, Keats felt, was the 'new leaf' he had looked to turn over: his excited recognition that these vivid, grotesque juxtapositions of human pleasure and misery provided food for his imagination gave him the most positive impulse he had felt for many months, and it would soon find focus and direction. Yet if we can sense Keats's creative energies stirring as the new year came in, it was still by no means certain that his relationship with Fanny Brawne would flourish — or that, if it did so, it would prove happy for either of them.

With Tom dead and George thousands of miles away, individuals with whom Keats had formerly been acquainted started to reappear. This phenomenon is distinctly odd, as if the retrospective mood encouraged by Tom's death was embodied by the arrival of figures Keats had long since consigned to the past. A cousin of George Felton Mathew, one Edward Kirkman, presented himself. Presumably he was an acquaintance from the old Mathew circle of 1815, but why was he at Wentworth Place now? On his way home along nearby Pond Street, Kirkman was beaten and robbed of his watch, a reminder that Hampstead's winding lanes could be dangerous territory. Other predators were circling too, lured by the share of Tom's legacy that Keats could now expect. Haydon, famished for the 'nectar & manna' of cash, kept on at him. Equally insistent were unwelcome visits from a man Keats refers to as 'Archer'. 'Archer above all people called on me one day,' he told the George Keatses on 16 December. And again, in the same letter, on Sunday, 3 January:

Kirkman . . . tells me too of abominable behaviour of Archer to Caroline Mathew—
Archer has lived nearly at the Mathews these two years; he has been amusing

Caroline all this time—and now he has written a Letter to M^rs M—declining on pretence of inability to support a wife as he would wish, all thoughts of marriage. What the worst is, Caroline is 27 years old—It is an abominable matter—He has called upon me twice lately—I was out both times—What can it be for—[23]

Keats no longer called at the Mathews' home on Goswell Street, but contact of some kind must have continued. He had once been close to Caroline, and now she had been jilted he felt for her. But who was Archer, and why should he attempt to call on Keats? It has been suggested that he was Archibald Archer, a well-known painter of portraits and historical subjects then at work on a picture of the Temporary Elgin Room. Archibald Archer changed addresses around now, which might suggest he was evading creditors as well as Caroline Mathew, although why any of this should have involved Keats is as obscure as how his address had been obtained in the first place.[24]

Another identification is possible. 'Archer of all people' was perhaps the former business partner of Thomas Mower Keats, acquainted with Keats and his brothers when they were at Cheapside in 1816–17 and quite possibly introduced by them to Anne and Caroline Mathew.[25] After the Keats/Archer partnership was dissolved in January 1817, John Archer had been involved 'these two years' with the Mathews family – the timing is exact, almost to the week. His attempt to contact Keats was most likely related to Thomas Mower Keats's bankruptcy in December 1818, when William Twysden, eldest son and heir of Sir William Twysden, defaulted on a £2,000 debt.[26] John Archer's otherwise mysterious visits to Keats may have been a mission to raise money on behalf of his former partner, and his address could readily have been ascertained from Abbey in Pancras Lane (Keats had called there on 9 December). Abbey's near-neighbour Joseph Keats, hatter, was also caught up in this bankruptcy of his brother Thomas Mower Keats, and with tragic consequences.

When his brother was bankrupted Joseph was seeking re-election to the Court of Common Council – the City of London's primary decision-making assembly. Wrongly fingered as a debtor, he found himself suddenly ineligible to stand and called on the *Morning Chronicle* to reassure voters: 'We are requested to state that the Mr. Keats, referred to in the case of Twysden, in the insolvent Debtors Court, Thursday, 17th Dec., a hatter in the City, is not Mr. Joseph Keats of Cheapside.' Joseph was eventually returned for Cheapside, but the stress had been great; within a month he was dead, 'universally and deservedly respected'. At auction his household effects revealed a man of considerable property, with a second home in Nightingale Lane, Clapham.[27]

Was Keats aware of any of these Cheapside upheavals? If he glanced at the London papers he would have seen reports of the Keats/Archer bankruptcy, and Abbey surely passed on the gist of what had happened when he called on 9 December and again, just after Joseph Keats's death, on 18 January. With Tom's affairs to arrange, and short of money himself, Haydon's incessant demands grated. 'I shall have a little trouble in procuring the Money,' Keats told him, 'and a great ordeal to go through—No trouble indeed to any one else—or ordeal either—I mean I shall have to go to town some thrice, and stand in the Bank an hour or two—to me worse than any thing in Dante.'[28] Banks were unbearable reminders of his stepfather William Rawlings, his mother's disappearance, the Chancery case and the break-up of the family. To go three times to the City and wait upon a clerk like Rawlings would be more tormenting than Dante's Hell, Lasinio's 'Triumph of Death' or the 'Doom' at St Stephen's.

The year closed with days of sunshine, white frost and winter haze. Wrapped up in his plaid against the cold, Keats went shooting on the Heath with Dilke, and on New Year's Day dined with the Brawnes. Mostly he kept indoors at Wentworth Place, however, nursing a slight return of his sore throat. He read over *Hyperion*, judging it 'scarce begun', and, with Mrs Dilke's old tabby cat curled up beside the fire, copied out for George and Georgiana his recent poems 'Fancy' and 'Bards of Passion and of Mirth', and a lyric he had written for their sister, 'I had a dove'. He added two *Examiner* extracts from Hazlitt's lecture on Godwin's novels, then closed his long letter in time for the Philadelphia mail.

The new year began with ten days at home – Keats was writing a little now and then, but generally felt low and discontented. Possibly he was again dosing himself with laudanum, easing his sore throat while succumbing to opium-induced lassitude or what he called an 'agonie ennuiyeuse'.[29] As at Margate in 1817, however, this seemingly fallow mood signalled imminent change, and at the full moon on 11 January 1819 he said he was moulting like a cat preparing for spring. It was another week before Keats actually stirred himself, telling his sister he would call on her at Pancras Lane before leaving for Hampshire.

In London on Sunday, 17 January, Keats visited Isabella Jones. She suggested he should write a poem on the superstitions of St Agnes' Eve, fast approaching on the 20th. As Keats knew from Robert Burton's seventeenth-century disquisition on 'Love-Melancholy' and 'Symptoms of Love', on that evening young girls should fast 'to know who shall be their first husband'.[30] Popular superstitions filled the folk calendar and, like other anniversaries woven deep into his imagination, complemented the patterns of circling, contrasts, and ebb and flow that made up the instinctual life of his poetry. More consciously, he saw that St Agnes' Eve held possibilities for a story that would mingle midwinter austerity with warm sensuality in a narrative of forbidden love charged with erotic tension and suspense. Perhaps he sensed as well how the frosty night, red-lipped pleasures and tender melancholy of his poem 'Fancy' might be adapted to create a colourful medieval world akin to that of Hunt's *Story of Rimini*, Coleridge's *Christabel*, Scott's *Marmion* and *The Lay of the Last Minstrel* – but here unmistakably *English* in atmosphere. Further prompts and suggestions emerged more gradually. He recalled the aisles and passages, archways, spiral stairs and little doorways from Scotland's ruined abbeys and Lincluden mansion at Dumfries. These elaborate structures and secret inner spaces might enable him to shape a narrative that would lead step by step into the passionate heart of his story in an old ancestral home stalked by dangers. Somewhere wound into this narrative, too, was his memory of a different household full of warmth, security and music – his school at Enfield. As he had done with *Endymion* and *Isabella*, Keats would carry these ideas away from London and, far from the city, give life to them as poetry. His fluctuating feelings for Fanny Brawne would also steady while they were separated, although for the moment Isabella Jones and St Agnes' Eve were uppermost in his mind.

With £20 in cash from Abbey, on Monday the 18th Keats was at the Angel Inn on the Strand to catch a morning coach to Chichester. Already in his knapsack were some sheets of thin paper for his poem. The sixty-two miles usually took eleven hours and, with the weather turning fine, they were on time as they hastened through Midhurst and on to solitary Singleton deep in the South Downs. Weary of winter sun flickering through bare trees, perhaps Keats gazed along the valley to East Dean where, many years after he passed this way, his great twentieth-century biographer Robert Gittings – like Keats, a watcher of the skies – pondered a rare planetary conjunction:

Three planets stand over our stable,
Jupiter, Saturn, Mars,
All come out of the east
With Venus opposed in the west
Four together a testament
Of heathenish portent,
Though no one looks or wonders
But we and a few astronomers.
When conjunction glows again
We shall be gone, our children's children

Old, forgetful, unable
To reckon such pallid forebears,
Who lived, bled, loved, and died,
As you and I did, you and I did.[31]

Across the generations come echoes of Keats and Hardy, poets long dead and gone exactly as we, too, shall be 'gone' at a future moment of planetary conjunction – returned to the changeful universe of life and death that this poem has momentarily escaped. In making his poem turn upon that Keatsian word 'gone', Gittings knowingly adapted a technique of time-shifting that he knew Keats, as he passed East Dean late on the afternoon of 18 January 1818, would shortly invent.

'What did Keats mean—by claiming that from his infancy he had no mother?' Gittings mused on another winter day at East Dean, speculating whether Frances kept her husband and Rawlings on the go at the same time. There is good reason to suspect that when Keats himself crossed the South Downs in January 1819 he was turning over similar thoughts as he pondered Burton's curious turn of phrase in *The Anatomy of Melancholy*: on St Agnes' Eve, young girls should fast 'to know who shall be their first husband'.[32] *First husband?* For Keats, the weeks after Tom's death had revived childhood scenes and memories. There would be no exact or easy alignment between what he recalled from his childhood and the poem now forming in his mind, but the themes of secret passion, a bold lover, a maiden whose dreams prove far from chaste, their love-making and elopement fit the outlines of what little we know about the personalities and relationship of Thomas and Frances Keates. In his epic fragment *Hyperion,* Keats had been concerned with inter-generational conflicts and successions, and we can sense similar preoccupations in the hatreds and rivalries of the new poem towards which he was now feeling his way. Whereas *Hyperion* was projected as statuesque, 'naked and Grecian' in manner, in *The Eve of St Agnes* Keats's lost parents would live again – no 'pallid forebears' but creatures of warm life who had lived, bled, loved and died before he reckoned himself out of his infancy.

Rooks Hill, with its windmill and gibbet, signalled the coach's descent from the Downs. Chichester's cathedral spire soared above the Roman city walls as the coach passed along prosperous North Street with its red-brick town-houses, Assembly Rooms and Buttermarket, then wheeled right at the Gothic market cross and entered the yard of the Dolphin Inn.

Keats was expected. Maria Dilke had written to her father-in-law: 'You will find him a very odd young man, but good-tempered, and good-hearted, and very clever indeed.'[33] Chichester was laid out on the original Roman grid plan, its streets aligned with the points of the compass, finding his way was easy. Keats struck out along East Street, already in sight of a little terrace of houses at the far end. At the front door he was welcomed by seventy-five-year-old Charles Dilke Snr, his wife, Sarah, and a bewhiskered Brown now in the fourth week of his stay. Perhaps William Dilke, a year younger than Keats, was there too. Their home was much larger than Wentworth Place, as appears from a contemporary auction catalogue:

> in the Basement, excellent Cellarage. Ground floor, a neat Entrance, Eating Room, 17 ft. 3 in. by 14 ft. 9 in., stucco cornice, and marble chimney piece, dadoes and papered, opening into a handsome breakfast Room, 18ft. 6 in. by 10 ft. 9 in. with a semi bay window, Kitchen, Scullery, Wash-house, and a Pantry, with a Servant's Room over the same. First floor, a handsome Drawing Room, 18 ft. 8 in. by 17ft. 6 in. stucco cornice, marble chimney piece, dadoed and papered in compartments, a Bed Chamber annexed, three airy attics, a good GARDEN, well planted with Fruit trees, and a Building with a Pit sunk for a Hot House.[34]

Keats was given an attic room with views over red-tiled roofs to the cathedral, bell tower and, at an angle up East Street, the market cross. Behind the house, beyond an orchard, were open fields. The Dilkes' home still stands on Eastgate Square, now converted into a shop, manicure parlour and, in Keats's attic, a hairdresser. Those marble chimneypieces have long gone, but the layout of rooms Keats knew can be traced.

Keats took up the Dilkes' routines. He attended 'old Dowager card parties', explored the twelfth-century cathedral and cloisters, and saw something of how the shattered ruins at Lincluden, Dundrennan, Glenluce, Crossraguel and Beauly might originally have appeared.[35] As a local resident, Robert Gittings understandably believed Chichester's medieval architecture and atmosphere were vital for *The Eve of St Agnes*, although Keats's poem also grew from a more protracted ferment. In 1819 the medieval aspect of Chichester was by no means unique, for similar buildings could still be found at places known to Keats like Canterbury, Oxford, Exeter and, above all, London. As with *Isabella* at Teignmouth, Chichester was a location where experiences, ideas and other prompts towards poetry – some dating from as far back as the Armourers' Hall, the school at Enfield and the ancient 'Moat' – started to coalesce and approach articulation. Old Mr Dilke's talk of heraldry and the byways and rivalries of family history were also an encouragement, and – as Keats's first line suggests – in all probability he began *The Eve of St Agnes* on 20 January 1819 at Chichester.[36]

Around now, too, he set down three stanzas of a lyric apparently related to the mingled romantic theme he intended for his longer poem. At first amorous and amusing –

> Hush, hush, tread softly, hush, hush, my dear,
> All the house is asleep, but we know very well
> That the jealous, the jealous old baldpate may hear,
> Though you've padded his night-cap, O sweet Isabel

– his poem darkens in its third verse:

> Lift the latch, ah gently! ah tenderly, sweet,
> We are dead if that latchet gives one little chink.

Possibly this was drawing on an encounter with Isabella Jones, although the edgy, erotic energy of his lovers' meeting in a 'house asleep' was also impelling Keats in a quite different direction. When he presented his copy of Hunt's 1819 *Literary Pocket Book* to Fanny Brawne, she transcribed this poem into it with a note: 'Written [illegible] twenty first of January' – that is, the Feast of St Agnes.[37] Whether or not Keats actually wrote his poem on that day is uncertain; what mattered to Fanny was that it set a 'latchet' – a fastener – on their love for each other.

On Saturday the 23rd Keats and Brown walked westwards along the old Roman road through Fishbourne, skirted sea marshes at Bosham Creek and Thorney Channel, and came to Emsworth with its merchants' houses and quays. Two more miles brought them to Havant and then Bedhampton, where they passed St Thomas's Church with its ancient yew trees and arrived at the Old Mill House, home of the Dilkes' son-in-law John Snook, his wife, Letitia, and their two sons, Henry, thirteen, and John, eleven.

Born on 7 October 1780, the son of John Snook Snr and Mary Livingston of Portsea, John Snook Jnr came from a large family of bakers and millers. Old Mr Dilke of Chichester was a former Bedhampton resident; he had done business with the Snooks to provision the navy, and their families were now close friends. All of them may have known John Keats, miller, of nearby Hayling Island. The Snooks had acquired the freehold of the Old Mill House and adjacent Bedhampton Mill at a sale on Christmas Eve 1796, and by the time John Snook Jnr married Letitia Dilke on 20 November 1804 he had taken over the business.

The eighteenth-century Old Mill House was elegantly proportioned with a large hallway and three parlours on the ground floor, three bedchambers with a drawing room on the second floor, and four attic lodging rooms. Outside was a garden bordered by a mill pond to the house front and, at the back, by Hermitage Stream. Bedhampton Mill was on the far side of the pond, a massive brick building with adjacent cottage, bakehouse, stable and yard. A powerful waterwheel drove the six pairs of millstones on which Snook's prosperous business turned.[38] A few yards below the mill's tailrace was the sea, so close that small ships could load flour directly from the mill's windows.

Bedhampton Mill has long been demolished and the Old Mill House is now separated from the coast by a busy road, yet it is still possible to recover a sense of the specialness of this place when Keats visited. From his attic room he could gaze out over the mill pond to meadows beyond, listening to water flowing through the sluices. Indeed, this waterside setting held auspicious significance for the intricately crafted poem he was now composing:

> St. Agnes' Eve—Ah, bitter chill it was!
> The owl, for all his feathers, was a-cold;
> The hare limp'd trembling through the frozen grass,
> And silent was the flock in woolly fold.
>
> (1–4)

In these first four lines alone Keats may have had in mind poor Tom from *King Lear*, Wordsworth's 'Resolution and Independence' and the opening 'chill' of Scott's *Marmion* – the poem he had presented to Tom at Margate. *Romeo and Juliet, Antony and Cleopatra, All's Well That Ends Well* and *Cymbeline* have all been suggested as Shakespearean models for Keats's poem alongside Boccaccio, Burton and Ann Radcliffe; and yet, as so often, in *The Eve of St Agnes*, Keats was also drawing directly upon his own experiences and circumstances.

At Bedhampton there was plenty of water. The neatly channelled mill pond recalled the school at Enfield and the New River, Keats's first 'stream of rhyme'. Hermitage Stream behind the house was tidal water from Langston Harbour, a reminder of the mysterious 'shadowy sound' that haunted 'On the Sea'. Located midway between fresh and salt water, the Old Mill House was perfectly placed to suggest the contrasted tones Keats meditated for his poem. Right from his early 'Imitation of Spenser' the steady surface of water had presented a threshold between real and ideal worlds, and *The Eve of St Agnes* would also be concerned with dreaming and waking, folklore and frosty actuality. Likewise, the tidal alternations of Hermitage Stream may have brought to mind a narrative of stealthy entry and furtive flight, the ebbing and flowing of voluptuous desire, and even a verse form that might artfully reconcile passion's 'purple riot' with the demands of narrative – Spenser's stanza from *The Faerie Queen*. Spenserian verse was associated with Keats's delighted discovery of poetry at Enfield; it was used by his early favourites James Beattie and Mary Tighe; and it enjoyed popular success in Byron's *Childe Harold*. Keats had not attempted this form since his 'Imitation of Spenser', but it was exactly suited to his present needs. The rhyme scheme a b a b b c b c c mounts towards a central couplet, then turns in a second sequence towards a closing couplet that takes its leave with a long, supple Alexandrine measure in its final line. Each stanza contained a pattern of gathering intensity, fulfilment and leave-taking that would be reflected in his poem's larger narrative structure. That Keats's genius was indeed responding to the tidal fluctuations of Hermitage Stream is suggested by one of his many masterstrokes in *The Eve of St Agnes*. A new moon appeared two days after his arrival at Bedhampton, and *The Eve of St Agnes* is illuminated throughout by 'St Agnes' moon' as it moves across a cold winter sky, setting six stanzas before the end. By pallid moonshine and turning tides, Keats told the time of his poem.

Keats's plot is simple. Young, virginal Madeline retires from an evening of 'argent revelry' hoping to dream of her lover and future husband, unaware that by a stratagem Porphyro is already hidden in a closet of her bedchamber. She undresses by moonlight and, in 'azure-lidded sleep', dreams of Porphyro until she wakens to find that the 'vision of her sleep' is an all-too-physical reality who melts into her dream as they make love before escaping into a stormy night. In a particularly deft manoeuvre Keats shifts his poem's time frame, and dispatches his lovers into the darkness of a distant past:

And they are gone—Aye, ages long ago
These Lovers fled into a night of Storms.[39]

(370–1)

Such a basic summary does no justice to the sustained narrative drive of his poem's forty-two stanzas, or to its rich Shakespearean tapestries of allure and danger, light and darkness, Christianity and paganism, 'foemen' and lovers, chill and warmth, uproar and silence, pallor, colour, youth, age, life and death. If one measure of Keats's achievement is his poem's finely wrought narrative, another is the assurance with which incipient conflicts are registered and held at bay. Porphyro and Madeline's love will outlive the hatred between their families, the Beadsman's icy penance and old Angela's 'palsy-twitch'd' demise. Every stanza discloses in vivid detail the imponderable contraries of Keats's life and the successive 'heart vexations' that coupled Tom's death with his passionate feelings for Isabella Jones, Jane Cox and, as yet somewhat less intensely, Fanny Brawne. Indeed, there is good reason to believe that the Old Mill House's resemblance to the school at Enfield had drawn Keats back to his school days and earliest recollections of his parents, and that *The Eve of St Agnes* reshapes those traumatic memories to create an alternative, romantic narrative of two lovers who got away.

The evidence for such an interpretation is James Rice's Teignmouth gift of Mateo Alemán's romantic comedy *Guzman de Alfarache*. Keats had read Alemán's opening pages closely, and they supplied rich material for *The Eve of St Agnes*. At the outset Guzman's mother is described frankly as a 'whore'. 'Young, faire, and full of wit', with 'cunning to serve two Masters, and to please two husbands', she is married to an old knight and, on first seeing Guzman's father, 'let him understand, his Addresses would not be indifferent to her'. Assisted by an old woman, Guzman's mother contrives to be taken to a bedchamber where his father is already 'hid in an adjoining room'. He promptly emerges to enjoy 'such a tender and lively Conversation' with her that his son owed his existence 'to that very Minute'.[40] That Keats marked all of these passages in his copy of the book has encouraged conjecture that he saw resemblances to his mother and her complicated relationships with men.[41] Is it possible, too, that Keats also highlighted those passages from *Guzman de Alfarache* because he recognised their potential for a narrative poem? In the book's opening pages he had found the story of a secret affair, an aged woman's 'stratagem' for love and a bedchamber with a hidden closet. Here, in outline, was his plot for *The Eve of St Agnes*.

If Keats saw something in Mateo Alemán's mother that resembled what he knew about Frances, the poem in which he placed her romantic alter ego, Madeline, was also associated with his father. As he was writing in his attic room at Bedhampton, memories of music at night at his school in Enfield helped Keats to create this compelling moment as Porphyro gazes on Madeline sleeping. Here is Keats's first draft:

>             festive          ~~Ball~~
> The boisterous midnight Clarions of the ~~feast~~
> ~~Sounded though faint and far away~~
> ~~Came Sound in his ears~~
> And kettle drums and far heard clarinet
> ~~Reach'd his scar'd ears~~
>
>                 in
> Affray'~~d~~ his ears though but ~~with~~ faintest tones:
>
>                     is
> The Hall door shuts again and all the noise ~~was~~ gone.[42]

He later revised these lines to read:

> The boisterous, midnight, festive clarion,
> The kettle-drum, and far-heard clarionet,
> Affray his ears, though but in dying tone:—
> The hall door shuts again, and all the noise is gone.
>
> (258–61)

That final line, Keats told Cowden Clarke, 'came into my head when I remembered how I used to listen, in bed, to your music at school', a sure indication
that the location of the Old Mill House had carried him back to his school
days.[43] A record of such first causes of great art would be 'enchanting', Cowden
Clarke added in an article in 1861, without attempting to explain how this
Enfield schoolboy had become a poet who – like Shakespeare in *Twelfth Night*
– mingled warmth and chill, passion and danger, as Porphyro and Madeline
meet by moonlight. Keats's revised phrase 'dying tone' echoes the languishing
music of Orsino's 'dying fall' in *Twelfth Night*, and may also whisper in that
fractured rhyme 'gone' of another departure scarred into his school memories.
The moment is picked up by his repetition of 'gone' at the end of *The Eve of St
Agnes* –

> And they are gone—Aye, ages long ago
> the ~~Stom~~
> These lovers fled into a ~~night of~~ Storms[44]

– as if Keats intended to blend family trauma with the romantic world of his
lovers, finding 'solution sweet' for Thomas and Frances in the different destinies of Porphyro and Madeline. There can be no precise likeness between
Keats's parents and the lovers of *The Eve of St Agnes*, and resemblances and
echoes traced here offer us only shadowy clues as to what may have swum into
Keats's imagination in that high room overlooking the water. There is one
further hint, however, that he was indeed romancing family history. It appears
in the final verses where Porphyro exclaims to Madeline, 'Awake! Arise! my
love, and fearless be, / For o'er the southern moors I have a home for thee.' His
first thought for these lines had been more tenderly intimate, and less misty
about his lovers' destination: 'Put on warm cloathing, sweet, and fearless be /
Over the bleak Dartmoor I have a home for thee.'[45] Across Dartmoor lay
Cornwall. In Keats's early draft, when Porphyro and Madeline vanish into
the dark they are bound for a home that family tradition told him was his
father's native place. In his revised version, Keats's 'southern moors' take his

lovers – and us – to Salisbury Plain and, beyond that, to Thomas and James Keates's Dorsetshire.

Keats's draft of *The Eve of St Agnes* shows how intensely he worked at the poem while at Bedhampton, his days varied only by meals and, in the evenings, 'a little Religion and politicts'.[46] 'Nothing worth speaking of happened,' he told George and Georgiana, except for a single excursion with Brown and young John Snook on 25 January – a wet Monday. They took a chaise with a 'leaden horse' on the long uphill road from Havant to Stansted Park, home of the Rev. Lewis Way and his wife, Mary Drewe, to see a chapel consecrated. Their curiosity had been roused by this newspaper advertisement: 'THE CONSECRATION of the CHAPEL in STANSTED PARK, will take place on Monday, the 25th instant, (being the holiday of the Conversion of St. Paul) . . . the ceremony, on this occasion, will be performed by the Right Rev. the LORD BISHOP of St. DAVID'S, or the Honourable and Right Rev. the LORD BISHOP of GLOUCESTER'.[47] Their interest piqued, they had evidently applied, as was required, for tickets. 'The Chapel is built in Mr. Way's park,' Keats explained, adding that its consecration was 'not amusing—there were numbers of carriages, and his house crammed with Clergy—they Sanctified the Chapel—and it being a wet day consecrated the burial ground through the vestry window. I begin to hate Parsons—they did not make me love them that day.'[48] Given his anticlerical opinions, it is surprising to find Keats there at all. 'I will not harm her, by the great S$^t$ Paul,' Porphyro says of Madeline in his draft of *The Eve of St Agnes*. Here, and in other details of imagery and architecture, Keats drew on the consecration service and what he had seen in Way's stately mansion. Grinling Gibbons's wood carvings and the chapel's three-arched, Gothic windows of stained glass may have been the originals of Keats's 'Casement high and tripple arch'd . . . / All gardneded with carven imageries' (208–9), although his brooding on his school days also points us to the three high windows and ornate brick designs of the old Enfield mansion.[49]

Stansted created another set of strange conjunctions with his past. Lewis Way had trained as a lawyer until an unexpected legacy, willed by a stranger, brought the fortune with which he purchased Stansted and founded a college to train ministers to convert Jews to Christianity – the new chapel represented the latest stage in that programme. Way was vice-president of the London Society for Promoting Christianity Amongst Jews, had travelled throughout Europe visiting synagogues and addressed the czar of Russia on his conversionist aims. So he was something of an international curiosity, but Keats's interest in him may have lain rather closer to home. He was the son of Benjamin Way of Denham Park, a former president of Guy's Hospital, and he had married Mary Drewe, daughter of the Rev. Herman Drewe of Combe Raleigh, a mile or so from Honiton in Devon. In August 1811 Mrs Way and her family were reported to be staying at Belmont House, Bedhampton, a short distance from the Old Mill House.[50] For some years John Hamilton Reynolds had been courting Eliza Powell Drewe, daughter of the Rev. George Powell Drewe of Exeter and quite possibly a relative of the Drewes of Combe Raleigh. There was also a Way link with Richard Woodhouse, who attended Eton with Lewis Way's orphaned cousins. Taken together, the Way associations at Guy's and in Bedhampton and a possible Way-Drewe-Reynolds-Woodhouse connection start to make sense of Keats's otherwise unlikely interest in a consecration ceremony conducted by two '*damnation* Bishops'.[51] This network extended further, too. The Way family came from Bridport, Dorset, midway between Honiton and Dorchester, all places associated with Keats's West Country foray in spring 1818. From Teignmouth, Keats and Tom had taken a cross-country route to meet the London coach at Honiton, when the coaching inn at Exeter was obvious, easier and quicker. A day into their journey, they had paused at Bridport for Tom to recuperate.[52] All of these matters may be no more than coincidences, but they are suggestive too – as if Keats's various migrations around England were following Way itineraries and associations now invisible to us. His proximity to the Jew-converter Lewis Way on 25 January 1819 makes his presence at Guy's Hospital, Bedhampton, Stansted, and even Honiton and Bridport align in a curious fashion with Abbey's recollection that after her marriages to Thomas Keates and William Rawlings, Keats's mother had lived '*as* the Wife of a Jew at Enfield, named Abraham'.[53] In *The Eve of St Agnes*, Keats had redeemed family tragedy with romance; given his hatred of 'Parsons', perhaps his decision to visit Stansted Chapel was, in some way, an attempt to make his own wayward life come to terms with his mother's so-called 'irregularities' after the death of her first husband.

# CHAPTER 19

# Ever Indolent

Back from Bedhampton, Keats was at Wentworth Place in the dark snowy days of early February. The intensity of composition had left him drained, and there were unmistakable signs that he was now chronically ill. Rainy Stansted had brought back the sore throat that had troubled him intermittently since autumn 1817, and its debilitating long-term effects were now becoming apparent. The exotic foods Porphyro had prepared to entice Madeline – 'jellies soother than the creamy curd, / And lucent syrops, tinct with cinnamon' (266–7) – also told of Keats's agonising need to soothe his throat. If one looks for a precise time at which his recurring but apparently superficial illnesses became something much worse, January 1819 appears most likely. In the coming weeks his bouts of intense activity and prolonged lethargy point to a deeper infection, pulmonary tuberculosis, starting to take hold.

With no word from America, he felt increasingly responsible for his sister and advised her on reading, music, games, health, plants, Tassie gems, drawing, pets and her confirmation. Abbey's decision to withdraw her from school particularly dismayed him, for she would have to endure Mrs Abbey's 'unfeeling and ignorant gabble'. '[T]he Keatses were ever indolent,' she had told Fanny, for 'it was born in them'.[1] As noted earlier, Fanny had shrugged this off – 'If it is born with us how can we help it' – and from now on Keats's relish for the 'delicious diligent indolence' of poetic creativity spoke up for Keatses while snubbing their persecutor. Indolence and the poetic life, both connected with his illness and recourse to opium, would preoccupy him throughout the coming spring.

A change came on Friday, 12 February, when he went to town. Among those he saw were Abbey, Woodhouse, the Wylies and John Taylor. Isabella Jones presented him with a brace of pheasants and suggested a superstitious subject for another poem, 'The Eve of St Mark', when, according to James Montgomery,

The ghosts of all whom DEATH shall doom
Within the coming year,
In pale procession walk the gloom,
Amid the silence drear.[2]

In the following week Keats set to work, adapting the four-stress octosyllabics of 'Fancy' and Coleridge's *Christabel* to his morbid theme:

Upon a Sabbath day it fell;
Twice holy was the Sabbath bell,
That call'd the folk to evening prayer.
(1–3)

He was aiming, he said later, at a 'spirit of Town quietude [and] the sensation of walking about an old county Town in a coolish evening'.[3] His poem is suffused with the romantic medievalism of Thomas Chatterton's *Aella*, from which the name of his heroine, Bertha, is taken, while the 'old Minster Square' and 'bishop's garden wall' are unmistakably recalled from Chichester. Further architectural details came from Stansted Chapel, and the fashionable interior of Bertha's home –

The parrot's cage and pannel square,
And the warm angled winter screen,
On which were many monsters seen,
Call'd doves of Siam, Lima mice,
And legless birds of paradise
(76–80)

– recalls Keats's description of Isabella's 'tasty' London apartment. Surrounded by shadows of 'wildest forms' cast by a fire's glare, Bertha sits to read the legend of St Mark and, beneath her text, this 'pious poesie' is added in 'smallest crow-quill size':

—'Als writith he of swevenis
Men han beforne they wake in bliss,
Whanne thate hir friendes thinke hem bounde
In crimpid shroude farre under grounde.'
(99–102)

Those shrouded corpses were taken directly from the 'Doom' on St Stephen's gateway, and as Keats's imagination took flight in Chatterton's Middle English he added this remarkable passage on the legend of St Mark's Eve:

Gif ye wol stonden hardie wight—
Amiddes of the blacke night—
Righte in the churche porch, pardie
Ye wol behold a companie
Appouchen thee Full dolourouse
For sooth to sain from everich house
Be it in City or village
Wol come the Phantom and image
Of ilka gent and ilka carle
Whom coldè Deathè hath in parle
And wol some day that very year
Touchen with foulè venìme spear
And sadly do them all to die—
Hem all shalt thou see verily—
And everichon shall by the thee pass
All who must die that year Alas[4]

Chatterton, Chaucer and Lasinio's engravings all helped to create this grim tableau of death, as did Keats's own frequent encounters with those whom 'coldè Deathè hath in parle'.

His new poem was soon well under way, and its eerie counterpointing of 'Town quietude' and a grotesque medieval Dance of Death promised much. But after 119 lines he dropped it. For Keats, early 1819 was a season of abruptly conflicting impulses. His manuscript of *Hyperion*, incomplete though not abandoned, stood as a reproach to any other composition he might attempt, and there were signs that he was tiring of Isabella Jones's expectation that he should write poems to order. After the strain of recent months he needed time to think and recuperate, yet he was distracted by anxieties about America, his sister, health and money. Abbey and Haydon were both impossible to deal with. These immediate worries were compounded by his brooding over Tom's death and his unfair treatment by critics. Unable to settle, he told George and Georgiana that he was 'not in great cue for writing lately'.[5] All of these factors weighed in his decision to leave off his poem, but most pressing were its superstitious subject matter and the date of St Mark's Eve: 24 April. This was the day following Thomas Keates's funeral fifteen years earlier, a coincidence that Keats would not have missed. Coming so soon after

Tom's death, and while he was enduring a chronically sore throat, a poem about those who would die in the coming year was too melancholy to contemplate. But he would return to 23 April and the Eve of St Mark in the autumn when, with sphinx-like oddity, he decided to set his comic fantasy poem *The Cap and Bells* on those two days.

Isabella's pheasants were given to Mrs Dilke and on 20 February made a Sunday dinner for the Dilkes, Keats, Brown, Rice and Reynolds. A new moon brought heavy snow on Thursday the 24th, St Mark's Eve, detaining Keats in town for several days – probably at Taylor's in Fleet Street. 'I have about every three days been to Abbey's and to the Lawers [*sic*]', he told Haydon, referring to his attempts to secure a third share of Tom's capital from their grandmother's legacy (he remained unaware of the £1,072 capital and £300 interest awaiting him in Chancery). Unfortunately, this encouraged Haydon to anticipate a loan, and when the dismal actuality of Keats's finances became apparent (he had less than he 'thought for') there was awkwardness for them both. As trustee for the Keats children, Abbey was now minded to delay any payments until Fanny, the youngest, came of age in 1824.[6]

If Keats heard too frequently from Haydon, there was not a word from George and Georgiana. *The Examiner* carried weekly reports of 'American Affairs', including the reformer William Cobbett's interventions from there in the Westminster election campaign. When voting for an MP commenced on 13 February, Keats began another letter to his brother: 'How is it that we have not heard from you . . .?' This letter would be continued, off and on, until 3 May, and Keats's fitful bouts of writing and silence reveal much about his erratic state of mind.[7] He told them about Bedhampton, his visits to London, the 'dull' Reynolds girls and Miss Brawne, an invitation to a dance, his recent poems, Stansted Chapel, drinking claret with Woodhouse, Isabella Jones, reviews and the Dilkes' plan to move to Westminster.[8] Visits to the theatre and the British Museum were mentioned alongside an account of a 'velocopede' (a primitive bicycle) and, with vicarious pleasure, extracts from Hazlitt's waspish pamphlet *A Letter to William Gifford*.

Keats evidently had plenty to say, yet the feeling that comes across is brittle and dissatisfied, nowhere more so than in his surprisingly sour reflections on Benjamin Bailey. Formerly a 'noble fellow' attached to Marianne Reynolds, Bailey's hasty courtship of Bishop Gleig's daughter had revealed no more romance in him than 'want of a wife'. Friendships for Keats often proved short-lived – Cowden Clarke, Mathew, Hunt and Haydon had once been close but were now shunned or out of touch. Still, Bailey had formerly been an esteemed friend, and this drastic alteration is puzzling unless Keats had a strong personal motive for it. Perhaps Taylor had told him of Bailey's fateful contributions to the 'Cockney School' essay.[9] Or had Bailey's and Archer's behaviour reminded Keats of a woman from whom he, too, had recently parted? After this letter Keats never again mentioned Isabella Jones, and by May she was unwell and obliged to quit London.[10] The lesson of Bailey's behaviour to Marianne Reynolds, Keats surmised, was that 'the man who redicules romance is the most Romantic of Men' and 'he who abuses women and slights them—loves them the most'. The upshot was that one should not take 'every thing literal', for '[a] Man's life of any worth is a continual allegory . . . Shakespeare led a life of Allegory; his works are the comments on it.'[11] Apparently self-effacing and invisible as a man, Shakespeare in his works comprehended all humankind. Burns, mired in a life of whoring and booze, became in his songs the most lyrical of lovers. And Keats? Physically compact, socially awkward, he had found in poetry a means to hoist himself up and attract greatness, and women, to his embrace – yet at different times he was so dissatisfied that he contemplated giving up poetry altogether.

Other figurative reversals this spring appear in his verse caricature of Brown's sturdy figure and balding head as 'a melancholy carle, / Thin in the waist, with bushy head of hair'. A less playful attack was unleashed on his former school friend Charles Wells. Keats had been to Bentley's to recover papers and correspondence, among them Wells's 'Amena' letters to Tom from Margate two years earlier. Seizing on this 'cruel deception' as a cause of Tom's fatal sickness, and forgetting his own earnest plea that men should bear up with each other, he vowed to 'harm him all I possibly can'.[12] He broke decisively with Wells, and continued to think of a defection from poetry. To amuse Georgiana, he parodied a petition for entry to a madhouse, explaining how he had originally committed to the 'art & mystery of poetry' by having 'cut, rebuffed, affronted, huffed & shirked, and taken stint, at all other employments' – surely a glance back at his own abandoned medical training. A few lines later he returned to that theme, pondering whether he should 'go to Edinburgh & study for a physician . . . it is not worse than writing poems, & hanging them to be flyblown on the Reviewshambles—Every body is in his own mess.' Among other novelties of the season were Abbey's frequent suggestions that he should go in for hatmaking – with Joseph Keats dead, there was a vacancy at the firm.[13]

Life to Keats in early 1819 seemed a 'mess', yet on one day he dined sociably with Taylor and William Hilton, and on another got a black eye while playing cricket.[14] At times he was also irritable, restless in himself and suspicious of others. Several of his letters from January to April contrive a further narrative, to the effect that he had been doing little or nothing: 'nothing particular passed' (2 January); 'Nothing worth speaking of happened' (14 February);

'During the evening nothing passed' (19 February); 'dined—and had a nap. I cannot bear a day annihilated in that manner' (17 March); 'I do not know what I did on Monday—nothing—nothing—nothing' (17 March). Haydon heard that he had been 'about nothing; being in a sort of qui bono temper, not exactly on the road to an epic poem'; his sister, Fanny, of his 'idleness' and that he had 'written nothing, and almost read nothing.'[15] We know that Keats was not entirely 'about nothing', so what was he covering up?

'We lead verry quiet lives here,' he told George and Georgiana. 'I never drink now above three glasses of wine—and never any spirits and water.' Keats relished the cool, throat-calming effects of claret and may have kept to his limit, although some evidence suggests otherwise. Haydon, never entirely trustworthy in his anecdotes, claimed that Keats had once been 'scarcely sober' for six weeks. If true, the most likely period was in these unsettled days of February and March when Keats apparently succumbed, as Haydon recalled, to a bout of despondency. His recourse to laudanum was never explicitly admitted, although Brown later came to the conclusion that he had done it to 'keep up his spirits'. That Brown warned Keats of the 'danger of such a habit' suggests that it was already a long-term one and, as we saw, the likelihood is that he had started dosing himself when caring for Tom. At two centuries' distance, it is difficult to appreciate how commonplace an opium habit was in Keats's lifetime. Guy's dispensed laudanum as a matter of course, and for a simple reason: it was the only painkiller that worked. Thomas De Quincey maintained that it had curative powers as the 'sole known agent' to 'arrest' pulmonary consumption, and Keats may well have believed likewise.[16] For everyday ailments, opium was a remedy so routine as not to be worth mentioning, although its effects often demanded expression.

Keats's black eye was a salutary instance. That evening, Thursday, 18 March, he had gone to bed, slept all night and woken late next morning

in a sort of temper indolent and supremely careless: I long after a stanza or two of Thompson's Castle of indolence—My passions are all alseep [sic] from my having slumbered to nearly eleven and weakened the animal fibre all over me to a delightful sensation about three degrees on this side of faintness . . . the fibres of the brain are relaxed in common with the rest of the body, and to such a happy degree that pleasure has no show of enticement and pain no unbearable frown.[17]

If Keatses 'were ever indolent', as Mrs Abbey said, in this mood of 'supreme carelessness' Keats was most fully himself – and at least part of his 'delightful sensation' arose from an exquisite sense of self-vindication. He referred to moods of 'indolence' throughout his letters, using the word to denote mental and physical laziness, withdrawal, passivity and, more positively, a 'numbness' – the feel of not to feel – that could herald renewed creativity.[18] The careless temper described in his letter on Friday the 19th was of the latter order. If, as seems likely, Keats had taken laudanum to comfort his eye, it is striking that he should have compared his feelings on waking to the pleasurable indolence, or *indolentia*, that James Thomson's allegorical poem *The Castle of Indolence* had associated with a poetic temper. In *Lyrical Ballads*, Wordsworth had deemed a 'wise passiveness' conducive to poetry, and more recently Coleridge's preface 'Of the Fragment of Kubla Khan' had endorsed opium's poetic efficacy.[19] Physically inert yet intellectually vital and creative, Keats's dream-like abstraction on 19 March also resembled the effects of laudanum described by contemporaries such as De Quincey. Doses of opium help to explain his unstable moods; his sense that poetry had been 'so distant lately'; his four weeks' silence when, 'in a rather low state of mind', he broke off his letter for America; and the sudden outpouring of brilliant poetry that ensued.[20] If one wished to find a case study of opium's effects beyond De Quincey's classic *Confessions of an English Opium-Eater*, Keats early in 1819 would make a fine example.

Like Coleridge and De Quincey, Keats found in opium a recreation that was also a stimulant for his imagination, and his subsequent encounter with Coleridge on Hampstead Heath was particularly fortunate. Keats had taken a Sunday morning stroll towards Highgate and met

> M$^r$ Green our Demonstrator at Guy's in conversation with Coleridge—I joined them, after enquiring with a look whether it would be agreeable—I walked with him a[t] his alderman-after dinner pace for near two miles I suppose In those two Miles he broached a thousand things—let me see if I can give you a list— Nightingales, Poetry—on Poetical sensation—Metaphysics—Different genera and species of Dreams—Nightmare—a dream accompanied by a sense of touch— single and double touch—a dream related—First and second consciousness—the difference explained between will and Volition—so my metaphysicians from a want of smoking the second consciousness—Monsters—the Kraken— Mermaids—southey believes in them—southey's belief too much diluted—A Ghost story—Good morning—I heard his voice as he came towards me—I heard it as he moved away—I had heard it all the interval—if it may be called so.[21]

What an interval! Keats's first and only encounter with the Sage of Highgate could not have come at a better moment. Poetry, poetical sensation and different kinds of dreams were all among his recent preoccupations, and in many ways this famous record of Coleridge's extraordinary, thousand-thinged voice foreshadowed Keats's own remarkable resurgence of creativity during May.[22] The conjunction of 'Nightingales, Poetry' in Coleridge's discourse was a happy one, for Keats had read Coleridge's conversational poem 'The Nightingale' with particular attention. But it was the dream-like succession of ideas and images from 'Nightingales, Poetry' to 'the Kraken—Mermaids' that struck Keats most powerfully; his journal-letters and spring odes of 1819 have a similarly sustained pliancy of thought, and dreams of different kinds would flow into the springtide of poetry that lay a little way ahead.

One such dream-vision had occurred on 19 March, when a laudanum-induced mood in which 'pleasure has no show of enticement and pain no unbearable frown' was readying him for composition. 'Neither Poetry, nor Ambition, nor Love have any alertness of countenance as they pass by me,' his letter continued, 'they seem rather like three figures on a greek vase—a Man and two women—whom no one but myself could distinguish in their disguisement.'[23] Here, described in his letter for America, is the origin of his 'Ode on Indolence' – a poem in which Keats explores his own unique 'poetical sensation'.

The five poems that he would write between now and late May – 'Ode on Indolence', 'Ode to Psyche', 'Ode to a Nightingale', 'Ode on a Grecian Urn' and 'Ode on Melancholy' – do not form a sequence, and no one has been able to establish the order in which they were written. They grew out of Keats's experiments with sonnet forms, and stand as independent yet interwoven meditations with similarities of theme, style and phrasing. In general terms the odes are concerned with ideas that had long preoccupied him: exile and home, solitude and society, beauty and suffering, joy and melancholy, transience and loss, and how a life of tragic contingencies spoils a nightingale's singing. Readers and critics alike have long agreed that these poems are among the greatest expressions of Romantic genius, but that consensus has consistently detached them from the life in and by which they were created. We need to be more sympathetically aware of how circumstances that shaped Keats's orphaned spirit became, in his 1819 odes, the forlorn life of all humankind.

That indolence was said to be Keats's birthright gave the passage from his letter – and the poem that grew from it – an intensely personal significance: the 'Ode on Indolence' amounted to his manifesto both as a poet and as a man. But when exactly was it written? The Shakespearean tenor of

The morn was clouded, but no shower fell,
Though in her lids hung the sweet tears of May

(45–6)

is no reason to date it to the end of that month, after the other odes had been composed. Equally, the protracted composition of *Endymion* and *Hyperion* shows that Keats often had difficulty in reviving a lapsed or interrupted impulse to write, and the likelihood is that he wrote his 'Ode on Indolence' immediately after his letter while still both overcome and fulfilled by *indolentia*. As he began to compose, he transformed the 'three figures on a greek vase' into a masque of hushed inquiry:

> O folly! What is Love? and where is it?
> And for that poor Ambition—it springs
>     From a man's little heart's short fever-fit;
> For Poesy!—no,—she has not a joy,—
>     At least for me,—so sweet as drowsy noons,
>         And evenings steep'd in honied indolence;
> O, for an age so shelter'd from annoy,
>     That I may never know how change the moons,
>         Or hear the voice of busy common-sense!
>                         (32–40)

Forsaking love, ambition and his 'demon Poesy', Keats contemplates an age as blissfully insulated from worldly 'annoy' as 'evenings steeped in honied indolence'. As his three figures return for a third time, the 'dim dreams', 'stirring shades, and baffled beams' of reverie gradually merge with a world of time and physical actuality:

> The open casement press'd a new-leaved vine,
>     Let in the budding warmth and throstle's lay;
> O shadows! 'twas a time to bid farewell!
>     Upon your skirts had fallen no tears of mine.
>                         (47–50)

His 'shelter'd' moment may have passed, but its personal import has been grasped: Keats's 'idle spright' is most creatively receptive when least distracted by love, ambition or hunger for fame. No longer 'dieted with praise' like a 'pet-lamb in a sentimental farce' (53–4), Keats announces that he will respond to and write out of the seemingly 'idle days' that were his richest inheritance as Thomas Keates's son:

> Ripe was the drowsy hour;
> The blissful cloud of summer-indolence

Benumb'd my eyes; my pulse grew less and less;
Pain had no sting, and pleasure's wreath no flower.

(15–18)

In such a mood successful composition begins, he now realised, and similar ventures into the heart of visionary *indolentia* would shape each of the odes yet to be written. Three of them, 'Ode to a Nightingale', 'Ode on a Grecian Urn' and 'Ode on Melancholy', adapted the pentameter lines and rhyme scheme of 'Indolence', opening each ten-line stanza with a quatrain rhyming a b a b and concluding with a sestet variously rhymed. The stanzaic architecture of these poems, enabling their sustained development of thought, was related to Keats's parallel endeavour to find a sonnet stanza that was 'more interwoven & complete' and better suited to the English language.[24] The new verse form of his odes, compact yet capable of multiple configurations, was ideal for tracing the prolonged ebb and flow of introspective life with all the concentrated power of the sonnet form.

Another floating and whirling daydream lay behind Keats's irregular fourteen lines on Dante's Paolo and Francesca. 'Why did I laugh tonight?', a sardonic sonnet transcribed in a letter on 19 March, voiced a chastened awareness that even amid pleasures 'the seed of some trouble is put into the wide arable land of events'.[25] News of the death of Haslam's father was expected at any moment.

After that sonnet, he left off his letter until mid-April. In the interim he visited Abbey on 2 and 3 April to withdraw £60 and £43.7s.7d., two extraordinarily large sums of money that exhausted the £500 deposited on 4 June 1818. A considerable portion of this went on debts, rent and living expenses, and a farewell party for the Dilkes on Saturday, 3 April. They were moving to be near their son at Westminster School, and over this weekend Mrs Brawne and her family returned to occupy their half of Wentworth Place. Fanny was now living immediately next door, and Keats joined them on Sunday the 4th for lunch. Far from being able to project an image of affluence, he was obliged from now on to call in various loans he had made.[26] His *Examiner* review of Reynolds's parody of Wordsworth's *Peter Bell*, written at mid-month, may have brought in a few shillings, but from now on his circumstances were desperately straitened.

After a long break Keats returned to his journal-letter on 15 April, once again rallying himself at the anniversary of his father's accident and death. Still 'at a stand in versifying' and unable to resume *Hyperion*, he was now far from entertaining the high hopes with which he had set about *Endymion* exactly two years before. 'I mean ... to look round at my resources and means,' he confided to George and Georgiana, 'and see what I can do without poetry.'[27] After his 'Ode on Indolence' this was hardly a mood in which to expect another release into composition, and yet that was exactly what happened. Within days of thinking to quit poetry, Keats wrote out this ballad in his letter:

**La belle dame sans merci—**

O what can ail thee knight at a[r]ms
   Alone and palely loitering?
The sedge has withered from the Lake
   And no birds sing!

O what can ail thee knight at a[r]ms
   So haggard and so woe begone?
The squirrel's granary is full
   And the harvest's done.

     a
I see ~~death's~~ lilly on thy brow
   With anguish moist and fever dew,
          a
And on thy cheeks ~~death's~~ fading rose
   Fast Withereth too—

I met a Lady in the ~~Wilds~~ Meads
   Full beautiful, a faery's child
Her hair was long, her foot was light
   And her eyes were wild—

I made a Garland for her head,
   And bracelets too, and fragrant Zones
She look'd at me as she'd did love
   And made sweet moan—

I set her on my pacing steed
   And nothing else saw all day long
For sidelong would she bend and sing
   A faery's song—

She found me roots of relish sweet
           manna
  And honey wild and ~~honey~~ dew
And sure in language strange she said
    I love thee true—

She took me to her elfin grot
              and sigh'd full sore
  And there she wept ~~and there she sigh'd full sore~~
And there I shut her wild wild eyes
    With kisses four.

And there she lulled me asleep
    And there I drean'd Ah Woe betide!
The latest dream I ever dreamt
    On the cold hill side

I saw pale kings and Princes too
    Pale warriors death pale were they all
They cried La belle dame sans merci
    Thee hath in thrall.

I saw their starv'd lips in the gloam
  ~~All tremble~~      gaped
    With horrid warning wide ~~agape~~
And I awoke and found me here
    On the cold hill's side

And this is way I ~~wither~~ sojourn here
    Alone and palely loitering;
Though the sedge is wither'd frome the Lak[e]
    And no birds sing— —..........[28]

Mysterious in origin and meaning, Keats's poem was a bleak pendant to *The Eve of St Agnes* in which Porphyro had played for Madeline an 'ancient ditty, long since mute, / In Provence call'd, "La belle dame sans merci"' (291–2). Forsaking the warmed interior of Madeline's chamber for a withered landscape, Keats, like James Macpherson in his Ossian poems, contrived to make the remote and ancient speak with powerful immediacy. If words such as 'ail', 'woe begone', 'withereth', 'meads', 'zone', 'elfin', 'thrall' and 'gloam' create an atmosphere of romantic medievalism, Keats's tale of erotic fixation and entrapment invokes the figure of Jane Cox that distracted him at Tom's deathbed. Fanny Brawne was, for the moment, most likely not involved in his obsessive fantasies, although it would not be long before she, too, awakened feelings of desire, danger and 'horrid warning'.

While Keats's 'knight at arms' was a medieval stand-in for his own sexual *tristesse*, an alternative version of 'La Belle Dame sans Merci' transformed that warrior into the Chaucerian figure of a 'wretched wight'. Derived from an Old English word, 'wiht', meaning 'a man', 'wight' can also suggest supernatural possession – akin to the 'carle / Whom coldè Deathè hath in parlè' in *The Eve of St Mark*. George Keats had a copy of this alternative version, as did Leigh Hunt, who published it in *The Indicator* with the first line 'Ah, what can ail thee, wretched wight'.[29] Most curious among this *Indicator* version's many enigmas is how it embellishes that English word 'wight' with recollections of Burns in a ballad stanza that owed a good deal to the Bard. Its three lines of four measures followed by one of two measures were technically identical to the first four lines of Burns's stanza in 'To a Mountain Daisy':

> Cauld blew the bitter-biting *North*
> Upon thy early, humble birth;
> Yet cheerfully thou glinted forth
>     Amid the storm.[30]

Keats varies his rhyme scheme and adds much greater emphasis to the short line, sometimes with three consecutive stresses ('made sweet moan', 'love thee true', 'cold hill side', 'no birds sing'). His lines sound slower and more laboured than Burns's, and their cumulative burden creates a sense of intractable inertia. That Burns should be a presence in both versions of 'La Belle Dame sans Merci' is perhaps less surprising when we recall how Keats had been thinking of the Bard as he walked slowly towards Iona's old kings and princes, whose effigies are now re-encountered in his ballad's dream-world:

> I saw pale kings, and princes too,
>     Pale warriors, death-pale were they all;
> Who cried, 'La belle Dame sans mercy
>         Hath thee in thrall!'

> I saw their starv'd lips in the gloom
>     With horrid warning gaped wide,

And I awoke, and found me here
    On the cold hill side.[31]

Keats had thought of Burns's miserable life tilling 'a few strips of Green on a cold hill', and he had encountered Iona as an island populated by the ghosts of all those called, like Burns, to venture on the road of the dead. In a singularly weird transposition Keats's 'wretched wight' in the *Indicator* version awakens from his dream of pale kings and warriors to realise his own enthralment on a 'cold hill side' identical to the one tilled by the passion-torn Bard. Was a similar fate now awaiting Keats too?

'La Belle Dame sans Merci' emerged from protracted imaginative gestation, when Keats was also meditating the interpenetration of love and grief, laughter and trouble, and the virtues of a 'honied indolence' quite unlike his ballad's desolate scene. These human concerns were continued in his letter for America, in a remarkable passage of philosophising about the world of 'mortal pains' he had experienced after his parents' deaths, at Guy's and most recently beside Tom's deathbed – a world in which man is 'destined to hardships and disquietude of some kind or other'. The language in which he lashed out at Bailey and Wells had now given way to a calmer, more accepting voice. Much as he had sought 'to know a Man's faults, and then be passive', he argues that 'the inhabitants of the world will correspond to itself' and that consequently we should brace ourselves to endure life's troubles. Dismissing the Christian idea of a 'vale of tears' from which we are 'to be redeemed by a certain arbitrary interposition of God and taken to Heaven', he gives us a 'vale of Soul-making' where 'intelligences or sparks of the divinity' acquire identities 'by the medium of a world like this': 'Do you not see how necessary a World of Pains and troubles is to school an Intelligence and make it a soul?' Recent events and anniversaries were much on his mind, and perhaps his thoughts turned to his youngest brother, Edward, whose untimely death meant that he had never developed a distinct personality. Had Edward Keats lived he would have been eighteen years old a few days hence; as it was, in Keats's 'faint sketch of a system of Salvation which does not affront our reason and humanity', his little brother Edward had disappeared like the shadow of a face in water.[32]

Keats's idea that pains and troubles were necessary to form a spiritual identity resembled Apollo's apotheosis at the climax of *Hyperion*'s third book, hurriedly resumed about now. With Hyperion's power waning, Apollo has encountered the 'awful Goddess' Mnemosyne, mother of the Muses, who initiates his divinity. What Apollo undergoes is the 'wondrous lesson' of what it means 'to feel and suffer in a thousand diverse ways', a preternatural amplification of the 'vale of Soul-making' he had explored in his letter. 'Knowledge enormous makes a God of me,' Apollo proclaims:

> 'Names, deeds, gray legends, dire events, rebellions,
> Majesties, sovran voices, agonies,
> Creations and destroyings, all at once
> Pour into the wide hollows of my brain,
> And deify me, as if some blithe wine
> Or bright elixir peerless I had drunk,
> And so become immortal.'—Thus the God,
> While his enkindled eyes, with level glance
> Beneath his white soft temples, stedfast kept
> Trembling with light upon Mnemosyne.
> Soon wild commotions shook him, and made flush
> All the immortal fairness of his limbs;
> Most like the struggle at the gate of death;
> Or liker still to one who should take leave
> Of pale immortal death, and with a pang
> As hot as death's is chill, with fierce convulse
> Die into life: so young Apollo anguish'd:
> His very hair, his golden tresses famed,
> Kept undulation round his eager neck.
> During the pain Mnemosyne upheld
> Her arms as one who prophesied.—At length
> Apollo shriek'd;—and lo! from all his limbs
> Celestial * * * * * * * * * *
> * * * * * * * * * * * * *

(iii.113–36)

In these impassioned lines Keats's own quest for knowledge is rendered incandescent with erotic energy: Apollo appears to 'die into life' in a moment of ecstatic release that prefigures Keats's insight, in his 'Ode on Melancholy', that 'in the very temple of Delight / Veil'd Melancholy has her sovran shrine' (25–6). Sexual desire, poetry and death had all been neurotically bound together for him since Tom's demise, and that these lines had a temporarily cathartic effect is indicated on his manuscript where *Hyperion* trails off into a starry ellipsis. Richard Woodhouse claimed that had Keats continued his poem it would have dealt with the Olympians' dethronement of the Titans and an ensuing war for Saturn's restoration.[33] However, 'Ode on Indolence' and 'La Belle Dame sans Merci' had shown him already elsewhere, drawn from epic conflicts of gods to more lyrical 'provings and alterations and perfectionings'.[34] As always with Keats, venturing poetically in one genre awakened a countering desire to set off in a contrary direction.

April drew to a close, and on the last day of the month he transcribed in his journal-letter two sonnets on an 'abatement' of his love of fame, and an 'irregular' sonnet 'To Sleep'. These were by way of a preface to another poem, announced as 'the first and the only one with which I have taken even moderate pains ... This I have done leisurely—I think it reads the more richly for it.' Sensing that his 'Ode to Psyche' needed further explanation, he reminded George and Georgiana that in antiquity Psyche 'was not embodied as a goddess' until her story was retold in Apuleius's Latin romance *The Golden Ass* (c. 155 AD). As usual Keats was drawing on Lemprière: 'PSYCHE, a nymph whom Cupid married and carried into a place of bliss, where he long enjoyed her company. Venus put her to death because she had robbed the world of her son; but Jupiter, at the request of Cupid, granted immortality to Psyche.' 'The word signifies the *soul*,' Lemprière added, and evidently Keats's interest in Psyche's immortality had been revived by his recent reflections on 'Soul-making'. He had already written about Psyche in 'I stood tip-toe', and his Teignmouth epistle to Reynolds had opened with Claude's 'Landscape with Psyche and the Palace of Amor' ('The Enchanted Castle'). Now, with Claude's painting currently on show at the British Institution, Keats revisited the Cupid-Psyche myth in an elaborately irregular 'Ode to Psyche' copied out to close his letter to America.[35]

Like *Hyperion*, 'Ode to Psyche' opens after a family row – albeit between bouts of passion, and in a mood of 'calm-breathing'. Now that Keats had abandoned *Hyperion*, his ode offered a glimpse of what might have appeared in a final book about the 'latest born, and loveliest vision far / Of all Olympus faded Hierarchy'. Forsaking Miltonic blank verse, Keats adopted a more inward, questioning voice:

Surely I dreamt to day; or did I see
The winged Psyche, with awaked eyes?[36]

He did so in order to quarrel with Milton, poet of 'On the Morning of Christ's Nativity', by way of recovering and enshrining antiquity's heathen inspiration. Having encountered his mythical lovers Cupid and Psyche 'in a forest thoughtlessly', somewhere between dream and reality, Keats proceeds in his third stanza to a belated lament for the Olympian gods and asserts his wish 'even in these days so far retir'd / From happy Pieties' to imagine an inviolable pagan sanctuary for Psyche. In so doing, Keats was deliberately addressing Milton's lines:

> The oracles are dumb,
> No voice or hideous hum
>     Runs through the arched roof in words deceiving.
> Apollo from his shrine
> Can no more divine,
>     With hollow shriek the steep of Delphos leaving.
> No nightly trance, or breathed spell,
> Inspires the pale-ey'd Priest from the prophetic cell.[37]

Milton had seen Christ's nativity ousting the paganism of classical myth; now, Keats dismisses that history of Christianity with his own bold revival of 'antique vows':

> O let me be thy Choir and make a moan
> Upon the midnight hours;
> Thy voice, thy lute, thy pipe, thy incense sweet
> From swinged Censer teeming;
> Thy shrine, thy Grove, thy Oracle, thy heat
> Of pale-mouth'd Prophet dreaming!

By petitioning a pagan spirit of 'holy . . . haunted forest boughs', Keats echoed the wistful classicism of his dedication sonnet 'To Leigh Hunt, Esq.' There, regretting 'a time, when under pleasant trees / Pan is no longer sought', his 'poor offerings' were tendered with the inspired devotion, and prophetic certainty, that he now dedicates to Psyche's cult. In vowing to 'build a fane' to the goddess 'in some untrodden region of [his] Mind', Keats abandoned the shrine, grove and oracle of classical tradition to create an ideal temple from an all-too-worldly haven for love:

> And in the midst of this wide-quietness
> A rosy Sanctuary will I dress
> With the wreath'd trellis of a working brain;
> With buds and bells and stars without a mane;
> With all the gardener, fancy e'er could feign
> Who breeding flowers will never breed the same—

This extraordinary celebration of creativity has been read in relation to Coleridge's theories of imagination, Shakespeare's profusion, contemporary theories of mind, even suburban horticulture. Most striking, though, is a hitherto-unnoted presence signalled by his phrase 'this wide-quietness'. Hunt's frequent use of such compound words had influenced Keats's earliest poems, and the reappearance of Hunt's manner here in 'Ode to Psyche' is revealing. Their early friendship may have cooled, but the romantic scene that surrounded Hunt in prison, 'papered . . . with a trellis of roses' and surrounded by a trellised flower-garden, had been woven deep into Keats's idea of imaginative life.[38] The misspelling, 'mane' for 'name', quirkily associated his 'rosy Sanctuary' with Hunt's prophetic cell in Horsemonger Lane, as did the thoughts of 'soft delight' and 'warm love' with which 'Ode to Psyche' concludes. In his early poem 'Remembered Friendship', Hunt had evoked his most deeply felt experiences as a schoolboy at Christ's Hospital – his friendships, his delight in classical mythology and the prospect from a dormitory window, when,

> For a while, before the gentle sweets
> Of sleep had clos'd our eyes, how oft we lay
> Admiring thro' the casement open'd wide
> The spangled glories of the sky.

One such glory was the moon 'bursting forth' from clouds, likened by Hunt to 'love resistless' and the birth of Cupid's mother, Venus: 'So Cytherea from the frothy wave / Rose in luxuriant beauty.'[39] That vision of Venus 'thro' the casement open'd wide' helped Keats transform the 'open casement' of 'Ode on Indolence' into the radiant conclusion of 'Ode to Psyche':

> A bright torch, and a casement ope at night,
> To let the warm Love in—

Suffused with heartfelt intimacy, these lines were a reminder on the threshold of spring that Fanny Brawne was now living next door. Hunt's schoolboy poem about Cytherea and the 'frothy wave' may seem remote from Lower Heath Quarter, Hampstead, but Keats's copy of Hunt's *Juvenilia*, with 'Remembered Friendship' starting on page twenty-five, was on his bookshelf at Wentworth Place.

'Ode to Psyche' was a complex, difficult poem to write, its engagement with 'shadowy thought' more driven yet also more elusive than the more conventionally 'stirring shades, and baffled beams' in 'Ode on Indolence'. It was also a much more literary poem. Besides Shakespeare, Milton and Coleridge, its many influences extend to William Adlington's translation of Apuleius's *The Golden Ass*, Spenser's 'Garden of Adonis' in *The Faerie Queene*, Mary Tighe's *Psyche* and Erasmus Darwin's *The Botanic Garden*. But it was Hunt's early poem and Keats's idea of Hunt's prison-sanctuary that yielded his vision of 'all soft delight / That shadowy thought can win'. In the odes yet to be written the interweaving of autobiography and poetic myth that began in his odes to Indolence and Psyche would be further explored and enriched, forming a series of intersecting 'life studies' that merged day-to-day life at Wentworth Place with the more elusive and untrodden regions of his mind.

May 1819 was a glorious month. Fine weather stretched from the 1st to the 18th, and again from a new moon on the 24th until Wednesday, 9 June. Newspapers reported 'lengthened fineness' of weather and 'luxuriant' fruit-blossoms with 'universal' indications of fruitfulness: 'there never was a season which gave greater promise of plenty than the present.'[40] Even *The Examiner* joined in Maytime's pleasures. With 'no foreign news worth mentioning', Hunt had leisure to dwell on spring's 'rapture' in his monthly *Examiner* column 'The Calendar of Nature':

> Towards the end of the month, indeed, as it stands at present, if a very great blight does not occur, the treasures of summer are almost all laid open. The grass is in its greenest beauty; the young corn has covered the more naked fields; the hedges are powdered with the snowy and sweet-scented blossoms of the hawthorn, as beautiful as myrtle-flowers; the orchards give us trees, and the most lovely flowers at once; and the hedge-banks, woods, and the meadows, are sprinkled in profusion with the cowslip, the wood-roof, the orchis, the blue germander, the white anemone, the lily of the valley, the marsh-marygold, and the children's favourites, daisies and butter-cups, whose colours start in an instant to one's mind. The dragon-fly carries his long purple-shining body along the air; the butterflies enjoy their merry days; the bees send out their colonies; the birds sing with unwearied love, while their partners are sitting; the later birds of passage arrive; the cattle enjoy the ripe and juicy herbage, and overflow with milk; most of the trees complete their foliage, filling the landscape with clumps and crowning woods, that 'bosom' the village steeples; the distance echoes with the cheerful bark of the dog; the ladies are abroad in their spring dresses; the farmer does little, but leisurely weed his garden, and enjoy the sight of his flowering industry; the sun stops long, and begins to let us feel him warmly; and when the vital sparkle of the day is over, in sight and sound, the nightingale still continues to tell us its joy; and the little glow-worm lights up her trusting lamp, to shew her lover where she is.[41]

Keats luxuriated in the sunshine too. 'O there is nothing like fine weather,' he wrote to his sister on May Day, and launched into an extempore song that gambols from 'Two or three Posies / With two or three simples' to 'Two or three dove's eggs / To hatch into sonnets' (1–2, 27–8). Just five short letters survive from this month. Three of them concerned welcome news received from George and Georgiana. Instead of heading for Birkbeck's Illinois settlement, they had struck south to Louisville where they met up with Charles Briggs, a school friend from Enfield. They were weary, harassed but settled. An introduction to American naturalist John James Audubon had led to a business agreement: George would invest in a steamboat, *The Henderson*, plying the Ohio and Mississippi rivers. The letter Keats received gave no hint of the disaster that was about to unfold. Unaware that Audubon was insolvent and that he had no stake in the steamboat, George had effectively handed his capital directly to Audubon's creditors. Perhaps this was a deliberate swindle. Certainly it was an unfortunate coincidence of Audubon's desperation and George's naivety about doing business in the pioneering midwest.[42] For the moment Keats knew nothing of this, however, and word of George's plight would take another two months to reach him.

Meanwhile, he took stock of his own options. Brown had loaned him money, but as he would vacate Wentworth Place over the summer Keats would be obliged to do so too. He thought of making 'a voyage', wrote to Sarah Jeffrey about lodgings near Teignmouth and even contemplated going on an Indiaman or joining Simon Bolivar's insurgents in South America. *The Examiner* had reported on South American volunteers, and George's transatlantic venture still appeared to be a success. Keats could well have gone to South America too but James Rice, once more in ill-health, had proposed 'a Month ... at the back of the Isle of Wight'. Keats fell in readily with this plan.[43]

May's days were rendered all the more poignantly idyllic by Keats's awareness that change was coming. Warmth made him feel better, he was seeing Fanny Brawne every day and, although none of his letters mentioned it, shortly after the appearance of *The Examiner* of 9 May he composed three odes to greet the spring. Returning to the ten-line stanza of his 'Ode on Indolence', 'Ode on Melancholy', 'Ode to a Nightingale' and 'Ode on a Grecian Urn' take different but related approaches to the meaning of poetry's 'diligent indolence' in 'a world of pains and troubles'. All three respond like Hunt's 'Calendar of Nature' to a 'seasonable month', noticing the beauty of grass, hawthorn, fruit trees, and 'unwearied' birdsong. Keats imagines the nightingale singing now as it had done in 'ancient days' (64), and the 'happy melodist' in 'Ode on a Grecian Urn' is, like Hunt's birds, 'Forever piping songs for ever new' (23–4). Line by line these poems echo what Hunt had written in *The Examiner*, augmenting seasonal pleasures with a more urgent awareness of Hunt's caveat, 'if a very great blight does not occur'. Working as an undersong to what Hunt termed 'the healthy intoxication of the season' was Keats's awareness that spring's forwardness, and his own imminent departure from Hampstead, rendered its pleasures inescapably transient. The beautiful autumnal constellation, Libra, was already visible in the night sky over Wentworth Place.

In just such a mingled mood Keats composed 'Ode on Melancholy'. His first stanza is burdened by 'mysteries' of sorrow, its Gothic thoughts of poison, suicide, death and oblivion derived from his medical training and hours of poring over Burton's *Anatomy of Melancholy*. His own melancholy, in this extraordinary spring of 1819, proved to be a gift of nature,

> when the melancholy fit shall fall
> Sudden from heaven like a weeping cloud,
> That fosters the droop-headed flowers all,
> And hides the green hill in an April shroud.
>
> (11–14)

Then, Keats writes, the 'morning rose', 'rainbow', 'globed peonies' and even the 'rich anger' of a mistress will 'glut sorrow' with beauty. Beauty, this ode proclaims, is sorrow's true domain:

> She dwells with Beauty—Beauty that must die;
> And Joy, whose hand is ever at his lips
> Bidding adieu . . .
>
> (21–3)

Does this scene of alloyed happiness and mortal fragility depict a farewell kiss, hand at lips bidding adieu, or an attempt to conceal tubercular coughing? Framed by a window of Wentworth Place, Keats's adieus to Fanny with hand at lips might appear to be both, his 'April shroud' a glimpse both of the misty Heath and a reminder of last farewells from years long past. 'Ay, in the very temple of Delight,' his poem assures us, 'Veil'd Melancholy has her Sovran shrine.' If the imagery of 'Ode on Melancholy' speaks for experience, its 'temple of Delight' was also a measure of how far Keats had ventured since he first encountered poetry as a child – simultaneously Lackington's Temple of the Muses at Finsbury, and an Oxford brothel he had visited in autumn of 1817.

Like 'Ode on Melancholy', the double-edged enquiries of 'Ode on a Grecian Urn' delve back to the British Museum and Keats's two sonnet encounters with the Elgin Marbles. His 'heifer lowing at the skies' has long been recognised as a slab from the Marbles – already glimpsed, as we have seen, in his Teignmouth epistle to Reynolds. As he contemplates the 'leaf-fring'd legend' (5) with which the urn is decorated, it appears to depict two lovers who seem to enjoy an unchanging paradise of erotic anticipation:

Bold lover, never, never canst thou kiss,
  Though winning near the goal—yet, do not grieve;
    She cannot fade, though thou hast not thy bliss,
  For ever wilt thou love, and she be fair!

             (17–20)

'More happy love! more happy, happy love! / Forever warm and still to be enjoy'd' is apparently the urn's meaning – elated 'far above' cloying human passion, winningly 'shelter'd from annoy' and time's passing. More readily chastened than in the earlier 'Ode on Indolence', however, his poem turns next to contemplate a stark image of lost community in the 'little town' forever 'emptied of this folk':

And, little town, thy streets for evermore
  Will silent be; and not a soul to tell
    Why thou art desolate, can e'er return.
             (38–40)

Like eternity, the urn is said to 'tease us out of thought'; it is an enduring witness to human suffering encountered day by day and also, I think, to an earlier experience of desolate silence linked, as in *The Eve of St Agnes*, with memories of his father's death and London's empty streets at night. Two years had passed since he had quit medicine for poetry, and attempted to compose upon Haydon's 'union of Nature with ideal beauty' in the Elgin Marbles. Then, he had been confronted with 'unwilling sleep' and words that 'tell me I must die'; now, approaching the conclusion of 'Ode on a Grecian Urn', thoughts of 'old age' and 'waste' (46) lead on to the famously enigmatic lines that conclude his poem:

'Beauty is truth, truth beauty,'—that is all
  Ye know on earth, and all ye need to know.
             (49–50)

These eighteen words opened the way for nineteenth-century aestheticism and readers like the Pre-Raphaelites and Stopford Brooke for whom Keats's poetry disclosed no interest in anything except beauty. During the twentieth century they provoked fierce argument between critics trying to fix the meaning of 'Beauty is truth, truth beauty' in one way or another.[44] And yet perhaps it is the two lines' hospitality to so many divergent readings that offers a clue to their negatively capable Keatsian wisdom. 'Beauty is truth, truth beauty': the phrase's measured authority might mimic a connoisseur like Richard Payne Knight, descanting on a classical vase in a manner that Keats,

according to *Blackwood's*, was not qualified to attempt. Yet his phrase is also
as riddlingly elusive as the pronouncements of the Fool in *King Lear*, or the
childish rhymes with which Keats quenched questions at Craven Street and
escaped with a laugh. Rhyme – poetry – had enabled Keats then, as it did now
in his 'Ode on a Grecian Urn', to keep all answers open – as alert to 'other woe'
as to what 'all ye need to know' might be.

'Ode to a Nightingale' begins, like 'Ode on Indolence', with a sensation of
'drowsy numbness' as of 'some dull opiate'. What follows deserves a place
alongside 'Kubla Khan' or De Quincey's *Confessions of an English Opium-
Eater* as one of the greatest re-creations of a drug-inspired dream-vision in
English literature. More than a figure of speech, Keats's 'dull opiate emptied to
the drains' frankly admits his own laudanum habit since nursing his brother.
Perhaps because of his medical experience, Keats sees no need for an awkward
apology such as Coleridge's defence of 'ill-health' and 'a slight indisposition' in
his preface to 'Kubla Khan'. Instead he turns the squalor of a sickroom into an
endlessly recessed vision of human suffering and its counterurge in his desire
to escape – literally, metaphorically – into an outdoor world of health and
happiness. His relish

> for a draught of vintage . . .
> Cool'd a long age in the deep-delved earth,
> Tasting of Flora and the country green,
> Dance, and Provençal song, and sunburnt mirth!
>                        (11–14)

is as pleasurably alive to the season as 'Two or three posies', and yet it tells us
also of his longing to salve the persistent soreness of his throat and to 'quite
forget' the insistent clamour

> Here, where men sit and hear each other groan;
> Where palsy shakes a few, sad, last gray hairs,
>     Where youth grows pale, and spectre-thin, and dies;
>         Where but to think is to be full of sorrow
>             And leaden-eyed despairs,
>     Where Beauty cannot keep her lustrous eyes,
>         Or new Love pine at them beyond to-morrow.
>                        (24–30)

As in all of his odes, verse measures and arrests time, but whereas the 'drowsy
hour' in 'Ode on Indolence' was haunted by three figures repeatedly passing,

32 In 'slipshod County', 20 The Strand, Teignmouth. Here Keats stayed with his brother Tom in the rainy spring, March–May 1818. In this house Keats worked on *Isabella, or the Pot of Basil*.

33 Charles Armitage Brown (1787–1842). A self-portrait of Brown as a young man around the time that he knew Keats.

34 Charles Wentworth Dilke (1789–1864). Dilke and his wife Maria were Keats's neighbours at Wentworth Place, Hampstead, 1817–18.

35  Maria Dilke (1789–1850).

a)

b)

36 a)  John Taylor (1781–1864) and b) James Augustus Hessey (1785–1870), publishers of *Endymion* (1818) and *Lamia, Isabella, The Eve of St Agnes, and Other Poems* (1820).

37  Joseph Severn (1793–1879), a self-portrait aboard the *Maria Crowther*, 1820.

38 James Henry Leigh Hunt (1784–1859), poet, journalist and critic, nicknamed 'Libertas' by Keats 'for showing truth to flatter'd state'. This pencil sketch by Thomas Charles Wageman was taken shortly after Hunt's release from prison in 1815.

39 William Hazlitt (1778–1830), critic, in a chalk drawing by William Bewick, 1825. Hazlitt has often been cited as a shaping force on Keats's thinking about poetry and creativity, although influence flowed the other way too. Keats and Leigh Hunt lay behind some of Hazlitt's ideas of Shakespeare and the theatre.

40  Charles Cowden Clarke (1787–1877), in a watercolour portrait by an unknown artist. Cowden Clarke taught Keats at Enfield, and encouraged his earliest poems. For Clarke, Chaucer and Shakespeare – visible as busts in this painting – represented traditional English liberties as well as supreme literary achievement.

41  John Hamilton Reynolds (1794–1852), poet, watercolour portrait by Joseph Severn, 1818. Leigh Hunt praised Reynolds, Percy Bysshe Shelley and Keats in his controversial 'Young Poets' article in *The Examiner*, 1 December 1816.

42 Lincluden Priory, Dumfries, from an engraving dated c. 1770. Keats visited here on 2 July 1818, en route with Charles Brown to the Scottish Highlands.

43 Derry-na-Cullen, the 'House under the Waterfall', on the Isle of Mull. On 23 July 1818 Keats and Brown breakfasted here, on their way to Iona.

44 Pale Warriors. Effigies of Scottish kings at Iona, seen by Keats on 24 July 1818.

45 A cathedral of the sea. Fingal's cave, Staffa, where Keats landed on 24 July 1818.

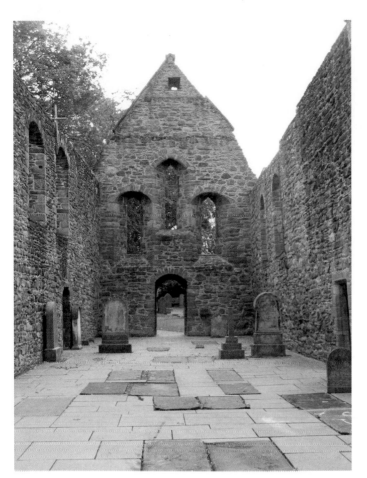

46 Interior of Beauly Priory, visited by Keats at the end of his Scottish tour, August 1818.

47 Charles Jeremiah Wells (c. 1800–79), a portrait by Thomas Charles Wageman. Wells was a friend of Tom Keats at Clarke's Academy, Enfield. At Margate in the summer of 1816, Wells wrote a series of amorous letters to Tom, signed by a fictitious Frenchwoman named Amena Bellafilla, in a poeticised language borrowed from the early poetry of Keats himself. Keats believed that this hoax had an adverse effect on his brother's health.

48 Tom Keats (1799–1818), a watercolour miniature painted by Joseph Severn.

49 Fanny Keats (1803–89), the poet's sister in middle age.

50 George Keats (1797–1841), watercolour miniature by Joseph Severn. This likeness shows George Keats as a young man, shortly before he emigrated to America in July 1818.

51 Benjamin Bailey (1791–1853), a miniature taken of Keats's friend as a young man. In Bailey's rooms at Magdalen Hall, Oxford, Keats wrote the third book of *Endymion*.

52 A watercolour of Keats's 'dear generous noble' friend James Rice (1792–1832). It was Rice who gave Keats a copy of Mateo Alemán's comic romance *The Rogue: or, The Life of Guzman de Alfarache*, inscribed 'John Keats From his Friend Js Rxxx 20th April 1818'. This book may well have suggested some of the plot of *The Eve of St Agnes*.

53 Richard Woodhouse (1788–1834), legal adviser to Taylor and Hessey and an astute and farsighted critic of Keats's poems. This portrait in oils is the only known likeness of Woodhouse.

54 Jack Randall sparring. Keats went to a prize fight between Randall and Ned Turner, 4 December 1818, immediately after the death of his brother Tom.

55 The home of Charles Dilke Snr and his wife Sarah, Chichester, seen here in May 2007. Keats stayed here 18–23 January 1819.

56 Lewis Way's chapel, Stansted Park, Hampshire. Keats was in the congregation when the chapel was consecrated, 25 January 1819.

57  The Old Mill House, Bedhampton, home of John and Letitia Snook. It was here that Keats wrote *The Eve of St Agnes* in January 1819. Seen here in May 2007.

58 The Hospital of St Cross, Winchester. When Keats visited in September 1819 he said it was 'a very interesting old place'.

59 Miniature of Fanny Brawne (1800–65), by an unknown artist, watercolour, c. 1833.

60 John Taylor's house at 93 Fleet Street, rear view. It was here Keats stayed before boarding the *Maria Crowther* to sail to Naples.

61 Villa di Londra, Via San Lucia, Naples. Keats and Joseph Severn stayed here 31 October–8 November 1820 on their way to Rome.

62 Apollo and (left) Melpomene, Muse of Tragedy, and right, Terpsichore, Muse of Dance. Façade of the Teatro San Carlo, Naples.

63 Eternal Road. The Via Appia, seen at the pass across Monte Grande. Keats passed this way with Severn on their way to Rome, November 1820.

64 James Clark, Keats's physician at Rome, in later life.

65 The Keats-Shelley House in Rome, seen here in the early twentieth century. Here John Keats died, 23 February 1821.

'Ode to a Nightingale' turns away to push deeper through 'verdurous glooms and winding mossy ways' – Keats's 'dark passages', akin to Wordsworth's in 'Tintern Abbey'. Here his poem conjures each sweet of the season amid 'embalmed darkness', fully aware that this loving enumeration of May's perfumes and 'dewy wine' is chased by time: violets are already 'fast fading', and a 'murmurous haunt of flies' presages an eve when the 'coming musk-rose' will have rotted. Whereas Wordsworth's dark passages yielded an intimation of blessedness and 'something far more deeply interfused', Keats dares to find something of far more immediate sensory fulfilment:

> Darkling I listen; and, for many a time
>   I have been half in love with easeful Death,
> Call'd him soft names in many a mused rhyme,
>   To take into the air my quiet breath;
> Now more than ever seems it rich to die,
>   To cease upon the midnight with no pain,
>     While thou art pouring forth thy soul abroad
>       In such an ecstasy!
>
>                   (51–8)

'When the vital sparkle of the day is over,' Hunt had written, 'in sight and sound, the nightingale still continues to tell us its joy.' Like Hunt, Keats follows his nightingale's song into a twilight zone, wishfully longing for continuity although painfully aware that its delight is as much on borrowed time as he is himself:

> Still wouldst thou sing, and I have ears in vain—
>   To thy high requiem become a sod.
>
>                   (59–60)

That stark monosyllable 'sod' shocks us with its sudden return to Burns's cold hillside, and its reminder that the London clay that had swallowed Keats's father, mother and brothers was waiting to absorb his own throbbing life force. Shadowed yet not wholly darkened by Tom's death, the 'melodious plot' of 'Ode to a Nightingale' flickers between a vision of eternity and 'this passing night', between a tender fantasy of 'beechen green' and – lingering from *Hyperion* – an epic sense of impending destruction. Its supreme achievement in reconciling those contraries with a darkling awareness, now, of his own imminent farewell tells us why this poem, more than his other odes, has echoed in so many later poems.

While Keats's sense of the perilousness of the moment in 'Ode to a Nightingale' is related to his own protracted ill-health, an inexorable advance of 'hungry generations' was also threatening as London's edges pushed outwards into surrounding villages and fields. Directly opposite the garden plot where Keats apparently wrote his poem, two houses were being erected – one of many such speculative enterprises at Hampstead in 1819, soon to be abandoned half-built, dingy and as if 'dying of old age before . . . brought up'. Builders and brickmakers were always passing to and fro.[45] If in the nightingale's 'high requiem' Keats imagined he heard a mass for himself, its 'plaintive anthem' was also an elegy for a landscape and way of life as ephemeral as the music he hears fading

> Past the near meadows, over the still stream,
>   Up the hill-side; and now 'tis buried deep
>     In the next valley-glades . . .
>                       (76–8)

The phrase 'buried deep', summoning all that lay behind Keats's orphaned recognition of his 'sole self', supplied a cue for his poem's closing lines. In a brilliant reversal of his childish game at Craven Street, he leapt from 'stream' and 'deep' to put two questions that would never require or receive an answering rhyme:

> Was it a vision, or a waking dream?
> Fled is that music:—Do I wake or sleep?
>                       (79–80)

Self-dramatising, even stagey, those questions invited his readers to re-enter the world of his poem. For Keats himself, they pointed beyond May's lyrics towards writing for the theatre.

CHAPTER 20

# Hope and Chance

As MAY's fine weather fled, Keats was 'unsetled' too, returning books and making 'a conflagration of all old Letters and Memorandums'. Among them, most likely, were letters from Isabella Jones. Unwell, she had left London for Tunbridge – and Keats noticed that she had vanished. If he was making ready to move out of Wentworth Place for the summer, his clearance of papers also signalled a deepening involvement with Fanny Brawne – 'a beautiful Girl whom I love so much'. At some time during June they had come to an 'understanding' and were engaged. Fanny recalled that Keats had 'wished to marry', although, unaware of funds held for him in Chancery, he had insufficient resources and no steady income. While he longed for her 'moistened and bedewed with Pleasures', circumstances dictated otherwise: if married life was to prove suitable to Fanny's 'inclinations and spirits', to secure 'nobler amusements; fortune favouring' he would have to act decisively and leave Hampstead. In summer he would take cheap accommodation on the Isle of Wight while agonisingly aware of the 'worst that can happen' – that in his absence she might fall in love with someone else. But Keats was determined. He needed money. Writing was now a necessity.[1]

Keats gave no indication that he considered his recent poems remarkable, although he did tell Sarah Jeffrey that 'the thing I have most enjoyed this year has been writing an ode to Indolence'. With no funds and a sore throat coming on again, he could neither walk nor take a coach to see his sister at Walthamstow. At Abbey's, too, 'cash-recourses' had stopped. Having produced a letter from George with news of the birth of a niece, Abbey put into his hand 'a Letter from my Aunt's Solicitor containing the pleasant information that she was about to file a Bill in Chancery against us'.[2] This letter was from Margaret, Midgley John Jennings's widow, who had heard of Tom's death and now hoped to extract a share of his inheritance. In Tom's estate were funds that had reverted from her husband to his mother, Alice Jennings, and then on her death to Tom. Abbey would not distribute Tom's estate while there was a chance that this new claim might succeed. The family quarrel had been dormant for some ten years; its sudden rekindling shook Keats, and would reverberate in his poetry this year. Until Margaret's claim was settled he could expect no more money from Abbey.

Seeing Keats desperate, Brown intervened. He must call in loans to friends, and against that security Brown would advance funds 'for the present'. Keats was owed more than £200, with a further £30 due from Haydon, whose affairs were 'more dreadful than ever'. Aware that Keats was thinking once again of employment with an apothecary, Brown urged him to 'make one more attempt in the Press'.[3] As usual, when the odds were stacked against him, Keats redoubled his efforts. On Monday, 14 June he sent a copy of 'Ode to a Nightingale' to James Elmes for publication in July's issue of *The Annals of the Fine Arts*. He was also projecting a fourth verse tale, *Lamia*, based on Burton's story of Lycius in *The Anatomy of Melancholy*:

> Lycius, a young man twenty-five years of age, ... going between Cenchreas and Corinth, met such a phantasm in the habit of a fair gentlewoman, which, taking him by the hand, carried him home to her house in the suburbs of Corinth, and told him she was a Phœnician by birth, and if he would tarry with her, 'he should hear her sing and play, and drink such wine as never any drank, and no man should molest him; but she being fair and lovely would live and die with him, that was fair and lovely to behold'. The young man, a philosopher, otherwise staid and discreet, able to moderate his passions, though not this of love, tarried with her awhile to his great content, and at last married her, to whose wedding, amongst other guests, came Apollonius, who, by some probable conjectures, found her out to be a serpent, a lamia, and that all her furniture was like Tantalus' gold described by Homer, no substance, but mere illusions. When she saw herself descried, she wept, and desired Apollonius to be silent, but he would not be moved, and thereupon she, plate, house, and all that was in it, vanished in an instant: 'many thousands took notice of this fact, for it was done in the midst of Greece'.[4]

*Lamia* gave Keats scope to dramatise the rival claims of passion and philosophy, and as his poem developed over the summer he came to think it had 'that sort of fire in it which must take hold of people in some way'.[5] He had written to Fanny Brawne of an adhesive 'fire' between them, and there is no doubt that his new poem grew from an uneasy sense that she had 'entrammelled' him exactly as Jane Cox and Isabella Jones had done previously.[6]

Indeed, Lamia's suburban 'palace' at Corinth was an irresistible reminder of Isabella's apartment with its fashionable furniture, where that enigmatic woman might be at home on one day and on the next, like Lamia, nowhere to be found.

What Brown had in mind, however, was potentially far more lucrative than a narrative poem. He proposed that they should collaborate on a play for the London stage, pitched squarely at Edmund Kean. Brown would supply the plot, Keats would write the script, and they would each take a half-share of the profits due to the authors. Brown's comic opera *Narensky* had enjoyed some success at Drury Lane; he knew of Keats's ambition as a dramatist, and to write for Edmund Kean would stretch his stagecraft. The partnership had promise. Brown suggested the melodramatic story of Otho the Great, first of the Holy Roman emperors. Kean's role was to be Otho's hot-blooded son Ludolph, in a plot of family conflict, passion, betrayal, madness and death that would be like a furnace for his fiery stage presence.

Keats was soon thinking excitedly of a 'revolution in modern dramatic writing'.[7] He had read about Otho in Gibbon's *Decline and Fall of the Roman Empire* and, many years before, in one of his schoolbooks, William Mavor's *Universal History*:

> Ludolphus engaged in a treasonable confederacy with Conrade duke of Franconia ... This unnatural revolt produced some serious hostilities, and occasioned the destruction of the city of Ratisbon: but, after some time, the prince was made sensible of his error, and took an opportunity, while his father [Otho] was hunting, to throw himself at his feet, and implore his clemency. 'Have pity', said he, 'upon your misguided child, who returns like the prodigal son to his father ...' To this affecting appeal Otho could only reply by a flood of tears and a paternal embrace; but when his agitation subsided, he assured the penitent of his warmest favour, and generously pardoned all his adherents. The bitter reproaches, however, which Ludolphus received from the Italians, in his subsequent expedition against Beranger, overwhelmed him with insupportable distress, and eventually brought him to an untimely grave.[8]

This passage from Mavor was Keats's starting point for scenes of power politics and pathos, historical pageant and venomous strategy. In June 1819 London saw repeated performances of plays such as *Brutus*, *Pizzaro* and Shakespeare's *Richard III* and *Julius Caesar*: as Hunt had been arguing for years, fresh material was badly needed. A new play about Otho the Great starring Edmund Kean might seize the prize that eluded Byron and Coleridge: a box-office smash. Keats resolved to set to with 'all my industry and ability', and drafted an opening scene in the last week of June. Kean would require a vigorous, muscular style, and for this Keats went to the seventeenth-century dramatist Philip Massinger whose *Duke of Milan* he was reading attentively. Massinger's work had seen a recent public revival, rescued from oblivion by Kean as Sir Giles Overreach in *A New Way to Pay Old Debts*. With what seemed to be realistic prospects of a money-spinner, Keats told Fanny Brawne, with Keanish swagger, that he would not return to London without a best-seller in his bag. Early on Sunday the 27th he and Rice took two outside seats on a heavily laden Portsmouth coach, and set out to 'live upon hope and Chance'.[9]

Their journey took them through Keats's old haunts at Southwark and on to Kingston, Guildford and Godalming. Also aboard were some French people, probably refugees, and Keats observed how 'there was a woman amongst them to whom the poor Men in ragged coats were more gallant than ever I saw a gentleman to a Lady at a Ball'. When they got down to walk up Hind Head Hill, 'one of them pick'd a rose, and on remounting gave it to the woman with—"Ma'mselle—voila une bell rose!"'. Three years ago Keats had marked a similar incident with a sonnet; what now caught his eye was dramatic gesture and effect.[10] Resuming their seats, the travellers went on to Petersfield and Portsmouth where Keats arrived wet, cold and throat-sore.

That evening or on Monday the 28th they crossed to Ryde, then went south to Shanklin and Eglantine Cottage on the High Street. Keats had been here before, in April 1817, and now had more time to enjoy 'a very pleasant Cottage window, looking onto a beautiful hilly country, with a glimpse of the sea'. The chasm of Shanklin Chine was just yards away, winding down to the beach where, two years before, he had started to compose his sonnet 'On the Sea'. Now, in high season, he saw hordes of tourists 'hunting after the pictur-esque like beagles'. Heavy thunder clouds loured overhead, and a 'ball of condensed electric matter' was seen at midday.[11]

Today Eglantine Cottage forms part of Keats Cottage Hotel, its original structure hidden behind a later, nineteenth-century frontage. The living room Keats shared with Rice has survived unchanged, as has the window through which he gazed 'over house tops and Cliffs onto the Sea, so that when the Ships sail past the Cottage chimneys you may take them for Weathercocks'. Keats's bedroom remains intact too, with its low ceiling and neat brick-lined fireplace. In one corner of his room was a hole through which a coffin could be lowered, as the stairs were too narrow – hence Keats's remark about his 'little coffin of a room at Shanklin'. Here, on the night of Tuesday the 29th, he wrote a letter of passionate 'rapsodies' to Fanny Brawne and was glad, next morning, not to have posted it. A calmer letter followed. From the first he was unsure how to address Fanny or how she would construe what he said, but he fell into a pattern of writing to her each week. As with his *Endymion* proofs, this correspondence coincided with quarterly phases of the moon, each letter being written and dispatched at the new moon, its first quarter and the full moon as if, as he said, she had absorbed him 'in spite of myself'.[12] If this was 'negative capability' of a kind, Keats was now living out his 'poetic romance' for real – and with more diligence, judgement and deliberation than was allowed by Matthew Arnold when he later despaired of Keats's sensual enervation.

Keats's third letter to Fanny, written under a full moon on 8 July, mentioned another celestial phenomenon: 'I have seen your Comet.'[13] News of a 'most magnificent Comet' had broken in the London papers on 5 and 6 July,

> not far from the star called (B) Beta Auriga, nearly in line with it and the very bright star called Capella . . . Probably the present comet has long traversed ethereal space, and is now rapidly making its way towards the sun, its foci, in which case it will become more brilliant in approaching the sun, but appear to sink towards the northern horizon, and very soon become invisible.[14]

Night after night Fanny's comet hung brightly overhead, apparently as stationary and unchanging as the stars yet in reality a transient visitor returned fleetingly from its long traverse of 'ethereal space'. As Keats's solitary yearning for Fanny took on an aspect of 'impossibility and eternity', contrasting aspects of her comet – brilliantly present, eternally vanishing – may have helped release his divided feelings into a sonnet, 'Bright Star':

Bright Star! Would I were steadfast as thou art!
    Not in lone splendour hung amid the night;
Not watching, with eternal lids apart,
    Like Nature's devout sleepless Eremite,
The morning waters at their priestlike task
    Of pure ablution round earth's human shores;
Or, gazing on the new soft fallen mask
    Of snow upon the mountains and the moors:—
No;—yet still steadfast, still unchangeable,
    Cheek-pillow'd on my Love's white ripening breast,
To touch, for ever, its warm sink and swell,
    Awake, for ever, in a sweet unrest;
To hear, to feel her tender-taken breath,
Half passionless, and so swoon on to death.[15]

Steadfast, unchanging, so intimately close as to 'touch', 'hear', 'feel' and then 'swoon on': the arc of Keats's feelings across the single sentence of his sonnet mirrors the trajectory of Fanny's comet, poised aloft yet also careering on towards the sun. This version of 'Bright Star', transcribed by Brown and dated '1819', came from a lost manuscript that may have been Keats's original draft – although exactly when he wrote it is unknown and probably unknowable. Different dates have been suggested, debated and argued over. For instance, it has been claimed that 'Bright Star' was a much earlier composition, possibly written for Isabella Jones in October 1818, although Keats's circumstances in July 1819, supported by Brown's dating, should encourage us to speculate otherwise. 'Bright Star' is as likely to have been composed now as at any other time: with Fanny's comet aligned dazzlingly with that 'bright star' Capella, Keats wrote to her of his 'swooning admiration of [her] beauty', of her 'Loveliness' and 'the hour of [his] death', in a letter aglow with images from his poem. And as he signed off – 'I will imagine you Venus tonight and pray, pray, pray to your star like a Hethen. Your's ever, fair star, John Keats' – he was yearning to make a radiant, comet-like traverse of the distance that separated him from Wentworth Place.[16]

Always given to 'bod[ing] ill', Keats knew that comets were traditionally seen as bad omens. Having taken one of Fanny's letters to bed with him, next morning he was horrified to find that her name on its sealing wax had been obliterated. Life at Shanklin had become oppressive too. Crowds of tourists irritated him. Damp air from the Chine chilled him. Rice's mysterious affliction made him edgy and melancholy: 'He was unwell and I was not in very good health: and I am affraid we made each other worse by acting upon each others spirits.'[17]

Despite thundery weather Keats managed to escape Eglantine Cottage and ventured along the coast as far as Bonchurch, returning to intensive work on *Otho the Great* and *Lamia*. Like *Isabella*, *Hyperion* and *The Eve of St Agnes*, *Otho* turns upon a family quarrel. Three opening scenes of fiendish complexity elaborated Mavor's account of treasonable confederacy so as to portray an inter-generational war. Determined that Prince Ludolph must marry his niece Erminia, Otho has forbidden his son to wed Auranthe, the sister of Conrad, duke of Franconia. Thwarted in love, Ludolph leads an insurrection against his imperial father. Having 'thrived as a rebel', Conrad, a Machiavellian villain 'calling interest loyalty', changes sides and secures in gratitude from Otho the 'golden fortune' of Ludolph's hand for Auranthe. Ludolph, meanwhile, awaits the 'thwart spleen' of his father's vengeance (I. i.42, 51, 91).

By Sunday, 11 July, Keats had completed a first act of nearly five hundred lines and, with Brown's arrival on the 20th, both were soon harnessed to their 'dog-cart' of composition and ready to begin the second act.[18] As the plot lumbers on, it is obviously in Conrad's interest to manage a reconciliation between Ludolph and Otho, and this is readily achieved in act two when the emperor discovers that his son, bizarrely disguised as a Saracen, has been covertly fighting rebels on his behalf. Hapless Erminia attempts to intervene from prison, warning Otho of Conrad's duplicity and Ludolph of Auranthe's betrayal (from the first act it has been clear that she loves Albert, a knight favoured by Otho). Ludolph and Auranthe's marriage is hastily patched up in act three, and the remainder of the play traces Ludoph's downfall as he discovers her treachery. She eventually commits suicide, 'fingers clenched and cold' (V.v.188), whereupon Ludolph immediately dies of grief.

Apart from sources in history books, *Otho the Great* owed a good deal to the destructive family feud ignited by John Jennings's death. The legal action threatened by Margaret Jennings was a recent reminder of this; so was Keats's renewed struggle with Abbey to secure funds for George, whose involvement with Audubon's speculation had drained his resources. Auranthe's hasty marriage to Ludolph, greeted with an astonished exclamation – 'Wife! So soon!' – was almost unquestionably Keats's recollection of family dismay at his mother's remarriage to Rawlings and its disastrous repercussions. While *Otho the Great* replayed the break-up of the Keats family as historical drama, other traumatic episodes from Keats's childhood would revive when he resumed composition of *Hyperion*.

Shakespeare's influence is evident throughout *Otho*, and Sir Walter Scott's sympathetic portrait of Saladin in *Ivanhoe* suggested Ludolph's otherwise inexplicable decision to disguise himself as a Saracen. An opening soliloquy by Conrad echoes Ben Jonson's *Volpone*, and subsequent exchanges with Auranthe convey some sense of dramatic tension and suspense. More generally, however, the scenes are overcrowded and the tortuous plot is difficult to follow. Early in August, Keats wrote to Fanny Brawne: 'I leave this minute a scene in our Tragedy and see you . . . through the mist of Plots speeches, counterplots and counter speeches—The Lover [Ludolph] is madder than I am—I am nothing to him.'[19] A month after Keats arrived at Shanklin, Fanny was being seen 'through' the dramatic story he had undertaken to ensure their future together: if he had been 'entrammelled' by his feelings for her, he had perhaps contrived to recover a measure of freedom in the world of his play. And as he was increasingly drawn into a life of writing, Fanny became less luminously present to him – more indistinct, misty, almost like an imagined character in his play.

In places *Otho* recalls *Hyperion*'s epic manner, as in '[t]he bruised remnants of our stricken camp' or Otho's 'Olympian oaths' (I.ii.127, I.iii.14) and its celestial imagery included skies 'portentous as a meteor' (III.i.65). Elsewhere, Keats's dramatic poetry grew comparatively austere and restrained –

> In wintry winds the simple snow is safe,
> But fadeth at the greeting of the sun
>                         (I.ii.26–7)

– and his dialogue focused on explaining characters and motives. By the time he reached his fourth act he was aiming for a more Shakespearean pathos and grandeur:

> O wretched woman! Lost, wreck'd, swallow'd up,
> Accursed, blasted! O, thou golden crown,
> Orbing along the serene firmament
> Of a wide empire, like a glowing moon;
> And thou, bright sceptre, lustrous in my eyes—
> There!—as the fabled fair Hesperian tree,
> Bearing a fruit more precious! graceful thing,
> Delicate, godlike, magic! must I leave
> Thee to melt in the visionary air,
> Ere, by one grasp, this common hand is made
> Imperial? I do not know the time
> When I have wept for sorrow; but methinks
> I could now sit upon the ground, and shed
> Tears, tears of misery. O, the heavy day!
>                         (IV.i.77–90)

Auranthe echoes Richard II on the death of kings, a speech that Keats had once associated with 'the death of Poets'. Was her tearful downfall in the final act a form of vicarious vengeance on women whom he felt had 'destroyed [his] freedom'?[20] A snatch of dialogue earlier in the play may suggest as much. Ludolph – 'madder than Keats' – is talking with Auranthe:

> *Ludolph:*        O, my bride, —my love,—
> Not all the gaze upon us can restrain
> My eyes, too long poor exiles from thy face,
> From adoration, and my foolish tongue
> From uttering soft responses to the love
> I see in thy mute beauty beaming forth!
> Fair creature, bless me with a single word!

All mine!
*Auranthe*: Spare me, spare me, my lord; I swoon else.
*Ludolph*: Soft beauty! by to-morrow I should die,
Wert thou not mine.        [*They talk apart*]
*First Lady*: How deep she has bewitch'd him!

(III.ii.5–14)

There are echoes here of Keats's correspondence with Fanny and his 'Bright Star' sonnet, while the idea of malign witchcraft – recalling 'La Belle Dame sans Merci' – connects with his other narrative of this summer: *Lamia*. By 11 July he had finished the first part of that poem, consisting of about four hundred lines.

Like *Otho the Great*, Keats's narrative in *Lamia* was a further approach to his Gordian knot theme of a lover ensnared and betrayed by a woman. His poem tells how Lycius, a young man from Corinth, was possessed by a lamia – a witch with a woman's mouth and eyes, and the body of a snake. Richard Woodhouse explained to John Taylor how Keats had adapted Burton's story:

Hermes is hunting for a Nymph, when from a wood he hears his name & a song relating to his loss—Mercury finds out that it comes from a serpent, who promises to shew him his Nymph if he promises to turn the serpent into a Woman; This he agrees to: upon which the serpent breathes on his eyes when he sees his Nymph who had been beside them listening invisibly—The serpent had seen a young Man of Corinth with whom she had fallen desperately in Love—She is metamorphosed into a beautiful Woman, the Change is quite Ovidian, but better,—She then finds the Youth, & they live together in a palace in the Middle of Corinth (described, or rather pictured out in very good costume) the entrance of which no one can see.[21]

In *Lamia*, Keats mastered the terse, epigrammatic manner of John Dryden's verse, its mingling of couplets and triplets mirroring the sudden transitions of Ovidian myth. He had been reading Dryden's translations of Ovid and, as Woodhouse hinted, his transformation of the snake into 'a lady bright' eclipsed Dryden's version of Pygmalion's statue becoming a living woman. In a 'dusky brake' reminiscent of the nightingale's sanctuary, Hermes discovers 'a palpitating snake, / Bright, and cirque-couchant' (i.45–6):

She was a gordian shape of dazzling hue,
Vermilion-spotted, golden, green, and blue;
Striped like a zebra, freckled like a pard,
Eyed like a peacock, and all crimson barr'd.

(i.47–50)

Keats's snake-woman, 'freckled like a pard', was apparently a recollection of Jane Cox's 'Leopardess' beauty.[22] This is not to say that Lamia is meant to 'represent' Jane Cox, although her association in Keats's overwrought imagination with Tom's fetid sickroom at Well Walk, overlaying earlier memories of dissections at Guy's, helps to explain why Lamia's lurid glamour was mingled with 'gloomier tapestries . . . touch'd with miseries' (i.53–4). Week by week at Guy's, Keats had dissected corpses in various multi-coloured states of nauseating decomposition. While Lamia's aspect is gloriously 'dazzling', she is also tainted by colours of putrefaction and death, a living-dead thing that is either a 'demon's mistress, or the demon's self'. From the moment of Lamia's feverish metamorphosis –

> Her eyes in torture fix'd, and anguish drear,
> Hot, glaz'd, and wide, with lid-lashes all sear,
> Flash'd phosphor and sharp sparks, without one cooling tear.
> The colours all inflam'd throughout her train,
> She writh'd about, convuls'd with scarlet pain:
> A deep volcanian yellow took the place
> Of all her milder-mooned body's grace.
>
> (i.150–6)

– the deadly outcome of Lycius's passion for her is assured.

In mid-July, Keats wrote again to Abbey about the perilous state of George's affairs. James Rice and John Martin arrived and for three days they smoked, drank and played cards, leaving Keats no opportunity to write until Sunday the 25th, when he worked all day at *Hyperion*. He had abandoned that poem in April, at the double anniversary of his father's death and his first composition towards *Endymion*. Now, as he gazed out over the Chine that had suggested the 'shady sadness' of Saturn's vale, he returned to *Hyperion* and began to reconstruct it as a vision related by Moneta/Mnemosyne, goddess of memory, mother of the Nine Muses, to a poet-dreamer (i.e. Keats himself). As the sole surviving Titan, Moneta is Saturn's priestess and chronicler 'of a war / Foughten long since by giant hierarchy / Against rebellion' (i.222–4). She is also the poet-dreamer's guide, and in Keats's restructured narrative she combines the roles of Virgil and Beatrice in Dante's *Divine Comedy* – a poem that Keats is known to have been reading this summer both in Cary's translation and the original Italian. To prepare for Moneta's vision of 'high tragedy', the poet-dreamer must undergo a rite of passage that Keats supplied from his own tragic history: in short, the epic narrative of *Hyperion* would now be prefaced by an introduction in which Keats would probe and question his own poetic identity.

Written between July and 21 September, *The Fall of Hyperion* revisited questions about the poet's calling which Keats had first broached in *Sleep and Poetry*. Since then, his thinking about suffering and a vale of soul-making had rendered *Hyperion*'s progressive optimism naively unsustainable; by gazing unflinchingly at the 'agony and strife of human hearts', the Dantesque vision of his new poem would show how suffering was essential to the attainment of poetic identity. Back in April 1817 he had deliberately travelled to Southampton on the night of his father's death to begin the 'trial' of *Endymion* that he hoped would confirm him as a poet; now, at the start of *The Fall of Hyperion*, in a remarkable passage of verse autobiography he would once again undergo a 'struggle at the gate of death' as his poet-dreamer commences an ascent to poetic selfhood. The poem opens 'among trees of every clime', close by an 'arbour' with remnants of a summer feast; here the dreamer tells us he 'ate deliciously' and 'pledging all the mortals of the world, / And all the dead whose names are in our lips, / Drank' (i.40, 44–6). Since childhood, eating had occasionally given comforting substance to Keats's sense of himself – literally putting the 'eat' into 'Keats'. As his new poem developed from this first scene of delicious feasting, it would address profound and troubling questions entailed by his fateful decision to 'get his living by poetry'.

July's dog days expired with a gigantic thunder cloud growling and muttering over Hampshire. Their time at Shanklin was almost over. On 5 August, Keats told Fanny he would shortly move with Brown to Winchester. He needed a library, and would receive her letters there more speedily. On Thursday, 12 August the two men were at Cowes, where they saw the regent in his yacht *The Royal George* – a 'silent, light, and graceful' scene that included the frigate *Hyperion*.[23] They crossed to Southampton and by Saturday the 14th were settled at Winchester in 'tolerably good and cheap Lodgings' near the cathedral. Released from his Shanklin coffin, Keats now had a large room in which he could walk up and down, and after six weeks of sea views his window opening onto a blank wall appeared curiously beautiful.[24] There were no crowds of tourists, no gossiping neighbours, and he enjoyed the quiet spaciousness of the cathedral, college and clear chalk streams that accompanied his daily walk across water meadows to the medieval Hospital of St Cross:

I go out at the back gate across one street, into the Cathedral yard, which is always interesting: then I pass under the trees along a paved path, pass the beautiful front of the Cathedral, turn to the left under a stone door way—then I am on the other side of the building—which leaving behind me I pass on through two college-like squares seemingly built for the dwelling place of Deans and Prebendaries—

garnished with grass and shaded with trees. Then I pass through one of the old city gates and then you are in one College-Street through which I pass and at the end thereof crossing some meadows and at last a country alley of gardens I arrive, that is, my worship arrives at the foundation of Saint Cross, which is a very interesting old place.[25]

Although it is now impossible to locate Keats's lodgings precisely, his route through the meadows can still be walked with pleasure despite the roar of traffic and signs warning 'No Public Access'.

Back at his lodgings, Keats dispatched business letters on behalf of George and set about *Otho*'s final act. It took him four days to tell Fanny Brawne of their arrival, in a letter that frankly admits to seeing her 'through a Mist'. 'Believe in the first Letters I wrote you,' he tells her. 'I assure you I felt as I wrote—I could not write so now.' Plunged into 'imaginary interests' that made him 'unloverlike and ungallant', he tells her that his 'heart seems now made of iron' and he 'can no more use soothing words to [her] than if I were at this moment engaged in a charge of Cavalry'.[26]

Unknown to Keats, on that very day citizens were gathering in St Peter's Fields, Manchester, to hear Henry 'Orator' Hunt call for political reform. They assembled peaceably, *The Examiner* reported, until local yeoman cavalry surged into the crowd at full gallop in an attempt to disperse them. There would be cause for soothing words in months and years ahead, for this was the sad sixteenth of August, notorious since 1819 as the bloodstained day of the Peterloo Massacre.

A week passed, and Keats fired off an abrupt letter to John Taylor. He needed an advance, for which Brown pledged security. He was determined to 'get a livelihood', he told Taylor, then launched into a 'hammering' tirade on his dislike of public favour and contempt for the literary world. This was pride and egotism, he granted, but it would enable him to 'write finer things than anything else could'. If this was meant to ingratiate him with Taylor, it didn't work: Taylor forwarded the letter to Woodhouse, who responded to him emolliently that Keats had meant not 'personal pride, but literary pride' and offered a loan of £50. Nothing better exemplifies Woodhouse's steady good wishes towards Keats than his observation: 'Whatever People regret that they could not do for Shakespeare or Chatterton, because he did not live in their time, that I would embody into a Rational principle, and (with due regard to certain expediencies) do for Keats.'[27]

A letter also went to Reynolds, on 'fine writing' and how 'Paradise Lost becomes a greater wonder'. Then followed a passage alarmingly like Haydon's deranged ramblings: 'The more I know what my diligence may in time probably effect; the more does my heart distend with Pride and Obstinacy—I feel it in my power to become a popular writer—I feel it in my strength to refuse the poisonous suffrage of a public'. As with Keats's excoriation of Bailey and Wells, to find him writing thus is an indication of intense stress. He had finished *Otho the Great* and Brown was now making a fair copy. It would be understandable if Keats had felt upbeat and confident – indeed, he may have started four promising but fragmentary scenes of a new play, *King Stephen*, around now. Yet his swerves between steady self-estimation and rant, feeling himself 'impelled', 'driven' and 'in the fever', signalled a coming crisis: 'My Mind is heap'd to the full,' he told Fanny, 'stuff'd like a cricket ball— if I strive to fill it more it would burst.' Reynolds had also heard how Keats's heart would 'distend with Pride and Obstinacy', and there was more to this sensation of inner swelling than a figure of speech. He was anxious about his health, and told Reynolds as much:

> I think if I had a free and healthy and lasting organization of heart and Lungs—as strong as an ox's—so as to be able [to bear] unhurt the shock of extreme thought and sensation without weariness, I could pass my Life very nearly alone though it should last eighty years. But I feel my Body too weak to support me to the height; I am obliged continually to check myself and strive to be nothing.

Here, in few words, was Keats's first overt acknowledgement that his heart and lungs were by no means fit and free of infection. As long ago as April 1817 at Carisbrooke, he had found himself unable to sustain 'extreme thought' without physical agitation. At Winchester his symptoms were little more than a persistent sore throat and cough, yet his feelings of inner distension betokened worse and he passed late August in 'reading, writing, and fretting'. Keats needed a jolt to get him out of this mood, and newspapers supplied it. Kean was to tour in America. No one else could play Ludolph. *Otho the Great* was 'labour in vain for the present'.[28]

It was in fact a setback with a silver lining. Hessey, who knew of Keats's hopes for *Otho*, advanced him £30, Haslam repaid a loan and Brown borrowed and forwarded funds from John Snook. The fine weather continued and as Keats walked up on Twyford Down he relished the pure late-summer air: like claret soothing his throat, it eased his lungs and calmed his heart. From here, east of the city, he could look back and see streets and old buildings mixed up with trees. And perhaps it was here, on the chalk upland, that Keats began the second part of *Lamia*.

Like Hunt's brisk May morning start to *The Story of Rimini*, the first part of *Lamia* had begun in an English landscape of 'rushes green', 'brakes' and 'cowslip'd lawns'. Keats's Crete was the Isle of Wight. Up on Twyford Down, a hunting horn's *taratantara* provided the startling sound he needed to disturb Lycius and Lamia, as they repose in their palace 'with eyelids closed, / Saving a tythe which love had open kept, / That they might see each other while they almost slept' (ii.22–5). What follows is as English as love's 'tythe':

> When from the slope side of a suburb hill,
> Deafening the swallow's twitter, came a thrill
> Of trumpets—Lycius started—the sounds fled,
> But left a thought, a buzzing in his head.
> For the first time, since first he harbour'd in
> That purple-lined palace of sweet sin,
> His spirit pass'd beyond its golden bourn
> Into the noisy world almost forsworn.
>
> (ii.26–33)

'Almost forsworn': those two words capture an ambiguous temper in the second part of *Lamia* as this moment of 'passion's passing' reveals Lycius, formerly 'tangled in her mesh', determined to 'entangle' Lamia in marriage and 'cruel grown' as she beseeches him to 'change his purpose':

>       He thereat was stung,
> Perverse, with stronger fancy to reclaim
> Her wild and timid nature to his aim:
> Besides, for all his love, in self despite,
> Against his better self, he took delight
> Luxurious in her sorrows, soft and new.
>
> (ii.69–74)

After the enchanted complicity of part one, *Lamia*'s second section presents a scene of antagonistic virtues, where contending claims of poetry and philosophy, art and rationalism orchestrate the lovers' ruin. Lamia, serpent and enchantress, now draws sympathy as, 'pale and meek', she sorrows in knowledge of what is to come, while Lycius appears perplexed, foolish, pompous but determined to show off his bride to Corinth's 'gossip rout' at their wedding feast (ii.146). Among their guests is austere Apollonius, Lycius's tutor, from whom Lamia has asked to be hidden. As the ceremony reaches its Bacchanalian meridian, all garlanded with green, Keats devised this exquisite tableau of impending destruction:

What wreath for Lamia? What for Lycius?
What for the sage, old Apollonius?
Upon her aching forehead be there hung
The leaves of willow and of adder's tongue;
And for the youth, quick, let us strip for him
The thyrsus, that his watching eyes may swim
Into forgetfulness; and, for the sage,
Let spear-grass and the spiteful thistle wage
War on his temples. Do not all charms fly
At the mere touch of cold philosophy?
There was an awful rainbow once in heaven:
We know her woof, her texture; she is given
In the dull catalogue of common things.
Philosophy will clip an Angel's wings,
Conquer all mysteries by rule and line,
Empty the haunted air, and gnomed mine—
Unweave a rainbow, as it erewhile made
The tender-person'd Lamia melt into a shade.

(ii.221–38)

With Shakespearean tact, Lamia is offered willow and adder's tongue, emblems of sorrow; Lycius is given a thyrsus, Bacchus's ivied wand of drunken oblivion; and Apollonius's brow is garlanded with piercing leaves of spear-grass and thistle, an anticipation of the 'cruel, perceant, stinging' gaze with which he will destroy Lamia and, with her, his pupil Lycius. From one perspective, Apollonius's 'cold philosophy' triumphs over imagination and poetry's enchantment just as, at another Immortal Dinner, Keats had agreed that Newton 'destroyed all the Poetry of the rainbow, by reducing it to a prism'. And yet the poem itself, which Keats was sure would 'take hold of people', has already exercised its own potent magic: with Lamia 'vanished', Lycius's arms are tragically 'empty of delight / As were his limbs of life' (ii.307–8). Rather than proposing a single definitive reading, Lamia, like the Grecian urn, offers to 'tease us out of thought' with alternative possibilities, asks us to accommodate conflicting impulses as Keats himself was obliged to do throughout this difficult summer of 1819. He had written Lamia with more deliberate judgement than hitherto, and the poem was unlike anything he had written before – unsentimental, forceful, powerfully visual.

Some of Lamia's dramatic effects made use of Keats's immediate surroundings. The homely 'lintel of their chamber door' (ii.14) may be a glimpse of his Winchester lodgings, while the 'fretted splendour of each nook and niche' (ii.137) comes from the cathedral, college and St Cross. Contrasting with the tranquillity of Cathedral Close, Corinth's 'thronged streets' (ii.63) and 'dazzling spokes' (ii.64) mingled Grecian antiquity with the hubbub of an English provincial city, anticipating the urban satire of *The Cap and Bells*.

After three weeks at Winchester, Keats wrote to tell Taylor that he had finished *Lamia* and was revising *The Eve of St Agnes*. As Brown was going to visit friends at Chichester and Bedhampton, he anticipated being alone for three weeks, although neither scenario turned out as expected. According to Brown's son Carlino, his father dashed over to Ireland, where he married Abigail Donohoe, housekeeper at Wentworth Place and 'a handsome woman of the peasant class', in a ceremony of dubious legality. Exactly how Brown contrived this marriage is unknown. Many years later his granddaughter stated that it took place in a Roman Catholic church, and that the birth certificate of her own father (Carlino) had been 'written by a RC priest' and described his mother as 'Abigail Brown née (or its equivalent) Donahoe'.[29]

In Brown's absence, Keats's solitude was interrupted by an urgent letter from George. His business venture with Audubon had completely failed, and he was in desperate need of funds. Keats saw the reality immediately: 'I cannot help thinking M^r Audubon a dishonest man—Why did he make you believe that he was a Man of Property? How is it his circumstances have altered so suddenly? In truth I do not believe you fit to deal with the world; or at least the american worrld [*sic*].'[30]

Audubon was already being pursued by five creditors, and George's remaining capital was further sunk by the great 'Panic' of 1819, America's first major financial crisis with bank failures, foreclosed loans, unemployment and depressed prices. Abbey was still withholding funds and cash would take months to reach George, but if Keats could dissuade his aunt from going to court all might yet be well. With thoughts of offering a poem to John Murray, on Friday the 10th he bundled up his manuscripts and hurried to London on an overnight coach. In the morning he went directly to Abbey and gave him a note from George. Appearing genuinely anxious and willing to expedite George's request for funds, Abbey fixed a meeting for Monday evening. Keats next went to 93 Fleet Street, where he met by chance Woodhouse and Hessey, telling them that he wanted immediate publication of *Lamia* and *The Eve of St Agnes*. Perhaps sensing one of Keats's moods of fits and starts, Hessey was discouraging. Woodhouse suggested that *Isabella* might sell better but Keats, fresh from composing *Lamia*, now thought *Isabella* 'mawkish' – simple and sentimental. That night he went to Covent Garden on a half-price ticket, then tumbled exhausted into bed.[31]

Sunday morning took Keats to Woodhouse's for breakfast. He had *The Eve of St Agnes* with him 'copied fair', and pointed out some recent changes.[32] An extra stanza clarified the legend of St Agnes' Eve, and a dramatic change of sentiment at the end now brought 'Old Angela in ... dead stiff & ugly'. Woodhouse supposed Keats was copying Byron's modish technique in *Don Juan*, provoking his reader by deliberately mingling passages of sentiment and sneering. A third revision caused Woodhouse genuine disquiet: in nine lines Keats had made Porphyro and Madeline's love-making much more explicit:

> See, while she speaks his arms encroaching slow,
> Have zoned her, heart to heart,—loud, loud the dark winds blow!

> For on the midnight came a tempest fell;
> More sooth, for that his quick rejoinder flows
> Into her burning ear: and still the spell
> Unbroken guards her in serene repose.
> With her wild dream he mingled, as a rose
> Marrieth its odour to a violet.
> Still, still she dreams, louder the frost wind blows ...[33]

Woodhouse was shocked. While there were no 'improper expressions' and 'all was left to inference', it was obvious that the poem was now 'unfit for ladies & indeed scarcely to be mentioned to them'. Unabashed, Keats responded that he did not want ladies reading his poetry — he wrote for men. He had been at fault for not writing clearly and comprehensibly: Porphyro would have appeared contemptible to abandon 'a maid, with that Character about her, in such a situation' without making love to her. Indeed, he would despise himself for having written as much.[34]

After six hours of discussion Keats accompanied Woodhouse to the Weymouth coach, then went on to dine with Georgiana's mother, brothers and aunt at Henrietta Street. Musing on their breakfast 'tête à tête', Woodhouse decided to relate 'these Keatsiana' to Taylor. He was the publisher's legal adviser, and a concerted response might make Keats see sense about *The Eve of St Agnes*. Taylor's reply to Woodhouse was unequivocal. He would publish nothing that 'can only be read by Men' and if Keats did not leave the passage as it originally stood, he should be obliged to admire his poems with 'some other Imprint'.[35] Impropriety would be damaging; diminished sales more so.

Monday morning, 13 September. Keats rose early and wrote affectionately to Fanny Brawne. He was in town, but loved her too much to come out to Hampstead. Already embroiled in 'downright perplexities', to see her would be 'venturing into a fire'. He posted his letter at Lombard Street, then took a coach to see his sister at Walthamstow. His return that afternoon coincided with Henry Hunt's triumphant arrival in the city. From Islington to the Strand, his route was lined with multitudes of citizens determined to oppose the outrage at Peterloo; suddenly the private vexations that had hurried Keats to London intersected with national distresses. He saw that ever since the 1790s a state-sponsored 'superstition', confounding social and political change with revolutionary conspiracy, had oppressed Britain. It had prejudiced reviewers against him, and now it had spawned violence at Peterloo. Keats knew that to 'literary fashionables' his name was no better than that of a Dorset weaver boy – as vulgar as the poor citizens so cruelly trampled at Manchester. If the violent example of French terror and warmongering had put a stop to liberal progress in Britain, as Keats believed was the case, he now detected renewed signs of 'change for the better' in a fundamental contest 'between right and wrong'.[36] All in all, Hunt's triumphant entry to London was a heartening sight.

At seven that evening Keats met Abbey who, like everyone he had seen so far, behaved in what appeared a 'most conciliating manner'. Abbey said he would contact solicitors, head off Margaret Jennings's claim and be 'expeditious' about George's affairs. This was all to the good, yet all was not quite as it seemed. Keats set off up Cheapside, turned back to post some letters, met Abbey again and walked with him through The Poultry to 'the hatter's shop he has some concern in—He spoke of it in such a way to me, I thought he wanted me to make an offer to assist him in it'.[37] What was going on here?

It appears that within minutes of their first discussion of George's crisis and the Jennings estate, Abbey had set off to visit Joseph Keats's widow at 74 Cheapside, where she was carrying on the hatter's shop 'in her own behalf'.[38] Knowing that Keats had no money, was Abbey trying to find him employment with a woman who might plausibly have been a relative? Or are we looking at an altogether murkier scenario where Abbey's responsibility for the Keats inheritance was entangled with business at a hatter's shop in which he was also concerned? Whatever the case, these Cheapside conversations were strange, and Keats himself felt uneasy: with most of his friends away, he found London 'a very odd place', with 'not one house I felt any pleasure to call at'.[39] On Wednesday the 15th, under cloudy skies, he took a morning coach back to Winchester.

Settled and solitary at Winchester, with quiet and time to think, Keats resumed his study of Italian and read Ariosto and Dante. Letters went in quick succession to Reynolds, Brown and Dilke, and on the 17th he began a journal-letter for America. While in London he had resolved to write for a periodical 'on the liberal side of the question' and thought of taking rooms in Westminster. The writing would bring in cash and might contribute to change for the better – he could not keep on applying to Brown for support. When he woke on the morning of Saturday the 18th he felt that, despite 'bad times and misfortunes', he was alert, well spirited, and must exert himself independently. Yet, throughout these mid-September days, he knew that although he had not gone to Hampstead to visit her he felt no less deeply about Fanny Brawne. They had been apart for twelve weeks and if, as was likely, Brown decided to winter at Wentworth Place, Keats would not join him: 'I like x x x x x x x x x and I cannot help it. On that account I had better not live there.'[40] As he approached his twenty-fourth birthday each week's *Examiner* came as a reminder of how much he valued his own independence. If he could not help liking Fanny Brawne he was also wary, frightened even, of compromising his freedom by living so near her. He was well aware of his own 'inconstant disposition' and, while he hoped to shake off his obstinate circumstances and marry Fanny, in many respects he was constitutionally unable to do so.

Having told George and Georgiana of his visit to London and his encounter with Abbey at Cheapside, Keats found memories of earlier times uppermost in his mind. Among papers not committed to the flames at Wentworth Place was his letter to Tom, begun a year ago at Derry-na-Cullen. In it were his descriptions of Mull, Iona's ruined cathedral and smashed columns in that sublime 'Cathedral of the Sea', Fingal's Cave. Transcribing these for George and Georgiana on the 18th seems to have prepared him for resuming *The Fall of Hyperion*, put aside since Shanklin. As the poet-dreamer 'ate deliciously' and drank deep, a 'cloudy swoon came on' (ii.40, 55). 'How long I slumber'd 'tis a chance to guess', but as 'sense of life returned' the poet-dreamer finds himself in 'an old sanctuary':

> So old the place was I remembered none
> The like upon the earth; what I had seen
> Of grey Cathedrals, buttress'd walls, rent towers
> The superanuations of sunk realms,
> Or nature's rocks hard toil'd in winds and waves,
> Seem'd but the failing of decrepit things
> To that eternal-domed monument—[41]

All of Scotland's wonders were diminished by this gigantic temple of Saturn, an 'eternal-domed monument' with an altar at its western extremity 'approach'd on either side by steps' to which the poet-dreamer proceeds 'sober-pac'd' along a marble pavement (ii.71, 90, 93). Keats now ventured into the shadowy terrain of his earliest childhood, as his poet-dreamer encounters Moneta in a 'domed monument' that strikingly recalls Lackington's Temple of the Muses on Finsbury Square. From 'white fragrant curtains', Moneta admonishes him:

> 'If thou canst not ascend
> These steps, die on that marble where thou art.
> Thy flesh, near cousin to the common dust,
> Will parch for lack of nutriment—thy bones
> Will wither in few years, and vanish so
> That not the quickest eye could find a grain
> Of what thou now art on that pavement cold.
> The sands of thy short life are spent this hour,
> And no hand in the universe can turn
> Thy hour glass, if these gummed leaves be burnt
> Ere thou canst mount up these immortal steps.'
>                              (i.107–17)

Inside Lackington's Temple of the Muses a wide staircase had led up to 'lounging rooms' and a series of book-lined galleries beneath a glazed dome. As that awe-inspiring building revives in Keats's poem, his poet-dreamer goes through a ritual initiation on 'immortal steps' of a 'domed monument' that Moneta describes as a 'temple'. What he endures is akin to Thomas Keates's 'mortal bruise' just a few yards from the Temple of the Muses, as he struggled at the gates of death beside Bunhill Fields:

> suddenly a palsied chill
> Struck from the paved level up my limbs,
> And was ascending quick to put cold grasp
> Upon those streams that pulse beside the throat:
> I shriek'd; and the sharp anguish of my shriek
> Stung my own ears—I strove hard to escape
> The numbness; strove to gain the lowest step.
> Slow, heavy, deadly was my pace: the cold
> Grew stifling, suffocating, at the heart;
> And when I clasp'd my hands I felt them not.
> One minute before death, my iced foot touch'd
> The lowest stair; and as it touch'd, life seem'd
> To pour in at the toes.
>                              (i.122–34)

In this suffocating experience of life-in-death, or death-in-life, Keats was almost certainly describing his own deadly coagulating sensations of inhaling cold air with tubercular lungs. 'Blood without the access of air coagulated,' he had scribbled down in his medical notebook. At a more symbolic level, his poet-dreamer had suffered and survived the terrible accident that dispatched Thomas Keates beneath the 'Doom' at St Stephen's:

> Then said the veiled shadow—'Thou hast felt
> What 'tis to die and live again before
> Thy fated hour. That thou hadst power to do so
> Is thy own safety; thou hast dated on
> Thy doom.'
>
> (i.141–5)

'I saw the sun rise,' Keats had written on arriving at Southampton on 15 April 1817, dating his own doom beyond the night that had claimed his father's life. The passage that follows, frequently interpreted as a chilling confrontation between Keats and the shade of his mother, is an exchange in which the poet-dreamer enquires why he alone should have survived when there are so many that 'feel the giant agony of the world'. Moneta replies that those who labour practically for 'mortal good'

> 'are no dreamers weak,
> They seek no wonder but the human face;
> No music but a happy-noted voice—
> They come not here, they have no thought to come—
> And thou art here, for thou art less than they.
> What benefit canst thou do, or all thy tribe,
> To the great world? Thou art a dreaming thing;
> A fever of thyself—think of the earth.'
>
> (i.162–9)

On being told that he deliberately 'venoms all his days, / Bearing more woe than all his sins deserve', the dreamer protests, 'sure a poet is a sage; / A humanist, physician to all men', and draws from Moneta this uncompromising clarification:

> 'The poet and the dreamer are distinct,
> Diverse, sheer opposite, antipodes.

The one pours out a balm upon the world,
The other vexes it.'

(i.198–202)

Back in the spring Keats's 'Ode on Indolence' had been his own mischievous manifesto for a life of deliciously indolent imagining; now, as he fears he has abandoned medical training for a more dubious 'balm', Moneta softens her voice to maternal tones and parts the veils that had 'curtain'd her in mysteries':

Then saw I a wan face,
Not pin'd by human sorrows, but bright blanch'd
By an immortal sickness which kills not;
It works a constant change, which happy death
Can put no end to; deathwards progressing
To no death was that visage; it had pass'd
The lily and the snow; and beyond these
I must not think now, though I saw that face—

(ii.256–63)

'I saw that face.' As with so much of Keats's poetry, his poet-dreamer's astonishing vision of an 'immortal sickness' originated in first-hand experience; his apprehension of 'a constant change' was a horrified contemplation of mortality suggested, perhaps, by an image that had once enchanted him – the chilly pallor of the moon's disc when seen behind hurrying clouds. Frances Keates's lingering winter deathbed and pale shrouded face may indeed have suggested Moneta's veiled lineaments, but we should not forget that John and Alice Jennings, Thomas Keates, Midgley John Jennings, Tom Keats and Edward Keats were also among his family's mighty dead. To them may be added scores of bereavements Keats had witnessed with Hammond and at Guy's. All were now gathered into Moneta's spectral embodiment of a disease that had made its catastrophic inroads amid a family conflict that had ruined them all. As his poet-dreamer petitions to know more, we can detect echoes of 'bad times and misfortunes' all too familiar to Keats:

'Shade of Memory!'
Cried I, with act adorant at her feet,
'By all the gloom hung round thy fallen house,
By this last temple, by the golden age,
By great Apollo, thy dear foster child,
And by thy self, forlorn divinity,

The pale Omega of a wither'd race,
Let me behold, according as thou said'st,
What in thy brain so ferments to and fro.'—
(i.282–90)


By invoking Moneta's 'dear foster child' Apollo, this anguished petition speaks as well of high tragedy in Keats's own 'fallen house', of a forlorn mother of his own 'wither'd race'. 'Wither' here means shrunken, emaciated and wasted by disease, a clear reference to the Keatses' dwindling tubercular deaths rather than 'the thunder of a war / Foughten long since by giant hierarchy / Against rebellion' (i.222–4). The parallels are not exact, of course, but they are perhaps sufficient to suggest that when Keats's poet-dreamer intuits a restless 'ferment' in Moneta's brain, her agitation at the imminent disclosure of tragic memories reflected turmoil in his own brain too.

# Consumption, 1819–1821

# CHAPTER 21

# Repasts

Even as Keats made progress with *The Fall of Hyperion* his ferment of thought was leading him in other, surprising new directions and by Tuesday, 21 September, the autumn equinox, he had set his poem aside. Hitherto his brilliance as a mimic had enabled him to adapt another poet's manner to make it his own, but now he felt that his blank verse was contaminated by Milton's Latin inflections in *Paradise Lost*. Thomas Chatterton was a poet Keats had long associated with autumn and, unlike Milton, Chatterton had written 'genuine English Idiom in English words'.[1] 'How beautiful the season is now,' he wrote to Reynolds,

> How fine the air. A temperate sharpness about it. Really, without joking, chaste weather—Dian skies—I never lik'd stubble fields so much as now—Aye better than the chilly green of the spring. Somehow a stubble plain looks warm—in the same way that some pictures look warm—this struck me so much in my sunday's walk that I composed upon it.[2]

Sunday was 19 September, when a new moon brought the fine autumnal weather and 'Dian skies' that Keats 'composed upon' in 'To Autumn':

> Season of mists and mellow fruitfulness,
>   Close bosom-friend of the maturing sun;
> Conspiring with him how to load and bless
>   With fruit the vines that round the thatch-eves run;
> To bend with apples the moss'd cottage-trees,
>   And fill all fruit with ripeness to the core;
>     To swell the gourd, and plump the hazel shells

With a sweet kernel; to set budding more,
And still more, later flowers for the bees,
Until they think warm days will never cease,
    For summer has o'er-brimm'd their clammy cells.

Who hath not seen thee oft amid thy store?
  Sometimes whoever seeks abroad may find
Thee sitting careless on a granary floor,
  Thy hair soft-lifted by the winnowing wind;
Or on a half-reap'd furrow sound asleep,
  Drows'd with the fume of poppies, while thy hook
    Spares the next swath and all its twined flowers:
And sometimes like a gleaner thou dost keep
  Steady thy laden head across a brook;
  Or by a cyder-press, with patient look,
    Thou watchest the last oozings hours by hours.

Where are the songs of spring? Ay, where are they?
  Think not of them, thou hast thy music too,—
While barred clouds bloom the soft-dying day,
  And touch the stubble-plains with rosy hue;
Then in a wailful choir the small gnats mourn
  Among the river sallows, borne aloft
    Or sinking as the light wind lives or dies;
And full-grown lambs loud bleat from hilly bourn;
  Hedge-crickets sing; and now with treble soft
  The red-breast whistles from a garden-croft;
    And gathering swallows twitter in the skies.

Thatch, moss, kernel, clammy, reap, swath, brook, hook, sallows, bleat, croft and swallows are all sturdy old words that Keats associated with Chatterton's native English.[3] Doubtless some of these quintessentially English words and images were harvested during his walk along water meadows towards Twyford Down although, like his spring odes, 'To Autumn' also responded to what Hunt was writing in *The Examiner* (copies were being forwarded by Dilke).[4] For five weeks *The Examiner* had reported the trampling of a 'less fortunate multitude' at Peterloo, and as recently as 5 September, Hunt's 'Calendar of Nature' had made the season itself an argument for social justice, beginning with this 'lesson' from *The Faerie Queen*:

SEPTEMBER.

Next him September marched eke on foot;
Yet was he heavy laden with the spoyle
Of harvest's riches, which he made his boot,
And him enriched with bounty of the soyle:
In his one hand, as fit for harvest's toyle,
He held a knife-hook; and in th'other hand
A paire of weights, with which he did assoyle
Both more and lesse, where it in doubt did stand,
And equal gave to each as justice duly scanned.

                                        SPENSER.


The poet still takes advantage of the exuberance of harvest and the sign of the Zodiac in this month, to read us a lesson on justice.

Autumn has now arrived. This is the month of the migration of birds, of the finished harvest, of nut-gathering, of cyder and perry-making, and, towards the conclusion, of the change of colour in trees. The swallows, and many other soft-billed birds that feed on insects, disappear for the warmer climates, leaving only a few stragglers behind, probably from weakness or sickness, who hide themselves in caverns and other sheltered places, and occasionally appear on warm days. The remainder of harvest is got in; and no sooner is this done, than the husbandman ploughs up his land again, and prepares it for the winter grain . . .

September, though its mornings and evenings are apt to be chill and foggy, and therefore not wholesome to those who either do not or cannot guard against them, is generally a serene and pleasant month, partaking of the warmth of summer and the vigour of autumn. But its noblest feature is a certain festive abundance for the supply of all creation. There is grain for men, birds, and horses, hay for the cattle, loads of fruit on the trees, and swarms of fish in the ocean. If the soft-billed birds which feed on insects miss their usual supply, they find it in the southern countries, and leave one's sympathy to be pleased with an idea, that repasts apparently more harmless are alone offered to the creation upon our temperate soil. The feast, as the philosophic poet says on a higher occasion,

The feast is such as earth, the general mother,
    Pours from her fairest bosom, when she smiles
In the embrace of Autumn. To each other
    As some fond parent fondly reconciles
Her warring children, she their wrath beguiles
    With their own sustenance; they, relenting, weep.

> Such is this festival, which from their isles,
>   And continents, and winds, and oceans deep,
>   All shapes may throng to share, that fly, or walk, or creep.
>                                                SHELLEY.[5]

Immediately below that stanza from Shelley's *Revolt of Islam* is the heading 'LAW. Surrey Sessions. *Tuesday Aug. 31*. Seditious Placards', returning Hunt's readers to controversial politics of the day.

Similarities between 'To Autumn' and Hunt's 'Calendar of Nature' extend beyond 'harvest's riches' and a reaper's 'knife-hook'. Migrating birds, cider-making, swallows and insects, warm days, and even the chill and fog all reappear in Keats's poem. As striking is the schooling Hunt extracts from Spenser as 'a lesson on justice'. Spenser's harvester, using a 'paire of weights' to apportion equally, is well judged for September because, as Hunt notes, the latter part of this temperate month lies under the constellation Libra – 'The Scales'. Keats had known about Libra since his schoolboy reading in Bonnycastle's *Introduction to Astronomy*, and in autumn 1819 Libra's scales also appeared in images of Peterloo. At the Manchester meeting banners had depicted Justice bravely brandishing her scales; after the atrocity, George Cruikshank's satirical cartoon 'Manchester Heroes' showed a smirking prince regent beneath a set of flagrantly unbalanced scales, urging on the cavalry: 'Cut them down, don't be afraid, they are not armed.' Against that scene of tyranny and persecution, Hunt's 'lesson on justice' at a time of seasonal plenty is apparent: the 'exuberance of harvest' – literally, *ex-uber*, from nature's breast – is a 'festive abundance' for all to share, as in Shelley's 'banquet of the free' from *The Revolt of Islam*. Only if such democratic sharing takes place, Hunt suggests, will divisions between England's 'warring children' be reconciled.

When we turn from Hunt's 'Calendar of Nature' to Keats's poem, its three richly laden stanzas appear as a harvest-home for England's 'less fortunate multitude': a lock of hair is 'soft-lifted' to float free on a 'winnowing wind'; a furrow is abandoned 'half-reap'd'; the gleaner – an archetype of poverty and exclusion – becomes a figure of steady purpose; and swallows, still gathering, announce their imminent departure while keeping at bay Keats's fateful word 'gone'. Under a new moon's Dian skies, such images of natural liberty assured Keats's poem a hearing even amid the noisy, disorderly debates ignited by the Manchester outrage.

Keats was gathering himself too. As the government laid plans for the 'Six Acts' to clamp down on seditious libel, limit public meetings and increase taxation on newspapers, he determined to secure cheap lodgings in London and seek Hazlitt's advice about writing for periodicals. Dilke was enlisted to find rooms in Westminster, and around Friday, 8 October, Keats moved into an apartment at 25 College Street adjacent to Westminster Abbey. If he had hoped to speak out for reform, that plan was abandoned almost at once. Saturday, 10 October found him at Hampstead, completely dazzled at seeing Fanny Brawne again, after three months. Two days later at College Street he had set himself to make a fair copy of some verses when a note came from her. "'T is richer than an Argosy of Pearles,' he replied, salvaging a favourite image from Kauffman's *Dictionary of Merchandize*; a three-day visit at Wentworth Place ensued, and by the new moon on Tuesday the 19th Keats had resolved to live once again with Brown at Hampstead. By Thursday the 21st he had moved in as a heavy fall of snow announced winter's onset. In 'a tremble' at his sudden capitulation to passion, perplexed by 'ill news' of George's speculations and with his own hopes at hazard as *Otho the Great* was sent to Robert Elliston, manager of Drury Lane, he turned vegetarian to purge his mind and body of 'mist'.[6]

November frequently brought Keats to London on 'Georges business', unaware that financial difficulties at Louisville had already forced his brother to take ship for England. On the 18th he saw his sister, Fanny, at Abbey's in Pancras Lane although he had little news for her. What passed between them is unknown. Neither could have realised that this poignantly nondescript encounter, watched by a guardian they both disliked, was the last time they would ever meet. Beyond that, Keats made occasional visits and had dinner with Hilton and Woodhouse at Taylor's, but other old friends had now lost touch. He saw nothing of Haydon, and had no time to visit the Royal Academy to view Severn's rendering of Spenser's 'Cave of Despair' entered for the Academy's Gold Medal for painting. 'You had best put me in,' he wrote bleakly to Severn at mid-month; two days later, resolving not to publish anything he had already written, he told Taylor he planned another poem with the 'colouring' of *The Eve of St Agnes* and, in due course, 'a few fine Plays'. Against the odds, Severn's painting won the Academy's Gold Medal for Historical Printing.

Suddenly, Keats seemed to have struck gold too. News came that Elliston had accepted *Otho* for the next season at Drury Lane, although Brown hoped it might yet be scooped up by Covent Garden for an earlier production. Keats's November despondency lifted, and he was now preparing 'some Poems to come out in the spring'. With Brown he resumed their old 'dog trot' routines, a turn of phrase that indicates they were once again collaborating – this time on a comic satirical poem, *The Cap and Bells,* or, as Keats preferred, *The Jealousies*, to be published under the pseudonym Lucy Vaughan Lloyd.

Begun without a plan, its Spenserian stanzas accumulated rapidly – Keats wrote as many as twelve each morning, and then Brown immediately made a fair copy. Set on 23 and 24 April, this poem is loosely patterned on the star-crossed lovers in Hunt's *Story of Rimini* as Princess Bellanaine is summoned to marry Emperor Elfinan – both of them are immortals, and each has a mortal lover. As Bellanaine's pageant approaches, Elfinan's 'dearest love' is revealed as Keats's heroine from 'The Eve of St Mark' – the seamstress 'Bertha Pearl' of Canterbury. Summoning his magician Hum, the emperor is told:

> 'Those wings to Canterbury you must beat,
> If you hold Bertha as a worthy prize.
> Look in the Almanack—*Moore* never lies—
> April the twenty-fourth,—this coming day,
> Now breathing its new bloom upon the skies,
>     Will end in St Mark's eve;—you must away,
> For on that eve alone can you the maid convey.'

Was this a joke about Isabella Jones turning over *Old Moore's Almanack* to discover yet another theme for a poem? Elfinan was about to be dispatched on a lover's quest more appropriate to honied St Agnes' Eve than the death-infected rituals of the Eve of St Mark. Keats's high-spirited satire skips from the prince regent and Lord Byron to this sly parody of Hunt's poetry:

> The morn was full of holiday; loud bells
> With rival clamours rang from every spire;
> Cunningly-station'd music dies and swells
> In echoing places; when the winds respire,
> Light flags stream out like gauzy tongues of fire;
> A metropolitan murmur, lifeful, warm,
> Came from the northern suburbs . . .
> (568–74)

His novelistic genius captures a hackney carriage's seedy interior with slack 'linsey-wolsey lining' and a Cheapside evening as Abbey locks up his premises in Pancras Lane and turns on the gas lamps:

> It was the time when wholesale houses close
> Their shutters with a moody sense of wealth,
> But retail dealers, diligent, let loose
> The gas (objected to on score of health),

Convey'd in little solder'd pipes by stealth,
And make it flare in many a brilliant form,
That all the powers of darkness it repell'th,
Which to the oil-trade doth great scaith and harm . . .

(208–15)

*The Cap and Bells* had terrific potential. Keats enjoyed writing it and his amusement stemmed in part from ranging affectionately over 'metropolitan murmurs', political and literary quarrels in *The Examiner*, the old Hunt circle at the Vale of Health, Hunt's poems and his own. If *The Fall of Hyperion* was a venture along some darker passages of his psyche, *The Cap and Bells* gives us a streetwise Keats as he walks by gaslight to an evening of drink and talk with friends. He could see how it might eventually be divided into cantos for publication, although he was now consciously living from day to day, 'fearful lest the weather should affect my throat which on exertion or cold continually threatens me'. On medical advice he had bought a warm greatcoat, laid out £3.6s.6d. on a pair of thick shoes, and on Christmas Day, wrapped up and well shod, went to dine with the Dilkes at Westminster.[7]

George arrived with the first week of 1820, in London to cash his one-third share of Tom's capital. Social events began on Sunday the 9th, when Keats and George had dinner with Georgiana's family. Two days later they went to a 'piano forte hop' at the Dilkes', and it may have been here that Reynolds's sisters informed George that Fanny Brawne was 'an artful bad hearted Girl'. Since the Christmas dinner invitation fiasco of 1818, relations between the Reynoldses and Fanny Brawne had been strained, and there may have been other jealousies and rivalries at work too. On the other hand, the Reynoldses also knew Keats's precarious resources and poor health and, in their eyes, it appeared irresponsible – if not exactly 'bad hearted' – to have entangled him. As the sisters formed a 'not very inticing row opposite', Keats cautioned his brother to 'mark them and form his Judgement of them'. Whether or not George knew of Keats's engagement to Fanny, he later admitted to '[k]nowing John's affection' for her and that this made him 'very much disposed to like her' – although his busy visit to London actually gave them little chance to become acquainted. Certainly Fanny thought that George did not like her and confessed him 'no favorite', although these remarks suggest she was influenced by George's financial dealings with his brother – as we shall see.[8]

On 12 January there was another dinner at Taylor's in Fleet Street; on Sunday the 16th Keats had a party for his 'old set' of Rice, Reynolds and Thomas Richards; and the following weekend there was a dinner at the

Dilkes, for Keats and his brother, Brown, Reynolds, Rice and Taylor. Then at 6am on Friday the 28th George caught the coach for Liverpool. He arrived there thirty-six hours later, immediately booked a passage on the *Courier* and sailed for America on Tuesday, 1 February. Keats would not hear of his safe arrival until April.

While in London, George had persuaded Abbey to cash Tom's remaining capital and, after clearing his debts and balancing accounts, this amounted to some £800, to be divided into three sums of around £260. The confusions and misunderstandings that ensued dismayed Keats, angered his friends and eventually led to a bitter quarrel between Dilke and Brown. In brief, Keats took just £100 of his share, leaving George some £440 in cash. This, with other remittances due to him, amounted to the £700 he seems to have taken back to America. Although this was no more than a just settlement of what George had been owed since summer 1818, his abrupt manner and bad timing did far more damage than he realised. Mistakenly thinking George had left with an even larger sum, Keats's friends were outraged and Brown recalled his distress years afterwards. 'You, John, have so many friends, they will be sure to take care of you!' George had apparently said in parting, words that Keats repeated to Brown at Wentworth Place, adding, 'That was not, Brown, fair—was it?' All he now possessed was £70 and when he handed this to Brown it was insufficient to clear his bills.[9] Looking back more than a year later, Fanny Brawne judged that George's behaviour had been 'extravagant and selfish': with a wife and family to support, 'as he could not get what he wanted without coming to England he unfortunately came'. She was seemingly echoing what Keats had said to her: 'George ought not to have done this he should have recollected that I wish to marry myself—but I suppose having a family to provide for makes a man selfish.' Still, Fanny felt that he was more blamed than he deserved, and with some reason. When George left London, Keats had seemed to be readying his poems for publication and there were hopes of staging *Otho the Great*, with its follow-up, *King Stephen*, awaiting completion. There may have been talk of warmer climates, for George wrote from Louisville with hopes of forwarding £200 to help Keats move to 'a more favorable clime': 'to Italy you must and shall go.' George had reason to suppose any 'inconvenience' to his brother would not last, and could not have foreseen the dreadful indirect consequences of his actions.[10]

Unmentioned in any of Keats's correspondence from January 1820 is the bitterly cold weather that swept across England from north and east. For three weeks temperatures were well below freezing, with a single day of unseasonably warm sun on the 15th. Day after day Keats covered the 'cursed cold distance' from Hampstead to the city wrapped up in his greatcoat, still acutely 'fearful lest the weather should affect [his] throat'.[11] Quitting his fireside for an outside seat on a coach put his health at hazard, although, ironically, a thaw on Monday the 24th put him in greatest danger for he left off his coat and caught an infection that flew to his lungs.

Six days after George's departure, at eleven o'clock on the evening of Thursday, 3 February, Keats came into Wentworth Place in a fever. Brown recorded what happened next:

I asked hurriedly, 'What is the matter,—you are fevered?' 'Yes, yes,' he answered, 'I was on the outside of the stage this bitter day till I was severely chilled,—but now I don't feel it. Fevered!—of course, a little'. He mildly and instantly yielded . . . to my request that he should go to bed. I followed with the best immediate remedy in my power. I entered his chamber as he leapt into bed. On entering the cold sheets, before his head was on the pillow, he slightly coughed, and I heard him say,—'That is blood from my mouth'. I went towards him; he was examining a single drop of blood upon the sheet. 'Bring me the candle, Brown; and let me see this blood'. After regarding it steadfastly, he looked up in my face, with a calmness of countenance that I can never forget, and said,—'I know the colour of that blood;—it is arterial blood;—I cannot be deceived in that colour;—that drop of blood is my death-warrant;—I must die.'[12]

George Rodd, a local surgeon, was sent for. He immediately bled Keats to reduce the inflammation on his lungs, a pointless procedure that further weakened his patient. By five in the morning Keats was asleep. The next day Rodd attended with Robert Bree, a distinguished physician and author of *A Practical Enquiry into Disordered Respiration*, first published in 1797 and many times reprinted. Bree pronounced that his lungs were uninjured – a diagnosis that satisfied Brown but not Keats himself, who 'could not reconcile the colour of that blood with their favourable opinion'. Medical training and long, harrowing months nursing Tom told him the bright drop of arterial blood was a symptom of pulmonary consumption, for which there was no cure. His doctors prescribed a sedative and another 'nerve-shaking' medicine.[13] He must remain confined in his room, keep to a scanty vegetarian diet, speak in a low voice and avoid any disturbance that might bring on another haemorrhage. Reading and writing poetry were forbidden. Georgiana's mother called soon after he was taken ill, and although other well-wishers followed there was one visitor he longed to see most of all.

At first he thought that Fanny's presence next door would transform his confinement into a 'pleasant prison'. Then the desperate actuality of their situation sank in. 'My dearest Girl,' he wrote sadly to her. 'According to all appearances I am to be separated from you as much as possible.' She could visit – he liked her to call in the evenings between six and eight – but even a few minutes together made him perilously 'nervous' and exposed her to the infection he breathed. Tuberculosis ran in the Brawne family too. With illness a barrier between them, they resorted to messages. Only Keats's side of this correspondence has survived; although most of his letters are undated it is possible to reconstruct some of their exchanges. When he told her that she was released from their engagement, she suspected it was at another's suggestion – possibly Brown's or, more likely, Reynolds's. 'Believe . . . my Love that our friends think and speak for the best,' he reassured her, 'and if their best is not our best it is not their fault.' She worried that he suspected her of emotional 'coldness'; he responded with heartfelt concern that she should 'not stop so long in the cold'. Again and again he lingered on the dangers of frost and a thaw: 'wear warm cloathing not only in a frost but in a Thaw', 'be very careful to wear warm cloathing in a thaw', 'be very careful of your cloathing – this climate requires the utmost care.' 'Be very careful of open doors and windows and going without your duffle grey,' he signed off at the end of one of these February messages, poignantly associating Fanny Brawne with Wordsworth's orphan Alice Fell, whose grief-stricken sobbing could only be pacified by a warm cloak of 'duffil grey'.[14]

To have her living close by yet beyond his embrace was terrible, as day by day he glimpsed her in the garden, watched her coming and going, listened for her footfall and the sound of her voice. For Fanny, too, Keats's proximity brought deep anguish, especially his increasingly suffocating demands: 'You could not step or move an eyelid but it would shoot to my heart—I am greedy of you—Do not think of anything but me. Do not live as if I was not existing— Do not forget me—But have I any right to say you forget me?'[15] At least part of Keats's misery lay in the strict regime of physical restraint imposed by his doctors. Since childhood he had always been vigorously active. He had conquered Ben Nevis. With Fanny he had enjoyed walks across the airy ridges of Hampstead Heath. Now their world shrank into Wentworth Place, where she could hear his incessant coughing as she tried to cope with the devastating knowledge that he was succumbing to the disease that had killed her father.

Keats's outpourings of passion and tenderness frequently hardened into jealous possessiveness. In three letters sent between late May and early July he lashed out as he had done as a child, when he had reportedly brandished a sword to prevent his mother going out. He continued to suspect that Fanny flirted with Brown, and even while Brown was nursing him at all hours Keats dictated that she would not 'make any long stay with me when M$^r$ Brown is at home'. Sometimes he felt so cut off from her that he might as well be dead, and likened himself to Lorenzo's ghost in *Isabella*. 'I wish I had even a little hope,' he confided, while acknowledging that 'there are impossibilities in the world'. Lying awake at night, he persuaded himself that he had failed in his great objective of poetic fame and immortality: '"If I should die," said I to myself, "I have left no immortal work behind me—nothing to make my friends proud of my memory—but I have lov'd the principle of beauty in all things, and if I had had time I would have made myself remember'd."'[16] Keats bordered on admitting the tragic defeat of his life's ambition, while still hoping that he might have time to make one more attempt at the press.

Gifts of jam and jellies arrived along with presentation copies of *Dramatic Scenes* and *A Sicilian Story* from their author, Barry Cornwall (Bryan Waller Procter). Hunt had likened Cornwall's 'naturally poetic temperament' to that of Keats in his own debut, and *A Sicilian Story* was based on the same tale from Boccaccio as *Isabella*. Published by the Olliers, Cornwall owed his popularity to what Hunt called the 'gentler part of genius' and a willingness to appeal to the female readers Keats had spurned.[17] As we shall see, Cornwall's presentation copies and a missed encounter with Taylor and Hessey's newest young poet, John Clare, would harden Keats's resolve to publish his own poems. Yet while he might once more range freely in the public world through publication, any physical expression of his longing for Fanny was impossible. In March she presented him with a ring on which their initials were engraved, a touching reminder of how his parents' initials embraced each other on his seal.[18] He could not kiss her, but he would put his lips to their names.

On Monday, 6 March, another freezing day, Brown reported that Keats was 'taken ... with violent palpitations at the heart' and too weak to get up. Dr Bree attended and swiftly rallied Keats with 'favourable hopes', confident that there was 'no pulmonary affection, no organic defect whatever'. Astonishingly, by Friday, Keats was walking in the garden, apparently 'out of danger' as he planned a trip to Hampshire and the coast – the first of several jaunts he contemplated even while knowing himself gravely ill. If 'the disease [was] on his *mind*', as Dr Bree assured him, a change of location might effect a cure; there was in fact good reason to believe that his symptoms had been brought on by years of mental agitation and anxiety. Keats had long acknowledged his own 'morbid temperament'; now those destructive moods were manifest in his alarming physical symptoms. His poetic ambition, longing for fame and frustrated sexual desire were consuming a body that was inadequate to contain or sustain them. 'My Mind has been the most discontented and restless one that ever was put into a body too small for it,' he told Fanny.[19]

While he belittled himself physically in this way for his 'dear Girl', he made light of his illness for his sister: 'The Doctor assures me that there is nothing the matter with me except nervous irritability and a general weakness of the whole system which has proceeded from my anxiety of mind of late years and the too great excitement of poetry.'[20] She should beware lest 'fretting injure [her] health'. These remarks, made when Keats felt himself 'slowly improving', are telling: if he believed that sexual frustration was one cause of his illness, he was also convinced – as was Cowden Clarke – that hostile reviews led to 'excitement' and 'irritability', stressful symptoms that could produce heart palpitations and haemorrhages. His doctor had advised that 'quietness of mind and fine weather' would restore him; the previous spring had eased his symptoms, and the coming one would do so too.[21] Still, given Keats's view of the matter, there may be more truth to Byron's jest – 'Johnny Keats' was 'snuff'd out by an article' – than His Lordship would have cared to acknowledge.

# CHAPTER 22

———

# A Now

STAYING QUIET at Hampstead, Keats missed Taylor's dinner to celebrate the success of John Clare's *Poems Descriptive of Rural Life and Scenery*. J.H. Reynolds, Dante's translator Henry Cary and Clare's amiable patron Lord Radstock attended this feast, but the twenty-six-year-old 'Peasant Poet' – 'a big boy who has never been used to company' – was particularly disappointed not to meet Keats.[1] On returning to his Northamptonshire home at Helpstone, Clare penned a letter asking Taylor to pass his 'sincere Respects to Keats'. On the coach he had read and liked Keats's first volume and *Endymion*, and could point out 'many beauties'.[2] Cornwall's and Clare's arrival on the literary scene help to explain Keats's sudden interest in publishing his third book. 'He wishes his Poems to be published as soon as convenient to yourself,—the volume to commence with St Agnes' Eve,' Brown advised Taylor in an upbeat letter on 13 March.[3] Keats was able to get to town for the first time in five weeks, dining with Taylor on the 14th and discussing his poems and Clare's. 'He was very sorry he did not see you,' Taylor let Clare know. 'When I read Solitude to him he observed that the description too much prevailed over the Sentiment' (the poem is indeed a protracted catalogue of rural observations, with little reflective thought).[4] Clare's reply sent compliments to Keats and airily assured Taylor that his own latest poem would be remarkable – 'above your thumbs & Keats too'.[5] The day after Clare wrote this, Keats was again afflicted with palpitations and ordered not to make the slightest exertion. Was this another manifestation of encroaching disease, or a spasm of nerves brought on by Clare's and Cornwall's successes? Either Keats did not take his symptoms seriously or, more likely, he refused to accept being confined to his rooms again. Just five days later he took a coach to Haydon's private showing of 'Christ's Entry into Jerusalem' at the Egyptian Hall, Piccadilly.

Six years in the making, Haydon's painting was the talk of the town. 'The room was full,' Haydon recalled, 'Keats and Hazlitt were up in a corner, really rejoicing.'[6] Keats had not seen Haydon recently, but his wish to be among the poets present was understandable. If Fanny's ring had revived memories of his parents, Haydon's painting with its portraits of Wordsworth, Hazlitt and himself also stirred memories. Beneath that vast canvas he had first met Haydon, felt himself encouraged by a 'great spirit' and set about planning his first book. With Haydon's masterwork glimmering in the candlelight, he had dined with Wordsworth and Lamb, Monkhouse and Ritchie. Now, more than three years later, to see Haydon's picture finished reawakened a sense of possible greatness that helped steel him against fears of failure, disease and despair. Keats's visit to the Egyptian Hall may have been reckless, but that was exactly the point: he had staked his life on reviving the energy and enthusiasm with which he had first committed himself to poetry. And, for a few days at least, it seemed to have worked.

Early in April, Keats appeared to be improving every day, so much so that he was able to go for walks with Brown and entertained ideas of joining him in Scotland 'for a change of exercise and air'. As in 1819, spring's return eased his chest, and it was probably now that Brown wrote to America that he was 'really recovered' and, astonishingly, could 'wallk [sic] five miles without weariness'.[7] Keats continued preparing his manuscripts, had readied them by Shakespeare's birthday on Sunday the 23rd and then, as with his corrected proofs for *Endymion*, sent his poems to Taylor at the full moon. On Thursday the 27th Taylor reported to Clare:

> I have got all Keats's MSS. in my hands now to make a Selection out of them for another Volume, as I did of yours; & I should like to write an Introduction too, as Editor, to speak about the unfair Reception he has met with from the Critics, & especially from the Quarterly Review; but perhaps I had better not.

Taylor and probably Woodhouse would have a role in determining what went into the forthcoming volume, although they would not necessarily be responsible for the final selection or the arrangement of the poems. Recalling his interview with William Gifford, Taylor immediately thought better of dragging up the past and reminding readers of Keats's 'unfair Reception'.[8]

Having dispatched his poems, Keats rethought his options for the summer. Brown would soon depart for Scotland. He was feeling stronger, but there was no question of repeating their rain-sodden footslog of 1818 – he could not afford to and, anyway, there were his poems to see through the press. Whatever else Keats decided to do, he would have to move. An escape from his sickroom at Wentworth Place might prove exactly the tonic he needed, and with Abigail O'Donoghue now heavily pregnant with Brown's child there was a further incentive to leave.

By Thursday, 4 May he had taken lodgings Hunt found for him at 2 Wesleyan Place, Kentish Town, just across Hampstead Heath.[9] This was a village on the road to Highgate, and its popularity as a summer retreat for consumptives had already lured Leigh Hunt there – his wife, Marianne, had the disease. Hunt would be nearby at his home in Mortimer Terrace, and Fanny Brawne just a few more minutes away. Brown advanced Keats a guinea for a week's rent and two days later a further £50. On the morning of Sunday the 7th they were both aboard a smack for Scotland when it sailed from London Bridge – Keats accompanied Brown as far as Gravesend, where he went ashore in good spirits. Was Brown's decision to go simply a matter of expedience, in that he needed rent and wished to be out of the way when his child was born? He was always a creature of habit, and to want to pass another summer in Scotland was wholly in character. Perhaps he could also see that other events were repeating themselves. He knew how ill Keats was, and that his brother had languished and died soon after their Scottish tour two years before. Having cared for Keats since February, perhaps he realised that his friend would not survive much longer and could not face nursing him on his deathbed.

'La Belle Dame sans Merci' appeared in Hunt's new *Indicator* magazine on 10 May over the signature 'Caviare', a year since Hunt's 'Calendar of Nature' had inspired 'Ode to a Nightingale'. Calm, fine days followed from mid-month, but if Keats had hoped his move away from Wentworth Place might have a calming effect he was disappointed. Mrs Brawne called in occasionally, but for a month he did not see Fanny at all. Hunt was preoccupied with his two weekly publications and his own ill-health; Reynolds was red-taped to the law; Cowden Clarke was now living at Ramsgate; and other friends were busy or away. Only Severn called regularly, and in warm spring air they rambled together on Hampstead Heath. Buoyed by his Royal Academy prize and portrait commissions, Severn's mood contrasted with Keats's and proved a welcome distraction – whenever Keats went to the Heath alone with a book his thoughts turned in 'happy misery' or 'miserable misery' to Fanny, haunted by visions of her in a 'shepherdess dress'.[10] He had always borne solitude badly, as his few days at Carisbrooke had shown, and from the first his relationship with Fanny had been volatile: last summer at Shanklin he had been so uneasy about her it had seemed impossible they could be happy together. Living on his own, with his mental resilience worn down by illness and fatigue, he found his immense resources of human sympathy and

selflessness starting to collapse as he brooded over an incident that had
been reported to him.

Late in May he wrote to Fanny of his shock on hearing that she had been to
town unchaperoned. Not the least of his agony was that he had expected this,
knowing her heart was preoccupied with the pleasures of the world. Probably
it had been no more than a visit to Mrs Dilke, entirely innocent and accept-
able, but to Keats it signalled that his fiancée was attending social gatherings
without him – vivacious, attractive and to all appearances 'available'.
Overwhelmed by misery, he persuaded himself that she had done so because
she no longer had Brown to flirt with. As he sat with her flowers on his table
and her ring on his finger, he realised that she could and would be happy
without him. If she could enjoy a party, smile at people and seek their admiration, Keats told her, she had never loved him nor ever would do. He even put
to her a sadistic idea that she must be his to 'die upon the rack' if he wished it,
to undergo 'agonies and uncertainties' he had endured himself and which
she was 'peculiarly made to create'. To recover his health, he assured her,
would be of no benefit if she was not completely his.[11]

Another letter followed, full of broodings on their time together at
Wentworth Place, his inability to recant his distrust of her, and his awareness
that the Reynolds girls and other envious friends had been gossiping and plotting against them. And then a third, vowing never to see or speak to Brown
'until we are both old men, if we are to be', and reproaching Fanny for those
she had 'smil'd with': 'you have amusements—your mind is away . . . you can
wait—you have a thousand activities—you can be happy without me. Any
party, any thing to fill up the day has been enough.'[12] It is a dreadful reversal
of the usual pattern – expressed by Byron's Donna Julia and Jane Austen's
Anne Elliot – that men forget women more easily because they can occupy
themselves with the world while women live quiet, confined lives.
Fanny evidently replied robustly, blaming the mischief-making of so-
called friends and regretting his ill-treatment of her 'in word thought
and deed'. Keats's stony apology – 'could I believe that I did it without any
cause' – hardly showed genuine contrition, nor were his closing words the
reaffirmation of affection that he evidently intended: 'do not believe me
such a vulgar fellow. I will be as patient in illness and as believing in Love as
I am able.'[13]

Four poems Keats wrote for Fanny are footnotes to his anguished *liber
amoris* in these letters, confessions of 'some one in Love as I am, with a person
living in such Liberty as you do': 'The Day is gone', 'I cry your mercy', 'What
can I do to drive away' and 'To Fanny'.[14] Keats's letters had been demanding,
needy and deliberately hurtful, and these poems tell us why: they dwell upon

the physical 'sweets' of her presence – albeit as pleasures that have 'faded', 'vanished' or been appropriated by another man:

> Who now, with greedy looks, eats up my feast?
>   What stare outfaces now my silver moon!
> Ah! keep that hand unravished at the least;
>     Let, let the amorous burn—
>     But, prithee, do not turn
>   The current of your heart from me so soon:
>     Oh save, in charity,
>     The quickest pulse for me.
>                       ('To Fanny', 17–24)

Echoing here are the 'unravish'd bride' of 'Ode on a Grecian Urn' and worries about Fanny's party-going, while his rival lover's devouring looks tap into formative anxieties about the withdrawal of food and nurture. Keats's letters to Fanny are full of the horrifying realisation that he would have to endure being abandoned all over again if she deserted him as he felt his mother had done sixteen years before. 'But, prithee, do not turn / The current of your heart from me so soon' (21–2) gives an elegantly Shakespearean cadence to Keats's ingrained suspicion that women were bound to betray him, and not for the first time he identified with Hamlet. 'Hamlet's heart was full of such Misery as mine is when he said to Ophelia "Go to a Nunnery, go, go!"'[15]

He tried to dislodge such thoughts, forcing himself to work. Early June was passed in reading proofs and correcting Taylor's and Woodhouse's amendments, restoring his masterly phrase 'bitter chill' to *The Eve of St Agnes* and, less fortunately perhaps, unable to resist Taylor's attempts to muffle sexual explicitness. A letter to Brown around the 21st has Keats world-weary, regretting an episode of bad behaviour and explaining why he turned down an invitation to dinner with Wordsworth, Southey, Lamb and Haydon: 'I was too careful of my health to risk being out at night.'[16] The sight of portraits at the British Institution revived his satirical wit; he had hopes of restarting *The Cap and Bells*, but was wary that doing so might bring on a 'relapse'.

As in February, it was a 'cursed cold distance' that produced the crisis Keats feared. His sister was now seventeen and he was planning to take his new book to her at Walthamstow. He set out on the morning of Thursday, 22 June, experienced a slight spitting of blood and immediately turned back. At Hunt's that evening, he was introduced to Shelley's friends John and Maria Gisborne, visiting from Italy, but was little inclined to conversation and soon went home. That night he suffered a second massive haemorrhage, sufficient to negate all his doctors' warm words about recovery. The reason for this major relapse is not as clear as it might be. Exertion probably caused his slight indisposition that morning. Was it meeting John Gisborne, another young man full of schemes for the future, that agitated and unsettled him as such encounters had often done before? A local surgeon, William Lambe, attended and Hunt – who was ill himself – took Keats to his home in Mortimer Terrace. When Severn called, he was reminded of poor Tom's shocking appearance when ailing at Well Walk; Hessey sent word to Clare that Keats was being treated with 'copious bleedings & active medicines'.[17] The eminent physician Dr George Darling was now consulted, and he pronounced that Keats must without fail winter in Italy. To stay in London would be fatal. From this time onwards even the promise of Keats's new book could not allay distress at the gravity of his condition. Only Clare put into words what Keats's publisher and friends were dreading: 'the symptons of his illness I think very alarming as we have people in the same way here often who creep on for a little time—but it generaly proves death has struck at the root—for they mostly go off.'[18]

To know he had been struck down on the anniversary of his mother's remarriage would have been a further shock. If he was aware of that dismal coincidence, in Hunt's home he found a temporary refuge, and here, at first, a more benign past revived. He had come back to the 'poet's house' he had celebrated in *Sleep and Poetry*. Here, once again, were the familiar portraits, prints and 'sacred busts' that adorned Hunt's studio at the Vale of Health, where he had stayed when planning his first book. 'Hunt amuses me very kindly,' he reported to Fanny Brawne, and a little later told his sister: 'Mr. Hunt does every thing in his power to make the time pass as agreeably with me as possible.'[19] A copy of Hunt's latest book arrived, *Amyntas, a Tale of the Woods, from the Italian of Torquato Tasso*. When Keats opened it, he read this:

To
**JOHN KEATS**, ESQ.
THIS TRANSLATION OF THE EARLY WORK
OF A CELEBRATED POET,
WHOSE FATE IT WAS
TO BE EQUALLY PESTERED
BY THE CRITICAL,
AND ADMIRED BY THE POETICAL,
IS INSCRIBED,
BY HIS AFFECTIONATE FRIEND,
**LEIGH HUNT.**

Keats's friendship with Hunt had been restored. He was kept busy with reading, walking and marking passages in a copy of Spenser for Fanny Brawne to read. Marianne Hunt cut a silhouette of him resting on two chairs. On one of these sweltering summer days he helped Hunt with copy for *The Indicator* by contributing to his prose poem, 'A Now, Descriptive of a Hot Day'. Hunt began with a Homeric description of dawn: 'Now the rosy- (and lazy-) fingered Aurora ...' Perhaps he intended to remind Keats of Hyperion – Aurora was his daughter – and of the opening of his 'Imitation of Spenser': 'Now morning from her orient chamber came ...' Several passages can be identified as Keats's and they suggest how, suddenly and unexpectedly, Hunt's sympathetic genius had enabled him to go back over his earliest years and write from them with astonishing immediacy. 'Now rooms with the sun upon them become intolerable; and the apothecary's apprentice, with a bitterness beyond aloes, thinks of the pond he used to bathe in at school.' Here Keats becomes Hammond's disgruntled apprentice once again, bottled up in the surgery, recalling happier Enfield days with feelings as bitter as the emetic aloe vera he was now taking as an 'active medicine'. More distant memories surfaced, of his sister as a little girl at her grandmother's door, 'hand held up over her sunny forehead'. Another Enfield scene came to mind, as the boys 'bathe all day long in rivers and ponds, and follow the fish into their cool corners, and say millions of "My eyes" at "tittle-bats"'. Part of Keats and Cowden Clarke's route between Enfield and Edmonton revived as 'a walled lane, with dust and broken bottles in it, near a brick-field', and, from as far back as Keats could remember, scenes from Keates's Livery Stables: 'horses ... stretching their yearning necks with loosened collars', 'the old stage-coachman' with 'a hoarse voice', 'the lounger, who cannot resist riding his new horse', and 'jockies, walking in great coats to lose flesh'.[20] Throughout Keats's letters and poems we have seen vivid glimpses of a novelist in the making, suggesting that in the 1830s and '40s he might have rivalled Dickens, then turned his awareness of life's ironies into moments of vision like Thomas Hardy's, or even joined Hunt, whose insights about consciousness and time prefigured Virginia Woolf's.[21]

There had been much in recent weeks to draw Keats into his past – Haydon's painting, Severn's company, Hunt's study – and in a dejected moment it occurred to him that if his book failed he might try 'the Apothecary line' again (actually to do so would be the grimmest defeat of all, for he would be admitting that Abbey had been right all along). In another ironic gesture of kindly intent, Horace Smith sent over his coach to bring Keats to dinner with his literary set at Elysium Terrace, Fulham. Keats had formerly winced at these 'fashionables'; now they welcomed him back into their circle. As they drank six bottles of Château Margaux in warm summer twilight, Keats recalled another evening there when Haydon and Shelley had quarrelled about religion and parted for ever.

Having launched his painting, Haydon now reappeared, badgering Keats to return a copy of Chapman's Homer while making it obvious that he thought he might 'go off' at any moment. A visit from Dilke gave 'more pain than pleasure' by reviving memories of the Brawnes' domestic arrangements and Brown's 'indecencies', which he imagined would continue at Wentworth Place while he wintered in Italy. Hunt had meant well by taking him in, but amid the uproar of children, music, singing, puns and streams of visitors he could most often be found staring from a window towards Hampstead.

On Monday, 26 June the *Morning Chronicle* announced as 'just published' 'LAMIA, ISABELLA, the EVE OF ST. AGNES, and other Poems. By John Keats, Author of "Endymion"'. Those narrative romances had been selected to begin the book, and 'other Poems' included the 1819 odes but not 'Ode on Indolence'. That poem's moment of gleeful self-vindication had passed, but its fruits were now apparent in the full list of contents:

Lamia
Isabella
The Eve of St Agnes
Ode to a Nightingale
Ode on a Grecian Urn
Ode to Psyche
Fancy
Ode ['Bards of Passion and of Mirth']
Lines on the Mermaid Tavern
Robin Hood
To Autumn
Ode on Melancholy
Hyperion, a Fragment

'Lines on the Mermaid Tavern' was the earliest poem represented here, 'To Autumn' the most recent. The book's opening group of three romance narratives culminates with *The Eve of St Agnes*, a midnight escape, and old Angela 'palsy-twitch'd' and dead. Next follows 'Ode to a Nightingale', first of three darkling ventures through landscapes of the imagination, reflecting that 'palsy shakes a few, sad, last gray hairs' (25) and speculating on art's role in a world subject to old age and 'other woe' hastened by time and change. 'Ode to

Psyche', concluding in an 'untrodden region' tended by 'the gardener Fancy' (51, 62), offers a link to fleeting pleasures of 'Fancy' and the nostalgic, Shakespearean England of 'Lines on the Mermaid Tavern' and 'Robin Hood'. Often said to be the slightest poem in this book, 'Robin Hood' announces its outlaw theme in a world where 'honey / Can't be got without hard money!' (47–8) and in so doing intersects neatly with the poem that follows. Foraging in the same callously material world, the 'gleaner' in 'To Autumn' is a representative of all those in whose names Hunt in *The Examiner* was calling for a revival of the spirit of Old England and Robin Hood. A note of valediction sounded at the close of 'To Autumn' carries through to the forlorn farewells of 'Ode on Melancholy' and 'Joy, whose hand is ever at his lips / Bidding adieu' (22–3). Keats, knowing himself bound to forsake Fanny Brawne, had intended his book to end here.

That Taylor and Hessey added *Hyperion* as a final poem destroyed the coherence of the twelve-poem volume that Keats had projected. It supplied a fragmentary coda, and tactlessly predicted that the poet would not live long enough to complete his epic and for it to appear in a volume of its own.[22] Yet Taylor, Hessey and Woodhouse had acted in his best interests, for with *Hyperion* Keats's third volume was evidently a much more substantial accomplishment than *Poems, by John Keats*.

The *Lamia* collection gathers together the extraordinary outpouring of the preceding year and a half in a powerful, coherent volume that contains eight of the greatest poems in the English language. With *Lyrical Ballads* (1798), Keats's third book is one of very few 'landmark' volumes in the English poetic tradition. It far surpasses *Endymion* and *Poems*, yet, touchingly, it is arranged on a principle Keats announced in his first book: once again, his 'short pieces in the middle' were written at 'an earlier period than the rest of the Poems'. Still marking time like his swallows, Keats was gathering himself and looking forward to what he might yet do.

By contrivance or coincidence, Keats's book had been published at the full moon, and advance copies arrived at Mortimer Terrace along with the issue of *The Indicator* containing 'A Now' and Keats's Paolo and Francesca sonnet. He should have been pleased, but when he opened his book he was taken aback. Not only had *Hyperion* been included against his wishes, but Woodhouse had prefaced the book with an 'Advertisement' to which Keats took angry exception:

> If any apology be thought necessary for the appearance of the unfinished poem of HYPERION, the publishers beg to state that they alone are responsible, as it was printed at their particular request, and contrary to the wish of the author. The

poem was intended to have been of equal length with ENDYMION, but the reception given to that work discouraged the author from proceeding.

*Fleet-Street, June 26, 1820.*[23]

Keats crossed this out in a presentation copy, writing above it: 'This is none of my doing—I was ill at the time.' Under its final sentence he added: 'This is a lie.' He had been involved in correcting proofs but was seriously ill when the 'Advertisement' was drawn up with its reference to *Endymion*'s reception and, most irksome, the suggestion that he had been 'discouraged'. Keats had confided that he 'fought under disadvantages' in his original preface for *Endymion*, only to have his words rejected by his publishers. Now they had repeated precisely the same appeal in his third book, just when he was confident he did not need any special pleading.

Copies moved quickly. Hessey had 160 subscribed; reviews came early and were almost wholly positive. Charles Lamb in *The New Times* set the tone, quoting from *Isabella* ('finest thing in the volume') and comparing Keats favourably with Coleridge, Chaucer, Dante and Spenser. *The Monthly Review* singled out *Hyperion* as 'decidedly the best'; Hunt in *The Indicator* quoted praisingly from the romances and *Hyperion* ('Milton could do no more'), noting as well evidence of 'the modern philosophy of sympathy and natural justice'. The *Guardian*, Gold's *London Magazine*, Baldwin's *London Magazine*, and the *New Monthly* were all well disposed, as were Barry Cornwall and Francis Jeffrey reviewing *Endymion* and *Lamia* in the *Edinburgh Magazine, and Literary Miscellany* and August's *Edinburgh Review*. All of these reviews quoted Keats extensively, and usually with approval. 'My book has had good success among literary people,' Keats notified Brown in mid-August, 'and, I believe, has a moderate sale.'[24]

Fanny Brawne heard nothing of that success. Instead, around the date of her twentieth birthday on 9 August, Keats told her he was sickened by 'the brute world' and 'more and more concentrated' in thoughts of her. He was unable to suppress his anxiety and the sudden arrival of any visitor made him agitated and nervous. To write the shortest of messages brought on a constricting tightness in his chest. 'The last two years taste like brass upon my Palate,' he wrote, deliberately poisoning all that they had meant to each other and all that he had achieved since *Endymion*: 'To be happy with you seems such an impossibility! it requires a luckier Star than mine! it will never be.'[25] Fanny's response to this, the last of Keats's letters to her that has survived, was to prove him wrong – thanks to Hunt's chaotic household.

# CHAPTER 23

## Regions of Poetry

Happily, escape routes were appearing. Alerted by John Gisborne to Keats's dangerous state of health, Shelley had immediately written, inviting him to 'take up ... residence' at Pisa. His letter arrived on Saturday, 12 August, shortly before an unpleasant accident came to light at Mortimer Terrace. Two days earlier, a note from Fanny had been delivered and Marianne Hunt had asked a maid to take it up to Keats's room. It did not immediately reach him, however. When it was eventually handed over on the Saturday, its seal broken, he could not bear to think that her words had been read by another and broke down and wept for several hours. Despite Hunt's entreaties, he left that evening, struggling along the lanes to Wentworth Place, where Mrs Brawne, seeing his dreadful condition, took him in. Here, surrounded by Fanny, her brother Sam and sister Margaret ('Tootts'), their dog, Carlo, and the cats, Keats found another temporary home and the happiest few days of his life – the only time, he later said, when his mind was at ease.[1]

Among several messages written with great effort the next morning, one went to Hunt with thanks for his 'many sympathies'. A response came immediately: 'I need not say how you gratify me by the impulse which led you to write ... for you must have seen by this time how much I am attached to yourself.'[2] A longer letter went to Brown in Scotland, mentioning his relapse and making a 'confession' that Brown, when he later published an edited version of this letter, was careful to omit. What was this mysterious 'confession' or, as Brown termed it, 'the secret'? Was it a reference to Keats's engagement to Fanny, or a plan that they would marry and live at Wentworth Place if he recovered?[3] Such matters could hardly have been news to Brown, and would not have required screening from Victorian readers. Keats introduced his disclosure with this curious passage:

I shall make some confession, which you will be the only person, for many reasons, I shall trust with. A winter in England would, I have not a doubt, kill me; so I have resolved to go to Italy, either by sea or land. Not that I have any great hopes of that,—for, I think, there is a core of disease in me not easy to pull out. (Note) xxxxxxxxxxxxxxx If I should die xxxxx I shall be obliged to set off in less than a month.*

Brown's asterisk refers to his note explaining the deletions: 'The omitted passage contained the secret. He went to Italy in pursuance of his physician's urgent advice.'[4] An obvious reason why Brown might have omitted this 'secret' was that it involved him, casting him in a light he did not wish posterity to see. Living now with the Brawnes, Keats had perhaps finally recognised that his suspicions about Brown and Fanny were groundless, and apologised for mistrusting his friend. That is certainly possible, but Keats's overriding concern in the letter was his own health. He was convinced that the 'Amena' affair had killed Tom, and believed sexual frustration was a cause of his own disease. Certainly he seems to be alluding to some kind of inner disorder: that this 'core of disease' was 'not easy to pull out' referred to the practice of deliberately blistering skin to draw out poison (as Keats is known to have done). I suspect he told Brown of the venereal infection he had tried to cure with mercury; that this had made him hold back from Fanny; and that stifled desire, as well as disease, was now flooding his lungs with blood. As he later admitted to Brown, 'I should have had her when I was in health, and I should have remained well.'[5]

As difficult to write was a letter gracefully deflecting Shelley's invitation. Keats banters a little about poetry, advising Shelley to '"load every rift"' of [his] subject with ore' and reminding him of his advice not to publish 'first-blights'. His reference to a 'mind . . . like a pack of scattered cards' recalls the younger poet of *Endymion*. Then, he had trusted that life, knowledge and experience would deal him a stronger hand; as he felt his chest tighten again, he knew he was at his last trump – 'sorted to a pip'. His only chance was a more benign winter climate than Pisa offered. As Keats's departure suddenly drew closer, he scrawled on a scrap of paper that was intended to serve as his will. His estate consisted 'in the hopes of the sale of books publish'd or unpublish'd'. Brown and Taylor were to be his first paid creditors, his tailor's bill was to be cleared and his books divided among his friends. Everything else he considered *in nubibus*, in a mist, including money held in Chancery. Abbey refused a loan, but did offer a small advance if Keats would call to see him.[6]

Dr James Clark, physician at Rome, had returned to Britain to marry and there was a chance that Keats could be introduced to him. The intermediary may have been Dr Darling, or Taylor's business acquaintances Thomas and George Underwood – they had published Clark's *Medical Notes on Climate, Diseases, Hospitals, and Medical Schools in France, Italy, and Switzerland.* Although in the event a meeting did not occur in England, Clark's *Medical Notes* had a decisive influence on Keats's plans: 'the consumptive patient may pass the winter at Rome full as well as at any other part of Italy, and perhaps, better. The best residence is somewhere about the Piazza di Spagna, which is well sheltered.'[7]

Taylor had been negotiating for Keats's passage. Influenced by Shelley's invitation, an early plan was for him to sail to Livorno and then, presumably, proceed to Pisa. Clark's book changed that. Taylor secured a berth aboard the 127-ton brigantine *Maria Crowther* for Naples and thence Keats would proceed overland to Rome. She would sail on Sunday, 17 September. Now certain of when he would set out, Keats wrote poste restante to Scotland. Would Brown accompany him to Italy?

On receiving Keats's letter early in September, Brown immediately turned south. In London, meanwhile, Keats's friends were worrying that he might have to make the voyage ill and alone. On 12 September, Haslam approached a mutual friend, Joseph Severn. There are various accounts of this episode, and from all of them it is clear that Severn readily agreed to go. A spell abroad would offer a way of offloading responsibilities for his illegitimate son Henry, now a year old and still unknown to his family. With Haslam's assistance, Henry would be placed in care.[8] Almost from the first there were doubts about Severn's suitability as Keats's companion, but the fact is that he stepped up to the task when no one else would do so – and he endured all that ensued. Rome might provide opportunities for his painting, but as Severn packed his bags there was no sense that accompanying a 'young poet' to Rome was a decisive advantage for him. Several times Severn welcomed signs that he took to indicate that Keats was recovering; equally, for all Severn knew Keats might well die before the *Maria Crowther* cleared British waters. The two men had long been friends and it could be argued that Severn's cheerful, carefree demeanour – deemed inappropriate by some – was exactly the kind of temperament Keats needed in a companion; certainly it enabled Severn himself to cope with distressing situations that would have defeated others. Severn's input is problematic, however, from a biographical point of view. Isabella Jones took exception to his egotistical correspondence: while his letters on the voyage and from Italy offer us glimpses of the last weeks of Keats's life, we have few other perspectives that might complement or modify what he allows us to see and hear. The tone and content of Severn's letters to his family are also markedly different from those addressed to Keats's friends.[9]

Haslam went to tell Keats the good news that Severn would go with him, slept at Wentworth Place and returned to town early on Wednesday the 13th to secure a second berth on the *Maria Crowther*. With preparations moving fast, Keats decided to face the moment when he would have to leave Fanny. They exchanged rings, and as Fanny cut locks of his hair for herself and his sister she noticed how very short it was (possibly an effect of taking mercury). Simple gifts followed. He gave her his miniature by Severn, and received from her a penknife, a pocket diary and his travelling cap newly lined with silk. She hoped that he would write to her; he asked her to write to his sister – she must avoid cold air. One can imagine the scene on that sunny afternoon: Keats thanked Mrs Brawne for her care and well-wishes, Sam and Tootts for their good cheer. As they parted, Fanny pressed into his hand an oval of polished white carnelian used to cool her fingers while doing needlework.[10] As he held it, he would be able to imagine her hand in his. That night he dined with Taylor and Haslam at 93 Fleet Street, and stayed there the next four nights. Alone at Wentworth Place, Fanny took out her copy of Hunt's *Literary Pocket-Book* and beside the second Wednesday in September set down four words: 'Mr. Keats left Hampstead.'

On Saturday, 16 September, Keats's passport was signed and, with Haslam and Woodhouse as witnesses, Keats transferred the copyright on his poems to Taylor and Hessey. He received £200 and, because his existing debts to them reduced this to just £30, Taylor guaranteed up to £120 payable at a bank in Rome.

All was now prepared. Keats woke on the 17th to fine weather and a fair wind, and in good time he went with Taylor, Haslam and Woodhouse to Tower Wharf where they greeted Severn and his brother Thomas.[11] Here too were the ship's master, Thomas Walsh, and another passenger, one Mrs Pidgeon. Their bags and boxes were stowed in a tiny cabin lined with five bunks, Keats being allotted an upper one. All around there was noise and bustle as the crew made ready. They cast off at seven and made steady progress down river, mooring at Gravesend about midday. Taylor, Haslam and Woodhouse went ashore at four that afternoon, while Keats remained on board to dine with Severn, the captain and Mrs Pidgeon. That night he lay listening to the river's whisper and footsteps passing overhead, sniffed astringent smells of rope, wood and pine tar, then fell soundly asleep.

On Monday, Severn went ashore to get provisions – apples, biscuits, a bottle of laudanum. Back at Wentworth Place, Fanny Brawne began the first of her many letters to Keats's sister, explaining that they had nursed her brother for six weeks and how all of his friends had exerted themselves for him: 'I am certain he has some spell that attaches them to him, or else he has fortunately met with a set of friends that I did not believe could be found in the world.'[12] At Gravesend the magic of Keats's personality was already at work, as Severn noted: 'full of his waggery—looked well—ate well—and was well.'[13] His high spirits were due in part to the fact that a blister applied to his chest while Severn was away had relieved his symptoms – at least, that was what he had convinced himself to believe. Severn's passport arrived, and then a fifth passenger, Miss Cotterell, a pretty eighteen-year-old with consumptive symptoms, bound to join her brother at Naples where she too hoped to find a cure. With their company complete, the *Maria Crowther* sailed on a favourable wind that evening. Captain Walsh was a 'good fellow', they had decided; 'if he makes us happy his object is gain'd.'[14] Keats retired to his bunk and, separated by a screen, the women to theirs. Severn sat up on deck until midnight, sketching a moonlit scene of the *Maria Crowther* viewed from the sea.

Keats had been to sea before, so life on the *Maria Crowther* would not have surprised him. He was soon accustomed to the rhythms of round-the-clock watches, ropes rumbling, sails flapping or straining at the yards, wood creaking and, below deck, the soft hiss of the wash along the hull, the slop of bilge water, oil lamps flickering and shadows jiggling. By Tuesday the 19th they were off Margate, Keats apparently improving and scanning a coastline swarming with memories. It was at Margate, on that clifftop and in Tom's company, that he had composed his poems for George – there, too, that he had written 'To Charles Cowden Clarke', the poem that had led to his meeting with Hunt. Then – as they rounded the Nore – Cowden Clarke's home came in sight just a few miles away in Ramsgate. Exactly a year after Keats had composed 'To Autumn', at Mortimer Terrace Hunt was writing a heartfelt *bon voyage* for his friend: 'Ah, dear friend, as valued a one as thou art a poet,—John Keats,—we cannot, after all, find it in our hearts to be glad, now thou art gone away with the swallows to seek a kindlier clime . . . farewell for awhile: thy heart is in our fields: and thou wilt soon be back to rejoin it.'[15]

There was nothing kindly about sea conditions in the Channel. All four passengers were seasick and retired to their bunks to recuperate with cups of tea. They scudded past Ramsgate – perhaps Cowden Clarke was gazing out from Belle Vue House and saw the *Maria Crowther* making headway for Dover. On the bright morning of Wednesday the 20th they were off Brighton, and Keats sensed a coming change of weather. At two that afternoon, as the storm came on, he lay calmly in his bunk listening to waves buffeting at the bows and crashing overhead; while the *Maria Crowther* battled against wind and tide, sea water poured into the cabin. 'Water parted from the sea,' Keats joked, thinking of that song in Fanny's *New London and Country Songster*:

Water, parted from the sea,
    May increase the river's tide,
To the bubbling fount may flee,
    Or thro' fertile valleys glide.


Though, in search of lost repose,
    Through the land 'tis free to roam,
Still it murmurs as it flows,
    Panting for its native home.

Those well-known lines and other sweet inland murmurs echoed in his head as the storm raged. Eventually the *Maria Crowther* was forced to put about and, with pumps at full stretch, ran with the wind some twenty miles before the storm blew itself out at daybreak. That night two ships were driven ashore at Brighton, one of them with its hull smashed and full of water.[16]

On the 22nd and 23rd they lay becalmed off Dungeness. Captain Walsh and Severn went ashore and set off across an expanse of gravel to New Romney, where Severn posted a journal-letter to Haslam reassuring him that 'Keats is without even complaining'. In truth, their voyage could scarcely have got off to a worse start. Keats was cramped and cold in his bunk, the cabin saturated with sea water and Miss Cotterell's cough a constant reminder of his own predicament. If cabin windows were closed she would faint; if they were opened, Keats started coughing and spitting blood. It took another five days before the *Maria Crowther* crept along towards Portsmouth, putting in there on Thursday the 28th – a day after the king had visited aboard his yacht the *Royal George*.[17]

Keats had passed through Portsmouth before, en route to Shanklin with James Rice, whose illness had worn at his nerves as Miss Cotterell's was now doing. While the *Maria Crowther* was made shipshape, Keats and Severn set off to visit the Snooks at the Old Mill House. He had visited Bedhampton with Brown in January 1819, rebounding from low spirits after Tom's death. From here they had set off on that wet Monday morning to Stansted, and Keats had returned to press on with *The Eve of St Agnes* in his high room between the sweet water of the mill pond and the salty flow of Hermitage Stream. On this second visit the Snooks found Keats in better health than they had expected, as he mimicked Miss Cotterell martyring herself to her illness with 'all the bustling wit of a man in saucy health'.[18] So sick was he of the voyage that a word might have sent him off back to London; when the Snooks told him that Brown, returned from Scotland, was staying with the Dilkes at Chichester his longing to stay grew stronger. That night Keats retired to the room where he had written of Porphyro and Madeline, and listened to the sound of the mill sluice, sharp and clear in the night air.

Next day, Friday the 29th, the *Maria Crowther* put to sea with a fair wind, heading west along the Solent in sight of the Isle of Wight and the landscape of runnels and freshes where Keats had begun *Endymion*. Overnight the breeze slackened, and by morning they were in a calm. He had resolved to write to Brown, to tell of his disappointment at not meeting him at Bedhampton, and this was the moment to do so. His letter soon turned to Fanny Brawne and how, even if he recovered, his love for the woman he most wanted to live for would occasion his death: 'Were I in health it would make me ill, and how can I bear it in my state.' 'I wish for death every day and night to deliver me from these pains,' he tells Brown, calling to mind the 'easeful death' of his 'Ode to a Nightingale', 'and then I wish death away, for death would destroy even those pains which are better than nothing.' As Keats confronted the finality of death with something like the acceptance of his 'vale of Soul-making', he was able at times to gaze stoically beyond a final separation: 'When the pang of this thought has passed through my mind, I may say the bitterness of death is passed.' Yet the thought of leaving Fanny was 'beyond every thing horrible—the sense of darkness coming over me,' he told Brown. 'I eternally see her figure eternally vanishing.' In another strange, Keatsian reversal Fanny has become Eurydice, consigned forever to the underworld as Orpheus gazes helplessly after her. 'Is there another Life? Shall I awake and find all this is a dream? There must be we cannot be created for this sort of suffering.'[19]

That night they may have put into Studland Bay, close by the port of Poole from where generations of Keates mariners had plied to the ports of Spain. Then, the wind again turning contrary, it seems likely that they put in to the Dorset coast a second time and Keats and Severn went ashore. When they came back on board, if Severn can be believed, Keats wrote out his sonnet 'Bright Star' on a blank page of the 1806 *Poetical Works of William Shakespeare*.[20] Severn knew this sonnet was not originally composed on this occasion, as appears from a later letter to Charles Brown asking, 'do you [know] the sonnet beginning—"Bright star—would I were stedfast as thou art"—he wrote this down in the ship.'[21] Possibly he was aware of Brown's transcriptions of Keats's poems, in which a different version of 'Bright Star' appears under the title 'Sonnet (1819)', but in subsequent retellings of their landing in Dorset, Severn elaborated one of the great scenes of Romantic myth. 'The present exquisite Sonnet was written under such interesting circumstances that I cannot forbear making them public,' Severn recalled. 'The stormy British sea, after a fortnight, had exhausted [Keats]; and on our arrival off the Dorsetshire coast ... we landed to recruit.' Severn goes on to explain how landing in Dorset helped Keats:

> The shores, with the beautiful grottoes which opened to fine verdure and cottages, were the means of transporting Keats once more into the regions of poetry;—he showed me these things exultingly, as though they had been his birthright. The change in him was wonderful, and continued even after our return to the ship, when he took a volume (which he had a few days before given me) of Shakespeare's Poems, and in it he wrote me the subjoined Sonnet.[22]

*Endymion* had associated 'Echoing grottos, full of tumbling waves / And moonlight' with sleep and 'silvery enchantment' that 'calm'd to life again' (i.453–64). Severn had heard Keats read the poem and possessed a copy, so it is possible he recollected those lines in describing how a shoreline encountered 'as though his birthright' had transported Keats into 'regions of poetry'. So it was that he 'wrote ... the ... Sonnet ... and never wrote again'. While not suggesting that 'Bright Star' originated at this moment, Severn's recollection embraces ideas of birth, a native place, renewed creativity and, finally, a sense of completion as a scene of 'birthright' forms a backdrop to what has become Keats's last poem.[23]

Exactly where all of this took place is unknown. The idea that it was at Lulworth Cove did not emerge until the 1880s and, for us, Severn's account is most tantalising for its suggestion that – wherever they landed – Keats knew the terrain because he had been there previously. If it *was* Lulworth Cove, the home of James Keates – brother of Thomas – was just a dozen miles away at Lower Bockhampton. In Severn's recollection, and quite plausibly in actuality, Keats last set foot in England in the region his father had come from. Further down the coast he would pass Lewis Way's Bridport and Teignmouth where he had spent the wet spring of 1818 with poor Tom and scrambled along the undercliff to Babbacombe and Kent's Cavern.

As the *Maria Crowther* sailed further south, difficulties seemed to recede. Apart from a storm and an encounter with two warships, they had a good wind across the Bay of Biscay. Off Cape St Vincent the sea was calm like oil, and they slipped through the Strait of Gibraltar in dawn sunshine with the African coast glowing like an amber flame.[24] Keats seemed to be improving, but two days later a haemorrhage brought on fever and violent sweating: to Severn, it was obvious that the foul air below deck and poor diet were dangerous. Thirty-five days after leaving Tower Wharf, the *Maria Crowther* entered the Bay of Naples and was immediately quarantined because of a typhus outbreak in London. Unable to go ashore, they would have to endure ten more days on board in weather that turned cold and wet. 'Keats is now in a doubtfull state,' Severn let Haslam know. 'I cannot guess what this climate will do.'[25]

# CHAPTER 24

---

# Eternal Road

TUESDAY, 31 October 1820. With Keats just turned twenty-five, they went ashore. Miss Cotterell's brother Charles helped settle them at the Albergo della Villa di Londra on the Via Santa Lucia, a wide, fashionable Neapolitan street between the Palazzo Reale and the Castel dell'Ovo at the harbour entrance. With six storeys and a magnificent view over the bay to Vesuvius, the Villa di Londra was a grand eighteenth-century palazzo favoured by foreign visitors.

Aware that Keats was suffering from the same complaint as his sister, Charles Cotterell chose his accommodation carefully – the street's proximity to the sea meant that fresh air would circulate. After weeks in a stifling cabin, the Villa di Londra seemed likely to give intervals of ease, and on the morning of 1 November, Keats revived sufficiently to begin 'a short calm letter' to Brown. It proved to be one of his most anguished attempts to 'relieve the load of WRETCHEDNESS'. Emotionally and imaginatively, he was still enduring the confinement of the voyage as his thoughts turned obsessively to the sick-room where he had been 'a prisoner' at Mortimer Terrace.[1] It was six months since Keats and Brown had parted, and nothing Brown had heard since could have prepared him for this self-lacerating letter. Yet even as Keats was going over and over the hopelessness of his plight he was thinking creatively – albeit not in his 'horribly vivid' imaginings of Fanny. Hunt's prose poem 'A Now' had lingered with him, particularly the way Hunt showed how that simple monosyllable 'now' possessed 'the very essence of wit' by virtue of 'bringing the most remote things together'.[2] The effect was similar to another partiality of Hunt's, punning; witty togetherings of unlike things that resembled Keats's instinct to resolve difference with rhyme. 'I was a prisoner at Hunt's,' he tells Brown, 'and used to keep my eyes fixed on Hampstead all day. Then there was a good hope of seeing her again—Now!—O that I could be buried near where she lives!'[3] For a moment Keats had succeeded in extricating himself from disease and thwarted passion to return to poetry and Hampstead where he imagined himself, like his nightingale, 'buried deep / In the next valley-glades' (77–8). The load of misfortune in this letter weighs so heavily that we can easily miss his implication that poetry might yet alleviate his suffering and write a different conclusion: 'It surprised me that the human heart is capable of containing and bearing so much misery. Was I born for this end?'[4]

That evening, Charles Cotterell and his sister called and stayed for dinner. Keats's mood lightened and, when they left, he repeated to Severn some of what he had written to Brown and went to bed 'much recovered'.[5] Next morning he slept long and late, woke in good spirits and made a pun in Italian. Fog and rain covered the city, although eventually the sky lifted and, with windows and shutters open, street clatter carried into their room. With Cotterell, Keats went by carriage along the Strada di Toledo, where the noisy life of Naples carried on with cries of 'Pane!', 'Panzarotti!', 'Acqua!' and 'Vino— Vino Rosso!' Here were men haggling over sardines; hungry children at pizza ovens; smoky stalls selling chestnuts; carpenters' benches and shoemakers' stools; water- and lemonade-sellers; dogs, chickens and a pig in the gutter; corner kitchens with steaming pots; dung-carts, carts full of grapes and wagonloads of melons; a bagpipe player with dancing puppets; two lawyers, arm in arm, coming back from court; a monk begging; labourers with striped red caps; letter-writers at portable desks; and then a funeral bier, all crimson and gold, followed by mourners in masks and white gowns.

They took a road up the Capo di Monte, from where they could scan the Bay of Naples down to the mountains of Sorrento. Keats had been surprised at roses still blooming in a cottage's garden, only to have his praise for this 'exquisite climate' punctured by discovering they had no scent. He started a rant about humbug – 'What is a rose without its fragrance?' – that lasted for the remainder of the drive until, halted close to the Capuan Gate, he watched a group of *lazzaroni* [beggars] at a cauldron scooping *maccheroni* and swallowing it in long unbroken strings: 'Glorious sight! How they take it in!'[6]

On Sunday, 5 November, Keats and Severn saw the Palazzo Reale and San Francesco di Paola with its long, semicircular colonnades embracing the Piazza Plebiscito. Soldiers were parading in front of King Ferdinand, who made the latest of many declarations of allegiance to his kingdom – a reminder that Naples was in the throes of a revolution.[7] Ferdinand was a scion of the Bourbon *ancien régime*, deposed in 1806 when Napoleon installed his brother Joseph as a more compliant monarch. After Waterloo, Ferdinand had returned to rule despotically until, three months before Keats and Severn arrived, an uprising of *Carbonari* – democratic revolutionaries – forced on him a new liberal constitution that limited his power. Where Naples led, others might follow. Dreading a resurgence of European revolution so soon after Napoleon's defeat, the Holy Alliance of Austria, Russia and Prussia had mobilised to quell the insurrection.

As Austrian soldiers marched south, *The Times* reported 'perfect unanimity' at Naples with the revolutionaries' 'constitutional spirit raised to the highest'. It would be easier for the Austrians to stop Vesuvius erupting than to suppress the citizens of Naples.[8] Keats agreed. Ferdinand's soldiers were 'not fighting men', and, anyway, gossip on the street said he had abdicated. As Keats followed these astonishing developments, his libertarian zeal revived.[9]

After the parade they went to the famous Teatro San Carlo, a few yards beyond the Palazzo Reale. As they approached, Keats noticed a fresco depicting the Nine Muses and his 'fore-seeing God', Apollo, and once in the auditorium he gazed up at Giuseppe Cammarano's celestial pageant of 'Apollo Introducing the Greatest Poets to the Goddess Minerva', its fresh, bold colours like a scene from an unwritten book of his epic. At each side of the stage was what looked like a statue of a soldier. Here, at last, after all they had endured on their voyage, was a thrilling vision of painting, poetry and music thriving in the midst of a liberal revolution. Or so it seemed for a few moments, until the orchestra struck up the overture to Pacini's opera *Il barone di Dolsheim*. The soldiers had not been statues, and as they sidled offstage, happy that the audience was passive, Keats exclaimed: 'we'll go to Rome for as I am to die I should not like to leave my ashes in the presence of a people with such miserable politicks'.[10]

On Wednesday, 8 November they left Naples, heading north in a horse-drawn *vettura* along a road lined with myrtle, laurel, cyclamen and Italian pines. On this first day they covered eighteen miles to Capua, formerly a thriving Roman town on the busy Via Appia, where they found a miserable inn for the night.[11] Next morning they made their way through throngs of ragged children and beggars, and started on the Via Appia, the 'eternal road' that would take them through vineyards and olive groves and over mountains reputed to be infested with *banditti*. Everywhere were remnants of deep antiquity: Roman buildings overgrown at the roadside; watchtowers precarious on craggy pinnacles; isolated crosses and chapels; and always, for Keats, looking up from the *vettura*, a changing skyline. From the Capuan plain they entered a landscape of hills and deep clefts overgrown with chestnut trees; their road climbed to the village of Cascano and then made a gradual descent towards the coast. Perhaps, like many travellers, they spent their second night at the lone inn near St Agatha,[12] then continued to Roman Minturnae, where they could see vestiges of an amphitheatre and an aqueduct, and so on along the beautiful coastline to Mola di Gaeta (Formia), where they may have spent the Friday night. The inn was said to be excellent.[13] As Keats knew from Lemprière, Cicero was assassinated here in 43 BC and his tomb, gardens and baths were popular attractions. Keats was sent back by Italy to his first encounters with the classics in Lemprière, *The Aeneid* and Chapman's Homer, finding in ruins a way of coming to terms with his deplorable situation.

When Keats and Severn woke on Saturday, 11 November they faced a dauntingly steep ascent into bandit country – wild, rugged, inaccessible. Most dangerous for Keats, however, was the drop in temperature as they came up from the coast, for at any moment cold air or a jolt of their carriage could induce a haemorrhage. He furled himself in a rug as they entered Itri with its massive citadel, then mounted the pass across the Monte Grande. Even in November wild flowers bloomed at the roadside, butterflies danced and lizards basked.

Down from the mountains, they came to another fertile valley of vines and groves of olives, oranges and lemons around Fondi, where the inn was said to have formerly been a nobleman's palace.[14] This was their fourth night on a journey most travellers completed in two or three days, sometimes faster. After Fondi they came to Terracina, where the Monti Ausoni plunge to the sea. Keats could see on the heights a ruined Sanctuary of Jupiter and, looming overhead as they rounded the headland, a massive cliff quarried by Roman engineers to open a way for the Via Appia. Keats's passport was visaed 'good for entry' to the Papal States, and they began a long straight stretch across the malarial Pontine Marshes. To their right was fenland, and distant mountains; on their left was the Decennovium – a canal, not unlike the New River, edged with bulrushes where herons stalked. The town of Mesa was some ten miles from Terracina. Perhaps they spent Sunday night here, close to the ruin of a Roman way station, before pushing on twenty-five miles to Velletri on the lower slopes of the Colli Albani.

Here they reached the last stage of their journey. As they started across the Colli Albani on Tuesday, 14 November, autumn had advanced and the air was chilly. All the way Severn had attempted to rally Keats's spirits, picking bunches of flowers from the wayside and laughing at his puns. From Albano they looked out across the Roman Campagna and glimpsed a dim outline of Rome itself. Ahead of them lay the long, unswerving descent of the Via Appia through a forlorn landscape that would shape Keats's state of mind in his final months. Charles Dickens came here in 1845 and likened the Campagna's 'mounds, and heaps, and hills, of ruin' and 'dark undulating surface' to 'a broad dull Lethe flowing round the walls of Rome, and separating it from all the world!'[15] As Dickens returned to Rome the descent along the Via Appia seemed like a passage into a 'ruined world' on which 'the sun would never rise again'.[16]

As Keats passed along the last dozen miles he too saw 'mounds and heaps' – and also fragments of columns, friezes and pediments; blocks of granite and marble; toppled arches, tumbled walls and broken aqueducts; and mile after mile of grave-like ridges overlaid with feathery grasses and flowers.[17] With Severn he watched as a crimson-cloaked cardinal shot birds attracted by the glint of a looking glass. With two footmen relentlessly reloading guns, this scene of slaughter amid the wreckage of Rome was another manifestation of 'eternal fierce destruction'.[18] They had travelled 140 miles through arduous terrain and, now, on the edge of Rome, this last suburban stretch surrounded them with the debris of antiquity. The sight of these ancient half-buried ruins would work upon Keats's imagination in the coming days.

They entered Rome through the Lateran Gate under the gaze of a stone satyr – two hundred years on, he still glares down at traffic and pedestrians passing below. Immediately ahead of them was the massive white façade of San Giovanni in Laterano, emblazoned with the words 'Christo Salvatori'. Their destination was the city centre, and they rattled along the narrow Via di San Giovanni towards the Colosseum, its weathered arcades all heaped up with rubble. Beyond lay a warren of medieval streets and Rome's chaotic street life: a portly signor arguing with a woman selling pancakes as a little boy fed the brazier with sticks; washerwomen at fountains; hawkers, musicians and singers, and children running alongside their *vettura* until they emerged at the Piazza di Spagna.

To arrive at Rome – a city ruined, buried and still living – was almost a home-coming for Keats. Here he had a feeling of his 'real life having passed' and that, like Rome, he was now lingering somewhere between the world of the living and whatever lay beyond. He had travelled to this boundary often, physically and imaginatively, and now felt better than he had on the voyage or at Naples, almost at one with a city that was leading a 'posthumous life' like his own.[19]

Their *vettura* paused at Dr Clark's apartment. Now returned to Rome after his marriage, Clark – the author of *Medical Notes* who specialised in treating consumption – had musical and literary interests, took the *Edinburgh Review*, and had read *Endymion* and the *Lamia* volume.[20] He had secured them rooms in a second-floor apartment at number 26 Piazza di Spagna. Known as the 'Casina Rossa' because of its deep red colour, the house dated from the sixteenth century and was renovated in 1724 during building of the Scalinata, the grandly sweeping steps leading up from the Piazza di Spagna to the Trinita dei Monti church and the fields beyond.

Leaving Clark and going to their own accommodation, Severn and Keats climbed the marble staircase, past the first-floor lodgings of Thomas Gibson, an elderly Englishman, and arrived at their second-floor rooms. They were met by their Venetian landlady, Anna Angeletti, and led into an inner hall designed to be cool and shady in summer. A curtain hung from a central archway to separate her quarters from the other rooms. To the front was Severn's sitting room, with a high ceiling and large windows overlooking Bernini's boat-shaped Fontana della Barcaccia. Leading off this to the right was a small lozenge-shaped bedroom with a red tiled floor. It had a window to the front, and another at the side giving onto the Scalinata. However the bed was placed, it would have been close up to a small fireplace carved with sprigs of foliage, fruit and satyrs. On the ceiling was a complex pattern of beams and laths, decorated with flowers and intersecting unevenly to give an irregular sequence of squares. The room still feels at odds with itself, full of clutter and angles, voices outside, and in the next room footsteps, hammering and the sound of water draining somewhere. This was to be Keats's. To the back a small closet, also overlooking the Scalinata, gave Severn space to set up his easel.[21]

Their most immediate need was for cash. Keats had Taylor's draft for £120 and having braced himself to go to the Roman banker Torlonias, he took their advice to draw and deposit the full amount to save the trouble and expense of a succession of small bills. This was sound advice: the proceeds of the draft were deposited with Torlonias, and Keats and Severn drew two sums on 15 and 23 November to cover rent and living expenses. (Severn calculated their rent at £4.16s. a week and a dinner at four shillings.)[22] This arrangement for funds worked well – for a while.

Clark had settled them in the healthiest part of the city for a consumptive patient, and after two weeks he gave a first opinion. Keats's stomach seemed to be the seat of his disease, and there was reason to suspect infection of his heart and lungs. His mental exertions also appeared to be a source of his complaints, and if his mind could be put at ease Clark thought he would do well. He advised Keats to hire a horse and ride whenever the weather was favourable.

Clark's diagnosis is baffling. He already knew Keats had advanced pulmonary consumption and had thus sought accommodation for him that would benefit a patient with infected lungs. Keats's palpitations may indeed point to a coronary disorder, and prolonged dosing with mercury, laudanum and other 'active' – or 'shattering' – medicines since autumn of 1817 is likely to have wrecked his stomach. Like blood-letting, all of these treatments were useless and did far more harm than good. Quite possibly Clark was trying to deflect

Keats's anxieties about the state of his lungs as a way of setting his mind at rest. Yet Keats understood his own symptoms very well, and a good deal of his anguish was caused by their resemblance to Tom's. Why Clark thought he might be persuaded to ignore them is not clear – perhaps he simply did not know the extent of Keats's medical knowledge and experience.[23]

On Clark's recommendation Keats took exercise on a 'little horse', as he had done as a boy at Moorfields. He rode up to the Pincio, an area of wooded gardens overlooking the city, where he met and befriended Lieutenant Isaac Elton of the Royal Engineers – another young consumptive escaping the English winter. Back at his lodgings, Clark had procured a piano and sheet music so that Keats could listen to Severn playing. Haydn's symphonies were a particular delight – the composer was 'like a child', Keats thought, 'for there is no knowing what he will do next'.[24] For a few moments Keats relived the freaks of a naughty boy at Edmonton, recalled on his Scottish tour in the summer of 1818:

Hurly burly
Get up early
And go
By hook or crook
To the brook.

Even though he was desperately ill and knew himself to be dying, there were days when the end dreaded by Severn and his London friends still seemed by no means inevitable – there might yet be a return to health, and his passport had been endorsed 'Good to go to England'. The combination of a tenacious will to live and the prospect of his imminent death – 'If I recover . . . and if I should not' – makes his last letter to Brown at the end of November unbearably painful:

Rome. 30 November 1820.

My dear Brown

'Tis the most difficult thing in the world to me to write a letter. My stomach continues so bad, that I feel it worse on opening any book,—yet I am much better than I was in Quarantine. Then I am afraid to encounter the proing and conning of any thing interesting to me in England. I have an habitual feeling of my real life having past, and that I am leading a posthumous existence. God knows how it would have been—but it appears to me—however, I will not speak of that subject. I must have been at Bedhampton nearly at the time you were writing to me from Chichester— how unfortunate—and to pass on the river too! There was my star predominant!

Flickering between 'how it would have been' and 'how unfortunate', between times when he was 'well, healthy, alert &c, walking with her—and now', Keats touched on 'the knowledge of contrast, feeling for light and shade ... necessary for a poem'. Even at this extremity, he was venturing back across the heat-stricken landscape of 'A Now' to the formative landscape of his child-hood between meadows and murk, city din and meadow calm.[25] His impulse to keep life in play had revived in jokes, waggery and puns on his long journey to Italy, enabling him to outface whatever malign power determined he should pass Brown on the Thames and then miss him a second time at Bedhampton.[26] Now the gentle sound of Bernini's fountain was mingling with ideas for a new poem on the river-goddess Sabrina in Milton's *Comus*, as if he were once again gazing down from the bridge into Salmons Brook.[27] He closes his letter by asking Brown to remember him to Hunt, George and his sister, adding, 'I can scarcely bid you good bye even in a letter. I always made an awkward bow.'[28] A more graceful farewell is impossible to imagine. He parts from Brown – as he had done, many times, from Cowden Clarke, Reynolds and others – by deliberately staging the awkwardness of bidding goodbye. With a reminder that his height always made it physically difficult for him to bow elegantly, he bids Brown a last adieu and allows his friend to glimpse his figure leaving but in no hurry to be gone.

So December came in, two years since Tom's death and four since Keats had celebrated Saturnalia with his brothers and friends. He had written his last letter, and for information about the remaining weeks of his life we have to rely on Severn and Dr Clark. Because post from Rome could take three or four weeks to reach London, Keats's friends had plenty of time to speculate on what they heard from Severn, although as the month wore on none of them was in any doubt about Keats's fate. 'Ever since I first read your account of his dreadful relapse,' Brown told Taylor, 'I have never been able to hope. It was then his death took place in my mind—and inwardly I mourned for him as lost.'[29] At Rome, however, Severn had begun by hoping for the best: Keats seemed to be convalescencing and improving day by day. At Hampstead, Fanny Brawne had almost the same impression.[30]

\* \* \*

***Wentworth Place. Monday, 4 December, afternoon.*** Fanny Brawne writes to Keats's sister. Brown has received her brother's letter of 1 November, but Fanny has not been shown its grim contents. She passes on more cheering news from Severn to Haslam – if Keats 'can but get his spirits good, he will answer for his being well in a moderate time'. Mindful of the worst, she adds, 'considering all things it is as well as we could have expected.'[31]

*26 Piazza di Spagna. Saturday, 9 December.* Keats wakes in unusually good spirits and then suddenly, without any apparent cause, is seized with coughing and haemorrhages two cups of blood. This is a sure sign that his tuberculosis is not in remission and Clark immediately takes eight ounces of blood from his arm to induce a lassitude and prevent a further relapse. Severn describes Keats's blood as 'black and thick in the extreme', no longer a warm, pulsing, red-bright force of life. Next morning he haemorrhages again, and Clark takes more blood. In a dismal spiral of despair Keats contemplates suicide. Severn now takes 'every destroying mean from his reach', including the laudanum that should and could have helped him to an easeful death like Tom's.[32] For nine days Keats coughs up blood with no change for the better, repeatedly enduring the horrors of drowning and suffocation as the disease makes cavities in his lungs and corrodes his arteries. His stomach is painfully distended by Clark's starvation diet of an anchovy with a morsel of bread a day, and Severn reports him 'in perpetual hunger or craving', delirious from lack of food and the fatal prospect of his disease.[33]

*Belle Vue House, Ramsgate. Tuesday, 19 December.* John Clarke, Keats's old schoolmaster at Enfield, dies aged sixty-three.[34]

*26 Piazza di Spagna. Sunday, 24 December.* Severn begins a letter to Taylor at 4.30 in the morning, telling him that Keats has changed for the worse. Taylor hears how with every cough and pain Keats remembers Tom's symptoms, convinced that 'the continued stretch of his imagination has killed him', that his illness has been caused by 'the exciting and thwarting of his passions' or that he had been poisoned in London.[35] Again and again Keats returns obsessively to his frustrations as poet and lover to explain why his body is destroying itself. Severn attempts to calm him by reading aloud from *Don Quixote* and Maria Edgeworth's novels, but Keats wishes for books difficult to find at Rome – Jeremy Taylor's *Holy Living and Holy Dying*, Plato and *The Pilgrim's Progress*. Clark now has very little hope of Keats and is sure he will die 'at some not distant period'.[36] His kindly interventions have saved expense, but Severn is now 'rather alarmed about money': their banker has refused further funds and their landlady has informed the police that Keats is dying of consumption. City law requires that after his death everything in their rooms – beds, sheets, curtains and even the wallpaper – must be burnt to prevent further infection. This news resolves Keats to ensure that all trace of him should be expunged. He tells Severn it is his last request that no mention is to be made of him in any review or newspaper, and that no engraving is to be taken from any picture of him.[37]

*26 Piazza di Spagna. Wednesday, 3 January 1821.* Dr Clark writes to an unknown friend in London:

he has had another attack of bleeding from the lungs which has weakened him greatly, and he is now in a most deplorable state—His stomach is ruined and the state of his mind is the worst possible for one in his condition, and will undoubtedly hurry on an event that I fear is not far distant and even in the best frame of mind would not probably be long protracted . . . When I first saw him I thought something might be done, but now I fear the prospect is a hopeless one—[38]

*26 Piazza di Spagna. Wednesday, 10 January.* Severn carries Keats from his bed into the living room to change him into clean clothes – he is too weak to walk. They sit talking and Severn senses Keats changing to 'calmness & quietude', accepting that he has already taken leave and is now existing in an 'absence of himself'.[39]

*26 Piazza di Spagna. Thursday, 11 January, one o'clock in the morning.* In a letter to Mrs Brawne, Severn sends an upbeat report of how he has 'perceived for the last 3 days symptoms of recovery—D$^r$ Clarke even thinks so—Nature again revives in him.'[40]

*Wentworth Place. Monday, 15 January 1821.* Brown to Severn:

He is present to me every where and at all times,—he now seems sitting by my side and looking hard in my face . . . So much as I have loved him, I never knew how closely he was wound about my heart. M$^{rs}$ Brawne was greatly agitated when I told her of—and her daughter—I don't know how,—for I was not present,—yet she bears it with great firmness,—mournfully but without affectation,—I understand she says to her mother, 'I believe he must soon die,—when you hear of his death, tell me immediately,—I am not a fool!' Poor girl! she does not know how desolate her heart will be when she learns that there is no hope, and how wretched she will feel,—without being a fool. The only hope I have rests on D$^r$ Clarke not considering the case in so gloomy a light as you do,—for his kindness ask him to receive a stranger's thanks. But you and I well know poor Keats' disease is in the mind,—he is dying broken hearted. You know much of his grief, but do you know how George has treated him? I sit planning schemes of vengeance on his head.[41]

*26 Piazza di Spagna. Monday, 15 January 1821.* Severn writes to Haslam: Keats is sinking daily of a confirmed consumption, with continual coughing of fawn-coloured phlegm, sometimes streaked with blood, night sweats, chattering teeth and great uneasiness in his chest. Dr Clark fears that next will be diarrhoea. Keats sees all this – his knowledge of anatomy makes every change in his condition ten times worse.[42]

*26 Piazza di Spagna. Thursday, 25 January.* Severn to Taylor: 'Another week and less and less hope.' Keats has described many parts of his life and various changes, all of them leading to the 'restless ferment' of emotions that is killing him. Since Keats's haemorrhage on 9 December, Severn has been with him constantly, shattered by tending him night after night without sleep. The bottle of opium Keats had relied upon to salve the misery of a protracted death has been given to Clark, for Severn no longer trusts himself to resist Keats's demands. Seeing Severn's exhaustion, Clark has found an English nurse to relieve him from his long hours of watching, has advanced money and taken it upon himself to sort out their problem at Torlonias. A young sculptor named William Ewing also comes to help, fetching iced jelly to cool Keats's throat. At eleven o'clock this evening Clark calls, and says he cannot survive another fortnight.[43]

On this day two years earlier, Keats went to the consecration at Stansted and returned to the Old Mill House to continue writing *The Eve of St Agnes*.

*26 Piazza di Spagna. Sunday, 28 January.* At three in the morning Severn draws a sketch of Keats to keep himself awake, noting how 'a deadly sweat was on him all this night'. Propped upon a pillow, Keats's emaciated face is pale in the candlelight, hair lank and matted with sweat, his shadow a black halo.

*Wentworth Place. Thursday, 1 February.* Fanny Brawne writes to Fanny Keats of Severn's good news in his letter to her mother of 11 January: 'for the first time he feels a hope, he thinks he shall bring him back to us.'[44]

*26 Piazza di Spagna. Thursday, 8 February.* Severn to Brown: 'The thought of recovery is beyond every thing dreadful to him. We now dare not perceive any improvement; for the hope of death seems his only comfort. He talks of the quiet grave as the first rest he can ever have.'[45]

*26 Piazza di Spagna. Wednesday, 14 February.* Severn to Brown:

To-night he has talked very much to me, but so easily, that he, at last, fell into a pleasant sleep. He seems to have comfortable dreams, without the night-mare. This will bring on some change,—it cannot be worse,—it may be better. Among the many things he has requested of me to-night, this is the principal one,—that on his grave-stone shall be this,—

HERE LIES ONE WHOSE NAME WAS WRIT IN WATER.[46]

*26 Piazza di Spagna. Sunday 11 February.* Severn writes to his sister Maria:

You will be glad to know that I am in good health and with the best prospects—yet still by the side of my dying friend—and there will I remain until he is no more for my dear Maria without me he would have died long since I have kept him alive and given him every chance of recovery—but I fear it is all over with him.[47]

### 26 Piazza di Spagna. Monday, 19 February. Severn to Maria:

I make bread and milk three times a day for Keats—for myself—sometimes tea—sometimes Chocolate—or Coffe—my dinner now I go out for—I have 1st dish macarona—it is like a dish of large white earth worms—made of Flour with butter &c—very good—my 2nd dish is fish—and then comes Roast Beef or Mutton—a cutlet of Pork or wild boar—their vegetables here are beautiful—cabbage—cauliflower—brocola spinach—every thing good—and very well cooked—and then I have pudding every day.[48]

### 26 Piazza di Spagna. Tuesday, 20 February. Severn to Maria:

poor Keats cannot last but a few days more I am now quite reconciled to his state—yet I fear I shall feel the miss of him—but here everybody is kind so that I should not feel it—a Gentleman has offered me the use of his study—Sir William Drummond has engaged me to paint a picture for him—at some future time—I have no doubt my dear Maria but here I shall be able to realise a great deal of Money by my Miniatures.

With a nurse attending Keats, Severn has been to see where he will be buried, in the cemetery field close to the city wall and the Pyramid of Caius Cestius. Any description of that locality, 'of the grass and the many flowers particularly violets, the flock of goats & sheep & the young shepherd', is of intense interest to Keats.[49]

On this day a young Spaniard, Valentin Llanos, visited Keats and spoke with him.[50]

### 26 Piazza di Spagna. Thursday, 22 February. Severn to William Haslam:

I have at times written a favorable letter to my sister—you will see this is best—for I hope that staying by my poor friend to close his eyes in death—will not add to my other unlucky hits—for I am still quite prevented from painting . . .—Poor Keats keeps me by him—and shadows out the form of one solitary friend—he opens his eyes in great horror and doubt—but when they fall upon me—they close gently and open and close until he falls into another sleep—The very thought of this keeps me by him until he dies.[51]

* * *

Having consigned his name to water, the element from which his poetry so often took life, Keats was ready to face death. Out of concern for Severn, who had never seen anyone die, he somehow managed to recover his old manner at Guy's and told him to be firm for it would not last long and he did not think he should be convulsed. Severn had put himself in the way of 'trouble and danger' by accompanying him and nursing him, and now Keats looked on his death as a release for them both: 'I shall soon be laid in the quiet grave—thank God for the quiet grave—O! I can feel the cold earth upon me—the daisies growing over me—O for this quiet—it will be my first.'[52]

# CHAPTER 25

# Terminalia

He is gone—he died with the most perfect ease—he seemd to go to sleep—on the 23ʳᵈ (Friday) at ½ past 4 the approaches of death came on—'Severn—S—lift me up for I am dying—I shall die easy—dont be frightened—thank God it has come'—I lifted him up in my arms—and the phlegm seemd boiling in his throat—this increased until 11 at night when he gradually sunk into death—so quiet that I still thought he slept—[1]

Casts were made of Keats's face, hand and foot, and the city authorities were informed of his death. On Sunday, 25 February 1821 Dr Clark with Dr Luby and an Italian surgeon performed an autopsy. Keats's lungs were entirely destroyed; they could not conceive how he had lived for the last two months. Any signs that his heart and stomach had been affected were not recorded. His body was then placed in a coffin, with gifts and unopened letters tucked into the winding sheet, to await burial on the morning of Monday the 26th. The burial party started from the Piazza di Spagna before daylight. His coffin was in one carriage; in another, Severn followed with the Rev. Richard Wolfe, an English chaplain, and two young architects, Ambrose Poynter and Henry Parke. They arrived at the Pyramid of Cestius just as dawn was breaking, and were joined at the cemetery by William Ewing, the sculptor Richard Westmacott, Dr Clark and Dr Luby, and an unknown man called Henderson. Dr Clark asked each of them to place a turf of daisies on the grave: 'this would be poor Keats's wish—could he know it.'[2]

Severn had been living at Dr Clark's, and it was here on Tuesday, 27 February that he gathered himself to write to Brown. He described Keats's last moments, but was too broken down to say more beyond mentioning that the police had been and that this was 'well looked to by Dʳ C.' Their furniture was burned, and the walls scraped and restored, all of which with Clark's help Severn paid for. When their landlady summoned Severn with a bill for broken crockery, he smashed the lot.[3]

Severn's letter reached Brown at Wentworth Place late on 17 March. He had expected this news, but when the blow actually came he proved utterly unprepared for it. Unable to face telling Fanny Brawne that evening, he decided to try to sleep and then do what had to be done. The following morning Brown wrote notes for Rice, Dilke, Abbey and then one for Taylor: 'Read the enclosed—it is all over. I leave to you the care of inserting his death in the papers,—word it as *you* please,—you will do it better than I can,—in fact I can't do it.'[4] Brown immediately had second thoughts about Abbey, suspecting he would leave Fanny Keats to read of her brother's death in the papers. He tore that message up, and dispatched a note to Haslam requesting him to call on Abbey without delay and make sure that she was told.[5] Then Brown went next door. The worst had been concealed from Fanny Brawne since Severn's letter of mid-December, and she was under the impression that 'he would live months at least if he did not recover'. The first shock was beyond words. '[I]t is enough she is now pretty well,' Brown confided to Severn on the 23rd,'—and thro'out she has shown a firmness of mind which I little expected from one so young, and under such a load of grief.'[6] With her mother she went into mourning and carefully waited nine days to be sure that Fanny Keats would have heard of her brother's death, before sending a letter.

The *Morning Chronicle* carried a first announcement on Thursday, 22 March: 'At Rome, on the 23d of February, of a decline, John Keats, the Poet, aged 25.' Other notices followed, in *The Examiner* on 25 March 1821, 'On Friday the 23d of February, at Rome, after a lingering illness, died John Keats the poet, aged 25,'[7] then in the *Liverpool Mercury* (30 March 1821), 'At Rome, aged 25, Mr. John Keats, author of a volume of beautiful poetry.'

As a boy Keats had lived on an edge where the metropolis merged with surrounding meadows; at the beginning of his story Thomas Keates, his father, was killed as he crossed that threshold back into the city. His son grew up in villages at Edmonton and Enfield amid a changeful landscape that allowed him to find a voice for his own unsettled, orphaned nature; time after time he ventured through this suburban terrain, finding in its most unconsidered corners material for his poems – a shadowy brook, a minnow, sugary cherries, snail horns, footsteps on gravel, a goldfinch, puddles in rain, a broken bottle. Throughout his life he was drawn to summits and shore-lines, casements and chasms, streams, beaches and caverns, as if he sought to station himself there to listen for greetings from the gathering dusk –

memories of music fled; 'Poor Tom's a-cold'; an old song in Gaelic of battles long ago. Death had delayed coming to him until late on Friday, 23 February, for this was the Roman festival of Terminalia, sacred to limits and extremities like this last darkling bridge on which John Keats paused, steadied himself as many times before, and stepped beyond tomorrow.

# Abbreviations

| | |
|---|---|
| AMBRH | *The Autobiography and Memoirs of Benjamin Robert Haydon*, ed. Tom Taylor, introd. Aldous Huxley (2 vols, London, 1926) |
| BC | John Lemprière, *Bibliotheca Classica; or, A Classical Dictionary* (4th edn, London, 1801) |
| BHCTT | *Benjamin Robert Haydon: Correspondence and Table-Talk*, ed. Frederick Wordsworth Haydon (2 vols, London, 1876) |
| BL | British Library |
| BLHC | Luther Brewer Leigh Hunt Collection, University of Iowa Libraries, Iowa City, Iowa |
| BLJ | *Byron's Letters and Journals*, ed. Leslie A. Marchand (13 vols, London, 1973–94) |
| BT | John Barnard, ' "The Busy Time": Keats's Duties at Guy's Hospital from Autumn 1816 to March 1817', *Romanticism*, 13.3 (2007), 119–218 |
| CBWN | 'Charles Brown's Walks in the North', originally published in the *Plymouth and Devonport Weekly Journal* (1, 8, 15 and 22 Oct. 1840), quoted from the text of 'Charles Brown's Walks in the North', in *The Letters of John Keats 1814–1821*, ed. Hyder Edward Rollins (2 vols, Cambridge, MA, 1958, reprinted 1972), i.421–42 |
| Colvin | Sidney Colvin, *John Keats, His Life and Poetry His Friends Critics and After-Fame* (London, 1917) |
| DM | Transcript of Charles Wentworth Dilke's marginalia in Richard Monckton Milnes, *Life, Letters, and Literary Remains, of John Keats* (2 vols, London, 1848) in the Houghton Library, at Keats*67m–163 |

| | |
|---|---|
| FBB | Joanna Richardson, *Fanny Brawne. A Biography* (London, 1952) |
| FF | John Barnard, 'First Fruits or "First Blights": A New Account of the Publishing History of Keats's *Poems* (1817)', *Romanticism*, 12.2 (2006), 71–101 |
| FH | Nicholas Roe, *Fiery Heart: The First Life of Leigh Hunt* (London, 2005) |
| Finney | Claude Lee Finney, *The Evolution of Keats's Poetry* (1936; 2 vols bound as one, New York, 1963) |
| HD | *The Diary of Benjamin Robert Haydon*, ed. W.B. Pope (5 vols, Cambridge, MA, 1960) |
| Houghton | The Houghton Library, Harvard University: Keats Collection |
| JK | Robert Gittings, *John Keats* (London, 1968) |
| JKCD | Nicholas Roe, *John Keats and the Culture of Dissent* (Oxford, 1997) |
| JKLY | Robert Gittings, *John Keats: The Living Year, 21 September 1818 to 21 September 1819* (London, 1954) |
| JMS | *The Journals of Mary Shelley*, ed. Paula R. Feldman and Diana Scott-Kilvert (2 vols, Oxford, 1987) |
| JSLM | *Joseph Severn, Letters and Memoirs*, ed. Grant F. Scott (Aldershot and Burlington, 2005) |
| KC | *The Keats Circle: Letters and Papers 1816–1878 and More Letters and Poems 1814–1879*, ed. Hyder Edward Rollins (2nd edn, 2 vols, Cambridge, MA, 1965) |
| KCH | *Keats: The Critical Heritage*, ed. G.M. Matthews (London, 1971) |
| KCL | King's College London |
| K&H | *Keats and History*, ed. Nicholas Roe (Cambridge, 1995) |
| KI | Robert Gittings, *The Keats Inheritance* (London, 1964) |
| KMA | Ian Jack, *Keats and the Mirror of Art* (Oxford, 1967) |
| K-SJ | *The Keats-Shelley Journal* |
| K-SMB | *The Keats-Shelley Memorial Bulletin* |
| LBsC | Leigh Hunt, *Lord Byron and Some of his Contemporaries* (2nd edn, 2 vols, London, 1828) |
| LCAB | *The Letters of Charles Armitage Brown*, ed. Jack Stillinger (Cambridge, MA, 1966) |
| LFBFK | *Letters of Fanny Brawne to Fanny Keats (1820–1824)*, ed. Fred Edgecumbe (London, 1937; 1939) |
| LHA | *The Autobiography of Leigh Hunt* (3 vols, London, 1850) |
| LHCCC | John Barnard, 'Leigh Hunt and Charles Cowden Clarke, 1812–1818', in *Leigh Hunt: Life, Poetics, Politics*, ed. Nicholas Roe (London, 2003), 32–57 |

LJK     *The Letters of John Keats, 1814–1821*, ed. Hyder Edward Rollins (2 vols, Cambridge, MA, 1958, reprinted 1972)

LLL     Richard Monckton Milnes, *Life, Letters, and Literary Remains, of John Keats* (2 vols, London, 1848)

LLP     Andrew Lang, *The Life of John Gibson Lockhart* (London, 1897), consulted in the proof copy held at the University of St Andrews Library with Lang's MS. notes on Lockhart and Keats

LMA     London Metropolitan Archives

Lowell     Amy Lowell, *John Keats* (2 vols, Boston, 1925)

LPBS     *The Letters of Percy Bysshe Shelley*, ed. F.L. Jones (2 vols, Oxford, 1964)

MC     *Morning Chronicle*

MJFS     *Memorials of John Flint South* (Fontwell, 1970)

MoK     Robert Gittings, *The Mask of Keats* (London, 1956)

MP     *Morning Post*

NYRB     *New York Review of Books*

PJK     *The Poems of John Keats*, ed. Jack Stillinger (London, 1978)

PMLA     *Publications of the Modern Language Association of America*

RN     William St Clair, *The Reading Nation in the Romantic Period* (Cambridge, 2004)

RoJK     Charles Cowden Clarke, 'Recollections of John Keats', in Charles and Mary Cowden Clarke, *Recollections of Writers* (London, 1878; Fontwell, 1969)

RoK     Charles Cowden Clarke, 'Recollections of Keats. By an Old School-Fellow', *Atlantic Monthly* (Jan. 1861), 86–100

RoW     Charles and Mary Cowden Clarke, *Recollections of Writers* (London, 1878; Fontwell, 1969)

Sharp     William Sharp, *The Life and Letters of Joseph Severn* (London 1892)

TKP     Jack Stillinger, *The Texts of Keats's Poems* (Cambridge, MA, 1974)

TLS     *Times Literary Supplement*

WJB     Walter Jackson Bate, *John Keats* (Cambridge, MA, 1963)

WNK     Carol Kyros Walker, *Walking North with Keats* (New Haven and London, 1992)

Unless indicated otherwise, Keats's poems and prefaces are quoted from *The Poems of John Keats*, ed. Jack Stillinger (London, 1978). Shakespeare's plays are quoted from *The Complete Works of Shakespeare. The Alexander Text* (1951; London, 2010).

# Notes

## Preface

1. W.M. Rossetti, *Life of Keats* (London, 1887), 208.
2. RoK, 88; LJK, ii.133.
3. WJB, viii, 580–1.
4. LJK, i.342; 'The Living Keats', NYRB (7 Nov. 1968), 28.
5. See LJK, i.323.
6. LJK, i.360.
7. LJK, ii.359.
8. LJK, ii.352.

## 1 Birthplaces

1. 'Inquisition taken the 27th day of April 1804 on Thomas Keates', LMA, CLA/041/1Q/02/017.
2. Fanny Keats's draft recollections about the origins of the Keats family, pencilled on a letter from Harry Buxton Forman of 1 Feb. 1886; Houghton, MS Eng. 1509.71. On her complexion, see George Keats to Fanny Keats, 28 April 1824, Houghton, MS Eng. 1509.89. Voyages of the mariner Keateses of Poole were widely reported in newspapers; see the shipping news in *The General Advertiser* (31 March 1752); *The Public Advertiser* (14 April 1753; 30 March 1758); *St James's Chronicle* (7 Jan. 1764).
3. For Hardy's recollection, see *The Collected Letters of Thomas Hardy*, ed. Richard Little Purdy and Michael Millgate (7 vols, Oxford, 1978–87), v.31. Robert Gittings noted the birth of Thomas Keates at Fordington in 1773, but did not follow it up: JK, 442. I am grateful to Robert Keats of Lanner, Cornwall, for sharing his records of Thomas and James Keates's early life and the poorhouse. Jane Keates's symptoms and death are recorded in 'Stinsford Burials 1750–1780', http://www.opcdorset.org/StinsfordFiles/StinsfordBurs1.htm. For Thomas Hardy's neighbours at Higher Bockhampton, see the 1841 and 1851 census returns for Stinsford. For Keats's sore throat, LJK, ii.200.
4. For Hunt on Keats, see LBsC, i.409; 'sphere in life', KC, i.274; 'earlier Misfortunes', LJK, i.293. For William Keates, see my essay 'John Keats and the West Country', *English Romantic Writing and the West Country*, ed. Nicholas Roe (Houndmills, 2010), 277–82; for John Keat of 'Mr. Keat's Livery Stables', *Daily Advertiser* (10 Feb. 1772), and frequently cited in other papers. For Keats connections at Corfe Castle, see Tom Driberg, *'Swaff': The Life and Times of Hannen Swaffer* (London, 1974), 6.
5. Bryan Waller Procter ('Barry Cornwall') to Leigh Hunt, 14 Sept. 1858, BLHC; Jean Haynes, 'Elizabeth Keats', K-SMB, 9 (1958), 21; Jean Haynes, 'Keats's Paternal Relatives', K-SMB, 15 (1964), 27–8; Edmund Blunden, *Leigh Hunt. A Biography* (London, 1930), 331; 'Keats's Father', MoK, 80–1. For Frederick Keats, see 'The New Sheriffs', *The Times* (1 Oct. 1856), 10. See also 'Keats's Father', MoK, 81. Frederick's descendant Anthony de Mancha Stevens tells me that according to

family tradition, related by his mother and grandmother, Sheriff Keats's family was 'closely related' to the poet. Personal conversation, 26 June 2006.

6. JKLY, 73–82.

7. For Jennings taking the Swan and Hoop, see Innholders' Company Court Minutes 1752–76, Guildhall Library MS 6648/5. Birth details from the flyleaf of the Jennings family Bible, by courtesy of Fernando Paradinas. Baptisms, Family Search database at https://www.familysearch.org/.

8. *The Diary of Samuel Pepys*, ed. Robert Latham and William Matthews (11 vols, London, 1970–83), ii.127; iii.93; *The Diary of John Evelyn*, ed. E.S. de Beer (6 vols, Oxford, 1955), iii.457; Moorfields c. 1792, from *Walks through London* (London, 1832), 58; Rictor Norton, *Mother Clap's Molly House: The Gay Subculture in England 1700–1830* (London, 1992), 76–8.

9. Patricia Allderidge, *Bethlem Hospital 1247–1997* (Chichester, 1997), 11–21.

10. Swan and Hoop details taken from an advertisement for the adjacent property at 20 The Pavement, Moorfields, *The Times* (8 Oct. 1804), 4; 'car park', see G.M. Matthews, 'The Living Keats', NYRB (7 Nov. 1968), 28.

11. S.M. Ellis, *Wilkie Collins, Le Fanu and Others* (London, 1951), 284. Trial of John Lightfoot and John Tyrell for theft with violence and highway robbery, 25 Oct. 1786, Proceedings of the Old Bailey, Ref: t17861025-16, online at http://www.oldbaileyonline.org/html_units/1780s/t17861025-16.html; trial of Richard Richardson for theft, 8 Dec. 1790, Proceedings of the Old Bailey, Ref: t17901208-21, online at http://www.oldbaileyonline.org/html_units/1790s/t17901208-21.html.

12. For Samuel Brawne, grandfather of Fanny Brawne, see FBB, 2; for Thomas Richards, father of Keats's printer and friend, LJK, i.121; for rent, KI, 73.

13. Innholders' Company Court Minutes 1752–76, Guildhall Library MS 6648/7.

14. RoJK, 121; 'Memoranda on the Keats Family', KC, i.303.

15. For Abbey, see LJK, i.62; for Joseph Keats, see auction of his property; MC (12 June 1819). For Abbey on women, KC, i.314. John Taylor's idea that Abbey came from Calne, like Alice Jennings (see JK, 32–3), was a mistake for Alne, Yorkshire, where Abbey's parents, Jonathan Abbey and Deborah Dodgson, were married on 18 June 1764.

16. 'Marriages in October 1794', Register of St George's, Hanover Square, City of Westminster Archives Centre, London. The register contains marriages of minors with the consent of parents or guardians; there is no such approval for Frances.

17. For the arrests, see *The Times* (15 May 1794), 2, (7 Oct. 1794), 3.

18. *The Poems of William Blake*, ed. W.H. Stevenson, text by David V. Erdman (New York, 1971).

19. John Thelwall, *Peaceful Discussion, and Not Tumultuary Violence the Means of Redressing National Grievances* (London, 1795), 9; *The Times* (31 Oct. 1795), 3.

20. LBsC, i.408. For Gittings's doubts, see JK, 4.

21. Brian Livesley, '"Little Keats" and his Congenital Diseases', a research paper consulted in typescript.

22. LJK, i.405.

23. Robert Gittings, 'Keats's Sailor Relation,' TLS (15 April 1960), 245; 'Ship News', *The Times* (12 Jan. 1795), 3, (11 March 1795), 3, (21 Sept. 1795), 3.

24. 'Advices from Admiral Duncan', *The Times* (20 July 1797), 2.

25. For the *Russell* and Camperdown, see 'Defeat of the Dutch Fleet', *The Times* (14 Oct. 1797), 2; *Glorious Victory: Admiral Duncan and the Battle of Camperdown* (Dundee, 1997). For De Winter's story, RoJK, 121. The anecdote may be a garbled report of the heroism of young sailor Jack Crawford; when the mast of the *Venerable* was shattered, under intense gunfire Crawford climbed the stump and nailed the admiral's colours to the top.

26. For the wounded, see National Archives, Kew, ADM 101/85/7 HMS *Ardent*; for Keats and his brothers, RoK, 87; KC, ii.164. 'Saturn' is lead acetate.

27. Willard B. Pope, 'The Family of John Keats', TLS (22 Dec. 1932), 977, who reports that an Ann Burch 'swore to an affidavit on June 29, 1825, that she was intimately acquainted with Thomas and Frances Keats before and after the birth of John Keats'. For bricks and tiles, see Hackney Archives, MS 4556/1.

28. 'Written in Disgust of Vulgar Superstition', 10.

29. For Haydon's recollection, see HD, ii.107. Residents of Craven Street, Hackney Archives, 'Shoreditch Land Tax Ledgers, 1795–1805' at H.A.D.P./LT 49–56 pt. For Croker's remarks, *Quarterly Review* (April–Sept. 1818), 204–8, reprinted in KCH, 112.

30. For Jennings, see Innholders' Company Court Minutes 1752–76, Guildhall Library MS 6648/7 and KC, i.303. For Keats and 'eat', LJK, ii.169.

31. For bankrupts, see *The Times* (23 April 1798), 2; frugality, Innholders' Company Court Minutes 1752–76, Guildhall Library MS 6648/7; gullibility, KC, i.314.

32. For 'Keates's Livery Stables', see MP (30 March and 20 April 1803). Jennings's move, Hackney Archives, 'Shoreditch Land Tax Ledgers, 1795-1805', and Jean Haynes, 'John Jennings: Keats's Grandfather', K-SMB, 13 (1962), 22. Thomas Keates's freehold, Innholders' Company Court Minutes 1752-76, Guildhall Library MS 6648/7.

33. RoJK, 121, 123.

34. 'Robert Mathews, Theft: Animal Theft, 16th February, 1803', Proceedings of the Old Bailey, Ref: t18030216-31. The trial was noticed in The Times (18 Feb. 1803), 3. See Criminal Register 1803, National Archives, Kew, HO26/9.

35. The Times (12 Sept. 1803), 3; (22 Feb. 1803), 2.

36. The Times (20 Oct. 1803), 2.

37. LJK, i.138. Pat Rogers, Grub Street: Studies in a Subculture (London, 1972), 45-70. For Keats's childhood in his poems, see, for example, 'I stood tip-toe upon a little hill' and The Fall of Hyperion.

38. For Keats's list of armour, see LJK, i.145.

39. LJK, i.139, 141.

40. For Lackington's Temple of the Muses, see Tim Chilcott, A Publisher and his Circle. The Life and Work of John Taylor, Keats's Publisher (London and Boston, 1972), 6-7.

## 2 School

1. When the schoolhouse was demolished in 1872, the façade was taken to the Victoria and Albert Museum in London, where, until recently, it was on display.

2. LJK, i.170, ii.149.

3. 'To Charles Cowden Clarke', l. 16.

4. William Robinson, The History and Antiquities of Enfield (2 vols, London, 1823), i.63; Mary Cowden Clarke, My Long Life: An Autobiographical Sketch (2 edn, London, 1896), 65.

5. Details from the Breton Estate Map of 1785 and the Enclosure map of Enfield, 1803.

6. A full history of the school is given in JKCD, 27-50.

7. The Times (17 Aug. 1802), 2; Gentleman's Magazine (Aug. 1802), 774.

8. 'You Can Be a Romantic and Still Think Revolting Thoughts', The Observer Review (8 June 1997). See also Graham Dalling, Enfield Past (London, 1999).

9. RoJK, 4.

10. LJK, i.155.

11. RoW, 34.

12. For Scott, see Patrick O'Leary, Regency Editor: The Life of John Scott (Aberdeen, 1983).

13. Edward Holmes's recollection: see KC, ii.164-5.

14. For Ryland and the living orrery, see William Newman, Rylandiana: Reminiscences Relating to the Rev. John Ryland (London, 1835), 117-22. For further discussion, JKCD, 34-9.

15. For the pond, see 'A Now, Descriptive of a Hot Day', The Indicator (28 June 1820), 300-3. After he left school, fights and cricket gave Keats two black eyes – 'during all my school days', he recalled, 'I never had one at all': LJK; ii.78.

16. He was buried in the nonconformist cemetery at Bunhill Fields.

17. LJK, ii.129.

18. 'On Sunday Mr. KEATS, Livery-stable keeper in Moorfields, went to dine at Southgate; he returned at a late hour, and on passing down the City road, his horse fell with him, when he had the misfortune to fracture his skull. It was about one o'clock in the morning when the watchman found him, he was at that time alive, but speechless; the watchman got assistance, and took him to a house in the neighbourhood, where he died about 8 o'clock': The Times (17 April 1804), 3. See also The Ipswich Journal (21 April 1804) and Gentleman's Magazine (May 1804), 482.

19. For Elizabeth Keats, see Jean Haynes, 'Elizabeth Keats', K-SMB, 9 (1958), 21; for 'Keat's Livery Stables', MP (7 June 1804).

20. Norman Kilgour, 'At "The Swan and Hoop"', K-SMB, 22 (1971), 52.

21. Fanny Keats's draft recollections pencilled on a letter from Harry Buxton Forman to Fanny Keats de Llanos, c. Feb. 1886, Houghton, MS. Eng. 1509.71. Letter of Fanny Keats de Llanos to Harry Buxton Forman, 3 March 1886, LMA, K/MS/02/47.

22. Letter of Fanny Keats de Llanos to Harry Buxton Forman, 3 March 1886. LMA, K/MS/02/47; and draft letter to solicitor Ralph Thomas, Feb. 1886, Houghton, MS. Eng. 1509.113.

23. Fanny Keats, list of answers to solicitor Ralph Thomas's questions, Madrid, 27 Feb. (1886?), LMA, K/MS/02035.

24. Smith, Payne and Smith, 'Register of Clerks 1801-9', The Royal Bank of Scotland Group Archives, SPS/179/1.

25. Fanny Keats to Harry Buxton Forman, 3 March 1886, LMA, K/MS/02/47.
26. HD, ii.107.
27. *The Times* (4 July 1804), 1, col. 2.
28. For Robert Potts and William Walter on short contracts at the Swan and Hoop, see Guildhall Library, 'Innholders Company Court Minutes 1752–76', MS 6648/7, 5 Sept. and 10 Oct. 1804.
29. KC, i.136.
30. RoJK, 121, 123; Sharp, 255.
31. RoJK, 144.
32. Edward Holmes's recollections, KC, ii.197–9; RoJK, 123.
33. That Jennings willed this sum in Feb. 1805 suggests that the Keats children were already separated from their mother and that he could foresee they would have to be provided for.
34. The nominal annual earnings of other occupations gives us a sense of the 'status value' of the sums Jennings had left: farm labourers, £40; builder, £55; surgeons, £217; solicitors and barristers, £340. See Peter H. Lindert and Jeffrey G. Williamson, 'Living Standards during the Industrial Revolution', *Economic History Review*, NS 36, 1 (Feb. 1983), 1–25.
35. KI, 8–11; JK, 21. For Danvers, see *A London Directory . . . Containing the Names and Residences of the Merchants, Manufacturers, and Principal Traders in London* (London, 1799), 50.
36. *Reports of Cases Argued and Determined in the High Court of Chancery, by William Brown* (4 vols, London, 1785–94), ii.19.
37. Smith, Payne and Smith, 'Register of Clerks 1801–9', The Royal Bank of Scotland Group Archives SPS/179/1.
38. KI, 13, 74.
39. KI, 74: '4th Paid Mr. Rawlings as per Bill 41.4.9.'
40. Reginald James Blewitt, *The Court of Chancery. A Satirical Poem* (London, 1828), ll. 1–2.
41. KI, 66–7, 69. 'Rawlings v. Jennings. Rolls. May 22d, July 29th, 1806.'
42. KI, 74–5.
43. MC (2 July 1805).
44. Fanny Keats's recollection, to Harry Buxton Forman, 3 March 1886, LMA, K/MS/02/47.
45. See his letter suggesting who might advance Leigh Hunt a loan: 'there is Keats, who certainly *can*', LPBS, i.550.
46. See her letters to Harry Buxton Forman at LMA, K/MS/02/47.
47. 'Enfield Middlesex Land Tax Assessment from Lady Day 1805 to Lady Day 1806'; 'Enfield Middlesex Land Tax Assessment 1806 to 1807', Enfield Local History Library.
48. LJK, i.236.
49. LJK, i.323; 'I stood tip-toe', ll. 237–8. Among Keats's other school friends were Charles Briggs (LJK, i.104, ii.110), James Peachey (LJK, i.197 and n.), Wade (KC, ii.264) and possibly William Haslam. Thomas Richards, clerk in the Ordnance Office, left the school when Keats arrived; his brother, the printer Charles Richards, was possibly also a pupil. Charles Wells and Richard Hengist Horne were friends of Tom's (LJK, i.83); Horne recalled Keats revisiting the school after he had left; see pp. 46–7 below.
50. RoJK, 201.
51. 'To Charles Cowden Clarke', ll. 60–7; RoK, 88.
52. RoK, 88.
53. *The Times* (12 Sep. 1805). The news of Trafalgar broke in *The Times* (7 Nov. 1805), 1.
54. KI, 21–3.
55. RoW, 16.
56. *Critical Essays on the Performers of the London Theatres* (London, 1807), 2, 16.
57. See especially *Critical Essays*, 50 n.
58. The Swan and Hoop was taken over by the victualler Joshua Vevers on Lady Day 1806 (i.e. 25 March). See 'St. Stephen Coleman Street Rotation Book 1792–1831', Guildhall Library MS 4494/1.
59. KI, 23–6.
60. George Keats's recollection in a letter to Fanny Keats, Feb. 1825, Houghton, MS. Eng. 1509.90; 'A Now, Descriptive of a Hot Day', *The Indicator* (28 June 1820), 300.
61. LJK, ii.46.
62. LJK, i.314.
63. LJK, i.312–13.
64. LJK, ii.149.
65. KC, i.305.
66. The Enfield Land Tax Assessment 1808–9 lists at Wilkinson's address 'Wid. Bright & ors', i.e. 'Widow Bright and others', Enfield Local History Library.
67. LJK, i.341.

## 3 Bridge

1. 'Keats's Sailor Relation', TLS (15 April 1960), 245.
2. KI, 26–8.
3. Sharp, 255; Fanny Keats to F. Holland Day, 26 Sep. 1889, Houghton, MS. Keats 4.12.8, 18.
4. KC, i.288. For brandy, see KC, i.305.
5. RoK, 87; JKCD, 45–50.
6. William Robertson, *The History of America* (6th edn, 3 vols, London, 1792), i.289; William Mavor, *Youth's Miscellany* (London, 1798), 105–13, 188–9; RoJK, 124.
7. See *The Examiner* (2 Oct. 1808), 625 and FH, 98–9.
8. RoK, 87. Cowden Clarke recalled that Keats read Andrew Tooke's *Pantheon* (1698, many times reprinted); Brown listed 'Baldwin's Pantheon' among Keats's books after his death; KC, i.258 and n.
9. LJK, i.341.
10. BC, entry under 'C. Cassius'.
11. RoK, 87.
12. Josiah Conder, *Eclectic Review* (Sept. 1817), KCH, 67.
13. 'On the Adversities of Keats's Fame', JSLM, 610.
14. LJK, ii.323.
15. LJK, i.224; KC, i.307.
16. KI, 29.
17. 'London Burial Index 1558–1872', www.englishorigins.com, 11 June 2009.
18. Fanny Keats de Llanos, draft of answers to solicitor Ralph Thomas, c. Feb. 1886, Houghton, MS. Eng 1509.112.
19. LJK, ii.123.
20. Information about Sandell from Jean Haynes, 20 Aug. 2009. LJK, ii.192, 18 Sept. 1819.
21. See Norman Kilgour, 'Mrs. Jennings' Will', K-SMB, 13 (1962), 24–7.
22. I draw upon KI, 32–4 for this account of the two funds available to the Keats children from midsummer 1810.
23. LMA, K/MS/01/006.
24. For Walton, see KI, 37.
25. Cowden Clarke thought Keats was born in 1796, as he told Milnes; KC, ii.146.
26. RoK, 88.
27. LJK, i.207. Keats may also have recollected Lemprière's note about Aeneas's 'submission to the will of the gods'.
28. RoK, 88.
29. LJK, i.170.
30. For the medal as a forgery, see WJB, 26 n.
31. Information on the medal and the hallmark is from personal correspondence with Harry Williams-Bulkeley, head of the Silver Department at Christie's UK, July 2009.
32. See Lowell, i.41–2.
33. *The Times* (23 July 1811), 1.
34. Autograph letter pasted into a presentation copy of *Life, Letters, and Literary Remains, of John Keats* (2 vols, London, 1848) from Milnes to Cowden Clarke. The Brotherton Collection, Leeds University. Cowden Clarke to Milnes, 20 Dec. 1846, KC, ii.168–9. See also JKCD, 89.
35. The son of Sampson and Elizabeth Hodgkinson, born 8 July and baptised 6 Aug. 1793, at St Sepulchre, London: Familysearch.org.
36. RoK, 90. The italics are Cowden Clarke's. Severn to Charles Brown, 15 April 1830, JSLM, 303. Benjamin Richardson, who knew Keats's fellow medical students Stephens and Mackereth, said the apprenticeship was 'apparently not by [Keats's] own choice'. See 'An Esculapian Poet: John Keats', *The Asclepiad* (London, 1884), 142.
37. See, for example, JK, 34.
38. Background information on the Hammond family is drawn from Phyllis G. Mann, 'John Keats: Further Notes', K-SMB, 12 (1961), 23–7; Gerald Hamilton-Edwards, 'John Keats and the Hammonds', K-SMB, 17 (1966), 31–6; J.G.L. Burnby, 'The Hammonds of Edmonton', Edmonton Hundred Historical Society, Occasional Paper, NS 26 (1973).
39. See Phyllis G. Mann, 'John Keats: Some Further Notes', K-SMB, 12 (1961), 25.
40. See a contemporary apprentice's indenture in V. Mary Cross, *A Surgeon in the Early Nineteenth Century: The Life and Times of John Green Crosse* (Edinburgh and London, 1968), 6.
41. PJK, 102–3.
42. RoK, 88.
43. Cross, *A Surgeon in the Early Nineteenth Century*, 14–30: 'The Young Apprentice'.

44. See Richard Hengist Horne's letter to the *Daily News* (8 April 1871).
45. See Colvin, 18; *The Life and Letters of Theodore Watts-Dunton* (2 vols, London and New York, 1916), i.152; Edmund Gosse, ' "Orion" Horne', in *Portraits and Sketches* (London, 1912), 101; Ann Blainey, *The Farthing Poet: A Biography of Richard Hengist Horne, 1802–1884: A Lesser Literary Lion* (London, 1968), 14.
46. 'A Now, Descriptive of a Hot Day', *The Indicator* (28 June 1820), 301.
47. LJK, ii.208.
48. KC, ii.148, 169. In LLL, i.20, Milnes alluded only to the 'termination' of Keats's apprenticeship.
49. *Daily News* (8 April 1871).
50. KC, ii.177.
51. HD, ii.107.
52. KC, i.277.
53. KC, i.277.
54. Mann, 'John Keats: Further Notes', 27; John Barnard, 'Keats, Andrew Motion's Dr. Cake, and Charles Turner Thackrah', *Romanticism*, 10.1 (2004), 5.
55. Cross, *A Surgeon in the Early Nineteenth Century*, 33–8; MJFS, 23
56. Bransby Blake Cooper, *The Life of Sir Astley Cooper, Bart.* (2 vols, London, 1843), i.236.
57. Charles Brown gives an account of Keats translating as an apprentice in *Shakespeare's Autobiographical Poems* (London, 1838), 133–4, adding that he had seen Keats 'deeply absorbed in the study of Greek and Italian' for which 'he allotted a portion of each day' as he had done for *The Aeneid*.
58. RoK, 88.
59. John Barnard, 'Charles Cowden Clarke's "Cockney" Commonplace Book', K&H, 70; Cowden Clarke had translated his portion of Virgil c. 28 Oct. 1812.
60. *The Examiner* (2 June 1811), 337, and FH, 146.
61. *The Examiner* (22 March 1812), 179, (26 April 1812), 259.
62. RoW, 16–17.
63. RoK, 88.
64. RoK, 88.
65. RoK, 88. Keats was quoting *The Faerie Queene*, II.xii.23.
66. Mary Cowden Clarke offers a detailed recollection of the path between Edmonton and Enfield and the old schoolhouse in *My Long Life*, 61–7, and in her letter to Alexander Main of Arbroath, 3 Aug. 1883, Keats-Shelley House Rome, MS. 5/62/172.
67. Colvin, 17.
68. Robert M. Ryan, *Keats: The Religious Sense* (Princeton, NJ, 1976), 50–1.
69. LJK, i.113: 'I am anxious too to see the Author of the Sonnet to the Sun.'
70. KC, i.274.
71. RoW, 16–17, 191–2.

## 4 Southwark

1. DM, on p. 9.
2. DM, on p. 20.
3. LCAB, 162.
4. Personal correspondence with Dee Cook, Archivist, The Worshipful Society of Apothecaries of London, Apothecaries' Hall, London, 16 Dec. 2008.
5. See Irvine Loudon, *Medical Care and the General Practitioner 1750–1850* (Oxford, 1986), 176–80.
6. KC, i.307.
7. KC, i.307.
8. Guy's Hospital Papers at KCL Archive, 'Dressers 1796–1834', TH/FP5/1.
9. 'Memoir of the Author's Life', in Joseph Henry Green, *Spiritual Philosophy: Founded on the Teaching of the Late Samuel Taylor Coleridge* (2 vols, London and Cambridge, 1865), i–v.
10. Guy's Hospital Papers, 'Pupils and Dressers Index 1723–1819', KCL Archive, TH/FP1/IN.
11. Loudon, *Medical Care*, 177; MJFS, 23; Guy's Hospital Papers, KCL Archive, 'Dressers 1796–1834', TH/FP5/1.
12. Samuel Wilks and G.T. Bettany, *A Biographical History of Guy's Hospital* (London and New York, 1892), 329. Guy's Hospital Papers, 'Pupils and Dressers 1755–1823', KCL Archive, G/FP1/1.
13. For George Cooper at Guy's, see 'George Cooper and Astley Cooper', in BT, 212–14.
14. MJFS, 81.
15. For Brown's dating of this poem, see KC, ii.55.

16. *The Examiner* (10 April 1814).
17. *The Examiner* (10 April 1814), 236, (24 April 1814), 257.
18. RoK, 95.
19. Cross, *A Surgeon in the Early Nineteenth Century*, 45.
20. Finney, 99.
21. Fanny Keats de Llanos to H. Buxton Forman, 2 May 1881 and 4 May 1883, LMA, K/MS/02/47. Thomas Parry, vicar of Walthamstow, to F. Holland Day, 18 Nov. 1889, Correspondence Relating to John Keats, 1889–1931, Houghton, b. MS. Am 800.14.
22. Hunt to Cowden Clarke, 16 Dec. 1814, reproduced in full in John Barnard, 'Leigh Hunt and Charles Cowden Clarke, 1812–1818', *Leigh Hunt: Life, Poetics, Politics*, ed. Nicholas Roe (London and New York, 2003), 41.
23. Richard D. Altick, *The Cowden Clarkes* (New York, London, Toronto, 1948), 29–33.
24. LJK, i.142.
25. KC, i.284–5.
26. RoK, 89.
27. RoJK, 127.
28. *The Examiner* (26 March 1815), 193, 203.
29. See JK, 47.
30. *The London Medical Repository*, 4.21 (1 Sept. 1815), 252–3.
31. *The Examiner* (16 July 1815), 456–7.
32. *The London Medical Repository*, 5.30 (1 June 1816), 533.
33. *The London Medical Repository*, 5.26 (1 Feb. 1816), 172.

## 5 Bright and Dark

1. See Spurgin's letter to Keats, 5 Dec. [1815], reproduced in Edward B. Hinckley, 'On First Looking into Swedenborg's Philosophy: A New Keats-Circle Letter', K-SJ, 9.1 (1960), 20–5, esp. the final paragraph. Hereafter, 'On First Looking into Swedenborg's Philosophy'.
2. KC, ii.218.
3. KC, ii.185.
4. *European Magazine and Literary Review* (Nov. 1816), 435. I am grateful to John Barnard for this reference. It considerably increases the range of Mathew's publications, and thus his sense of himself in relation to Keats.
5. KC, ii.185, 190.
6. KC, ii.191.
7. KC, ii.185.
8. KC, ii.221. For Severn, Holmes and Goswell Street, see Sue Brown, *Joseph Severn; A Life. The Rewards of Friendship* (Oxford, 2009), 29, to which the account of Severn and Keats in this book is indebted.
9. See 'On First Looking into Swedenborg's Philosophy'.
10. *European Magazine and Literary Review* (Oct. 1817), 360.
11. For Haydon on 1815, Napoleon and Wellington, see HD, ii.455, 457.
12. For Tyrell and Key, see Cooper, *The Life of Sir Astley Cooper*, ii.195.
13. *The Examiner* (25 June 1815), 413.
14. *The Examiner* (2 July 1815), 417.
15. LJK, ii.280–1, 210.
16. Cooper, *The Life of Sir Astley Cooper*, ii.196.
17. LJK, i.281, 102.
18. LJK, ii.102.
19. Guy's Hospital Papers at KCL Archive: 'Surgeons' Pupils of Guy's and St. Thomas's Hospitals 1812–1825', G/FP4/1; 'Guy's Hospital Entry of Physicians' and Surgeons' Pupils and Dressers, 1778/1813', G/FP3/1; 'Physicians' Pupils at Guy's', G/FP3/2.
20. Guy's Hospital Papers at KCL Archive: 'Guy's and St. Thomas's Hospitals Pupils and Dressers 1755–1823', G/FP1/1.
21. *Kent's Original London Directory* (London, 1817), 274.
22. Personal discussion with Ray Rackham, bookbinder at LMA, 24 March 2009.
23. Guy's Hospital Papers at KCL Archive: 'Anatomical Pupils 1814–21', TH/FP1/2; MJFS, 31; F.G. Parsons, *The History of St. Thomas's Hospital* (3 vols, London, 1932–6), iii.35.
24. For John Barnard on Keats's lecture courses, see BT, 201–3, and Donald C. Goellnicht, *The Poet-Physician: Keats and Medical Science* (Pittsburgh, PA, 1984), 23–4, 32.

25. William Allen, *The Substance of an Address to the Students at Guy's Hospital* (London, 1823); Wilks and Bettany, *A Biographical History of Guy's Hospital*, 387–91.
26. MJFS, 59–60.
27. MJFS, 32; Parsons, *The History of St. Thomas's Hospital*, iii.30.
28. Benjamin Golding, *An Historical Account of St Thomas's Hospital, Southwark* (London, 1819), 128; Cooper, *The Life of Sir Astley Cooper*, ii.411–13.
29. See Druin Burch, *Digging Up the Dead: Uncovering the Life and Times of an Extraordinary Surgeon* (London, 2007), 198–9.
30. Dates and times of Keats's lectures from *The Times* (25 Sept. 1815), 1, and MC (5 Oct. 1815), 1.
31. Burch, *Digging Up the Dead*, 196–7.
32. KC, ii.209. George Keats discovered his address in 1816 from an old school acquaintance, Charles Briggs; LJK, i.104.
33. 'Physical Society Guy's Hospital 1813–20', KCL Archive, G/S4/M9.
34. For Stephens's recollections, see KC, ii.206–14. Mackereth's memory of Keats as one of his 'great friends' comes via his son, J.W. Mackereth, 21 Oct. 1890, Houghton, MS. AM 800.14. See also William S. Pierpoint, *John Keats, Henry Stephens and George Wilson Mackereth: The Unparallel Lives of Three Medical Students* (London, 2010).
35. KC, ii.209–10; 'Index to Surgical Students Listed in Ludford Harvey's Journal 1807–26', St Bartholomew's Hospital Archives, X54/1.
36. *Poems by William Wordsworth* (2 vols, London, 1815), ii.159.
37. *The Examiner* (21 Aug. 1814), 542.
38. Quoted from *The Examiner* (5 May 1816), 282.
39. MJFS, 32–6.
40. *John Keats's Anatomical and Physiological Notebook*, ed. M.B. Forman (Oxford, 1934), 5, 10, 55, 56, 64.
41. Introductory lecture 'On Chemistry', quoted in Goellnicht, *The Poet-Physician*, 51–2.
42. *Lectures on the English Poets*, 'On Poetry in General', *The Complete Works of William Hazlitt*, ed. P.P. Howe (21 vols, London, 1930–4), v.9.
43. See Keats's review 'Mr Kean', *The Champion* (21 Dec. 1817), reproduced in *John Keats: The Complete Poems*, ed. John Barnard (Harmondsworth, 1973), 529–31, and compare *Lamia*, ii.229–37.
44. KC, ii.208–10.
45. KC, ii.208–11.

## 6 'J.K., and Other Communications'

1. KC, ii.211.
2. *The Examiner* (21 April 1816), 250.
3. 'Distressing Circumstance in High Life', *The Examiner* (21 April 1816), 249; *The Feast of the Poets* (London, 1814), 93–7, 107.
4. Leigh Hunt, *The Story of Rimini* (London, 1816), 15. Hereafter referred to as *Rimini*. All references are to the pages in this first edition.
5. *Rimini*, 18, 20, 22.
6. *Rimini*, 26.
7. *Rimini*, 28.
8. *Rimini*, 44.
9. *Rimini*, 44.
10. *Rimini*, 77.
11. See Richard Woodhouse's note to this poem: *The Manuscripts of the Younger Romantics*, gen. ed. Donald Reiman, *John Keats*, ed. Jack Stillinger (7 vols, New York and London, 1985–8), vol. 1, *Poems (1817): A Facsimile of Richard Woodhouse's Annotated Copy in the Huntington Library*, 80.
12. *Rimini*, 77–8.
13. *Rimini*, 111.
14. Leigh Hunt, *Foliage; or, Poems Original and Translated* (London, 1818), 17.
15. *The Letters of Charles and Mary Anne Lamb*, ed. E.J. Marrs (3 vols, Ithaca, NY, 1975–8), ii.209–10; BLJ, v.35; for Haydon's letter to Hunt, 21 Feb. 1816, see BL Add. Mss. 38108.
16. *Dublin Examiner* (June 1816), 131; *Monthly Review* (June 1816), 138, 146; *Eclectic Review* (April 1816), 380; *Quarterly Review* (Jan.–May 1816), 481.
17. *Memoirs, Journal, and Correspondence of Thomas Moore*, ed. Lord John Russell (6 vols, London, 1853–6), viii.215; LHA, ii.173.
18. *Address to That Quarterly Reviewer Who Touched Upon Mr. Leigh Hunt's 'Story of Rimini'* (London, 1816), 3. See LHCCC, 43, and FF, 77.

19. *The Times* (24 Dec. 1818).
20. *Rimini*, 13.
21. KC, ii.208, 211.
22. LBsC, i.413.
23. LJK, i.392; JSLM, 303. Brown believed Haslam and Keats had been schoolfellows, KC, ii.52, and Severn claimed to have known Keats 'as far back as 1813'. Spring 1816 remains the period from which their friendship can be dated with certainty.
24. LJK, i.392, ii.341.
25. See Brown, *Joseph Severn*, 33.
26. See BT, 204–5. Of these four dressers, Egerton went on to become an eminent eye surgeon and professor of surgery at the Calcutta Medical College Hospital.
27. BT, 208.
28. 'Aggregate of Cases Recorded in the Monthly Registry of the Repository of the Diseases of London, between the 20th of November 1815, and the 19th of May 1816', *The London Medical Repository* (London, 1816), 44–8.
29. This account of a dresser's duties is based on MJFS, 25–7, 125; Cross, *A Surgeon in the Early Nineteenth Century*, 41; Golding, *An Historical Account of St Thomas's Hospital*, 125–6.
30. For the different surgical abilities of Cooper and Lucas, see MJFS, 52–5.
31. Reported by R.H. Horne, 'Keats at Edmonton', *Daily News* (8 April 1871).
32. *The London Medical Repository*, 21 (Sept. 1815), 251.
33. KC, ii.211.
34. *The London Medical Repository*, 34 (1 Oct. 1816), 345.
35. Coleridge's line from 'The Eolian Harp', 'The stilly murmur of the distant sea', is echoed in 'the still murmur of the honey bee' in the verse epistle 'To my Brother George', written shortly after the sonnet.
36. See Dorothy Hewlett, *A Life of John Keats: Revised and Enlarged Edition* (London, 1938), 377–81.
37. George A.R. Wilson, 'John Keats and Joshua Waddington: Contemporary Students at Guy's Hospital', typescript at KCL Archive, G/EPH3/9.
38. 'Letter VI. To B.F. Esq', *The Examiner* (11 Aug. 1816), 504.
39. LJK, i.105
40. 'Harry Brown to his Cousin Thomas Brown, Jun. Letter 1', *The Examiner* (30 June 1816), 409.

## 7 An Era

1. LJK, i.82.
2. RoK, 91.
3. See BT, 205–12.
4. LJK, i.113.
5. LJK, i.114.
6. Hunt to Cowden Clarke, 17 Oct. 1816, LHCCC, 45–6.
7. MC (24 and 30 Sept. 1816).
8. Hunt to Cowden Clarke, 17 Oct. 1816, LHCCC, 46.
9. Hunt to Cowden Clarke, 17 Oct. 1816, LHCCC, 46.
10. RoK, 91.
11. *The Examiner* (6 Oct. 1816), 631.
12. *The Letters of William and Dorothy Wordsworth*, ed. E. De Selincourt, Second Edition, *The Middle Years, Part II, 1812–1820*, rev. Mary Moorman and Alan G. Hill (Oxford, 1970), 578. 'To Benjamin Robert Haydon', *The Examiner* (20 Oct. 1816), 663.
13. *The Times* (1 Feb. 1819, 5 April 1820).
14. HD, ii.38.
15. AMBRH, i.13.
16. AMBRH, i.66–7.
17. *The Examiner* (17 March 1816), 163.
18. *The Examiner* (17 March 1816), 174.
19. *The Examiner* (2 Feb. 1812), 77. Haydon's article ran over three weeks, from 26 Jan. to 9 Feb.
20. BHCTT, i.133 n.
21. AMBRH, i.v.
22. BHCTT, i.33; *Life of Benjamin Robert Haydon*, ed. Tom Taylor (3 vols, London, 1853), i.171–2.
23. HD, ii.54–60.
24. LBsC, i.409–10.
25. LBsC, i.407–8.

26. *Feast of the Poets* (London, 1814), 125–6.
27. AMBRH, i.251.
28. RoK, 91.


## 8 Wild Surmises

1. RoK, 91.
2. *The Examiner* (25 Aug. 1816), 537.
3. The Harvard Manuscript of the sonnet, from which this transcript is taken, is the earliest and may well be Keats's first draft. For a facsimile and discussion, see *John Keats: Poetry Manuscripts at Harvard. A Facsimile Edition*, ed. Jack Stillinger (Cambridge, MA, and London, 1990), 12–13; RoK, 90; TKP, 116–17.
4. KC, i.4–6; *The Letters of John Hamilton Reynolds*, ed. Leonidas M. Jones (Lincoln, NE, 1973), 60.
5. LJK, ii.245.
6. For the Zetosophian Society, see Joseph Grigely, 'A Romantic Literary Circle', K-SMB, 33 (1982), 49–61.
7. LJK, ii.245.
8. LJK, i.204.
9. Houghton, Keats-Holman b MS Am 800.48, three volumes of manuscript notes on persons connected with Keats. For Miss Martin, see LJK, ii.66. With James Cawthorne, Martin had published Reynolds's *Safie* and Hunt's *Feast of the Poets*.
10. For Dilke and Brown, see William Garrett, *Charles Wentworth Dilke* (Boston, 1982) and E.H. McCormick, *The Friend of Keats: A Life of Charles Armitage Brown* (Wellington, New Zealand, 1989). Other Zetosophians included Keats's acquaintances Frank and William Squibb and, possibly, the painter Archibald Archer. More obscure associates were Edward Hardisty, John Burchell and William Seymour: see Grigely, 'A Romantic Literary Circle', 50–2.
11. LJK, i.114–15.
12. For this discussion of Keats's duties as a dresser, I am indebted to the excellent analysis by John Barnard in BT, 199–214, especially 206–14.
13. In short: Friday, 1 Nov. Keats met Cowden Clarke; Friday, 8 Nov. Keats and Cowden Clarke were to meet Haydon, but he cancelled to see *Timon of Athens* at Drury Lane; Monday, 18 Nov. Tom's birthday, Keats was at home with his brothers; Tuesday, 19 Nov. in the evening, Haydon sketched Keats; Wednesday, 11 Dec. Keats was with Hunt at the Vale of Health; Tuesday, 17 Dec. in the evening, Keats was at home with his brothers, Cowden Clarke, Haydon and Severn; Wednesday, 18 Dec. at Hunt's; Wednesday, 25 Dec. at home with his brothers; Monday, 30 Dec. evening, at Hunt's.
14. RoK, 87.
15. LJK, i.103
16. Quoted in correspondence from Willard B. Pope, TLS (22 Dec. 1932), 977.
17. HD, ii.107.
18. Haydon notes both Tom's and George's stories together in his journal entry for 7 April 1817: HD, ii.107.
19. KI, 78.
20. Keats loaned small sums amounting to some £230, 'which might have gradually formed a library to my taste'. See LJK, ii.54, 145.
21. This account of Keats's finances in Oct. 1816 is based on KI, 1–2, 44–8, and FF, 79–80.
22. LJK, ii.141.
23. RoK, 91.
24. *The Examiner* (3 Nov. 1816), 694.
25. *Lectures on Painting and Design* (1844), 318.
26. HD, i.351, 383.
27. HD, i.383, 397–8.
28. HD, i.452, 456–7.
29. HD, ii.54–5.
30. HD, ii.64–5.
31. LJK, i.116. Monday the 11th is another possible date for this projected meeting with Haydon; *Timon* was also staged that evening, and would have obliged him to cancel. Keats's pattern of engagements this autumn always kept Monday evenings free, however, and Friday the 8th is the more likely date for this episode.
32. LJK, i.121 n., and FF, 77.
33. LJK, ii.121.

34. *The Times* (14 Nov. 1816).
35. TKP, 122; LJK, i.121. Keats's draft, his fair copy and Tom Keats's transcript are all dated Dec. 1816.
36. LJK, i.121.
37. Leonidas M. Jones, *The Life of John Hamilton Reynolds* (Hanover and London, 1984), 101–7.
38. RoK, 91.
39. RoK, 92. Cowden Clarke mistakenly located the apartment in The Poultry, the eastern continuation of Cheapside, and he has Ironmongers' Hall instead of Mercers' Hall (which bordered Ironmonger Lane). The passageway below the apartment was probably Bird in Hand Alley. Cowden Clarke's passageway leading to the Queen's Head Tavern is Queen's Head Alley off Paternoster Row at the western extremity of Cheapside.
40. MC (24 Dec. 1817).
41. LJK, i.117.
42. LJK, i.119.
43. *William Wordsworth: The Critical Heritage Volume I, 1793-1820*, ed. Robert Woof (London and New York, 2001), 972–3.
44. *The Letters of William and Dorothy Wordsworth*, ed. E. De Selincourt, Second Edition III, *The Middle Years, Part II, 1812-1820*, rev. Mary Moorman and Alan G. Hill (Oxford, 1970), 360–1.

## 9 Saturnalia

1. 'Addressed to Haydon', i.10; LJK, i.118, 121.
2. Lawrence M. Crutcher, 'Finding the Family', K-SR, 25.1 (2011), 4–9, and *The Keats Family* (Louisville, KY, 2009), 13–15, 48 n. See also Louis A. Holman's manuscript notes on people in the Keats circle: Houghton, b. MS Am 800.48.
3. *The Examiner* (3 Nov. 1816), 694, (1 Dec. 1816), 761–2.
4. For Hunt's poem, see *Foliage; or Poems Original and Translated* (London, 1818), cxxv; for Stephens, KC, ii.211; for 'young poets', a Google search on 24 June 2011 turned up 'Young Poets Network', 'Yale Young Poets', 'Young Poet Laureate', 'Young Poets Society', 'Ted Hughes Young Poets Award', 'Young American Poets', 'Advice to Young Poets', 'New Generation Young Poets' and 'Young Poets of America'.
5. For 'ruin', see *The Examiner* (29 Sept. 1816), 610, and 'Spa-Fields Meeting', *The Examiner* (8 Dec. 1816), 777–81; flag, *The Examiner* (8 Dec. 1816), 778.
6. *The Examiner* (1 Dec. 1816), 760, (15 Dec. 1816), 785–7, (22 Dec. 1816), 801–3.
7. Arthur H. Beavan, *James and Horace Smith* (London, 1899), 136–8; *Shelley and his Circle 1773-1822*, ed. K.N. Cameron, Donald Reiman et al. (10 vols, Cambridge, MA, 1961–2002), v.404; LHA, ii.201, 202.
8. For 'necessity', see *The Examiner* (24 March 1811), 177; argument, LPBS, i.77; 'oblivion', LPBS, i.517; Harriet, LPBS, i.389–90, and FH, 211.
9. LPBS, i.517–18.
10. JMS, i.150; drowning, *The Times* (12 Dec. 1816), 2.
11. Leigh Hunt to J.W. Dalby, 29 June 1836, BLHC; RoK, 91.
12. KMA, 132–3. Keats's seaweed image resembles the fronds and leaves of Keats's doodles in his medical notebook and the curious embellishment in the Guy's register book; see p. 92 above.
13. HD, ii.328.
14. For Cowden Clarke on Keats's appearance, see RoK, 86, 99.
15. LJK, i.121.
16. BLHC, MS. LH94tay2.
17. RoK, 99.
18. LJK, ii.121, 323.
19. The publishing background of Keats's *Poems* (1817) is explored in illuminating detail by John Barnard in FF. This account is indebted to Barnard's essay.
20. For Shelley, see RN, 508. For Keats's likely costs, see John Barnard's revised figures based on the account in FF, 79. An edition of five hundred copies would have cost Keats £47.12s.7d.
21. LJK, ii.113.
22. John Dix, *Pen and Ink Sketches of Poets, Preachers, and Politicians* (London, 1846), 144.
23. KC, i.277; C. and J. Ollier to George Keats, *The Athenaeum* (7 June 1873), 725; LJK, ii.334–5. See also FF, 75–6.
24. KC, i.307.
25. For Abbey, see KC, i.307–8; for business failure, see 'Partnerships Dissolved', MP (28 Jan. 1817), 'T.M. Keats and Co., London, hat-manufacturers'.
26. KC, ii.154; RoK, 92.

27. TKP, 120.
28. TKP, 24–5.
29. TKP, 24–5, 120.
30. For Shelley, see LPBS, i.525; for Cowden Clarke, RoK, 92.
31. Both sonnets are quoted from *The Examiner* (21 Sept. 1817), 599.
32. RoK, 92.
33. See FF, 99, n. 162.

## 10 Lancet

1. See LPBS, i.527; MC (25 Jan. 1817); *The Examiner* (26 Jan. 1817), 53–4, 60; *The Times* (3 Feb. 1817), 3. Papers relating to the case are reproduced in Thomas Medwin, *The Life of Percy Bysshe Shelley: A New Edition*, introd. H. Buxton Forman (London, 1913).
2. *The Examiner* (19 Jan. 1817), 42.
3. HD, ii.80–7.
4. LJK, i.242; AMBRH, i.253–4; LJK, i.135, 138, 144.
5. *The Examiner* (23 Feb. 1817), 124; LJK, ii.167.
6. 'Hymn to Intellectual Beauty', stanza 7, *The Examiner* (19 Jan. 1817), 41.
7. FF, 89.
8. HD, ii.84; JMS, i.164.
9. JMS, i.164; LBsC, i.410. That Hunt goes on to describe 'Mr. Keats's first juvenile volume' is further evidence that the proof of the volume was handed round to Hunt's guests. Godwin's diary for this day indicates that one of the Gattie brothers may have been present, along with Charles Cowden Clarke and the journalist Walter Coulson.
10. LPBS, i.532, 534; *The Examiner* (2 March 1817), 139.
11. See FF, 78.
12. RoK, 92.
13. My account of the publication of Keats's poems and the Shakespeare vignette is indebted to John Barnard's account in FF.
14. *The Examiner* (29 Aug. 1813), 547.
15. LBsC, i.413.
16. See 'God of the golden bow', l. 25. *The Manuscripts of the Younger Romantics*, gen. ed. Donald Reiman, *John Keats*, ed. Jack Stillinger (7 vols, New York and London, 1985–8), vol. 6, *The Woodhouse Poetry Transcripts at Harvard*, 18. Hereafter cited as *Woodhouse Poetry Transcripts*.
17. *The Examiner* (2 March 1817), 138, (16 March 1817), 173. See also RoK, 92–3.
18. *The Examiner* (9 March 1817), 145.
19. FF, 90.
20. 'Architectural Innovation. No. CLXXXIV. Progress of Architecture in England in the Reign of James II', *Gentleman's Magazine* (June 1814), 557–60; *The Picture of London, for 1816* (London, 1816), 107–113; Saint Fond's response, quoted in J. Mordaunt Crook, *The British Museum* (London, 1972), 62.
21. *The Original Picture of London, Enlarged and Improved* (London, 1826), 294.
22. Quoted from the text in *The Examiner* (9 March 1817), 155.
23. Quoted from the text in *The Examiner* (9 March 1817), 155.
24. Richard Woodhouse's gloss on the poem, from *Woodhouse Poetry Transcripts*, 18.
25. Haydon seems not to have received a presentation copy at this time, and only acknowledged that 'Keats has published his first Poems' in a diary entry for 17 March 1817 (HD, ii.101). Perhaps Keats had his copy specially bound in green leather, like the ones presented some time later to Cowden Clarke and Georgiana Wylie. See FF, 101, n. 200.
26. *The Champion* (9 March 1817), 78–81, and *The Examiner* (9 March 1817), 155.
27. LJK, i.122; RoK, 93; *The Fall of Hyperion*, i.190.
28. 'Charles Brown: Life of John Keats' in KC, ii.56.
29. *Index of English Literary Manuscripts*, Vol. 4: *1800–1900: Part 2, Hardy-Lamb* (London and New York, 1990), 343. Copies given to Charles Brown and Isabella Jane Towers were not inscribed.
30. LJK, i.127; KC, ii.267; Patrick O'Leary, *Regency Editor: The Life of John Scott* (Aberdeen, 1983), 98; KC, i.308.
31. Edmund Blunden, *Keats's Publisher: A Memoir of John Taylor (1781-1864)* (London, 1936), 25; C.H. Reynell, quoted in *ibid.*, 42.
32. The three reviews are reproduced in KCH, 45–54.

33. LJK, i.123–5. These events are reconstructed from three letters: Keats to Reynolds, 9 March 1817; Haydon to Keats, undated but circa March 1817; Keats to Reynolds, 17 March 1817.
34. Thomas Medwin, *The Life of Percy Bysshe Shelley: A New Edition*, introd. H. Buxton Forman (London, 1913), 179; LJK, i.170.
35. LJK, i. 126–7.
36. DM, annotating LLL, i. 188.
37. HD, ii.106–8.
38. For the agreement, see Blunden, *Keats's Publisher*, 42; for Keats's inscription, Caroline F.E. Spurgeon, *Keats's Shakespeare: A Descriptive Study* (Oxford, 1928), opposite p. 2; 'great good', LJK, i.125.

## 11 Strange Journeys

1. The coach timetable and route are taken from *Cary's New Itinerary* (London, 1817).
2. LJK, i.170.
3. LJK, i.154.
4. LJK, i.128, 140.
5. For troop ships, see *The Times* (15 April 1817), 2; LJK, i.132. I am grateful to Damian Walford Davies and Robert Barber for information about the tides at Southampton on 15 April 1817; LJK, i.132.
6. LJK, i.132; *Endymion*, iv.411.
7. LJK, i.132, 133.
8. LJK, i.132.
9. LJK, i.262.
10. LJK, i.262, where Ernest De Selincourt's remark on 'Nature's cruelty' is quoted. For the 'throat of Orcus', see book six of *The Aeneid*.
11. LJK, i.133.
12. LJK, i.158.
13. LJK, i.134.
14. LJK, i.13.
15. LJK, i.138.
16. LJK, i.135.
17. LJK, i.139, 141–2.
18. *The Athenaeum* (7 June 1873), 725.
19. For sales, see the original preface to *Endymion*, PJK, 738–9; 'nettle leaf', LJK, i.142; see also Charles E. Robinson, 'Percy Bysshe Shelley, Charles Ollier, and William Blackwood', *Shelley Revalued: Essays from the Gregynog Conference*, ed. Kelvin Everest (Leicester, 1983), 215 n. 19, and RN, 611. In 1824 Charles Ollier publicly praised *The Eve of St Agnes* as 'one of the most enchanting gems of literature': see Hyder E. Rollins, 'Charles Ollier and Keats', *Notes & Queries* (March 1953), 118.
20. LJK, i.142–3. In Rollins's view, James Ollier was the brother who wrote the letter disclaiming any connection with Keats.
21. LJK, i.142.
22. 'On Mr. Kean's Iago', *The Round Table: A Collection of Essays on Literature, Men and Manners* (2 vols, Edinburgh, 1817), i.57.
23. KC, i.307; LJK, i.142, 292.
24. LHA, ii.202–3.
25. LJK, i.169–70.
26. LJK, i.148.
27. LJK, i.146–7.
28. HD, i.392–3, 395.
29. Robert Gittings, 'More about Mrs. Jones', MoK, 45–7.
30. See MoK, 45–7; 'Frances Cairnes Murray' on the website www.the peerage.com; and 'Jones, of Bealanamore and Headfort', *A Genealogical and Heraldic History of the Commoners of Great Britain and Ireland* (4 vols, London, 1836), iii. 267–9.
31. W.G. Moss, *History and Antiquities of the Town and Port of Hastings* (London, 1824), 148; MoK, 47; JKLY, 233; and 'Fashionable Changes', MP (23 July 1814). See also Blunden, *Keats's Publisher*, 96–7. The Hon. Mrs Jones died at Hastings, aged eighty-six, in 1827: see *The Age* (11 Feb. 1827), 48.
32. Gittings Papers, West Sussex Record Office, Chichester, Add. MS. 46508.
33. Blunden, *Keats's Publisher*, 96–7.
34. JKLY, 230; LJK, i.402–3.
35. LJK, i.403; *Lamia*, i.8.

36. Woodhouse's transcript of 'You say you love' is annotated 'from Miss Reynolds' in ink, followed by 'and Mrs. Jones' in pencil (John Taylor had a copy taken from a manuscript in the possession of Mrs Jones, and Woodhouse had seen and noted variant lines in it). *The Manuscripts of the Younger Romantics*, gen. ed. Donald Reiman, *John Keats*, ed. Jack Stillinger (7 vols, New York and London, 1985–8), vol. 3, *Endymion (1818), a Facsimile of Richard Woodhouse's Annotated Copy in the Berg Collection*, 224. Hereafter, *Endymion Facsimile*.
37. JKLY, 230–5; Blunden, *Keats's Publisher*, 96–7.
38. 'Ceylon' in *The Times* (11 Jan. 1819).
39. The inquest into Isabella Jones's terrible death is noted in *Jackson's Oxford Journal* (18 March 1843).
40. LJK, i.147; subscription, *The Times* (29 March 1821), 1; Taylor's poems, Mabel A.E. Steele, 'The Authorship of "The Poet" and Other Sonnets', K-SJ, 5 (Winter 1956), 75–6.
41. LJK, i.402.

## 12 Fellowship

1. *The Examiner* (1 June 1817), 345.
2. *The Examiner* (6 July 1817), 428–9, (13 July 1817), 443–4.
3. PJK, 125 n., LJK, i.218.
4. LJK, i.218 n; for a summary of neo-Platonic and other interpretations, see Newell F. Ford, 'The Meaning of "Fellowship with Essence" in *Endymion*', PMLA, 62.4 (Dec. 1947), 1061–76.
5. *Critical Essays*, 30–1.
6. LJK, i.218.
7. LJK, i.125–6.
8. See 'Dilke and the Keats Circle', in William Garrett, *Charles Wentworth Dilke* (Boston, 1982), and, for meetings with the Keats brothers, KC, ii.104–5. The story that Brown and Dilke actually built the house is untrue. The rate books link two names, Burke and Robinson, with the house from November 1815 to June 1816; it seems likely that they purchased an interest in the two parts but did not occupy the house, and then sold it on to Brown and Dilke, who moved in between June and October 1816. I am grateful to Ken Page for this information.
9. KC, ii.105.
10. KC, i.lvi.
11. Gillian Iles, 'New Information on Charles Brown', K-SJ, 40 (1991), 161–2.
12. See Keats's 'Character of C.B.', PJK, 326–7, and LCAB, 1.
13. LJK, i.159.
14. LHCCC, 49; LJK, i.135, ii.11 n.; MC (27 Aug. 1817); MP (27 Aug. 1817).
15. RoK, 93.
16. LJK, i.207. Keats may also have recollected Lemprière's note about Aeneas's 'submission to the will of the gods'.
17. LJK, i.148–9.
18. See the *New DNB* entry on George Robert Gleig (1796–1888); *Quarterly Review* (Oct. 1864), 447; LLP, 34.
19. Bailey to R.M. Milnes, KC, ii.270.
20. *The Manuscripts of the Younger Romantics*, gen. ed. Donald Reiman, *John Keats*, ed. Jack Stillinger (7 vols, New York and London, 1985–8), vol. 4, *Poems, Transcripts, Letters &c. Facsimiles of Richard Woodhouse's Scrapbook Materials in the Pierpoint Morgan Library*, 196. Hereafter cited as *John Keats, Poems, Transcripts, Letters*.
21. See *The Picture of London, for 1816* (London, 1816), 107–13.
22. LJK, i.150, 154, 161, 167. For Paris, see Charles Brown to C.W. Dilke, 20 Jan. 1830, LCAB, 304.
23. LJK, i.162–3.
24. LJK, i.154, 166, 168.
25. See Hewlett, *A Life of John Keats*, 242, for Thomasine Leigh, 'to whom, her grand-daughter said, according to family gossip, Bailey had proposed'.
26. KC, ii.271–2.
27. LJK, i.168–71; Lowell, i.515–16.

## 13 'Z'

1. LJK, i.159, 171; Rossetti, *Life of John Keats*, 24 and n; B.W. Robinson, 'An Esculapian Poet: John Keats', *The Asclepiad* (London, 1884), 143.
2. Richard Carmichael, *Observations on the Symptoms and Specific Distinctions of Venereal Diseases [and] the Uses and Abuses of Mercury* (London, 1818), 13–14; James Bedingfield, *A Compendium*

*of Medical Practice* (London, 1818), 293–4; 'Sir Astley Cooper on Syphilis', *The Lancet*, 1823–4 (3rd edn, 2 vols, London 1826), 394, 395, 397, 399. For Gittings's view, JK, 449.

3. 'Sir Astley Cooper on Syphilis', 392; JK, 449; Motion, *Keats* (London, 1997), 197.
4. LJK, i.172, 174.
5. George Keats's recollection, KC, i.288; Carmichael, *Observations on the Symptoms*, 215; Abbey, KC, i.305; Hunt, LBsC, i.408–9.
6. JK, 449.
7. LJK, ii.321.
8. Oxford University Archives, UR3/1/2/1. For yawning bishops, see LJK, i.178.
9. Oxford University Archives, UR3/1/1/1.
10. KC, ii.292.
11. LJK, i.210.
12. LJK, i.123; *An Essay on the Principles of Human Action: Being an Argument in Favour of the Natural Disinterestedness of the Human Mind* (London, 1805), 1, 263.
13. LJK, i.173–4.
14. LJK, i.184.
15. LJK, i.184–5.
16. LJK, i.186.
17. *Eclectic Review* (Sept. 1817), reprinted JKCH, 67; *Edinburgh Magazine and Literary Miscellany (Scots Magazine)* (Oct. 1817), reprinted JKCH, 71–4. Keats's response, LJK, i.180.
18. This and subsequent extracts in this paragraph are from 'On the Cockney School of Poetry. No I', *Blackwood's Edinburgh Magazine* (Oct. 1817), 38–41.
19. Andrew Lang, MS letter to Edmund Gosse, 24 April 1896, bound into LLP at pp. 48–9.
20. For Keats's suspicions of Ollier, see DM, annotating LLL, i.198. For Hunt, *The Examiner* (2 Nov. 1817), 693; LJK, i.217 and n.
21. LJK, i.168, 181–2.
22. For Kosciusko, see MC (31 Oct. 1817) and *The Examiner* (2 Nov. 1817), 690–1.
23. *The Examiner* (9 Nov. 1817), 705; LJK, i.183.
24. JMS, i.185.
25. LLP, 199.
26. LLP, 196.
27. 'Chatterton', *Notes and Queries* (24 Aug. 1872), 157.
28. *The Examiner* (9 Nov. 1817), 715–17.
29. See 'Bristowe Tragedie or the Dethe of Syr Charles Bawdin', ll.373–6, in *The Complete Works of Thomas Chatterton*, ed. Donald S. Taylor (2 vols, Oxford, 1971), i.19.
30. LJK, i.186.
31. LJK, i.189.
32. *A Picturesque Promenade Round Dorking, in Surrey* (London, 1822), 237–9.

## 14 Immortal Dinners

1. LJK, i.192 n. For the mild air at Teignmouth, see *Croydon's Guide to the Watering Places on the Coast between the Exe and the Dart* (Teignmouth, 1817), 16.
2. LJK, i.118; *Princeton University Library Chronicle*, 38 (Winter–Spring 1977), plate 40, opposite p. 236. See also *William Wordsworth: The Critical Heritage, Volume 1,1793-1820*, ed. Robert Woof (London and New York, 2001), 973.
3. LJK, i.203.
4. T.O. Mabbott, 'Haydon's Letter Arranging for Keats to Meet Wordsworth', *Notes and Queries* (10 May 1941), 328–9.
5. *The Letters of William and Dorothy Wordsworth, The Middle Years, Part II, 1812-1820*, 405, 406.
6. KC, ii.142–3.
7. Stanley Jones, 'B.R. Haydon on Some Contemporaries: A New Letter', *Review of English Studies*, 26.102 (May 1975), 189.
8. See also Penelope Hughes-Hallet, *The Immortal Dinner. A Famous Evening of Genius and Laughter in Literary London, 1817* (London, 2000), 69.
9. MC (19 Dec. 1817). That Lamb saw the verses in the trial report is suggested by his letter to Mary Wordsworth, 18 Feb. 1818, where he speaks of being so much in company he is 'never C.L. but always C.L. and Co'. See *The Letters of Charles and Mary Lamb*, ed. E.V. Lucas (3 vols, London, 1938), ii.226.

10. See Wordsworth's letters to Lord Lonsdale of 13 Dec. 1817, 1 Jan. 1818, and 23 March 1818, *The Letters of William and Dorothy Wordsworth, The Middle Years, Part II, 1812–1820*, 404–5, 407, 443.

11. MP (16 Dec. 1817); MC (16 Dec. 1817); LJK, i.191.

12. LHA, ii.17.

13. LJK, i.193. See also John Barnard, ' "The Immortal Dinner" Again', *Charles Lamb Bulletin*, NS 127 (July 2004), 70–6.

14. *Riches: or, The Wife and Brother, a Play* (London, 1810), 13–14.

15. *The Poetical Works of Coleridge, Shelley, and Keats. Complete in One Volume* (Paris, 1829); John Keats, *Poems, Transcripts, Letters*, 259 and n.

16. *The Poetical Works and Other Writings of John Keats*, ed. H. Buxton Forman (8 vols, New York, 1938–9), v.227.

17. *Critical Essays on the Performers of the London Theatres* (London, 1807), 2, 16.

18. 'Fine Arts', *The Times* (13 Dec. 1817), 3.

19. LJK, i.192. West was seventy-nine in 1818.

20. LJK, i.196 and Jones, *Life of John Hamilton Reynolds*, 128–9.

21. *The Champion* (4 Jan. 1818), *The Poetical Works and Other Writings of John Keats*, v. 247.

22. LJK, i.193.

23. 'On Posthumous Fame', *Round Table*, i.76.

24. See *The Letters of Charles and Mary Lamb*, ii.221.

25. For Haydon's dinner, unless otherwise indicated quotations are from HD, ii.173–6.

26. For Scott's response to *Poems* (1817), see p. 154. Mrs Scott (Caroline Colnaghi) was also an early admirer and wrote to Haydon on 19 July 1817 of the 'true poetry' in *Poems*. See *The Letters of John Keats*, ed. M.B. Forman (4th edn, London, 1952), xv.

27. Joseph Ritchie to Richard Garnett, Houghton, b MS. Keats 10 (881).

28. AMBRH, i.271.

29. LJK, i.198.

30. Haydon to Wordsworth, 16 Oct. 1842, *Haydon Correspondence*, ii.54.

31. *Haydon Correspondence*, ii.54; LJK, i.198; Barnard, ' "The Immortal Dinner" Again', 72–5.

32. See *The Letters of Charles and Mary Lamb*, ii.228.

33. See, for example, 'House of Commons', MP (28 Feb. 1815); 'House of Lords', MC (1 March 1816).

34. See Wordsworth's letter to John Kingston, 2 Feb. 1818, *The Letters of William and Dorothy Wordsworth, The Middle Years, Part II, 1812–1820*, 421.

35. Charles Lamb, 'The South-Sea House', *Essays of Elia* (London, 1883), 3.

36. *The Poetical Works and Other Writings of John Keats*, v.247–56.

37. His premises at 236 Piccadilly are listed in *Kent's Original London Directory* (London, 1816), 274. Reddell had sold up and auctioned his stock in Nov. 1817: MC (30 Oct. 1817).

38. LJK, i.200–1, ii.13.

39. LJK, i.198, 231, 232.

40. LJK, i.232–3.

41. LJK, i.238–9.

42. LJK, i.197.

43. LJK, i.251, 265; RoK, 97; *The Letters of Sara Hutchinson, 1800–1835*, ed. Kathleen Coburn (London, 1954), 133.

44. LJK, i.202.

45. LJK, i.216. See also David Worrall, *The Politics of Romantic Theatricality, 1787–1832: The Road to the Stage* (Basingstoke, 2007), 44–6, and Malcolm Morley and George Speaight, 'The Minor Theatre in Catherine Street', *Theatre Notebook*, 18 (1964), 117–20.

46. Thomas Landseer, *Life and Letters of William Bewick* (2 vols, London, 1871), i.41.

47. LJK, i.204–7.

48. LJK, i.204, 208.

49. LJK, i.207.

50. LJK, i.210.

51. LJK, i. 210.

52. *John Keats. Poetry Manuscripts at Harvard. A Facsimile Edition*, ed. Jack Stillinger (Cambridge, MA, and London, 1990), 60–1.

53. LJK, i.211; 'Father of', as in the Harvard manuscript of the poem.

54. LJK, i.214–15.

55. LJK, i.214–15.

56. 'On Shakespeare and Milton', *The Selected Writings of William Hazlitt*, ed. Duncan Wu (9 vols, London, 1998), ii.206–7, 208, 213.

57. See *The Examiner* (21 Dec. 1817), 800–3, (28 Dec. 1817), 817–19, (4 Jan. 1818), 1–3.
58. LJK, i.222.
59. See Richard Woodhouse's note on the poem in *Woodhouse Poetry Transcripts,* 416.
60. *Robin Hood: A Collection of All the Ancient Poems, Songs and Ballads,* ed. Joseph Ritson (2 vols, London, 1795), i.xi–xii.
61. *Selected Writings of William Hazlitt,* ii.297; for Reynolds's sonnet, see JKCD, 147–8.
62. LJK, i.227, and see Hyder E. Rollins, 'Charles Ollier and Keats', *Notes and Queries* (March 1953), 118.
63. LJK, i.239.
64. *The Selected Writings of William Hazlitt,* ii.241.
65. *The Selected Writings of William Hazlitt,* ii.278–9.
66. See the early sonnet 'Oh Chatterton!'.
67. LJK, i.237 and *Croydon's Guide to the Watering Places,* 22.
68. KI, 49.
69. LJK, i.236; KC, i.12.
70. LJK, i.282; MP (3 March 1818). See also *Life and Times of Frederick Reynolds* (2 vols, London, 1827), ii.249.

## 15 Dark Passages

1. LJK, i.244. For damage at Honiton, see MC (10 March 1818); for delays to mail coaches, MC (7 March 1818) and MP (9 March 1818). Storm at Teignmouth reported in the *Royal Cornwall Gazette* (14 March 1818).
2. *Croydon's Guide to the Watering Places*; LJK, i.241.
3. Keats was echoing the review of his *Poems* in the *Eclectic Review* (Sept. 1817), where the 'promise' of his poetry was said to vanish like 'the Will o' the Wisp'. KCH, 68.
4. LJK, i.248.
5. LJK, i.249–51.
6. To James Hessey, conjecturally dated to March 1818. *The Letters of John Hamilton Reynolds,* ed. Jones, 11.
7. LJK, i.256–7. On slang in this letter, see JK, Appendix 4.
8. LJK, i.259.
9. For Keats and Claude, see KMA, 128–9, 220–1. See also Robert Woof and Stephen Hebron, *John Keats* (Grasmere, 1995), 127. LJK, i.260.
10. LJK, i.262.
11. LJK, i.262–3.
12. LJK, i.258, 264, 265.
13. LJK, i.266–7.
14. RN, 611.
15. Lowell, ii.579.
16. LJK, i.262, 270–1.
17. LJK, i.274.
18. From Woodhouse's clerk's transcript of Keats's letter to Reynolds, 3 May 1818, in *Woodhouse Poetry Transcripts,* 241.
19. LJK, i.279.
20. See Robert Gittings on Keats and Hamlet in JK, 209–10.
21. LJK, ii.174.
22. See 'Richard Woodhouse: Notes on Keats's Life', KC, i.274.
23. See 'Keats's Source for *Isabella*', in *Woodhouse Poetry Transcripts,* 354–8.
24. LJK, i.293, 341–2, ii.12
25. LJK, i.342; 'Incidents of my Life', JSLM, 583
26. LJK, i.281.
27. LJK, i.281.
28. LJK, i.284.
29. 'Autumnal Musings', *Poems by Mrs. I.S. Prowse* (London, 1830), 4.
30. LJK, i.290.
31. LJK, i.287.
32. Morris Birkbeck, *Letters from Illinois* (London, 1818), 4; LJK, i.287.
33. LJK, i.286, 293.
34. LJK, i.287, 291, 341, 343. For the four-month tour, see LJK, i.342.
35. JKCD, 79–81.

36. Olive M. Taylor, 'John Taylor, Author and Publisher 1781–1864', *The London Mercury*, ed. J.C. Squire, 12.69 (July, 1925), 258.
37. Lyle H. Kendall, Jr., 'John Murray to J.W. Croker: An Unpublished Letter on Keats', K-SJ, 12 (Winter 1963), 8.
38. KC, i.20, 26–7, 228.
39. LJK, i.292–4.
40. *British Critic* (June 1818), JKCH, 91–6; *The Champion* (June 1818), KCH, 87–90.
41. *The Times* (3 April 1818), 3 and *The Examiner* (12 April 1818), 236.
42. LJK, i.301.
43. LJK, i.402.
44. See KI, 44–6 and 78, and George Keats's letter of 10 April 1824 at KC, i.276–81. For snuff, LJK, i.289–91.
45. LJK, i.295–7.
46. Details about the Brawne and Ricketts families are from FBB.
47. LJK, i.312–13.
48. LJK, i.297.
49. LJK, i.302 n., 317 n., 327 n., 346 n.

## 16 Walking North

1. KC, ii.212.
2. *Gore's General Advertiser* (28 May 1818) and records of emigrants and ship's manifest for the *Telegraph* in the National Archives of the United States. I thank Carol Kyros Walker for generously sharing this information.
3. *Traveller's Guide through Scotland, and its Islands. Illustrated by Maps, Views of Remarkable Buildings, &c.* (7th edn, 2 vols, Edinburgh, 1818), hereafter *Traveller's Guide through Scotland*. See WNK, 17.
4. CBWN, 423.
5. *The Examiner* (5 July 1818), 418.
6. See Carol Kyros Walker's good suggestion, WNK, 12.
7. See LJK, i.311, and CBWN, 424–5.
8. LJK, i.299.
9. *The Excursion, Being a Portion of The Recluse, A Poem* (London, 1814), 172.
10. LJK, i.300–1.
11. CBWN, 429.
12. LJK, i.301.
13. Brown noted Keats's expression in his projected life of the poet, but then deleted the passage. See E.H. McCormick, *The Friend of Keats. A Life of Charles Armitage Brown* (Wellington, New Zealand, 1989), 21
14. CBWN, 431.
15. For the Oak Inn, see WNK, 158, n. 5; for Keswick, CBWN, 431–3; LJK, i.306.
16. LJK, i.307.
17. LJK, i.309, CBWN, 435.
18. LJK, i.308–9. For Brown on Dumfries, see CBWN, 439.
19. LCAB, 37, and LJK, i.330–1.
20. LJK, i.323.
21. LJK, i.436.
22. CBWN, 439.
23. LJK, i.312–15.
24. KC, ii.54.
25. LJK, i.344.
26. LJK, i.318; *Traveller's Guide through Scotland*, i.238.
27. LJK, i.318–19.
28. LJK, i.319.
29. LJK, i.321–2.
30. LJK, i.328–9.
31. LJK, i.331.
32. LJK, i.331.
33. LJK, i.323, 331.
34. LJK, i.322–3, 331–2.
35. LJK, i.325.

36. LJK, i.332. For 'Resolution and Independence', see *William Wordsworth*, ed. Stephen Gill (Oxford, 1984), 260–4.

37. LJK, i.325.

38. 'For a' that and a' that' and 'The Fornicator. A New Song' from *The Poems and Songs of Robert Burns*, ed. James Kinsley (3 vols, Oxford, 1968), ii.762–3; i.101–2.

39. LJK, i.332.

40. LJK, i.334.

41. LJK, i.334–5.

42. Thanks to John Strachan for information about the Broughton rules.

43. *The Times* (4 July 1818).

44. LJK, i.336–7. For Enfield, see act four of *The Stranger: A Comedy. Freely Translated from Kotzebue's German Comedy of Misanthropy and Repentance* (2nd edn, London, 1798), 48.

45. LJK, i.338.

46. LCAB, 39; LJK, i.39.

47. Carlisle Bishops' Register, DRC 1/8, 379. My thanks to Jim Grisenthwaite of Cumbria County Council for this information.

48. LJK, i.337–8.

49. LJK, i.339.

50. Equivalent to roughly £310 in 2010.

51. LJK, i.346.

52. LJK, i.345.

53. LJK, i.341–2.

54. LJK, i.346.

55. KC, i.34.

56. KC, i.25.

57. KC, i.34–5.

58. KC, i.246. For 'Hunt delivered', see *Blackwood's Edinburgh Magazine* (July, 1818), 456.

59. KC, i.35.

60. Derry-na-Cullen was inhabited and worked as a farm until the 1940s; it is now an isolated ruin beside a tumultuous stream, surrounded by forests. See also LCAB, 40 and LJK, i.347.

61. LJK, i.348.

62. 'The War of Caros: A Poem', *The Poems of Ossian* (2 vols, Edinburgh, 1805), i.249.

63. See WNK, 199 n.

64. LJK, i.348–50.

65. LJK, i.351, 352, 362.

66. LJK, i.357–8.

67. LJK, i.354.

68. LJK, i.351–8, 264.

69. LJK, i.354.

70. *Hyperion*, i.22.

71. LJK, i.362.

72. Here I am indebted to Angus Graham-Campbell's fine essay 'Beauly Priory and *The Eve of St Agnes*', K-SMB, 26 (1975), 5–10.

73. LJK, i.361–2.

74. LCAB, 41 n., 43.

## 17 Sleepless Nights

1. Sir Charles Dilke, *Papers of a Critic* (2 vols, London, 1875), i.5.

2. Dilke, *Papers of a Critic*, i.5.

3. LJK, i.406.

4. LJK, i.386.

5. LJK, i.364, 365, 368, 375, 386, 391.

6. Brown, *Life of Keats*, KC, ii.73; LJK, i.369, 391.

7. LJK, i.366, 367, 372–3, 393.

8. LJK, i.366, 369, 394, 369.

9. All quotations are from 'Cockney School of Poetry. No IV', *Blackwood's Edinburgh Magazine* (Aug. 1818), 519–24.

10. LJK, i.368; *The Times* (21 Sept. 1818).

11. For Hessey on Keats, see Blunden, *Keats's Publisher*, 56.

12. LJK, i.394–6.

13. LJK, i.370, 395.
14. LJK, i.396.
15. 'Nature withheld Cassandra in the skies', quoted from Woodhouse's transcript, *Woodhouse Poetry Transcripts*, 257.
16. LJK, i.207.
17. LJK, i.374.
18. LJK, i.380.
19. LJK, ii.108.
20. *The Examiner* (3 Jan. 1819).
21. *Hyperion*, iii.5, 6; LJK, i.391.
22. 'THE QUARTERLY REVIEW, No. XXXVII. Will be published on SATURDAY the 26th', MP (24 Sept. 1818); KC, i.44.
23. JKCH, 110–14.
24. MC (Saturday, 3 Oct. and Thursday, 8 Oct.).
25. 'The Quarterly Review,—Mr. Keats', *The Examiner* (11 Oct. 1818), 648–9; KC, i.42.
26. MC (27 July 1821). For a full discussion of Cowden Clarke's letter to the *Morning Chronicle*, to which my account is indebted, see John Barnard, 'Keats's Sleepless Night: Charles Cowden Clarke's Letter of 1821', *Romanticism*, 16.3 (2010), 267–78. See also RoK, 96.
27. LJK, i.374.
28. LPBS, ii.284, and BLJ, viii. 102.
29. Barnard, 'Keats's Sleepless Night', 274.
30. KC, i.52–3; MC (13 and 30 Oct. 1818).
31. LJK, i.392–8.
32. LJK, i.402–3. For Mrs Green as the wife of Lieutenant-Colonel Thomas Green of the 6th Regiment, Native Infantry, Madras Regiment, see JKLY, 32 and KC, i.76. See also an alternative conjunction of Mrs Jones and Mrs Green in 'Extract of a Letter from Ceylon, Dated Candy, June 16, 1818': 'Amongst the ... officers who have already died of the fever are Captain Jones ... and many others; ... Poor ... Mrs. Jones ... and Mrs. Green are widows.' *The Times* (11 Jan. 1819).
33. LJK, i.402–3.
34. Thanks to Simon Bainbridge for the link between busts of Napoleon and Holland House. Hazlitt's Sarah Walker also owned a small bronze bust of Napoleon, smashed by her would-be lover.
35. LJK, i.402–3.
36. LJK, i.380–1.
37. LJK, i.387.
38. See Barnard, 'Keats's Sleepless Night', 274.
39. LJK, i.374.
40. LJK, i.387; TKP, 230.
41. LJK, i.405.
42. DM, annotating LLL, i.240.
43. LJK, ii.16–17 and n.; for Rice, see LJK, i.406–7. P. Fenbank, obviously a pseudonym, has been identified as Richard Woodhouse or Keats's Teignmouth friend Marian Jeffrey: LJK, ii.16–17 n.
44. KC, ii.64–5.


## 18 ditto, ditto

1. See LCAB, 250, for Keats's living expenses with Brown.
2. Information from Wentworth Place maintenance officer Mr John May, Oct. 2009. Mr Albert Lee, caretaker of the house in 1965, told curator Christina M. Gee of the original water supply through interconnecting wooden pipes. I am grateful to Ken Page for further details about amenities in the house.
3. See Fanny Brawne's letter to Fanny Keats, 7 May 1822, LFBFK, 47. Further details about Wentworth Place and its garden from *The Times* (26 Oct. 1821): 'HAMPSTEAD.—To be Let, on Lease, a small Cottage, pleasantly situate, containing 2 parlours, 3 bed rooms, and 2 kitchens; together with a large sized garden, well stocked with ornamental and useful trees; terms 50l. per annum; fixtures about 20l.; taxes moderate; the greater part of the furniture may be taken at a valuation.' This was probably Dilke's advertisement as it refers to three bedrooms and Brown only had two, and the garden was Dilke's rather than Brown's, although they shared the use of it. My thanks to Ken Page for this information.
4. LJK, ii.8.
5. LJK, i.411–12.

6. MP (7 Dec. 1818); MC (7 Dec. 1818).
7. LJK, ii.80 and RoK, 95.
8. See LJK, i.411 and 413–14.
9. LJK, i.412.
10. LJK, i.411, 412.
11. LJK, ii.8.
12. DM annotating LLL, i.240.
13. LFBFK, 1.
14. See FBB, 22–3, and LFBFK, 1, 36, 39.
15. LJK, ii.13.
16. LJK, ii.59.
17. LJK, ii.132.
18. LFBFK, 41, 25–6.
19. LJK, ii.59.
20. LJK, ii.65, 82.
21. LJK, i.415.
22. LJK, ii.19.
23. LJK, ii.7, 27–8.
24. JK, 271.
25. As proposed by Robert Gittings to Jean Haynes, 29 June 1964. Haynes Papers in LMA at K/MS/04/028/2.
26. 'Law Intelligence', MP (18 Dec. 1818); 'Bankrupts', MP (25 Jan. 1819); 'Bankrupts', The Examiner (24 Jan. 1819), 55.
27. 'Mirror of Fashion', MC (21 Dec. 1818); 'Died', The Times (14 Jan. 1819); 'Sales by Auction', MC (12 June 1819 and 7 Sept. 1820).
28. LJK, ii.32.
29. LJK, ii.32.
30. Robert Burton, The Anatomy of Melancholy, ed. Holbrook Jackson (1621; New York, 2001), 'The Third Partition', 181.
31. 'Conjunction 1980', Gittings Papers, West Sussex Record Office, Chichester, Add. MS. 45, 537. I am grateful to John Gittings for permission to quote Robert Gittings's poem.
32. 'Standing Apart', script for BBC Radio 3, broadcast 23 Feb. 1971, Gittings Papers, West Sussex Record Office, Chichester, Add. MSS. 42, 137.
33. Lulke, Papers of a Critic, 18.
34. Emlyn Thomas, Georgian Chichester. Volume 1 (Middleton on Sea, 2000), 63.
35. LJK, ii.59.
36. For old Mr Dilke's interests, see Houghton, Keats-Holman bMS Am 888.48 volume 1, an annotated list of persons significant to Keats.
37. The poem in the Literary Pocket Book appears in JKLY, 58–9.
38. Poster advertising the sale of the Old Mill House and Bedhampton Mill, 24 Dec. 1796, at Havant Museum; 'Flour Mill at Bedhampton', notice of sale in The Times (30 April 1864).
39. Quoted from Keats's draft of The Eve of St Agnes, John Keats Poetry Manuscripts at Harvard. A Facsimile Edition, ed. Jack Stillinger (Cambridge, MA and London, 1990), 130–1.
40. Mateo Alemán, The Rogue, or, The Life of Guzman de Alfarache, tr. James Mabb (3rd edn, London, 1634), 22.
41. See JK, 210.
42. John Keats Poetry Manuscripts at Harvard, 116–18.
43. RoK, 94.
44. John Keats Poetry Manuscripts at Harvard, 130–1.
45. John Keats Poetry Manuscripts at Harvard, 126.
46. LJK, ii.60.
47. Sussex Weekly Advertiser (18 Jan. 1819).
48. LJK, ii.63.
49. John Keats Poetry Manuscripts at Harvard, 102, 110. The fullest account of Keats at Stansted is in JKLY, 75–82.
50. MP (26 Aug. 1811).
51. Diary of John Marsh, 23 Jan. 1819. West Sussex Record Office, MF 1169. He attended the consecration and recorded high winds and rain on the day.
52. A.M.W. Stirling, The Ways of Yesterday Being the Chronicles of the Way Family from 1307 to 1885 (London, 1930); Phylliss G. Mann, 'New Light on Keats and his Family', K-SMB, 11 (1960), 33–8.
53. KC, i.305.

## 19 Ever Indolent

1. LJK, i.198, ii.41.
2. James Montgomery, 'The Vigil of St. Mark', *The Poetical Works of James Montgomery* (3 vols, London, 1836), i.254.
3. LJK, ii.201.
4. See JKLY, 86–92; LJK, i.402. For Keats's continuation of the Chatterton passage, see PJK, 633–4.
5. LJK, ii.62.
6. LJK, ii.41, 42–3, 54. See also KI, 52.
7. *The Examiner* (7 and 14 Feb. 1819), 83–4, 93–4, 102.
8. LJK, ii.58–66.
9. As Gittings conjectured; JK, 291.
10. Blunden, *Keats's Publisher*, 96–7.
11. LJK, ii.67.
12. LJK, i.210, ii.90–1.
13. LJK, ii.69, 70, 77.
14. LJK, ii.78.
15. LJK, ii.20, 42, 51, 58, 66, 77.
16. See LJK, ii.42, 51, 64; AMBRH, i.301–2; KC, ii.73; *Confessions of an English Opium-Eater 1821–1856*, ed. Grevel Lindop, *The Works of Thomas De Quincey* (21 vols, London, 2000–2003), ii.98, 249.
17. LJK, ii.78–9
18. See Alethea Hayter, *Opium and the Romantic Imagination* (London, 1968), 308–11, and *Christabel: Kubla Khan, A Vision: The Pains of Sleep, by S.T. Coleridge, Esq.* (London, 1816), 52.
19. See Hayter, *Opium and the Romantic Imagination*, 307.
20. LJK, ii.91.
21. LJK, ii.88–9. This was Sunday, 11 April.
22. For Keats's meeting with Coleridge, see LJK, ii.88–9.
23. LJK, ii.78–9.
24. LJK, ii.108.
25. LJK, ii.79, 81, 91.
26. See Garrett, *Charles Wentworth Dilke*, 11; KI, 38 and LCAB, 306.
27. LJK, ii.84.
28. LJK, ii.95–6.
29. KC, ii.120; *The Indicator* (10 May 1820), 248.
30. 'To a Mountain-Daisy', *Poems, Chiefly in the Scottish Dialect* (Kilmarnock, 1786), 171.
31. *The Indicator* (10 May 1820), 248.
32. LJK, ii.101–3, 210.
33. *Endymion Facsimile*, 426.
34. LJK, ii.103–4.
35. LJK, ii.105–6; BC; KMA, 128–9.
36. 'Ode to Psyche' is quoted from the letter to the George Keatses, 30 April 1819, LJK, ii.106–8.
37. *The Poetical Works of John Milton* (4 vols, London, 1807), iv.21.
38. LHA, ii.148.
39. *Juvenilia: or, a Collection of Poems. Written between the Ages of Twelve and Sixteen, by J.H.L. Hunt* (London, 1802), 28–9.
40. 'Monthly Agricultural Report', MC (1 May and 1 June 1819); 'The Season', *Bristol Mercury* (17 May 1819).
41. 'Calendar of Nature. *(From the Literary Pocket-Book.)* May', *The Examiner* (9 May 1819), 297, 303–4.
42. LJK, ii.56–7, 109–10.
43. LJK, ii.111–20.
44. For a helpful summary of various interpretations, see *The Poems of John Keats*, ed. Miriam Allott (London, 1970), 537–8.
45. LJK, ii.252–3.

## 20 Hope and Chance

1. LJK, ii.112, 122, 126, 127, 138, 128; LFBFK, 26.
2. LJK, ii.116, 141, 120.

3. HD, ii.226; LJK, ii.120, 206.

4. Burton, *The Anatomy of Melancholy*, 'The Third Partition', 46–7.

5. LJK, ii.189.

6. LJK, ii.160.

7. LJK, ii.139.

8. William Mavor, *Universal History, Ancient and Modern*, vol. 17, *The History of the Empire of Germany* (New York, 1804), 23.

9. MC (27 Jan. 1816); LJK, ii.123.

10. LJK, ii.125. 'To a Friend Who Sent me Some Roses', composed 29 June 1816.

11. LJK, ii.123, 130; *Hampshire Chronicle and Courier* (19 July 1819).

12. LJK, ii.125, 133, 141.

13. LJK, ii.126.

14. 'A New Comet', MP (5 July 1819); 'New Comet. To the Editor of the Times', *The Times* (5 July 1819).

15. *The Manuscripts of the Younger Romantics*, gen. ed. Donald Reiman, *John Keats*, ed. Jack Stillinger (7 vols, New York and London, 1985–8), vol. 7, *The Charles Brown Poetry Transcripts at Harvard Facsimiles Including the Fair Copy of 'Otho the Great'*, 62.

16. For 'Bright Star' and Isabella Jones, see JKLY, 25–36; for the dating of the sonnet, cf. WJB, 618–19.

17. LJK, ii.129, 134, 156.

18. LJK, ii.135.

19. LJK, ii.137.

20. LJK, ii.123, 139–40.

21. LJK, ii.164.

22. LJK, i.395.

23. *Hampshire Chronicle and Courier* (16 Aug. 1819).

24. LJK, ii.137, 139, 141, 142.

25. LJK, ii.209.

26. LJK, ii.140–1.

27. LJK, ii.143–4, 150–1.

28. LJK, ii.141, 146, 147, 149, 185.

29. LJK, ii.157, 159 n.; KC, i.lvi; Mona Osborne to Horace Fildes, letters of 9 and 17 Feb. and 3 March 1937, Alexander Turnbull Library, National Archives, Wellington, New Zealand, at FILD 000054[3].

30. LJK, ii.185.

31. LJK, ii.192.

32. LJK, ii.162.

33. *Woodhouse Poetry Transcripts*, 220.

34. LJK, ii.163.

35. LJK, ii.165, 182–3.

36. LJK, ii.160, 186, 193–5; *The Examiner* (Sept. 1819), 604–5.

37. LJK, ii.192.

38. As advertised in MC (Monday, 21 June 1819).

39. LJK, ii.187.

40. LJK, ii.189, 177.

41. LJK, ii. 171, as transcribed by Keats for Woodhouse.

## 21 Repasts

1. LJK, ii.167, 212.

2. LJK, ii.167.

3. LJK, ii.212.

4. LJK, ii.180, 218.

5. *The Examiner* (5 Sept. 1819), 574.

6. LJK, ii.174, 177, 179, 181, 222–5, 229.

7. LJK, ii.232–8.

8. LJK, ii.232–8, 241. For Tom's capital, see KI, 51. Fanny as 'bad hearted', 'Supplement', KC, ii.20. Fanny on George, LFBFK, 25.

9. For George and Keats's finances, see KI, 51; KC, i.217–18, 278; KC, ii.102.

10. LFBFK, 26–7; LJK, ii.295–6.

11. LJK, ii.243, 237.

12. Brown, *Life of Keats*, KC, ii.73.

13. Brown, *Life of Keats*, KC, ii.74; LJK, ii.262.
14. LJK, ii.257, 258, 252, 261, 262, 265, 273.
15. LJK, ii.290.
16. LJK, ii.257, 263, 269.
17. See Richard Marggraf Turley, ' "Slippery Steps of the Temple of Fame": Barry Cornwall and Keats's Reputation', *Keats-Shelley Review*, 22 (2008), 64–81. For Hunt on Cornwall, see *The Examiner* (23 and 30 May 1819), 333–4, 345–6.
18. LJK, ii.270.
19. LJK, ii.270, 273–5.
20. LJK, ii.287.
21. LJK, ii.261, 289.


## 22 A Now

1. R.W. King, *The Translator of Dante: The Life, Work and Friendships of Henry Francis Cary (1772-1844)* (London, 1825), 134; Jonathan Bate, *John Clare. A Biography* (London 2003), 169.
2. *The Letters of John Clare*, ed. Mark Storey (Oxford, 1985), 36–7.
3. LJK, ii.276.
4. Quoted by John Goodridge, 'Junkets and Clarissimus: The Clare-Keats Dialogue', *Keats-Shelley Review*, 25.1 (2011), 35.
5. *The Letters of John Clare*, 38.
6. AMBRH, 282.
7. LJK, ii.295.
8. For Taylor to Clare, see Goodridge, 'Junkets and Clarissimus: The Clare-Keats Dialogue', 37.
9. LJK, ii.288.
10. LJK, ii.290, 292.
11. LJK, ii.290–1.
12. LJK, ii.303–4.
13. LJK, ii.290–4, 303–4.
14. LJK, ii.312.
15. LJK, ii.312.
16. LJK, ii.298–9.
17. For Severn, see LJK, ii.306; for Hessey's letters to Clare of 27 and 30 June, see Goodridge, 'Junkets and Clarissimus: The Clare-Keats Dialogue', 41.
18. *The Letters of John Clare*, 78.
19. LJK, ii.301, 309.
20. *The Indicator* (28 June 1820), 301.
21. See my essay 'Leigh Hunt, Charles Lamb, and Virginia Woolf', *Romantic Presences in the Twentieth Century*, ed. Mark Sandy (Farnham, 2012), 1–17.
22. On this, see especially R.S. White, *John Keats: A Literary Life* (Basingstoke, 2010), 217.
23. *Lamia, Isabella, The Eve of St. Agnes, and Other Poems* (London, 1820).
24. KC, i.116 n., 118; KCH, 149–240; LJK, ii.321.
25. LJK, ii.311–12.


## 23 Regions of Poetry

1. Joseph Severn, 'On the Adversities of Keats's Fame', JSLM, 612; KC, i.191.
2. LJK, ii.310, 313 n., 316–17.
3. LFBFK, 21; FBB, 70–1.
4. LJK, ii.321.
5. LJK, ii.351.
6. LJK, ii.319, 331, 334–6; 'Keats's Bank Account at Rome', held at the Keats-Shelley House, Rome.
7. LJK, ii.327; James Clark, *Medical Notes on Climate, Diseases, Hospitals, and Medical Schools in France, Italy, and Switzerland* (London, 1820), 76.
8. See the discussion in JSLM, 26–8.
9. For Isabella Jones on Severn, see JSLM, 149–51.
10. Severn, 'On the Adversities of Keats's Fame', JSLM, 613.
11. Taylor brought along his apprentice, William Smith Williams, later a reader for Smith and Elder, publishers, and a good friend to the Brontë sisters: see Blunden, *Keats's Publisher*, 79.

12. LFBFK, 2–3.
13. LJK, ii.341.
14. JSLM, 98.
15. *The Indicator* (20 Sept. 1820), 399–400.
16. MC (25 Sept. 1820).
17. Details of the voyage thus far are from Severn's journal–letter to Haslam, 17–21 Sept. 1820, LJK, ii.340–4. See also JSLM, 108–9.
18. LJK, ii.347.
19. LJK, ii.345–6.
20. See TKP, 228–30.
21. Letter dated 19 Sept. 1821, JSLM, 172.
22. 'Sonnet by the Late John Keats', *The Union Magazine*, 1.2 (Feb. 1846), 157.
23. For a full account of Keats's landing in Dorset and the 'Bright Star' myth, see my essay 'John Keats and the West Country', *English Romantic Writers and the West Country* (Basingstoke, 2010).
24. JSLM, 108–9, 641–2.
25. LJK, ii.348.

## 24 Eternal Road

1. LJK, ii.351–2; JSLM, 109.
2. *The Indicator* (28 June 1820), 302.
3. LJK, ii.351.
4. LJK, ii.352.
5. LJK, ii.354.
6. Charles MacFarlane, *Reminiscences of a Literary Life* (London, 1917), 14–15.
7. See *The Times* (27 Nov. 1820), 2.
8. *The Times* (27 Nov. 1820), (4 Dec. 1820), (20 Nov. 1820).
9. JSLM, 644.
10. JSLM, 644.
11. The account of the journey to Rome in the following pages makes use of three sources: Henry Coxe, *Picture of Italy; Being a Guide to the Antiquities and Curiosities of That Classical and Interesting Country* (London, 1815); Selina Martin, *Narrative of a Three Years' Residence in Italy 1819–22* (London, 1828); Henry Matthews, *The Diary of an Invalid; Being the Journal of a Tour in Pursuit of Health in Portugal, Italy, Switzerland and France in the Years 1817, 1818 and 1819* (London, 1820).
12. See Coxe, *Picture of Italy*, 282.
13. Martin, *Narrative*, 55.
14. Martin, *Narrative*, 54–5.
15. Charles Dickens, *American Notes and Pictures from Italy* (London, 1957; rpt. 1966), 396, 408.
16. Coxe, *Picture of Italy*, 397.
17. These sights are noted in Coxe, *Picture of Italy*, 396.
18. JSLM, 644–5; LJK, ii.359.
19. LJK, ii.359.
20. Sharp, 106.
21. Sally Brown, 'Suppose me in Rome', *Keats and Italy. A History of the Keats-Shelley House in Rome* (Rome, 2005), 22–5.
22. KC, i.191; JSLM, 119; 'Keats's Last Bank Account', K-SMB, 2 (1913), 94–5.
23. See LJK, ii.358–9.
24. JSLM, 646–7
25. LJK, ii.360.
26. See JSLM, 98, 99, 110. Anthony Burgess's novel *Abba Abba* (1977) has Keats plotting a new poem at Rome. My thanks to Michael O'Neill and Tim Webb for this reference.
27. For Sabrina, see 'My Tedious Life', JSLM, 648.
28. LJK, ii.359–60.
29. LCAB, 72.
30. JSLM, 112.
31. LFBFK, 9–10.
32. JSLM, 113.
33. JSLM, 114, 648.
34. *The Times* (22 Dec. 1820).
35. JSLM, 116–17; KC, ii.92.

36. JSLM, 118.
37. JSLM, 119–20; LJK, ii.368.
38. LJK, ii.366–7.
39. KC, i.188–9.
40. KC, i.188–9.
41. LCAB, 67–8.
42. LJK, ii.370; JSLM, 649.
43. LJK, ii.371–3, JSLM, 139, 144, 151; Sue Brown, *Joseph Severn, A Life: The Rewards of Friendship* (Oxford, 2009), 100–1.
44. LFBFK, 14–15.
45. KC, ii.90.
46. KC, ii.91.
47. JSLM, 125.
48. JSLM, 128.
49. JSLM, 130, 650.
50. See Daniel Griffin, *The Life of Gerald Griffin Esq. by his Brother* (London, 1843), 190.
51. JSLM, 135–6
52. LJK, ii.378.

## 25 Terminalia

1. JSLM, 136–7, from a draft at the Keats-Shelley House, Rome.
2. LJK, ii.379 and n.; JSLM, 139. For the Rev. Richard Wolfe at Rome, see Martin, *Narrative*, [356]. See also 'Keats's Funeral', dictated by Ambrose Poynter to his daughter Miss H.M. Poynter at LMA, KPM/K 770 3/4.
3. KC, ii.94–5; JSLM, 650.
4. LCAB, 73.
5. KC, i.231.
6. See LFBFK, 20 and LCAB, 75.
7. *The Examiner* (25 March 1821), 184.

# Index